CONSTRUCTION MANAGEMENT AND MACHINERY

CONSTRUCTION MANAGEMENT AND MACHINERY

B.L. Gupta
M.Sc (Maths) M.E. Civil Engg. (Roorkee)

and

Amit Gupta
B.E. (Hons) I.R.S.E.

STANDARD PUBLISHERS DISTRIBUTORS

1705-B, NAI SARAK, POST BOX No.: 1066, DELHI-110006
Phones : 23262700, 23285798, Fax: 23243180
www.standardpublishers.com email: stpub@vsnl.com

Published by :
A. K. Jain
For Standard Publishers Distributors
1705-B, Nai Sarak, Delhi-110006.

First Edition	:	1994
Second Edition	:	1998
Third Edition	:	2005
Fourth Edition	:	2008
Reprint	:	2010
Reprint	:	2012
Reprint	:	2013
Reprint	:	2015
Reprint	:	2017
Reprint	:	2019

Price: Rs. 300-00

ISBN : 81-8014-121-7
ISBN : 978-81-8014-121-8

Laser Typesetting by : Bhargave Laser Printers, Delhi.
Printed by : Prabhat Offset Press, Delhi.

Preface to the Fourth Edition

Construction industry is one of the major industries all over the world. In India it is the second largest industry providing employment to workers after agriculture. Scientific and technological advancement is taking place in leaps and bounds through out the world in all fields of life. Hence to keep abreast with the new technologies technical universities and boards have incorporated changes in their syllabi. Hence keeping the needs of the students in mind authors have fully revised and enlarged their text on construction management and accounts.

In the revised version of the book 10 chapters on the construction equipment and machinery, 100 solved examples and about 400 objective type questions have been added. In the present text some problems appeared in the UPSC examinations have also been solved.

Authors have tried to provide the best possible material in simple and lucid language to the students preparing for degree, diploma and other competitive examinations. It will also prove useful to the people engaged in field duties. Authors have consulted many standard works on the subject and express their gratitude to all of them. We are thankful to all those who in any form helped us in preparing this text.

Though every effect has been made to eliminate errors of all types, yet some errors might have been left un noticed. Authors sincerely request the readers to bring any mistake observed by them to the notice of the publishers for the improvement of the book. Any constructive criticism for the improvement of the text is welcome. Authors express their gratitude to M/s Standard Publishers Distributors who in a very short period have brought out this text in such a nice get up.

B.L. GUPTA
AMIT GUPTA

CONTENTS

1

The Construction Industry in India

1.1. INTRODUCTION

India has a glorious past in the field of construction work. The earliest known organised construction of dwellings at Mohen-Jo-doro dates back to 3000 B.C. The monoments of cave temples at Ellora and Ajanta are the testimony of the skill and craftsmanship in construction of the early days. During British regime, the construction activities remained confined to a limited sphere of construction of some irrigation works, roads and cities etc.

From the very beginning of the existence of the human being on this planet, man has been constantly devising means of safeguarding himself against the onslaught of nature and wild animals. In the ancient times man used to live on trees, machans and in caves. With the advancement of knowledge and civilization man started constructing huts and then houses and started living in groups. With the passage of time, new techniques of construction developed and construction activity turned into a Industry. Thus construction industry is the single largest important undertaking in the economy of a country. Thus the basic needs of human beings from very beginning are as:

(*a*) Food (*b*) Clothing

(*c*) Sheltre

After independence, the Government of India adopted a policy of planned investment in the form of five year plans for the quick development of the country. In all the five year plans more than 50% expenditure incurred is related to construction work in one form or the other such as dams, power and irrigation projects, Roads, establishment of heavy industries, Communications, housing and urban development etc. Thus the construction is the second largest economic activity in India next to agriculture only. The volume and scope of construction industry can be directly linked with the population and size of the country and plays a critical role in alround development of the country. With the increase in population, the need for housing and industry also increases. At the end it can be concluded that national development is directly linked with the development of construction activities.

1.2. CONCEPT OF MANAGEMENT

It is a well known fact that an single individual can not do all the works, so he joined hands with other people to achieve his goals. With the passage of time, the needs of the man also increased which gave birth to the idea of organised activities to achieve his goal. Thus management is an organisation in which different class of people work together to produce qualitative and economical products with the available resources such as capital, material and equipment etc.

1.3. EMPLOYMENT GENERATION IN CONSTRUCTION SECTOR

In India Construction activity is the largest activity after agriculture and employs very large work force. Though there is no reliable data on the employment is construction industry, but about 5% of the total labour force of the country may be assumed safely. In addition to this figure, additional 5 to 10% may be assumed employed in other construction related industries as cement, brick, steel and construction equipment manufacturing industries etc. Thus the total work force working in actual construction activities and related fields come to 10 to 15% of the total work force in the country. Studies carried out by some agencies have shown that construction industry has given birth to the development over 250 industries in other sectors. Thus the construction sector has given a substantial boost to the economy with its substantial contribution to national income, GDP, and employment generation.

The National Building organisation (NBO) has shown that every one million rupees invested in construction sector generated 3000 man days of semiskilled and skilled labour and 1300 man days of technologists and managerial employment. In housing sector, it has been estimated that every one million rupees invested, generated 30623 man days for direct employment and 32996 man days for indirect labour employment. It has been estimated that by the end of 2002, the production of cement and steel crossed the limit of 100 million tonnes and 30 million tonnes respectively.

1.4. AGENCIES ENGAGED IN CONSTRUCTION ACTIVITIES

In India construction activity is one of the most wide spread activities involving from small builders in villages and towns to large private companies, Public undertakings and various state agencies. Thus following agencies are involved in the construction activities.

(*a*) Individuals

(*b*) Private companies and other enterpreneurs.

(*c*) Public undertakings such as Railways, National Building Construction organisation, National Projects of Construction Corporation, Fertilizer Corporation of India, Airport Authority of India, Oil and Natural gas Commission of India etc.

(*d*) Government and its agencies such as Central and state governments Public works departments and various other agencies as urban development authorities and municipalities, Military Engineering services etc.

Apart from the enormous construction work being undertaken in the country, Indian firms are also engaged in large construction projects of different kinds in foreign countries involving more than 1000 crores of rupees in competition of other advanced countries.

1.5. ROLE OF GOVERNMENT IN CONSTRUCTION SECTOR AND ORGANISATIONS OF CONTRACTORS

In India, most of the construction works are government controlled. They are financed by the government. Even industrial and housing sectors get financial support from banks and institutions regulated by the government. The construction activities are also governed by the government by controlling the finance allotted to different execution agencies. Many a times delay taken place in giving timely decisions and bureaucratic red tapism cause great difficulties in the execution of a project and many a times cost exceeds many fold of the original estimated cost.

In India, the contractors and construction agencies in general are a unorganised lot. The contractor's organisations are very few. Most of the contractors have no technological and management back ground. There are only few construction agencies in India who have technological and managerial organisational set up and have necessary equipment to handle the major projects.

The main organisation of contractors is known as BAI, (Builders Association of India). It has 10,000 direct and 15,000 affiliated members and about 70 centres throughout India.

1.6. CLASSIFICATION OF CONSTRUCTION WORKS

The classification of construction works may be made depending upon the following factors.

1. Cost of Construction. In this category, construction works may be classified as:

(*a*) *Minor works.* If the estimated cost of construction of work is less than Rs. 20,000/- then the work is called as *minor work.*

(*b*) *Medium works.* If the cost of construction of the work is between Rs. Twenty thousand and Rs. one lakh then the work is known as *medium work.*

(*c*) *Major works.* If the cost of construction of work is greater than Rs. One lakh, then it is called *major work.*

2. Based on life of work. In this category construction works are classified as follows:

(*a*) *Temporary work.* If the work is made of cheaper materials and is of temporary nature and can be dismentaled easily, then such a construction is called as *temporary work*

(*b*) *Semi permanent work.* If the life span of the work is short and can be dismentaled and replaced then it is called as semi permanent work

(*c*) *Permanent work.* If the structure is of long life and durable then it is called *permanent work.*

3. Based on the nature of work. In this category, construction works may be classified as follows:

(*a*) *Original work.* All new construction works are classified as *original works.*

(*b*) *Repair works.* Any repair of an old work is called repair work.

Now a days the rehabilitation of old buildings in big cities, monuments and important structures affected by environmental factors is gaining importance. The repair of monumental works need special technique and materials. For such works some specialists have given the name as FORENSIC ENGINEERING.

4. Based on the type of structural members and equipment used. Under this category, construction works are classified as follows:

(*a*) *Light construction.* The construction works which have light structural members and consequently light foundations and do not need heavy machinery and equipment for their construction are called *light construction.* Residential and commercial buildings, warehouses schools, village and city roads, light industrial buildings, small water supply and sewage works etc. are classified as light construction works.

(*b*) *Heavy Construction.* Structures having heavy structural members and heavy foundations which require heavy machinery and equipment and large quantities of materials, labour and heavy investment for their construction are called as *heavy construction.* Construction of dams, bridges irrigation works, railways, high ways, oil pipe lines, thermal and hydropower generation works, docks and harbour, tunnelling etc. are classified under this category.

(*c*) *Industrial Construction.* The works which need specialised equipment and machinery and special technology and know how for their construction are known as *Industrial construction.* The construction work for atomic power plants, steel and fertilizer plants, oil refineries, chemical plants are classified under this category.

1.7. STAGES OF CONSTRUCTION OF A PROJECT

The various stages in the construction of a project may be classified under the following heads:

1. Conceptual or Initial stage
2. Study and Evaluation stage
3. Design stage
4. Awarding of contract for construction stage
5. Construction stage
6. Utilization and maintenance stage

1. Conceptual stage. It is the stage at which an project is conceived to be undertaken to achieve certain aims. Thus either due to the efforts of individuals or to satisfy the social and public needs many construction projects were under taken. What ever may be the source of originating idea for starting a welfare project, needs to be promoted with the user agencies to generate sufficient interest for its further consideration and development to reach the completion stage.

2. Study and evaluation stage. After the initial conception of any project, it is further studied and analysed regarding the cost of the project and benefits that will accure from it. Before finally accepting the proposal, preliminary surveys are carried out and rough estimates are prepared to study the feasibility and economic viability of the project. If it is a social welfare project, then the social utility of the project will be of main consideration. After the acceptance of the project, sources of funding are found out. In case of a Government project, an administrative approval is accorded and a budget provision is made at this stage. In a private organisation a decision is taken to undertake the project and arrangements are made to raise funds for its completion. Thus after taking decision of the construction of the project, following points are studied:

(*a*) Availability of land where the project is to be constructed.
(*b*) Finances required for its completion.
(*c*) Necessity for its construction at present.
(*d*) Future utility of the project.
(*e*) Type of construction to be adopted
(*f*) Returns from the project.

3. Design stage. This is an very important stage for the implementation of the project. At this stage necessary field surveys and investigations are carried out. At this stage generally following investigations are made.

(*a*) Topography of the area
(*b*) Bearing capacity of soil
(*c*) Position of ground water table
(*d*) Access to the site
(*e*) Availability of construction material and required labour near the site of work
(*f*) Local weather conditions.

Thus after the field investigations and surveys carried out, site and alignment finalised, the process of land equisition and obtaining approval of local authorities goes on simultaneously. Any economy that can be effected in the cost of the project depends mainly on the decisions taken at the design stage on the basis of site investigations and other related data. Any change made after the approval of the design will prove more expensive.

4. Awarding of Contract for Construction. At this stage necessary tender documents are prepared and tenders called, and evaluated. Finally the work is awarded to the contractor, whose terms of execution are more favourable. Preference is given to a contractor who has executed similar work successfully in the past. In case the work is to be executed departmentally, the internal orders are issued authorising expenditure and preparations are made for its execution.

5. Construction stage. At this stage maximum coordination is required between the various agencies connected with the implementation of the project. This stage needs the maximum skill from the project manager so that the project may be completed well in time as per approved design. Proper safety measures should be adopted during the construction. The work should be cost effective. Problems encountered during the construction due to the variations in site conditions should be referred to the designer for suitable changes in the design.

6. Utilization and maintenance. Some projects can be put to use even after completion some of its parts. After putting the full project to use, the factors regarding its maintenance should be considered carefully. The performance, the nature and extent of maintenance and repair are good indicator of the quality of construction and provide a valuable feed back for the use in the construction of other similar new projects. Many projects completed with great efforts at huge cost failed to give fullest benefits due to non provision of continuous maintenance facilities to them. The line diagram of various stages of construction is shown in Fig. 1.1.

1.8. CONSTRUCTION TEAM

It is a well known fact that for the construction of any project a group of persons or team with specific duties to be performed by each group is needed. Thus the construction team includes the followings:

1. Owner
2. Engineer/Architect/Consultant
3. Contractor or Builder

The functions of each team or constituent of the construction depend upon the type and size of the work and the method of execution of the work. Each constituent has to discharge his responsibility and cooperate with other constituents to complete the construction work with out delay and escalation in construction cost. Usually delay and accidents take place due to the un-coordinated efforts by the different constituents.

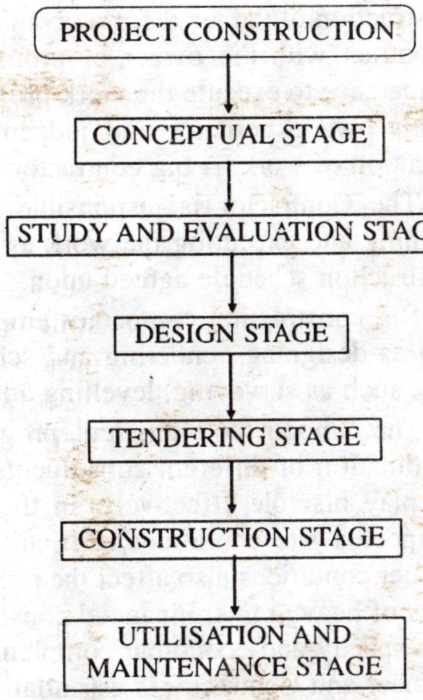

Fig. 1.1. Various stages of Construction.

1.9. FUNCTIONS OF EACH CONSTITUENT

Following are the functions of each constituent:

1. Owner. The owner may be an individual, group. private or public body who promotes the work and provides finances for the execution of the work. After completion of the work, the owner arranges for its proper utilization and maintenance.

2. Engineer/Consultant/Architect. May be an individual person or group of persons or a company who give the technical advice about the project to the owner.

Engineer. He is a professional man and is responsible for the safe and economical design and construction of the work under his supervision. His field activities are as follows:

(*a*) Field investigations for the proposed project.
(*b*) To prepare the plans and design of the work.
(*c*) To prepare estimates and specifications.
(*d*) To work out the quantities of construction materials and the cost of the project.
(*e*) To obtain approval of construction plans from the local authorities.
(*f*) To float tender, their evaluation and approval of the lowest tender.
(*g*) Supervision, control and inspection of the quality and progress of the work done by the contractor.
(*h*) Measurements of works done and their payment.

In case the work is executed departmentally, then he is responsible to arrange construction materials, equipment and labour etc. If necessary for the proper design, the engineer may be assisted by architect and other specialists.

The cost of construction is affected significantly by the specifications and design requirements. Thus an engineer has a very important responsibility to ensure the minimum cost of construction of the project. He may examine a number of proposals and designs and select the most economical and viable project. Some times builders may be asked to submit their designs along with tenders and the most suitable and economical design may be selected.

Consultant. A consultant is a specialist in his field. A consultant may be appointed for a highly specialized project to help the owners and contractors in the execution of a highly specialized job. His appointment is optional. In Government departments generally Chief Engineer of the department acts as consultant.

Architect. An architect is a technical person. Usually he is involved in the building construction projects. He designs the buildings to give aesthetic look to the building and proper and economical use of the available space.

Builder/Contractor. A Contractor for Civil Engineering works may be an individual person or a group of persons or a company who under takes the construction of the work. He offers to under take the construction of the work for a given amount of money. In case the tender is accepted in his favour, he signs a contract with the owner or promoter to execute the construction work. He must have the skill and competence to execute the work properly as per design and specifications. A small contractor usually relies on his own experience and judgement or on the advice of his experienced mistries in tendering and execution of work. A big contractor may take the advice of qualified engineers.

The Contractor is responsible for procuring of materials not supplied by the owner, organising, planning and executing the work as per drawings and specifications laid down in the contract and as per construction schedule agreed upon.

Big construction companies employ engineers, who deal with office work involved in large contracts such as designing, tendering and scheduling. The site engineers are concerned with the execution of the work such as surveying, levelling and giving lay outs for the construction.

The Smooth and efficient progress of any construction project, large or small depends upon the coordination of different constituents involved in the project. Each constituent should know his job well and play his role effectively. In the construction work, there is always a degree of uncertainty due to unexpected site conditions, difficulties in the procurement of construction materials and labour. Local weather conditions also affect the progress of work as progress of earth dam construction is very less in the zones of heavy rains. Financial constraints are a major hurdle in the speedy progress of the project. Hence for a speedy and economic completion of a work, the constant liasion and interaction among the owner, Engineer and Contractor is essential.

1.10. RESOURCES OF CONSTRUCTION INDUSTRY

The resources needed for a construction industry are as follows:

1. Money
2. Man
3. Material
4. Machine and equipment
5. Management

1. **Money.** It is the first and foremost item required for any project. It should be arranged before starting the work. Money should be supplied regularly as and when required for the proper progress of the work. Insufficient available funds for the project will cause delay in the completion of the work, resulting in escalation in the cost of the project and also depriving the people from the benefits expected from the project. Thus irregular and insufficient supply of money will cause delay in the completion of the project and wastage of time and energy. It will also deprive the people from the benefits expected from the project.
2. **Man.** For the successful completion of any project man power both skilled or unskilled is very important. It is economical and dependable both being the oldest resource. According to planning, from labour to skilled supervisory staff is required for the successful completion of any project.
3. **Materials.** It has been estimated that for any work or project usually the cost of material is about 50% of the total cost of the project. Thus construction materials should be available with in 1 to 1.5 km radius of the site of work for economical completion of the work as the cost of cartage of materials affects the total cost of the project to a great extent. The supply of materials should be regular in sufficient quantity as per need. While stacking and storing the materials, proper care should be taken to avoid their deterioration.
4. **Machines and equipments.** For major works different kinds of machines are needed for different activities. On major projects it is economical interms of money and time both. The Engineer in-charge of machines should have sufficient knowledge about the machines and equipment needed for a particular activity and most economical machine/equipment should be chosen. The machine/ equipment chosen should be available as and when needed for the work.
5. **Management.** It is a sort of administration, whose functions are to plan, organise, control and coordinate the use of different resources to achieve the desired goal. Infact management is an art of

arranging various activities and group of people to achieve the common goal. Thus an executive must have managerial skill.

1.11. EDUCATION FOR CONSTRUCTION MANAGERS

In the present era science and technology is developing in leap and bound all over the world in all fields. Now a days the construction of projects is becoming more complex and costly than before. The complex nature of the work requires more skill in the management of every phase of construction work. Such management skill hardly been imparted to an Engineer during his study or training period.

To day the large industrial projects are handlled as ready made tools requiring coordination of project engineering and management activities on site and at corporate office. This is further necessitated by the substantial increase in oversees construction exports and international contracting. A large number of public sectors like Railways, National Building organisation and private firms are engaged in construction activities in foreign countries. Thus the construction management as a professional function has assumed greate importance.

The difference between the management of construction and construction management is very delicate and is difficult to explain. However they are explained as follows:

management of construction confines to the management of actual construction, while construction management involves the whole process starting right from the conceptual stage to the completion of the project construction. Thus the task of a construction manager is much more complex than the general contractor. The construction manager is more involved during the pre-design and design stages of the project construction. This early involvement differentiates the tasks of construction manager and general contractor most notably.

The pre-design phase or exploratory phase needs more involvement of the project manager. The environmental effect studies also require special skills for the site selection and zoning etc. The design phase also puts heavy responsibility on the construction manager. During construction phase also construction manager has to administer contract, cost control and schedule etc.

Thus to be a successful project manager, he needs famaliarity with the modern techniques and theories of management and engineering.

In India at present very few institutions offer construction management. Only National Institute of Management and Research Pune is Conducting post graduate course in Construction management.

1.12. CONSTRUCTION SECTOR FOR 21ST CENTURY

As the construction is critical to improve the standard of living of the people, it needs to be more faster, active and cost conscious. In the recent past construction activities have increased manifold, becoming progressively more complex and capital intensive. Thus the expected growth of construction work demands sophisticated managerial talent to manage these big projects properly.

QUESTIONS

1. Construction and National Development are linked inseparably with regard to our country. Comment.
2. How the construction sector in India is helping to solve the problem of unemployment.
3. Give the various stages of construction of a project.
4. Name the different constituents of a construction team and discuss the importance of coordination between them.
5. Discuss the different resources of construction work.
6. How can the construction management education improve the efficiency of the construction industry.
7. Differentiate the tasks of construction manager and a general contractor.
8. Give the present condition of constructional infrastructure in India. Suggest remedial measures keeping the economic conditions of the country in mind.

9. Write short notes on the followings:
   (*a*) Role of government in the construction industry.
   (*b*) Construction sector for 21st century.
   (*c*) Condition of construction workers in India.

OBJECTIVE TYPE QUESTIONS

1. Construction industry in India provides employment about...percent of the total labour force of the country.
   (*a*) About 8% (*b*) About 12%
   (*c*) About 15% (*d*) About 5%
2. In each five year plan the lay out of construction industry is kept about... percent of G.D.P. of the country.
   (*a*) More than 60% (*b*) Abut 50%
   (*c*) Less than 35% (*d*) About 40%
3. The second largest employment generating industry in the country is
   (*a*) Petrochemical industry (*b*) Cement industry
   (*c*) Construction industry (*d*) Leather industry
4. The largest employer sector in India is
   (*a*) Power sector (*b*) Petro-chemical sector
   (*c*) Automobile sector (*d*) Agriculture sector
5. The over all coordinating person in a construction team is
   (*a*) The project manager (*b*) The contractor
   (*c*) The Engineer (*d*) The owner
6. The classification of construction works can be done as
   (*a*) Temporary and permanent works (*b*) Light and heavy construction works
   (*c*) Minor and Major works (*d*) All the above
7. In a construction project, the most important stage is
   (*a*) Design stage (*b*) Conceptual stage
   (*c*) Contract awarding stage (*d*) Construction stage
8. The difference between management of construction and construction management is...
   (*a*) Actual supervision and design of project
   (*b*) Financing the construction and design and supervision
   (*c*) Management of actual construction and the whole process from inception to completion
   (*d*) Both are the same
   (*e*) All the above
9. In a construction project the environmental studies are important due to
   (*a*) It affects the health of the people
   (*b*) It increases the pollution
   (*c*) It displaces the people and causes health hazards
   (*d*) None of the above
   (*e*) All the above
10. The specialised training in construction management is given in
   (*a*) Many government departments
   (*b*) In many Engineering colleges
   (*c*) In few institutions only
   (*d*) Only in National institute of construction management and research Pune.

ANSWERS

1. (*d*)	4. (*d*)	7. (*d*)	10. (*c*)
2. (*b*)	5. (*a*)	8. (*c*)	
3. (*c*)	6. (*d*)	9. (*c*)	

2

Feasibility Report

2.1. INTRODUCTION

The feasibility report is prepared during the initial phase of the project. The feasibility report of the project contains the results of detailed technical and economical analysis carried out to evaluate the viability of the project, so that the owner may take decision on the investment to be incurred, so that the project can be properly planned and implemented. For the implementation of the project, the updating and validation (legalision) of the feasibility is required. The project can be implemented as per technical and economical stipulations made in the feasibility report. Some times due to the delay in the implementation, cost updating of the project becomes necessary.

2.2. SCHEMATIC DIAGRAM FOR FEASIBILITY STUDY

It can be shown as follows:

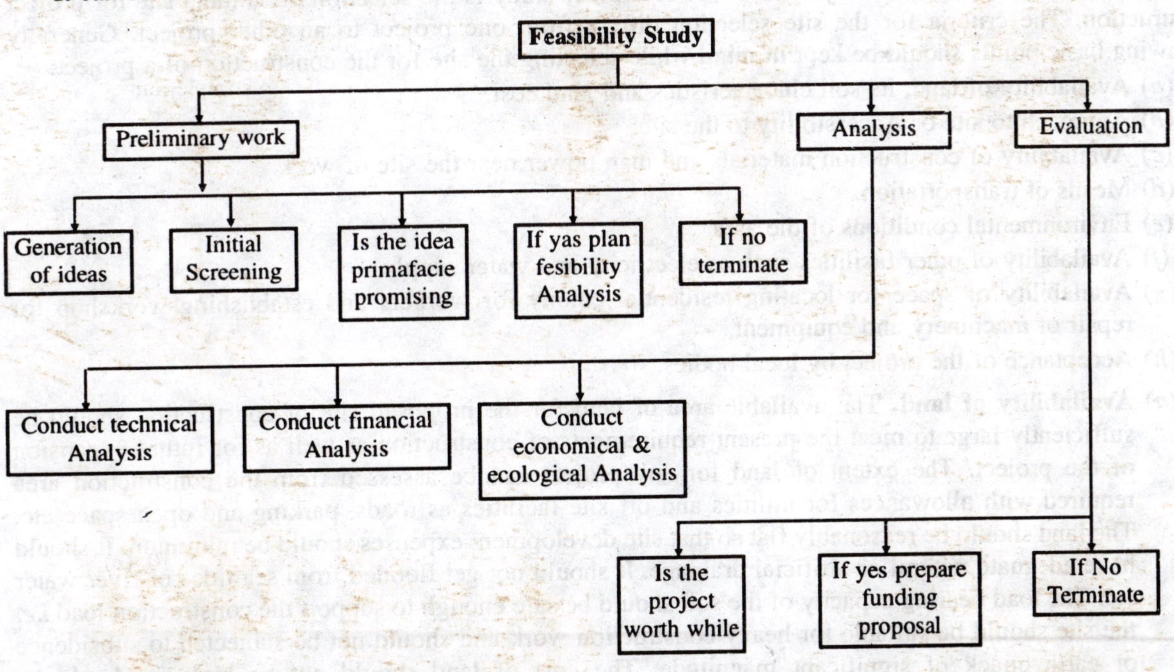

2.3. FACTORS AFFECTING THE VIABILITY OF THE PROJECT

The viability of a project is affected or depends on the following factors:

(*a*) Technical analysis
(*b*) Financial analysis
(*c*) Economic analysis
(*d*) Ecological analysis

2.4. TECHNICAL ANALYSIS

In the technical part of the feasibility study the alternate methods of selection of best available technology and course of action are identified. In this study following works are carried out.

1. Location of suitable site
2. Selection of appropriate method of construction
3. Selection of suitable equipment for construction
4. Drawing specifications of construction materials
5. Determining the availability of different resources.

While selecting the most appropriate technology, the safety of workers and environmental impact on the surrounding vicinity must be kept in view. Selection of appropriate method of construction depends on the availability of resources and detailed economic evaluation of various alternative methods.

2.4.1. Features of New Technology introduced in the field of Construction

Followings are the features of the new technology in the field of construction.

(*a*) It is quite expensive
(*b*) It is of high degree of automation
(*c*) It needs highly trained personnel and sophisticated management culture.

Therefore while selecting the new technology for the project, the above noted points should be kept in mind. The adoption of new technology depends on the size of project and its duration of completion.

2.5. OBJECTIVES OF FEASIBILITY STUDY

One of the most important objective of the feasibility study is the selection of suitable site for project construction. The criteria for the site selection differs from one project to an other project. Generally following basic points should be kept in mind while selecting the site for the construction of a project:

(*a*) Availability of land, its soil characteristics and land cost.
(*b*) Approach to site or Accessibility to the site.
(*c*) Availability of construction materials and man power near the site of work.
(*d*) Means of transportation.
(*e*) Environmental conditions of the area.
(*f*) Availability of other facilities such as electricity and water supply.
(*g*) Availability of space for locating residential colony for workers and establishing workshop for repair of machinery and equipment.
(*h*) Acceptance of the project by local bodies.

(*a*) **Availability of land.** The available area of land for the proposed site of construction should be sufficiently large to meet the present requirements of construction as well as for future expansion of the project. The extent of land for any project can be assessed from the construction area required with allowances for utilities and off site facilities as roads, parking and open space etc. The land should be reasonably flat so that site development expenses should be minimum. It should have adequate natural or artificial drainage. It should not get flooded from sea tides or river water etc. The load bearing capacity of the soil should be safe enough to support the construction load *i.e.* the site should be suitable for heavy construction work and should not be subjected to subsidence or earth quack of significant magnitude. The cost of land should not be high, it should be competitive with other alternative sites. Preferably land should be government owned and be available for development work. It should not involve heavy displacement of persons. As rehabilitation of persons is a gigantic and very expensive work. Thus all these informations or data should be collected at the feasibility stage.

(*b*) **Accessibility to the site.** The site should be accessible in all parts of the years. The location of the site should be such that it may be approachable by road and rail. The site should be near the national high way and railway siding.

(*c*) **Availability of construction materials.** If the materials of construction are available with in a radius of 1.5 km of the site of construction, then the cartage cost will be minimum.

(*d*) **Availability of man power.** If the unskilled, semi skilled and skilled labour in sufficient number is available near the site of work, then the cost of project will reduce to a great extent. In case the skilled and semi skilled labour is not available and it is difficult to attract the labour from out site, then arrangement to train the local people have to be made. Along with training local people, out side trained and experienced people have to be attracted by providing housing and other facilities. This will increase the cost of the project as this expenditure has to be added to the cost of the project. Thus while selecting the site of construction, the cost of man power, cost of training of labour and cost of other facilities etc. also should be taken into account at the time of comparing merits of alternative locations.

(*e*) **Transportation.** The cost of transpiration is one of the major factors which influence the selection of the site of construction. As already stated above that the availability of raw materials needed in bulk with in a radius of 1.5 km of the site of work makes the project most economical. In case the quality of raw material is likely to deteriorate during transportation, then such projects as sugar factory should be located centrally near the source of raw material. To make the project economical, the site should be so selected which has easy access to the most economic mode of transportation. At the time of studying the relative merits of alternative sites, the cost of transportation of raw materials, machines and equipment, cement etc. should be taken into account.

(*f*) **Availability of other facilities.** In case of projects which require high consumption of water and electricity, in such cases the selection of site is governed by the availability of these facilities. The cost of pumping water to the site and its treatment and the availability of electricity always influence the selection of the site of the project. Thus while selecting the site, these factors should be considered on economic basis.

(*g*) **Acceptability by local authorities.** Now a days more attention is paid to the pollution of environment. Thus the location of the project should be such that it should not affect the surrounding environment by any kind of pollution.

Besides the above factors, economic factors are the most important factors for the site selection of a project. If the basic conditions are met, then the economics of potential sites should be evaluated in detail and the decision may be taken in favor of the most economically viable site.

2.6. FINANCIAL ANALYSIS

The financial analysis of a feasibility study may be classified in the following two groups:

1. Estimation of capital cost requirement
2. Sources of financing

1. Capital Cost of Project

The cost incurred in the completion of all components of the project is known as *capital cost.* Estimation of capital cost of a project gives the basic information necessary for deciding the pattern of financing and viability of the project. A owner arranges his resources according to the estimated cost of the project. If the cost of a project over runs substantially, then it may be difficult to arrange the additional resources and the implementation of the project may be delayed, which may further escalate the cost of the project.

On the other hand over estimation of the cost of project also is undesirable. If the cost is over estimated the promoters may divert the resources to other purposes and the financial institutions will have to make un necessary higher commitments. The capital cost estimation depends on the following elements.

(*a*) Project and Engineering management cost.
(*b*) Management and supervision during the construction.
(*c*) Engineering fee.
(*d*) Payment for technology cost.
(*e*) Construction equipment used.
(*f*) Commissioning expenditure.
(*g*) Preliminary and Pre operative expenses.
(*h*) Contingency expenses.
(*i*) Miscellaneous fixed assets.
(*j*) Working cost.
(*k*) Operating cost etc.

The list of above elements may change from project to project. The total funds will be required in phases as per requirement of the project schedule. The sum of all the capital cost of the items plus the working and operating cost will give the idea of total funds required for the project.

Working cost. The expenditure incurred for maintaining various inventories in the form of raw material or construction materials, operating supplies and maintenance etc. is known is working cost.

Operating cost. The expenditure incurred in repair and maintenance cost of the project after its completion is known as *operating cost.*

2. Sources of Financing

Basically the sources for funding the required fund may be classified into the following two categories:

(*a*) Internal source. For small projects internal sources of financing are used.
(*b*) External source. For big projects external sources of financing are used.

The capital cost of the project basically is arranged through equity and long term debts.

2.7. ECONOMIC ANALYSIS

The economic analysis is required at the time of feasibility stage of the project. The economic analysis checks the economic viability of the project. In some cases it has been observed that though the project is technically feasible but economically unviable. The economic feasibility of a project can be assessed by the following methods.

1. Return on investment method
2. Net present value method
3. Pay back period method
4. benefit cost ratio method
5. Internal rate of return method

The best alternative which can give the best results in term of economy may be determined by the above methods. The economic analysis is known as social cost benefit analysis.

2.8. ECOLOGICAL ANALYSIS

In the recent past more and more emphasis is put on pollution control. Now great emphasis is put on the treatment of effluent and its disposal so that the environmental pollution may not take place. The process of effluent treatment and disposal is quite expensive and differs from industry to industry depending upon the nature and quality of effluent. Thus in recent years the environmental concerns have assumed a great significance. The ecological analysis should be carried out for major projects which have significant ecological implications such as chemical, drug, leather processing industries and thermal power plants, irrigation project etc.

The guide lines of central and state pollution control boards should be considered during the feasibility study of the project and cost provision for suitable treatments be made for various prospective locations.

QUESTIONS

1. What do you mean by the feasibility report? Discuss fully.
2. Discuss in brief various criterions for the site selection for a project.
3. Draw the flow diagram for the feasibility study of a project.
4. Explain the significance of the following analysis during the feasibility study.
   (*a*) Technical analysis (*b*) Economic analysis
   (*c*) Financial analysis (*d*) Ecological analysis
5. For estabilishing a sugar factory near your city, prepare a feasibility report.
6. Prepare a feasibility report for estabilishing a drug factory near your city. Relevant data required may be assumed.

OBJECTIVE TYPE QUESTIONS

1. In the construction projects the importance of environmental impact studies is due to:
   (*a*) It increases pollution (*b*) It affects the health of the people
   (*c*) It displaces large number of people (*d*) It causes health hazards
2. The feasibility report of a project is prepared
   (*a*) After completion of the project (*b*) During intermediate phase
   (*c*) During initial phase (*d*) During final phase
3. The viability of a project depends on
   (*a*) Financial analysis (*b*) Ecological analysis
   (*c*) Economic analysis (*d*) Technical analysis
   (*e*) On all the analysis
4. The site selection for any project is influenced by
   (*a*) Availability of land, soil characteristics and cost of land
   (*b*) Accessibility to the site
   (*c*) Availability of man power and material of construction near the site of work
   (*d*) Transportation and availability of other facilities
   (*e*) All of the above
5. The main element of capital cost estimate are
   (*a*) Management and supervision cost
   (*b*) Project and Engineering management cost
   (*c*) Cost of construction equipment and contingencies
   (*d*) All the above
6. The source of financing a construction project is by
   (*a*) External source (*b*) Internal source
   (*c*) Both (*a*) and (*b*) (*d*) None of the above
7. The economic viability of a project can be assessed by
   (*a*) Return on investment and internal rate of return
   (*b*) Benefit cost ratio
   (*c*) Pay back period and net present value
   (*d*) All the above
   (*e*) Non of the above
8. Identify the incorrect statement/statements
   (*a*) The feasibility report is prepared in the initial phase of the project
   (*b*) The site selection for a project depends upon the availability and cost of land
   (*c*) Chemical and leather industries do not pollute the environment

(*d*) Accessibility to site is one of the main requirement of site selection for a project

9. Identify the correct statement/statements
   (*a*) Thermal power plant and drug industry do not have any effect on environment.
   (*b*) Characteristics of soil of site and cost of land have no influence on the site selection of a project
   (*c*) Technical analysis of a project is an important factor for determining the viability of the project.
   (*d*) Selection of appropriate method of construction does not depend on the availability of resources.
   (*e*) Rehabilitation of people displaced from the site of a project is not a big problem.
   (*f*) Economic analysis of a project is also called as social cost benefits analysis.
10. The feasibility report consists of
    (*a*) Preliminary work studies (*b*) Analysis studies
    (*c*) Evaluation studies (*d*) All the above
11. Under analysis studies following studies are carried
    (*a*) Technical (*b*) Financial
    (*c*) Economical (*d*) Ecological
    (*e*) All the above
12. In technical analysis, works are done
    (*a*) Selection of suitable site (*b*) Selection of suitable equipments
    (*c*) Assessing resources availability (*d*) Drawing specifications of materials
    (*e*) All the above
13. Identify the correct statement/statements
    (*a*) New technology in the field of construction is quite expensive
    (*b*) New technology is high degree of automation
    (*c*) It needs highly trained personal and sophistical management
    (*d*) All the above

ANSWERS

1. (*d*)	5. (*d*)	9. (*c*), (*f*)	13. (*d*)
2. (*c*)	6. (*c*)	10. (*d*)	
3. (*e*)	7. (*d*)	11. (*e*)	
4. (*e*)	8. (*c*)	12. (*e*)	

3

Constructin Planning

3.1. INTRODUCTION

Planing is the most important constituent of the construction management. In the simplest sense planning is the mental process deciding about the future line of action. Thus deciding what to do, when to do and who will do and where, is known as planning. At the planning stage of a project, various alternative methods of execution of work are studied and the decisions taken not only about the work as a whole, but for each part of the work regarding the time of inception and time of completion, materials, labour, machines and equipment required and also arrangements to be made for the other requirements of the other construction facilities required from time to time. Thus planning is the course of action to achieve the desired results taking into consideration the present needs and future requirements. Planning also has to keep in mind the likely uncertaintities in the execution of work due to various unforeseen factors such as weather, price fluctuations, non availability of labour and difficulties in Procuring construction materials.

3.2. STEPS INVOLVED IN PLANNING

Following steps are involved in the effective planning:

1. Identifying the likely problems to be encountered in the execution of the work and obtaining necessary information useful in the execution of the work.
2. Ascertaining alternative feasibility of execution of work and selection of the optimum plan.
3. Fixing the time of starting the execution of work.
4. Deciding the time of delivering the materials at site.
5. Deciding the quantities and duration of various type of machines and equipment.
6. Deciding the number of different types of labourers for various works and duration of their employment.
7. Estimation of financial help if needed.
8. Estimation of the duration of completion of the work.
9. Evaluation of the effectiveness of plan adopted.

3.3. OBJECTIVES OF PLANNING

The main objectives of planning of a work is to execute the project or work most economically is terms of money and time both. The effective planning depends upon the following factors.

1. Proper design of each element of the project.
2. Proper selection of machinery and equipment for the execution of the project. In big projects the use of larger capacity plants has been found economical.
3. Proper arrangement of repair of machinery and equipment near the site of work to keep them ready for work.

4. Procurement of required materials well in advance.
5. To ensure employment of trained and experienced staff on the project.
6. To provide welfare schemes for the staff and workers such as medical and recreational facilities.
7. To provide incentives to good workers.
8. To arrange constant flow of funds for the completion of the project.
9. To provide proper safety measures such as proper ventilation, light and water drainage etc.
10. Proper arrangements for communication and feed back etc.

3.4. PRINCIPLES OF PLANNING

Followings are the general principles of planning:

1. The plan should be readily understandable. It should be in simple and lucid language. It should be able to convey the correct message, how ever complex the situation may be.
2. The plan should be realistic.
3. The plan should be flexible.
4. The plan should be comprehensive.
5. The plan should be such as it can be used as the basis for monitoring and controlling the project.

3.5. DIFFERENCE IN DIFFERENT TYPES OF PLANNING

The difference between different types of planning is due to the following two factors:

1. Mode of operation
2. Objectives

The plans may differ from one another when their objectives and mode of operations are different from each other. The technique of preparing a plan has no effect on it. Thus the difference between two plans can be judged by their objectives and mode of execution, but not on technique adopted to prepare them. For example the difference between the objectives of setting up a sugar factory and constructing a dam is quite obvious. Thus these two plans are quite different from each other.

3.6. STAGES OF PLANNING

Usually the stages of planning are as follows:

1. Pre planning.

(*a*) During this stage of planning objectives are clearly spelt out.
(*b*) A general frame work of the project is to be formulated.
(*c*) Justification for the construction of the project is to be laid down.
(*d*) A cost-benefit analysis is to be carried out.
(*e*) Cost analysis of all alternative sites is to be done.

Thus this stage of planning is before a decision finally is taken to undertake a project.

2. Detailed planning. The planning at this stage includes the following items:

(*a*) Preparation of detailed design.
(*b*) Preparation of detailed working drawings.
(*c*) Preparation of drawing specifications.
(*d*) Working out the quantities of materials.
(*e*) Breaking the project into different activities.
(*f*) Detailing the sequence of operation of various activities and allotting time duration to different activities.

3. Monitoring and control.

(*a*) In this phase, the progress of construction is monitored as per proposed scheduled.
(*b*) Updating the schedule according the actual progress of work.

(*c*) Preparing the revised forecasts regarding the availability of various resources.

3.7. TYPES OF PLANS

Usually following types of plans are prepared:

(*a*) **Standing plans.** These plans are used repeatedly and include procedures, rules and management's policies.

(*b*) **Single use plans.** These plans are designed to accomplish a specific objective with in a relatively short time *i.e.* these plans are single purpose plans as those of budgets and programmes for a specific project.

(*c*) **Strategic plan.** These plans are concerned with the broad matters, which may vitally affect the development of the organisation. In this phase, economic, technological and environmental factors are included. In this phase more emphasis is placed upon predicting the future behaviour of external variables and formation of alternative actions in the light of expected events.

(*d*) **Administrative plan.** This plan focuses more on the accomplishment of the objective of the project and is concerned with factors with in the control of the organisation. This plan is less subjective than strategic plan.

3.8. STAGES OF PLANNING BY DIFFERENT AGENCIES

3.8.1. Planning by the Owner

1. The owner of a project may be an individual or a group of individuals or central or state governments or their agencies. In case, the owner is an individual or a group of individuals, they appoint an engineer to investigate and plan the project for him or for them as the case may be.
2. After proper investigations, the engineer prepares approximate estimate and determines the quantum of money required for the completion of the work.
3. In case owner is government, then the detailed plans and estimates are prepared and approval of the competent authority is obtained.
4. After obtaining the approval, the tenders are invited to complete the work and an agreement is made between the government and the contractor.

3.8.2. Planning by the Contractor

The contractor has to plan at the following two stages:

1. Pre tender stage planning
2. Contract stage planning

1. Pre tender stage planning. The planning under taken by the contractor after the receipt of tender notice and before submitting the bid is known or called as *pre tender planning*. This planning enables the contractor to give reasonable and proper bid and prepares him to take up the work speedily with out loss of time if his bid is accepted. Planning at this stage involves the following steps.

(*a*) Careful study of tender documents and drawings to find out the quantities of each item of work, time limit and other conditions of work.

(*b*) To work out the quantities of materials required for different items.

(*c*) To determine the availability of required materials near the site of work. If not, from where they can be procured economically.

(*d*) To determine the availability of required labour, machinery and equipment and other facilities such as repair of machines, testing facilities and camp office etc.

(*e*) *Execution of work.* Examining the mode of execution of the work as manually or mechanically, so that the work can be completed most economically.

(*f*) To decide the amount of the bid and to submit the tender.

2. Contract planning. After the acceptance of the tender, the contractor further needs intensive planning. This stage of planning is known as *contract planning*. In this planning, the pretender stage planning work is fully utilised in working out the details so that work may proceed economically with out any delay and difficulty. Delay in execution of the work results in heavy loss of money and time. The beneficiaries are also deprived of benefits due from the project.

3.8.2.1. Steps in Tender Stage Planning

Contract stage planning involves the following steps:

(*a*) Studying the alternative methods of construction, considered at the pre tender stage to choose the most economical method and to decide about sub contracting.

(*b*) Working out the quantities of materials required at each stage of the work, locating sources of their supplies and their comparative cost from different sources and capacities of the suppliers.

(*c*) Working out the requirement of construction labour, supervisory and managerial staff at various stages of work and arranging their selection and recruitment.

(*d*) Working out the details of requirement of machinery and equipment at various stages of work and arranging for them.

(*e*) Arranging repair and maintenance of machinery and equipment and their servicing facilities.

(*f*) Planning for the location and other details of camp office, service roads, layout of site, temporary accommodation for labour and staff, facilities of drinking water etc.

(*g*) Planning and arranging for transport of labour to the site of work and back and other related matters.

(*h*) To study the interdependence of different items of work and to decide their proper sequence of operations.

(*i*) To finalise the work programme of each item of work and to decide the dates of their starting and completing.

To ensure the optimum utilisation of resources, a number of alternative methods and sequences of operations may be considered. The ultimate aim is to keep the cost of the work to a minimum and effect greatest economy. The final form of work should be put in the form of charts and diagrams, so that it may be easily understood by those responsible for its implementation and ensuring its progress.

The information in the final work programme should be clear and definite as the target dates of important activities such as the dates of placement of supply orders, delivery of materials, issue of working drawing, requirement of staff etc. The requirements of money, materials, machines and equipment at various stages of work should also be indicated, so that they may be arranged timely, with out loss of time and without affecting the progress of the work.

3.9. ADVANTAGES OF PLANNING TO THE CONTRACTOR

1. A properly drawn programme in construction with cost control can prevent the money loss and help to relieve the financial burden of the contractor.
2. The job studied in detail to draw up a net work or bar chart shows that the contractor knows about the job.
3. From the programme drawn earlier, labour requirement week by weak for each operation can be calculated easily.
4. From the programme various schedules can be prepared easily.
5. The programme provides a standard, by which actual work can be measured.
6. A programme provides a pre conceived plan for the whole job as well as for various stages of the work.

3.10. ADVANTAGES TO THE CLIENT

By the planning of the project, the client will know the exact time after which he will get the benefits, he expects from the construction of the project or work. He will also know the period for which his investment will remain unproductive.

3.11. ADVANTAGES TO THE ARCHITECT/ENGINEER

Generally the programme of construction is prepared by the contractor in close consultation with the architect. After preparing the programme of construction, the draft of programme and targets laid down for different operations should be put up before the architect/engineer for his approval. In this way architect/engineer will know the full picture of the progress of the project.

3.12. LIMITATIONS OF PLANNING

Usually following limitations are observed of the planning of a project:

1. Planning is expensive
2. Planning delays action
3. Planning develops a false sense of security
4. The effectiveness of plan depends upon the correctness of the assumptions.

3.13. CONSTRUCTION STAGES

At the time of preparing plans for big projects, they can be divided into several small stages or operations in order to get good progress of their completion. To achieve this aim several operations may be started simultaneously together or independently. The construction stages can be divided according to the type of project. Construction stages of few Civil Engineering works are shown below:

A. Stages of a highway project. In this case construction stages may be as follows:

1. Going to the site of construction.
2. Placing machines at the appropriate locations on the site of work.
3. Cleaning site of work or construction.
4. Earth work:
   (*a*) In cutting (*b*) In filling
5. Construction of drainage work such as culvert etc.
6. Procurement of road materials.
7. Construction of road and shoulders on both sides of the road.
8. Removing of remaining materials from the construction site.
9. Removing machinery and equipment from the construction site.

B. Water supply project. In this case there may be following stages:

1. Clearing of reservoir site.
2. Procurement of construction materials at site
3. Excavation of foundations of different works of the project:
4. Construction works:
   (*a*) Construction of dam (*b*) Construction of pumping station
   (*c*) Construction of tunnel
5. Laying of pipe line
6. Construction of filtre and sediment tank etc.

C. Construction of Cement Concrete retaining wall. In this case there may be following stages:

1. Excavation of foundations:
   (*a*) Machine or mechanical excavation
   (*b*) Manual excavation
2. Erection of form work
3. Preparation of reinforcement

4. Mixing of concrete
5. Pouring or placing of concrete in the form work
6. Filling of earth behind the retaining wall.

3.14. SHORT-TERM PLANNING

This type of planning is carried out at site in more detail and the work is divided into different sub heads. Usually short term planning is done for works which can be completed in about four to six weeks time. First planning for six weeks work is done and then four week work is planned. At the end of this four week period, further planning is done for the remaining work. In this system of short term planning, the workers are provided with weekly plan of work, so that the plan may be executed effectively.

3.15. DEGREE OF DETAILS TO BE GIVEN DURING SHORT TERM PLANNING

In order to execute the plan effectively, full details of any work or activity should be given in detail. The details of activities of the construction of retaining wall and a four storyed residential building are shown below:

A. Activities of retaining wall

1. Excavation work
   (*a*) Mechanically (*b*) Manually
2. Erection of form work
3. Preparing of reinforcement
4. Placing of reinforcement
5. Pouring of concrete
6. Filling earth behind the retaining wall.

B. Construction of building

1. Excavation of foundation:
   (*a*) Manually (*b*) Mechanically
2. Erection of form work for columns
3. Preparation of reinforcement
4. Placing reinforcement for columns
5. Construction of brick masonry
6. Pouring of concrete in columns
7. Placing form work for beam and columns
8. Placing reinforcement in beam and columns
9. Pouring concrete in beams and columns
10. Curing of concrete
11. Fixing door and windows
12. Plastering on both sides
13. Painting and varnishing
14. Cleaning of site etc.

QUESTIONS

1. What is meant by construction planning? What data should be collected under this head?
2. Enumerate the stages of planning.
3. What are the objectives of planning of a construction project? What informations are to be collected for this
4. Discuss the advantages of planning of a construction project.
5. Discuss the difference between pre tender and contract stage planning.
6. Enumerate the stages of planning by different agencies.

OBJECTIVE TYPE QUESTIONS

1. While planning a project which aspects should be kept in mind.
   (*a*) Design considerations
   (*b*) Man power considerations
   (*c*) Past, present and future aspects of the project
   (*d*) Financial considerations
2. In the execution of a project, the main objective of planning is
   (*a*) Completion of project most economically and well in time
   (*b*) Completion of the project safely and economically
   (*c*) Completion of project only economically
   (*d*) Completion of project only in time
3. Planning is important as it is advantageous to
   (*a*) Client (*b*) Architect and Engineer
   (*c*) Contractor (*d*) To all
4. In the execution of a project, the role of planning stages involved are
   (*a*) During construction (*b*) During design and commissioning
   (*c*) At tendering stage only (*d*) All of the above
5. In the planning process of a project the stages involved are
   (*a*) Pre planning (*b*) Detailed planning
   (*c*) Monitoring and control (*d*) All the above
6. The planning is to be done by
   (*a*) By the contractor only (*b*) By the owner only
   (*c*) By the architect only (*d*) By owner and contractor both
7. The difference between different types of planning depends upon
   (*a*) Objectives of the project (*b*) Climatic condition of the area
   (*c*) Mode of operation (*d*) Both of (*a*) and (*b*)
8. Identify the incorrect statement/statements
   (*a*) The plan of a project depends upon its objectives
   (*b*) The plan of a project depends upon its mode of operation
   (*c*) The technique of preparing a plan has a marked effect on it
   (*d*) The technique of preparing a plan has no effect on it.
9. The types of plans are
   (*a*) Standing plan (*b*) Strategic plan
   (*c*) Administrative plan (*d*) Single use plan
   (*e*) All the above
10. Identify the incorrect statement/statements
    (*a*) Standing plans are used for rules and policies of the management
    (*b*) Strategic plans are concerned with broad matters which vitally affect the development of the organization
    (*c*) Administrative plans focus more on the accomplishment of the objective of the project
    (*d*) Administrative plan is more subjective than strategic plan

ANSWERS

1. (*c*)	4. (*d*)	7. (*d*)	10. (*d*)
2. (*a*)	5. (*d*)	8. (*c*)	
3. (*d*)	6. (*d*)	9. (*e*)	

4

Construction Management

4.1. INTRODUCTION

Now a days construction activity has taken the shape of a industry of multiple activities. It is a well known fact that an single individual can not do all the activities, so he joined hands with other people to achieve his goal. The passage of time gave birth to the idea of organised management. Thus management is an organisation in which different class of people work together to produce qualitative and economical products with the available resources such as capital, material and equipment.

Infact management is a sort of administration, whose function is to plan, organise, control and coordinate the use of other resources to achieve the desired goal. Thus management is an art of arranging various activities and group of people to achieve the common goal. Therefore an executive must have a managerial skill.

4.2. NECESSITY OF CONSTRUCTION MANAGEMENT

Management is essential to have proper coordination between different agencies engaged on the work and to check the following activities.

1. To effect economy in the cost of construction by adopting the new techniques of construction and supervision.
2. To check the wastage of material and labour.
3. To arrange the completion of the work in the minimum possible time duration.
4. To improve the quality and speed of work by adopting modern equipment and machinery etc.
5. To have proper coordination between different agencies and categories of persons engaged in the work using modern techniques of management.

In short the aim of management is to effect maximum possible economy in the cost and time of construction of the project.

4.3. OBJECTIVES OF CIVIL ENGINEERING CONSTRUCTION MANAGEMENT

Followings are the objectives of construction management:

1. The work should be planned and organised properly.
2. The work should be completed with in the specified estimated cost and time.
3. The work should be properly supervised by qualified and trained staff.
4. The quality and workmanship of the work should be good.
5. The work should be executed as per specifications.
6. The work should be executed most economically.
7. There should be proper coordination and team spirit between different categories of workers, so that every worker may work efficiently to achieve the common goal.

4.4. FUNCTIONS OF MANAGEMENT

Following are the functions of management:

1. Planning
2. Organising
3. Staffing
4. Directing
5. Controlling
6. Coordinating
7. Communicating

4.4.1. Planning

The managerial function of planning is to answer the following quarries:

(*a*) What to do (*b*) When to do

(*c*) How to do

The answer of the above quarries is *known as planning*. The planer relies on sound judgement based on knowledge and experience. Thus planning is important as it provides:

1. It provides direction.
2. It provides unifying frame work
3. It provides performance standard
4. It reveals future opportunities and threats.

In planning of construction work, various alternative methods of executing the work are studied and decision is taken not only about the whole work, but for each component of it, regarding the time of inception and completion, materials, machines and equipment, labour and finances needed etc. and the arrangements to be made for the provision of construction facilities from time to time. Planning also takes care of the likely uncertainties to be encountered in the execution of the work due to various unpredictable factors such as weather, price fluctuations, difficulties in procurement of materials, non availability of labour due to festival and cropping season etc. The planer also has to take the decision, whether the work is to be done manually or mechanically. After deciding the mode of execution of work, he decides about the time of starting the work and arranges for required resources such as money, machines, labour and materials etc.

Strategies. An strategy specifies the central concept or purpose of the work or enterprise as well as the means by which it intend to carry that purpose. In short an strategy is an important type of plan.

4.4.1.2. Steps in project planning

Generally following steps are recognised in the planning of a project:

1. To define the objectives of the project in definite words.
2. To establish intermediate goals and stages to attain the final target.
3. To develop and forecast the means of achieving the goals.
4. To evaluate the organisation's resources as financial, managerial and operational to carryout the activities. Also to determine what is feasible and what is not.
5. To determine the alternative courses of action to accomplish the goals.
6. To test for the consistency with company's policy.
7. To choose an alternative which is not only consistent with its goals and concept but also one which can be accomplished with the evaluated resources.
8. To decide on a plan.

4.4.2. Organising

This function of a organisation relates to the creation of an organisational set up capable for the execution of the planned activity and defining the responsibility of each individual employed in the organisation. The type of organisation would depend upon the type and volume of work as well as on the method of execution.

A large contracting firm may have an elaborate organisation with tendering, planning, design, drafting, costing and procurement etc. stationed at the head quarter. The field work is assigned to the site engineers assisted by other staff. In small contracting firms, the engineer manages both office as well as the field work.

In government departments dealing with construction work, officers at different levels are assigned responsibilities of getting works executed with in their jurisdiction. They are assisted by subordinate staff members, whose duties and responsibilities are well defined. Each unit is responsible for the complete execution of work. Certain activities such as architectural work, design, estimates and procurement of stores may be centralised.

The organisational structure should as simple and balanced as far as possible. A man should have only one boss immediately above him and one officer should have five to seven subordinates under him directly responsible to him.

4.4.3. Staffing

In a construction organisation the selection of right persons for different jobs should be selected very carefully, so that work may be completed as per schedule. This function of management not only relates to the proper selection of staff in requisite number as laid down in the organisational structure, but also includes in service training not only to keep them upto date in their routine work, but they should be trained to handle fresh and complicated problems and to shoulder greater responsibilities.

4.4.4. Directing

This function of management involves motivation, guidance, supervision and leading the employees of the organisation. This function can be achieved by establishing the effective communication between the employees and the management to develop awareness of the planned programmes and means and methods to be employed to implement them.

The object of directing is to ensure that each employee knows, what exactly he is supposed to do and how and when to do it. In a construction organisation at every level, from top managers to the work mistries perform this function. In such organisations the employees are kept aware of the planned programme in the form of bar charts or net work diagrams, drawings, estimates, detailed specifications and other details of the work. The work is executed under the guidance and supervision of the senior staff members.

4.4.5. Controlling

This function of management relates to monitoring the progress achieved in comparison with planned programme and identifying the area of deficiency so that remedial measures may be taken to rectify the deficiency.

4.4.5.1. Aims of Controlling

In a construction work the aims of controlling are as follows:

(*a*) To check the quality of work, so that it is completed as per scheduled specifications.

(*b*) To monitor the physical progress of each activity so that the work may be completed as per time schedule.

(*c*) To keep control on the use of machines and material and labour output for each item of work to avoid wastage if any.

(*d*) To control the expenditure on each item of work to complete the work as per cost estimate.

4.4.5.2. Steps in Control Process

Controlling can be accomplished in the following steps:

1. To establish the standard targets in terms of time.

2. To measure performance against the standard as set above in step 1.
3. To identify the deviation from the targets.
4. To correct the measures.

4.4.6. Coordinating

This function of management relates to harmonising the approach and actions of various employees or groups of employees to achieve a common objective. In any organisation there is bound to be a difference of opinion about their sphere of work and targets set for them. In a construction organisation a large number of inter related and inter dependent activities are carried out simultaneously. In such cases it is essential that the actions of various groups involved do not cause hindrance in the progress of any activity. For example in a reinforced cement concrete work, it is essential that the mixing of cement concrete should not be started before the completion of placement of reinforcement in its place. Thus in a large construction work, there are many such interdependent activities which need careful coordination to achieve the specified goal.

4.5. CONSTRUCTION ECONOMY

The construction economy can be achieved at design and supervision level. It can be classified into two categories as follows:

A. At the level of designer/engineer
B. At the level of contractor

A. At the level of designer/engineer

A designer or engineer can effect economy on the following aspects:

1. **Repeated use of form work.** The design of the structure should be such that the same form work may be used repeatedly.
2. **Simple design.** The design of the structure should be as simple as possible.
3. **Minimum requirement of machines and equipment.** The design of the structure should be such that for its execution minimum machinery and equipment is required.
4. **Minimum labour requirement.** The design of the structure should be such that no special equipment is required for its execution and the requirement of labour also should be minimum.
5. **Use of local material.** As far as possible local materials should be used in the construction which will reduce the cost of the structure.
6. **Language of specifications.** Specifications to be given to the contractor should be written in simple language and should be complete, specifying the results expected from the contractor.
7. **Simple specifications.** Specifications should be such with which the contractor is familiar.
8. **Skilled supervision.** The supervision of the work should be carried by experienced supervisors who understand the problem of the project and can take decisions on the spot.

B. At the level of contractor

Contractor can control the cost on the following aspects. Before bidding, the contractor should study the following aspects well as they influence the cost of the project to a great extent.

1. Topography of the site.
2. Geology of the area of the site.
3. Climatic conditions of the site.
4. Sources of construction materials and their availability.
5. Access to the site.
6. Availability of labour.
7. Local services as power, fuel and water.
8. Housing facility for staff.

9. Storage facilities for the materials and equipment at the site.
10. Using alternate construction equipment having higher efficiency and capacity with low operating cost.
11. Employing trained and experienced staff.
12. Adopting safety measures at the site to reduce accidents.
13. Providing servicing and maintenance of equipment facilities near the site of work.
14. Providing telephone facility at site for communication between the head quarter office and key personel on the project.
15. Giving incentives to workers as bonus to accelerate the speed of work.
16. Holding periodic meetings of key personnels, contractors and engineers to discuss and solve any difficulty developed in the execution of the work.

4.6. SCIENTIFIC METHODS OF CONSTRUCTION MANAGEMENT

Scientific management is an approach to management where the methods and procedures adopted are not based on traditional thumb rules, but are carefully planned and analysed in advance. The aim of scientific management is to organise and execute the work, ensuring maximum productivity out of each worker.

The scientific management methods of industrial organisations are equally applicable to construction industry with advantage. The variableness and uncertainties are inherent in the very nature of the construction industry. Thus to carry out the systematic and economical construction work, scientific planning techniques are to be adopted in the construction work. In the construction industry generally following two methods are adopted which are known as *new work*.

1. Critical path method (CPM)
2. Programme Evaluation and Review Techniques (PERT)

These methods have been discussed in detail in subsequent chapters.

4.7. PRINCIPLES OF SCIENTIFIC MANAGEMENT

Following are the principles of scientific management.

1. Work study
2. Task planning
3. Selection and training of staff
4. Tools and materials
5. Management and workers relation.

1. **Work study.** Under this head a systematic and objective study of the factors which influence the operational efficiency of workers of handling an activity of the work is under taken to determine the best method to execute a job and to find out the standard time in which the job can be completed.
2. **Task planning.** After ascertaining the productivity of each worker, the task is planned in such a way that there should be no snags in the job and it is executed systematically. The job may be planned using PERT or CPM technique discussed subsequently fully in chapter 7 and 8.
3. **Selection and training of the staff.** Scientific management requires that the workers be selected keeping in view the skill training and experience required for the job. Workers must be placed on work depending upon their aptitude, suitability and personal liking. They should be provided training in the latest techniques and methods related to their jobs to update their knowledge and skill. It will not only help the worker, but the productivity will also increase.
4. **Tools and materials.** Adequate materials and tools must be provided to the workers, so that work may not suffer due to the shortage either of the two.
5. **Management and workers relation.** The relations between the management and workers should be cordial. If their relations are not cordial, even the best planned job may be ruined. To have

cordial relations it is essential that the attitude of both management as well workers should be positive. This aspect is further discussed in detail in chapter on organisation.

4.8. ROLE OF CONSTRUCTION MANAGEMENT

Till the recent past, all the Civil Engineering projects were labour intensive. In those days management laid emphasis on the proper utilisation of labour force to get optimum progress in the construction in the most economical manner. But now a days due to the technological advancement in all spheres through out the world, new dimensions have been added to the construction industry also. Now a project is considered as a group of activities having inter dependence. The work may be executed in the most systematic manner utilising the services of specialists for specilised work and using the latest knowledge and skill available. In the absence of using latest techniques and skill, the progress of the work may be hampered. The ''most systematic manner'' involves the adoption of new techniques to control the activities with in time at a specified cost. As stated above the techniques adopted to control activities are CPM and PERT.

Further the use of latest machinery and equipment in the construction industry has improved the quality of construction and reduced the time of construction. With the use of equipment and machinery the construction has become easier, of high quality and can be completed well with in time schedule. The use of computer for finding out the solution of complex problems of the structure further has made the process easy.

QUESTIONS

1. Define construction management and also discuss its necessity.
2. What are the objectives of construction management?
3. Discuss the functions of Construction management.
4. Discuss the Construction economy fully.
5. Explain the principles of scientific management.

OBJECTIVE TYPE QUESTIONS

1. The management is essential for
   (*a*) To check the wastage of labour and material
   (*b*) To effect economy in the cost of construction
   (*c*) To improve the quality and speed of work
   (*d*) To complete the work with in minimum time
   (*e*) All the above
2. The objectives of construction management are
   (*a*) To organise and plan the work properly
   (*b*) To execute the work as per specifications
   (*c*) To ensure the quality and workmanship of the work
   (*d*) To execute the work most economically
   (*e*) All the above
   (*f*) Non of the above
3. The functions of the management are
   (*a*) Planning (*b*) Organising
   (*c*) Directing (*d*) Controlling
   (*e*) All the above
4. The principles of scientific management are
   (*a*) Work study (*b*) Task planning
   (*c*) Management and workers relations (*d*) Selection and training of staff
   (*e*) All the above
5. Identify the incorrect statement/statements
   (*a*) Geology of site of work does not influence the cost of construction

(*b*) Climatic conditions influence the cost of construction to a great extent
(*c*) Availability of construction materials near the site reduces the cost of the project substantially
(*d*) Local services, power, and water have no influence on the cost of construction
(*e*) Topography of the site affects the cost of the project substantially.

6. Identify the correct statement/statements
(*a*) The repeated use of form work on a project has no influence on the cost of the construction.
(*b*) The use of local materials has no influence on the economy of the project
(*c*) The construction work can be supervised by any worker
(*d*) Proper and easy access to the project site influence the cost of the project
(*e*) Adopting safety measures at the site of work is not essential
(*f*) To effect economy the design of structure should be as simple as possible.

7. Management is necessary for
(*a*) To effect economy in the cost of construction
(*b*) To improve quality and speed of work
(*c*) To check wastage of material and labour
(*d*) To develop proper coordination between different agencies etc.
(*e*) All the above

8. Planning provides
(*a*) Direction (*b*) Unifying frame work
(*c*) Performance standards (*d*) Future opportunities
(*e*) All the above

9. The aims of controlling are
(*a*) To check the quality of work (*b*) To monitor the physical progress of each activity
(*c*) to keep control on the use of machines (*d*) To control the expenditure
(*e*) All the above

10. Identify the correct statement/statements
(*a*) Language of specifications have no effect on construction economy
(*b*) Topography, climatic conditions and geology of site have no effect on the cost of the project
(*c*) Holding of periodic meetings of management and workers does not enhance the progress of work
(*d*) Use of scientific methods on construction have no effect on the cost of the project
(*e*) All are correct
(*f*) None of the above is correct

ANSWERS

1. (*e*)	4. (*e*)	7. (*e*)	10. (*f*)
2. (*e*)	5. (*a*), (*d*)	8. (*e*)	
3. (*e*)	6. (*d*), (*f*)	9. (*e*)	

5
Scheduling

5.1. INTRODUCTION

All construction works consist of a sequence of different activities, which usually start with the preparation and setting out of the sites. After site preparation, foundation, sub structure, super structure fittings, finishing and a number of other activities are taken up. Most probably the last activity is demolishing the temporary structures, removing the construction machinery and clearing up the site. The number of activities increases with the progress of work and decreases as the work reaches completion stage. The sequence of activities depends upon the method of construction adopted. Some of the activities may be of critical nature and if the scheduled of programme is not adhered, then the construction programme may be seriously disrupted and delayed. Thus to have control over the work, different techniques are adopted. For the construction of a small building the general sequence of activities are as follows:

1. Earth work in excavation
2. Lime concrete and brick work in foundation
3. Damp proof course
4. Precasting of R.C.C. lintels
5. Casting of R.C.C. columns
6. Preparation of chowkhats
7. Brick work in super structure
8. Earth work in filling
9. Sanitary work
10. R.C.C. roof slab
11. Preparation of door panels
12. Glazed windows
13. Preparation and fixing window grils
14. Lime concrete in roof etc.
15. Plastering
16. Flooring
17. Electric work
18. Sanitary work
19. Colour and white washing
20. Painting of doors and windows
21. Sanitary and electric fittings
22. Cleaning up the site etc.

5.2. SCHEDULING

A construction schedule is a graphic representation which shows the phasing rate of construction with the starting and completing dates of each activity and the sequential relationship among various operations in a construction project.

In other words, scheduling can also be defined as the mechanical process for setting various planned activities in order by fixing the starting and finishing dates for each activity of the work to execute the whole work in a systematic and orderly manner.

Thus a schedule is a time table for the execution of a project assigning definite timings for individual constructional activities leading to the completion of the work.

5.3. USE OF SCHEDULING

Following are the use of scheduling:

1. The quantity of work involved, labour, material, equipment and money required at each stage of work can be determined by scheduling.
2. The actual progress of the work can be checked from time to time by scheduling.
3. The project can be carried out in a systematic manner by the use of scheduling.

5.4. ADVANTAGES OF SCHEDULING

For any important construction work the planning and scheduling is indispensable. Following are the advantages of scheduling:

1. By studying the schedule of the work, alternative methods of execution can be examined and the most economical method can be selected. Further the effect of likely constraints can be evaluated at the planning stage only.
2. It gives clear picture of quantity and type of materials, man power and equipment required at different stages of execution of work and duration of supply of material.
3. As the time of starting of each activity is known, the arrangement of adequate resources as man power, material, money and equipment etc. can be done in advance.
4. The resource utilisation can be optimised and the available resources can be directed to various activities to the best advantage.
5. The actual progress of each activity can be monitored with reference to the planned programme. If there is any delay in any activity the remedial measures can be taken to speed it up before it can cause difficulty in the other related activities.
6. As the inter relationship of various activities at different stages is known, their priorities can be fixed properly to the best advantage.
7. The effect of any change such as modification in original plan or weather conditions can be properly evaluated and the programme of construction can be suitably amended.
8. Total time of completion of the work can be known from scheduling.
9. The last but the most important advantage of scheduling is that the work may be executed in a most efficient way with out wastage of time and any input, resulting in maximum possible economy.

5.5. PREPARATION OF CONSTRUCTION SCHEDULES

The procedure of preparing construction schedule is as follows:

1. The work or project is divided into a number of operations and their inter dependence or relationship is studied. After the carefull study of their interdependence the sequence of operation is decided.
2. The quantity of work involved in each operation is to be determined.
3. The time required for the completion of each operation as well as the completion of total project is determined. This can be done by knowing the quantum of work involved and the rate of performing each activity.

5.6. CLASSIFICATION OF SCHEDULING

Schedules can be classified into groups according to the requirement for which it is required as follows:

1. Construction schedule
2. Materials schedule
3. Labour schedule
4. Equipment schedule
5. Financial schedule
6. Control schedule
7. Organisational schedule
8. Summary schedule

5.6.1. Construction Schedule

It is a roaster prepared for the construction of different activities or items of work for the completion of a certain project. Before preparing the construction schedule following informations must be known.

1. Various operations to be done in a particular project.
2. Quantum of work to be done in each operation.
3. Unit of measurement.
4. Rate of progress or rate of completing the work with due allowance for weather conditions.
5. Number of labourer required (both skilled and unskilled).
6. Number and type of machines and equipment required.
7. Date of starting the work.
8. Date of completing the work.
9. Correlation between different operations.

On the top of each schedule following information should be clearly written on the left hand side:

(*a*) Name of the project
(*b*) Name of the Owner/Contractor/Engineer
(*c*) Location of the project

Use of Construction Schedule. Same as advantages of the scheduling.

Example 5.1. *Prepare a construction schedule for the construction of a road project with the following data:*

(*a*) Length of the road = 1200 km
(*b*) Width of the road = 30 m
(*c*) Construction of culverts = 12 Nos.
(*d*) Earth work for filling = 15×10^4 m^3
(*e*) Area of 8 m wide and 0.25 cm thick road surface is 12.5×10^4 m^2
(*f*) For the above road project an area of 65 hectare is to be cleared.

Note. In the execution of the above project only tentative values of different quantities have been assumed. For the execution of the project, following works will be done.

1. Moving on the site. Under this head following works are to be done:

(*a*) Erection of silos for stroing aggregate at site.
(*b*) Erecting silos for storing cement at site.
(*c*) Arrangements for storing equipment and machines.
(*d*) Arrangement for suitable office work.
(*e*) Arrangement for establishing testing labouratory.
(*f*) Servicing arrangements of equipment and machines near the site of work.
(*g*) Arrangements for other miscellaneous works etc.

Let time required for above actives be one weak.

2. Clearing and grubbing the site. Let buldozers employed for this task, complete the work in 8 weeks.

3. Construction of drainage work. Let 12 weeks are required to complete 12 culverts on the road site.

4. Earth filling. Let earth filling can be completed in 27 weeks.

5. Concreting the rod. Let 15 weeks are required for concreting work.

6. Clearing the site. After the completion of the project, let two weeks are require to move the equipment and machines from the site.

The construction schedule of this work is shown in Fig. 5.1.

5.6.2. Equipment use schedule

To decide the type, number and dates on which a particular equipment will be needed, equipment use schedule has to be prepared before the start of the project, so that it is arranged well in advance and brought

Job No. ______________ Year ______________

Project ______________ Date ______________

Owner ______________

Location ______________

ESTIMATED PROGRESS

ACTUAL PROGRESS

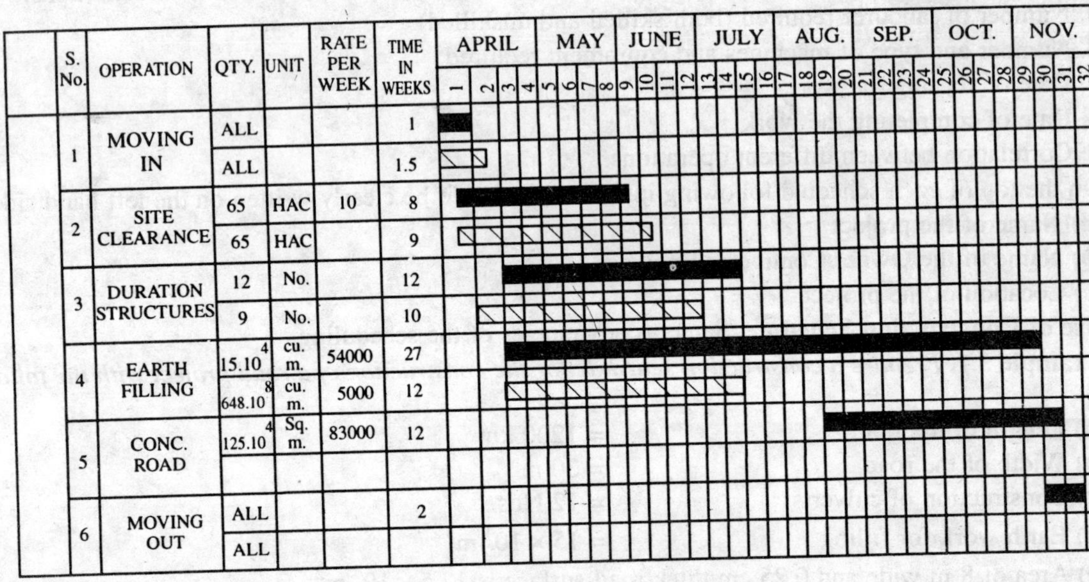

Fig. 5.1. Construction Schedule

(Equipment use report)

JOB NO. ______________.

PROJECT ______________.

OWNER ______________.

LOCATION ______________.

DATE OF CLOSING WEEK______________.

YEAR ______________.

WORKING

IDLE

UNDER REPAIR

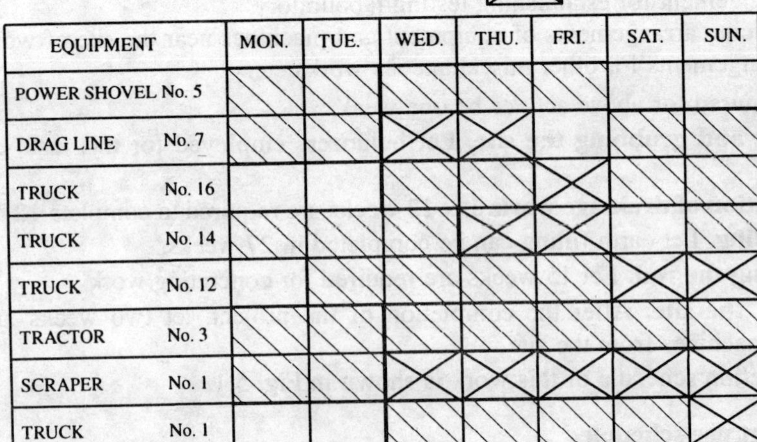

Fig. 5.2. Equipment use Schedule

at site as and when needed. The aim of this schedule is to derive maximum advantage of the equipment when at site and remove it from the site when its job is over. This will save money. Fig. 5.2.

5.6.3. Labour schedule

The aim of this schedule is to decide the number of skilled and unskilled labour required for the execution of different operations on different dates. With the help of this schedule required labour can be arranged well in time. It is difficult and costly to arrange skilled labour as and when required. It helps in reducing the labour cost. A labour schedule can be prepared from the construction schedule.

5.6.4. Material schedule

This schedule should be prepared well in advance of the start of the work. This schedule may be prepared from the construction schedule. To avoid delay in the execution of the work, all construction materials should reach the site of work well in advance, at least before the start of the work. In case materials stored at site long before its use, it is likely to deteriorate in its quality. For example cement will lose its strength by 50% if stored for six months. Thus at the time of preparing material schedule following points must be kept in mind.

1. The materials should be delivered at site at least one week earlier than its use.
2. Materials at site should not remain un used for long. If they allowed to remain unused for long they will detoriate.

5.6.5. Financial schedule

The estimated amount of money which the owner or contractor has to provide to finance the project can be obtained from construction schedule. In most of the cases of construction contracts, it is specified that the owner will pay about 90% cost of the completed work during each month for each job to the contractor.

5.6.6. Control schedule

At the end of a fixed date the incharge of the project has to send the progress report of the project to the head quarter. In order to complete the project with in specified time limits, the chief executive plans to provide resources as equipment, machines and money etc.

5.6.7. Equipment use schedule

After the purchase of the equipment for a particular project, the owner gets a mark punched or painted on the equipment or machine to identify it from others. The owner should have full knowledge of the equipment purchased by him. Usually following information is sent to the owner.

1. Cost of the equipment
2. Efficiency of each equipment or machine
3. Record of their repair
4. Details of expenditure on repair
5. Duration of effective use of the equipment.
6. Details of fuel consumption by the equipment.
7. Details of servicing of the equipment.

With the above information, the efficiency and working capacity of the equipment can be compared with the figures supplied by its manufacturers. This schedule is useful at the time of purchase new equipment. The specimen of a equipment use schedule is shown in Fig. 5.2.

5.7. PROJECT CONTROL

During the construction stage every project needs proper supervision and control. The details of supervision vary depending upon the type of the project. The supervision of small projects. comparatively is simpler and easy, but for the big and complex projects such as the construction of a dam is difficult. Hence different officers are made responsible for its construction and supervision. Their areas of work also have to be decided.

Due to the fixation of boundaries of the field work of different officers, developing of difference of opinion and groupism between them is natural. Thus control of such tendencies is of paramount importance. If such tendencies allowed to grow, the progress of work will decline. To mitigate this problem, periodic meetings of different officials is essential, so that they can discuss their problems and a way out may be found out. A specimen of construction organisation is shown below:

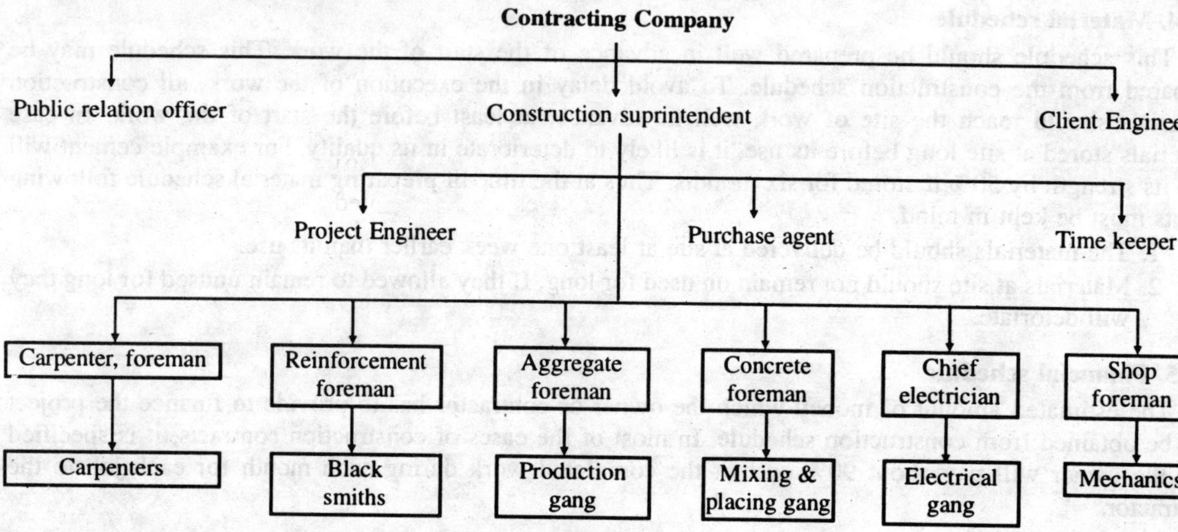

Fig. 5.3.

5.8. CONSTRUCTION COST CONTROL

In every field, cost is an important factor. Thus cost control should be carried out through out construction duration of any project. Planning and supervision are primarily aimed at achieving the maximum economy in the cost of construction.

In a project, a contractor may suffer loss due to the following reasons:

1. By offering low bid.
2. Due to Insufficient knowledge of job conditions.
3. Due to the increase in the cost of the materials.
4. Due to the increase in the wages of labour.
5. Due to bad weather
6. Due to faulty selection of construction equipment.
7. Due to poor supervision of the work.

Thus to have cost control, it is essential to keep the following records:

1. Cost Control record. Under this head following records are kept:

(*a*) Quantity of materials purchased and their source of purchase.
(*b*) Mode and amount of payment.

2. Details of labour engaged. Under this head following record is kept:

(*a*) Number of labourer engaged on a particular job.
(*b*) Category of labourer engaged in each operation as skilled or unskilled etc.
(*c*) Daily wages of each category of labour.
(*d*) Total number of each category of labourer employed.

(e) Total amount of money paid to each category of labour.
(f) Total period for which different category of labour engaged on each job.
(g) Details of payment made every week.
(h) Number of labour employed on each operation and money paid to them.

5.9. METHODS OF SCHEDULING

Scheduling can be done by different methods depending on the size of the project. Usually following methods are employed:

1. Bar charts or Gantt charts
2. Milestone charts
3. Net work analysis.

5.9.1. Bar charts

Bar chart is an graphical representation of completion of various activities of a project. This technique of representation of activities was introduced by HENRY GANTT around 1919.

A bar chart consists of two coordinate axis. The activities are represented on y-axis and time required to complete the activity is represented on x-axis. Each bar represents one specific activity of the project. The beginning and end of each bar represents the time of start and time of finish of that activity. The length of the bar shows the time required to complete that activity. The degree of details of the activities and scale of time depends upon the intended use of the chart.

5.9.1.1. Symbols used in bar charts

In a bar chart usually following symbols are used:

1. The planned programme is shown by a thick line.
2. The actual progress of work obtained is shown by a heteched line.
3. The planned start and finish are shown by small vertical lines.
4. Float represents flexibility range with in which the start and finish times of a activity can fluctuate without affecting the total duration of the project. In bar charts it is represented by doted horizontal line.
5. The dependency of one activity on an other activity is shown by vertical doted line. These symbols are shown in Fig. 5.4.

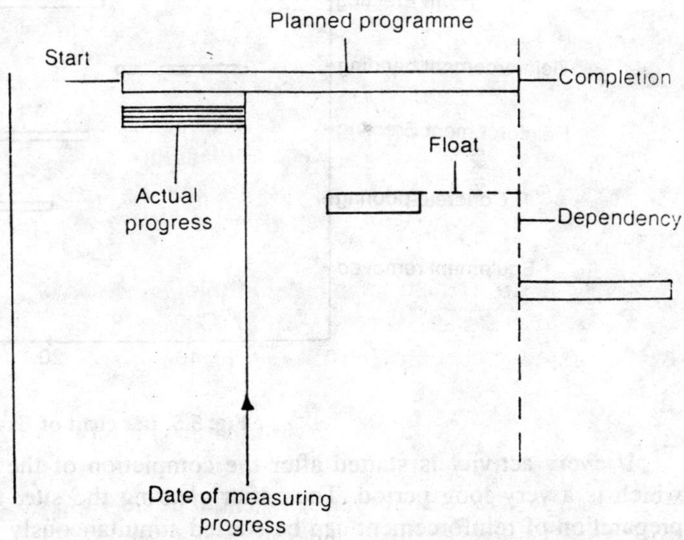

Fig. 5.4. Symbols used in Bar chart

5.9.1.2. Steps in preparing a bar chart

In preparing a bar chart following steps are involved.

1. Divide the project into different activities as far as possible.
2. List out the activities.
3. Determine the inter relationship amongst these activities.
4. Arrange the activities in a systematic way.
5. Determine the quantum or quantity of work and the time required to complete it.
6. Draw the bar chart on a suitable scale.

In all projects some activities may be started simultaneously, while others can only be started after completing the previous activities. The activities which can be started simultaneously are shown starting from the same point and running parallel to the other activities, while activities which can only be started after the completion of the previous activity, can start from the end point of the previous activity. The method of preparing a bar chart is shown from the following example.

Example 5.2. *For constructing a R.C.C. retaining wall, time taken in completing the different activities is estimated as follows. Prepare its bar chart and find out the most economical duration of the project.*

Item of work	*Time required in weeks*
1. Clearing of site	5
2. Excavation of foundations	20
3. Erection of form work	15
4. Reinforcement preparation	10
5. Reinforcement erection in position	5
6. Pouring of concrete and finishing	12
7. Removing equipment and clearing the site	6

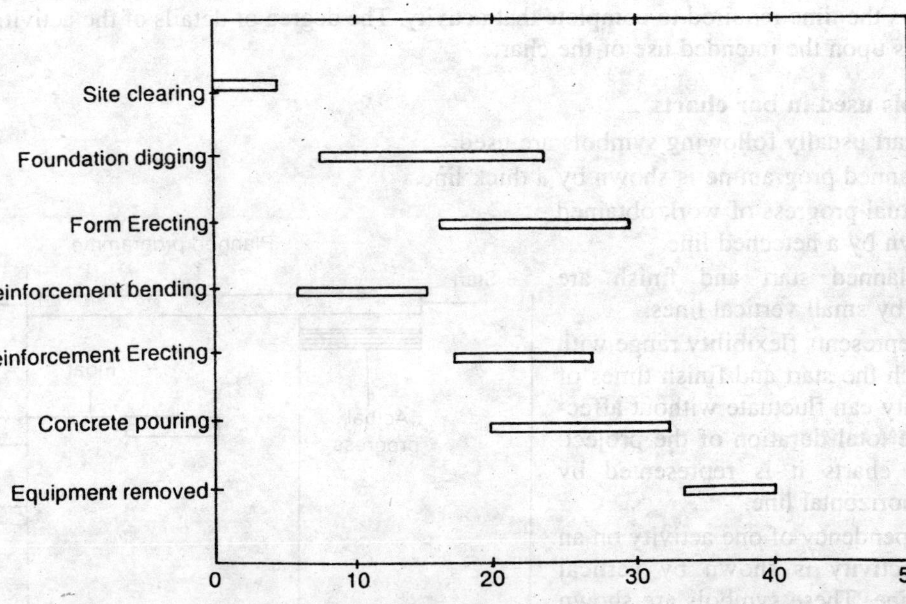

Fig. 5.5. Bar chart of Example 5.2

If every activity is started after the completion of the previous activity, it will take 73 weeks time, which is a very long period. Thus after clearing the site, the activities of excavation of foundation and preparation of reinforcement can be started simultaneously as they have no inter dependence relation. Thus they can be started independent of each other. After half excavation of foundation, putting form work in position may be started. The placement of reinforcement be started after the start of the work. Let placing of reinforcement may be started after 3 weeks of the start of foundation and pouring concrete after placing of reinforcement. The bar chart of this project is shown in Fig. 5.5.

Example 5.3. *For the construction of a residential building, the activities are performed as shown in given table.*

Activity	*Duration in weeks*
A	3
B	4
C	6
D	5
E	3
F	4
G	6

After the completion of activity A, the activities B and C can be performed simultaneously. Activity D can start only after the completion of activity B. Activity E can start after the completion of activities B and C. Activity F can start after completion of activities D and E. The last activity G can start only after the completion of activity C only.

Prepare the bar chart of the above construction and find out the total time taken for the completion of the project.

Solution. The bar chart of the construction is shown in Fig. 5.6.

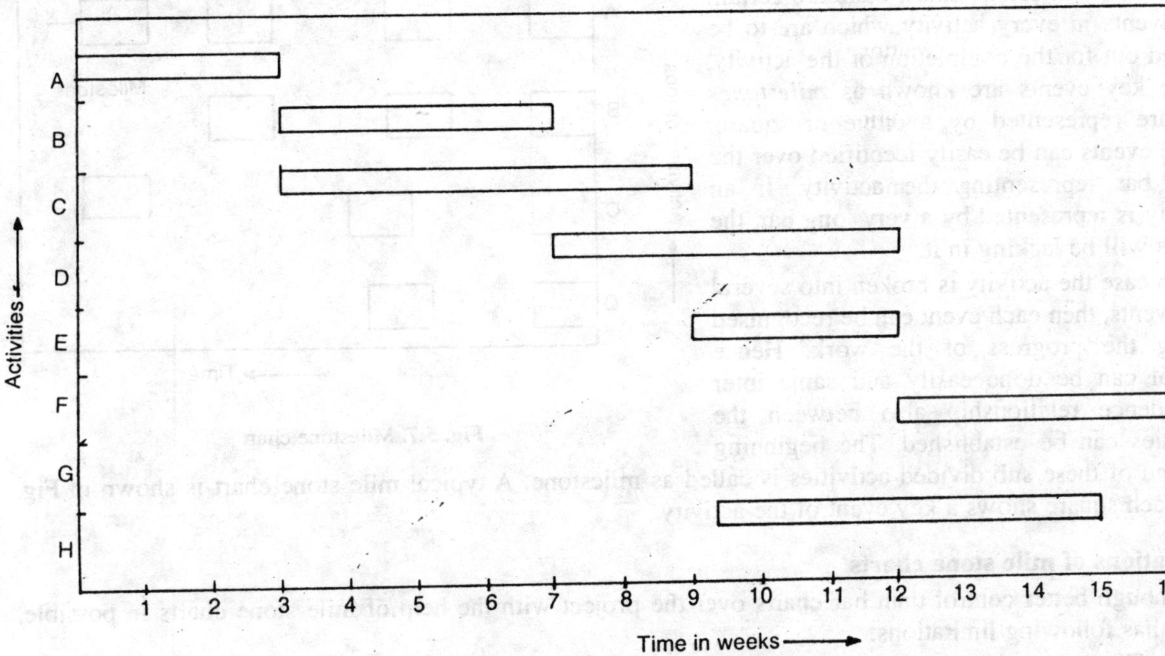

Fig. 5.6. Bar chart of Example 5.3

(*ii*) The total time of construction is 16 weeks.

5.9.1.3. Limitations of bar charts

Though bar chart is simple to construct and understand and widely used for scheduling, yet it has a number of limitations as follows:

1. It can be used only for small projects.
2. It is difficult to depict or show complicated interdepencies of various activities of the project. This is a serious limitation of the bar chart.
3. Bar chart does not indicate the actual progress of the work as it only represents the time which has elapsed. Thus the progress of work can not be monitored scientifically.
4. From bar chart, it is not possible to know the maximum or peak progress necessary for its completion. It gives the impression that the rate of progress of any activity is uniform.
5. Delays in the work are not detected till the allotted time is over and work remains incomplete.
6. It does not indicate the critical activities of the project.
7. It gives some idea of the physical progress of the project only and the financial aspects involved are not known whether the cost of the project is within the estimated cost or it has escalated.
8. In case of variation from the planned programme it is difficult to find out the alternative course of action to be adopted to complete the work in time.

9. Bar chart is only a static representation of the planned programme. It does not indicate the dynamic happenings on the construction site of a complex project.
10. The feed back obtained from a bar chart is only approximate.
11. The sequence of operations under one activity is not clearly known as various functions under each activity are shown by one bar chart only. Hence no effective control over the project is possible.

5.10. MILESTONE CHARTS

It is an modification of the original bar chart. In the milestone chart, there are certain key events in every activity which are to be carried out for the completion of the activity. These key events are known as *milestones* and are represented by a circle or square. These events can be easily identified over the main bar representing the activity. If an activity is represented by a very long bar, the details will be lacking in it.

In case the activity is broken into several key events, then each event can be recognised during the progress of the work. Hence control can be done easily and same inter dependence relationship also between the activities can be established. The beginning and end of these sub divided activities is called as milestone. A typical mile stone chart is shown in Fig. 5.7. Each square shows a key event of the activity.

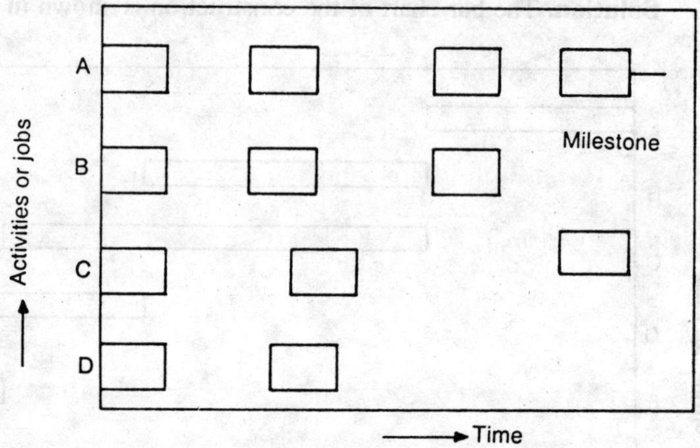

Fig. 5.7. Milestone chart

Limitations of mile stone charts

Though better control than bar charts over the project with the help of mile stone charts in possible, still it has following limitations:

1. The interdependencies between the mile stones is not possible.
2. The relationship between two specific mile stones with in an activity only is revealed by the mile-stone chart, but the relationship between milestones contained in different activities is not indicated.

5.11. DEVELOPMENT OF NETWORK

To over come the deficiency of milestone chart, network system was introduced. The main deficiency of mile stone chart was its inability to depict the interrelationship of two mile stones. This deficiency has been removed effectively by the use of PERT net work. In the PERT net work, the mile stone to mile stone chart can be considered as event along the main task as the PERT net work is always event oriented.

In the development of PERT network, the mile stones of each bar or task have been joined serially by arrows and the mile stones of other tasks are also joined by arrows which have inter relationship with each other.

5.11.1. Advantages of the net work developed

Following advantages of the net work developed have been noted:

1. The net work developed shows clearly the interrelationship between the mile stones or events.
2. In the case of developed net work, the designation of tasks has become redundant and the project is viewed as a single unit, consisting of a number of events (mile stones) and not a number of tasks. This helps in controlling the project to a great extent.
3. Net work can be used even for highly complicated projects consisting of large number of activities.

4. It directly indicates the time required in between the two mile stones or activities. This is useful for rescheduling if need aries.
5. In uncertain situations, net work diagram allows the use of probability theory for time estimation. The use of net works has been discussed in subsequent chapters fully.

5.12. LINE OF BALANCE (L.O.B.) TECHNIQUE

Actually it is a planning techniques for repetitive works. In this technique the required resources for each stage or operation are determined so that subsequent operations of the activities are not disturbed and the target output achieved. This technique can be applied to construction projects involving repetitive activities such as construction of tunnels, multi stories buildings and housing colonies etc.

In repetitive type activities of construction, the cost and time efficiencies can be achieved by adopting standard designs for different units of the project. It can be achieved by constraining resources and balancing the crews with each other. By such planning the continuity in the placement of repetitive units, maximising the productivity of equipment and labour can be achieved. This technique can be used for selecting, assembling and interpreting the essential factors involved in the construction from the initial stage to the completion stage in the graphical form against time. This technique has been found highly effective in determining the areas of weakness and attending the items requiring immediate attention.

5.13. CONSTRUCTION OF LINE OF BALANCE

The term line of balance is used in the context of construction which involve repetitive activities such as building works and utilities, housing projects etc. which can be built at such a rate that they support and balance each others requirement and also meet the agreed rate of completion of the project.

For the use of line of balance in any construction project some stages are to be identified in the whole sequence of operations, scheduling and monitoring process such that the whole project progresses at these stages as per plan. This technique may use these stages as milestones for the balancing requirements of other milestones and the project as a whole. In case of a mass construction project the volume of work to be completed at important stages to meet the agreed progress can be judged or determined by the use of LOB. By the use of LOB following two things can be achieved:

1. At each important stage, work will be completed as per requirement. This will ensure proper utilisation of resources at the required time only.
2. The work can be completed as per commitment.
3. LOB also allows some buffer time between any two stages.

5.14. SCHEDULING USING LINE OF BALANCE (LOB)

For preparing a schedule with the help of LOB, following procedure may be adopted:

1. First prepare a logical diagram of the work.
2. Determine or estimate the minimum duration (man hour) required to complete each operation.
3. To avoid interference between two operations, choose suitable buffer time.
4. To meet the project completing schedule, calculate the required targeted out put.
5. Complete the LOB schedule.
6. Study the schedule and assess the possible alternatives to get the best balanced schedule.

The basic approach is to determine the available resources and calculate the rate of construction that can be achieved.

Example 5. *Prepare the schedule of staff quarters project where seven units of dwellings are to be constructed.*

Solution. First a bar chart for the construction of a single unit showing various activities is drawn. The work of each gang is balanced in such a way that continuity in the work of each gang is maintained. This bar chart of logic diagram is shown in Fig. 5.8.

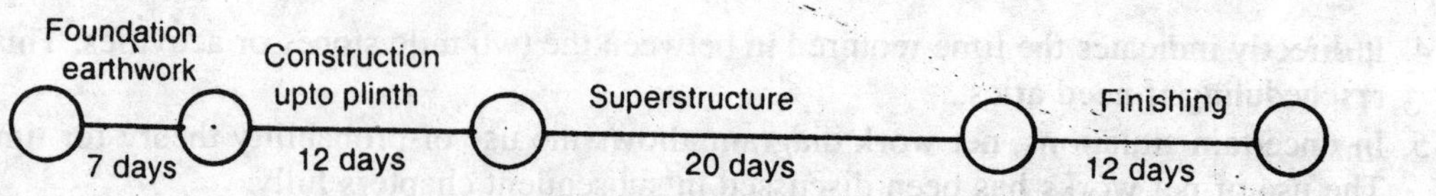

Fig. 5.8. Logic diagram

A buffer or margin in the completion time of each activity should be provided to take care of any error in determining the completion time of different activities. For simplicity let us keep a buffer time of 3 days in the completion of each activity. Now prepare the logic diagram with buffer for one unit of construction as shown in Fig. 5.9.

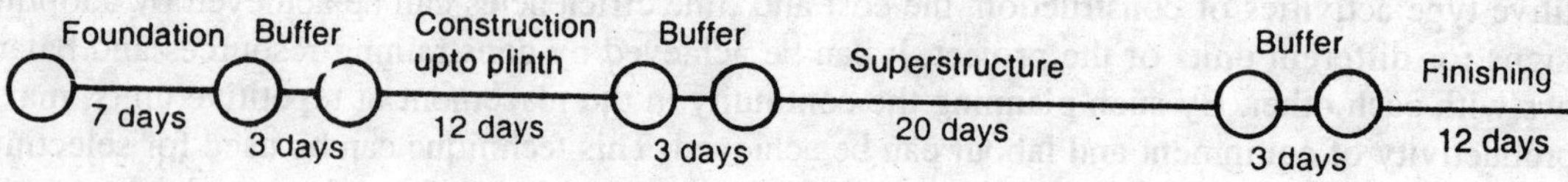

Fig. 5.9. Logic diagram (Bar chart) with buffers

From the logic diagram with buffers shows that a total time of 60 days is required to complete one sequence of activities for a building. The target out put of the project can be expressed in terms of completion of one building. This rate is expressed diagramatically in Fig. 5.10. In the diagram the progress of the work is plotted on *y*-axis and the passage of time on *x*-axis.

Now the hand over dates are drawn for each of the seven units. The first one will be handed over on the 60th day, the second on 67th, 3rd an 74th and so on *i.e.* one unit is to be handed over every week.

The logic diagrams with buffers are drawn for the construction of each of the seven units to match the hand over schedule as shown in Fig. 5.10. The starting and finishing points of each activity such as earth work, foundation structure, super structure and finishing etc. of all units are joined by sloping lines. These lines form series of bands, which are the *line of balance schedules* for each gang. Here all the sloping lines are parallel to the hand over line. Each activity is proceeding at the same rate as the hand over schedule.

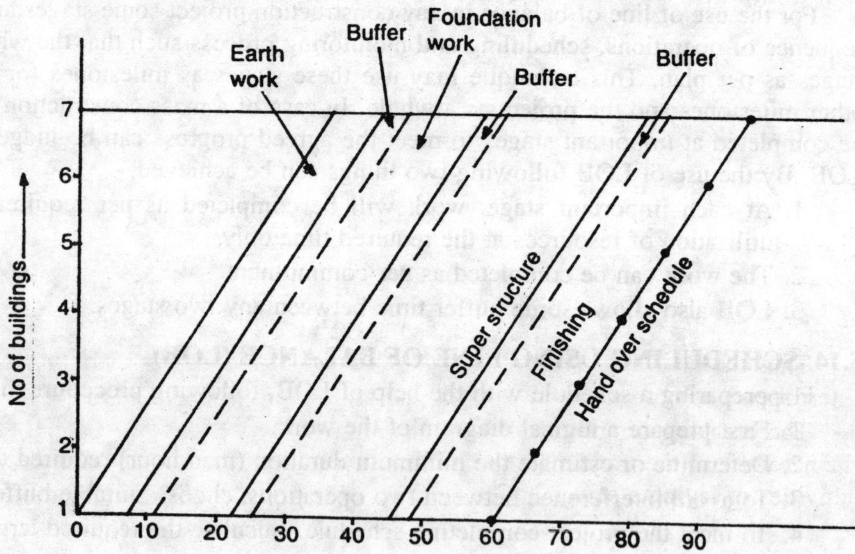

Fig. 5.10. Logic diagram

To provide a margin for error and to ensure that one gang does not interfere with an other an buffer of 3 days has been provided for each activity.

5.14.1. Advantages of line of balance technique

1. The Combination of the principles of line of balance and the logic of net work analysis gives a very detailed picture of any repetitive work.
2. As in the line of balance technique only one net work is used for each type of unit, hence it reduces

the labour of net work planning and scheduling.

3. This technique provides an effective and simple tool for programming for procuring construction materials and subsequently their use in the construction.
4. The activities lagging behind schedule can be identified easily by proper monitoring the work and corrective measures can be taken at the earliest.

5.16. WORK BREAK STRUCTURE

The process of breaking a major project into its major and sub systems and discrete activities which can be identified easily is called *work break system.* First of all the major project is identified in terms of its end activities or items and then it is split into various systems, sub systems, components and element as shown in Fig. 5.11.

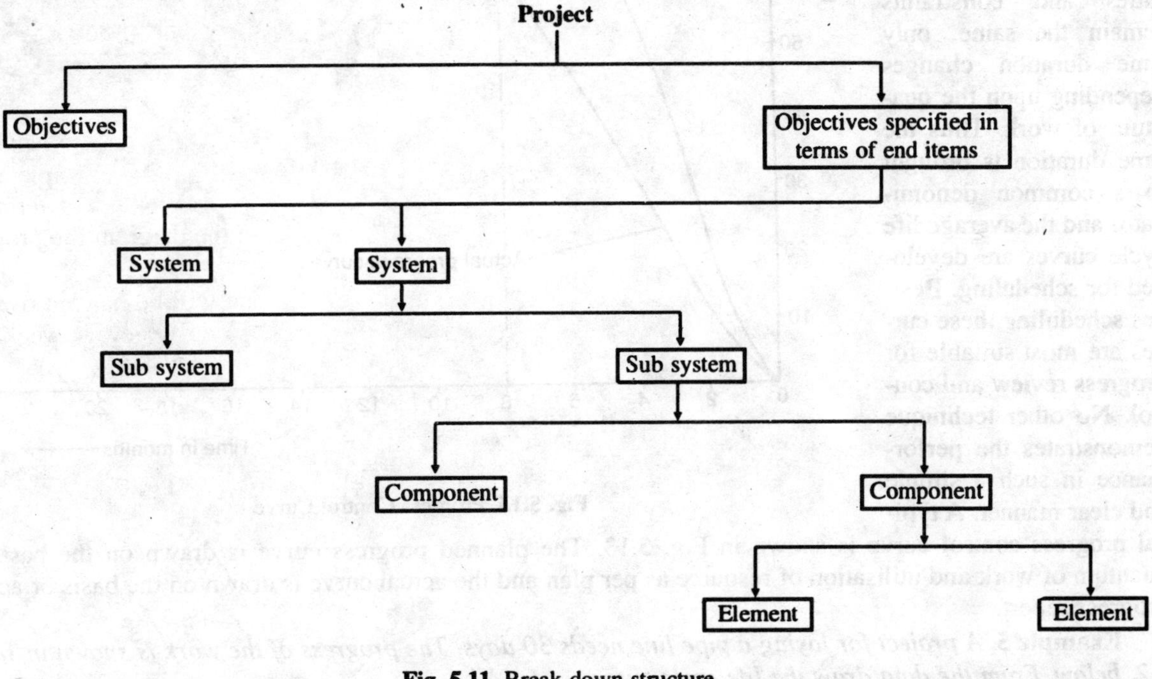

Fig. 5.11. Break down structure

Thus the breakdown structure is a good tool to identify the functional elements of a project and their interdependence or relationship.

The breaking or splitting the project into various functional elements, will not only help in preparing the net work of the project but will also be usefull in planning and preparing schedule of the activities. The activities of laying a sewer line may be split as follows:

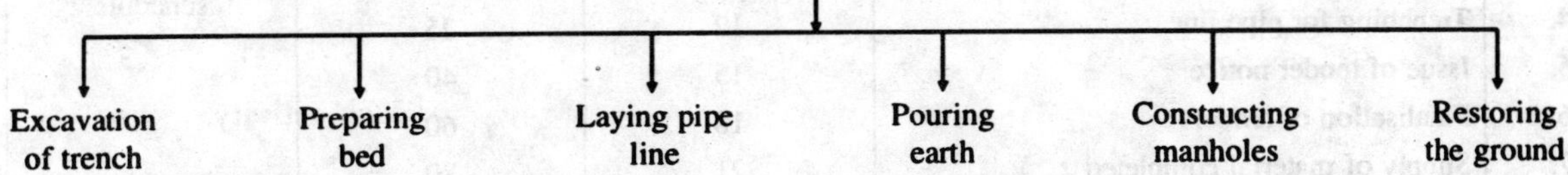

Fig. 5.12. Break down diagram of a sewer line

5.16. LIFE CYCLE CURVES

Normally life cycle curves are used after the over all time schedule has been decided by the use of bar chart. For using a life cycle curve for a particular type of work, the empirical relationship between percentage progress and time has to be established by examining a number of works of identical sequence of work and constraints. While sequence of activities and constraints remain the same, only time duration changes depending upon the quantum of work. Thus the time duration is brought to a common denominator and the average life cycle curves are developed for scheduling. Besides scheduling these curves are most suitable for progress review and control. No other technique demonstrates the performance in such a simple and clear manner. A typical progress control curve is shown in Fig. 5.13. The planned progress curve is drawn on the basis of quantum of work and utilisation of resource as per plan and the actual curve is drawn on the basis of actual progress report.

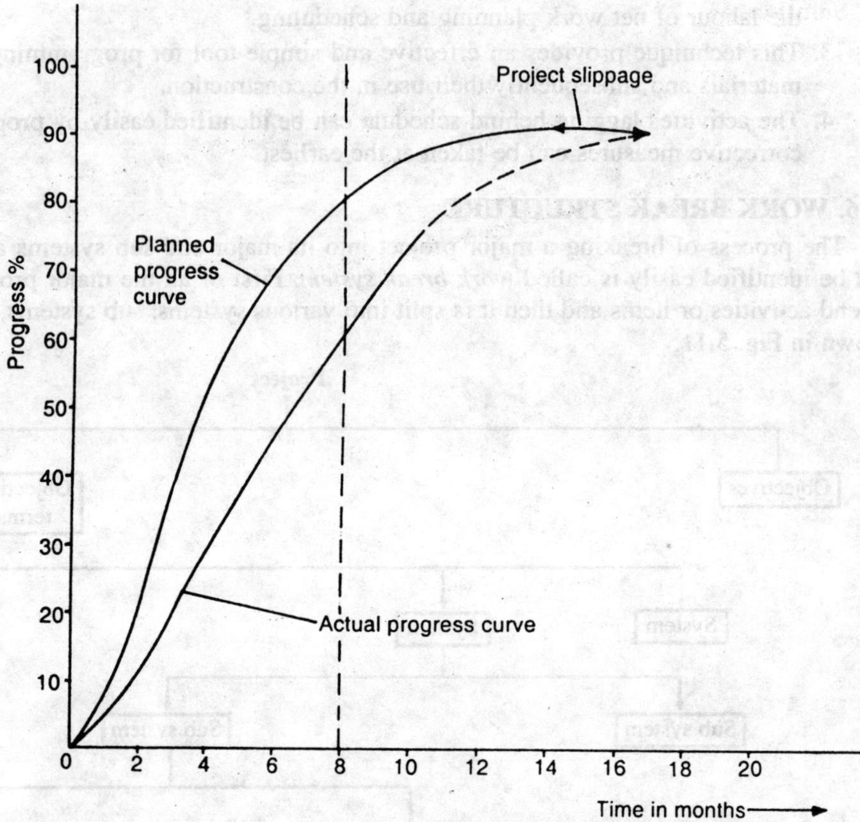

Fig. 5.13. Progress Control Curve

Example 5. *A project for laying a pipe line needs 30 days. The progress of the work is shown in Table 5.2. below. From the data draw the life cycle curve.*

Table 5.2.

Item No.	*Description*	*Time in weeks*	*Percentage of progross*	*Remark*
1.	Survey work for laying the pipe line	3	2	Work done as per schedule
2.	Finalisation of specifications	6	8	
3.	Pegging the alignment	9	15	
4.	Trenching for pipe line	12	25	
5.	Issue of tender notice	15	40	
6.	Finalisation of tenders	18	60	
7.	Supply of material completed	21	80	
8.	Laying of pipe line completed	24	90	
9.	Back filling the trenches	27	95	
10.	Clearing the site	30	100	

Solution.

The curve is shown in Fig. 5.14.

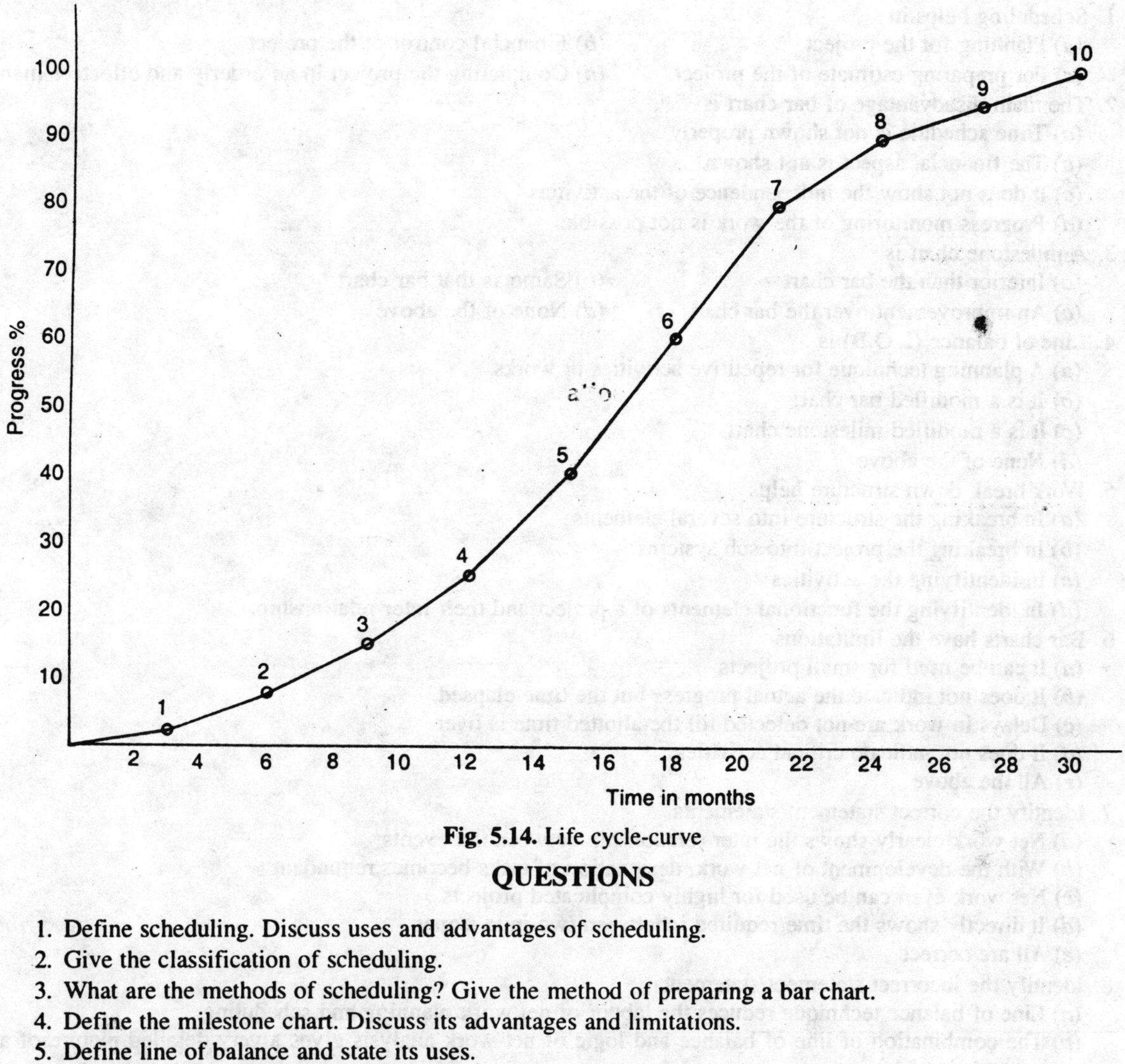

Fig. 5.14. Life cycle-curve

QUESTIONS

1. **Define scheduling. Discuss uses and advantages of scheduling.**
2. **Give the classification of scheduling.**
3. **What are the methods of scheduling? Give the method of preparing a bar chart.**
4. **Define the milestone chart. Discuss its advantages and limitations.**
5. **Define line of balance and state its uses.**
6. **Give step wise procedure of preparing a schedule with the help of line of balance.**
7. **Prepare the bar chart for the following operations:**

(*a*) Preparation of question paper	**10 days**
(*b*) Printing of question paper	**3 days**
(*c*) Sending question paper to different centres	**7 days**
(*d*) Examination	**1 days**
(*e*) Returning answer books to headquarters	**6 days**

8. **Prepare the bar chart for preparing conference hall chairs**

(*a*) Preparation of drawings of all parts	**3 days**
(*b*) Preparation of legs	**4 days**
(*c*) Preparation of seats	**3 days**
(*d*) Preparation of backs	**2 days**
(*e*) Joining all parts	**3 days**

(*f*) Polishing the chairs 2 days

OBJECTIVE TYPE QUESTIONS

1. Scheduling helps in
   (*a*) Planning for the project
   (*b*) Financial control of the project
   (*c*) For preparing estimate of the project
   (*d*) Completing the project in an orderly and effective manner
2. The main disadvantage of bar chart is
   (*a*) Time schedule is not shown properly
   (*b*) The financial aspect is not shown
   (*c*) It does not show the independence of the activities
   (*d*) Progress monitoring of the work is not possible
3. A milestone chart is
   (*a*) Inferior than the bar chart
   (*b*) Same as that bar chart
   (*c*) An improvement over the bar chart
   (*d*) None of the above
4. Line of balance (L.O.B) is
   (*a*) A planning technique for repetitive activities or works
   (*b*) It is a modified bar chart
   (*c*) It is a modified milestone chart
   (*d*) None of the above
5. Work break down structure helps
   (*a*) In breaking the structure into several elements
   (*b*) In breaking the project into sub systems
   (*c*) In identifying the activities
   (*d*) In identifying the functional elements of a project and their inter relationship.
6. Bar charts have the limitations
   (*a*) It can be used for small projects
   (*b*) It does not indicate the actual progress but the time elapsed
   (*c*) Delays in work are not detected till the allotted time is over
   (*d*) It does not indicate critical activities
   (*e*) All the above
7. Identify the correct statement/statements
   (*a*) Net work clearly shows the inter relationship between the events
   (*b*) With the development of net work, designation of tasks becomes redundant
   (*c*) Net work even can be used for highly complicated projects
   (*d*) It directly shows the time required inbetween two mile stones
   (*e*) All are correct
8. Identify the incorrect statement/statements
   (*a*) Line of balance technique reduces the labour of net work planning and scheduling
   (*b*) The combination of line of balance and logic of net work analysis gives a very detailed picture of any repetitive work
   (*c*) It provides a very effective and simple tool for completion project
   (*d*) All are correct

ANSWERS

1. (*d*)	3. (*c*)	5. (*d*)	7. (*e*)
2. (*c*)	4. (*a*)	6. (*e*)	8. (*d*)

6

Net Work Techniques in Construction Management

6.1. INTRODUCTION

Every project is composed of jobs, activities and functions or tasks which are interrelated with each other in one form or the other. In order to complete the project in time all these activities and functions have to be completed well with in time. Every project has one specific purpose *i.e.* it should start at a specified time and finish at the stipulated period.

It has been observed that many a times a project is over run in time and cost. The reasons for this over runs may be due to inadequate planning at the out set of the projects. It has been felt that conventional planning and control techniques of planning, scheduling and monitoring are not satisfactory for large and complex projects. To overcome this difficulty net work planning was developed during 1958-1960 solving two different problems. The net work approach to action planning is a major advancement in management science. In the net work technique the projects are broken down to individual jobs or events and arranged in a logical net work. These individual jobs are given time estimates for their execution. The network helps in identifying those events which control the completion of the project. PERT and CPM are two such tools that have been accepted in recent years. PERT stands for Program Evaluation and Review Technique. This technique was developed during the control of completion of POLARIS MISSILE PROGRAMME, which was a research and development project. As it was a new project and was never tried in the past, so neither cost nor time could be estimated accurately. Thus the completion time of the project had to be based on probability. Thus contractors were asked to furnish their optimistic time, pessimistic time and most likely times. Then these estimates were assessed mathematically to determine the probable completion time and the procedure was called PERT. This system involves a probabilistic approach and is best suited to research and development work in which major uncertainties exist.

CPM technique was developed during the same period of 1958-60 by an German Construction Company during the Construction of a major chemical plant in America. Such projects need both cost and time to be estimated accurately. As the contractor had previous experience of constructing such projects, so he was confident to estimate the cost and time in a deter-ministic manner. The method of planning and controlling developed originally was called project planning and scheduling (PPS), which was later named critical path method (CPM). Thus CPM involves deterministic approach and is used for repetitive type of projects.

6.2. DEFINITIONS

1. Activity. Any portion of a project which consumes resources and has a definite beginning and an end is called an *activity* as placing concrete in a beam and column. It needs time for its performance.

An activity is denoted by an arrow. The tail of the arrow shows the start and head of the arrow shows the finish of the activity. The length of the arrow has no significance. The description of the activity is shown above the arrow and number below the arrow indicates duration in time units as shown in Fig. 6.1.

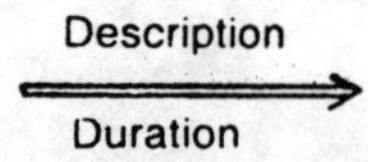

Fig. 6.1. Representation of an activity

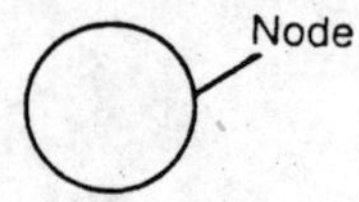

Fig. 6.2. Representation of an event

2. Event. The commencement or completion of an activity is termed or called an event. It does not need time *i.e.* It does not consume resources by itself. The events are represented by nodes. The shape of nodes may be circular, square, rectangular or oval. Thus an event is that particular instant of time at which some specific part of a plan is to be achieved. It is indicated on the net work by a number which is enclosed by a simple geometric figure such as a circle or square or a triangle etc. An event is also called as node or connector. Fig. 6.2.

4.2.1. Difference between an activity and event

Activity

1. An activity stands for time consuming part of the project.
2. It represents a job.
3. Activities are denoted by arrows.

Event

1. It is called a node.
2. It is either a beginning or end of a job.
3. Events are denoted by circles or rectangles.

Though the difference between an activity and a event is given above. How ever their difference is indicated by the following examples in table 6.1.

Table 6.1.

S. No.	*Activity*	*Event*
1.	Excavate trench	Trench or foundation excavated
2.	Prepare specifications	Specifications prepared
3.	Mix Concrete	Concrete mixed
4.	Drive piles	Piles are driven
5.	Erect the scaffolding	Scaffolding erected
6.	Cure the concrete floor	Concrete floor cured
7.	Set the question paper	Question paper set
8.	Fix the door frame	Door frame fixed etc.

Net Work

The graphical and logical plan or model of a project which lists out the sequence of various operations (with inter dependence) required to be performed for the final achievement of the project objectives is known as *the net work.*

6.3. PLANNING FOR NET WORK CONSTRUCTION

Net works can be constructed depending upon the end configuration of the plan by either of the three methods:

1. Forward planning. In this method the planner starting from the initial event builds up all the events and activities in logical sequence till the end event is reached. In this method the planner asks the following questions by himself.

(*a*) What event should come next?

(*b*) What are dependent events?

(*c*) What events can be taken up simultaneously.

The answer of these questions is not easy in complex situations.

2. Backward planning. In this method of planning, the planner starting from the end event arranges the events and activities till the initial event is reached. Keeping the goal in mind, the planner asks by himself what events and activities should have taken place to achieve a particular event.

3. Combined planning. Actually in practice combination of both forward planning and backward planning is followed. In this case the planner at any stage makes trial for forward and backward planning till he gets a satisfactory solution of the problem. In this case the planner at any stage must ask following questions by himself.

(*a*) Before starting a particular event, what events must be completed?

(*b*) What event or events should follow a particular event?

(*c*) What activities can be accomplished simultaneously.

6.4. MODES OF NET WORK CONSTRUCTION

Basically there are following two modes of a net work:

1. Activity oriented diagram
2. Event oriented diagram

1. Activity oriented diagram. An activity oriented diagram is one in which emphasis is given to the activities of the project. These diagrams are used in critical path method net works. The activities are arranged in logical and sequential order. As the diagramming proceeds additional activities are selected as per nature of the work or project. Generally in activity oriented diagrams the importance of events is minimised. Fig. 6.3. shows an activity based diagram.

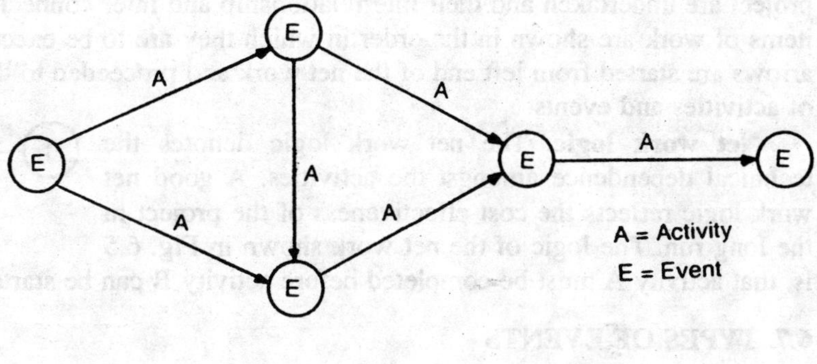

Fig. 6.3. Activity oriented diagram

2. Event oriented diagrams. The event oriented diagram is one in which emphasis is given to the events of the project. The events to be included in the plan are chosen first and the interest is focussed on the start or finishing events rather than the activities. The activities which take place in between the events are not specified. The events in such net works fall in a logical sequence where ambiguities are not caused. Only the completed event is recorded. It is under stood that the start

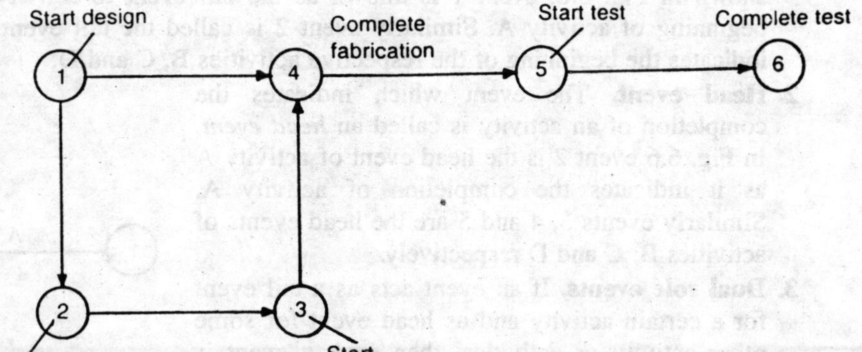

Fig. 6.4. Event oriented diagram

event must have taken place before the end event occurs. Then the events are connected by arrows to show their inter dependence for accomplishing the project. The event oriented diagrams are used in PERT programs. An event oriented diagram is shown in Fig. 6.4.

6.5. PROPERTIES OF EVENT

An event has the following three properties:

(*a*) An event is either start or completion of an operation or activity. It should be readily understood by all concerned with the project.

(*b*) An event represents an significant, note worthy and recognizable point in the project. The events act as control points in the project.

(*c*) An event is an instantaneous accomplishment, requiring no resources or time for itself.

An event must satisfy the following requirements:

(*a*) A significant event must be specific, positive, tangible and meaning full to the project.

(*b*) It should be distinguishable as a specific point in time.

(*c*) It should be readily under stood by all concerned with the project.

6.6. NET WORK DIAGRAM

A Net work diagram is a graphical representation of the sequences in which various activities in a project are undertaken and their interrelationship and inter connections shown. In the diagram, the various items of work are shown in the order in which they are to be executed. As a convention the first arrow or arrows are started from left end of the net work and proceeded to the right. Fig. 6.3 and 6.4 show net work of activities and events.

Net work logic. The net work logic denotes the technical dependence amongst the activities. A good net work logic reflects the cost effectiveness of the project in the long run. The logic of the net work shown in Fig. 6.5 is, that activity A must be completed before activity B can be started Fig. 6.5.

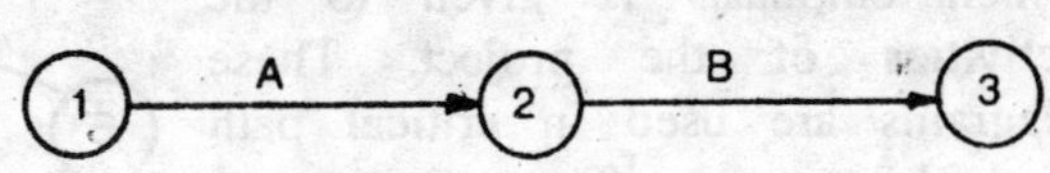

Fig. 6.5. Net work logic

6.7. TYPES OF EVENTS

Events can be classified as follows:

1. Tail event
2. Head event
3. Dual role events
4. Brust and merge events

1. **Tail event.** An event which shows or marks the beginning of an activity is known as tail event. As shown in Fig. 6.6, event 1 is known as the tail event to activity A as it indicates the start or beginning of activity A. Similarly event 2 is called the tail event to activities B, C and D as it indicates the beginning of the respective activities B, C and D.

2. **Head event.** The event which indicates the completion of an activity is called an *head event*. In Fig. 6.6 event 2 is the head event of activity A as it indicates the completion of activity A. Similarly events 3, 4 and 5 are the head events of activities B, C and D respectively.

3. **Dual role events.** If an event acts as a tail event for a certain activity and as head event for some other activity or activities, then such a event is called an dual role event. In Fig. 6.6, event 2 is the dual role event as it acts as the head event for

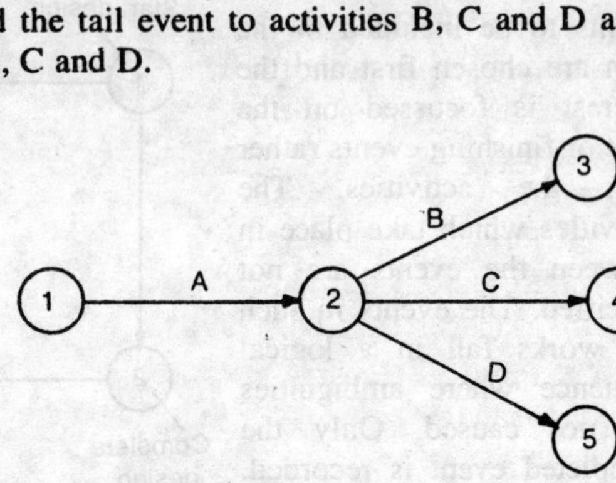

Fig. 6.6. Types of events

activity A and tail event for activities B, C and D.

4. Brust event. In arrow diagram the node from which a number of activities emerge or diverge is called a brust event or brust node as shown in Fig. 6.7. In Fig. 6.7 event 1 is a burst event.

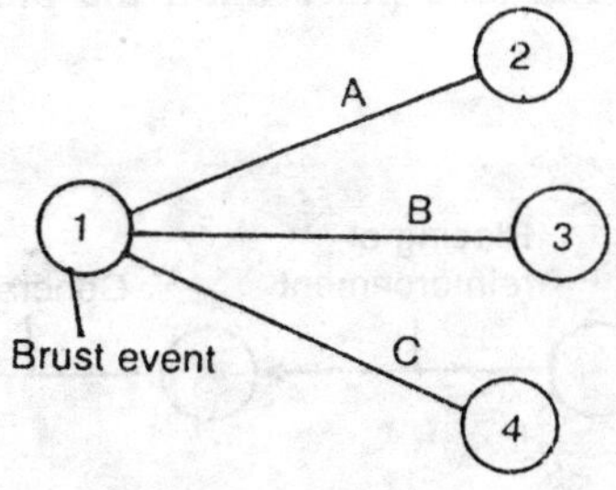

Fig. 6.7. Brust events

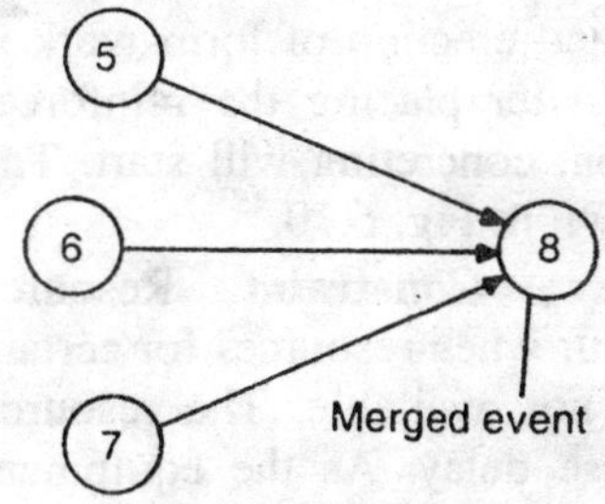

Fig. 6.8. Merged event

6. Merged event. In a arrow diagram the node to which some activities converge is called a merged event or node. In Fig. 6.8 node 8 is the merged node.

7. Successor event. The event that follows a particular event in the sequence of their completion of a net work is called a successor event of that particular event. Event 2 of Fig. 6.6 is the successor event of event 1.

8. Predecessor event. The event that occurs before a particular event in the sequence of their completion in the net work is called a predecessor event of that particular event as in Fig. 6.6, event 1 is said the predecessor event of event 2. Similarly event 2 is the predecessor event of events 3, 4 and 5.

9. Parallel or Concurrent activities. The activities which can be carried out simultaneously and independently of each other are called parallel activities. As shown in Fig. 6.6, activities B, C and D can be started simultaneously after completing the activity A. Hence these activities B, C and D are said to be parallel activities.

10. Serial activities. The activities which can be performed one after the completion of the other sequentially are called serial activities as shown in Fig. 6.9. Activity C can only be started after the completion of activities A and B. Activity C can not be started before the completion of activity B and activity B can not be started before the completion of activity A.

Fig. 6.9. Serial activities

6.8. CONSTRAINTS IN THE DEVELOPMENT OF A NET WORK

After finalising the list of activities of a project they are connected with each other to determine the relationship between the activities. During deriving the sequence, certain restrictions with respect to physical construction, availability of resource, equipments, labour, safety considerations and management aspects may be imposed. These restrictions are known as *Constraints*. There are five constraints as follows:

1. Physical Constraint
2. Safety Constraint
3. Resource Constraint
4. Labour Constraint
5. Management Constraint

1. Physical Constraint. In some situations there may be some restrictions for the start of a particular activity and this particular activity itself may be a cause of restriction for the start on other activities related to it. In the list of activities, each activity should be put to the following three questions. The answers obtained of these questions determine the relationship and sequence of the activities.

(a) What activities must proceed this activity?

(b) What activities must follow this activity?

(c) What activities can be done simultaneously with this activity?

For example placing of concrete in the beam of a roof can not take place untill the preparation of reinforcement and erection of form work is not complete. After placing the reinforcement in position, concreting will start. The network is shown in Fig. 6.10.

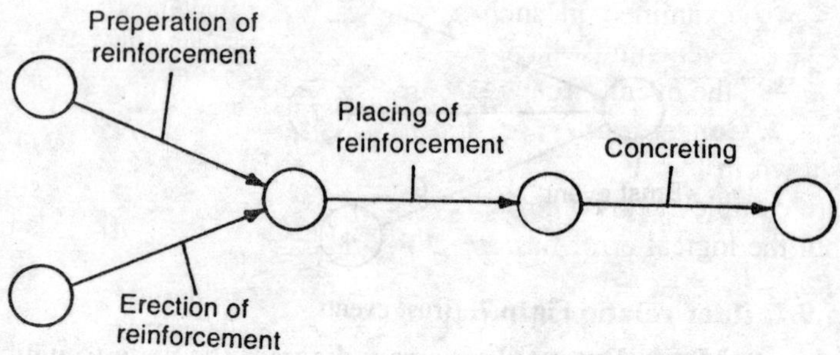

Fig. 6.10. Physical Constraints

2. **Resource Constraint.** Resource Constraints occur when resources for certain operations are not available. The resource constraints cause delay. As the equipment required for a certain activity is not available for a certain date. During this period certain activities have to be delayed till the equipment is available and some concurrent activities may proceed.

3. **Safety Constraint.** Some times safety constraints disturb the sequential operations, which could otherwise be started simultaneously. For example ground floor concreting operation may be postponed while steel frame work is being assembled first over head.

4. **Labour or crew Constraint.** Non availability of trained mistry some times cause resource constraint. For example non availability of an welder, welding activities have to be stopped and the sequence of work has to be altered.

5. **Management Constraint.** Management constraints may occur when the management wants certain activities to be completed in a certain sequence, which normally could be taken up simultaneously.

All these aspects must be studied carefully by the planner at the stage, the project is broken down into its activities while considering the various chains of activities that must be maintained.

6.9. ERRORS IN NET WORKS

Some times errors creep in the net work due to either constructional mistake or conceptual mistake during the period of drawing the net work.

1. **Construction errors.** Constructional errors may be of the following two types:

(a) **Looping error.** Some times due to the constructional mistake in the direction of arrow an impossible situation in the logic of the net work develops the formation of a loop as shown in Fig. 6.11.

(b) **Dangling error.** It is a hanging error of a activity whose duration has no effect on the completion

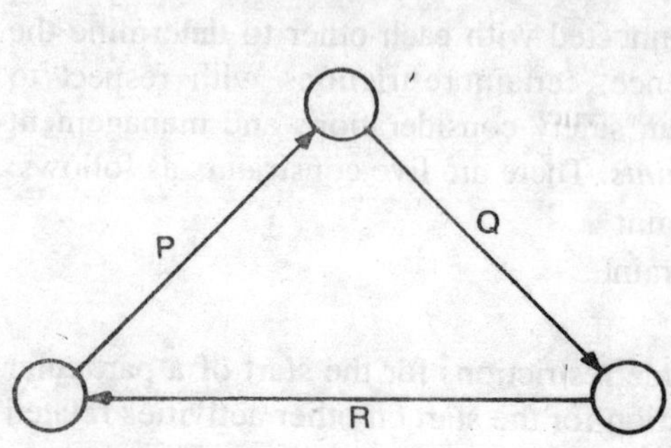

Fig. 6.11. Looping error

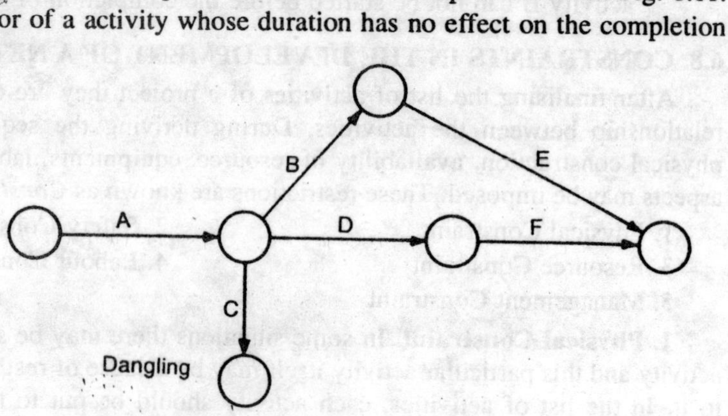

Fig. 6.12. Dangling error

of the project. As a matter of fact a project is complete when all its activities are complete, but the duration of activity C has no effect on the duration of the project as shown in Fig. 6.12. This is a dangling error.

To avoid dangling or hanging error the net work must be examined in such a manner that all events except first and final events must have at least one entering and one leaving activity with the event circle.

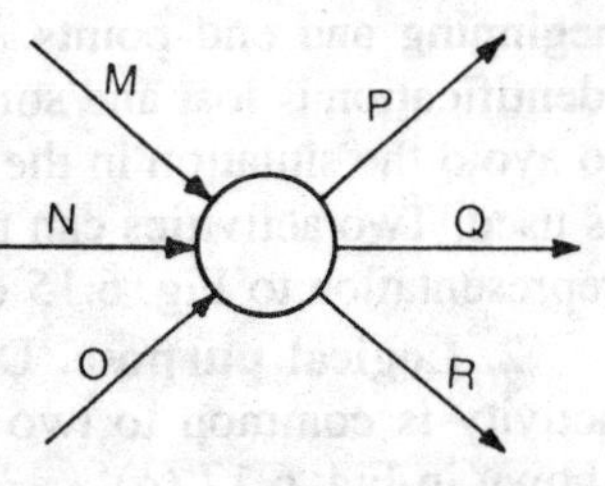

Fig. 6.13. Wagon wheel error

2. Conceptual error. This error is also known as wagon wheel error. As shown in Fig. 6.13 each of the activity P, Q and R can not start untill all the three activities M, N and O are completed. But in reality it is not the case. There is no visible error in the construction of the diagram, but the logical error has crept into it.

6.9.1. Inter relationship between events

The completion of a project, which has been split into a number of activities, passes through a number of events. These events must occur at a definite time and in a particular order. In preparing a event oriented net work diagram following questions regarding the sequence of events must be kept in mind.

(*a*) What event or events must be completed before a particular event under consideration can be started?

(*b*) What event or events must follow a particular event under consideration?

(*c*) What activities can be accomplished simultaneously?

6.10. DUMMY ACTIVITIES

It is an artificial operation in the network. It requires neither time nor any resource. It is merely a device to identify the dependence amongst the operations. A dummy activity usually is denoted by a dotted arrow as shown in Fig. 6.14. The main objective of using a dummy is to show the logical relationship between different activities. In Fig. 6.14 four activities OPQR are shown, in which activities O and P can be started simultaneously, but activity R can not be started untill activity O is completed *i.e.* event 2 is reached. This inter dependence is shown by dummy activity 2-3 by dotted arrow.

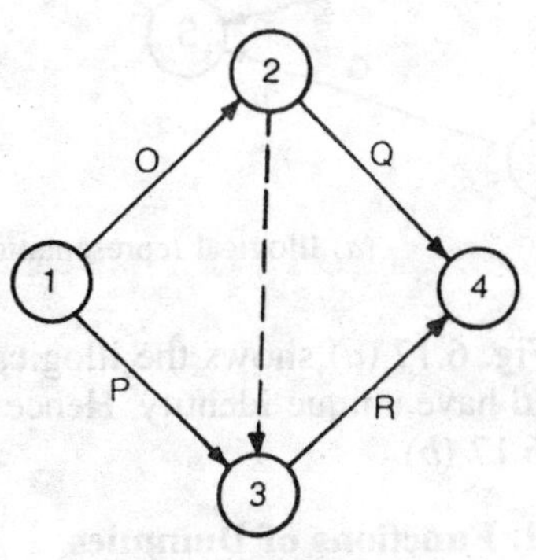

Fig. 6.14. Representation of dummy activity

6.11. USE OF DUMMY ACTIVITIES

The use of dummies is done for two purposes in a net work:

1. Grammatical purpose
2. Logical purpose

1. Grammatical purpose. In a project some times a situation arises when two activities have the same

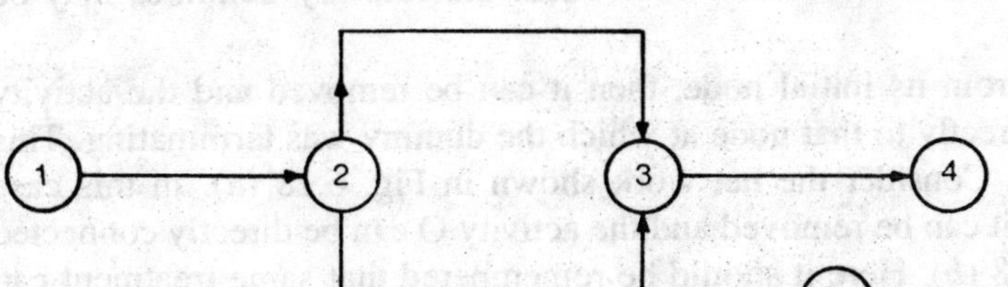

Fig. 6.15. Incorrect representation

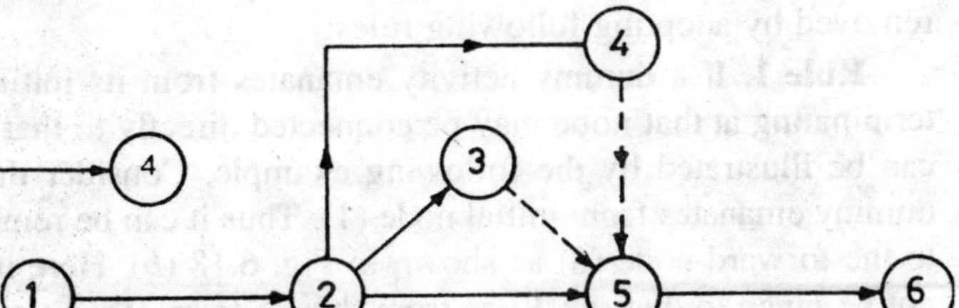

Fig. 6.16. Correct-representation using dummies

beginning and end points. In such situations when net work is used for computation, uniqueness in the identification is lost and some inconvenience is felt and errors in the computations are likely to occur. Thus to avoid the situation in the net work when two activities have the same beginning and end point a dummy is used. Two activities can not have the same starting and end events. Thus to give the correct grammatical representation to Fig. 6.15 dummies may be used as shown in Fig. 6.16.

2. Logical purpose. Dummies are also used to represent the logic of the network clearly where an activity is common to two sets of operations running parallel to each other. Let us consider the case as shown in Fig. 6.17 (*a*)

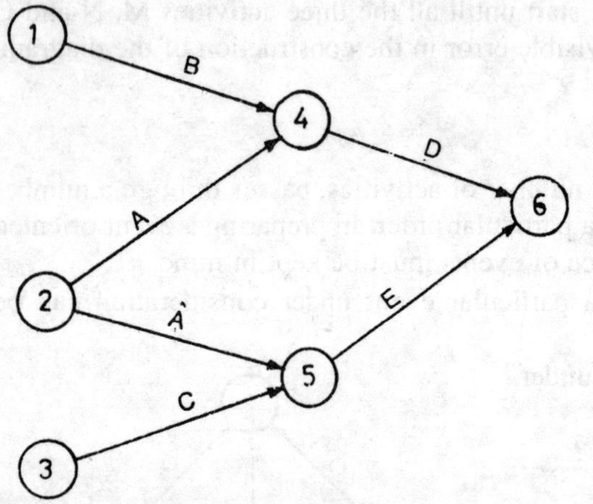

(*a*) Illogical representation

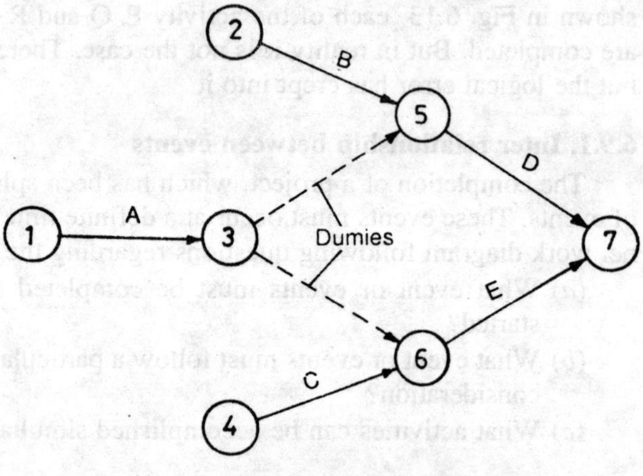

(*b*) Logical representation

Fig. 6.17.

Fig. 6.17 (*a*) shows the illogical representation of activities as activity A can not have dual identity. It should have unique identity. Hence the uniqueness can be maintained by introducing dummies as shown in Fig. 6.17 (*b*).

6.11.1. Functions of Dummies

The functions of dummies are as follows:

1. The dummies maintain the logic of the net work diagram perfectly.
2. The dummies keep the numbering system of the net work unique.

6.12. RULES FOR PROVISION OF DUMMIES

During the development of a net work providing dummies at the correct position is a very difficult job. Provision of redundant dummies in the net work may create confusion. To avoid this confusion the simple rule is that in initial stage of developing a net work the liberal use of dummies may be made as per requirement of the interrelationship between various activities and between various sets of activities. In this condition some unnecessary dummies might have been introduced. These unnecessary dummies may be removed by adopting following rules:

Rule 1. If a dummy activity emanates from its initial node, then it can be removed and the activity terminating at that node may be connected directly to that node at which the dummy was terminating. This can be illustrated by the following example. Consider the net work shown in Fig. 6.18 (*a*). In this case dummy emanates from initial node (1). Thus it can be removed and the activity O can be directly connected to the forward node (3) as shown in Fig. 6.18 (*b*). Here it should be remembered that same treatment can not be given to dummy P_1 as from this node an other activity Q also emanates from same node (2).

Rule 2. If only a dummy terminates into a node, then the dummy may be removed and the two nodes

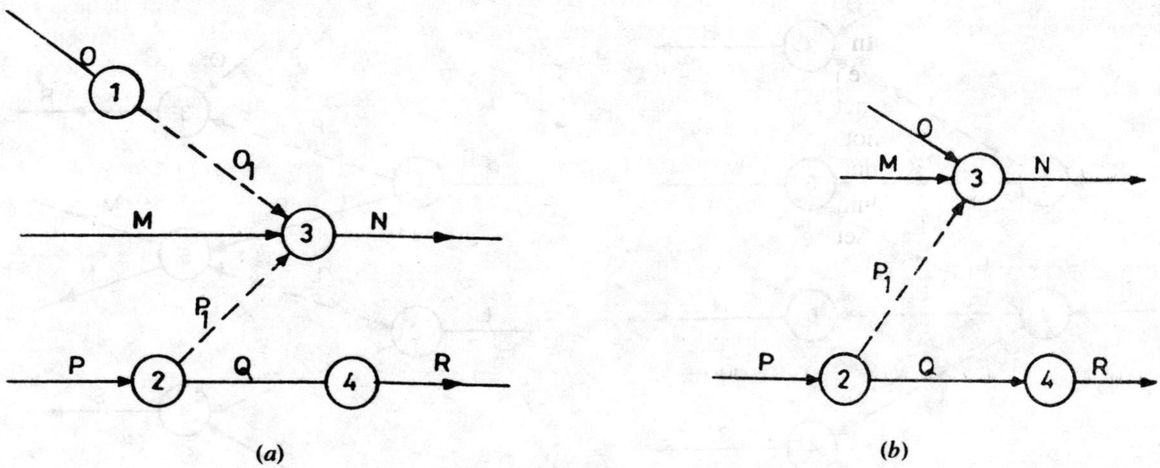

Fig. 6.18

at the two ends of the dummy can be merged into one. Consider Fig. 6.19 (*a*). In the Fig. activity M is joined to activities P, Q, R by dummies M_1, M_2 and M_3 respectively. Dummy M_2 only terminates into node

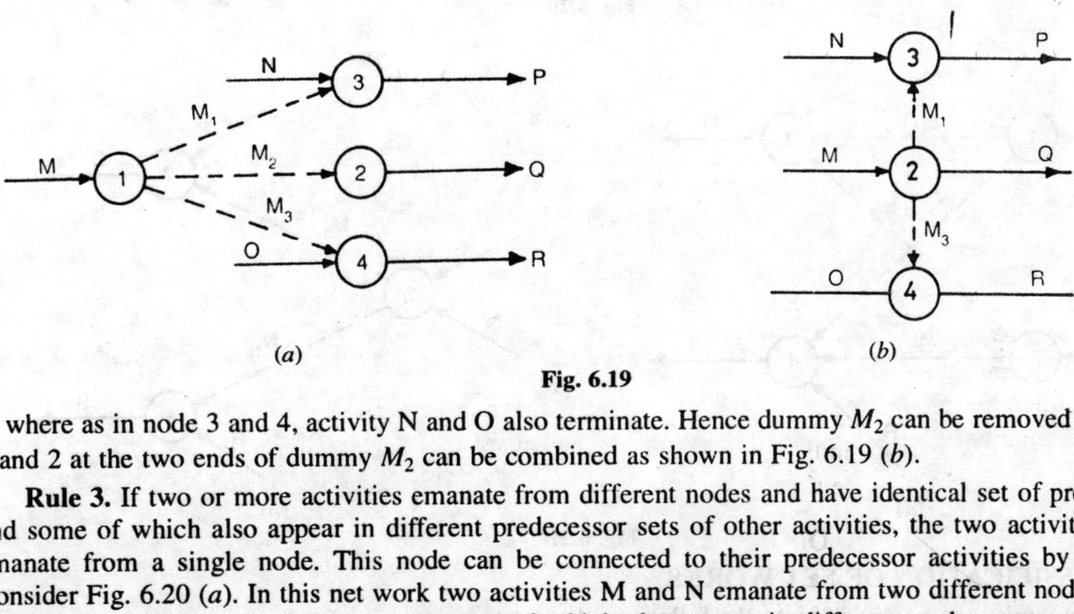

Fig. 6.19

2, where as in node 3 and 4, activity N and O also terminate. Hence dummy M_2 can be removed and nodes 1 and 2 at the two ends of dummy M_2 can be combined as shown in Fig. 6.19 (*b*).

Rule 3. If two or more activities emanate from different nodes and have identical set of predecessors and some of which also appear in different predecessor sets of other activities, the two activities should emanate from a single node. This node can be connected to their predecessor activities by dummies. Consider Fig. 6.20 (*a*). In this net work two activities M and N emanate from two different nodes 5 and 6 and have identical sets of predecessors somě of which also appear in different predecessor sets of other activities. In such a case activities M and N can be made to emanate from a single node (5) to which the predecessor activities can be joined through dummies as shown in Fig. 6.20 (*b*), in which two dummies P_2 and L_2 completely have been eliminated.

Rule 4. If two or more activities terminate into two different nodes and have identical set of successors, the latter having other predessors as well, the two activities should terminate into one single node. This node can be connected to their successors through appropriate dummies. Consider Fig. 6.21 (*a*) in which two activities M and N terminate into two different nodes 1 and 2. Each one of these activities, have identical set of successors Q and S and having their other predecessors P and R respectively. In such a case both M and N can be made to terminate into one common node (2) and connected to their successors through M_1 and N_1 as shown in Fig. 6.21 (*b*). In this way two dummies M_2 and N_2 have been eliminated.

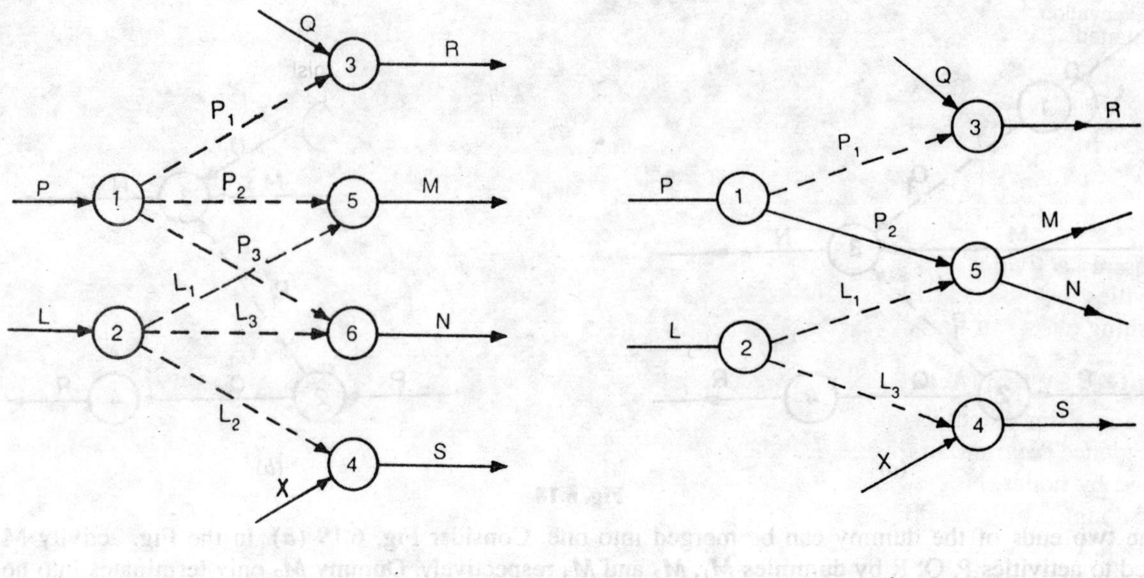

Fig. 6.20

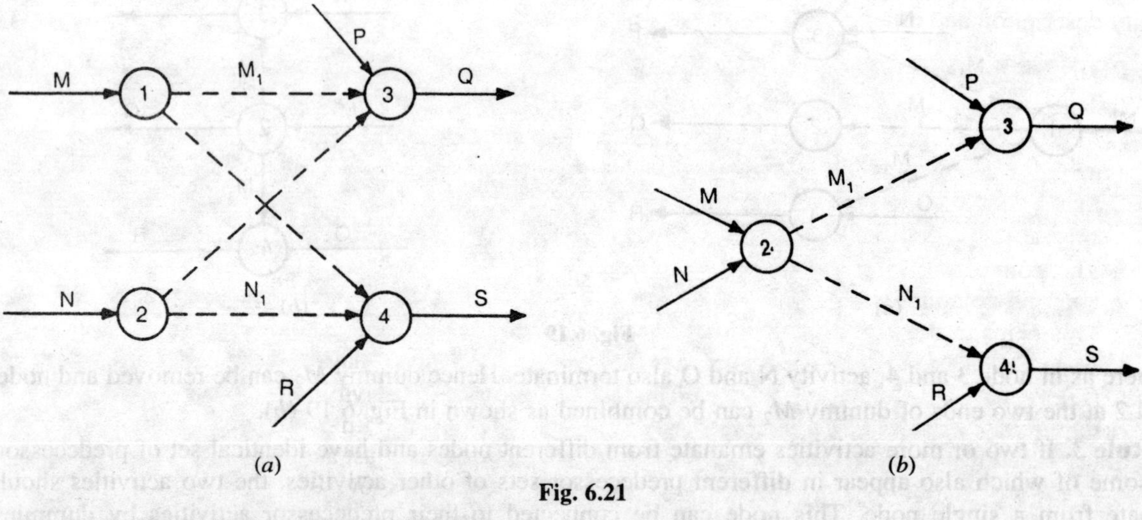

Fig. 6.21

6.13. CLASSIFICATION OF NET WORKS

The net works can be divided into the following three categories:

1. Activity on arrow or Arrow diagram (A-O-A) net work.
2. Activity on node or precedence diagram (A-O-N) net work.
3. Event oriented net works (Pert type).

1. Activity on arrow (A-O-A) Net-Work

This system consists of arrows and nodes. The arrows represent the activities and nodes represent the event as start or finish. The name of activity or symbol is written on the upper side of the arrow and the time duration of the activity on the lower side of the arrow. The node or circle situated at the tail end of the arrow is called tail event or I node and represents the instant of time when the activity will start and the node situated at the head end of the arrow is known as head event or J node. It represents the instant of time when the activity will finish. This system uses dummies to maintain the unique system of numbering for

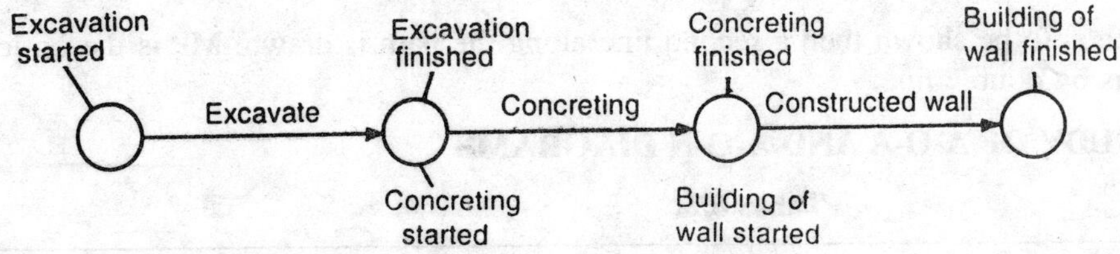

Fig. 6.22

different activities and to keep logical sequence of activities as shown in Fig. 6.22. In Fig. 6.22 starting and finishing events of the job have been shown.

2. A-O-N System (Activity on the node system) Diagram

Some times activity on the node system is also called precedence diagram. In this system the activities are represented by nodes. Nodes usually are represented by square or rectangle or circles. Other conventional shapes may also be used. One of the most common types of node representation is shown in Fig. 6.23. In this system arrows only show the interdependence or precedence relationship of activities. When square or rectangular nodes are used, the activity description and other details are written as shown in Fig. 6.23 For details please refer chapter 9.

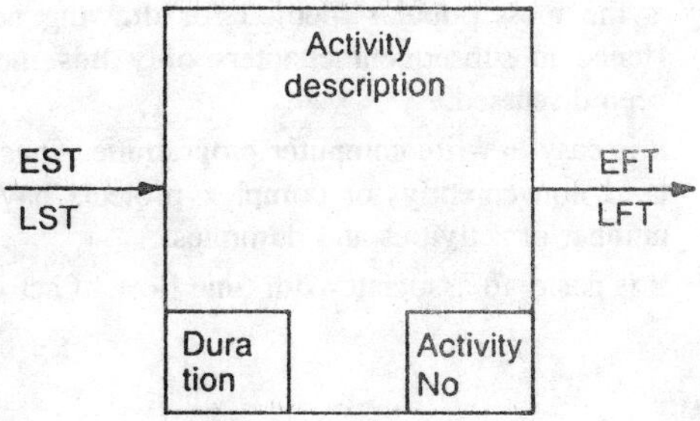

Fig. 6.23.

6.14. POINTS TO BE KEPT IN MIND WHILE DRAWING A-O-N DIAGRAM

While drawing a A-O-N diagram following points should be kept in mind:

1. In this system, events have no place, while activities have their place with durations. Numbering of activities are same as in A-O-A system.
2. Start of an activity must be linked to the end of all activities which must be completed before the start of that activity may take place.
3. The connecting lines run from left to right direction. The vertical lines drawn to connect the appropriate nodes, preferably should join on the left hand side of the box as close as possible to it. This helps in drawing a clear and easily understandable and manageable diagram in size.
4. In case when a number of activities start simultaneously, an activity called DEBUT represented by (D) is provided as the first activity. This activity may not exist in the list. Debut activity has zero duration (Do). Similarly a finish activity (F) is provided as the last activity, it also has zero duration as shown in Fig. 6.24. The corresponding A-O-A diagram is shown in Fig. 6.25.

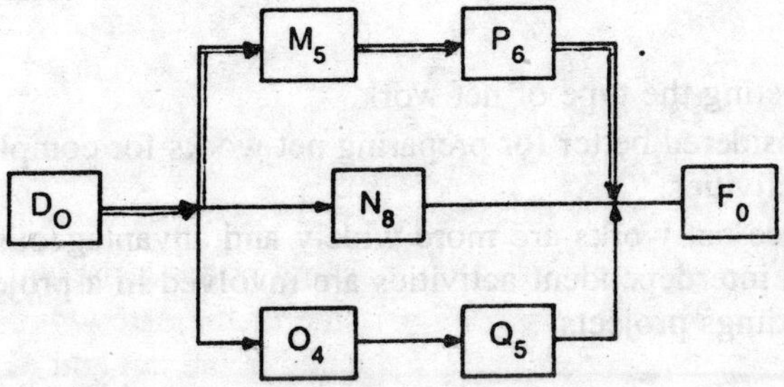

Fig. 6.24

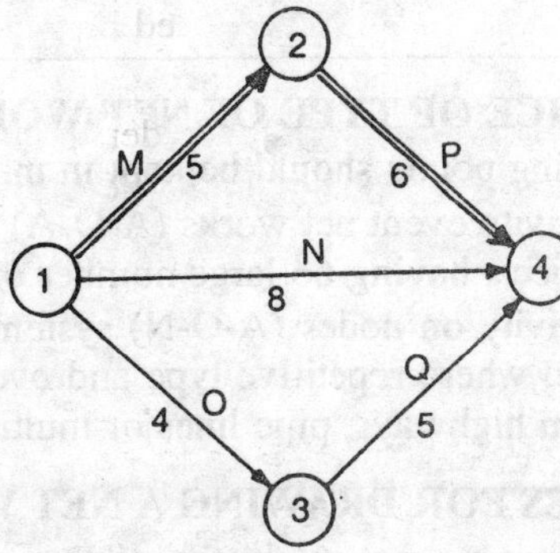

Fig. 6.25

In case their critical path is to be shown then a second line along the path is drawn. MP is the critical path shown in both diagrams by double line.

6.15. COMPARATIVE STUDY OF A-O-A AND A-O-N DIAGRAMS

Table 6.2.

A-O-A System	*A-O-N System*
1. This system was the first method of CPM net work to be introduced and developed. Now a days this system is the most popular method for drawing net works. Hence in subsequent chapters only this method has been discussed.	1. This system of net work Completely eliminates the use of dummy activities.
2. It is easy to write computer programme. Thus it can be used conveniently for complex projects having large number of activities and dummies.	2. In this system activities can be shown distinctly which are to be allowed to over lap each other or separated by a time delay.
3. It is easier to associate with time flow of activities	3. In this system all activity times as early start time (EST), Late start time (LST), Early finish time (EFT) and late finish time (LFT) etc. are written on the diagram. This facilitates efficient scheduling and control. Hence this system is self sufficient.
4. Event times as earliest occurrence time and latest occurrence time (EOT & LOT) depicted on the diagram itself are main parameters which facilitate the calculation of all activity times as (EST, EFT, LST and LFT) and all floats (TF, FF, IF and INTF) in a separate table. The critical path and project duration are identified with the help of EOT & LOT only.	4. In this system the revision and modification can be done easily with out affecting most of the activities *i.e.* only few activities only have to be modified to accommodate the change in duration, logic and sequence of activities.
5. The main difficulty or draw back of this system is the introduction of dummy activities which require experience and judicious judgement.	5. Pre operations and post operations of the activities under consideration are distinctly visible.
6. Due to increase in the number of dummies, number of calculations due to the increase in paths also increase.	6. In this system simple notations are used as in engineering flow charts. Hence it can be understood easily by non specialists also.
7. In construction projects when there are overlapping activities, large number of activities and dummies have to be incorporated.	7. This system can be employed advantageously in projects having a large number of overlapping or intermediate activities in the net work, as in highways, pipe lines and multi-storeyed buildings projects etc. Thus this system is preferred to A-O-A system for projects having several parallel strings of repetitive and some times overlapping activities.

6.16. CHOICE OF TYPE OF NET WORK

Following points should be kept in mind while selecting the type of net work.

1. Activity event net works (A-O-A) system is considered better for preparing net works for complex projects having no large number of repetitive activities.
2. Activity on nodes (A-O-N) system or precedence net works are more widely and advantageously used where repetitive type and overlapping and interdependent activities are involved in a project as in highways, pipe lines or multistoreyed buildings projects.

6.17. RULES FOR DRAWING A NET WORK

For drawing a net work, the rules are based on Common sense. Following points should be kept in mind while drawing a new work:

1. In a net work there must be only a single node and the initial node must have only out going arrows.
2. A net work can have only one final node and the final node will have only incomming arrows.
3. No activity can start untill its tail event has occurred.
4. An event can not take place or occur untill all the activities leading to it are completed.
5. An event can not occur twice, *i.e.* there can not be any net work path looping back to previously occurred event. No event is dependent for its occurrence upon the occurrence of a succeeding event. Hence the net work shown in Fig. 6.26 is wrong.

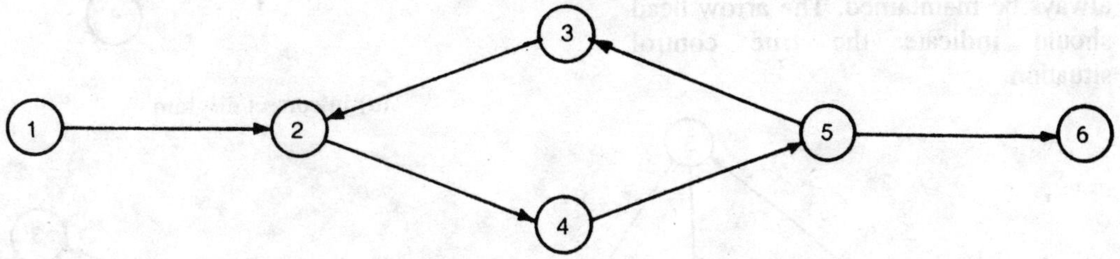

Fig. 6.26. In correct net work

6. There must not be any dead end left except the final node. The final node has only incoming arrows. There must be only single final node if there are more than one final nodes then the net work is wrong as shown in Fig. 6.27 having two final nodes.
7. An arrow in a net work should represent the singular situation. The individuality and separate entity of an activity must be maintained in a net work diagram. Particular arrow can emanate from a single event only.

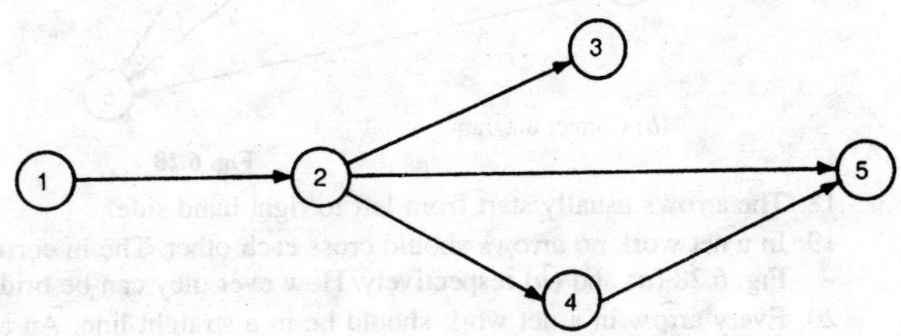

Fig. 6.27. Incorrect Network

8. The number of arrows should be equal to the number of activities in the project.
9. The net work should be drawn in such a way that all activities are completed to reach the end objective.
10. All constraints and interdependencies should be shown properly on the net work by appropriate dummies.
11. Arrows used in a net work are not vectors. Their length is not proportional to time or any resource required to complete that activity. Thus there is no relation between the length of the arrow and duration of the activity or any resource required.
12. As far as possible the length of all arrows should be kept equal. The length should be chosen suiting the drafting requirements.
13. In a net work an arrow shows the logical inter dependency of one activity on the other activity. The geometry of the arrow in the net work has no significance. The geometry of the arrow should look beautiful.
14. The head of the arrow in a net work shows the direction of progress of the work.
15. All net works should be drawn on the principle of logical interdependence of one activity on the other activity.

16. The orientation of angle between two arrows should be chosen to suit the drafting convenience. The angle between two arrows joining or leaving nodes should be as large as possible, so that there may be sufficient space available for the addition of other relevant information in the diagram.
17. The logic of the net work should always be maintained. The arrow head should indicate the true control situation.

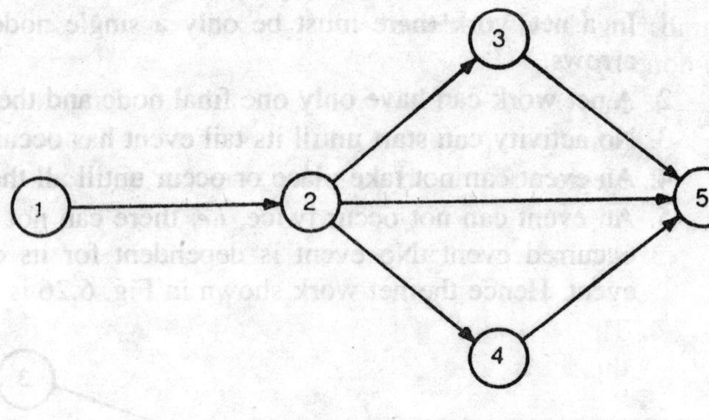

(*a*) In correct diagram

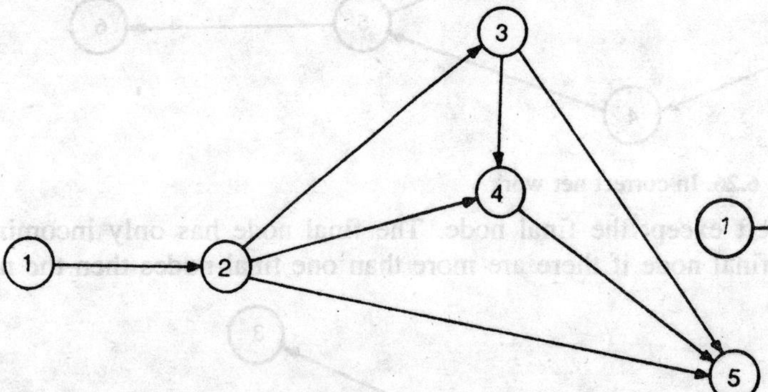

(*b*) Correct diagram

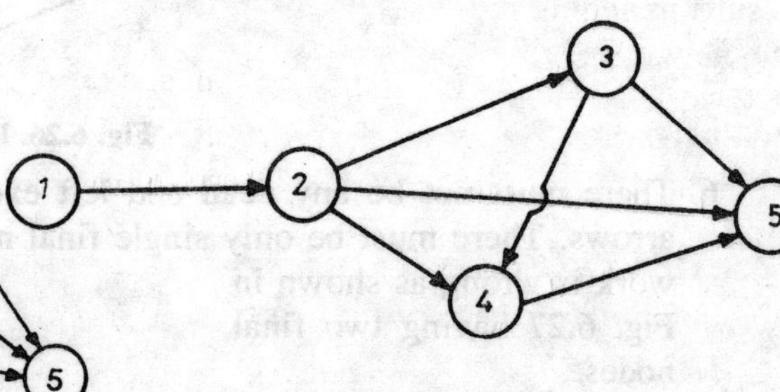

(*c*)

Fig. 6.28

18. The arrows usually start from left to right hand side.
19. In a net work no arrows should cross each other. The in correct and correct net work are shown in Fig. 6.28 (*a*) and (*b*) respectively. How ever they can be bridged as shown in Fig. 6.28 (*c*).
20. Every arrow in a net work should be in a straight line. An arrow should never be an curved one. Incorrect and correct arrows are shown in Fig. 6.29 (*a*) and (*b*) respectively.

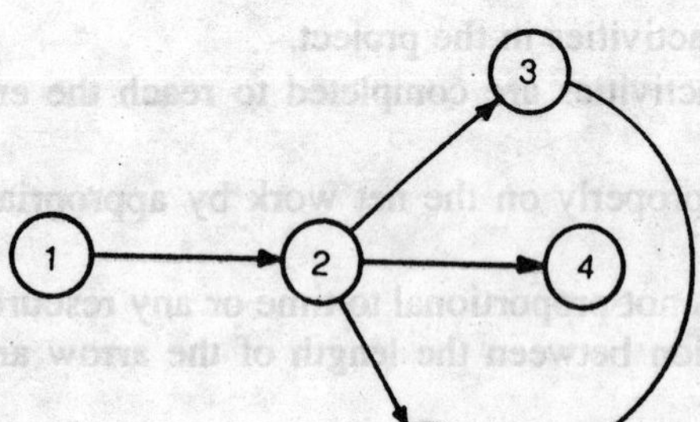

(*a*) In correct diagram

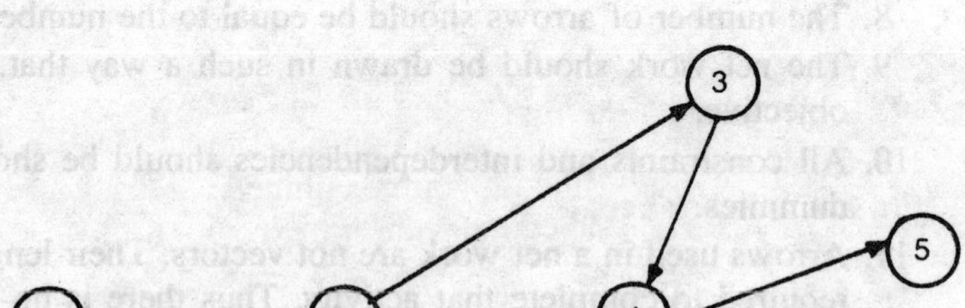

(*b*) Correct diagram

Fig. 6.29.

6.18. D.R. FULKERSON'S RULE FOR NUMBERING THE EVENTS

The numbering of node points or events is very essential. The activities joining the nodes generally are identified by node numbers or event numbers on the net work on either end of the activity arrow. Thus the numbering should be done very carefully so that logical sequence could be maintained. The numbering can be done by D.R. FULKERSON'S rule in the following sequence.

1. In a net work there must be only one or single initial event, from which arrows can only emerge or come out. No arrow will enter in it. This initial event is given number (1).
2. Neglect all the arrows emerging out of the initial event number (1). This will provide one or more new initial events. These events are numbered as 2, 3, 4 etc.
3. Again neglect all the arrows emerging out of these new numbered events. This will create some more new initial events.
4. This operation is repeated untill the last event is reached, which has no emerging arrows. Number this event as usual.

6.19. SKIPPING NUMBERING

In a net work, as a rule the tail event is given a lower number than the head event. In drawing net works for large projects extensive modifications to the initial net work are to be made frequently. This results in adding more events. To over come the difficulty of developing a loop or confusion in numbering the new events, the numbering is assigned in the multiple of 10, as 20, 30, 40 etc. to the events of initial net work and then assign the number 1 to 9 *i.e.* 11 19, 31, 34 etc. which lie between the number of immediate predessor event and immediate successor event. The procedure is illustrated with solved example 4.

6.20. DEVELOPMENT OF A NET WORK

In the development of a net work of a proposed project following procedure is found useful.

1. Setting objective. The objective specifies the task to be undertaken and policy of its execution. This specification defines the project and determines the way of its execution. Thus during the planning of a project the first and the fore most step is:

(*a*) To define the project.

(*b*) To decide the way of its execution.

2. Plan break down. After deciding the objective of the task, it is planned either by forward pass method or backward pass method. This operation of planing will give the list of activities/events to be performed to achieve the desired objectives and also the stages in the project execution. To obtain the list of activities or events, following points need careful examination.

(*a*) What are the likely difficulties, which have to be over come.

(*b*) What facilities will be helpful in the removal of the above difficulties.

(*c*) What safe guards have to be taken in using the facilities. The result of the above three questions will provide the list of activities or events.

3. Sequencing. Arranging the logical completion of activities is called sequencing. After obtaining the list of activities or events, they are examined carefully and activities with definite similarities are grouped in suitable sub groups in serial order of execution.

4. Location of nodes. The placement of activities and events which represent the initial relationship amongst them is called location nodes. This relationship results from the proposed use of resources such as money, man power, material etc. during a period of time. For obtaining the relationship among the events or activities, the planner must ask himself the following questions regarding the sequence.

(*a*) What event or events must be completed before a particular events can occur?

(*b*) What event or events should follow this particular event?

(*c*) What events can be accomplished simultaneously.

In this way the logical sequence of events may be obtained. While locating the nodes, following points should be kept in mind.

(*a*) The first event must be located by the extreme left or first node.

(*b*) Events occurring earlier must be represented to the left side with respect to the events occurring later.

(*c*) Serial events must be represented by nodes along a horizontal plane while simultaneous events are represented up or down the vertical plane.

(*d*) No event should be located in position to the left of the vertical axis of any preceding event.

5. Drawing of arrows. After locating the nodes, the events having close and direct relationship are joined together by arrows representing activities to be performed for passing from one stage of the project to the other stage. These activities should occur in a logical sequence. Regarding the sequence of activities the planner should ask himself the following three questions.

(*a*) What activity or activities should be completed before the start of a particular activity?

(*b*) What activity or activities should follow this particular activity?

(*c*) What activities can be accomplished simultaneously.

6. Checking the net work diagram. At this stage the diagram should be checked for the followings:

(*a*) Content (*b*) Sequence

(*c*) Sense (*d*) Degree of details

(*a*) **Contents.** The contents or the operations of the net work must be complete. There should be no missing operation.

(*b*) **Sequence.** It is essential to check a network diagram that it is drawn in a logical sequence with desired level of accuracy. Particular attention should be paid to multiple events. The checking must ensure that the net work correctly represents the sequence.

(*c*) **Sense.** In a net work loops or cycles should not exist. If they are found, they should be removed. In a net work there should be no dead ends except the last event. If they exist, they should be rectified.

(*d*) **Degree of details.** In a net work an arrow should always represent a singular situation but an event may represent commencement of more than one operation. If in a net work, there are sufficient details then the ratio of total events to total activities should be from 1.0 to 1.6 *i.e.*

$$\frac{\text{Event}}{\text{Activity}} \text{ ratio} = \frac{\text{Total No. of event}}{\text{Total No. of activities}} = 1.0 \text{ to } 1.6$$

7. Redrawn. If at the time of checking of a net work, some errors are found then the errors should be removed and the diagram redrawn by introducing dummies if found necessary.

8. Numbering the net work. After drawing the final network, the events are numbered by D.R. Fulkerson's rule.

Example 1. *Draw a net work with and with out dummies for the operations to be done in the construction of a house:*

(*a*) *Construction of a wall.*

(*b*) *Preparing wood work and their fixing.*

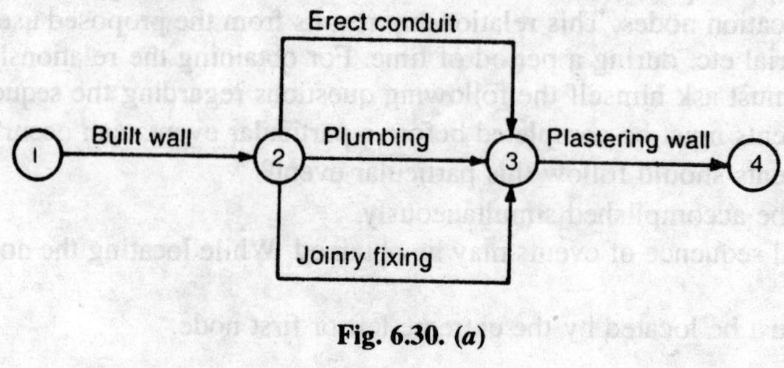

Fig. 6.30. (*a*)

(*c*) *Electric fitting.*
(*d*) *Plumbing fittings*
(*e*) *Plastering of walls.*

Solution. With out the use of dummies the net work for the above operations is shown in Fig. 6.30.

From the study of the Fig. 6.30. It will be seen that three activities plumbing, electric fittings and joinry fitting have been shown by a single activity 2-3. Activity 2-3 does not indicate that what unique activity it shows. Thus the net work drawn does not give clear picture of the work. This ambiguity can be removed by the use of dummies. The correct and clear net work for the above activities is shown in Fig. 6.30 (*b*).

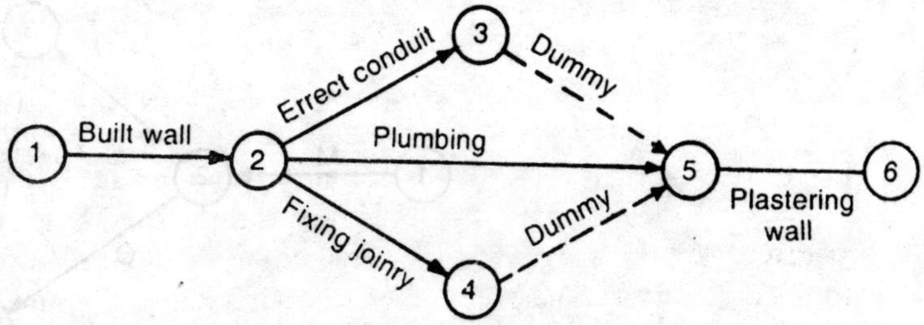

Fig. 6.30. (*b*)

Example 2. *To build a concrete retaining wall only two gangs, one for erecting form work and the other for placing concrete in place and finishing are available. Draw the net work of this work with the use of dummies.*

Solution. It is a well known fact that before placing concrete in situ it is essential that form work must be completed. The procedure is shown in Fig. 6.31.

In the Fig. letters ABC show form work activities while letters LMN show pouring of concrete.

1. First of all, the form work gang after completing the erection work in part 1-2 will come to point 4.
2. Now the concreting gang will pour concrete in portion 1-2 *i.e.* in A.
3. During the period concreting gang will pour concrete in 1-2, the form work gang will complete form work in 4-5 and revert to 2-3 and complete form work. During the period form work is completed in 2-3, concrete will be completed in 4-5.
4. After completing the form work in 2-3, the form work gang will come to 5-6 and work there. In the mean time the concrete gang will complete concrete work in 2-3. Thus in one part form work and in the other concreting will continue. This example illustrates clearly the use of dummies and inter dependence of one activity on the other activity.

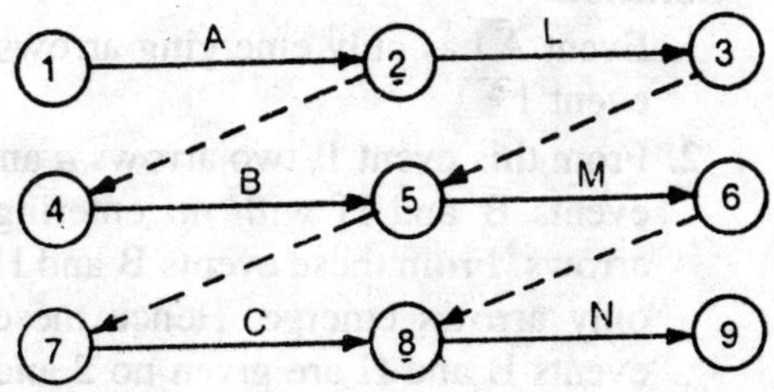

Fig. 6.31.

Example 3. *Draw a net work for the following events.*

1. *Start car from house.*
2. *Park the car in a garage.*
3. *Complete the out side cleaning.*
4. *Complete the inside cleaning.*
5. *Take car from the garage.*
6. *Park the car in the house.*

Solution. Its net work is shown in Fig. 6.32 (*a*). It is assumed that out side and inside cleaning is done simultaneously. In the Fig. 6.32 these activities are shown by N and O. Activities *P* and *Q* consume zero

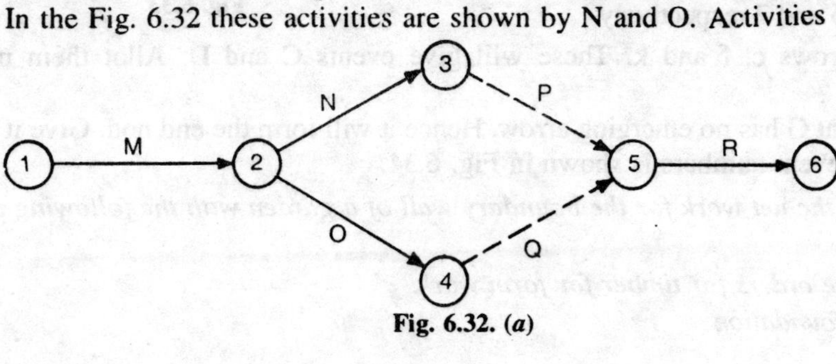

Fig. 6.32. (*a*)

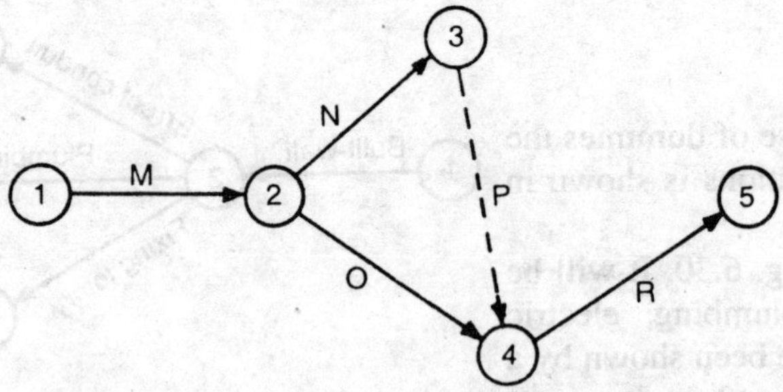

Fig. 6.32. (*b*)

time in their completion, but they show the condition that event 5 can be started only after the completion of event 3 and 4. These activities P and Q are known as dummy activities. How ever a better net work can be drawn as shown in Fig. 6.32 (*b*) having only one dummy and avoiding event 5. Event 3 and 4 can occur simultaneously. Dummy Q has been eliminated.

Example 4. *Number the events of the net work shown in Fig. 6.33 by the Fulkerson method.*

Solution.

1. Event A has only emerging arrows from it, no arrow enters into it. Hence it is taken as the starting event 1.
2. From this event 1, two arrows *a* and *b* emerge. Deletion of these arrows *a* and *b*, generates two new events B and H with no entering arrows. From these events B and H only arrows emerge. Hence these events B and H are given no 2 and 3 respectively.
3. From the newly numbered event 2 and 3, arrows c, d, e and f emerge. Deleting these arrows we get new events E and J, which have emerging arrows.
4. From Fig. 6.33, it will be clear that deleting arrows e and f, the event K has only one entering arrow, hence event K can not form an initial event. Give number 4 and 5 to events E and J. respectively.
5. Now delete arrows g, d and h. These will give events F and K. Give them no 6 and 7 respectively.

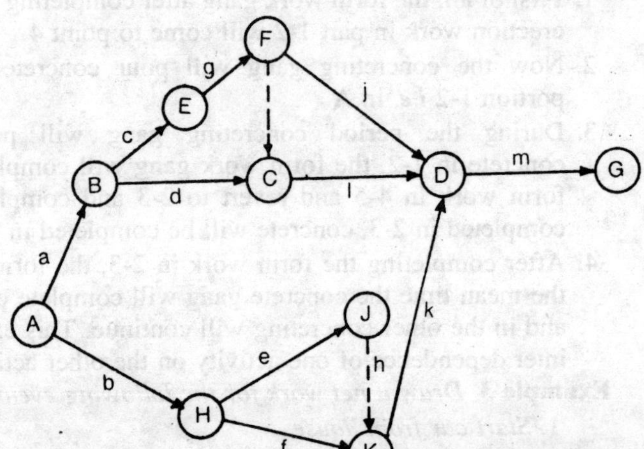

Fig. 6.33

6. Now delete arrows c, f and k. These will give events C and D. Allot them number 8 and 9 respectively.
8. Finally the event G has no emerging arrow. Hence it will form the end nod. Give it number 10. The net work with event numbers is shown in Fig. 6.34.

Example 5. *Draw the net work for the boundary wall of a garden with the following activities.*

1. *Setting out.*
2. *Placing purchase orders for timber for form work.*
3. *Excavating the foundation.*

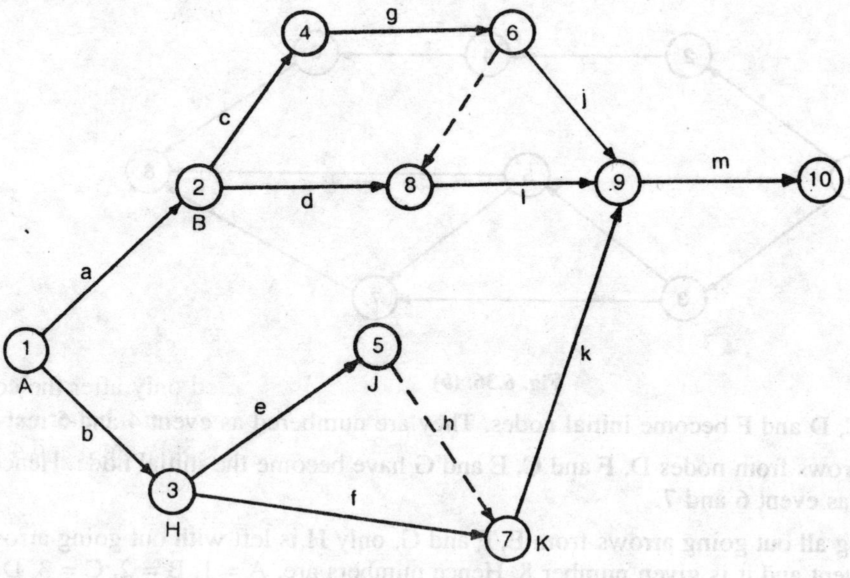

Fig. 6.34

4. *Preparation of form work.*
5. *Erecting the form work.*
6. *Pouring of concrete and finishing.*

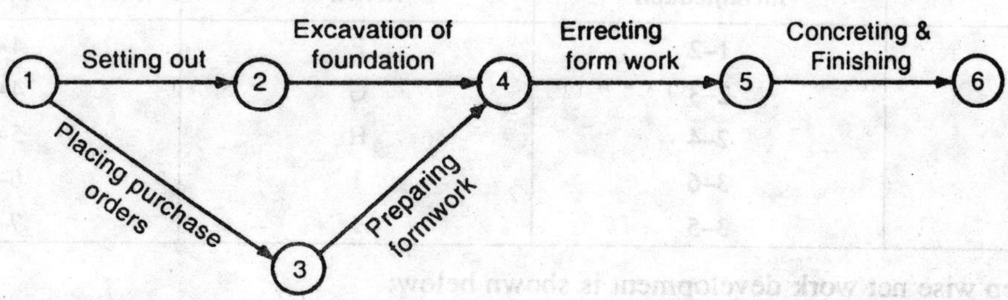

Fig. 6.35.

Solution. The diagram of the work is shown in Fig. 6.35. In this example setting out and placing purchase orders can be placed simultaneously. Similarly activity (3) and (4) also can be done simultaneously.

Example 6. *Number the following net work shown in Fig. 6.36 by Fulkerson's rule.*

Solution. Step by step solution of the problem is as follows:

1. The event A has only emerging or out going arrows. No arrow enters into it. Hence it is given number 1.
2. Deleting all arrows from node no 1, we get B and C as initial nodes. B is numbered as event no 2 and C as event no. 3.
3. Now deleting arrows from

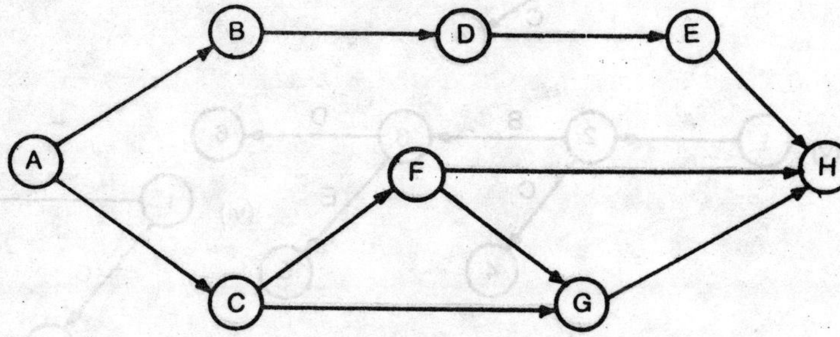

Fig. 6.36. (*a*)

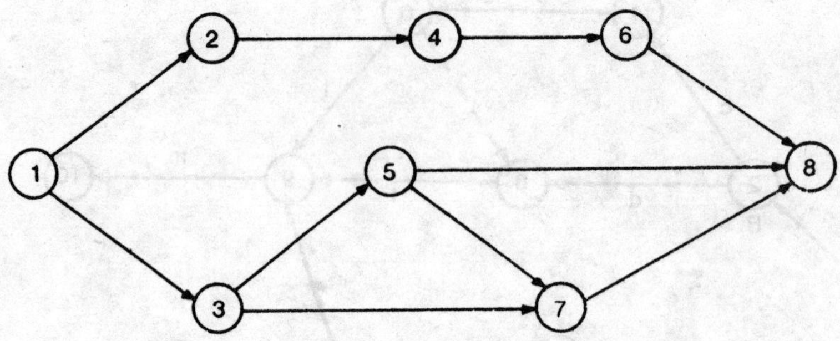

Fig. 6.36. (*b*)

nodes B and C, D and F become initial nodes. They are numbered as event 4 and 5 respectively.

4. Deleting all arrows from nodes D, F and C, E and G have become the initial node. Hence E and G are numbered as event 6 and 7.
5. Finally deleting all out going arrows from E, F and G, only H is left with out going arrows. Hence it is the last event and it is given number 8. Hence numbers are, A = 1, B = 2, C = 3, D= 4, F = 5 E = 6, G = 7 and H = 8. These are shown in Fig. 6.36 (*b*).

Example 7. *Draw the network step by step from the data of table 6.3.*

Table 6.3.

Activity	*Identification*	*Activity*	*Identification*
A	1–2	F	4–5
B	2–3	G	4–7
C	2–4	H	5–8
D	3–6	I	6–8
E	3–5	J	7–8

Solution. Step wise net work development is shown below:

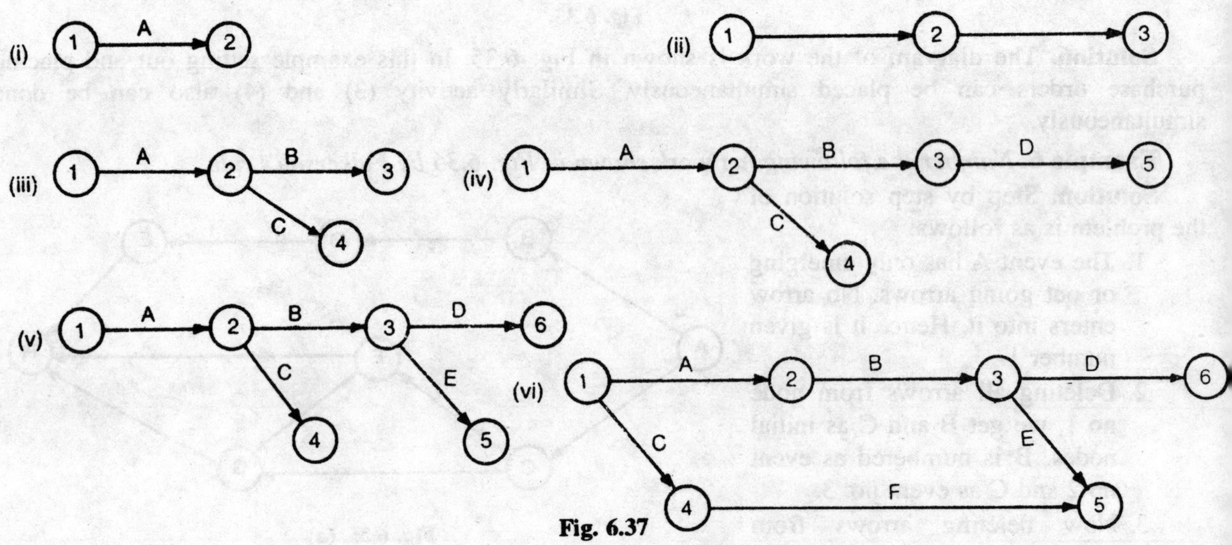

Fig. 6.37

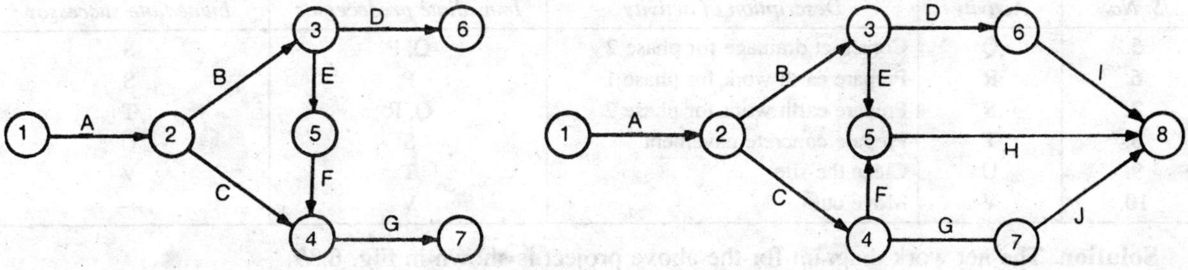

Fig. 6.37.

Example 8. *Draw a net work for the erection of a shed. The various activities involved are as shown in the following table 6.4.*

Table 6.4.

S. No.	*Name of activity*	*Description of activity*	*Pre requisite*
1.	M	Erect site work shop	—
2.	N	Fence the construction site	—
3.	O	Prepare reinforcement	O
4.	P	Excavate foundation	N
5.	Q	Fabricate steel works	M, O
6.	R	Install concrete plant	N
7.	S	Place reinforcement	O, P
8.	T	Place concrete in foundation	S, R
9.	U	Paint steel work	Q
10.	V	Erect steel work	T, U
11.	W	Give finishing touch	V

Solution. The net work of the above project is shown in Fig. 6.38.

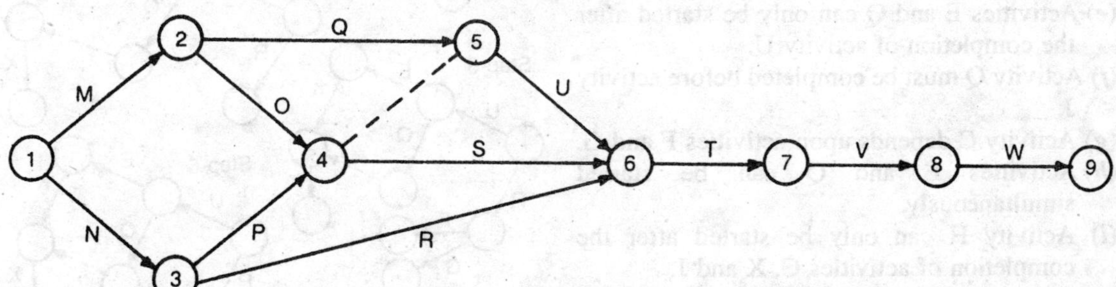

Fig. 6.38.

Example 9. *Draw the net work for a high way for the activities shown in the following table 6.5.*

Table 6.5.

S. No.	*Activity*	*Description of activity*	*Immediate predecessor*	*Immediate successor*
1.	M	Move in	—	N
2.	N	Clear land for phase 1	M	O, P
3.	O	Clear land for phase 2	N	Q
4.	P	Construct drainage for phase 1	N	Q, R

S. No.	Activity	Description of activity	Immediate predecessor	Immediate successor
5.	Q	Construct drainage for phase 2	O, P	S
6.	R	Prepare earth work for phase 1	P	S
7.	S	Prepare earth work for phase 2	Q, R	T
8.	T	Prepare concrete pavement	S	U
9.	U	Clean the site	T	V
10.	V	Move out	V	—

Solution. The net work diagram for the above project is shown in Fig. 6.39.

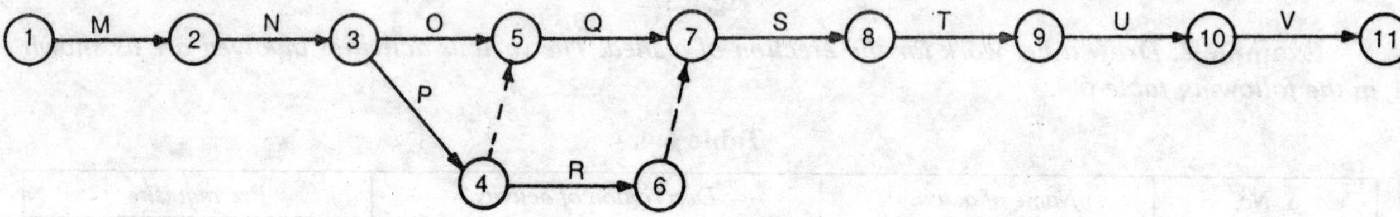

Fig. 6.39. Net work diagram for a high project.

Example 10. *Prepare the net work with the help of following activities and logic.*

1. There are total 11 activities in the project as U, R, E, Q, K, X, J, H, G, F and C.
2. Logic
   (*a*) Activities U and R can be started simultaneously.
   (*b*) Activity K can only be started after activity E.
   (*c*) Activity X depends on activities Q and K.
   (*d*) Activities F and G can only be started after the completion of activity R, but they can be started simultaneously.
   (*e*) Activities E and Q can only be started after the completion of activity U.
   (*f*) Activity Q must be completed before activity J.
   (*g*) Activity C depends upon activities F and G.
   (*h*) Activities E and Q can be started simultaneously.
   (*i*) Activity H can only be started after the completion of activities C, X and J.
   (*j*) Activity H is the last activity.

Solution. The logical and step wise construction of the problem is shown in Fig. 6.40.

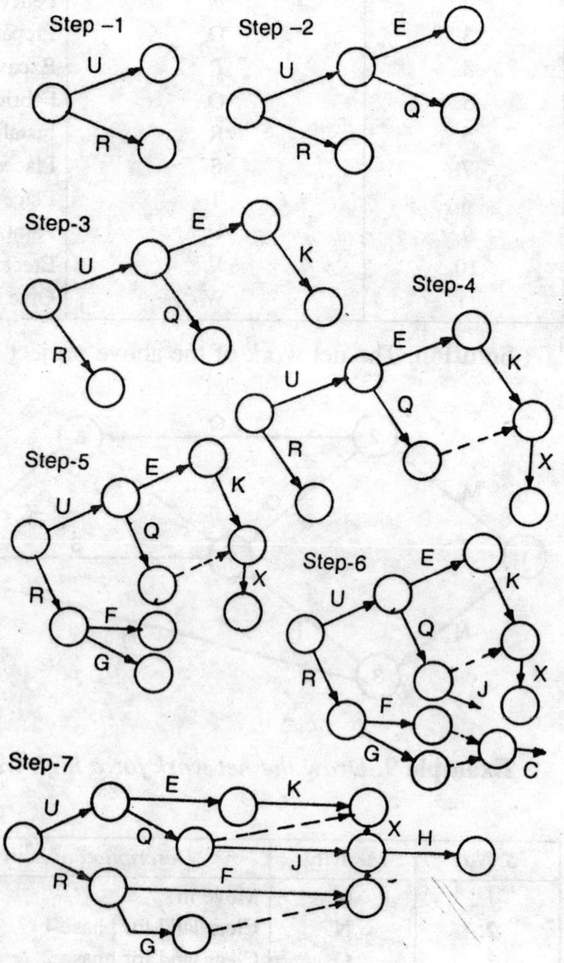

Fig. 6.40.

Example 11. *Draw the net work for the events A, B, C, D, E, F, G, H, I, J and K with the following logic.*

Logic:

1. A and K events are the initial and last events respectively.
2. Event J can be started after the completion of event F.

3. Events C and D can be started simultaneously after event B is completed.
4. Event D must be completed before event G.
5. Events E and F can only be started after event C.
6. Event E must be completed before event F.
7. Event Q can only be started after the completion of event C and event G must be completed before event H.
8. Event H must be completed before event J.
9. Event F must be completed before event H.
10. Event K starts after the completion of event J.

Solution. The logical net work of the problem is shown in Fig. 6.41.

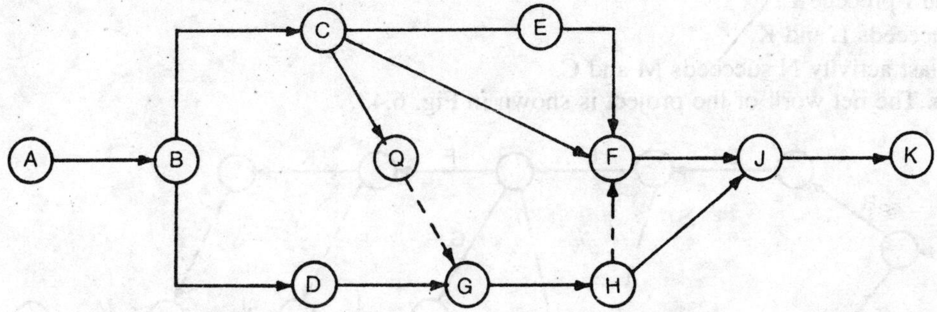

Fig. 6.41.

Example 12. *A construction project has twelve activities A, B, C... to L. Prepare the net work of the project with the following logic.*

1. A and B can be performed in parallel independently.
2. A must be finished before the start of the activities C, D and E.
3. F can not be stated until D is finished.
4. G follows activities C and D.
5. H and I can not be started till F is completed.
6. E and H precede J.
7. G and I precede K.
8. L depends on the completion of J and K.

The project is complete when L and B are complete.

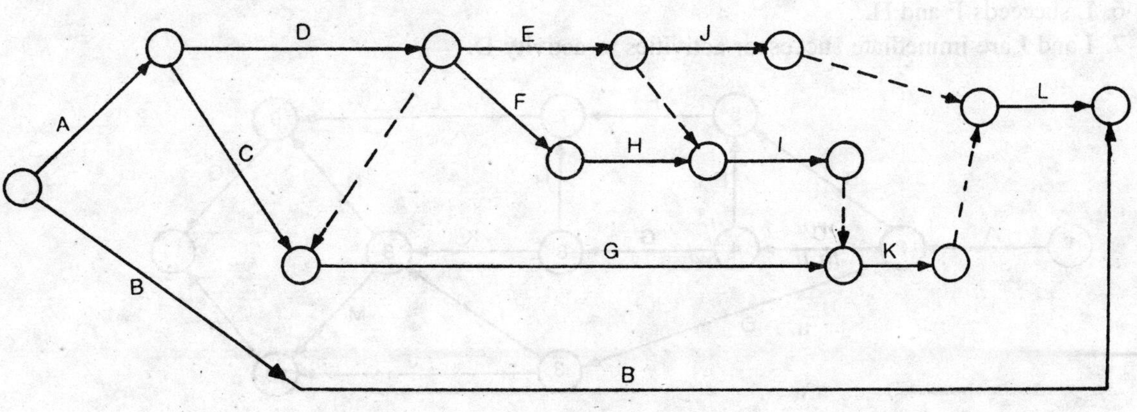

Fig. 6.42.

Solution. The net work of the project is shown in Fig. 6.42.

Example 13. *A project has fourteen activities A to N. Draw the net work of the project with the following logic.*

1. A is the first activity.
2. Activities B and C can be performed in parallel and are intermediate successor of A.
3. D, E and F follow B.
4. G follows E.
5. H follows D, but it can not be started till E is complete.
6. J and I succeed G.
7. F and J precede K.
8. H and I precede L.
9. M succeeds L and K.
10. The last activity N succeeds M and C.

Solution. The net work of the project is shown in Fig. 6.43.

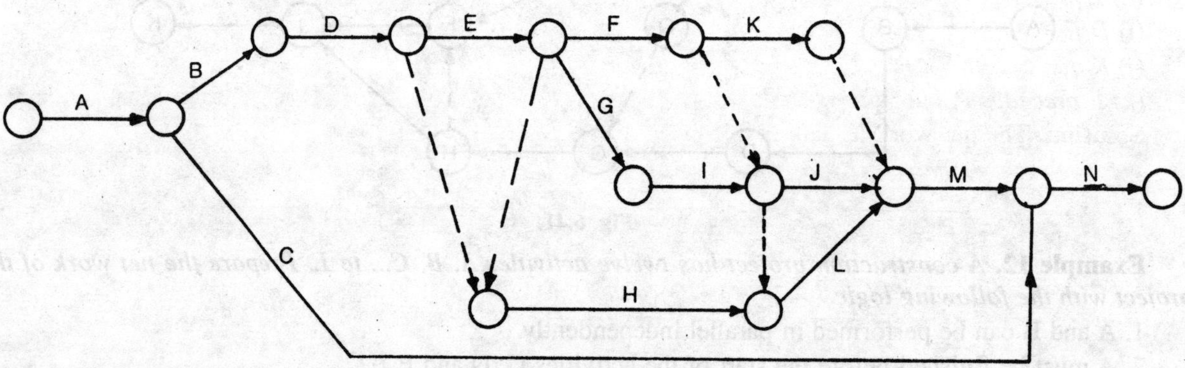

Fig. 6.43.

Example 14. *A project has sixteen activities. Draw its net work with the following logic.*

1. A is the first activity.
2. B, C and D follow A and can be done simultaneously.
3. E and G can not be started till C is completed.
4. F is the immediate successor to activities B and E.
5. Activities H and K succeed activity G and can start simultaneously.
6. L succeeds F and H.
7. I and J are immediate successor activities to activity D.

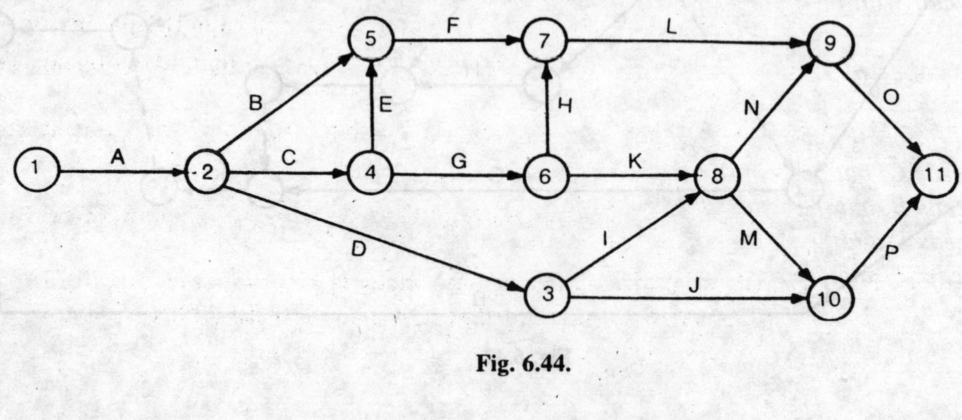

Fig. 6.44.

8. M and N are immediate successor to activity I and K. However both M and N can be performed simultaneously.
9. O and P are the last activities. Activity O is the immediate successor to N and L and activity P is the immediate successor to M and J. Draw the net work and number the events.

Solution. The net work of the project is shown in Fig. 6.44.

Example 6.15. *Draw the net work representing the following activity relationship using minimum number of dummies.*

(*a*) *A, B, and C are the initial activities*
(*b*) *Q, M and R are finishing activities*
(*c*) *E follows D but precedes N.*
(*d*) *H precedes N but follows D.*
(*e*) *F and L follow K and B.*
(*f*) *F precede M*
(*g*) *Q follows P, L and N*
(*h*) *L precedes R but follows C*
(*i*) *D follows G*
(*j*) *K and D follows A*
(*k*) *F precedes P, but follows G.* [UPSC, Engg. Services, 1986]

Solution. The net work is shown in the following Fig. No. 6.45

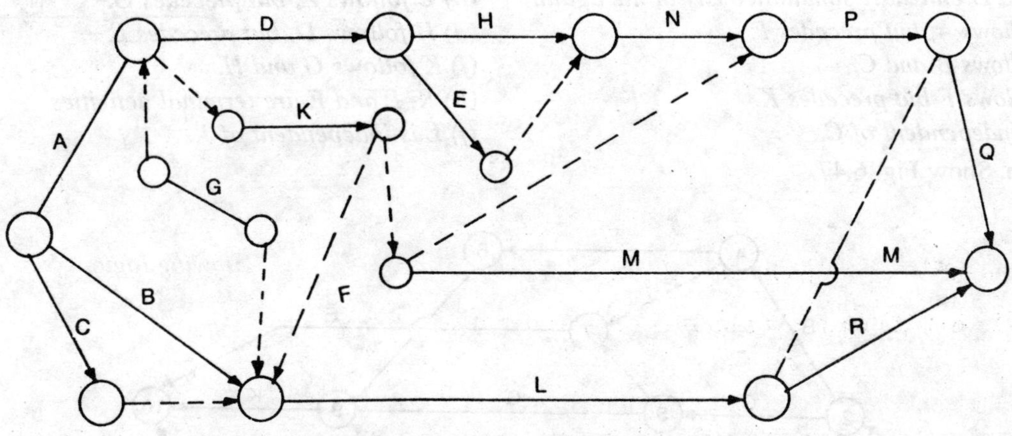

Fig. 6.45.

Example 6.16. *In a project there are 11 events as A, B, C, D, E, F, G, H, J, K, L, M. A is the first and M is the last event. With the following logic draw the diagram.*

Logic:

(*a*) *B occurs after A.*
(*b*) *C succeeds B and precedes L and restrains G.*
(*c*) *D occurs after B but before K and restrains C.*
(*d*) *F succeeds C, but precedes G and restrains E.*
(*e*) *E succeeds B, but precedes J.*
(*f*) *G succeeds F and precedes H.*
(*g*) *H precedes L and constrainst J.*
(*h*) *L occurs after J but before K.*
(*i*) *M succeeds K.* [UPSE Engg. Services, 1997]

Solution.

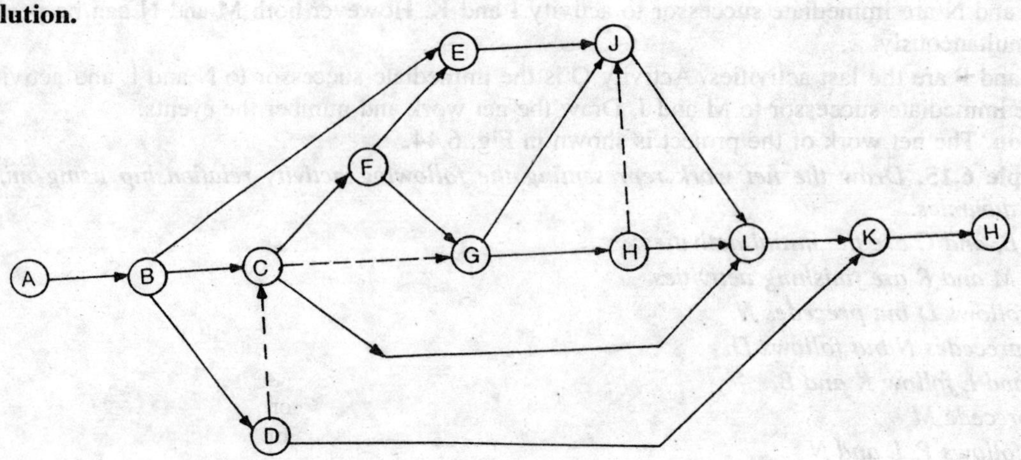

Fig. 6.46.

Example 6.17. *A construction project has 11 activities as A, B, C, D, E, F, G, H, J, K, and L. With the given logic draw the net work.*

Logic:

(*a*) *A and D can start simultaneously at the again.*
(*b*) *C follows A, but precedes G.*
(*c*) *B follows A, but precedes F.*
(*d*) *H follows D, but precedes L.*
(*e*) *E follows B and C.*
(*f*) *K follows G and H.*
(*g*) *J follows F but precedes K.*
(*h*) *K, L and E are terminal activities.*
(*i*) *F is independent of C.*
(*j*) *L is independent of J.*

Solution. Show Fig. 6.47.

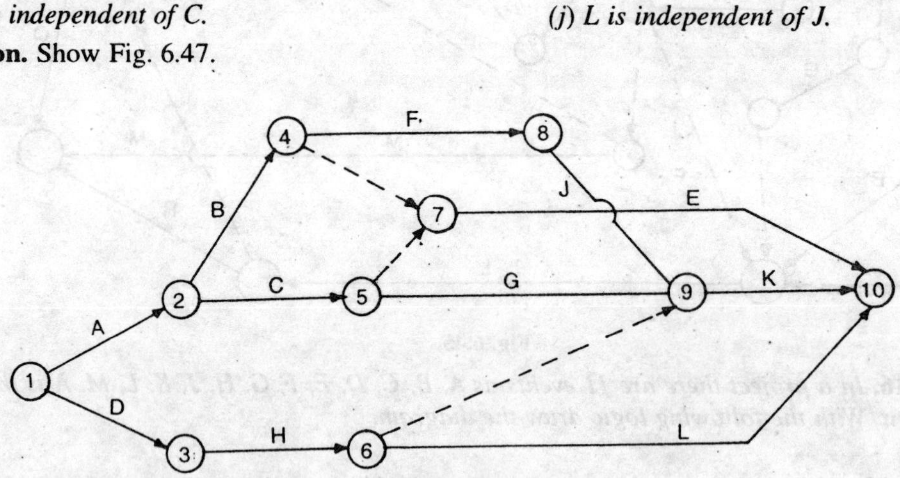

Fig. 6.47.

QUESTIONS

1. Define activity and event and draw activity and event based net works.
2. What is a net work? Discuss different types of scheduling net works with examples.
3. What is a dummy? Write down its uses. How and where a dummy should be used.
4. Discuss the rules of drawing a net work fully.
5. Discuss the D.R. fulkerson's method of numbering the events of a net work.
6. How do A-O-A net works differ from A-O-N net works.

7. Discuss the advantages and disadvantages of net work analysis over other techniques.
8. Separate out the activities and events from the following list.
   (*a*) Survey the site
   (*b*) Clean the site
   (*c*) Maps prepared
   (*d*) Invitation cards dispatched
   (*e*) Type the minutes
   (*f*) Audit the account
   (*g*) Building inaugurated
   (*h*) Assemble parts
   (*i*) Electric design completed
   (*j*) Start interior decoration.
   (*k*) Cure concrete cubes
   (*l*) Start testing cubes
   (*m*) Materials at site received
   (*n*) Payments made
   (*o*) Specifications prepared
   (*p*) Install pumps
   (*q*) Prepare estimates.
9. A project consists of eight activities M, N, O. P, R, S and T. Draw the net work and number the events if
   (*a*) Activities M, N and Q can start simultaneously.
   (*b*) Activities O and P can start concurrently and depend on the completion of M and N both.
   (*c*) Activities R and S are also concurrent and depend on the completion of activity O.
   (*d*) Activity T depends on the completion of P, Q, and R.
   (*e*) The project is complete on the completion of activities S and T.
10. A project has following fourteen activities. Draw the net work with the following logic
   (*a*) A is the first and N the last activity.
   (*b*) Activities B and C can be started simultaneously after the completion of activity A.
   (*c*) Activities D, E and F follow activity B.
   (*d*) Activity G follows activity E.
   (*e*) Activity H follows activity D, but it can not be started till E is completed.
   (*f*) Activities I and J succeed activity G.
   (*g*) Activities F and J precede activity K.
   (*h*) Activities H and I precede activity L.
   (*i*) Activity M succeed activities L and K.
   (*j*) The last activity N succeeds M and C.
11. Draw the net work for the following activities and number the events.
   (*a*) Activities B and C follow activity A.
   (*b*) Activity E follows activity B and preceeds activity J.
   (*c*) Activity C preceeds G and F.
   (*d*) Activity M follows activity H.
   (*e*) Activity G follows F and preceeds activity N.
   (*f*) Activity L follows both activities J and K and merge with M and N at the last event.
   (*g*) Activity J follows activity E.
   (*h*) Activity C preceeds F and D.
   (*i*) Activity D follows both B and C.
   (*j*) Activity G and H follow activity F.

   Time taken by each activity is shown in table below:

Activity	A	B	C	D	E	F	G	H	I	J	K	L	M
Time in days	2	7	5	6	4	3	10	6	5	3	8	2	9

12. Draw the net work with the following logic:
   (*a*) Activities A and B can be carried out simultaneously.
   (*b*) Activities D follows activity C.
   (*c*) Activity F depends on activity E and D.
   (*d*) Activities I and K can not be started untill B is completed. However they can be started simultaneously.
   (*e*) Activities C and E follow activity A and can be started simultaneously.
   (*f*) Activity E must be finished before activity G.
   (*g*) Activity J depends on the completion of activities I and K.

(*h*) Activity H can be started on completion of activities J, F and G.
(*i*) H is the last activity.

13. A project consists 12 activities as shown in below. With the data of the given table draw the net work of the project.

S. No.	*Activity*	*Identify*
1.	A	1 – 2
2.	B	2 – 4
3.	C	2 – 3
4.	D	2 – 7
5.	E	3 4
6.	F	3 – 5
7.	G	4 – 6
8.	H	5 – 6
9.	I	5 – 7
10.	J	7 – 8
11.	K	6 – 8
12.	L	8 – 9

14. There are six activities in a construction net work. Draw the net work with the following logic
(*a*) A precedes D (*b*) B precedes D and E
(*c*) C precedes E (*d*) D precedes F
(*e*) E precedes F.

15. A building project consists of eleven activities. For the following restrictions draw the net work.
A → B, A → C, A → D, B → E, C → F, C → G, D → H, E → I, F → J, G →, H → K.
Hint. (A → B means A is restriction on start of B).

16. Draw the net work from following date

S. No.	*Activity*	*I node*	*J node*
1.	A	1	2
2.	B	1	3
3.	C	1	4
4.	D	2	5
5.	E	3	5
6.	F	5	6
7.	G	4	6
8.	H	6	7
9.	I	4	7

17. From the following date draw the arrow diagram.
(*a*) A and D can start simultaneously.
(*b*) F follows A
(*c*) K follows A but precedes L
(*d*) G follows D, but precedes J
(*e*) G follows F, but precedes H
(*f*) M follows H, but precedes L
(*g*) J and L terminate at the same time.

OBJECTIVE TYPE QUESTIONS

1. Identify the correct statement/statements:
(*a*) In a net work arrows should flow from left to right direction
(*b*) No two arrows should cross each other
(*c*) No loop should be formed in a net work
(*d*) All are correct

2. Identify the correct statement/statements
   (*a*) A net work has only one initial node
   (*b*) From the initial node arrows only come out
   (*c*) In the initial node arrows only enter into it
   (*d*) In the initial node arrows enter into it and emerge as well
   (*e*) All are correct
   (*f*) None of the above is correct
3. Identify the incorrect statement/statements
   (*a*) A event net work has only one final node
   (*b*) From the final node arrows only emerge
   (*c*) From the final node arrows can emerge as well enter into it
   (*d*) In a final node arrows only can entre
   (*e*) All are incorrect
4. Identify the true and false statements of the followings:
   (*a*) In a net work diagram the time flow usually is shown from right to left direction
   (*b*) In a net work diagram the time flow usually is shown from left to right direction
   (*c*) The inter dependence and constraints should be shown in the net work by using dummies
   (*d*) In a net work keeping individuality of each activity is not essential
   (*e*) No activity can start until its tail event has occurred
   (*f*) Formation of a loop in a net work is permitted
   (*g*) Length and direction of an arrow is most significant.
5. Identify the incorrect statement/statements
   (*a*) Dummies do not maintain the logic of the diagram perfectly
   (*b*) Dummies maintain the logic of the diagram perfectly
   (*c*) Dummies keep the numbering system of the net work unique
   (*d*) The dummy activity is shown by broken line arrow
6. Precedence net works is also known as
   (*a*) A-O-A net work (*b*) A-N-O net work
   (*c*) A-O-N net work (*d*) A-A-O net work
7. Precedence net works are best suited in cases when
   (*a*) There are large number of over lapping activities
   (*b*) There are many critical activities
   (*c*) A-O-A net works are to be avoided
   (*d*) The project is to be executed efficiently
8. In the given net work, the activity Z is
   (*a*) Dependent on only activity M
   (*b*) It can be executed independently
   (*c*) It is dependent on N only
   (*d*) It is dependent on both M and N activities

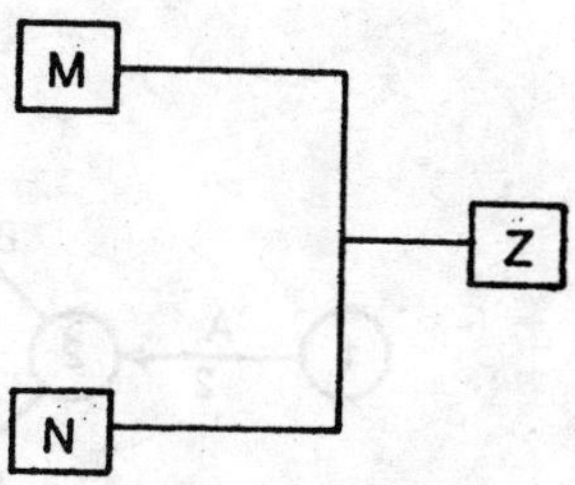

Fig. Q. 8.

9. In a precedence net work there are
   (*a*) Many dummy activities (*b*) Many serial activities
   (*c*) Many parallel activities (*d*) There is no dummy activity

ANSWERS

1. (*d*)	4. True (*b, c, e*)	7. (*a*)
2. (*a, b*)	5. (*a*)	8. (*d*)
3. (*b, c*)	6. (*c*)	9. (*d*)

Q. 9.

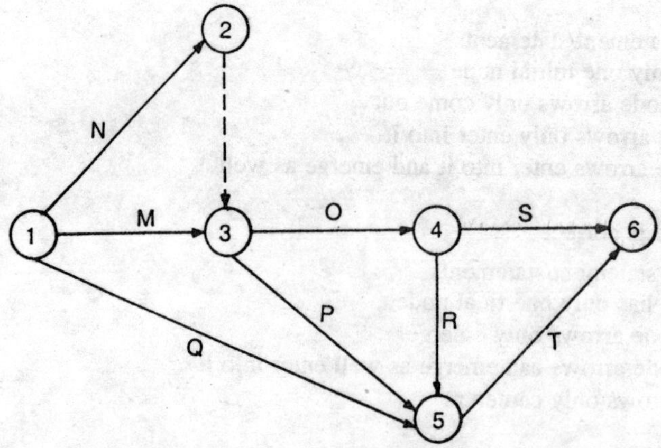

Fig. 6.48

Q. 10.

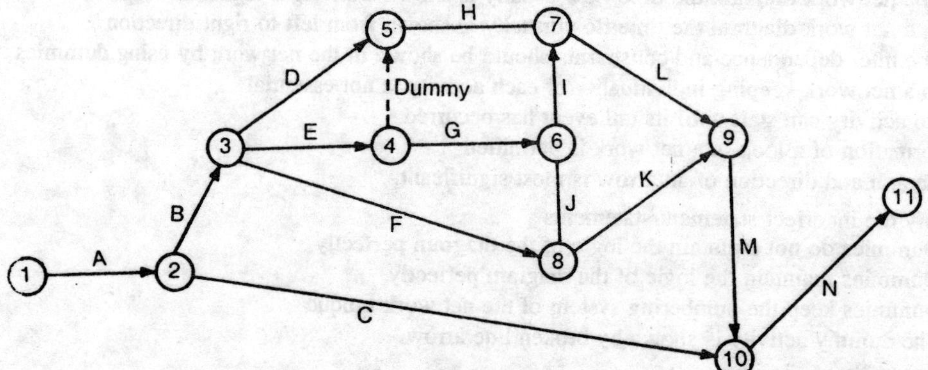

Fig. 6.49

Q. 11.

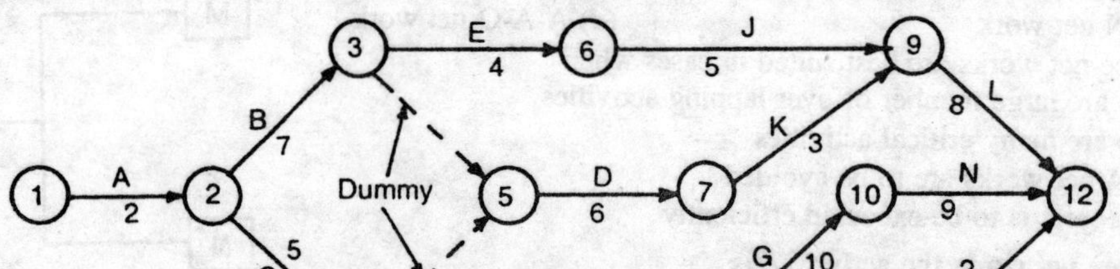

Fig. 6.50

Q. 12.

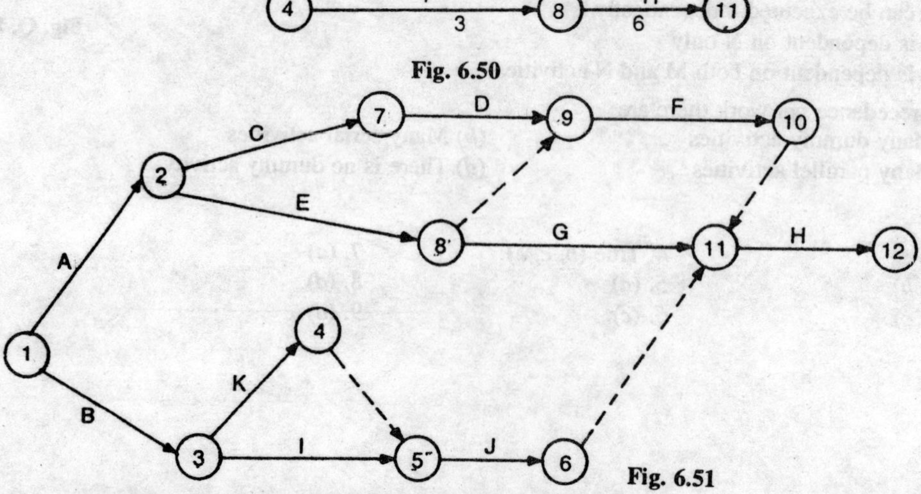

Fig. 6.51

Q. 13.

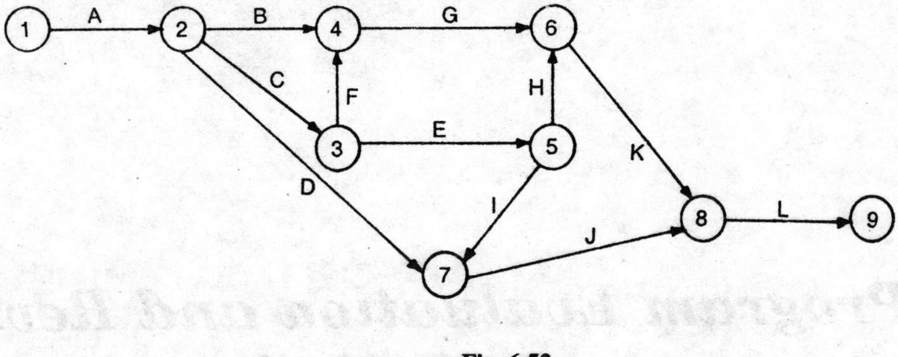

Fig. 6.52

Q. 14.

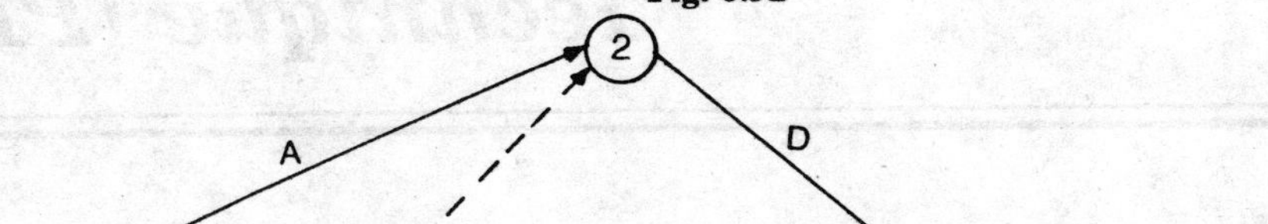

Fig. 6.53

Q. 15.

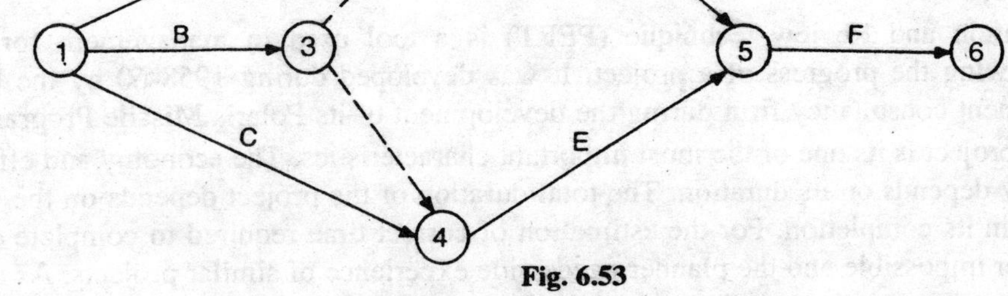

Fig. 6.54

Q. 16.

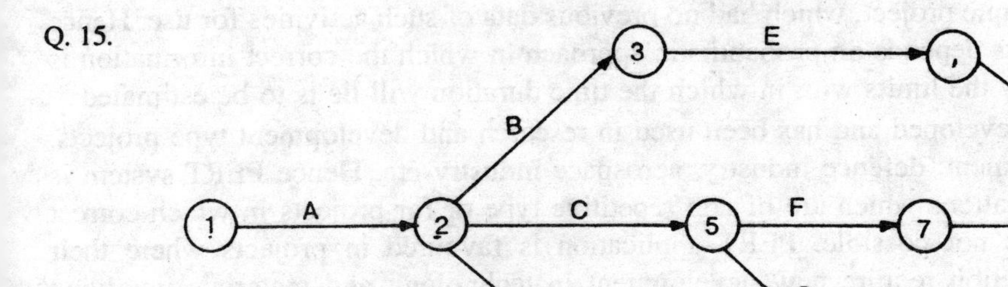

Fig. 6.55

Q. 17.

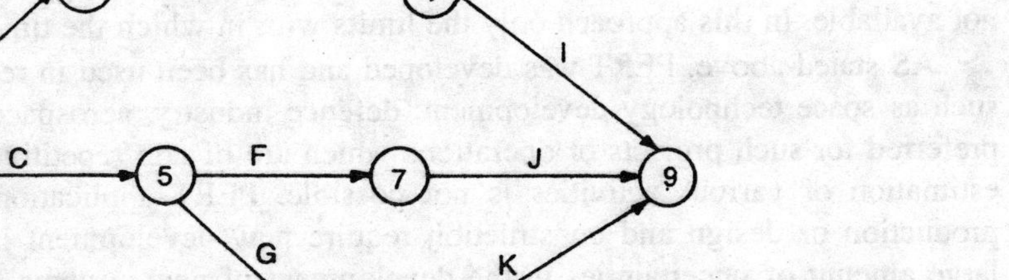

Fig. 6.56.

7

Program Evaluation and Review Technique (PERT)

7.1. INTRODUCTION

Program. Evaluation and Review technique (PERT) is a tool used in management for planning, controlling and reviewing the progress of a project. It was developed during 1958-60 by the U.S. Navy alongwith a management consultancy firm during the development of its Polaris Missile Program.

Duration of any project is its one of the most important characteristics. The economy and effectiveness of any project usually depends on its duration. The total duration of the project depends on the time taken by individual events in its completion. For the estimation of correct time required to complete each event is very difficult, rather impossible and the planner needs vide experience of similar projects. As a matter of fact PERT was developed for a unique project, which had no previous data of such activities for use. Hence the time estimation of such projects depends on probabilistic approach in which the correct information is not available. In this approach only the limits with in which the time duration will lie is to be estimated.

AS stated above, PERT was developed and has been used in research and development type projects, such as space technology development, defence industry, aerospace industry etc. Hence PERT system is preferred for such projects or operations which are of non repetitive type or for projects in which correct estimation of various activities is not possible. PERT application is favoured in projects where their production or design and construction require new development in technology and materials involving large amount of uncertainties in the development of new systems. These uncertainties may be about the time required for development of engineering materials, design and research etc.

As there is no past history available for such projects to base net work construction and time estimates, in such situations the project management has to fall back on probability approach.

In other words PERT may be defined as a technique that statistically presents knowledge about activities and their uncertainties. PERT is a manager's tool, which gives direction and technique etc. These points are explained elaborately below.

1. A Manager's tool. PERT works as a tool to define and coordinate various operations involved in the project.

2. A Direction. PERT gives the direction to the Manager what must be done to accomplish the objectives of the project successfully.

3. A Profile. PERT can not take decision itself, but it helps the manager to take a decision.

4. A Way. PERT suggests a way to synchronize the various activities of the project.

5. A Technique. PERT presents statistical information about uncertainties and computation times of various activities connected with the project.

6. A method. PERT focusses the attention of the management to take decisions on the following types of problems.

(*a*) To take decision on the latent (hidden) problems which require quick decision.

(*b*) On procedure and adjustments regarding time and resources.

(*c*) It focusses the attention of the management on minimising the production delays, interruption and conflicts.

At the end it can be said that PERT keeps the management informed with all types of information, favourable or unfavourable.

7.2. TIME ESTIMATES

Taking all uncertainties into account the time estimates may be categories into the following three categories.

1. The optimistic time estimate
2. The pessimistic time estimate
3. The most likely time estimate

1. The optimistic time estimate

The shortest possible time in which an activity can be performed or completed under ideal conditions is known as the *optimistic time estimate*. This time is denoted by t_o. In the estimation of optimistic time ideal conditions of working have been assumed having no problems and adverse conditions.

2. The pessimistic time estimate

The maximum time required to complete an activity is called or known as the pessimistic time. This is denoted by t_p. It is the best guess of time. In the estimation of this time, it is assumed that the activity has been completed under abnormal situations but not highly unusual situations as fire hazzards, earth quack or floods etc.

3. The most likely time estimate

Most often the time required to complete an activity under normal conditions is called *most likely time estimate*. It is represented by t_L. This time lies in between the optimistic and pessimistic time estimates. This time estimate reflects normal conditions.

These time estimates usually are expressed in days, weeks and months. They usually represent calendar dates and not actual working days.

7.3. SHAPE OF PROBABILITY DISTRIBUTION CURVE

The shape of the probability distribution cure associated with the three time estimates of PERT as discussed above is shown in Fig. 7.1.

From the curve it will be seen that there is a peak corresponding to the most likely time (t_L). This peak may take up any position with in the range of the distribution to conform to the characteristics of the activity under consideration. This range is approximately defined by the optimistic time (t_o) and pessimistic time (t_p). As these time estimates represent extreme cases having little chances of being realized, hence these times have very little probability. Usually 1% chance is assigned to these extreme time estimates. These extreme estimates approximately define the range of distribution of feasible activity distribution. The curve shown in Fig. 7.1 is known as unimodal curve as it has a single hump. This curve is symmetrical about the apex point *Q*. Such curves are also called normal distribution curves. It is not necessary that a frequency distribution curve may be normal. It may have skewness to the right of most likely time or to the left of it. Thus it may be concluded that a wide range in time estimates represents greater uncertainty and less confidence in our ability to estimate the correct time that the activity will need to complete it.

7.4. BETA DISTRIBUTION CURVE

The beta distribution is a typical type of probability distribution, which is not symmetrical about its apex point. The beta distribution curve gives fairly satisfactory results for most of the PERT activities. The beta distribution may be skew to the left or to the right of most likely time as shown in Fig. 7.2 (*a* and *b*).

The originators of PERT technique were interested in finding that type of probability distribution which may satisfy the following conditions:

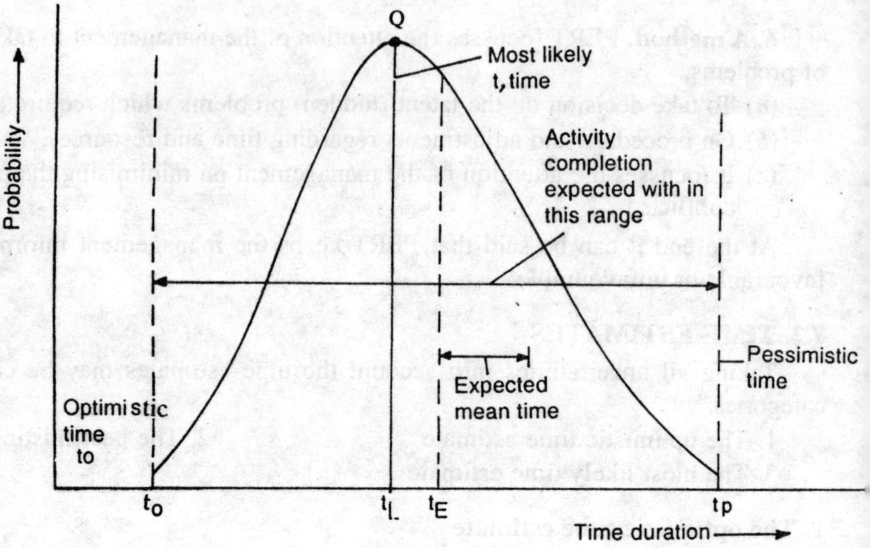

Fig. 7.1.

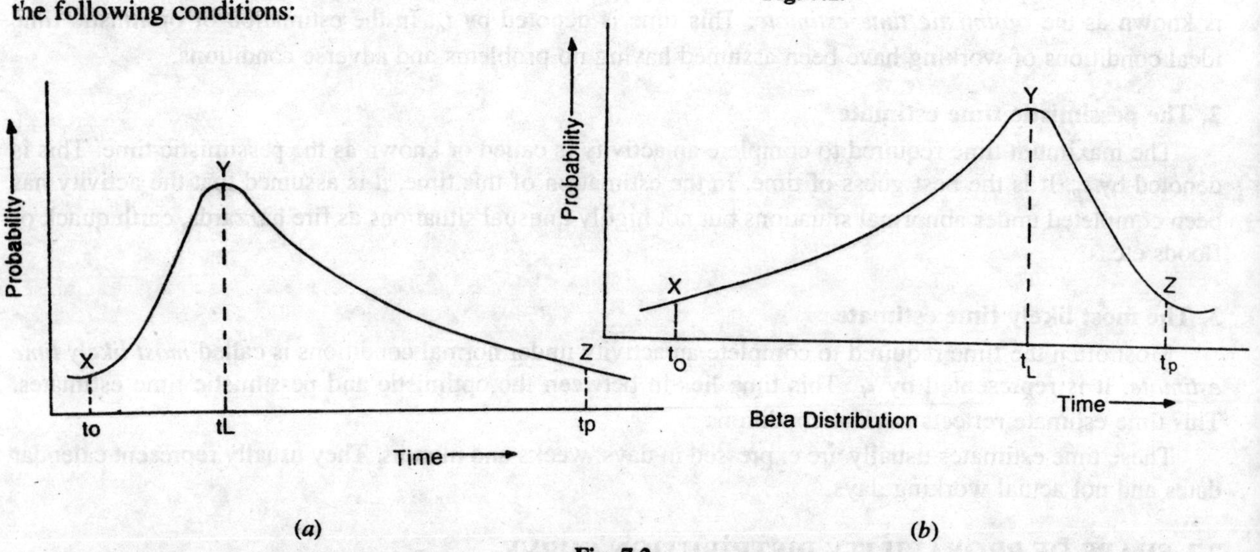

(*a*) (*b*)

Fig. 7.2.

(*a*) The distribution should have a small probability of reaching the most optimistic time (shortest time).

(*b*) The distribution should have a small probability of reaching the more pessimistic time (longest time).

(*c*) The distribution should have only one most likely time (unimodal) which should be free to move between the two extermities mentioned in *a* and *b* above.

(*d*) The distribution should be such that the quantum of uncertainty in estimating times can be measured easily.

The above mentioned four requirements are met with the beta distribution. Hence it can be concluded that the beta distribution curve will fairly fit into the analysis of PERT net work. From the beta distribution curve, the expected time, standard deviation and variance of each activity of PERT net work can be determined as follows:

1. Expected time. It is an weighted average of three times (optenistic time, pessimistic time and most likely time). It is denoted by t_E. The three times estimates are identified on beta distribution curve. If the exact shape of the probability distribution curve is known, the average or expected time can be calculated accurately. As precise curves are never available, specially for non repetitive jobs, approximation has to be adopted. In calculating the expected time, a weightage of 1 is given to the optimistic time t_o, 4 to the most likely time t_L and 1 to the pessimistic time t_p.

(*i*) Thus $$t_E = \frac{t_o + 4\,t_L + t_p}{6} \qquad \text{...(7.1)}$$

(*ii*) Standard deviation $$\sigma = \frac{t_p - t_o}{6} \qquad \text{...(7.2)}$$

(*iii*) Variance of an activity $$\sigma^2 = \left[\frac{t_p - t_o}{6}\right]^2 \qquad \text{...(7.3)}$$

As already stated, variance is the measure of uncertainty. Greater the value of variance, greater will be the uncertainty.

From equation 7.2 it will be seen that standard deviation is 1/6th of the range $(t_p - t_o)$. Thus lesser the range, more certain becomes the duration of the activity. In the limiting case, when the three time estimates coincide at one point then the certaintity duration of an activity occurs. The duration of an activity becomes certain when standard deviation and variation both vanish, which is the case of CPM. Thus PERT is a general case where as CPM is a particular case of PERT.

Example 7.1. *Plot the frequency distribution curve from the following data.*

In a certain construction project 60 concrete piles are to be driven for the construction of a bridge. For constructing the piles different parties having the same number of workers were engaged. The time-taken for constructing each pile is shown in the following Table 7.1.

Table 7.1.

10	13	16	11	12	10
12	11	14	13	11	12
14	10	9	15	13	11
8	12	11	12	12	13
11	16	15	16	9	12
13	18	12	11	15	–
12	14	10	14	13	9
15	18	13	17	10	–
17	17	19	16	14	–
14	12	15	11	13	–

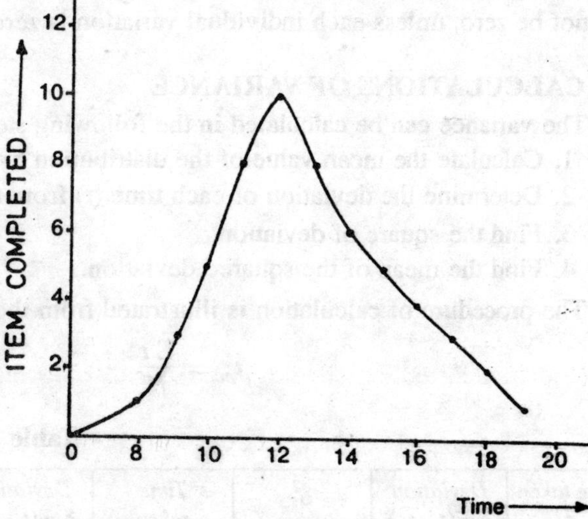

Fig. 7.3

Solution. From the above table 7.1, it will be seen that the minimum time taken to complete a pile is 8 days which represents optimistic time t_o and maximum time is 19 days which represents pessimistic time t_p. The number of piles completed in 8, 9, 10, 11, 12, 13, 14, 15, 16, 17, 18 and 19 days respectively are shown in Table 7.2 below and the curve in shown in Fig. 7.3.

Table 7.2.

No. days of completion	*No. of piles completed duing these days*	*Days of completion*	*No. of piles completed during these days*
8	1	15	5
9	3	16	4
10	5	17	3
11	8	18	2
12	10	19	1
13	8		
14	6		

7.5. MEAN, VARIANCE AND STANDARD DEVIATIONS

Mean time. It can be defined as the algebraic sum of time durations taken by various activities divided by the number of activities or jobs. It may be denoted by t_m.

$$\therefore \quad t_m = \frac{\Sigma t}{n} \qquad \ldots(7.4)$$

Deviation δ. It is defined as the difference between the time under consideration (t) and the mean time t_m

$$\text{Thus} \quad \delta = t - t_m \qquad \ldots(7.5)$$

Variance. It is defined as the mean of squared deviation. It is denoted by σ^2. Variance usually is used in statistical calculations to measure the variability of the distribution.

$$\therefore \quad \sigma^2 = \frac{\Sigma \delta^2}{n} = \frac{\Sigma(t - t_m)^2}{n} \qquad \ldots(7.6)$$

The value of variance can never be negative as it is the square of the of the deviation. Its value also can not be zero, unless each individual variation is zero.

7.6. CALCULATIONS OF VARIANCE

The variance can be calculated in the following steps:

1. Calculate the mean value of the distribution by equ^n. (7.4).
2. Determine the deviation of each time (t) from the mean time (t_m) *i.e.* calculate ($t - t_m$).
3. Find the square of deviation.
4. Find the mean of the squared deviation.

The procedure of calculation is illustrated from the table 7.3 of example 7.1.

$$t_m = \frac{\Sigma t}{N}$$

Table 7.3.

Time taken t	*Deviation* $\delta = (t - t_m)$	δ^2	*Time taken*	*Deviation* $\delta = (t - t_m)$	δ^2	*Time taken* t	δ $(t - t_m)$	δ^2
10	– 3.05	9.303	16	+ 2.95	8.703	12	– 1.05	1.103
12	– 1.05	1.103	14	+ 0.95	0.903	11	– 2.05	4.203
14	+ 0.95	0.903	9	– 4.05	16.403	13	– 0.05	0.003
8	– 5.05	25.503	11	– 2.05	4.203	12	– 1.05	1.103
11	– 2.05	4.203	15	+ 1.95	3.803	9	– 4.05	16.403

Time taken t	*Deviation* $\delta = (t - t_m)$	δ^2	*Time taken*	*Deviation* $\delta = (t - t_m)$	δ^2	*Time taken* t	$\delta\ (t - t_m)$	δ^2
13	– 0.05	0.003	12	– 1.05	1.103	15	+ 1.95	3.803
12	– 1.05	1.103	10	– 3.05	9.303	13	– 0.05	0.003
15	+ 1.95	3.803	14	– 0.05	0.003	10	– 3.05	9.303
17	+ 3.95	15.603	19	+ 5.95	35.403	14	+ 0.95	0.903
14	+ 0.95	0.903	15	+ 1.95	3.803	13	0.05	0.003
13	– 0.05	0.003	11	– 2.05	4.203	10	– 3.05	9.303
11	– 2.05	4.203	13	– 0.05	0.003	12	– 1.05	1.103
10	– 3.05	9.303	15	+ 1.95	3.803	11	– 2.05	4.203
12	– 1.05	1.103	12	– 1.05	1.103	13	– 0.95	0.903
16	+ 2.95	8.703	16	+ 2.95	8.703	15	+ 1.95	3.803
18	+ 4.95	24.503	11	– 2.05	4.203	18	+ 4.95	24.503
14	+ 0.95	0.903	14	+ 0.95	0.903	17	+ 3.95	15.603
18	+ 4.95	24.503	17	+ 3.95	15.603	12	– 3.05	9.303
17	+ 3.95	15.603	16	+ 2.95	8.703	9	– 4.05	16.403
12	– 1.05	1.103	11	– 2.05	4.203	16	+ 2.95	8.703
267		152.360	270		135.060	246		130.860

$$\Sigma t = 783$$

$$\therefore \quad t_m = \frac{\Sigma t}{N} = \frac{783}{60}$$

$$= 13.05$$

$$\Sigma \delta^2 = \frac{418.28}{60}$$

$$\therefore \quad \sigma^2 = \frac{\delta^2}{N} = \frac{418.28}{60}$$

$$= 6.971$$

$\therefore$ Standard deviation $\quad \sigma = \sqrt{6.971} = 2.64$

From Fig. 7.3 of example 7.1, the most likely time t_L is 12 days. While mean time $t_m = 13.05$. Corresponding to the most likely time the talest peak is called mode. As the distribution is not symmetrical about the peak, both mean and mode do not coincide. In normal distribution curve *i.e.* in symmetrical curves mean and mode coincide with each other.

7.7. CRITICAL PATH

The path that connects the events with zero slack or minimum slack time in a net work is called the critical path. All the events along a critical path are considered to be critical in the sense that any delay in their occurrence will result the delay in the scheduled completion of the project. Eventually a critical path is the longest path connecting the initial and end event. Usually it is denoted by a thick line on the net work.

7.8. EXPECTED TIME FOR ACTIVITIES IN SERIES

In a net work, if there are a number of activities in series then the expected time for the path along the activities is the sum of the expected time (t_E) for each activity. Alternatively, the optimistic time (t_o), the most likely time (t_L) and pessimistic time (t_p) of the path are calculated first by taking the sum of all t_o, t_L and t_p respectively and the t_E is calculated by the same formula 7.1. The procedure is illustrated by the following example.

Example 7.2. *For the following net work having four activities in series determine the expected time. The optimistic, most likely and pessimistic times are noted on the activities.*

Fig. 7.4

First method. Calculate the value of t_E by the formula,

$$t_E = \frac{t_o + 4t_L + t_p}{6}$$

The computations are shown in Table 7.4 below.

Table 7.4

Activity	t_o	t_L	t_p	t_E
1 – 2	6	7	8	7
2 – 3	7	8	12	8.5
3 – 4	5	11	13	10.33
4 – 5	3	4	7	4.33

Hence total expected time $t_E = 7.0 + 8.5 + 10.33 + 4.33 = 30.16$

Alternatively.

$$\Sigma t_o = 6 + 7 + 5 + 3 = 21$$

$$\Sigma t_L = 7 + 8 + 11 + 4 = 30$$

$$\Sigma t_p = 8 + 12 + 13 + 7 = 40$$

$$\therefore \quad \Sigma t_E = \frac{\Sigma t_o + 4 \times \Sigma t_L + \Sigma t_p}{6}$$

$$= \frac{21 + 4 \times 30 + 40}{6} = 30.16$$

Thus the expected time t_E from both the methods is same.

Example 7.3. *Calculate the expected time t_E for the following net work. The most optimistic, most likely and pessimistic time for each activity have been shown on the diagram. 1 is the initial event and 10 is the end event. Also find the critical path for the net work.*

Solution. In this diagram there are four paths to reach from event 1 to event 10 as follows:

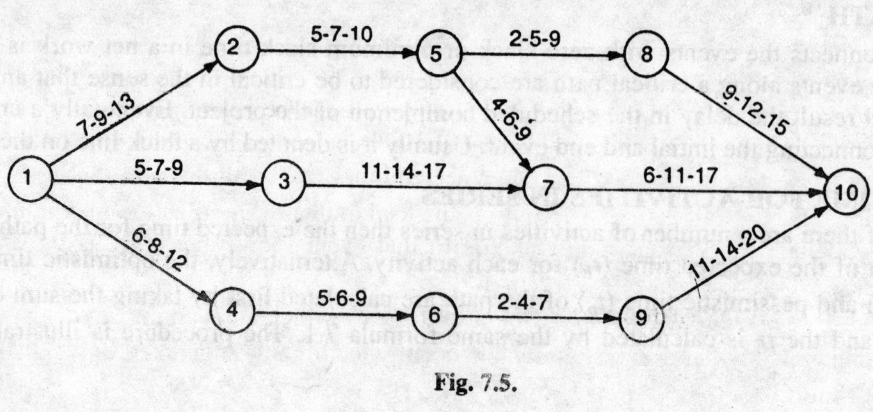

Fig. 7.5.

Path A 1-2-5-8-10

Path B 1-2-5-7-10

Path C 1-3-7-10

Path D 1-4-6-9-10

For each path the expected time t_E is calculated in the following Table 7.5.

Table 7.5.

Activity	*Optimistic time* t_o	*Most likely time* t_L	*Pessenistic time* t_p	*Expected time* t_E
1 – 2	7	9	13	9.33
1 – 3	5	7	9	7.0
1 – 4	6	8	12	8.33
2 – 5	5	7	10	7.16
3 – 7	11	14	17	14.0
4 – 6	5	6	9	6.33
5 – 7	4	6	9	6.16
5 – 8	2	5	9	5.16
6 – 9	2	4	7	4.16
7 – 10	6	11	17	11.16
8 – 10	9	12	15	12.0
9 – 10	11	14	20	14.5

From the above table $\Sigma\, t_E$ is determined for each path as follows:

$\therefore$ $\Sigma\, t_E$ for Path 1-2-5-8-10 = 9.33 + 7.16 + 5.16 + 12.0 = 33.65

$\Sigma\, t_E$ for Path 1-2-5-7-10 = 9.33 + 7.16 + 6.16 + 11.16 = 33.81

$\Sigma\, t_E$ for Path 1-3-7-10 = 7.0 + 14.0 + 11.16 = 32.16

$\Sigma\, t_E$ for Path 1-4-6-9-10 = 8.33 + 6.33 + 4.16 + 14.5 = 33.32

From the above calculations it can be seen that path 1-2-5-7-10 takes the maximum time to reach the event 10 from event (1) *i.e.* $\Sigma\, t_E = 33.81$ units of time. Hence it is the critical path.

(*b*) Thus critical path is 1-2-5-7-10 path. Hence duration of the project = 33.81 units of time.

Sofar we have considered activity oriented time durations, but PERT is an event oriented net work and the importance is for the occurrence of events. PERT oriented net work time duration will be illustrated in the next example.

7.9. DEFINITIONS

1. **Earlier expected time (T_E).** It is the time when an event can be expected to occur. The earliest expected time is denoted by TE. Usually it is put above or below that particular node (event circle) in the net work. It is computed by adding the expected times (t_E) of all the activities along the path leading to that event. If more than one activity paths lead to that event, then the maximum value of the sum of t_E's along the various paths leading to that event should be taken as the T_E for that particular event.
2. **Latest allowable occurrence time (T_L).** The latest time by which an event must occur to keep the project on schedule is known as latest allowable occurrence time. It is denoted by T_L. Thus it is an another event time.

, When ever a project is started, a decision is taken regarding completion time of project and accepted figure is known as scheduled completion time. It is also called contractual obligation time and denoted by T_S.

Thus $T_S = T_L$ ...(7.7)

3. **Slack.** It can be defined as the difference between the latest allowable time T_L and the earliest expected time T_E of an event. It is denoted by S. Slack can be positive zero and negative.

Thus $S = T_L - T_E$ ...(1)

4. **Positive stack.** If latest allowable occurrence time is more than the earlier expected time *i.e.* $T_L > T_E$, it is an indication of an ahead schedule condition *i.e.* the work will be completed earlier than schedule.
5. **Zero slack.** It occurs when $T_L = T_E$ for an event. it is an indication of a an schedule condition.
6. **Negative slack.** When T_L is less than T_E. It happens when schedule time of completion T_S is less than T_E. This indicates the condition that the work of the project is behind the schedule.

7.10. DETERMINATION OF EARLIEST EXPECTED TIME T_E.

The earliest expected time T_E is calculated by adding the expected times (t_E) of all the activities along the path leading to that event. If there are more than one paths leading to that event, then the maximum value of the sums of expected times (t_E) along the various paths leading to that event will be taken as the earliest expected time T_E of that particular event. The procedure is illustrated by the help of the following examples.

Example 7.4. *Find the earliest expected times T_E of all the events of the net work shown below in Fig. 7.6 The three time estimates t_o, t_L and t_p are shown on the activities of the net work and the activity expected time t_E is written below the arrow of the activity.*

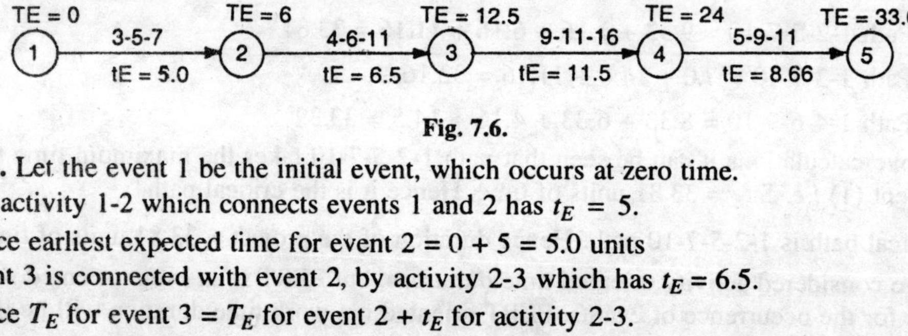

Fig. 7.6.

Solution. Let the event 1 be the initial event, which occurs at zero time.

The activity 1-2 which connects events 1 and 2 has $t_E = 5$.

Hence earliest expected time for event 2 = 0 + 5 = 5.0 units

Event 3 is connected with event 2, by activity 2-3 which has $t_E = 6.5$.

Hence T_E for event 3 = T_E for event 2 + t_E for activity 2-3.

$\therefore$ T_E for 3 = 5.0 + 6.5 = 11.5

Similarly T_E for event 4 = 11.5 + 11.5 = 23.0

T_E for event 5 = 23 + 8.66 = 31.66.

Thus it is concluded that the earliest expected time for any event is the sum of the activities expected times (t_E) of the activity path leading to the event under consideration. The earliest expected time is written above circle of the event.

Example 7.5. *Find the earliest expected times of all the events of the net work shown in Fig. 7.7.*

Solution. The event (1) is the initial event,

hence T_E for event (1) is zero.

Event 5 has two activity paths.

Path (*i*) 1-2-3-5

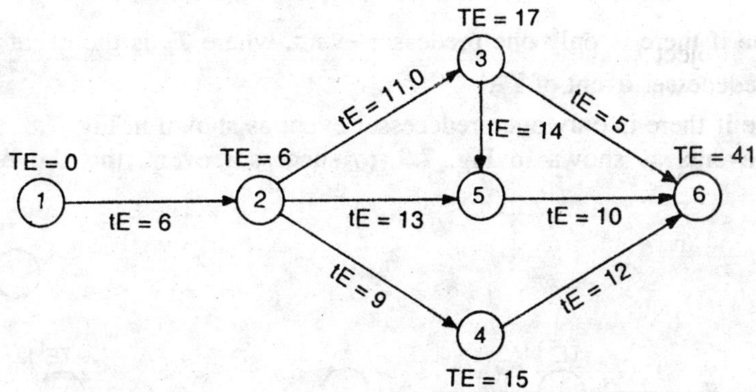

Fig. 7.7.

Path (*ii*) 1-2-5

In both paths the event 1 and 2 are common. The time computations along each path leading to event 5 are as under:

Event	T_E
1	0
2	6
3	6 + 11 = 17
4	6 + 9 = 15

5 along the path 1-2-3-5 = 6 + 11 + 14 = 31

5 along the path 1-2-5 = 6 + 13 = 19.

From the above figures, it will be seen that T_E for event 5 along the two activity paths is different. How ever no event can be considered to have reached untill all the activities are completed leading to that event. Hence event 5 can not be considered to have occurred untill all the activities along the paths are completed.

Thus the greater value of two T_E will be the earliest expected times for event 5. Thus the T_E for event 5 will be 31.

Event 6 can be reached along four paths as follows:

Paths	T_E
(*i*) Path 1-2-3-6	22
(*ii*) Path 1-2-3-5-6	41
(*iii*) Path 1-2-5-6	29
(*iv*) Path 1-2-4-6	27

Thus the earliest expected time for event 6, will be the largest value.

Hence T_E for event 6 = 41. The $T_{E's}$ are marked on the Fig. 7.7.

7.11. RULE FOR EVALUATING THE EARLIEST EXPECTED TIME T_E

The method for evaluating the earliest expected time T_E is suitable for small net works, but for large or complicated net works in which an event under consideration may have many predecessor events, it is time consuming. In such cases it is better to formulate a rule for computation of T_E with out frequent reference to the net work diagram. For such cases T_E for any event can be determined by the following rule.

$$T_E \text{ (successor event)} = T_E \text{ (predecessor event)} + t_E \text{ (activity)}$$

It can be expressed symbolically as follows:

$$T_E^j = T_E^i + t_E^{ij} \qquad \ldots(7.8)$$

This relation is true if there is only one predessor event, where T_E^j is the event for which T_E is to be calculated. T_E^i is the predecesser event of T_E^j.

Equation 7.8 is true if there is only one predecesser event as shown in Fig. 7.8. In case there are more than one predecessor events as shown in Fig. 7.9, to successor event, the above relation needs some

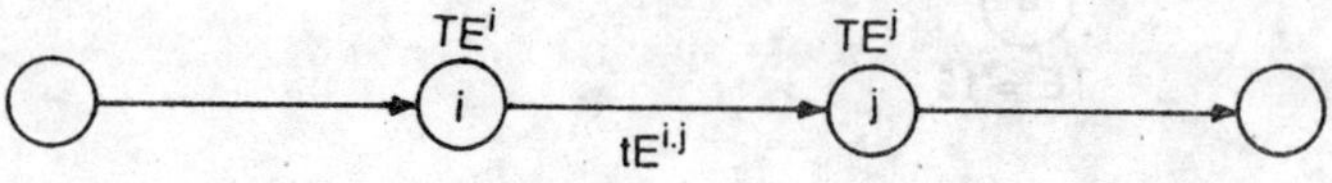

Fig. 7.8

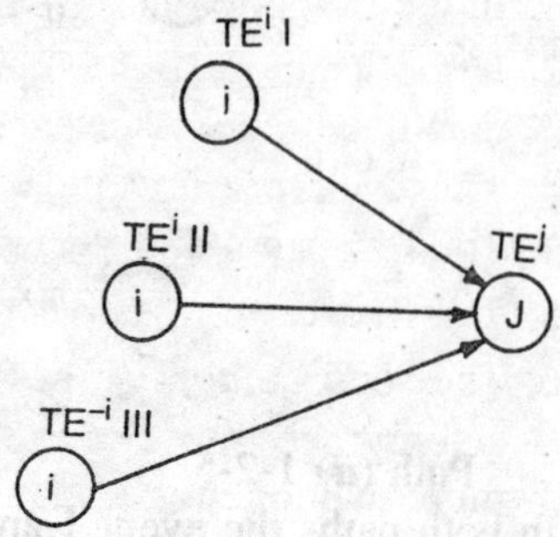

Fig. 7.9

modification as the event j can not occur unless all activities leading to it are completed. In this case the T_E will be equal to the maximum value of $(T_E^i + t_E^{ij})$ along the different activity paths. Thus

$$T_E^j = T_E^i + t_E^{ij} \text{ max} \qquad \ldots(7.9)$$

This rule is explained with the help of example 7.6.

Example 7.6. Find the earliest expected time T_E for all the events shown in the net work of Fig. 7.10.

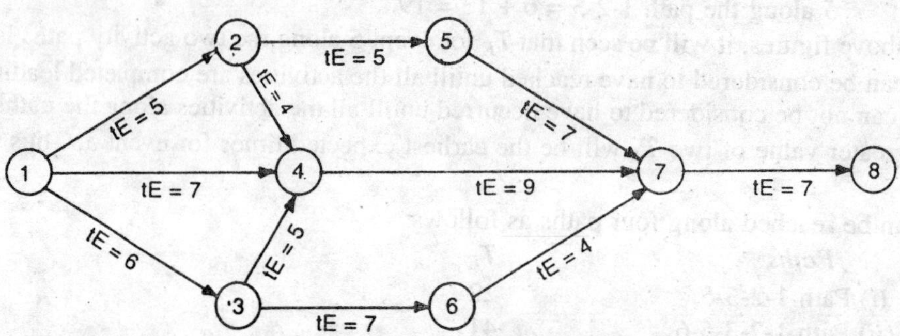

Fig. 7.10.

Solution. In the net work of Fig. 7.10, events 1 is the initial event, hence T_E^1 is zero.

For event 2, $T_E^2 = 0 + 5 = 5$

For event 3, $T_E^3 = 0 + 6 = 6$

For event 4, $T_E^4 = 5 + 4 = 9$ for 1–2–4 path $= 0 + 7 = 7$ for 1–4 path

$= 6 + 5 = 11$ for 1–3–4 path

The value for path 1-3-4 is the largest value of 11. Hence $T_E^4 = 11$.

For event 5, $T_E^5 = 5 + 5 = 10$

For event 6, $T_E^6 = 6 + 7 = 13$

For event 7, $T_E^7 = 5 + 5 + 7 = 17$ for path 1–2–5–7 $= 11 + 9 = 20$ for path 1–4–7

$= 6 + 7 + 4 = 17$ for path 1–3–6–7

Of these values 20 is the largest value, hence $T_E^7 = 20$.

For event 8, $T_E = 20 + 7 = 27$.

The net work can be redrawn to incorporate the T_E values of each event.

These computations can also be done in tabular form as shown in table 7.6 below.

1. In the first column that event is entered for which T_E is to be determined.
2. In the second column, the predecessor to the event of 1st column is entered. In case there are more than one predecessor events, then all of these are written one above the other.
3. Third column shows the activity between events of column (1) and (2).
4. The fourth column shows the expected time t_E of the activity of column (3).
5. The fifth column shows the T_E of event of column (2).
6. The sixth column shows the sum of T_E of the predecessor event plus the expected time t_E of the activity between that event and its predecessor event (*i.e.* the sum of column (4 + 5). If there are more than one predecessor events, then there will be more than one T_E in column 6. In such cases largest value of time T_E will be taken for that event. The computation of example 7.6 is shown in Table 7.6 below.

Table 7.6.

Event (1)	*Predecessor event* (2)	*Activity ij* (3)	Expected time of activity t_E^{ij} (4)	T_E^i (5)	T_E^j (6)
1	–	–			0
2	1	1 – 2	5	0	5
3	1	1 – 3	6	0	6
4	1	1 – 4	7	0	7
	2	2 – 4	4	5	9
	3	3 – 4	5	6	11
5	2	2 – 5	5	5	10
6	3	3 – 6	7	6	13
7	4	4 – 7	9	11	20
	5	5 – 7	7	10	17
	6	6 – 7	4	13	17
8	7	7 – 8	7	20	27

Example 7.7. *Find the T_E for each event of the net work shown in Fig. 7.11 in the tabular form.*

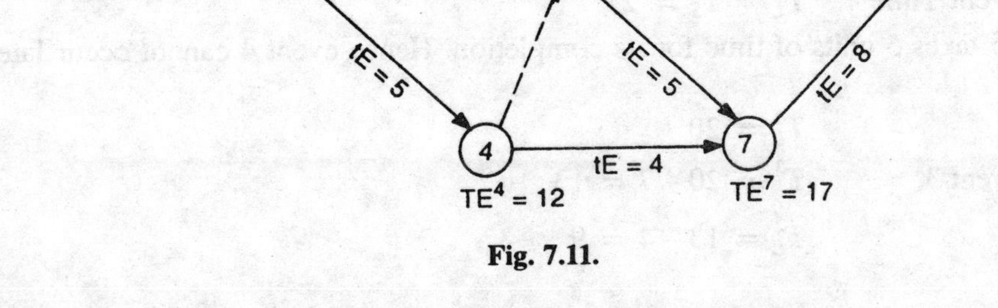

Fig. 7.11.

Solution. In the net work, 2-6 and 4-6 are the dummy activities, which do not take up any time. The computation is shown in Table 7.7 below.

Table 7.7.

Event	*Predecessor event*	*Activity ij*	Expected time of activity t_E^{ij}	T_E^i	T_E^j
(1)	(2)	(3)	(4)	(5)	(6)
1	0	–	–	–	0
2	1	1 – 2	5	0	5
3	1	1 – 3	7	0	7
4	3	3 – 4	5	7	12
5	2	2 – 5	6	5	11
	3	3 – 5	5	7	12
6	2	2 – 6	0	5	5
	3	3 – 6	4	7	11
	4	4 – 6	0	12	12
7	4	4 – 7	4	12	16
	6	6 – 7	5	12	17
8	5	5 – 8	5	12	17
	6	6 – 8	7	12	19
	7	7 – 8	8	17	25

In the computation of the earliest expected time T_E, we started from the initial event and proceeded along the net work and ended with the end or final event of the net work. This process is known as *forward pass* in which the net work is processed from the initial event to the final event. The value of T_E is shown on the net work of Fig. 7.11 itself.

7.12. LATEST ALLOWABLE OCCURRENCE TIME

An other important event time is the latest allowable occurrence time. Almost all projects are time bound. Therefore for each event some time limit is allotted by which time that event must occur. The latest time by which an event must occur to keep the project on schedule is called the *latest allowable occurrence time.* It is denoted by T_L. The time by which a project has to be completed usually is called the schedule completion time or contractual obligation time. It is denoted by T_S. Thus it refers to the latest time of the last event, *i.e.* $T_S = T_L$. The procedure of calculation of T_L is illustrated by the simple net work of Fig. 7.13 having 5 events and 4 activities.

Fig. 7.12.

Let us assume that schedule completion time T_S for the project is 25 units. It signifies that the last event 5 must occur latest by 25 units of time after the start of the project.

Thus the last event Time $T_L^5 = T_S = 25$

The activity 4-5 takes 5 units of time for its completion. Hence event 4 cannot occur later than 25 – 5 = 20 units of time.

Thus $T_L^4 = 20$

Similarly for event 3, $T_L^3 = 20 - 7 = 13$

For event 2, $T_L^2 = 13 - 4 = 9$

For initial event $T_L^2 = 9 - 5 = 4.0$

These values of latest occurrence time for each event are indicated below the corresponding event circles Fig. 7.13.

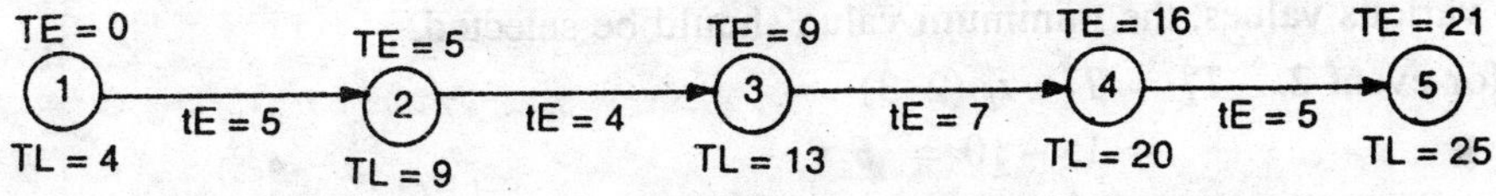

Fig. 7.13

Example 7.8. *Find the latest allowable occurrence time of all events of the net work shown in Fig. 7.14.*

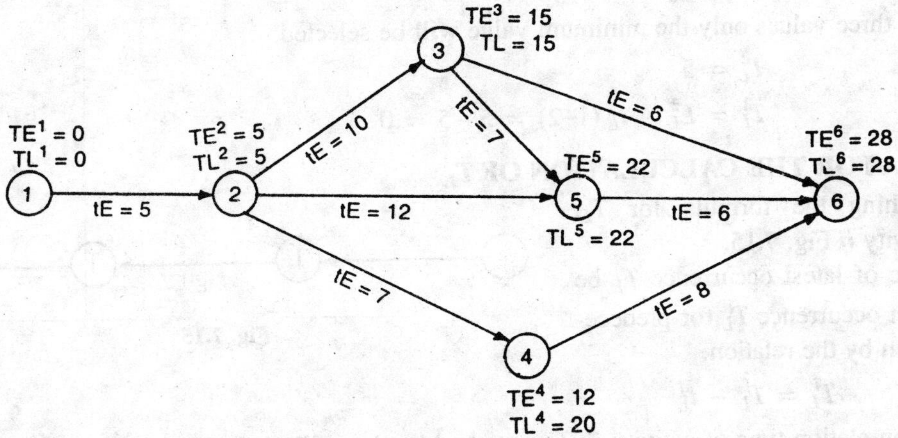

Fig. 7.14

Solution. First we should calculate earliest expected time T_E.

$$T_E^1 = 0$$
$$T_E^2 = 5$$
$$T_E^3 = 15$$
$$T_E^4 = 12$$
$$T_E^5 = \frac{22}{17}$$
$$T_E^6 = 21$$
$$= \frac{28}{20}$$

Let us assume that schedule completion time T_S for project is 28 units of time. The latest occurrence time T_L for the last event is also 28 units.

For event 5, latest occurrence time is given by the relation.

$$T_L^5 = T_L^6 - t_E \text{ for } 5-6$$
$$= 28 - 6 = 22 \text{ units}$$

For event 4, $T_L^4 = T_L^6 - t_E\,(4-6) = 28 - 8 = 20$ units

Event 3 has two successor events 5 and 6.

Hence $T_L^3 = T_L^6 - t_E\,(3-6)$

$= 28 - 6 = 22$

$T_L^3 = T_L^5 - t_E\,(3-5) = 22 - 7 = \underline{15}$

Out of the various values, the minimum value should be selected.

Similarly for event 2, $T_L^2 = T_L^3 - t_E\,(2\text{–}3)$

$= 15 - 10 = \underline{5}$

$= T_L^5 - t_E\,(2\text{–}5)$

$= 22 - 12 = 10$

also $= T_L^4 - t_E\,(2\text{–}4)$

$= 20 - 7 = 13$

Out of these three values only the minimum value will be selected.

Hence $T_L^2 = 5$

$T_L^1 = L_L^2 - t_E\,(1\text{–}2) = 5 - 5 = 0$

7.13. FORMULA FOR THE CALCULATION OF T_L

For establishing the formula for T_L, Consider an activity *ij* Fig. 7.15.

Let the value of latest occurrence T_L be known. The latest occurrence T_L^i for predecessor event is given by the relation.

Fig. 7.15

$$T_L^i = T_L^j - t_E^{ij} \qquad \ldots(7.10)$$

where t_E^{ij} is the completion time of activity *ij*. The method has been illustrated by the following example.

Example 7.9. *Find the value of T_L of all the events of net work shown in Fig. 7.17 using the above formulation.*

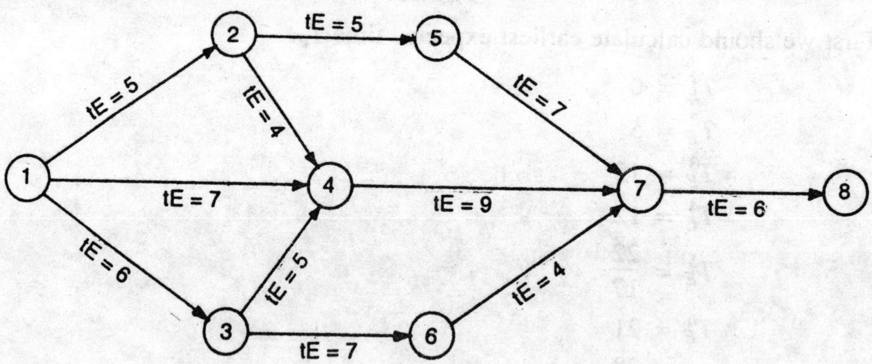

Fig. 7.16

Solution. For the given net work no scheduled completion time T_S has been given. Hence where no schedule completion of the final event is given, it should be assumed equal to earliest expected time T_E. Hence $T_S = T_L = T_E$.

In this case first we have to calculate the earliest expected time T_E for all the events and then T_L.

1st earliest expected times T_E.

$T_E^1 = 0$

$T_E^2 = 5$

$$T_E^3 = 6$$
$$T_E^4 = 11 \text{ For Path (1–3–4)}$$
$$T_E^4 = 7 \text{ For Path (1–4)}$$
$$T_E^4 = 9 \text{ For Path (1–2–4)}$$
$$T_E^5 = 10$$
$$T_E^6 = 13$$
$$T_E^7 = 17 \text{ For Path (1–3–6–7)}$$
$$= 20 \text{ For Path (1–3–4–7)}$$
$$= 17 \text{ For Path (1–2–5–7)}$$
$$T_E^8 = 20 + 6 = 26$$

Thus T_S of the project is 26 units.

$\therefore$ $$T_S = T_E^8 = 26$$

Hence $$T_L^8 = 26$$

Event 7 has one successor event only.

$\therefore$ $$T_L^7 = T_L^8 - t_E\,(7\text{–}8)$$
$$= 26 - 6 = \underline{20}$$

Event 6 has one successor event only

$\therefore$ $$T_L^6 = T_L^7 - t_E\,(6\text{–}7) = 20 - 4 = 16$$

Events 5 also has one successor event only

$\therefore$ $$T_L^5 = T_L^7 - t_E\,(5\text{–}7) = 20 - 7 = \underline{13}$$

Event 4 also has one successor event only

$\therefore$ $$T_L^4 = T_L^7 - t_E\,(4\text{–}7) = 20\ 9 = 11$$

Event 3 has 2 successor events 4 and 6.

$\therefore$ $$T_L^3 = T_L^6 - t_E\,(3\text{–}6) = 16 - 7 = 9$$
$$T_L^3 = T_L^4 - t_E\,(3\text{–}4) = 11 - 5 = \underline{6}$$

Out of these values, minimum value is to be selected

Hence $$T_L^3 = \underline{6}$$

Event 2 also has 2 successor events 4 and 5.

$\therefore$ $$T_L^2 = T_L^4 - t_E\,(2\text{–}4) = 11 - 4 = \underline{7}$$
$$T_L^2 = T_L^5 - t_E\,(2\text{–}5) = 13 - 5 = 8$$

$\therefore$ $$T_L^2 = 7$$

Event 1 has 3 successor events 2, 3 and 4.

$\therefore$ $$T_L^1 = T_L^2 - t_E\,(1\text{–}2) = 7 - 5 = 2$$
$$T_L^1 = T_L^3 - t_E\,(1\text{–}3) = 6 - 6 = \underline{0}$$
$$T_L^1 = T_L^4 - t_E\,(1\text{–}4) = 11 - 7 = 4$$

Out of the three values least value will be selected.

Hence $$T_L^1 = \underline{0}$$

The values of T_L accepted is under lined.

Example 7.10. *Find out the latest allowable occurrence time T_L of each event of the net work shown in Fig. 7.17 using the back ward pass method in tabular form.*

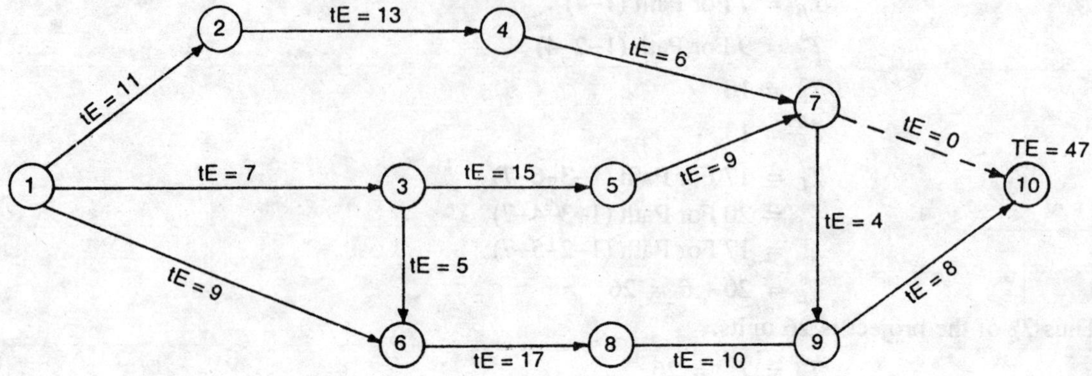

Fig. 7.17

Solution. In the net work earliest expected time T_E is given as 47 weeks. As no schedule completion time is given, T_E will be assumed as the scheduled time T_S.

Thus $$T_S = T_E = 47$$

In the 1st column of the table 7.8 predecessor events *i* are entered starting from the higher order. In the second column successor events (*j*) are entered. In the third column activity (*i-j*) are entered. In column 4 the expected time of activities t_E is entered and in the last column the value of latest allowable time T_L is entered as shown in Table 7.8. The procedure is self explanatory.

Table 7.8.

Predecessor event (i)	*Successor events (j)*	*Activity (i – j)*	*Activity (i – j) expected time t_E*	T_L^j	T_L^i
(1)	(2)	(3)	(4)	(5)	(6)
10	–	–	–	–	47
9	10	9 – 10	8	47	39
8	9	8 – 9	10	39	29
7	10	7 – 10	0	47	47
	9	7 – 9	4	39	35
6	8	6 – 8	17	29	12
5	7	5 – 7	9	35	26
4	7	4 – 7	6	35	29
3	5	3 – 6	5	12	7
	6	3 – 5	15	26	11
2	4	2 – 4	13	29	16
1	6	1 – 6	9	12	3
	3	1 – 3	7	7	0
	2	1 – 2	11	16	5

7.14. COMBINED TABULAR COMPUTATION FOR T_E and T_L

In practice or actual calculations in most of the cases both earliest expected time T_E and latest allowable occurrence time T_L have to be computed. The earliest expected time T_E is calculated by forward pass method starting from the initial event. For such calculations predecessor event (*i* event) forms the basis. On the other hand for calculating the latest allowable occurrence time T_L back ward pass method starting from the end event is adopted. For such computations successor events (j events) from the basis. In the tabular from both the T_E and T_L can be calculated easily. The format is shown in Table 7.9.

Table 7.9.

Event No	*Earliest expected time T_E*				*Latest allowable occurance time T_L*			
	Predecessor event (i)	*Duration of activity t_E*	T_E^i	T_E	*Suceessor event*	t_E^{ij}	T_L^i	T_L
(1)	(2)	(3)	(4)	(5)	(6)	(7)	(8)	(9)

In the table in column events are entered for which T_E and T_L are to be calculated. The next 4 columns are used for calculating T_E by forward pass method. In the second column predecessor events of the first column events are entered. In the third column duration of activity linking the events of first and second columns is entered. In the fourth column T_E of the event in the first column is entered. This value of T_E is obtained by adding the T_E of the event in the second column with the activity time t_E linking these two events entered in column (3). If there are more than one value of T_E for the event, then the maximum of all the values should be selected as the T_E of that event and written in column 5. In this way T_E of the events is calculated starting from the initial event. This constitutes the forward pass computation.

The next 4 columns (6 to 9) are used for computation of latest allowable occurrence time T_L by back ward pass method. It starts from the bottom of the table and goes upwards. The column (1) of the table is common for both backward and forward pass computations. The sixth (6) column contains the successor events of the events of column (1). The seventh (7) column contains the duration of activity linking the events of column (1) and (6). The 8th column is for T_L of events of column (1).

The value of T_L is obtained by subtracting the activity duration in the 7th column from the T_L of the successor event of column (6). The minimum value of various T_L for a particular event should be selected and written in column 9. The procedure is illustrated by the following example.

Example 7.11. *Find the earliest expected time T_E and latest allowable occurrence time T_L of all the events of the net work shown in Fig. 7.18.*

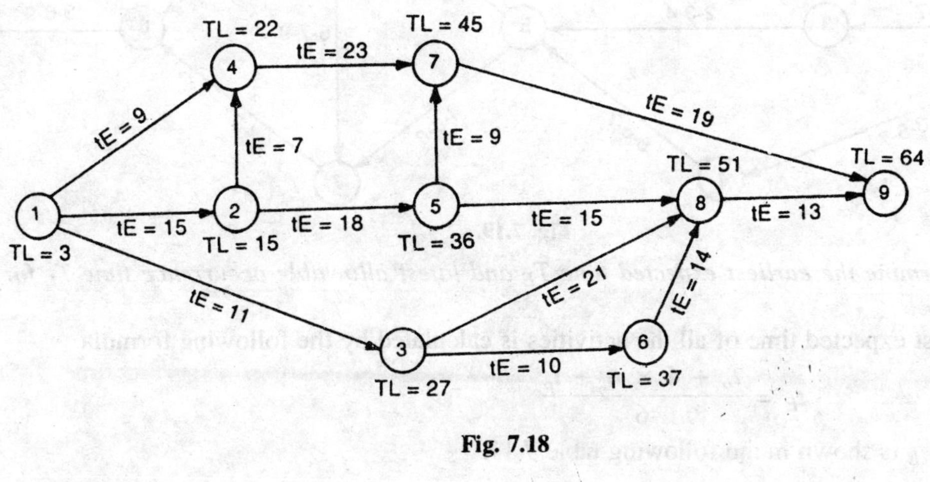

Fig. 7.18

Solution. First earliest expected time will be determined using forward pass method starting from the initial event.

Table 7.10.

Event	*Earliest expected time*					*Latest allowable occurance time*			
	Predecessor event	*Activity ij*	t_E	T_E^i	*TE*	*Successor event*	t_E^{ij}	T_L^i	T_L
1	–	–	0	–	0	2	12	3	3
						3	11	16	
						4	9	13	
2	1	1 – 2	12	12	12	4	7	15	15
						5	18	18	
3	1	1 – 3	11	11	11	6	10	27	27
						8	21	30	
4	2	2 – 4	7	19	19	7	23	22	22
	1	1 – 4	9	9					
5	2	2 – 5	18	30	30	7	09	36	36
						8	15	36	
6	3	3 – 6	10	21	21	8	14	37	37
7	5	5 – 7	15	45	45	9	19	45	45
	4	4 – 7	23	42					
8	6	6 – 8	14	35	45	9	13	51	51
	5	5 – 8	15	45					
	3	3 – 8	21	42					
9	8	8 – 9	13	58	64	–		64	64
	7	7 – 9	19	64					

Example 7.12. *In the net work of Fig. 7.19, the optimistic time, t_o most likely time t_L and pessimistic time t_p are given on the diagram. For this diagram determine expected time for each activity.*

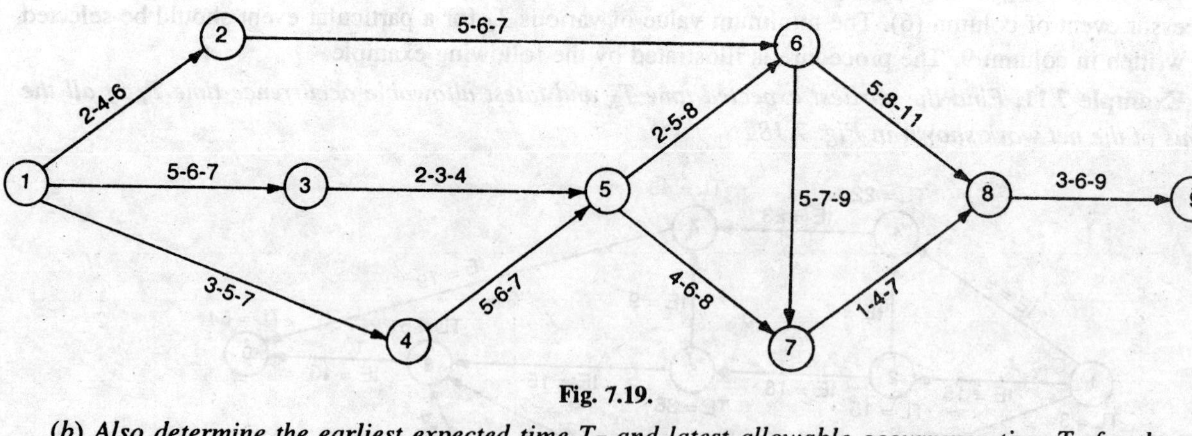

Fig. 7.19.

(b) Also determine the earliest expected time T_E and latest allowable occurrence time T_L for the net work.

Solution. First expected time of all the activities is calculated by the following formula.

$$t_E = \frac{t_o + 4 \times t_L + t_p}{6}$$

The value of t_E is shown in the following table 7.11.

Table 7.11.

Activity	t_o	t_L	t_p	t_E
1 – 2	2	4	6	4
1 – 3	5	6	7	6
1 – 4	3	5	7	5
2 – 6	5	6	7	6
3 – 5	2	3	4	3
4 – 5	5	6	7	6
5 – 6	2	5	8	5
5 – 7	4	6	8	6
6 – 7	5	7	9	7
6 – 8	5	8	11	8
7 – 8	1	4	7	4
8 – 9	3	6	9	6

The net work is redrawn and expected time of each activity is shown on it.

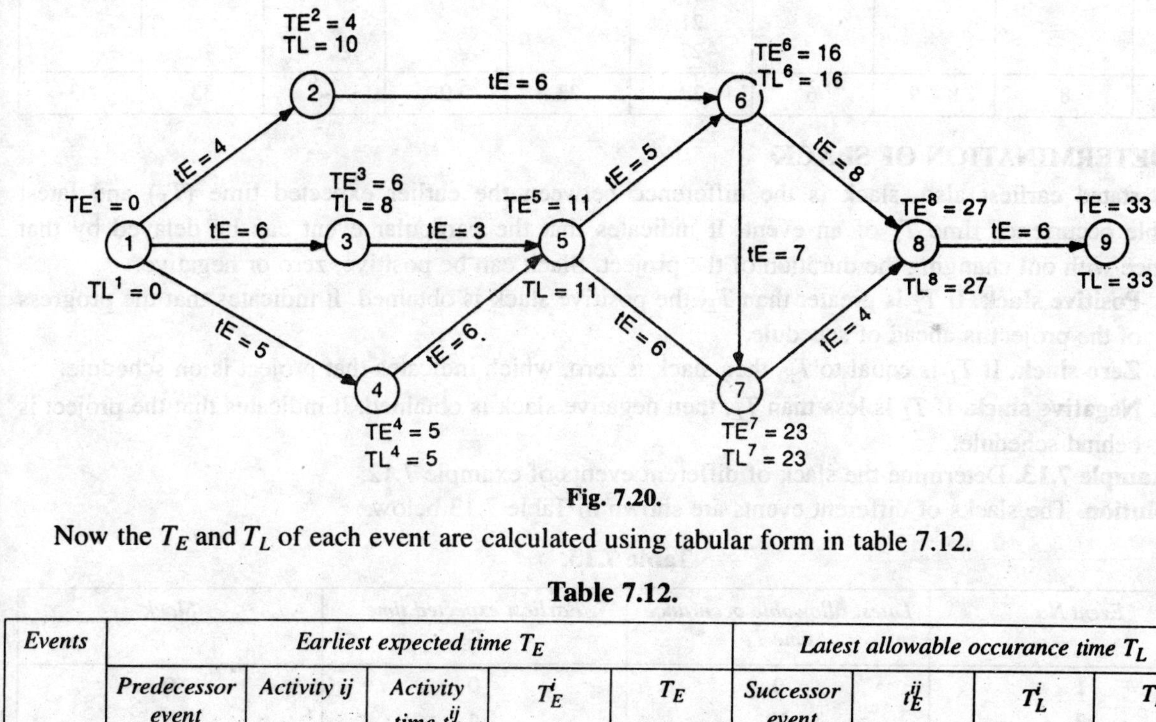

Fig. 7.20.

Now the T_E and T_L of each event are calculated using tabular form in table 7.12.

Table 7.12.

Events	*Earliest expected time* T_E					*Latest allowable occurance time* T_L			
	Predecessor event	*Activity ij*	*Activity time* t_E^{ij}	T_E^i	T_E	*Successor event*	t_E^{ij}	T_L^i	T_L
1	–	–	–	0	0	2 3 4	4 6 5	6 2 <u>0</u>	0
2	1	1 – 2	4	4	4	6	6	13 <u>10</u>	10
3	1	1 – 3	6	6	6	5	3	14 <u>8</u>	8

Events	*Earliest expected time T_E*					*Latest allowable occurance time T_L*			
	Predecessor event	*Activity ij*	*Activity time t_E^{ij}*	T_E^i	T_E	*Successor event*	t_E^{ij}	T_L^i	T_L
4	1	1 – 4	5	5	5	5	6	11 5	5
5	3 4	3 – 5 4 – 5	3 6	9 11	11	6 7	5 6	14 11	11
6	2 5	2 – 6 5 – 6	6 5	10 15 16	16	7 8	7 8	16 19	16
7	5 6	5 – 7 6 – 7	6 7	15 17 17 23	23	8	4	23	23
8	6 7	6 – 8 7 – 8	8 4	18 24 19 21 27	27	9	6	27	27
9	8	8 – 9	6	33	33	0	–	33	33

7.15. DETERMINATION OF SLACK

As stated earliest also, slack is the difference between the earlier expected time (T_E) and latest allowable occurrence time T_L of an event. It indicates that the particular event can be delayed by that difference with out changing the duration of the project. Slack can be positive, zero or negative.

1. **Positive slack.** If T_L is greater than T_E, the positive slack is obtained. It indicates that the progress of the project is ahead of schedule.
2. **Zero slack.** If T_L is equal to T_E, then slack is zero, which indicates that project is on schedule.
3. **Negative slack.** If T_L is less than T_E, then negative slack is obtained. It indicates that the project is behind schedule.

Example 7.13. Determine the slack of different events of example 7.12.

Solution. The slacks of different events are shown in Table 7.13 below.

Table 7.13.

Event No	*Latest allowable occurance time T_L*	*Earliest expected time T_E*	*Slack*
1	0	0	0
2	10	4	6
3	8	6	2
4	5	5	0
5	11	11	0
6	16	16	0
7	23	23	0
8	27	27	0
9	33	33	0

From the above table it will be seen that event 2 and 3 have slacks. It indicates that event 2 can occur upto 6 units of time late and event 3 for 2 units of time with out causing any delay in the completion of the project.

7.16. CRITICAL PATH

As stated earlier also, the critical path is the path which connects all the events having zero or minimum slack in a net work. As events on the critical path are considered critical events and delay in their completion or occurrence will cause a delay in the scheduled completion of the project. Time wise the critical path is the longest path in the project net work. In PERT system the critical path takes into accounts the slack of each event. In the net work, the critical path is distinctly marked usually by a thick line. The determination of critical path is illustrated by the following examples.

Example 7.14. Determine the critical path for the net work shown in Fig. 7.21.

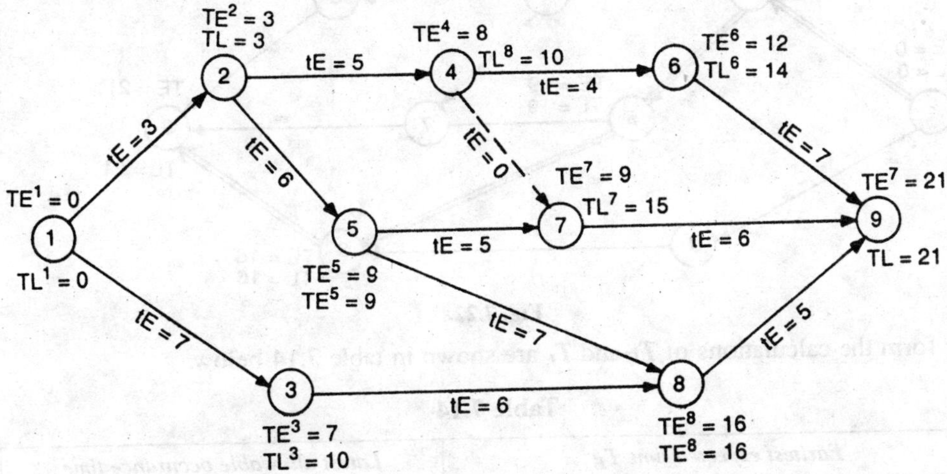

Fig. 7.21.

Solution.

Earliest occurance time T_E	*Latest allowable time T_L*
$T_E^1 = 0$	$T_L^9 = 21$
$T_E^2 = 3$	$T_L^8 = 16$
$T_E^3 = 7$	$T_L^7 = 15$
$T_E^4 = 8$	$T_L^6 = 14$
$T_E^5 = 9$	$T_L^5 = 10$
$T_E^6 = 12$	$= \underline{9}$
$T_E^7 = \frac{8}{\underline{14}}$	$T_L^4 = \frac{10}{15}$
$T_E^8 = \frac{13}{\underline{16}}$	$T_L^3 = 10$
$T_E^9 = 19$	$T_L^2 = \frac{3}{5}$
$= \frac{21}{18}$	$T_L^1 = \frac{0}{3}$

∴ Slack

Event	T_L	T_E	*Slack*	*Event*	T_L	T_E	*Slack*
1	0	0	0	6	14	12	2
2	3	3	0	7	15	14	1
3	10	7	3	8	16	16	0
4	10	8	2	9	21	21	0
5	9	9	0				

Hence critical path is the path joing zero events *i.e.* 1- 2-5-8-9.
This is shown on net work Fig. 7.22.

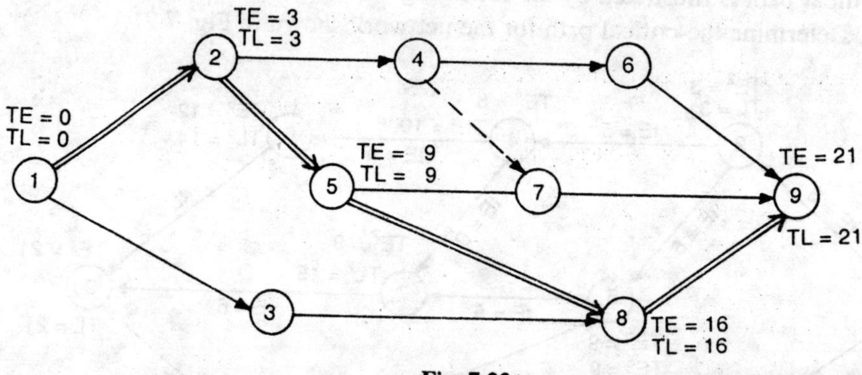

Fig. 7.22.

In tabular form the calculations of T_E and T_L are shown in table 7.14 below.

Table 7.14

Event	*Earliest expected time T_E*					*Latest allowable occurance time*				*Slack col (10-6)*
	Predessor events	*Activity (ij)*	*Activity time t_E^{ij}*	T_E^i	T_E	*Saccessor event*	t_E^{ij}	T_L^i	T_L	
(1)	(2)	(3)	(4)	(5)	(6)	(7)	(8)	(9)	(10)	(11)
1	–	–	–	0	0	2 3	3 7	0 3	0	0
2	1	1 – 2	3	3	3	4 5	5 6	5 3	3	0
3	1	1 – 3	7	7	7	8	6	10	10	3
4	2	2 – 4	5	8	8	6 7	4 0	10 15	10	2
5	2	2 – 5	6	9	9	7 8	5 7	10 9	9	0
6	4	4 – 6	4	12	12	9	7	14	14	2
7	5 4	5 – 7 4 – 7	5 0	14 8	14	9	6	15	15	1
8	5 3	5 – 8 3 – 8	7 6	16 13	16	9	5	5	16	0
9	8 7 6	8 – 9 7 – 9 6 – 8	5 6 7	21 20 19	21	0	–	21	21	0

Example 7.15. *The schedule completion time for the project as shown in Fig. 7.23 is given 53 weeks. Find the slack for each event and also the critical path.*

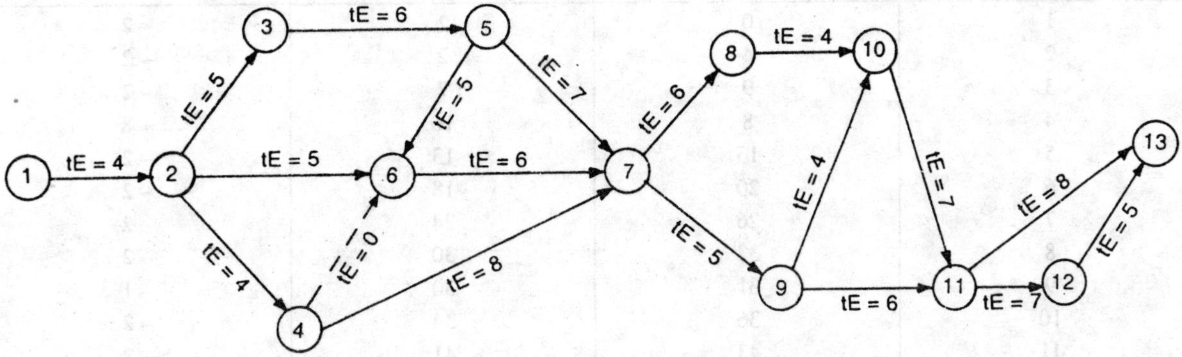

Fig. 7.23

Solution. The calculations are shown in table 7.15 below.

Table 7.15.

Event	Earliest Expted time T_E					Latest allowable occurance time T_L			
	Prdecessor event	Activity ij	Activity time t_E^{ij}	T_E^i	T_E	Successor event	t_E^{ij}	T_L^i	T_L
1	–	–	–	0	0	2	4	2	2
2	1	1 – 2	4	4	4	3	5	2	2
						4	4	12	
						6	5	13	
3	2	2 – 3	5	9	9	5	6	7	7
4	2	2 – 4	4	8	8	7	8	16	16
5	3	3 – 5	6	15	15	6	5	13	13
						7	7	17	
6	2	2 – 6	5	9	20	7	6	18	18
	4	4 – 6	0	8					
	5	5 – 6	5	20					
7	4	4 – 7	8	16	26	8	6	24	24
	5	5 – 7	7	22		9	5	25	
	6	6 – 7	6	26					
8	7	7 – 8	6	32	32	10	4	30	30
9	7	7 – 9	5	31	31	10	4	30	30
						11	6	35	
10	8	8 – 10	4	36	36	11	7	34	34
	9	9 – 10	4	35					
11	9	9 – 11	6	37	43	12	7	41	41
	10	10 – 11	7	43		13	8	45	
12	11	11 – 12	7	50	50	13	5	48	48
13	11	11 – 13	8	51	55	–	–	53	53
	12	12 – 13	5	55					

Calculations of Slack

Event	T_E	T_L	*Slack*
1	0	2	– 2
2	4	2	– 2
3	9	7	– 2
4	8	16	+ 8
5	15	13	– 2
6	20	18	– 2
7	26	24	– 2
8	32	30	– 2
9	31	30	– 1
10	36	34	– 2
11	43	41	– 2
12	50	48	– 2
13	55	53	– 2

∴ Critical path is 1-2-3-5-6-7-8-10-11-12-13. As shown in Fig. 7.24.

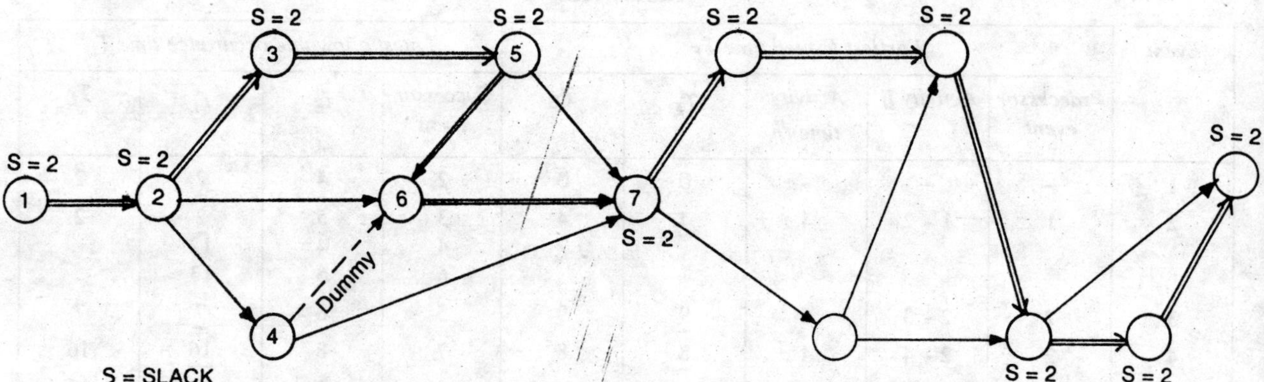

Fig. 7.24.

7.17. PROBABILITY OF ACHIEVING THE COMPLETION TIME OF A PROJECT

Many a times it becomes necessary to know the probability of completing the given project with in the scheduled time T_S. The answer of this question can be sought by applying the probability theory to the net work analysis.

In the last article 7.15 we learnt about the determination of critical path. A critical path is along a number of activities of the net work and it is the longest path time wise *i.e.* it takes more time. Assuming the β distribution of the activities in article 7.4 the expected or mean time (t_E) could be calculated from equation 7.1, reproduced below:

$$t_E = \frac{t_o + 4t_L + t_p}{6} \qquad \ldots(7.1\ a)$$

The expected time t_E shows that there are fifty-fifty-chances that activity *ij* will be completed with in this time t_E. Fig. 7.25 shows β distribution with

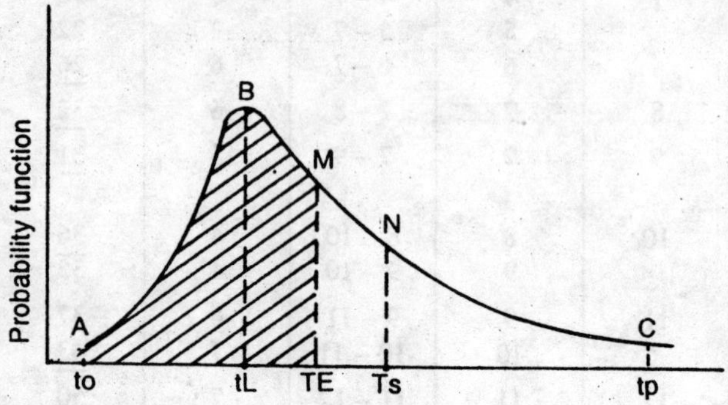

Fig. 7.25. Beta Distribution

t_O, t_L, t_p and t_E marked on it. If a vertical line is drawn through t_E, the shaded area to the left will be half of the total area of the curve. Thus the activity *ij* for which this curve has been drawn has fifty percent probability that it will be completed with in time t_E. The probability of completion of the activity with in some other time t_S will be equal to the area under the curve upto vertical line through t_s divided by the total area.

$$\text{Probability} = \frac{\text{Area under ABN}}{\text{Area under ABC}}$$

Also we know that the earliest expected time T_E of the last event is the sum of all activities along the critical path. The variation of t_E (individual activities) is assumed as beta distribution or random probability distribution, where as the variation of T_E for the whole project as normal distribution for all practical purposes. The assumption of normal distribution is based on central limit theorem. The normal distribution probability curve has an area equal to unity. if an event has a probability of 1, it is certain to occur. In case the value of probability is zero, it will never occur. Closer the probability to 1, more certain is the occurrence of the event.

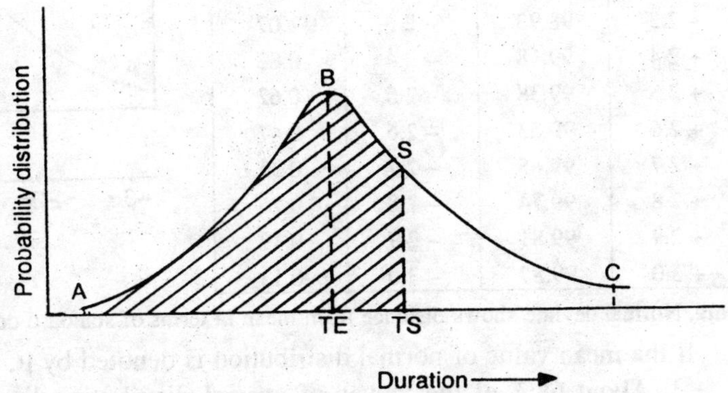

Fig. 7.26. Normal Distribution

Further a standardized normal curve has standard deviation equal to 1, and is symmetrical about the mean value of earlier expected time T_E.

Fig. 7.26 shows the normal distribution probability curve.

Normal distribution functions are shown in Table 7.16 below:

Table 7.16. Standard normal distribution function

Normal deviation Z (+)	*Probability percent (Pr)*	*Normal deviation* Z (–)	*Probability percent (Pr)*
0	50.0	0	50
+ 0.1	53.98	– 0.1	46.02
+ 0.2	57.93	– 0.2	42.07
+ 0.3	61.79	– 0.3	38.12
+ 0.4	65.54	– 0.4	34.46
+ 0.5	69.15	– 0.5	30.85
+ 0.6	72.57	– 0.6	27.43
+ 0.7	75.8	– 0.7	24.20
+ 0.8	78.81	– 0.8	21.19
+ 0.9	81.59	– 0.9	18.41
+ 1.0	84.13	– 1.0	15.87
+ 1.1	86.43	– 1.1	13.57
+ 1.2	88.49	– 1.2	11.51
+ 1.3	90.32	– 1.3	9.68
+ 1.4	91.92	– 1.4	8.03
+ 1.5	93.32	– 1.5	6.68
+ 1.6	94.52	– 1.6	5.48

Normal deviation Z (+)	*Probability percent (Pr)*	*Normal deviation* Z (–)	*Probability percent (Pr)*
+ 1.7	95.54	– 1.7	4.46
+ 1.8	96.41	– 1.8	3.59
+ 1.9	97.13	– 1.9	2.87
+ 2.0	97.72	– 2.0	2.28
+ 2.1	98.21	– 2.1	1.79
+ 2.2	98.61	– 2.2	1.39
+ 2.3	98.93	– 2.3	1.07
+ 2.4	99.18	– 2.4	0.82
+ 2.5	99.38	– 2.5	0.62
+ 2.6	99.53	– 2.6	0.47
+ 2.7	99.65	– 2.7	0.35
+ 2.8	99.74	– 2.8	0.26
+ 2.9	99.81	– 2.9	0.19
+ 3.0	99.87	– 3.0	0.13

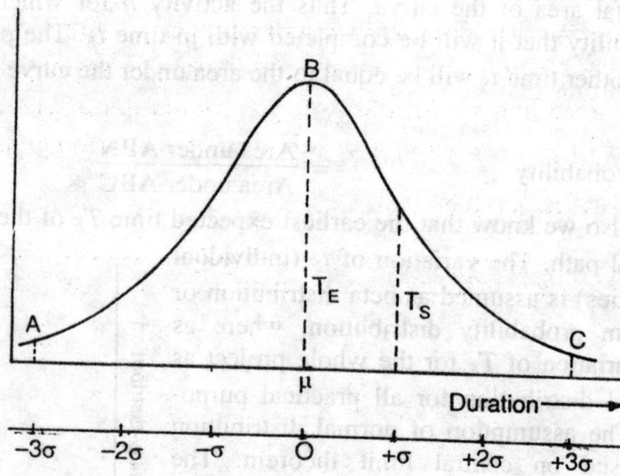

Fig. 7.27.

Note. Normal deviate shows distance from mean in terms of standard deviation σ.

If the mean value of normal distribution is denoted by μ, then it is proved that.

1. About 68% of the values of normal distribution lie with ± σ from the average, where σ is the standard deviation. It means that the area of the curve between $x = \mu - \sigma$ to $x = \mu + \sigma$ is 68% of the total area.
2. About 95% of all values lie with in ± 2 σ from the average *i.e.* between the area of the curve $x = \mu - 2\sigma$ to $x = \mu + 2\sigma$ is 95%.
3. The area of the curve between $x = \mu - 3\sigma$ to $x = \mu + 3\sigma$ is 99.7% Fig. 7.27.

7.18. PROCEDURE FOR FINDING THE PROBABILITY OF MEETING THE SCHEDULE TIME OF COMPLETION

The above properties of the normal distribution curve and % probability given in table 7.16 can only be used if the random curve obtained from a given net work is reduced to the normalized form. This can be done by making the T_E value for the end event coincide with the modal value of the normal distribution curve. The procedure adopted is explained steep by step in the following paragraph.

Step 1. Determine the standard deviation σ corresponding to critical path in the net work

$$\therefore \quad \sigma = \sqrt{\text{Sum of varinces along the critical path}} = \frac{(t_p - t_o)}{6} \quad \ldots(7.11)$$

Step 2. Knowing the standard completion time T_s and the earliest expected time T_E of completion, determine the difference of $T_S - T_E$ and express it in terms of probability factor or normal deviate z by the relation.

$$Z = \frac{T_S - T_E}{\sigma} \quad \ldots(7.12)$$

Step 3. From the normal distribution table 7.16 find the percentage probability corresponding to the value of z.

When $z = 0$ the chances of completing the project in time are fifty-fifty.

When z is positive the chances of completing the project in time are more than 50%.

When z is negative the chances of completing the project in time are less than 50%.

The procedure is illustrated with the following examples.

Example 7.16. *A project is expected to be completed in 28 days along the critical path and has a standard deviation of 4 days. Find the probability of completing the project with in (a) 28 days (b) 32 days and 24 days.*

Solution. Earliest expected time $T_E = 28$ days

Standard deviation $\sigma = 4$

(*a*)For project to be completed in 28 days *i.e.* $T_S = 28$,

Normal deviate $$Z = \frac{T_E - T_S}{\sigma} = \frac{28-28}{4} = 0$$

From the probability table, for Z = 0, probability = 50%

(*b*) For the project to be completed in 32 days *i.e.* $T_S = 32$

Normal deviate $$Z = \frac{32 - 28}{4} = 1.0;$$ the probability is 84.13%.

(*c*) For $T_S = 24$, the variate $Z = \frac{(24 - 28)}{4} = -1.0$, the probability is 15.8%

Example 7.17. *Along the critical path of a net work of a certain project the earliest completion period comes as 48 days. The variance is of 16 days. Find the completion time for the project for probabilities (i) 96%, (ii) 72.6%, (iii) 38.2%, (iv) 20%.*

Solution. Standard deviation $\sigma = \sqrt{\text{varience}} = \sqrt{16} = 4$

(*i*) For 96% Probability from table 7.16 variate Z = 1.75 (from interpolation)

Now $$Z = \frac{T_S - T_E}{\sigma}$$

or $$\sigma \cdot Z = T_S - T_E$$

$$\therefore \quad T_S = T_E + \sigma \times Z = 48 + 1.75 \times 4 = 48 + 7 = 55 \text{ days}$$

(*ii*) For 72.6% probability, from table 7.16 the value of z = 0.6.

$$\therefore \quad T_S = Z \cdot \sigma + T_E = 4 \times 0.6 + 48 = 2.4 + 48 = 50.4 \text{ days}$$

(*iii*) For 38.2% probability, from table 7.16 the value of z = – 0.3

$$\therefore \quad T_S = \sigma \cdot Z + T_E = -0.3 \times 4 + 48 = 48 - 1.2 = 46.8 \text{ days}$$

(*iv*) For 20% probability, the value of z = – 0.85 by interpolation

$$\therefore \quad T_S = -0.85 \times 4 + 48 = -3.40 + 48 = 44.6 \text{ days}$$ **Ans.**

Example 7.18. *Fig. 7.28 shows the net work of a construction project. The three time estimates*

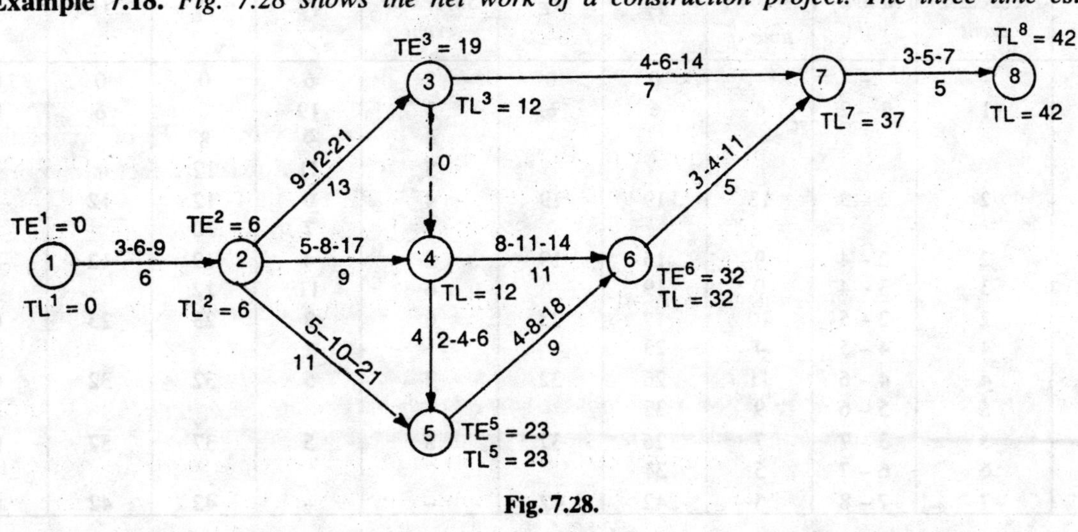

Fig. 7.28.

optimistic time t_o most likely time t_L and pessimistic time t_p are marked on the fig it self. Determine:

(i) Critical path.

(ii) Probability of completion of project in 45 days.

(iii) Time duration that will give 95% probability of its completion in time.

Solution. The completion of t_E and σ^2 are shown in table 717 below:

Table 7.17.

Activity	t_o	t_L	t_p	$t_E = \dfrac{t_0 + 4_L + t_p}{6}$	$\sigma^2 = \left(\dfrac{t_p - t_o}{6}\right)^2$
1 – 2	3	6	9	6	1
2 – 3	9	12	21	13	4
2 – 4	5	8	17	9	4
2 – 5	5	10	21	11	7.1
3 – 4	0	0	0	0	0
3 – 7	4	6	14	7	2.78
4 – 5	2	4	6	4	0.44
4 – 6	8	11	14	11	1.0
5 – 6	4	8	18	9	5.44
6 – 7	3	4	11	5	1.78
7 – 8	3	5	7	5	0.44

$$\Sigma\sigma^2 = 27.88$$

$$\therefore\ \sigma = \sqrt{\sigma^2}$$

$$= 5.083 \approx 5.1$$

To find the critical path, the values of earlier expected time T_E and latest allowable occurrence time T_L are to be determined. The values of T_E and T_L are determined as shown in Table 7.18 below. For the last event T_L is taken equal to T_E.

Table 7.18.

Event No.	*Earlier expected time T_E*					*Latest allowable occurance time T_L*				*Slack $(T_L - T_E)$*
	Predecessor event	*Activity ij*	*Activity time t_E^{ij}*	T_E^i	T_E	*Successor event*	T_E^{ij}	T_L^i	T_L	
1	–	–	–	0	0	2	6	0	0	0
2	1	1 – 2	6	6	6	3	19	6	6	0
						4	9	8		
						5	11	12		
3	2	2 – 3	13	19	19	4	0	12	12	– 7
						7	7	30		
4	2	2 – 4	9	15	19	5	4	19	12	– 7
	3	3 – 4	0	19		6	11	12		
5	2	2 – 5	10	17	23	6	9	23	23	0
	4	4 – 5	4	23						
6	4	4 – 6	11	26	32	7	5	32	32	0
	5	5 – 6	9	32						
7	3	3 – 7	7	26	37	8	5	37	37	0
	6	6 – 7	5	37						
8	7	7 – 8	5	42	42	–	–	42	42	0

From the table the slack is zero for events 1, 2, 5, 6, 7, 8. Hence the critical path is 1-2-5-6-7-8.

Standard daviation along the critical path = $\sqrt{15.76} \approx 4.0$

(*b*) Standard deviation $\sigma = \sqrt{\sigma^2}$

$= 4.0$

Now variate $Z = \dfrac{T_S - T_E}{\sigma}$

$= \dfrac{45 - 42}{4} = \dfrac{3}{4} = 0.75$

From table 7.16, the probability of completing the project in 45 days is 77.3%.

(*c*) For 95%, probability the value of Z from the table 7.16 is 1.65 by interpolation.

$\sigma Z = T_S - T_E$

$\therefore \quad T_S = T_E + \sigma Z = 42 + 1.65 \times 4$

$= 42 + 6.6 = 48.6$ days **Ans.**

Example 7.19. *A project is composed of seven activities, whose time estimates are shown in Table 7.19 below. From this data,*

(i) Draw the net work of the project and draw its critical path.

(ii) Determine its variance and standard deviation.

(iii) Findout the probability of completing the project in 22 weeks.

(iv) Find out the time duration for 85% probability of its completion

Table 7.19

Activity ij	*Time estimates in weeks*			*Expected time* t_E
	Optimistic time t_o	*Most likely time* t_L	*Pessimistic time* t_p	
1 – 2	2	2	8	3
1 – 3	2	5	8	5
1 – 4	3	3	9	4
2 – 5	2	2	2	2
3 – 5	3	6	15	7
4 – 6	3	6	9	6
5 – 6	4	7	16	8

Solution. The net work of the project is shown in Fig. 7.29.

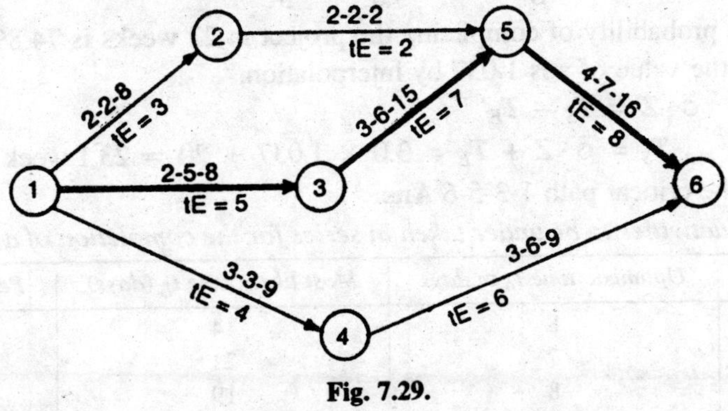

Fig. 7.29.

The variance and standard deviation are calculated in table 7.20.

Table 7.20.

Activity *ij*	*Optimistic time* t_o	*Most likely time* t_L	*Pessemestic time* t_p	*Most Expected time* t_E	*Variance* $\left(\frac{t_p - t_o}{t}\right)^2$	$\sigma = \sqrt{\sigma^2}$
1 – 2	2	2	8	3	1	1
1 – 3	2	5	8	5	1	1
1 – 4	3	3	9	4	1	1
2 – 5	2	2	2	2	0	0
3 – 5	3	6	15	7	4	2
4 – 6	3	6	9	6	1	1
5 – 6	4	7	16	8	4	2

(*iii*) For determining the critical path we have to determine the earlier expected T_E and latest allowable occurrence time T_L of the project, which are calculated in the table 7.21 below. The value of T_L is taken equal to T_E.

Table 7.21.

Event No	*Earlier expected time* T_E					*Latest allowable occurance time* T_L				*Slack* $(T_L - T_E)$
	Predecessor event	*Actually ij*	*Activity time* t_E	T_E^i	T_E	*Successer event*	t_E^{ij}	T_L^i	T_L	
1	–	–	–	0	0	2	3	7	0	0
						3	5	0		
						4	4	10		
2	1	1 – 2	3	3	3	5	2	10	10	7
3	1	1 – 3	5	5	5	5	7	5	5	0
4	1	1 – 4	4	4	4	6	6	14	14	10
5	2	2 – 5	2	5	12	6	8	12	12	0
	3	3 – 5	7	12						
6	4	4 – 6	6	10	20	–	–	20	20	0
	5	5 – 6	8	20						

Slack is zero for events 1, 3, 5 and 6. Hence critical path will be along 1, 3, 5 and 6.

The variance $\Sigma\,\sigma^2$ along the critical path 1-3-5-6 = 1+ 4 + 4 = 9

∴ Standard deviation $\sigma = \sqrt{9} = 3.0$

∴ Variate $Z = \dfrac{T_S - T_E}{\sigma} = \dfrac{22-20}{3.0} = \dfrac{2}{3} = 0.67$

For variate 0.670, the probability of completing the project in 22 weeks is 74.8%.

For 85% probability, the value of z is 1.037 by interpolation.

∴ $\sigma \cdot Z = T_S - T_E$

∴ $T_S = \sigma \cdot Z + T_E = 3.0 \times 1.037 + 20 = 23.1$ week

Say 23 weeks along the critical path 1-3-5-6 **Ans.**

Example. 7.20. *Four activities to be under taken in series for the completion of a project are as follows:*

Activity	*Optimisic time* t_o *in days*	*Most likely time* t_L *(days)*	*Pessimistic time* t_p *(days)*
P	8	14	22
Q	7	21	32
R	8	19	28
S	28	40	52

Estimate the time required at 95%. Probability and 5% probability to complete the work. Which of the above four activities has the most reliable time estimate? [UPSC, Civil Services, 1999]

Solution. The activities *P, Q, R, S* can be shown in series as follows:

Fig. 7.30

The expected time t_E of each activity is determined by the relation.

$$t_E = \frac{t_o + 4\,t_L + t_p}{6}$$

$$\therefore \qquad T_E \text{ for } P = \frac{8 + 4 \times 14 + 22}{6} = 14.33$$

$$t_E \text{ for } Q = \frac{7 + 4 \times 21 + 32}{6} = 20.5$$

$$t_E \text{ for } R = \frac{8 + 4 \times 19 + 28}{6} = 18.67$$

$$t_E \text{ for } S = \frac{28 + 4 \times 40 + 52}{6} = 40.0$$

Standard deviation $\sigma = \dfrac{t_p - t_o}{6}$

Variance $\sigma^2 = \left(\dfrac{t_p - t_o}{6}\right)^2$

These values are shown in tabular form in Table 22 below.

Table 7.22.

Activity	*Optimum time t_o*	*Most likely time t_L*	*Pessimistic time t_p*	*Expected mean time t_E*	*Standard deviation* $\sigma = \left(\dfrac{t_p - t_o}{6}\right)$	*Variance* σ^2	*Remark*
P	8	14	22	14.33	2.33	5.44	Most reliable
Q	7	21	32	20.5	4.17	17.36	
R	8	19	28	16.67	3.33	11.11	
S	28	40	52	40.0	4.0	16.0	

Expected mean time of the project $T_E = 14.33 + 20.5 + 16.67 + 40.0 = 91.5$

Variance of the project $\sigma^2 = 5.44 + 17.36 + 11.11 + 16.0 = 49.91$

Standard deviation along critical path

$$\sigma = \sqrt{\sigma^2} = \sqrt{49.91}$$

$$= 7.06 \text{ app.}$$

From table 7.16 prbbability factor z for 95% probability = 1.65 by interpolation.

The probability factor $z = \dfrac{\text{Given project duration – Expected duration calculated}}{\text{mean standard deviation calculated}}$

Let x be the project completion duration, then

$$z = \frac{x - T_E}{\sigma} = \frac{x - 91.5}{7.06}$$

or $7.06\, z = x - 91.5$

or $7.06 \times 1.65 = x - 91.5$

or $x = 91.5 + 7.06 \times 1.65$

$= 91.5 + 11.65 = 103.15$ days say 103 days

Probability factor z for 5% probability $= -1.65$

$\therefore$ Thus time period for 5% probability $x = 91.5 - 1.65 \times 7.06$

$= 91.5 - 11.65$

$= 79.85$ days $= 80$ days

As the variance of activity p is least, hence it has most reliable time estimates. **Ans.**

Example 7.21. *A father finds that his teenage daughter uses the telephone. She takes no less than 5 minutes for a call and some times as much as an hour. Fifteen minutes calls are more frequent than any other duration calls. If daughter's phone calls were a PERT project activity, then*

1. *What would be the phone call's expected duration?*
2. *What estimate would you give for its variance?*
3. *In scheduling the project, how much time would you allocate for the phone call?*

[UPSC, Engg. Services, 1981]

Solution. Here optimistic call time $t_o = 5$ minutes

Most likely call time $t_L = 15$ minutes

Pessimistic call time $t_p = 60$ minutes

1. Expected duration of call $t_E = \dfrac{t_o + 4\, t_L + t_p}{6}$

$$= \frac{5 + 4 \times 15 + 60}{6} = \frac{125}{6}$$

$= 20.83$ minutes

2. Variance of Phone call $= \left(\dfrac{t_p - t_o}{6}\right)^2 = \left(\dfrac{60 - 5}{6}\right)^2$

$= 84.09$ minutes

3. Time allocation for phone call in scheduling the project = Expected time

$= 20.83$ minutes say 21 min. **Ans.**

Example 7.22. *A project consists of 8 activities, code named based on the type of work as A, C, E, K, P, R, T and Y. A and E are initial activities. T follows C, R follows P, A preceeds K, R preceeds Y, P follows E and K is followed by C. The a, m, b durations have been estimated as under. What is the probability of the project being completed in 28 months.*

Activity	A	C	E	K	P	R	T	Y
a(t_o) *in months*	5	3	4	6	6	$2\frac{1}{2}$	$7\frac{1}{2}$	5
m(t_L)	6	3	8	12	7	$3\frac{1}{2}$	$9\frac{1}{2}$	7
b(t_p)	7	3	10	14	8	$7\frac{1}{2}$	$14\frac{1}{2}$	9

[UPSC Engg. Services, 1990]

Solution. The net work of the given activities is drawn as shown in Fig. 7.31 below.

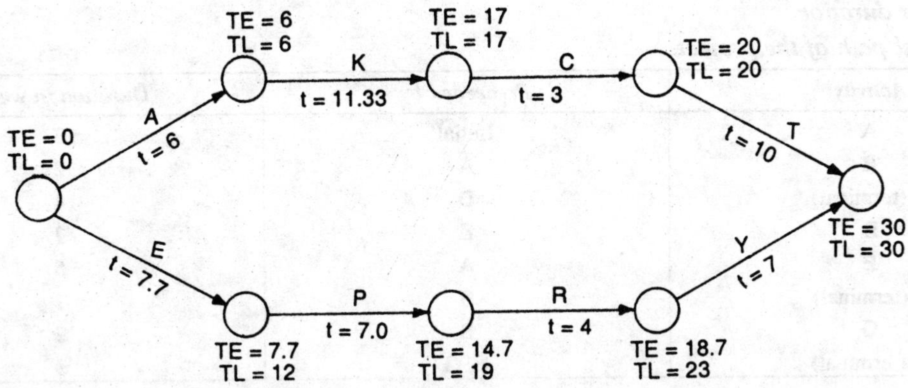

Fig. 7.31.

The expected time t_E of each activity is calculated in tabular form below.

Table 7.23.

Activity	*Optimum time t_o months*	*Most likely time t_L months*	*Pessimistic time month t_p*	*Expected time* $t_E = \frac{t_o + 4t_L + t_p}{6}$	*Standard deviation* $\sigma = \frac{t_p - t_o}{6}$	*Variance* $\sigma^2 = \left(\frac{t_p - t_o}{6}\right)^2$
A	5	6	7	6	0.333	0.111
C	3	3	3	3	0	0
E	4	8	10	7.67	1.0	1.0
K	6	12	14	11.33	1.333	1.778
P	6	7	8	7.0	0.333	0.111
R	$2\frac{1}{2}$	$3\frac{1}{2}$	$7\frac{1}{2}$	4.0	0.833	0.694
T	$7\frac{1}{2}$	$9\frac{1}{2}$	$14\frac{1}{2}$	10.0	1.167	1.362
Y	5	7	9	7.0	0.667	0.444

The earliest occurrence time T_E and latest occurance time T_L of all activities are determined and marked on the network.

On the basis of slack the critical path is along 1-2-4-6-8 and the duration of the project is 30.333 months.

Project variance $= 0.111 + 1.778 + 0 + 1.362 = 3.26$ months

Project standard deviation along critical path $\sigma = \sqrt{3.26} = 1.8$

The scheduled completion time T_S given as 28 months.

$\therefore$ Deviate factor $z = \dfrac{T_S - T_E}{\sigma}$

$$= \frac{28 - 30.333}{1.8} = -\frac{2.333}{1.8} = -1.296$$

for deviate factor $z = -1.296 \approx 1.3$

From table 7.16 For deviate $z = -1.3$, the probability = 9.68%.

Hence the probability of completion of project in 28 months is 9.68% **Ans.**

Example 7.23. *A net work consists of the following activities. The duration of each activity is shown against each activity. Draw the network and determine,*

(a) Project duration

(b) Critical path of the project.

Activity	*Preceeded by*	*Duration in weeks*
A	Initial	3
B	A	2
C (terminal)	D	4
D	E	2
E	A	5
F (terminal)	B	1
G	B	2
H (terminal)	E, G	3

[UPSC, Civil Services, 1973, 1987]

Solution. The net work for the given activities and conditions is drawn as shown in Fig. 7.32.

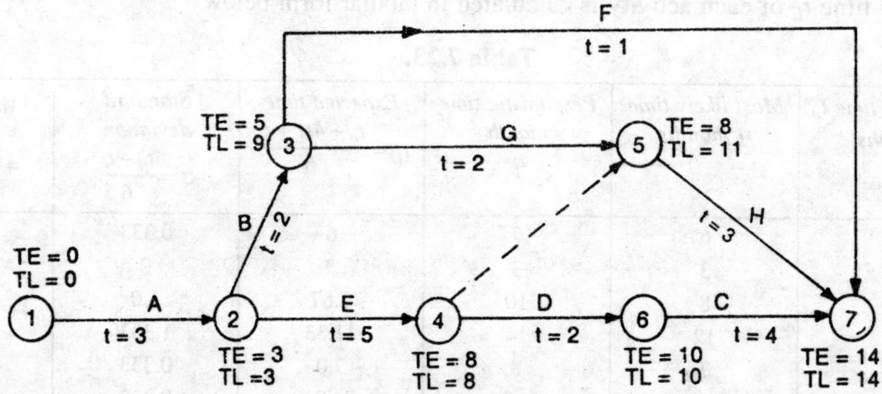

Fig. 7.32

The earliest occurrence time T_E and latest occurrence time T_L is determined to find out slack, for determining the critical path. The values of T_E and T_L are marked on the network.

The slack is zero along 1-2-4-6-7, hence the critical path is along 1-2-4-6-7 and marked by thick line.

The project duration is 14 weeks. **Ans.**

Example 7.24. *A project is consisted of seven activities A to G. Their interdependence is as follows:*

Activity	A	B	C	D	E	F	G
Preceeding activities	–	–	A	B	A	B	C & D
Succeeding activities	C & E	D & F	G	G	–	–	–

The time estimates in days for each activity are as follows:

Activity	*Three time estimates*	*Normal distribution function data*	
		Z (+)	*Probability %*
A	6 – 9 – 18	0.8	78.81
B	5 – 8 – 17	0.9	81.59
C	4 – 7 – 22	1.0	84.13
D	4 – 7 – 16	1.1	86.43
E	4 – 7 – 10	1.2	88.49
F	2 – 5 – 8		
G	4 – 10 – 22		

Draw the net work and determine the probability of completing the work or project in 35 days.

[UPSC, Engg. Services, 1995]

Solution. The network for the given activities is drawn as shown in Fig. 7.33.

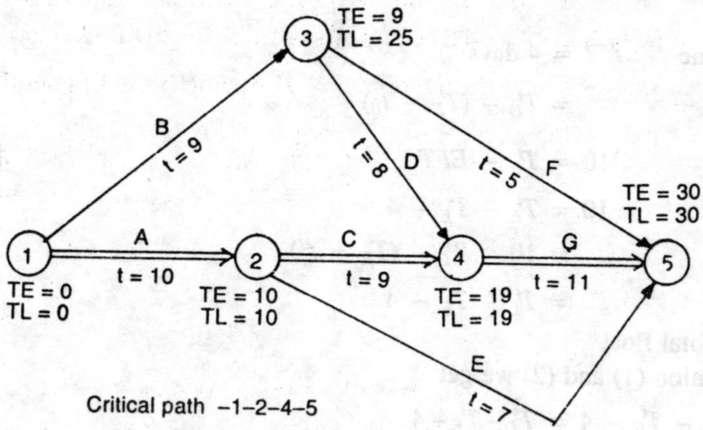

Fig. 7.33.

The expected time t_E for each activity is calculated as follows in the table below.

Activity	*Three time estimates*	*Expected time t_E*	*Standard deviation σ*	*Variance σ^2*
A	6 – 9 – 18	10	2	4
B	5 – 8 – 17	9	2	4
C	4 – 7 – 22	9	3	9
D	4 – 7 – 16	8	2	4
E	4 – 7 – 10	7	1	1
F	2 – 5 – 8	5	1	1
G	4 – 10 – 22	11	3	9

The earliest and latest times T_E and T_L are calculated and marked on the network.

The slack along 1-2-4-5 are zero. Hence the critical path is also along 1-2-4-5.

The duration of the project = 30 days

The standard deviation $= \dfrac{t_p - t_o}{6}$

The variance of the project = sum of variance along the critical path

$= 4 + 9 + 9 = 22$

∴ Standard deviation of the project along the critical path $\sigma = \sqrt{22}$

The duration of completion of the project given t_s = 35 days

∴ Variate $Z = \dfrac{T_S - T_E}{\sigma}$

$$= \frac{35 - 30}{4.69} = \frac{5}{4.69} = 1.006$$

∴ Probability for variate z = 1.006, from table 7.16 = 85.74% **Ans.**

Example 7.25. *An activity in a CPM net work has a duration of 4 days. The free float for the activity* *is 10 days and total float also is 10 days. Find the maximum delay that can be allowed for the activity from occurrence of the preceeding event*

[GATE 1999, ARCH]

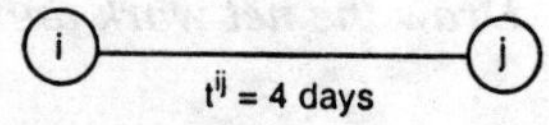

Fig. 7.34

Solution.

Given activity time $t^{i-j} = 4$ days

Free float $= T_E^j - (T_E^i + t_{ij})$

$10 = T_E^j - EFT$ $\quad [\because T_E^i = 0, \therefore EFT = 4]$

$\therefore \quad 10 = T_E^j - T_E^i - 4$ ...(1)

Total float $= 10 = T_L^j - (T_E^i + t^{ij})$

$= T_L^j - T_E^i - 4$ ...(2)

As free float = Total float

$\therefore$ Equating equation (1) and (2) we get

$$T_E^j - T_E^i - 4 = T_L^j - T_E^i - 4 \qquad ...(3)$$

$$T_E^j = T_L^j$$

By definition latest occurrence time T_{L_i} = Latest occurrence time $T_L^j - t^{ij}$ ...(4)

Latest occurrence time of head event = 4 + 10 = 14 ...(5)

$\therefore$ By equation 4 and 5.

Latest occurrence time of tail event – Earliest occurrence time of tail event = 10.

Hence maximum delay in the occurrence of the preceding event

(*i*) $L_T^i - T_E^i = 10$ days. **Ans.**

Eample 7.26. *In a particular construction project the event relationship is as follows: Event A is the initial event and F is the find event.*

Event	B	C	D	E	F
Preceeded by	A	A, B	B, C	C	D, E

For the various activities of the project, the optimistic time t_o, the most likely time t_L and pessimistic time t_p in days are as follows:

Activity	t_o	t_L	t_p
A – B	2	6	10
A – C	4	8	12
B – C	2	4	6
C – D	0	0	0
B – D	2	3	4
C – E	3	6	9
D – F	6	10	14
E – F	1	3	5

Draw the net work and show on it the critical path. Calculate the probability of finishing the project in (i) in 22 days and in (ii) 18 days. [UPSC, Civil Services, 1989]

Solution. First let us find the expected time t_E, standard deviation and variance in the tabular form as follows:

Table 7.24

Activity	t_o	t_L	t_p	$t_c = \frac{t_0 + 4t_L + t_p}{6}$	*S.D.* $\sigma = \left(\frac{t_p - t_o}{6}\right)$	*Variance* $= \left(\frac{t_p - t_o}{6}\right)^2$
A – B	2	6	10	6	1.33	1.77
A – C	4	8	12	8	1.33	1.77
B – C	2	4	6	4	0.67	0.449
C – D	0	0	0	0	0	0
B – D	2	3	4	3	0.33	0.109
C – E	3	6	9	6	1.0	1.0
D – F	6	10	14	10	1.33	1.77
E – F	1	3	5	3	0.67	0.449

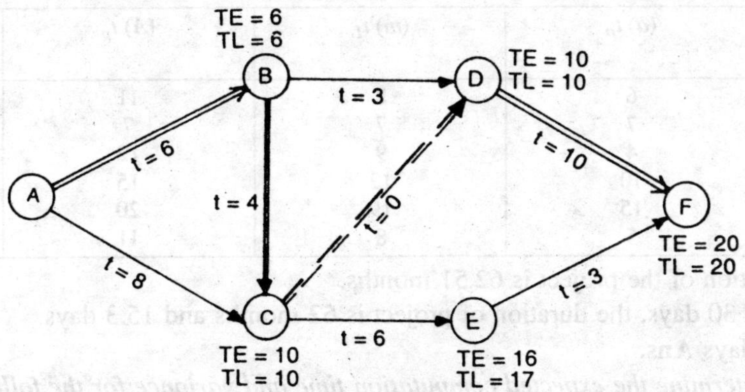

Fig. 7.35.

Critical path is along A-B-C-D-F.

The project duration = 20 days

Variate $z = \frac{T_s - T_E}{\sigma}$

∴ Variance along the critical path = 1.77 + 0.449 + 0 + 1.77 = 4.004

∴ Standard deviation $\sigma = \sqrt{\text{variance}} = \sqrt{4} = 2.0$

∴ Variate or probability factor for completion period 22 days,

$$z = \frac{T_S - T_E}{\sigma}$$

(*i*) $T_S = 22$, then $z = \frac{22 - 20}{2} = 1.0$

From table 7.16 the probability of completion of project in 22 weeks is 84.13%.

(*ii*) For completion period 18 days, $T_S = 18$

Hence probability factor $= \frac{18 - 20}{2} = -1.0$

From table 7.16 for probability factor –1.0, the probability of completion of project is 15.81%. **Ans.**

Example 7.27. *Six activities are to be under taken in series for the completion of a project and have been assessed to have the following* t_o, t_L and t_p *time estimates in months. What is the probable range of the project duration (write in months and days).*

Activities/times	1	2	3	4	5	6
t_o	6	7	4	10	15	5
t_L	8	7	9	12	19	8
t_p	11	7	12	15	20	11

[UPSC, Civil Services, 1986]

Solution. The network of the project is shown below in Fig. 7.36.

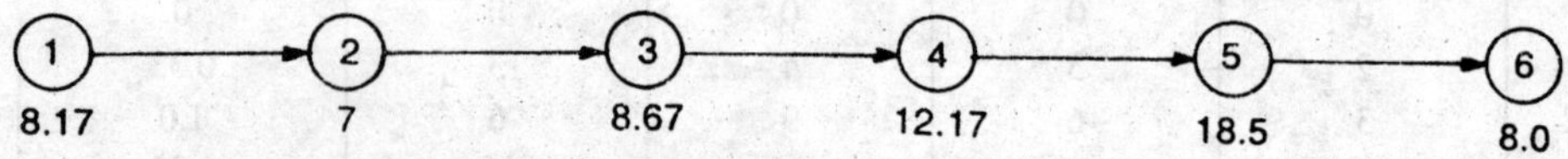

Fig. 7.36

Table

Activity	(*a*) t_o	(*m*) t_L	(*A*) t_p	$t_E = \frac{t_o + 4 \times t_L + t_p}{6}$
1	6	8	11	8.17
2	7	7	7	7
3	4	9	12	8.67
4	10	12	15	12.17
5	15	19	20	18.5
6	5	8	11	8.0

The probable duration of the project is 62.51 months.

Taking a month of 30 days, the duration of project is 62 months and 15.3 days.

Say 5 months 15 days **Ans.**

Example 7.28. *Determine the expected computation time and variance for the following project:*

Activity	A	B	C	D	E	F	G	H
Predecessors	–	A	–	–	D	C	B, C	E, C
Optimistic time	1	2	3	2	2	2	2	3
Most likely time	4	5	6	2	3	4	9	3
Pessimistic time	7	8	9	2	7	6	10	3

[UPSC, Civil Services, 1984]

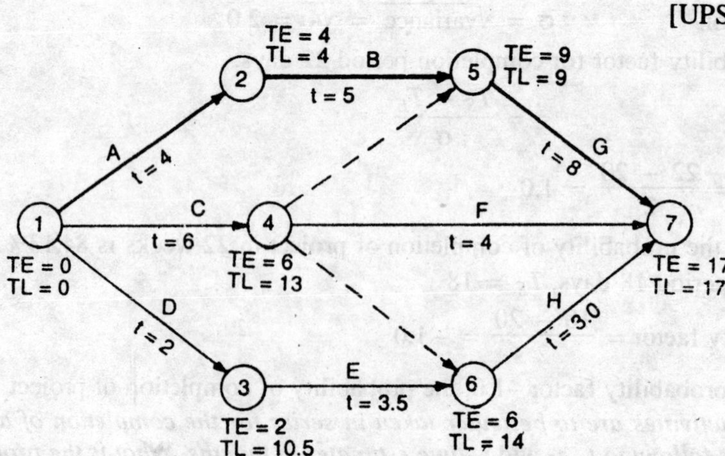

Fig. 7.37

(*iii*) The expected time and variance is calculated in tabular form as below:

Table 7.25

Activity	*Optimistic time t_o*	*Most likely time t_L*	*Pessenestic time t_p*	*Expected time* $t_E = \frac{t_o + 4\,t_l + t_p}{6}$	*Varience* $\sigma^2 = \left(\frac{t_p - t_o}{6}\right)^2$	*Standard duration* $\sigma = \left(\frac{t_p - t_o}{6}\right)$
A	1	4	7	4	1	1.0
B	2	5	8	5	1	1.0
C	3	6	9	6	1	1.0
D	2	2	2	2	0	0
E	2	3	7	3.5	0.7	0.833
F	2	4	6	4	0.444	0.67
G	2	9	10	8	1.78	1.30
H	3	3	3	3	0	0

Critical path is along 1-2-5-7.

The total expected time of the project = 17 days

Variance of the project along critical path $\sigma^2 = 1 + 1 + 1.78 = 3.78$

$= 3.78$

Standard deviation of the project along the critical path $= \sqrt{3.78} = 1.95$

Example 7.29. *Following information applies to a particular project:*

Event 0 is the initial event

Event 1 is preceded by event 0

Event 3 is preceded by event 1

Event 4 is preceded by event 1

Event 2 is preceded by event 1

Event 3 is preceded by event 2 and 1

Event 4 is preceded by event 3 and 1

Event 5 is preceded by event 4.

For the various activities in the project, the expected times are as follows:

Activity	0 – 1	1 – 3	1 – 2	2 – 3	1 – 4	3 – 4	4 – 5
Duration days	3	16	6	8	10	5	3

Draw the arrow diagram for this project. If the schedule completion time is equal to the earliest expected time for the end event, calculate the slack of each event and identify the critical path.

[UPSC, Engg. Services, 1984]

Solution. The arrow diagram of the project is shown in Fig. 7.38

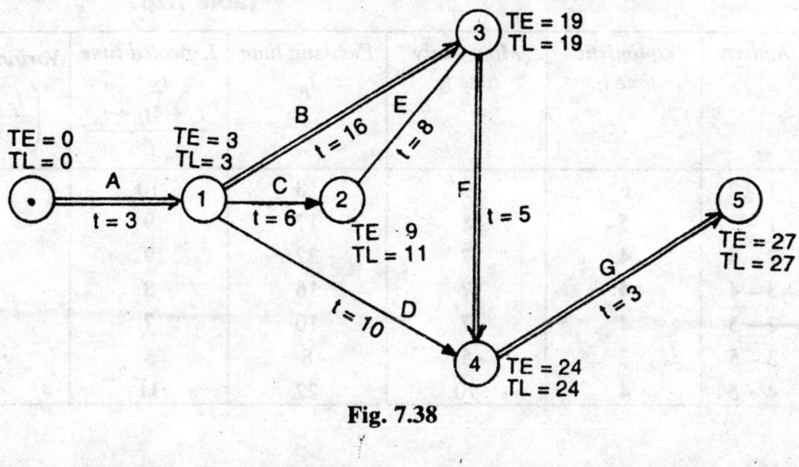

Fig. 7.38

Earliest Expected times

$T_E^0 = 0$	$T_L^5 = 27$	Slack $(T_L - T_E)$
$T_E^1 = 3$	$T_L^4 = 24$	Event 0 – 0
$T_E^2 = 9$	$T_L^3 = 19$	1 – 0
$T_E^3 = 17$	$T_L^2 = 11$	2 – 2
$= \underline{19}$	$T_L' = 5$	3 – 0
$T_E^4 = 13$	$= 3$	4 – 0
$= \underline{24}$	$T_L^0 = 0$	5 – 0
$T_E^5 = 27$		

Event	T_L	T_E	*Slack*
0	0	0	0
1	3	3	0
2	11	9	2
3	19	19	0
4	24	24	0
5	27	27	0

The critical path is along the events 0-1-3-4-5. Event 2 has a slack of 2 days.

The duration of the project = 27 days. **Ans.**

Example 7.30. *For the network shown in the following Fig. 7.39, the time estimates in days for each activity are indicated. Determine the critical path and the probability of completing the project in 36 days. The probability for various values of the probability factor z is as:*

Z	1.0	1.1	1.2	1.3
Pr	84.13	86.43	88.49	90.32

[UPSC, Engg Services, 1992]

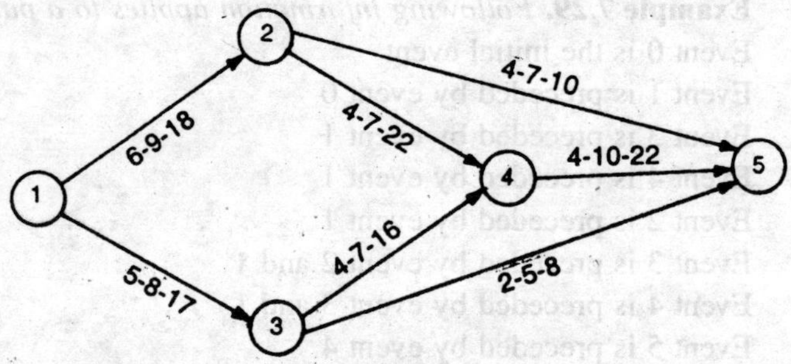

Fig. 7.39

Solution. The expected time, variance and standard deviation are determined in tabular form in table 7.26

Table 7.26

Activity	*Optimistic time* t_o	*Most likely time* t_L	*Pessistic time* t_p	*Expected time* $t_E = \frac{t_o + 4t_L + t_p}{6}$	*Variance* $\sigma^2 = \left(\frac{t_p - t_o}{6}\right)^2$	*Standard deviation* $\sigma = \left(\frac{t_p - t_o}{6}\right)$	*Remarks*
1 – 2	6	9	18	10	4	2	
1 – 3	5	8	17	9	4	2	
2 – 4	4	7	22	9	9	3	
3 – 4	4	7	16	8	4	2	
2 – 5	4	7	10	7	1	1	
3 – 5	2	5	8	5	1	1	
4 – 5	4	10	22	11	9	3	

For critical path, float is determined in the tabular form in table 7.27

Table 7.27

Activity	*Duration of activity*	*Earliest start time EST (T_E^i)*	*Earlist finish time EFT*	*Latest start time LST*	*Latest finish time LFT (T_L^i)*	*Float*	*Remarks*
1 – 2	10	0	10	0	10	0	critical
1 – 3	9	0	9	2	11	2	
2 – 4	9	10	19	10	19	0	critical
2 – 5	7	10	17	23	30	13	
3 – 4	8	9	17	11	19	2	
3 – 5	5	9	14	25	30	16	
4 – 5	11	19	30	19	30	0	critical

The critical path is along 1-2-4-5.

The duration of the project = 30 day.

Duration of completion of project = 36 day

(*ii*) The probability factor $z = \dfrac{T_S - T_E}{\sigma}$

where T_S is the duration of completion given and σ is standard deviation.

Variance along critical path = 4 + 9 + 9 = 22

Standard deviation along critical path = $\sqrt{22}$ = 4.69

$$\therefore \quad z = \frac{T_S - T_E}{4.69} = \frac{36 - 30}{4.69}$$

$$= \frac{6}{4.69} = 1.28$$

For probability factor 1.28, the probability of completion the project during 36 days is 89.95 ≈ 90.0% **Ans.**

Example 7.31. *In the following net work 7.40, the optimistic time, most likely time and pessimistic time estimates are given for each activity. If 10 and 100 are the start and end event, find the critical path for the project.*

[UPSC, Engg. Services, 1993]

Solution. The expected time, variance and standard deviation is determined in tabular form in table 7.28.

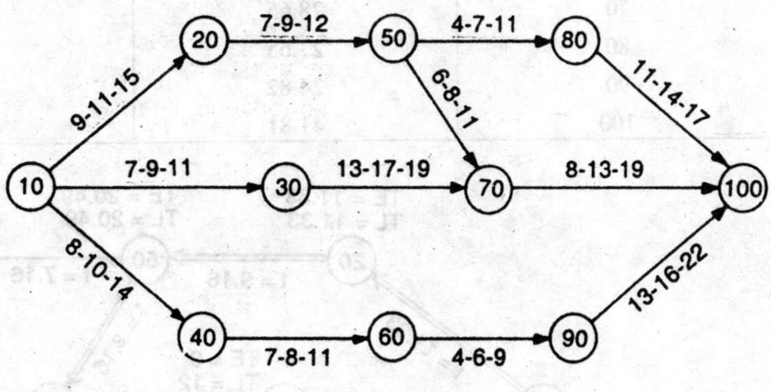

Fig. 7.40

Table 7.28

Activity	*Optimistic time t_o*	*Most likely time t_L*	*Pessistic time t_p*	*Expected time $t_E = \dfrac{t_o + 4t_L + t_p}{6}$*	*Variance $\sigma^2 = \left(\dfrac{t_p - t_o}{6}\right)^2$*	*Standard deviation $\sigma = \left(\dfrac{t_p - t_o}{6}\right)$*
10 – 20	9	11	15	11.33	1	1
10 – 40	8	10	14	10.33	1	1

Activity	*Optimistic time* t_o	*Most likely time* t_L	*Pessistic time* t_p	*Expected time* $t_E = \frac{t_o + 4t_L + t_p}{6}$	*Variance* $\sigma^2 = \left(\frac{t_p - t_o}{6}\right)^2$	*Standard deviation* $\sigma = \left(\frac{t_p - t_o}{6}\right)$
10 – 30	7	9	11	9.0	0.444	0.67
20 – 50	7	9	12	9.16	0.70	0.833
30 – 70	13	17	19	16.67	1.0	1.0
40 – 60	7	8	11	8.33	0.444	0.67
50 – 70	6	8	11	8.16	0.7	0.833
60 – 90	4	6	9	6.16	0.7	0.833
70 – 100	8	13	19	13.16	3.36	1.833
80 – 100	11	14	17	14.0	1.0	1.0
90 – 100	13	16	22	16.5	2.25	1.5
50 – 80	4	7	11	7.16	1.36	1.17

The earlier expected time T_E and latest start time T_L are determined as follows:

Event	T_E	T_L	*Slack*
10	0	0	0
20	11.33	11.33	0
30	9.0	12.0	3.0
40	10.33	10.82	0.5
50	20.49	20.49	0
60	18.66	19.15	0.5
70	28.65	28.65	0.0
80	27.65	27.81	0.21
90	24.82	25.81	0.5
100	41.81	41.81	0

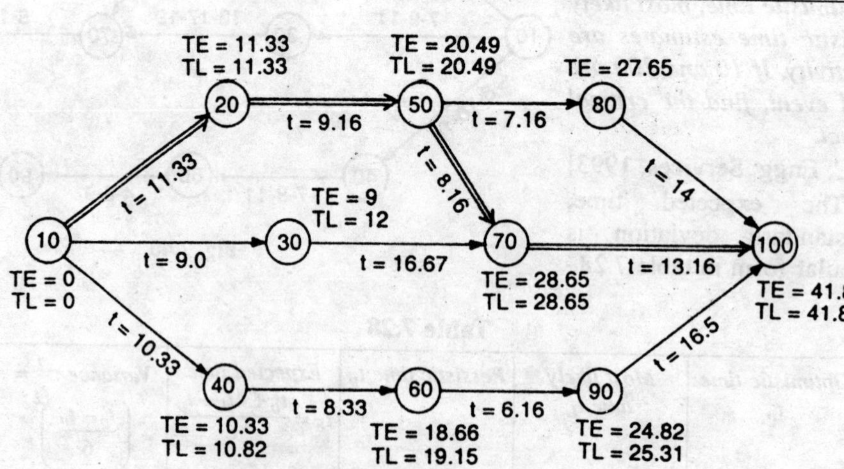

Fig. 7.41

Hence critical path along 10-20-50-70-100.

QUESTIONS

1. Define PERT and give its significance in detail.
2. What different time estimates are used in PERT? Explain their significance.
3. Explain the method of calculation of earliest expected T_E and latest allowable occurrence time T_L in PERT? With an example.
4. Define slack. How many types of slack you know? Explain.
5. How the probability of completion time for a project can be determined? Explain step by step.
6. The three time estimates of three activities A, B, C are given as follows. Determine the expected time t_E. Which of the activity has more reliable time estimate.

Activity	*Optimistic time*	*Most likely time*	*Pessimistic time*
A	11	13	15
B	7	8	12
C	6	11	13

[**Ans.** Activity A is more reliable as it has maximum earlier expected time of 13 days.]

7. The net work of a project is shown below in Fig. 7.42. The three time estimates optimistic, most likely and pessimistic times are shown on the net work itself. Determine the most reliable or critical path of the net work.
[**Ans.** 1-2-4-5-7 and 1-2-3-6-7 both are critical path as both have T_E = 27 days.]

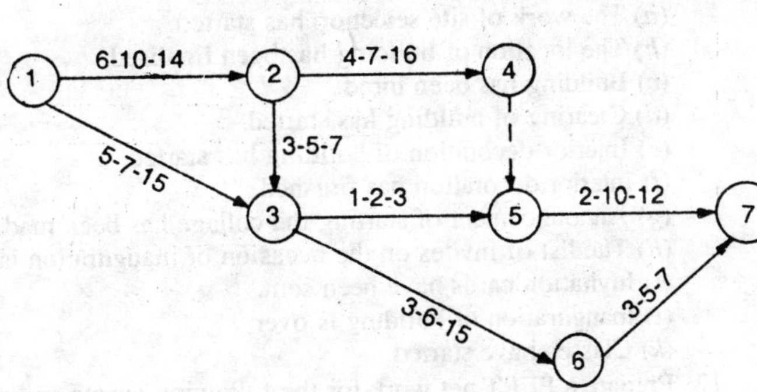

Fig. 7.42

8. Draw the PERT net work of a project with following events:
   (*a*) A is the starting and K the end event.
   (*b*) J is successor event to F.
   (*c*) C and D are successor events to B.
   (*d*) D is a predecessor event to G.
   (*e*) E and F occur after event C.
   (*f*) E preceeds F.
   (*g*) C restrains the occurrence of G and G preceeds H.
   (*h*) H preceeds J.
   (*i*) F restrains the occurance of H.
   (*j*) K succeeds event J.
9. The three time estimates t_o, t_L and t_p are shown on the net work of the project in Fig. 7.43. Compute the following for the project.

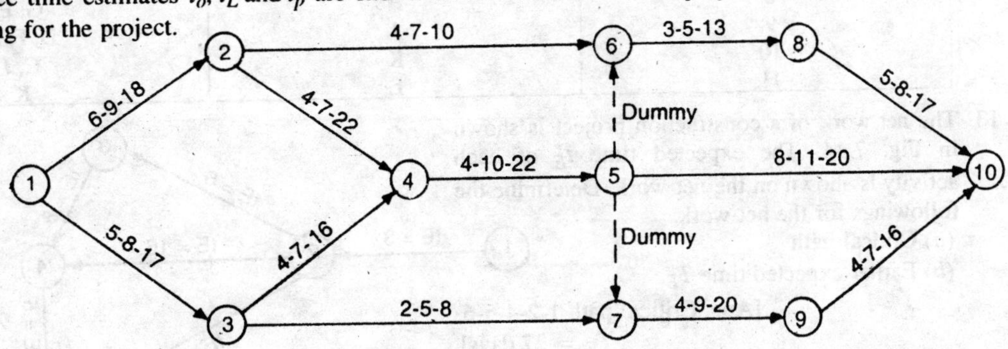

Fig. 7.43.

   (*a*) The expected or average time t_E.
   (*b*) The earliest expected time T_E.

(*c*) The latest allowable occurance time T_L.

(*d*) Slack for each event.

10. For the following two projects, state the problem in terms of events and draw the event oriented net work.

(*a*) Conducting an examination:

(*i*) Design question paper	7 days
(*ii*) Printing of question paper	2 days
(*iii*) Distribution of question papers to different centres	4 days
(*iv*) Answering the question paper	1 days
(*v*) Collection of answer books at head office	4 days

(*b*) Holding a conference

(*i*) Ask the members for a suitable date by mail	6 days
(*ii*) Inform date to members	2 days
(*iii*) Send agenda and other relevant material to each member by mail	4 days
(*iv*) Arrange conference room	2 days
(*v*) Arrange refreshment	1 day

11. To start a new collage a suitable building is to be hired. Draw the PERT net work if the following events are involved in it.

(*a*) The work of site selection has started.
(*b*) The location of building has been finalised.
(*c*) Building has been hired.
(*d*) Clearing of building has started.
(*e*) Interior decoration of building has started.
(*f*) Interior decoration has finished.
(*g*) Announcement of starting the collage has been made.
(*h*) The list of invites on the occasion of inauguration is complete.
(*i*) Invitation cards have been sent.
(*j*) Inanguration of building is over
(*k*) Classes have started.

12. Prepare a PERT net work for the following events and number them according to D.R. Fulkerson's rule:

S. No.	*Event*	*Preceding event*
1.	A	Start
2.	B	A
3.	C	B
4.	D	B
5.	E	D
6.	F	B
7.	G	E
8.	H	G, E
9.	J	D, F, H
10.	K	C, J
11.	L	K

13. The net work of a construction project is shown in Fig. 7.44. The expected time t_E of each activity is shown on the net work. Determine the followings for the net work.

(*a*) Critical path

(*b*) Earlier expected time T_E.

[Ans. Critical path 1-2-4-5-6,
T_E = 27 days]

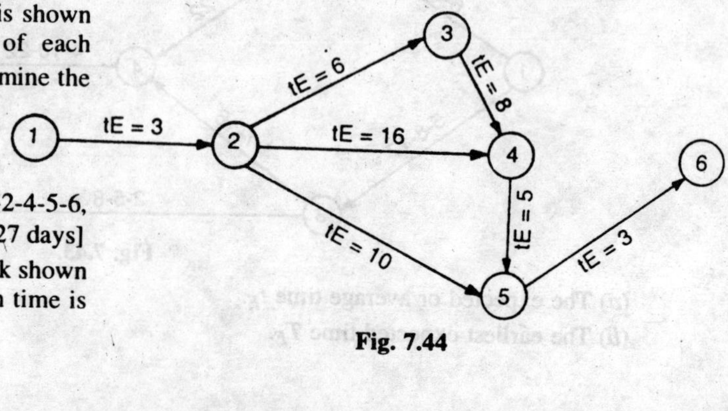

Fig. 7.44

14. Determine the critical path of the net work shown in Fig. 7.45, if the scheduled completion time is 22 weeks.

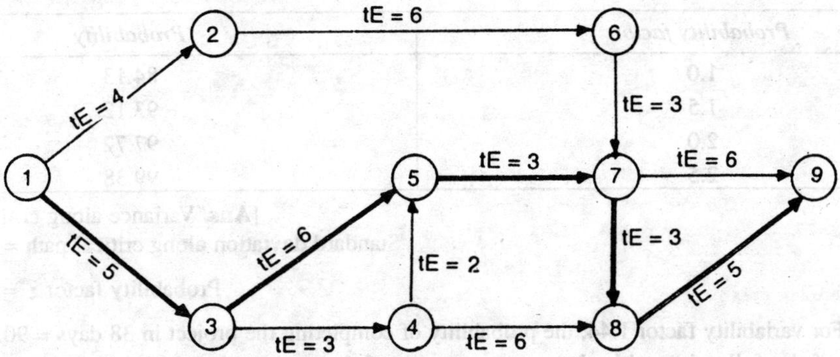

Fig. 7.45. **[Ans. Critical path (1-3-5-7-8-9)]**

15. A project can be completed in 50 weeks. The total variation of all activities is found 16. Find the duration of completion of the project with probabilities of
   (*a*) 95% (*b*) 75%
   (*c*) 40% **[Ans. (*a*) = 57 weeks, (*b*) = 53 weeks, (*c*) 49 weeks]**
16. The three time estimate optimistic time t_o, most likely time t_L and pessimistic time t_p are shown on the net work of a project shown in Fig. 7.46. For the net work, find out the followings.

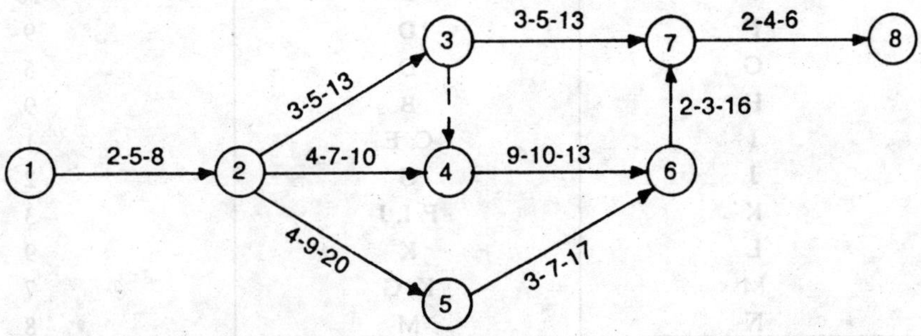

Fig. 7.46.

   (*a*) Expected time t_E
   (*b*) Variance for each activity
   (*c*) Slack for each event
   (*d*) Critical path
   (*e*) If the scheduled completion time is 36.5 days. Find the percent probability of completion.
17. The net work of an project is shown in Fig. 7.47. If the completion time of the project T_S is 38 days. Determine the slack of each event. Also determine the critical path. What is the probability of comple- ting the project in 38 days. Following values of probability factor may be used.

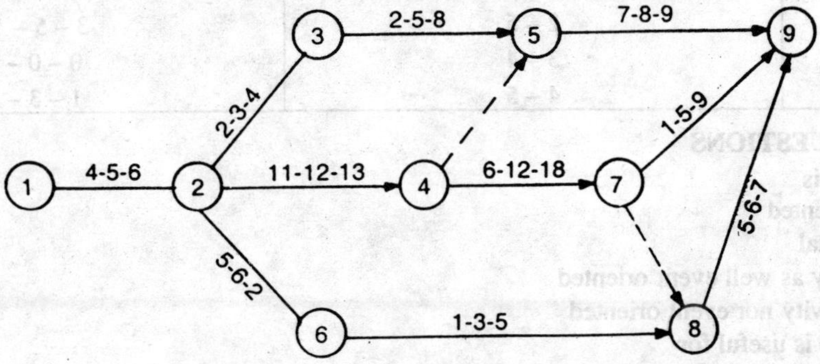

Fig. 7.47.

Probability factor	*Probability*
1.0	84.13
1.5	93.12
2.0	97.72
2.5	99.38

[**Ans.** Variance along critical path = 4.33

Standard deviation along critical path = $\sqrt{4.33}$ = 2.082

Probability factor $z = \frac{38.35}{2.08} = 1.44$

For variability factor 1.44, the probability of completing the project in 38 days = 90.22% say 90%]

18. From the data of the following table draw the net work of the project and determine the various paths and critical path. Also determine the duration of the project.

S. No.	*Activity*	*Preceeding activity*	*Expected completion time in days*
1.	A	None	5
2.	B	A	2
3.	C	A	6
4.	D	B	12
5.	E	D	10
6.	F	D	9
7.	G	D	5
8.	H	B	9
9.	I	C, E	1
10.	J	G	2
11.	K	F, I, J	3
12.	L	K	9
13.	M	K, G	7
14.	N	M	8

19. Draw a pert net work from the following data and find the expected mean time, variance and standard deviation for the project.

S. No.	*Activity*	*Three time estimates in days*
1.	0 – 1	2 – 3 – 10
2.	0 – 2	4 – 5 – 6
3.	1 – 2	0 – 0 – 0
4.	1 – 3	6 – 7 – 8
5.	1 – 4	1 – 5 – 9
6.	2 – 5	3 – 5 – 17
7.	3 – 4	0 – 0 – 0
8.	4 – 5	1 – 3 – 5

OBJECTIVE TYPE QUESTIONS

1. PERT net work is

(*a*) Activity oriented

(*b*) Event oriental

(*c*) Both activity as well event oriented

(*d*) Neither activity nor event oriented

2. PERT technique is useful for

(*a*) Non repetitive type projects in which correct time estimates can not be made

(*b*) Repetitive type of projects in which correct time estimates can be made
(*c*) It can be used for non repetitive and repetitive type projects.
(*d*) It can neither be used for non repetitive nor for repetitive type projects.

3. PERT technique can be used for
(*a*) Research and development projects
(*b*) It can be used for repetitive type projects as small housing construction project
(*c*) It can be used for Research and development project as well as repetitive type project
(*d*) It can be used for none of the above works

4. Identify, which of the following is not a PERT Event
(*a*) Assemble units (*b*) Income tax form completed
(*c*) List of necessary equipment completed (*d*) Assembly of units started

5. Identify, which of the following is a PERT event
(*a*) Blue prints started (*b*) Report is being written
(*c*) Write a report (*d*) Blue prints are being prepared

6. In PERT technique, the time estimate of activities and probability of their occurance follow
(*a*) Binomial distribution (*b*) Normal distribution
(*c*) Poisson's distribution (*d*) β distribution

7. The area under β distribution curve is divided into two equal parts by a vertical ordinate through
(*a*) Expected time (*b*) Optimistic time
(*c*) Most likely time (*d*) Pessimistic time

8. PERT technique is based on
(*a*) Probabilistic approach (*b*) Deterministic approach
(*c*) On both the approaches (*d*) None is applicable

9. In PERT technique time estimates used is
(*a*) optimistic time (*b*) Pessimistic time
(*c*) Most likely time (*d*) All the above
(*e*) None of the above

10. Identify the incorrect statement/statements
(*a*) In a construction project larger the variance lesser the variability and better the control
(*b*) In a PERT net work, the path which connects events of zero or minimum slacks is called the critical path
(*c*) Critical path is the longest path in terms of time units
(*d*) The difference between the latest allowable time T_L and the earliest expected time T_E is called SLACK
(*e*) In a net work there can be only one critical path
(*f*) There can be more than one critical paths in a net work

11. Slack may be
(*a*) Positive (*b*) Zero
(*c*) Negative (*d*) All the three
(*e*) None of the above

12. Zero slack indicates that the project is
(*a*) On schedule (*b*) Behind the schedule
(*c*) Ahead of the schedule (*d*) All the above

13. In a beta distribution curve the curve is symmetrical about
(*a*) Optimistic time t_0 (*b*) Pessimistic time t_p
(*c*) Most likely time t_L (*d*) Expected time t_E

ANSWERS

1. (*b*)	5. (*a*)	9. (*d*)	13. (*d*)
2. (*a*)	6. (*d*)	10. (*a, e*)	
3. (*a*)	7. (*a*)	11. (*d*)	
4. (*a*)	8. (*a*)	12. (*a*)	

Q. 8.

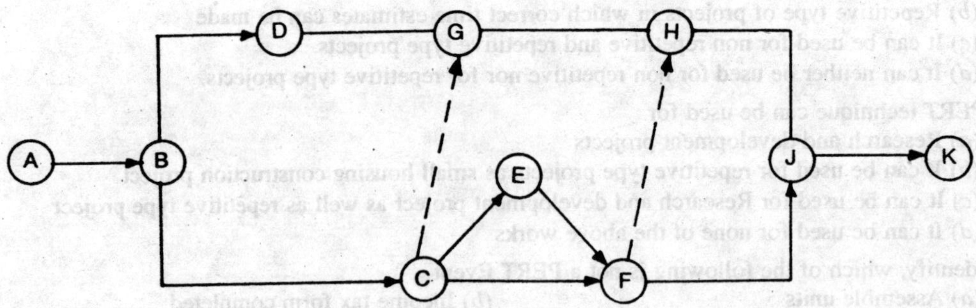

Fig. 7.48

Q. 9

Activity	t_o	t_L	t_p	t_E	T_E	T_L	*Slack*
1 – 2	6	9	18	10	$T_E^1 = 0$	$T_L = \frac{3}{5}$	3
1 – 3	5	8	17	9	$T_E^2 = 10$		
2 – 4	4	7	22	9	$T_E^3 = 9$		
3 – 4	4	7	16	8	$T_E^4 = \frac{19}{17}$	$T_L^2 = \frac{13}{26}$	3
2 – 6	4	7	10	7	$T_E^5 = 30$	$T_L^3 = \frac{14}{25}$	5
3 – 7	2	5	8	5	$T_E^6 = 17$ $\underline{30}$	$T_L^4 = 22$	3
4 – 5	4	10	22	11	$T_E^7 = 14$ 30	$T_L^5 = 36$ $\underline{33}$	
5 – 6	0	0	0	0	$T_E^8 = 36$	$T_L^6 = 33$	3
5 – 7	0	0	0	0	$T_E^9 = 40$	$T_L^7 = 30$	0
6 – 8	3	5	13	6	$T_E^{10} = 42$ 45 $\underline{48}$	$T_L^8 = 39$	3
5 – 10	8	11	20	12		$T_L^9 = 40$	0
7 – 9	4	9	20	10		$T_L^{10} = 40$	0
8 – 10	5	8	17	9			
9 – 10	4	7	16	8			

[Ans. Critical path 1-3-4-5-10]

Q. 10 (*a*).

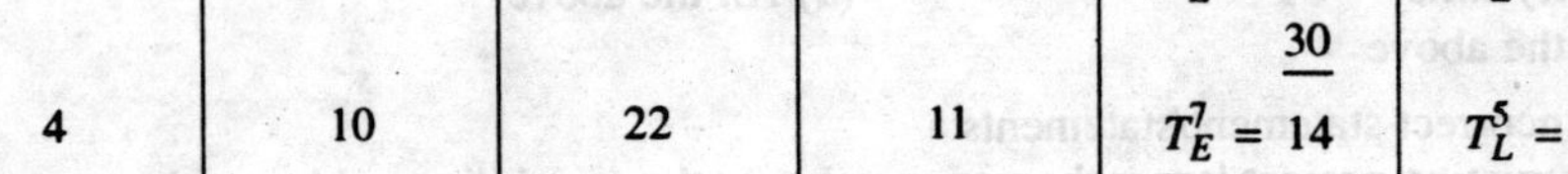

Fig. 7.49 (*a*)

Q. 10 (*b*).

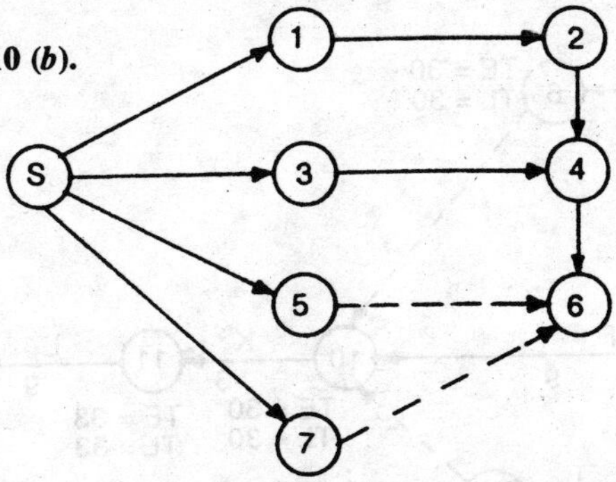

Fig. 7.49 (*b*)

[**Ans.** (*a*) It can be written in terms of events:
Event (1) Question paper prepared
Event (2) Question paper printed
Event (3) Question papers sent to various centres
Event (4) Question papers answered
Event (5) Answer books collected at the head office
(*b*) Event (1) Members, choice of date obtained by mail
Event (2) Members inform the date of conference
Event (3) Agenda of conference prepared
Event (4) Agenda and relevant material sand to members by mail
Event (5) Conference room arranged
Event (6) Refreshment arranged
Event (7) Conference started.]

Q. 11.

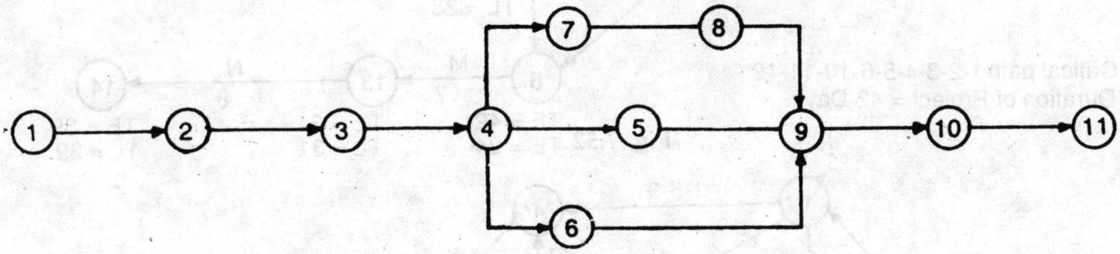

Fig. 7.50

Q. 12.

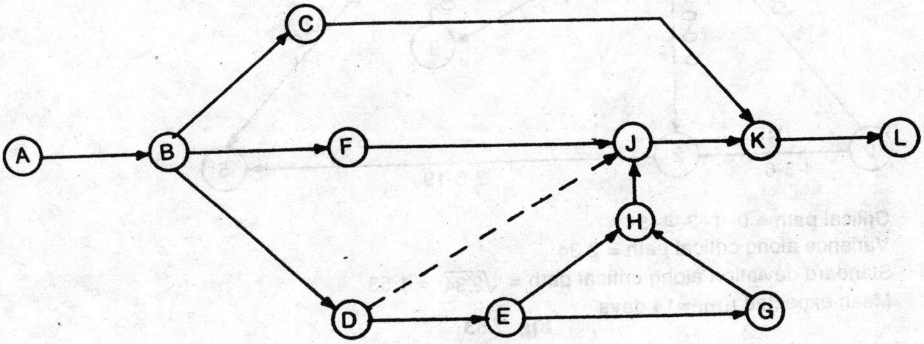

Fig. 7.51

Q. 16.

Activity	t_E	*Varience*	*Standard devidation*	*Slack*
1 – 2	5	1	1	0
2 – 3	6	2.78	1.67	0
2 – 4	7	1	1	12
2 – 5	10	7.11	2.67	1
3 – 7	6	2.78	1.67	0
3 – 4	0	0	0	0
4 – 6	10	1	1	0
5 – 6	8	5.44	2.33	0
6 – 7	5	5.44	2.33	0
7 – 8	4	0.44	0.663	0

[**Ans.** Critical 1-2-5-6-7-8, Slacks along C.P. are zeros.
(*e*) Probability % = 93.3%, Variance along C.P. = 9 Standard deviation = 3, Variate $z = 1.5$, Percent probability = 93.3%]

Q. 18.

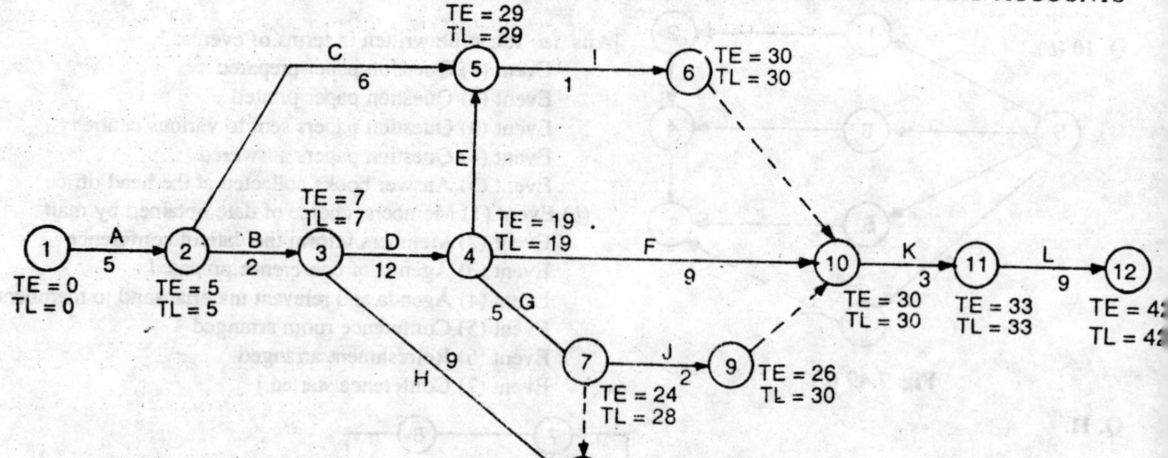

Critical path 1-2-3-4-5-6-10-11-12
Duration of Project = 42 Days.

Fig. 7.52

Q. 19.

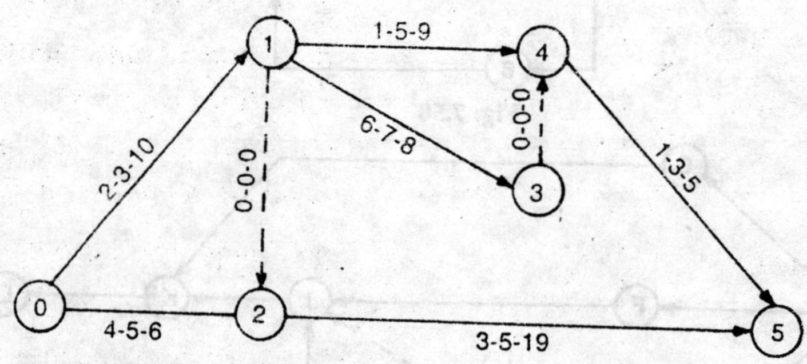

Critical path = 0–1–3–4–5
Varience along critical path = 2.34
Standard deviation along critical path = $\sqrt{2.34}$ = 1.53
Mean expected time= 14 days

Fig. 7.53

8

Critical Path Method Net Work Analysis

8.1. INTRODUCTION

The critical path method, abbreviated as CPM was developed independently of PERT in 1957 by DUPONT and SPERY RAND corporation of GERMANY, for application to industrial situations like construction, manufacturing and maintenance etc. Since then it has gained vide acceptance by construction industry with application in the massive structures such as bridges, dams, tunnels, power plants, highways, multi-storyed buildings etc.

CPM net works usually are used for repetitive type projects where fairly accurate estimates of times can be made for completion of each activity and the cost estimate can be made with fair degree of accuracy. How ever CPM technique is not suitable for Research and Development project. CPM technique can be applied usefully to the following types of projects.

1. Construction of multi-storyed buildings.
2. Construction of a new bridge across river Brahmputra
3. Manufacture of a new automobile
4. Repair of a car or locomotive
5. Extension of a factory building
6. Shifting of an manufacturing unit to a new site.

The above noted projects are more or less unique in nature. The projects either are repetitive nature such as repair of a car or similar nature of projects which have been executed in the past. How ever they are also of the nature which neither have been built in the past nor would be build in future as the construction of new bridge across the river Brahmputra is not likely to be under taken in the same form. But the activities required to complete the bridge can be listed easily and earlier experience and knowledge can be used for getting information regarding execution, duration, resources and cost etc. of these activities. Hence the results so available will be more reliable than PERT.

8.2. DIFFERENCE BETWEEN CPM AND PERT NET WORKS

The difference between the CPM and PERT net works is shown in tabular form below in table 8.1.

Table 8.1. Difference between CPM and PERT net works

C.P.M. net works	*PERT net works*
1. Basically it has deterministic approach in the design of net work	1. Basically it has probabilitistic approach in the design of net work.
2. It is activity oriented net work	2. It is event oriented net work

C.P.M. net works	*PERT net works*
3. For each activity only one time estimate is required	3. For each activity three time estimates pessimistic time t_p, optimistic time t_o and mostly likely time t_L are required.
4. Cost of the project is the prime governing factor. There is an optimum duration of the project at which the cost is minimum. This can be obtained by crashing the project net work. Thus Time and Cost both are controlling factors.	4. In this technique, it is assumed that the cost is directly proportional to the time. Thus toget the minimum cost the duration of the project is reduced to the minimum. Thus it is time controlling net work.
5. The critical path is that path which joins the critical activities of the net work having zero total float.	5. The critical path is the path which joins the critical events having zero or minimum slacks at each event. The critical events may have positive, zero or negative slacks depending upon the project scheduled completion time.
6. It is found useful for repetitive type of activities net works where past experience is adequately available.	6. It is recommended for non repetitive type of activities such as Research and Development projects where no past experience is available or where great uncertainty lies in the time estimates.

8.3. CPM APPLICATION

CPM technique has several levels of application in project management namely:

1. Planning 2. Scheduling and
3. Controlling

1. **Planning.** It is the most important part in a project management. In the planning stage the logical sequence in which the activities must be performed is decided. It should also be ensured that all activities are shown, scope of project has been interpreted correctly and resources required for each job are applied. Resources may be time, money and man power, and equipment etc.
2. **Scheduling.** In scheduling, the time required for the execution of each activity or operation and the time order in which each operation has to be carried to meet the plan objectives is determined. Scheduling is to be done not only in respect of operations, but also in respect of resources.
3. **Controlling.** It is the process in which the deviations between the plan and actual performances are reviewed after the start of the project and these deviations corrected. In CPM technique controlling is required not only in respect of physical progress of work, but also in respect of cost.

8.4. CPM NET WORKS

As mentioned earlier also, CPM net works generally are activity oriented while PERT net works are event oriented. Hence it is the activities that are planned and monitored. Activities usually are operations which take time to complete them and resources are spent over them. The junctions between activities are known as *events.* An event is a point in time, *i.e.* a event does not need time for its accomplishment. It represents the beginning or completion of some activities or group of activities. In CPM net works each activity is represented by an arrow and sequence in which the activities are performed is shown by the sequence of arrows. In CPM networks the activities are lebelled or numbered for reference.

In CPM net work planning a tentative list of activities that have to be performed in order to accomplish the project objectives is prepared and the net work is formed. The process of drawing the net work consists of following steps:

1. Preparing the list of activities of project.
2. Answering the three basic questions with regard to each activity.
3. Drawing the net work. The interdependence can be shown by dummies.

The three basic question are as follows:

(*a*) What activity or activities must preceed this activity.

(*b*) What activity or activities can not be started till the completion of this activity.

(*c*) What activity or activities can be performed simultaneously with this activity.

8.5. TIME ESTIMATION

In the estimation of time duration of the various activities two approaches may be adopted as follows:

1. Probabilitistic approach 2. Deterministic approach

PERT technique follows the probabilistic approach, in which the three time estimates, optimistic time (t_o), most likely time (t_L) and pessimistic time (t_p) for each activity are made. From these three time estimates the expected time (t_E) is calculated. This expected time duration has the same degree of uncertainty as in the range of the three time estimates.

CPM technique follows the deterministic approach in which, it is assumed that enough information is available for each activity and only one single time estimate of time duration is sufficiently accurate to give reasonably good results. Hence no uncertainties are taken into consideration. The activity duration is represented by (t^{ij}), where i represents the predecessor event and j the successor event.

8.6. EARLIEST EVENT TIME

The earliest event time or earliest occurrence time is the earliest time at which an event can occur. It is the time by which all activities leading to the event under consideration are completed. It is denoted by the term (T_E) as in the case of PERT also. The term earliest event time is analogous to the term earliest expected time (T_E) used in PERT analysis except that the degree of uncertainty inherent in the word "expected" is not there.

In the CPM net work, the time of completion of each activity (t^{ij}) is known. Hence the earliest occurrence time T_E can be calculated easily. It can be calculated by adding up the duration of all activities leading upto that event.

8.7. RULE TO CALCULATE THE EARLIEST EVENT TIME T_E

The earliest event occurrence time T_E can be calculated by the following equation

$$T_E^j = T_E^i + t^{ij} \qquad ...(8.1)$$

where,

$T_E{}^j$ = Earliest occurrence time for the head event

$T_E{}^i$ = Earliest occurrence time for the tail event

ij = Activity under consideration

t^{ij} = Time of completion of activity ij.

The procedure of calculation of earliest event time is illustrated by the following example.

Example 8.1 *Find the earliest event time of all the events of the simple net work given in the Fig. 8.1.*

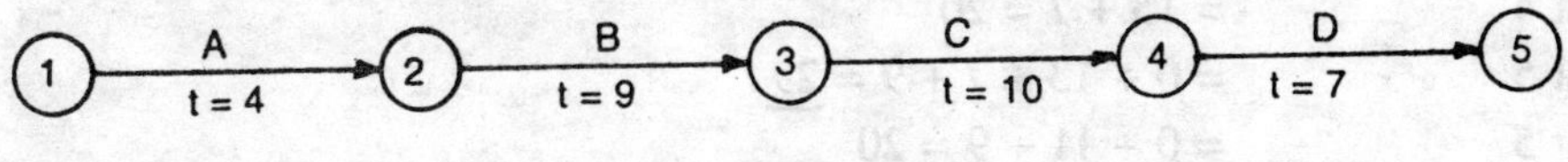

Fig. 8.1

Solution. For the given net work event (1) is the first event. Hence value of T_E will be 0

Thus $T_E^1 = 0.$

Event 2 occurs after the completion of activity A

Hence $T_E^2 = T_E^1 + t^{ij} = 0 + 4 = 4$

Event 3 occurs after the completion of activity B

Hence $T_E^3 = T_E^2 + t^{ij} = 4 + 9 = 13$

Event 4 occurs after the completion of activity C

Hence $T_E^4 = T_E^2 + t^{ij} = 13 + 10 = 23$

Event 5 occurs after the completion of activity D

Hence $T_E^5 = T_E^4 + t^{ij} = 23 + 7 = 30$

These event times are entered at the top of the node as shown in Fig. 8.2.

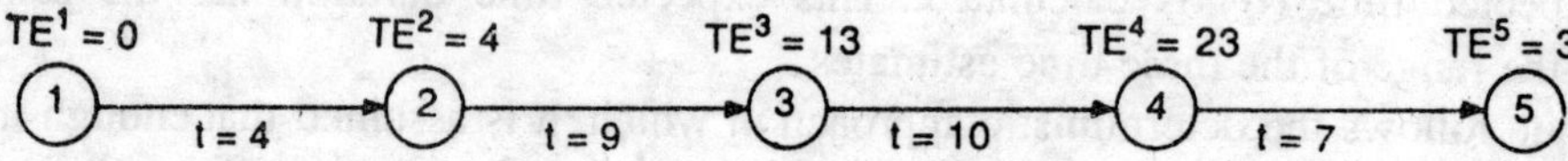

Fig. 8.2

Example 8.2. *Find the earliest event time for all events of the net work given in Fig. 8.3.*

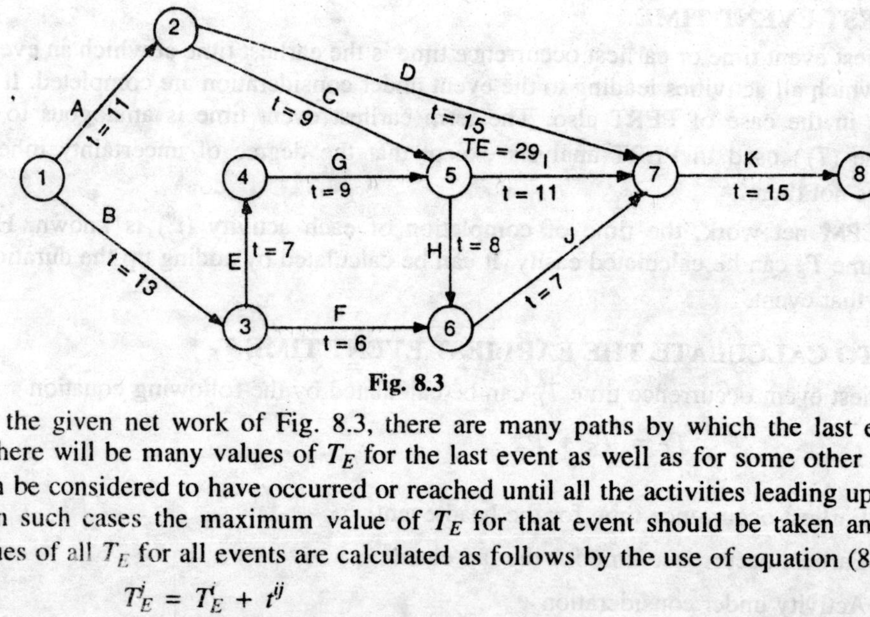

Fig. 8.3

Solution. In the given net work of Fig. 8.3, there are many paths by which the last event can be reached. Hence there will be many values of T_E for the last event as well as for some other events. How ever no event can be considered to have occurred or reached until all the activities leading upto this event are completed. In such cases the maximum value of T_E for that event should be taken and others are ignored. The values of all T_E for all events are calculated as follows by the use of equation (8.1)

$$T_E^j = T_E^i + t^{ij}$$

$T_E^1 = 0$, as the event (1) is the first event

T_E for event 2 $= 0 + 11 = 11$

T_E for event 3 $= 0 + 13 = 13$

T_E for event 4 $= 13 + 7 = 20$

T_E for event 5 $= 0 + 13 + 7 + 9 = \underline{29}$

T_E for event 5 $= 0 + 11 + 9 = 20$

T_E for event 6 $= 13 + 7 + 9 + 8 = \underline{37}$

T_E for event 6 $= 0 + 13 + 6 = 19$

$$T_E^7 = T_E^2 + 15 = 11 + 15 = 26$$

$$T_E^7 = T_E^5 + 11 = 29 + 11 = 40$$

$$T_E^7 = T_E^6 + 7 = 37 = \underline{44}$$
$$T_E^8 = T_E^7 + 15 = 44 + 15 = 59$$

The Computations of earliest event times T_E can be done on the net work itself by entering the values of T_E for each node near that node itself. If there are more than one T_E value from different paths, all the

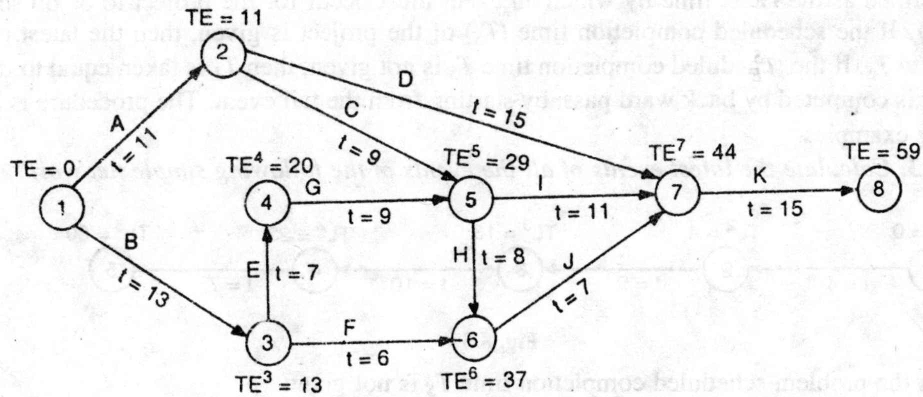

Fig. 8.4

values are written near the node first and after getting all values of T_E for that node, the largest value of all should be retained for that node and the rest, deleted.

In large and complicated net works, the calculations usually are done in tabular form to avoid mistake that might creep in.

8.7.1. Procedure of Tabular form

For calculating the earliest event time seven columns are made as shown in Table 8.2.

Table 8.2.

S. No.	*successor event j*	*Predecessor event i*	*Activity i-j*	*Activity time or duration* (t^{ij})	T_E^i	T_E
1.	1	0	–	–	0	0
2.	2	1	1 – 2	11	11	11
3.	3	1	1 – 3	13	13	13
4.	4	3	3 – 4	7	20	20
5.	5	2	2 – 5	9	20	29
		4	4 – 5	9	29	
6.	6	3	3 – 6	6	19	37
		5	5 – 6	8	37	
7.	7	2	2 – 7	15	26	44
		5	5 – 7	11	40	
		6	6 – 7	7	44	
8.	8	7	7 – 8	15	59	59

In the first column serial no of events is entered. In second column successor event *j* or head event is entered. In the third column the predecessor event is entered. If there are more than one predecessor event for a successor event, all the predecessor events are entered one after the other down the column.

In the 4th column activity connecting the events of column 2 and 3 are entered. The fifth column contains the activity duration corresponding to activity of column four. The sixth column contains T_E values of the events calculated for all paths. The T_E value is obtained from equation 8.1. If there are more than one value of T_E for an event, the largest of all is taken as T_E of that event and entered in the sixth column. The procedure is illustrated by solving example 8.2 by this method in table 8.2.

8.8. LATEST ALLOWABLE OCCURRENCE OR LATEST EVENT TIME

It can be defined as the latest time by which an event must occur for the project to be on schedule. It is denoted by T_L. If the scheduled completion time (T_S) of the project is given, then the latest event time T_L will be equal to T_S. If the scheduled completion time T_S is not given, then T_L is taken equal to the earliest event time T_E. It is computed by back ward pass, by starting from the tail event. The procedure is illustrated by the following examples.

Example 8.3. *Calculate the latest events of all the events of the following simple net work.*

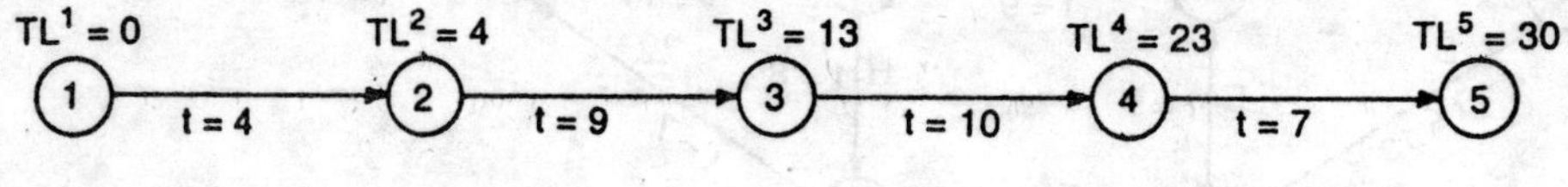

Fig. 8.5

Solution. In the problem scheduled completion time T_S is not given.

Hence it is taken equal to the earliest Event time T_E.

Hence $\quad T_L^5 = T_E^5 = 30$

T_L^4 is obtained by subtracting the activity duration of activity 4-5 from the value of T_L^5.

$\therefore \quad T_L^4 = 30 - 7 = 23$

Similarly $\quad T_L^3 = T_L^4 - t^{3-4} = 23 - 10 = 13$

$$T_L^2 = 13 - 9 = 4$$

$$T_L^1 = 4 - 4 = 0$$

8.8.1. Rule to determine the latest event time

The latest event time is equal to the difference of latest time of succeeding event and the duration of the activity between these two events.

i.e. $\quad T_L^i = T_L^j - t^{ij} \quad$ ...(8.2)

If there are more than one value of latest event time T_L, then the lowest value of the T_L should be attopted and others should be discarded. The procedure is illustrated by the following example.

Example 8.4. *Calculate the latest event times for all events of the net work of example 8.2.*

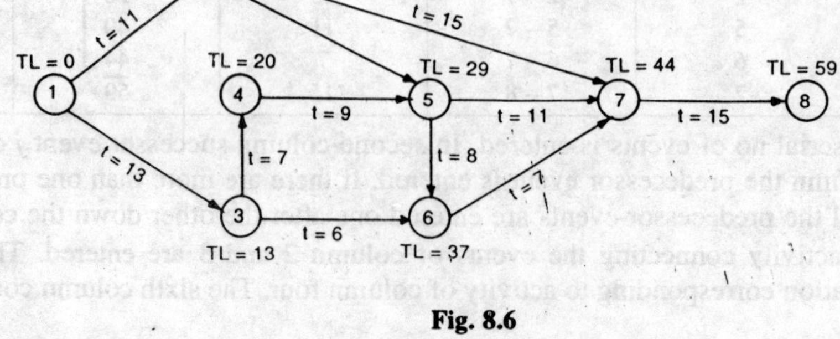

Fig. 8.6

Solution. Taking the value of $T_L^8 = T_E^8 = 59$. Calculated in example 8.2.

$\therefore \quad T_L^7 = T_L^8 - t^{(7-8)} = 59 - 15 = 44$

T_L for event 6, $\quad T_L^6 = T_L^7 - t^{6-7} = 44 - 7 = 37$

T_L for event 5, $\quad T_L^5 = T_L^6 - t^{5-6} = 37 - 8 = \underline{29}$

T_L for event 5, $\quad T_L^5 = T_L^7 - t^{5-7} = 44 - 11 = 33$

Lower of the two values is accepted *i.e.* $T_L^5 = 29$

T_L for event 4, $\quad T_L^4 = T_L^5 - t^{4-5} = 29 - 9 = 20$

T_L for event 3, $\quad T_L^3 = T_L^6 - t^{3-6} = 37 - 6 = 31$

Also $\quad T_L^3 = T_L^4 - t^{3-4} = 20 - 7 = \underline{13}$

T_L for event 2, $\quad T_L^2 = T_L^7 - t^{2-7} = 44 - 15 = 29$

Also $\quad T_L^2 = T_L^5 - t^{2-5} = 29 - 7 = \underline{22}$

Lower of the two values is taken *i.e.* $T_L^2 = 22$

T_L for event 1, $\quad T_L^1 = T_L^3 - t^{1-3} = 13 - 13 = 0$

Also $\quad T_L^1 = T_L^2 - t^{1-2} = 22 - 11 = 11$

Lower of the two values is taken *i.e.* $T_L^1 = 0$.

The values of latest event time T_L are shown on the net work of Fig. 8.6.

8.9. COMBINED TABULAR COMPUTATION

For complete analysis of a net work both the earliest occurrence event time T_E and latest event time T_L have to be computed. They can be computed separately as shown above or both can be computed in tabular format which is easy and less time consuming. The earliest occurrence event time is calculated by forward pass method and the latest occurrence event time by the back ward pass method. The method is illustrated by the following example.

Example 8.5. *Determine the earliest occurrence time* T_E and *latest event time* T_L *of net work of Example 8.4.*

Solution. The calculations are shown in Table 8.3 below:

Table 8.3.

Event	*Earliest expected time* T_E					*Latest allowable occurance time* T_L			
	Predessor event	*Activity*	*Activity time* t^{ij}	T_E^{ij}	T_E	*Successor event*	t^{ij}	T_L^i	T_L
1	0	–	–	–	–	2 3	11 13	9 $\underline{0}$	0
2	1	1 – 2	11	11	11	5 7	9 15	$\underline{20}$ 29	20
3	1	1 – 3	13	13	13	4	13	13	13
4	3	3 – 4	7	20	20	5	9	20	20
5	2 4	2 – 5 4 – 5	9 9	20 $\underline{29}$	29	6 7	8 11	$\underline{29}$ 33	29
6	3	3 – 6 5 – 6	6 8	19 $\underline{37}$	37	7	7	37	37

Event	*Earliest expected time T_E*					*Latest allowable occurance time T_L*			
	Predessor event	*Activity*	*Activity time t^{ij}*	T_E^{ij}	T_E	*Successor event*	t^{ij}	T_L^i	T_L
7	2	2 – 7	15	26	44	8	15	44	44
	5	5 – 7	11	40					
	6	6 – 7	7	<u>44</u>					
8	7	7 – 8	15	59	59	–	–	59	59

Example 8.6. *Determine the earliest expected time T_E and latest occurrence time T_L for all events in a tabular form of the net work shown in Fig. 8.7.*

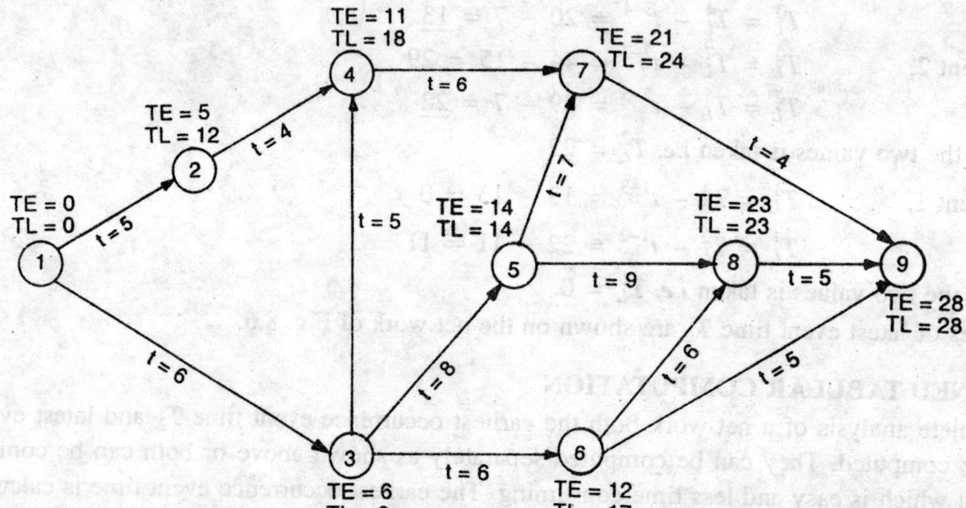

Fig. 8.7

Table 8.4.

Event	*Earliest expected time T_E*					*Latest allowable occurance time T_L*			
	Predessor event	*Activity*	*Activity time t^{ij}*	T_E^{ij}	T_E	*Successor event*	t^{ij}	T_L^i	T_L
1	–	–	–	–	0	2	5	7	0
						3	6	<u>0</u>	
2	1	1 – 2	5	5	5	4	6	12	12
3	1	1 – 3	6	6	6	4	5	13	6
						5	8	<u>6</u>	
4	2	2 – 4	4	9	11	7	6	18	18
	3	3 – 4	5	<u>11</u>					
5	3	3 – 5	8	14	14	7	7	17	14
						8	9	<u>14</u>	
6	3	3 – 6	6	12	12	8	6	17	17
						9	5	<u>23</u>	
7	4	4 – 7	6	17	21	9	4	24	24
	5	5 – 7	7	<u>21</u>					

Event	Earliest expected time T_E					Latest allowable occurance time T_L			
	Predessor event	Activity	Activity time t^{ij}	T_E^{ij}	T_E	Successor event	t^{ij}	T_L^i	T_L
8	5	5 – 8	9	23	23	9	5	23	23
	6	6 – 8	6	18					
9	6	6 – 9	5	17	28	–	–	28	28
	7	7 – 9	4	25					
	8	8 – 9	5	28					

The values of T_E and T_L are shown on Fig. 8.7.

8.10. ACTIVITY TIMES

As already stated that critical path method (CPM) net works are activity oriented. Apart from two event occurring times T_E and T_L, activity times are also useful in the analysis of a net work.

8.11. CLASSIFICATION OF ACTIVITY TIMES

The activity times may be classified as follows:

1. Earliest start time (EST)
2. Earliest Finish time (EFT)
3. Latest start time (LST)
4. Latest finish time (LFT)

1. Earliest start time (EST). It is the earliest time by which an activity can start. Thus it is equal to the earliest event time of the tail event of the activity. It is denoted by EST.

Thus EST = Earliest event time at its tail. If the activity is denoted by $(i - j)$, then earliest event time of tail event = $T_E{}^i$

$$\therefore \quad EST = T_E^i \qquad \ldots(8.3)$$

2. Earliest finish time. It is earliest time by which an activity can be completed. An early finish is said to occur if the activity starts at its earliest start time (EST) and takes the estimated duration of the activity for its completion.

Thus earliest finish time (EFT) = Earliest start time + Activity duration

$$\text{Thus} \quad EFT = EST + t^{ij}$$

$$= T_E^i + t^{ij} \qquad \ldots(8.4)$$

3. Latest start time (LST). It is the latest time by which an activity can start with out delaying the completion of the project as a whole. For no delay condition it should be equal to the latest finish time (LFT) minus activity duration.

$$\therefore \quad LST = LFT - \text{activity duration}$$

$$= LFT - t^{ij} \qquad \ldots(8.5)$$

4. latest finish time (LFT). It is the latest time by which an activity can be completed with out delaying thê completion of the project.

Thus it will be equal to the latest allowable occurrence time of the head event of the activity.

$$\therefore \quad LFT = \text{Latest event time at the head of actvity arrow}$$

$$\text{or} \quad LEF = T_L^j \qquad \ldots(8.6)$$

From the above four definitions of four times of an activity, the earliest start time and the latest finish times are equal to the earliest event time (T_E^i) at its tail and the latest event time (T_L^j) at the head respectively, the values of which are already known. Thus the earliest finish time and its latest start time can be determined simply by adding activity time to T_E^i and subtracting activity time from T_L^j respectively.

The procedure is illustrated from the following example.

Example 8.6. *Determine the values of (EST), (EFT), (LST) and (LFT) for the following net work.*

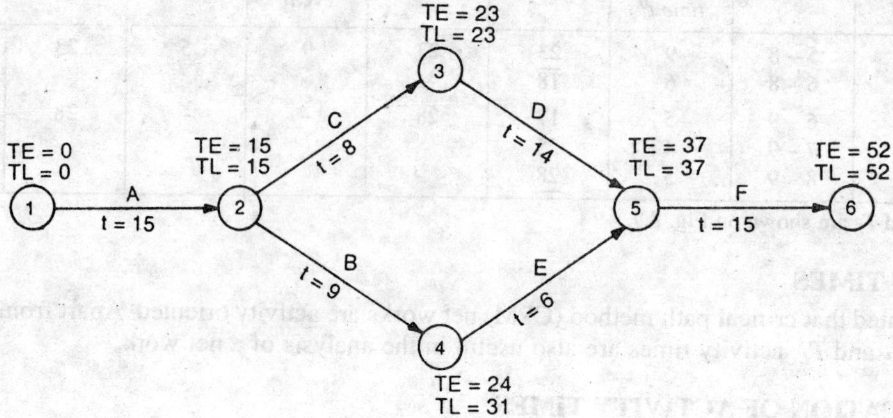

Fig. 8.8

T_E's

For activity 1-2,

$$T_E^2 = 0 + 15 = 15$$
$$T_E^3 \; T_E^2 + 8 = 15 + 8 = 23$$
$$T_E^4 = T_E^2 + 9 = 15 + 9 = 24$$
$$T_E^5 = T_E^3 + 14 = 23 + 14 = 37$$
$$T_E^5 = T_E^4 + 6 = 24 + 6 = 30$$
$$T_E^6 = T_E^5 + 15 = 37 + 15 = 52$$

For activity 1-2,

$$EST = T_E^i + 0 = 0$$
$$EFT = T_E^i + 15 = 0 + 15 = 15$$
$$LST = T_L^j - t^{ij} = 15 - 15 = 0$$
$$LFT = T_L^j = 15$$

Consider activity 2-4

(*i*) $EST = T_E^i = T_E^2 = 15$

(*ii*) $EFT = T_E^i + t^{ij} = 15 + 9 = 24$

(*iii*) $LST = T_L^j - t^{ij} = T_L^4 - t^{2-4} = 31 - 9 = 24$

(*iv*) $LFT = T_L^j = T_L^4 = 31$

The above four activity times usually are written on activity arrow along with activity name and time (t^{ij}) as shown in Fig. 8.9. A, B, etc. EST and EFT are written on the top of the arrow and the activity duration t^{ij}, LST, LFT are written below the arrow.

Fig. 8.9

8.12. FLOAT

It is associated with activity times. It is analogous to slack, which is associated with event times. As the CPM is activity oriented float is used in CPM instead of slack. Slack denotes the flexibility range with in which an event can occur *i.e.* the slack is the difference between the earliest event time and latest event occurrence time. Similarly float denotes the range with in which an activity start time or its finish time may fluctuate with out affecting the total duration of the project.

8.13. CLASSIFICATION OF FLOATS

Floats may be classified into the following four categories:

1. Total float
2. Free float
3. Independent float
4. Interfering float

1. Total float. The time span by which the starting or finishing time of an activity can be delayed with out affecting the overall duration of the project is *known as total float*. Some times it is observed that in certain activities there is a difference between the maximum available time for their completion and the actual time required to complete them. This difference is called as total float.

Consider an activity $i-j$. The time duration available for this activity is equal to the difference between its earliest start time T_E^i and latest finish time of head event T_L^j.

Hence maximum available time $= T_L^j - T_E^i$

Activity time required $= t^{ij}$

$\therefore$ Total float $(F_T) =$ Time available – time required

or Total float $F_T = (T_L^j - T_E^i) - t^{ij}$ ...(8.7)

$= T_L^j - (T_E^i + t^{ij})$ ...(8.7 *a*)

or $= T_L^j - t^{ij} - T_E^i$ ...(8.7 *b*)

but $T_L^j - t^{ij} = LST$

and $T_E^i = EST$

$\therefore$ $F_T = LST - EST$ ...(8.8)

Similarly $F_T = LFT - EFT$ ...(8.9)

Equation 8.7 can be used directly to determine the total float of an activity *ij*. For example, for activity 2-4 of Fig. 8.8, the total float

$$F_T = LST - EST = 22 - 15 = 7, \quad (LST = (T_L^4 - t^{2-4})$$

It means that even if the starting of this activity is delayed by 7 days the project completion time will not be affected. Thus total float for each activity is a measure of its particular relationship to all other activities in the project.

2. Free float. It is the duration by which an activity can be delayed with out delaying any succeeding activity or with out affecting the total float of the succeeding activity. Free float is a part of the total float. The concept of free float is based on the possibility that all the events occur at their earliest times.

Consider two activities $i - j$ and its successor activity $j-k$. The earliest start time for activity $i-j = T_E^i$ and for $j-k = T_E^j$. Let the duration for activity $i-j$ be t^{ij}. The activity $i-j$ will be completed by $(T_E^i + t^{ij})$ time and activity $j-k$ can not start because its EST is greater than $(T_E^i + t^{ij})$. The difference between these two is the free float of activity $i-j$.

$\therefore$ Free float for $i-j = T_E^j - (T_E^i + t^{ij})$ ...(8.10)

But $(T_E^i + t^{ij})$ is the early finish time (EFT) of the activity $i-j$. Where as T_E^j is the early start time for activity $j-k$.

$\therefore$ Free float F_F for ij = EST for successor event. – EFT of present activity

or F_F for $ij = T_E^j - EFT$ ...(8.11)

Hence free float for an activity *ij* is the difference between its earliest finish time and the earliest start time of its successor activity. It can be determined by taking the defference between the head event time (T_E^j) and early finish time of the activity *ij*.

From equation 8.10, F_F for $ij = T_E^j - T_E^i - t^{ij}$ ...(8.12)

In equation 8.11 T_E^j is the earliest start time (EST) for successor activity and T_E^i is the EST for the present activity *ij* and t^{ij} is the activity duration.

Thus free float is the excess time available over the required time when the activity in question and its successor activity start as early as possible.

Again from Total float we know that

$$F_F = T_E^j - (T_E^i + t^{ij}) \quad \text{...(8.13)}$$

or

$$F_F = (T_E^j - T_E^i) - t^{ij} \quad \text{...(8.14)}$$

$\therefore$

$$T_E^i + t^{ij} = T_E^j - EFT \quad \text{...(8.14 a)}$$

Substituting this value in equation (8.12)

$$F_F = T_F^j - (T_L^j - F_T)$$

$$= F_T - (T_L^j - T_E^j) = F_T = S_j) \quad \text{[where } S_j \text{ is the slack]...(8.15)}$$

Equation 8.15 suggests an other method of determining the free float.

From equation 8.15, *the fre float is equal to the difference of the total float and slack of head event.*

Thus free float can be determined from equation 8.13, 8.14 and 8.15 respectively.

3. Independent float. The excess of minimum available time over the required duration of the activity is known as independent float

$$\therefore \quad F_{1D} = \text{Minimum available time} - \text{activity time.}$$

or

$$F_{1D} = (T_E^j - T_L^i) - t^{ij} \quad \text{...(8.16)}$$

The independent float is a part of the free float.The independent float is *equal to free float minus tail event slack.*

4. Interfering float. *The difference between the total float and the free float is known as interfering float. It is denoted by F_{1T}.*

Thus

$$F_{1T} = T_L^j - T_E^j = S_j \quad \text{...(8.17)}$$

where S_j is the slack of head event *j*. Thus interfering float is equal to the head event slack.

8.14. SUMMERY OF FLOAT

Floats are as follows:

1. **Total float (F_T).** The total float of an activity is the excess of minimum available time over the activity time.

   i.e. $F_T = (T_L^j - T_E^i) - t^{ij}$ or $(LFT - EFT)$ *or* $(LST - EST)$ ...(8.7)

2. **Free float.** The free float of an activity is the excess of available time over the activity time, when all activities start as early as possible.

   Thus $F_F = (T_E^j - T_E^i) - t^{ij}$ ...(8.10)

   That is free float is equal to (Total float – slack of head event).

3. **Independent float.** Independent float of an activity is the excess of minimum available time over the activity time. Thus

   $$F_{1D} = (T_E^j - T_L^i) - t^{ij} \quad \text{...(8.16)}$$

   i.e. Independent float = Free Float – Tail Event Slack

4. **Interfering float of an activity.** It is the difference between the total float and free float. Thus *it is equal to the slack of the had event.*

$$\therefore \qquad F_{1T} = F_T - F_F = S_j \qquad \text{...(8.17)}$$

8.15. USE OF FLOATS

The knowledge of total float is usefull for the following purposes:

1. The start or finish of non critical activities can be delayed upto the time limit of total float. The delay may either be due to non availability of construction resources such as construction materials, labour, equipment, money or bad weather etc. The delay up to the limit of total float will not affect the completion schedule of the project.
2. The resources of non critical activities of the project during the period of total float may be diverted to critical activities. This diversion of resources during the total float period will not affect the completion schedule of the project.
3. In case of paucity of resources, the non critical activities may be started late upto the time limit of total float period.

8.16. PROCEDURE OF CALCULATING FLOATS

1. First draw the net work and calculate earliest expected time T_E and latest allowable occurrence time T_L and write these times adjacent to the node as shown in Fig. 8.8.
2. Prepare the table as shown in Table 8.5.
   This table contains 10 columns.
   Column (1) contains the activities as 1-2, 1-3, 2-5 etc.
   Column (2) contains activity duration
   Column 3 contains earliest start time (EST) of the activity
   Column 4 contains earliest finish time EFT of the activity
   Column 5 contains latest start time LST of the activity
   Column 6 contains latest finish time LFT of the activity
   Column 7 is for total float which is equal to LST-EST or LFT-EFT. From both equations it should be equal. It is a column (6-4) or column (5-3). Column 8 is for free float which is equal to earliest start time EST of succeeding activity minus EFT of activity under consideration or total float minus head event slack. For example free float for actually 1-3 is, the EST of activity (3-4) or (3-6) minus EFT of activity (1-3) *i.e.* Free float is equal to total float minus head event slack.
   Column 9 is for independent float which is equal to free float minus tail event slack.
   Column 10 is for interfering float which is equal to total float minus free float.

8.17. DETERMINATION OF FLOATS

The method of determination of floats is illustrated with the help of the following example.

Example 8.7. *Determine the activity times and floats of all activities of the net work shown in Fig. 8.10.*

Solution. The calculations are shown in table 8.5. The values of T_E, T_L and critical activities are shown on Fig. 8.10 itself.

Table 8.5.

Activity (i – j)	*Activity duration* t^{ij}	*Earliest*		*Latest*		*Total float* F_T *Cl. (6-7)*	*Free float* F_F	*Independent float* F_{1D}	*Interefering float* F_{1T}
		Start time EST	*Finish time (EFT)*	*Start time LST*	*Finish time (LFT)*				
(1)	(2)	(3)	(4)	(5)	(6)	(7)	(8)	(9)	(10)
1 – 2	11	0	11	8	19	8	0	0	8
1 – 3	13	0	13	0	13	0	0	0	0

Activity (i – j)	*Activity duration* t^{ij}	*Earliest*		*Latest*		*Total float* F_T Cl. (6-7)	*Free float* F_F	*Independent float* F_{1D}	*Interefering float* F_{1T}
		Start time EST	*Finish time (EFT)*	*Start time LST*	*Finish time (LFT)*				
(1)	(2)	(3)	(4)	(5)	(6)	(7)	(8)	(9)	(10)
2 – 5	8	11	19	21	29	10	29 – 19 = 10	10 – 8 = 2	8
2 – 7	13	11	24	31	44	20	44 – 24 = 20	20 – 8 = 12	8
3 – 4	7	13	20	13	20	0	20 – 20 = 0	0	0
3 – 6	6	13	19	31	37	18	29 – 29 = 0	10	8
4 – 5	9	20	29	20	29	0	29 – 29 =0	0	0
5 – 6	8	29	37	29	37	0	37 – 37 = 0	0	0
5 – 7	11	29	40	33	44	4	44 – 40 = 4	4	7
6 – 7	7	37	44	37	44	0	59 – 44 = 0	15	– 15
7 – 8	15	44	59	44	59	0	59 – 59 = 0	0	0

Note: Free float = EST of successor event minus EFT of the activity under consideration.

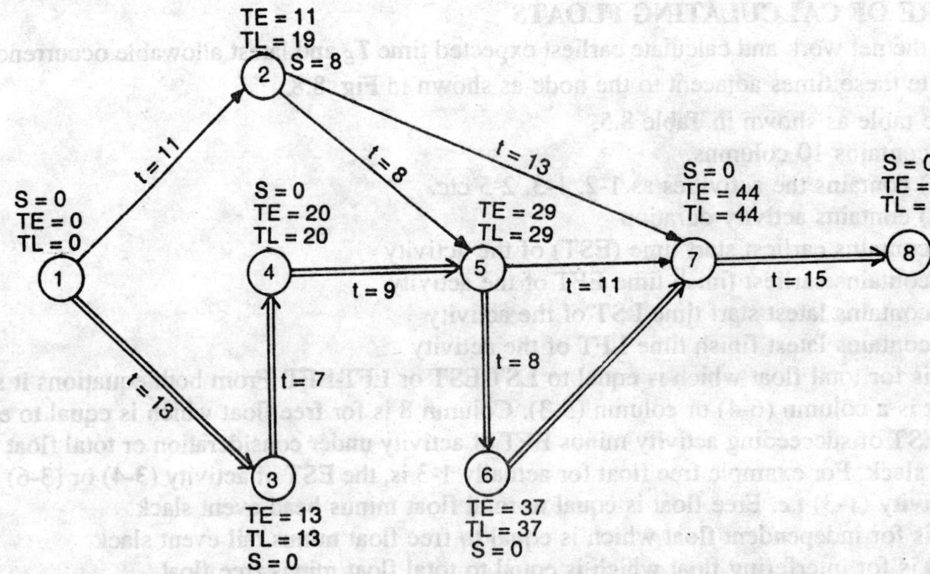

Fig. 8.10.

Independent float = Free float minus – tail event slack

Interfering float = Free float – slack of tail event

Thus the critical activities are those whose total float is zero

Hence in this case critical activities are 1-3, 3-4, 4-5, 5-6, 6-7, 7-8.

8.18. CRITICAL ACTIVITIES

Out of various floats discussed in artical 9.11, total float is the most useful. By definition total float is the difference between maximum available time and the duration of the activity. There may be three values of the total float as follows:

1. **If the time availability is less than the duration of the activity, then the value of total float may be –ve.**
2. **If the time availability is equal to the activity duration, then total float is zero.**

3. If the time availability is more than activity duration, then total float is positive.

The nature of total float is very useful with regard the criticality of the activity. On the basis of degree or nature of float, the activities can be classified as follows:

1. **Super critical activity.** When the value of total float is negative, then activity is called super critical. Such activities need special attention and action.
2. **Critical activity.** When the value of the total float is zero, then the activity is known as critical activity. Such activities need more than normal attention with freedom of action.
3. **Sub critical activity.** When the value of total float is positive then the activity is known as sub-critical activity, such activities need normal attention and allow some freedom of action.

8.19. CRITICAL PATH

The critical path of a net work is the longest path in the net work and the duration of this path gives the duration or completion time of the project. Critical path joins all those activities which are critical. In case of PERT technique the critical path joins the events having zero or minimum slacks while in CPM technique the critical path joins all critical activities which have total float equal to zero. The activities which have total float as zero, control the project duration and form continuous chain starting from first node and ending at the last node.

From the above discussion, following points can be concluded.

1. Critical path starts from the initial event and ends at the last event of the net work. All events and activities lying along the critical path are critical for the completion of the project.
2. In PERT technique, the critical path passes through all those events whose slack is zero. Although it is an necessary condition, but it is not sufficient. In this case though events may be critical, but the activity joining them may not be critical. Thus for determining the critical path total float concept is more use full, as it provides both the necessary and sufficient condition for the activity to be critical. This explains the basic difference in approach for determining the critical path through PERT and CPM techniques. Thus the concept of determining the critical path by CPM technique (Total float = zero) is more rational.
3. There can be more than one critical path in a network. Depending upon the total float value, degree of criticality can be assigned to a particular path.
4. Critical activities have no flexibilities in their start time or finish time. The procedure is illustrated by examples.

Example 8.8. *A building project consists of 9 activities. The duration of completion of various activities of the building project are shown in following table 8.6. compute*

(a) Event times

(b) Activity times

(c) Floats

(d) Also determine the critical path.

Table 8.6. Activity durations

Activity	A	B	C	D	E	F	G	H	I
Duration	3	6	4	7	10	6	4	5	8

Solution. First draw the net work with the activity times Fig. 8.11.

(*a*) Computation of event times

The earliest event time T_E and latest occurrence times T_L are computed in the tabular form in table 8.7 below:

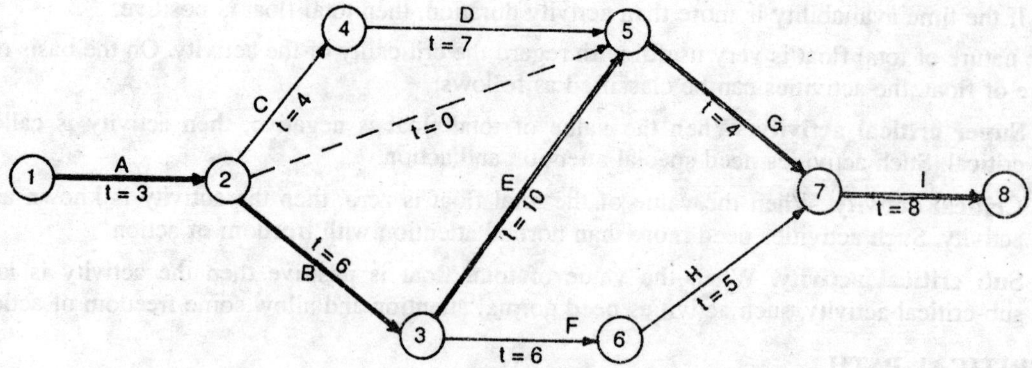

Fig. 8.11.

Table 8.7.

Event number	*Earliest event time T_E*					*Latest event time*				*Slack*
	Predecessor event	*Activity i-j*	*Activity time t^{ij}*	T_E^i	T_E	*Successor event*	t^{ij}	T_L^i	T_L	
1	–	–	–	0	0	2	3	0	0	0
2	1	1 – 2	3	3	3	3	6	3	3	0
						4	4	8		
						5	0	19		
3	2	2 – 3	6	9	9	5	10	9	9	0
						6	6			
4	2	2 – 4	4	7	7	5	7	12	12	5
5	2	2 – 5	0	3	19	7	4	19	19	0
	3	3 – 5	10	19						
	4	4 – 5	7	14						
6	3	3 – 6	6	15	15	7	5	18	18	3
7	5	5 – 7	4	23	23	8	8	23	23	0
	6	6 – 7	5	20						
8	7	7 – 8	8	31	31	–	–	31	31	0

(*b*) computation of activity times and floats

The earliest start time (EST), earliest finish time EFT, latest start time LST and latest finish time of each activity and floats are tabulated in Table 8.8 below:

The EST of each activity is equal to T_E^i, while EFT is equal to $T_E^i + t^{ij}$.

LFT is equal to T_L^j while LST = $T_L^j - t^{ij}$.

Table 8.8.

Activity (i – j)	*Duration of activity t^{ij}*	*Earliest*		*Latest*		*Total float F_T (LST-EST) Col (5-3)*	*Free float F_F*	*Independen-t float F_{ID}*	*Interfaring float F_{IT}*
		Start time EST = T_E^i	*Finish time EFT*	*Start time (LST)*	*Finish time LFT)*				
(1)	(2)	(3)	(4)	(5)	(6)	(7)	(8)	(9)	(10)
1 – 2	3	0	3	0	3	0	0	0	0
1 – 3	6	3	9	3	9	0	0	0	0

Activity (i – j)	*Duration of activity* t^{ij}	*Earliest*		*Latest*		*Total float* F_T *(LST-EST) Col (5-3)*	*Free float* F_F	*Independen-t float* F_{1D}	*Interfaring float* F_{1T}
		Start time $EST = T_E^i$	*Finish time EFT*	*Start time (LST)*	*Finish time LFT)*				
(1)	(2)	(3)	(4)	(5)	(6)	(7)	(8)	(9)	(10)
2 – 4	4	3	7	8	12	5	0	0	5
2 – 5	0	3	3	19	19	16	16	16–5 =11	0
3 – 5	10	9	19	9	19	0	0	0	0
3 – 6	6	9	15	12	19	3	0	0	3
4 – 5	7	7	14	12	19	5	5	0	0
5 – 7	4	19	23	19	23	0	0	0	0
6 – 7	5	15	23	18	23	3	0	0	0
7 – 8	8	31	31	23	31	0	0	0	0

Total float = (LST – EST)
Free float = EST of successor activity – EFT of activity under consideration.
Independent float = Free float – slack of tail event.
Interfering float = Total float – free float.
Critical path is along 1-2-3-5-7-8.

Example 8.9. *Determine the float of all activities and the critical path of the net work shown in Fig. 8.12.*

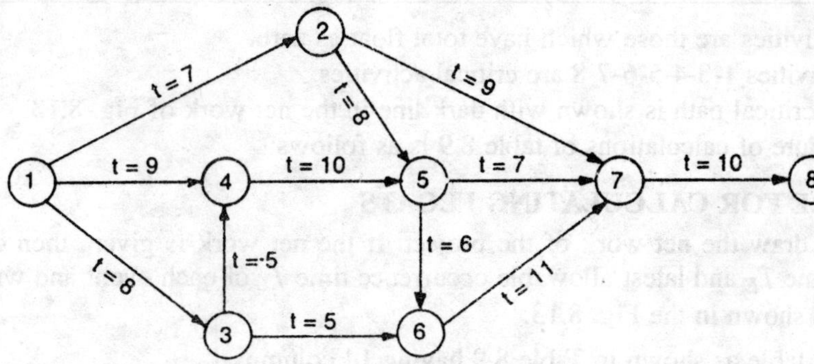

Fig. 8.12.

Solution. First the values of T_E and T_L are determined and marked on the net work as shown in Fig. 8.13. Other calculations are shown in table 8.9.

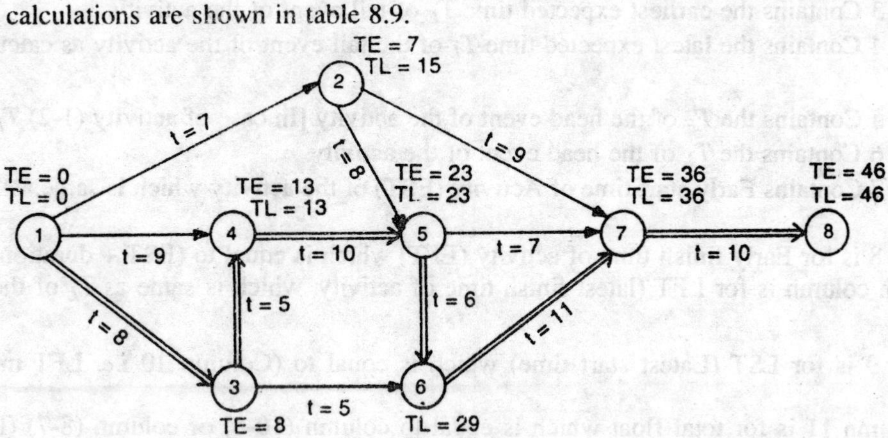

Fig. 8.13.

Table 8.9.

Activity i-j	Duration t^{ij}	Tail event		Head event		Activity times				Floats			
		T_E^i	T_L^i	T_E^j	T_L^j	EST T_E^i	EFT $T_E^i + t_{ij}$	LST Col. (10-2)	LFT T_L^j	Total float	Free float	F_{ID} indepe-ndent	T_{IT} Interer-ing
(1)	(2)	(3)	(4)	(5)	(6)	(7)	(8)	(9)	(10)	(11)	(12)	(13)	(14)
1 – 2	7	0	0	7	15	0	7	8	15	8	0	0	8
1 – 3	8	0	0	8	8	0	8	0	8	0	0	0	0
1 – 4	9	0	0	13	13	0	9	4	13	4	4	4	0
2 – 5	8	7	15	23	23	7	15	15	23	8	8	0	0
2 – 7	9	7	15	36	36	7	16	27	36	20	20	12	0
3 – 4	5	8	8	13	13	8	13	8	13	0	0	0	0
3 – 6	5	8	8	29	29	8	13	24	29	16	16	16	0
4 – 5	10	13	13	23	23	13	23	13	23	0	0	0	0
5 – 6	6	23	23	29	29	23	29	23	29	0	0	0	0
5 – 7	7	23	23	36	36	23	30	29	36	6	6	6	0
6 – 7	7	29	29	36	36	29	36	29	36	0	0	0	0
7 – 8	10	36	36	46	46	36	46	36	46	0	0	0	0

∴ Critical activities are those which have total float as zero.

Hence Activities 1-3-4-5-6-7-8 are critical activities.

Hence the critical path is shown with dark line in the net work of Fig. 8.13.

The procedure of calculations of table 8.9 is as follows:

8.20. PROCEDURE FOR CALCULATING FLOATS

1. First of all draw the net work of the project. If the net work is given, then calculate the earliest expected time T_E and latest allowable occurrence time T_L of each event and write them adjacent to the node as shown in the Fig. 8.13.

2. Prepare the table as shown in Table 8.9 having 14 columns.

   Column 1 Contains the activities as 1-2, 2-3 etc.

   Column 2 Contains the duration of activities.

   Column 3 Contains the earliest expected time T_E^i of tail event of the activity.

   Column 4 Contains the latest expected time T_L of the tail event of the activity as calculated on net work.

   Column 5 Contains the T_E^j of the head event of the activity [In case of activity (1-2) T_E of 2 is put]

   Column 6 Contains the T_L of the head event of the activity.

   Column 7 Contains Early start time of Activity (EST) of the activity which is same as T_E of the tail event.

   Column 8 is for Early finish time of activity (EFT) which is equal to (EST + duration of activity).

   The 10th column is for LFT (latest finish time of activity, which is same as T_L of the head event (T_L^j)

   Column 9 is for LST (Latest start time) which is equal to (Column 10 *i.e.* LFT minus activity duration.

   The column 11 is for total float which is equal to column (10-8) or column (8-7) (LFT-EFT) or (LST-EST)

The column 12 is for free float, which is equal to Total float minus head event slack.
The column 13 is for independent float which is equal to free float minus tail event slack.
Column 14 is for interfering float, which is equal to total float minus free float.

Example 8.10. *The construction of a culvert consists of 15 activities. The activities and their expected times are shown in Table 8.10. From the data of the table 8.10, determine the activities time EST, EFT, LST and LFT.*

(*b*) *Compute the total float and draw the critical path on the net work.*

Table 8.10. Expected time of activities

S. No.	*Activity i-j*	*Description of activities*	*Duration* t^{ij}
1.	1 – 2	Base slab	4
2.	2 – 3	North apron	5
3.	2 – 4	North side wall	6
4.	2 – 5	South apron	6
5.	3 – 6	Dummy	0
6.	3 – 10	North approaches	16
7.	4 – 6	Dummy	0
8.	4 – 8	South side wall	8
9.	5 – 8	Dummy	0
10.	5 – 10	South approaches	10
11.	6 – 7	North wing wall	7
12.	7 – 8	Dummy	0
13.	7 – 9	North roof	15
14.	8 – 9	South wing wall	8
15.	9 – 10	South roof	15

Solution. The calculations of time estimates are shown in 8-11 on the pattern of table 8.9.

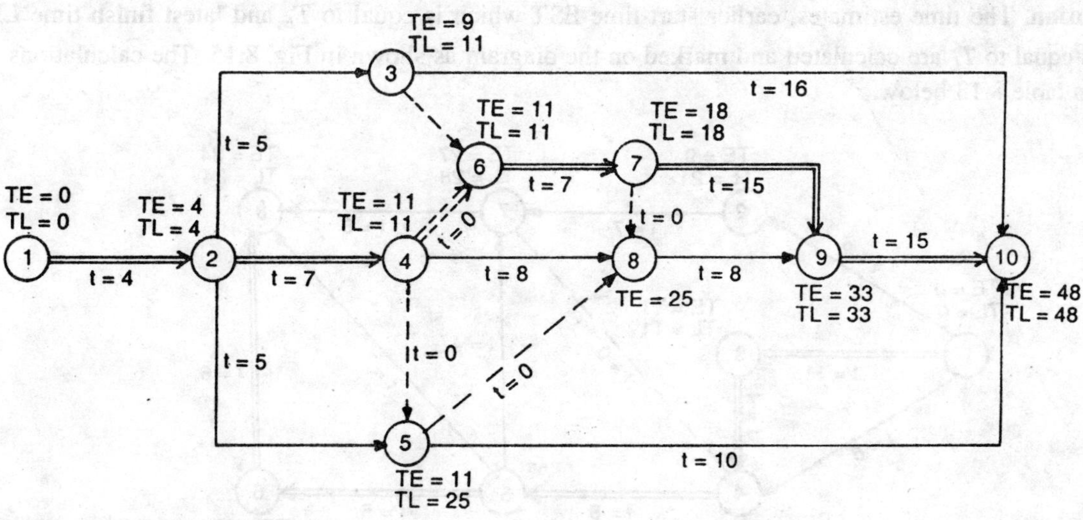

Fig. 8.14

Table 8.11.

Activity i-j	*Duration* t^{ij}	*Tail event* T_E^i	*Tail event* T_L^j *Col (2+3)*	*Head event* T_E^j	*Head event* T_L^j	*Activity times EST*	*EFT*	*LST*	*LFT*	*Total Float*
(1)	(2)	(3)	(4)	(5)	(6)	(7)	(8)	(9)	(10)	(11)
1 – 2	4	0	4	0	4	0	4	0	4	0
2 – 3	5	4	9	6	11	4	9	6	11	2
2 – 4	7	4	11	7	11	4	11	4	11	0
2 – 5	5	4	9	20	25	4	9	20	25	16
3 – 6	0	9	9	11	11	9	9	11	11	2
3 – 10	16	9	25	32	48	9	25	32	48	23
4 – 6	0	11	11	11	11	11	11	11	11	0
4 – 8	8	11	19	17	25	11	19	17	25	6
5 – 8	0	9	9	0	25	9	9	25	25	16
5 – 10	10	9	19	38	48	9	19	38	48	29
6 – 7	7	11	18	11	18	11	18	11	18	0
7 – 8	0	18	18	25	25	18	18	25	25	7
7 – 9	15	18	33	18	33	18	33	18	33	0
8 – 9	8	19	27	25	33	19	23	25	33	10
9 – 10	15	33	48	33	48	33	48	33	48	0

Critical path will be 1-2-4-6-7-9-10. The diagram is shown in Fig. 8.14.

Example 8.11. *The activities and their expected time of a project are shown in Table 8.12. From the table draw the net work and determine the activity times and floats. Also determine the critical path and its duration.*

Table 8.12.

Activity	1 – 2	1 – 3	1 – 4	2 – 7	3 – 4	4 – 5	4 – 7	5 – 6	5 – 7	5 – 8	6 – 8	7 – 8
Duration in days	9	11	6	7	4	8	0	5	4	7	6	6

Solution. The time estimates, earlier start time EST which is equal to T_E^i and latest finish time LFT, which is equal to T_L^j are calculated and marked on the diagram as shown in Fig. 8.15. The calculations are shown in table 8.13 below.

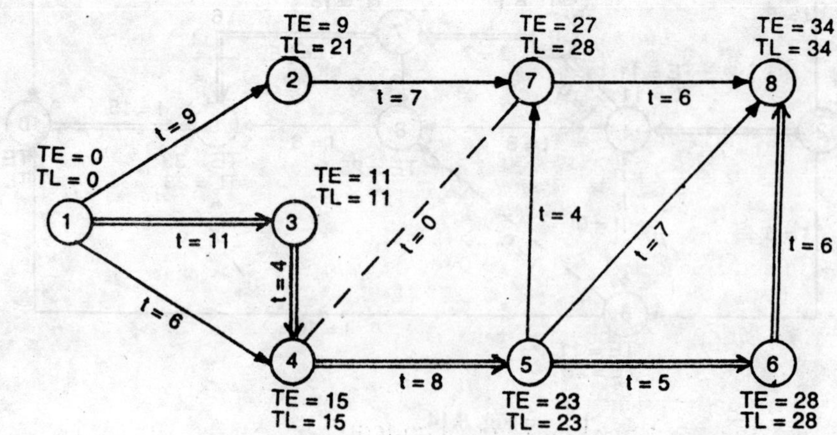

Fig. 8.15

Table 8.13.

Activity i-j	*Activity Duration t^{ij}*	*Tail event*		*Head event*		*Activity times*				*Floats*			
		T_E^i	T_L^i	T_E^j	T_L^j	*EST*	*EFT*	*LST*	*LFT*	*Total*	*Free*	*Independent*	*Interfering*
(1)	(2)	(3)	(4)	(5)	(6)	(7)	(8)	(9)	(10)	(11)	(12)	(13)	(14)
1 – 2	9	0	0	9	21	0	9	12	21	12	0	0	12
1 – 3	11	0	0	11	11	0	11	0	11	0	0	0	0
1 – 4	6	0	0	15	15	0	6	9	15	9	9	9	0
2 – 7	7	9	18	27	28	9	16	21	28	12	11	– 1	1
3 – 4	4	11	11	15	15	11	15	11	15	0	0	0	0
4 – 5	8	15	15	23	23	15	23	15	23	0	0	0	0
4 – 7	0	15	15	27	28	15	15	28	28	13	12	12	1
5 – 6	5	23	23	28	28	23	28	23	28	0	0	0	0
5 – 7	4	23	23	27	28	23	27	24	28	1	0	1	1
5 – 8	7	23	23	34	34	23	30	27	34	4	4	4	0
6 – 8	6	28	28	34	34	28	34	28	34	0	0	0	0
7 – 8	6	27	28	34	34	27	33	28	34	1	1	0	0

The critical path is along the critical activities 1-3-4-5-6-8 shown by thick lime on the net work.

Total duration of the critical path = 34 days **Ans.**

Example 12. *The three time estimates optimistic, most likely, and pessimistic times of each activity of a project are given below:*

Activity	*Optimestic time t_o*	*Most likely time t_L*	*Pessemestic time t_p*
1 – 2	2	5	14
1 – 3	3	12	21
2 – 4	5	14	17
3 – 4	2	5	8
3 – 5	6	15	30
4 – 5	1	4	7

(*i*) *Draw the net work.*

(*ii*) *Find the expected time and variance of each activity.*

(*iii*) *Calculate the early and late occurrence times for each event.*

(*iv*) *Determine the expected duration of the project.*

(*v*) *Calculate the total float for each activity.*

(*vi*) *Find the variance and standard deviation of the entire project.*

[UPSC Civil Services, 1982]

Solution.

(*i*) The net work is drawn as shown in Fig. 8.16 below.

(*ii*) Expected time and variance is calculated in tabular form in table 8.14.

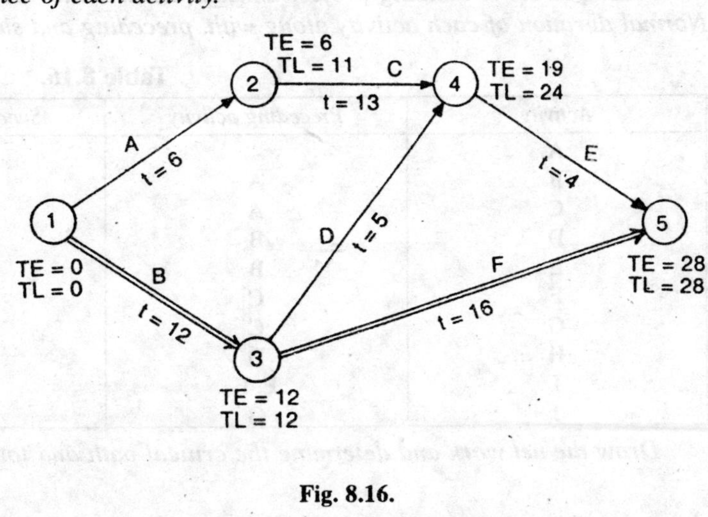

Fig. 8.16.

Table 8.14.

Activity	Optimistic time t_o	Most likely time t_L	Pessimistic time t_p	Expected time $t_E = \frac{t_o + 4t_l + t_p}{6}$	Standard deviation $\left(\frac{t_p - t_o}{6}\right)$	Variance $\sigma^2 = \left(\frac{t_p - t_o}{6}\right)^2$	Remark
1 – 2	2	5	14	6	2	4	
1 – 3	3	12	21	12	3	9	
2 – 4	5	14	17	13	2	4	
3 – 4	2	5	8	5	1	1	
3 – 5	6	15	30	16	4	16	
4 – 5	1	4	7	4	1	1	

(*iii*) The activities time earliest start time EST, Earliest finish time EFT, Latest start time LST and latest finish times LFT and total float are shown in table 8.15.

(*iv*) Expected duration of the project is 28 days.

(*v*) Total float is calculated in the tabular form as follows:

Table 8.15.

Activity	Duration	Earliest start time EST (T_E^i)	Earliest finish time EFT ($T_E^i + t^{ij}$)	Latest start LST ($T_L^i - t_{ij}$)	Latest finish time (LFT) j T_L	Total float
1 – 2	6	0	6	5	11	5
1 – 3	12	0	12	0	12	0
2 – 4	13	6	19	11	24	5
3 – 4	5	12	17	19	24	7
3 – 5	16	12	28	12	28	0
4 – 5	4	19	23	24	28	5

Critical path is along = 1-3-5.

Duration of project = 28 days.

Variance of project along critical path 1-3-5 = 9 + 16 = 25

Standard deviation along critical path = $\sqrt{25}$ = 5.0

Total variance of project = 35.

Example 13. *A building project consists 10 activities A, B, C etc. as listed in the table 8.16 below. Normal duration of each activity along with. preceding and succeeding activities are also given.*

Table 8.16.

Activity	Preceding activity	Succeding activity	Exstimated duration
A	–	B, C	5
B	A	D, E	2
C	A	F, G	6
D	B	H	4
E	B	I	4
F	C	I	2
G	C	J	3
H	D	–	8
I	E, F	–	7
J	G	–	7

Draw the net work and determine the critical path and total projection duration.

[UPSC, Engg. Services, 1991]

Solution. The net work of the project is drawn as shown in Fig. 8.17.

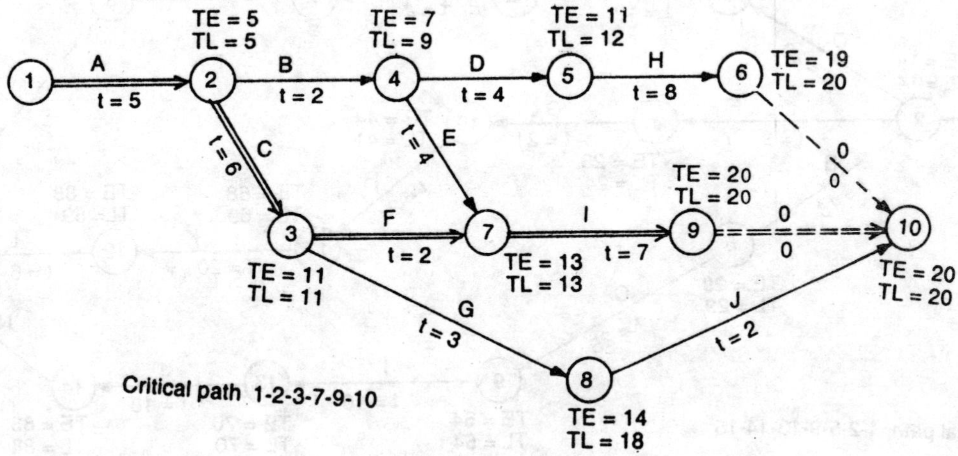

Fig. 8.17.

The earliest occurrence time T_E and latest occurrence time T_L are determined and marked on the diagram.

For determining the critical path total float may be determined as follows.

Table 8.17.

Activity	*Activity duration*	*Earliest start time (T_E^i) EST*	*Earliest finish time EFT*	*Latest Start time LST*	*Latest finish time LFT*	*Float (LFT – EFT)*	*Remark*
(1)	(2)	(3)	(4)	(5)	(6)	(7)	(8)
A (1 – 2)	5	0	5	0	5	0	critical
B (2 – 4)	2	5	7	7	9	2	
C (2 – 3)	6	5	11	5	11	0	critical
D (4 – 5)	4	7	11	8	12	1	
E (4 – 7)	4	7	11	9	13	2	
F (3 – 7)	2	11	13	11	13	0	critical
G (3 – 8)	3	11	14	15	18	4	
H (5 – 6)	8	11	19	12	20	1	
I (7 – 9)	7	13	20	13	20	0	critical
J (8 – 10)	2	14	16	18	20	4	

The critical path is along 1-2-3-7-9-10

Duration of the project = 20 days. **Ans.**

Example 14. *The details of activities of a construction job are given below. Determine job completion time, critical activities and total float for each activity.*

Activity	A	B	C	D	E	F	G	H	I	J	K	L	M	N	P
Predeceser	–	A	B	A	D	A	F	–	–	B, I	H	K	E	J, C	M, G
Duration (days)	14	15	25	20	12	9	21	24	16	18	20	6	8	7	10

[UPSC, Civil Services, 1984]

Solution. The net work of the project is shown in Fig. 8.18 and calculations in table 8.18.

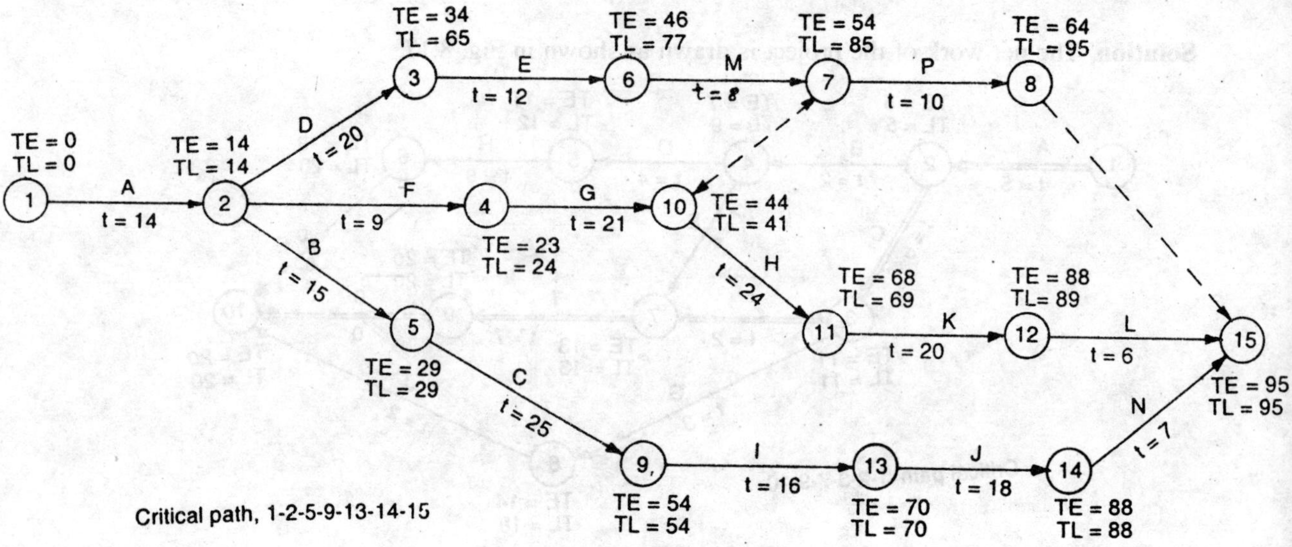

Fig. 8.18.

Table 8.18.

Activity	*Activity duration*	*Earliest start time EST* (T_E^i)	*EArliest finish time EFT*	*Latest start time LST*	*Latest finish time LFT* (T_L^i)	*Float*	*Remarks*
(1 – 2) A	14	0	14	0	14	0	critical
(2 – 3) D	20	14	34	45	65	31	
(2 – 4) F	9	14	23	11	24	1	
(2 – 5) B	15	14	29	14	29	0	critical
(3 – 6) E	12	34	46	65	77	31	
(5 – 9) C	25	29	44	29	54	10	
(6 – 7) M	8	46	54	77	85	31	
(7 – 8) P	10	54	64	85	95	31	
(4 – 10) G	21	23	44	20	45	1	
(10 – 11) H	24	44	68	45	69	1	
(11 – 12) K	20	68	88	69	89	1	
(12 – 15) L	6	88	94	89	95	1	
(9 – 13) I	16	54	70	54	70	0	critical
(13 – 14) J	18	70	88	70	88	0	critical
(14 – 15) N	7	88	95	88	95	0	critical

Critical path is along 1-2-5-9-13-14-15.

Critical activities are A, B, C, I, J and N.

Total duration of the project = 95 days

Floats are shown in the table 8.18 **Ans.**

Example 15. *The net work of a civil construction project is shown in Fig. 8.19.*

(*a*) *Calculate all activity times as EST, EFT, LST and LFT.*

(*b*) *All float of each activity in a tabular form.*

(*c*) *Determine the critical path and duration of the project.*

Solution. The net work of the project is shown in Fig. 8.19.

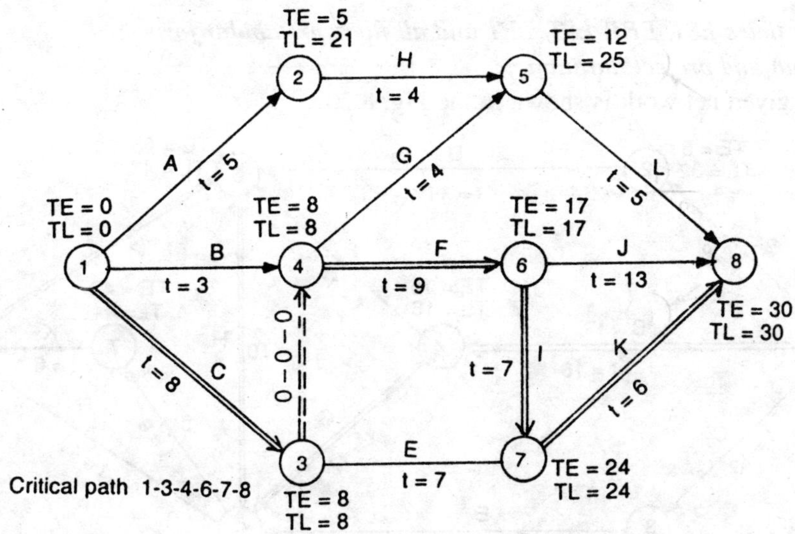

Fig. 8.19.

1. The earliest occurrence time T_E and latest occurrence time T_L of each activity is calculated and put near the node of each activity as shown on the net work. Fig. 8.19
2. The activities time EST, EFT, LST, LFT and floats are calculated as shown in table 8.19 below.

Total float	= (LFT – EFT) or (LST – EST)
Free float	= Total float – Head event slack
Independent float	= Free float – Tail end event slack
Interfering float	= Total float – Free float.

Table 8.19.

Activity	*Activity duration*	*Earliest start time EST (T_E^i)*	*Earliest finish time EFT*	*Latest start time LST*	*Latest finish time LFT*	*Total float*	*Free float*	*Indepent float*	*Intering float*	*Remarks*
(1 – 2) A	5	0	5	16	21	16	0	0	16	
(1 – 3) C	8	0	8	0	8	0	0	0	0	critical
(1 – 4) B	3	0	3	5	8	5	5	5	0	
(2 – 5) H	4	5	9	21	25	16	3	– 13	13	
(3 – 7) E	7	8	15	17	24	9	9	9	0	
(4 – 6) F	9	8	17	8	17	0	0	0	0	critical
(4 – 5) G	4	8	12	21	25	13	0	– 13	13	
(5 – 8) L	5	12	17	25	30	13	13	13	0	
(6 – 7) I	7	17	24	17	24	0	0	0	0	critical
(6 – 8) J	13	17	30	17	30	0	0	0	0	critical
(7 – 8) K	6	24	30	24	30	0	0	0	0	critical

The critical path is along 1-3-4-6-7-8 and 1-3-4-6-8 – both.

Duration of project = 30 days.

Example 16. *For the given CPM net work determine,*

(a) All activity times EST, EFT, LST, LFT and all floats in tabular form.
(b) Critical path and project duration.

Solution. The given net work is shown in the Fig. 8.20.

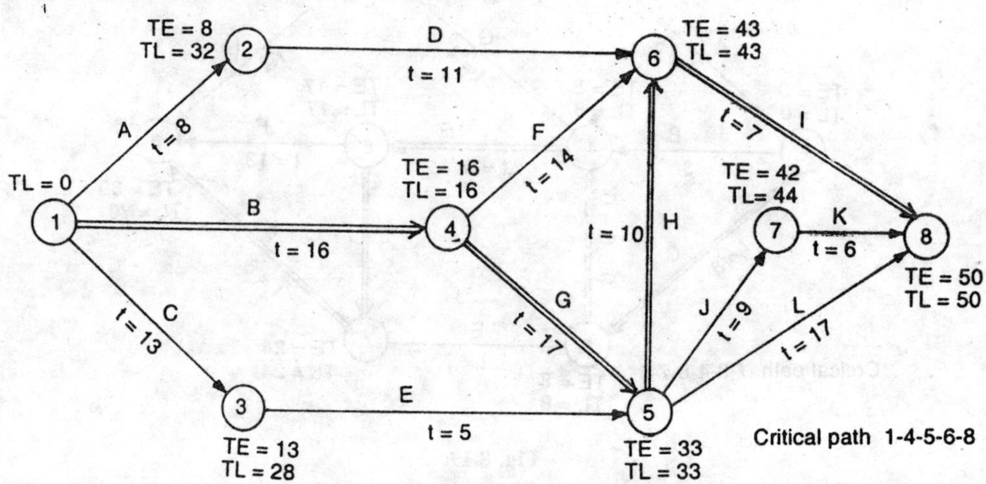

Fig. 8.20.

The earliest occurrence time T_E and latest occurrence time T_L are calculated and shown on the net work. Slacks are also calculated. The activity times EST, EFT, LST, LST and floats are shown in Table 8.20.

Table 8.20.

Activity	*Activity duration*	*Earliest start time EST* (T_E^i)	*Earliest finish time EFT*	*Latest start time LST*	*Latest finish time LFT* (T_L^j)	*Total float*	*Free float*	*Indepent float*	*Intering float*	*Remarks*
1 – 2	8	0	8	24	32	24	0	0	24	
1 – 3	13	0	13	15	28	15	0	0	15	
1 – 4	16	0	16	0	16	0	0	0	0	critical
2 – 6	11	8	19	32	43	24	24	0	0	
3 – 5	5	13	18	28	33	15	15	0	0	
4 – 5	17	16	33	16	33	0	0	0	0	critical
4 – 6	14	16	30	29	43	13	13	13	0	
5 – 6	10	33	43	33	43	0	0	0	0	critical
5 – 7	9	33	42	34	44	2	0	0	2	
5 – 8	17	33	50	33	50	0	0	0	0	critical
6 – 8	7	43	50	43	50	0	0	0	0	critical
7 – 8	6	42	48	44	50	2	2	0	0	

Critical path 1-4-5-6-8 and 0-1-4-5-8.

Total duration of project = 50 days.

Example 17. *For the given PERT net work of the Fig. 8.21.*

(i) Determine the expected mean time, variance and standard deviation of the project.
(ii) What time you are sure (90%) that the project will be finished in time.

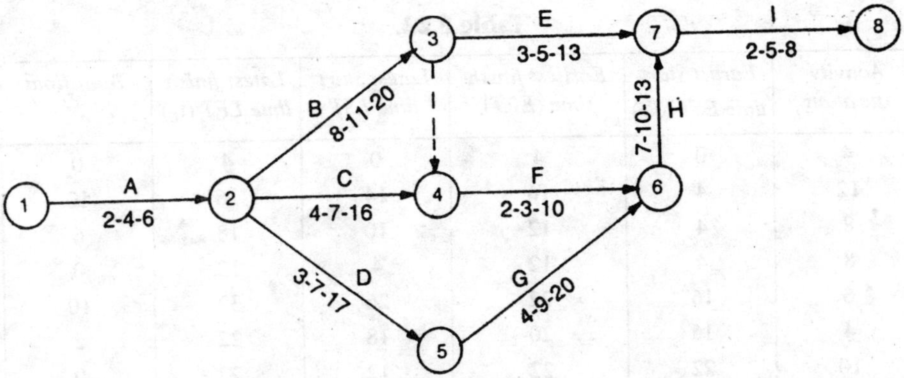

Fig. 8.21.

Solution. The expected mean time, variance and standard deviation of each activity is determined in tabular form in table 8.21.

Table 8.21.

Activity	*Optimistic time* t_o	*Most likely time* t_L	*Pessinistic time* t_p	*Expected time* $t_E = \frac{t_o + 4t_L + t_p}{6}$	*Variance* $\sigma^2 = \left(\frac{t_p - t_o}{6}\right)^2$	*S.D,* $\sigma = \frac{t_p - t_o}{6}$
A	2	4	6	4	0.444	0.67
B	8	11	20	12	4	2
C	4	7	16	8	4	2
D	3	7	17	8	5.44	2.33
E	3	5	13	6	2.78	1.67
F	2	3	10	4	1.78	1.33
G	4	9	20	10	7.11	2.67
H	7	10	13	10	1	1
I	2	5	8	5	1	1

For determining the duration of the project, the critical path has to be determined. It is determined after determining the activity times EST, EFT, LST, LFT and total float which is determined in tabular form as shown in table 8.22.

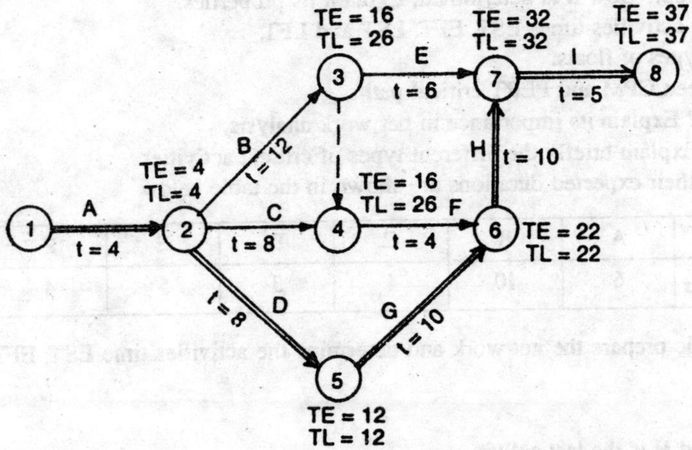

Fig. 8.22.

Table 8.22.

Activity	*Activity duration*	*Earlist start time EST (T_E^i)*	*Earliest finish time (EFT)*	*Latest start time LST*	*Latest finish time LFT (t_L)*	*Total float*	*Remark*
(1 – 2) A	4	0	4	0	4	0	critical
(2 – 3) B	12	4	16	14	26	10	
(2 – 4) C	8	4	12	10	18	6	
(2 – 5) D	8	4	12	4	12	0	critical
(3 – 7) E	6	16	22	26	32	10	
(4 – 6) F	4	16	20	18	22	2	
(5 – 6) G	10	22	22	12	22	0	critical
(6 – 7) H	10	32	32	22	32	0	critical
(7 – 8) I	5	32	37	32	37	0	critical

Variance of project $\sigma^2 = 0.444 + 5.44 + 7.11 + 1 + 1 = 14.994$

∴ Standard deviation of project= $\sqrt{14.994} = 3.88$

Critical path = 1-2-5-6-7-8.

Duration of project = 37 weeks.

Let project time be T_s

$$\text{Coefficient of probability factor } z = \frac{T_S - T_E}{\sigma}$$

$$\therefore \quad T_s = \sigma \cdot Z + T_E$$
$$= 1.32 \times 3.88 + 37$$
$$= 5.13 + 37 = 42 \text{ days.}$$

[From table 7.16, for 90% probability $Z = 1.32$

For 90% probability, the project will be completed in 42 days. **Ans.**

QUESTIONS

1. What is float? Differentiate between float and slack.
2. What is a critical path? How it is determined. Explain its properties.
3. Explain briefly the activities times EST, EFT, LST and LFT.
4. Explain different types of floats.
5. Differentiate between CPM and PERT critical paths.
6. What is total float? Explain its importance in net work analysis.
7. Define criticality. Explain briefly the different types of critical activities.
8. The activities and their expected durations are shown in the table below

Activities i-j	A	B	C	D	E	F	G	H
Duration t^{ij} in days	6	10	4	3	5	4	8	10

With the given logic prepare the net work and determine the activities time EST, EFT, LST, LFT. Draw the critical path also.

Logic:

(*a*) A is the first and H is the last activity.

(*b*) Activity B and C can be started simultaneously.

(*c*) Activity D can only be started after the completion of activity B.
(*d*) Activity G can not be started untill activity B is completed.
(*e*) Activities E and F can be started after the completion of activities C and D.
(*f*) Activity H can be started after the completion of activities G and F.

9. The activities and their completion time in days is shown in table below:

Activties	A	B	C	D	E	F	G	H	K	L	M	N
Duration in days	3	6	4	7	10	6	4	5	8	4	8	12

Logic:

(*a*) Activity A and N are the first and last activity
(*b*) After the completion of activity A, activities B and C can be started simultaneously.
(*c*) Activity D follows B and activities E and F follow activity C.
(*d*) Activity G can be started after the completion of activities D and E.
(*e*) Activity H follows activity F. Activities K and M can be started simultaneously after the completion of activity H.
(*f*) N is the last activity and can be started after the completion of activity L and M.

Determine the activities times and draw the critical path.

10. The activities and their duration of a project is shown in Table below. Draw the net work and determine the floats and draw the critical path.

Activities	U	R	E	Q	K	X	J	H	G	F	C
Duration in weeks	3	5	2	4	4	6	3	8	3	1	6

Logic:

(*a*) Activity K will start after activity E
(*b*) Activity X depends on Q.
(*c*) Activities K, F, and G can not start before the completion of activities R and E.
(*d*) Activities R and Q will follow activity U.
(*e*) Activity G should be completed before activity J.
(*f*) Activities C can start after the completion of activities F and G.
(*g*) Activities E and Q can start simultaneously.
(*h*) Activity H shall start only after the completion of activities C, X and J.
(*i*) H is the last activity.

11. Compute the earliest time T_E, latest occurrence time T_L and total float from the data of the following table. Also determine the critical path

Activity	A	B	C	D	E	F	G	H	I	J
Estimated time in days	5	2	6	4	4	2	3	8	7	2

12. For a certain project, following data is available. Draw the net work and determine the activities time and floats:

Activity	*Duration*	*Preceeding activity*
A	10	–
B	5	–
C	4	–
D	6	A and B
E	10	A and C
F	8	A, B and C

13. The activities and their duration of a project is shown in the following table.

Activity	A	B	C	D	E	F	G	H	I	J
Time in days	5	6	4	9	7	4	3	4	8	12

Logic:

(*a*) Activities A, B and C can be started simultaneously.

(*b*) Activities D and E can be started after the completion of activity A.

(*c*) Activity F can be started only after the completion of activity B.

(*d*) Activity G can be started after the completion of activity C.

(*e*) Activity I can be started after the completion of activity D.

(*f*) Activity H can be started after the completion of activity G.

(*g*) Activity J can only be started after the completion of activity E, F and H.

Project will be completed after the completion of activities I and J.

Draw the net work and determine the activity times EST, EFT, LST and LFT.

Find out the total float and mark the critical path.

14. Prepare the net work of a project from the data given in the following table and determine the followings.

(*a*) Earliest and latest activity times for all activities.

(*b*) Which activities are critical?

(*c*) If activity (2-3) would have taken 6 days instead 3 days, how it would have increased the completion time of the project.

(*d*) The slack of activities (3, 5), (4, 6) and (7, 8).

Activity	*Nodes*	*Estimated duration in days*
A	1 – 2	2
B	2 – 3	3
C	2 – 4	5
D	3 – 5	4
E	3 – 6	1
F	4 – 6	6
G	4 – 7	2
H	5 – 8	8
I	6 – 8	7
J	7 – 8	4

15. The net work of a project is shown below. The estimated duration of each activity is shown on the net work itself. Determine all the floats for each activity and establish the critical path also.

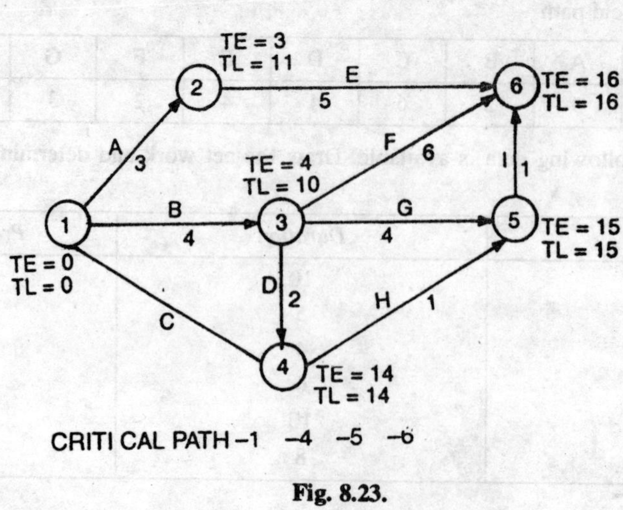

Fig. 8.23.

16. Find the critical path of the given net work Fig. 8.24.

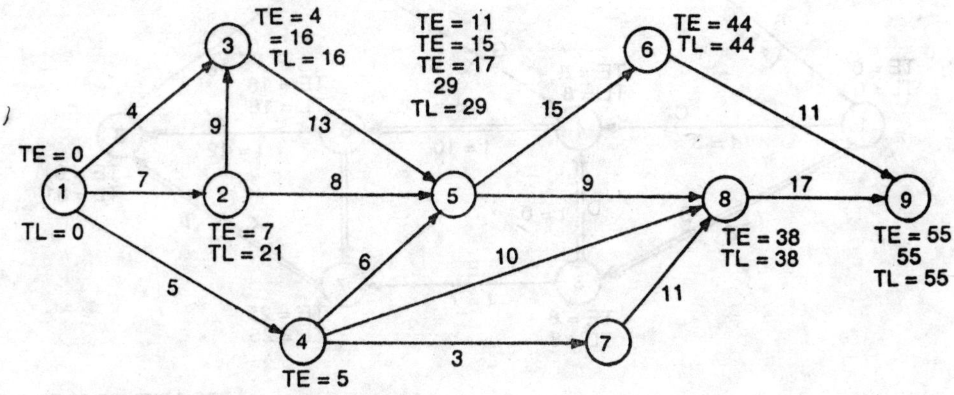

Critical path = 1-2-3-5-6-9 and 1-2-3-5-8-9

Fig. 8.24.

17. The net work of a construction project is shown in the following diagram of Fig. 8.25 for this diagram determine the following:

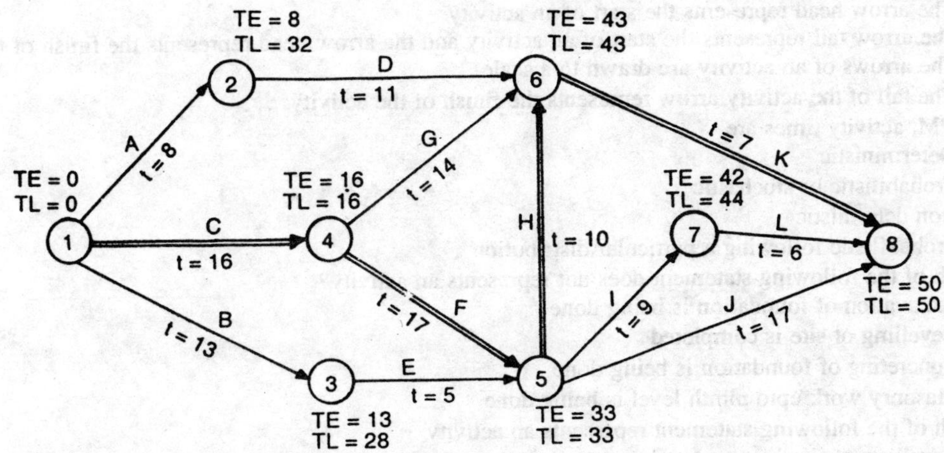

Fig. 8.25.

(*a*) All activities times and floats for all activities.
(*b*) Critical path and duration of the project

[Ans. Duration of project = 50 days
Critical path 1-4-5-6-8]

18. For the following CPM net work find the following:
(*a*) All activities times and floats in tabular form.
(*b*) Critical path and duration of the project.

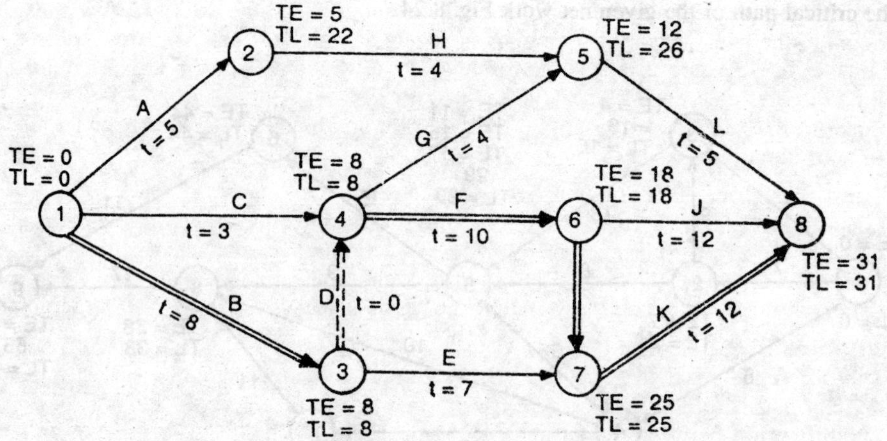

[**Ans.** Duration of project = 31 days
Critical path 1-3-4-6-7-8]

Fig. 8.26.

OBJECTIVE TYPE QUESTIONS

1. CPM net work is
   (*a*) Event oriented (*b*) Activity oriented
   (*c*) Both event as well as activity oriented (*d*) Neither event nor activity oriented.
2. In a CPM net work which is correct
   (*a*) The arrow head represents the start of an activity
   (*b*) The arrow tail represents the start of an activity and the arrow head represents the finish of the activity.
   (*c*) The arrows of an activity are drawn to a scale.
   (*d*) The tail of the activity arrow represents the finish of the activity.
3. In CPM, activity times are
   (*a*) Deterministic
   (*b*) Probabilistic or stochastic
   (*c*) Non determistic
   (*d*) Probabilistic following a particular distribution
4. Which of the following statement does not represents an activity?
   (*a*) Excavation of foundation is being done
   (*b*) Levelling of site is completed
   (*c*) Concreting of foundation is being done
   (*d*) Masonry work upto plinth level is being done
5. Which of the following statement represents an activity
   (*a*) Levelling of site is completed
   (*b*) Excavation of foundation is completed
   (*c*) Masonry work upto plinth level is completed
   (*d*) Masonry work of super structure is being done
6. The area under β distribution curve is divided into two equal pats by the ordinate through the
   (*a*) Pessimistic time (*b*) Optimistic time
   (*c*) Most likely time (*d*) Expected time
7. The earliest finish time (EFT) of an activity is
   (*a*) Equal to earliest event time for the node from which the activity arrow originates
   (*b*) Equal to earliest start time of an activity plus the activity time (duration)
   (*c*) Equal to earliest start time of an activity minus the activity time
   (*d*) Less than the event time for the node at which the activity arrow terminates.
8. The latest start time (LST) of an activity is

(*a*) More than the latest occurrence time for the event at which the activity arrow ends or terminates
(*b*) Equal to the latest occurrence time for the event at which the activity arrow ends or terminates
(*c*) Equal to the latest occurrence time for the event at which the activity arrow terminates minus the activity time or duration
(*d*) Equal to the latest occurrence time for the event at which the activity arrow terminates plus the activity time or duration.

9. The latest finish time (LFT) of an activity is
(*a*) Equal to the latest occurrence time for the event at which the activity arrow ends or terminates.
(*b*) Equal to the latest occurrence time for the event from which the activity arrow originates
(*c*) More than the latest occurrence time for the event at which the activity arrow terminates
(*d*) Less than the latest occurrence time for the event at which the activity arrow terminates.

10. Identify the correct statement
(*a*) The difference between the earliest finish time of an activity and the earliest start time of its successor activity is called total float
(*b*) The difference between the latest start time LST and the earliest start time of an activity is called total float.
(*c*) The difference between the latest allowable occurrence time and the earliest occurrence time for the head event of the activity is called total float.
(*d*) The excess time between the finishing and starting time of the two successive time is called the total float.

11. Identify the correct statement
(*a*) The difference between the latest start time and earliest start time of an activity is called free float.
(*b*) The difference between the latest allowable occurrence time and the earliest occurrence time for the head event of the activity is called free float
(*c*) The difference between the earliest finish time and earliest start time of its successor activity is called free float
(*d*) The excess time between the finishing and starting of two successive activities is called free float

12. The independent float of an activity is
(*a*) The excess time between the finishing and starting of two successive activities
(*b*) The difference between its earliest finish time and the earliest start time of its successor activity
(*c*) The difference between the latest start time and the earliest start time of the activity.
(*d*) The difference between the latest allowable occurrence time and the earliest occurrence time for the head event of the activity

13. Identify the correct statement
(*a*) The difference between the latest start time and the earliest start time of an activity is known interfering float
(*b*) The difference between the latest allowable occurrence time and the earliest occurrence time for the head event of the activity is known interfering float
(*c*) The excess time between the finishing and starting of two successive activities is known interfering float
(*d*) The difference between the earliest finish time and the earliest start time of its successor activity is called interfering float

14. Identify the correct statement
(*a*) When ever the total float of an activity is zero, its independent float is also zero, but its free float need not to be zero
(*b*) When ever the total float of an activity is zero, then both free float and independent float of the activity are zero
(*c*) When ever the total float of an activity is zero, its free float is also zero, but the independent float need not to be zero
(*d*) When ever the total float of an activity is zero, then both its free float and independent float need not to be zero

15. Which of the following statement is correct
(*a*) Free float is determined to identify the activities which can be delayed with out affecting the total float of the preceding activity

(*b*) Free float is determined to identify the activities which can be delayed with out affecting the total float of the succeeding activity
(*c*) Free float is determined to establish the priorities
(*d*) Free float is determined to identify the activities which can be delayed with out affecting total float of both preceding as well as succeeding activities.

16. Which of the following statement is correct
(*a*) The independent float only affects preceding activities
(*b*) The independent float only affects succeeding activities
(*c*) The independent float affects only a particular activity
(*d*) The independent float affects both preceding as well succeeding activities

17. The time by which a particular activity can be delayed with out affecting its succeeding and preceding activities is known as
(*a*) Interfering float (*b*) Independent float
(*c*) Total float (*d*) Free float

18. Slack times or simply slack refers to
(*a*) An event (*b*) An activity
(*c*) Both for event and activity (*d*) None of the above

19. In a net work critical path is
(*a*) Always the longest path (*b*) Always the shortest path
(*c*) May be shortest path (*d*) May be longest path
(*e*) None of the above

20. The interfering float for an activity is the difference between its
(*a*) Total float and free float (*b*) Free float and independent float
(*c*) Total float and independent float (*d*) Non of the above

21. When the latest allowable occurrence time is more than earliest expected time, it is called
(*a*) Negative slack (*b*) Positive slack
(*c*) Zero slack (*d*) None of the above

22. When latest allowable occurrence time is less than its earliest expected time, it is called as
(*a*) Positive slack (*b*) Negative slack
(*c*) Zero slack (*d*) None of the above

23. Which of the following statement is correct
(*a*) When the project is on its scheduled time then it indicates positive slack
(*b*) When the project is on its scheduled time, them it indicates negative slack
(*c*) When the project is on its scheduled time, it indicates zero slack
(*d*) All the above

24. A sub critical activity shows
(*a*) Resources are insufficient (*b*) Resources are just sufficient
(*c*) Resources are more than required (*d*) None of the above

25. Positive slack shows
(*a*) Excess resources (*b*) Insufficient resources
(*c*) Just enough resources (*d*) None of the above

ANSWERS

1. (*b*)	8. (*c*)	15. (*b*)	22. (*b*)
2. (*b*)	9. (*a*)	16. (*c*)	23. (*c*)
3. (*a*)	10. (*b*)	17. (*b*)	24. (*a*)
4. (*b*)	11. (*c*)	18. (*a*)	25. (*a*)
5. (*d*)	12. (*a*)	19. (*a*)	
6. (*d*)	13. (*b*)	20. (*a*)	
7. (*b*)	14. (*b*)	21. (*b*)	

Ans. Q. 8.

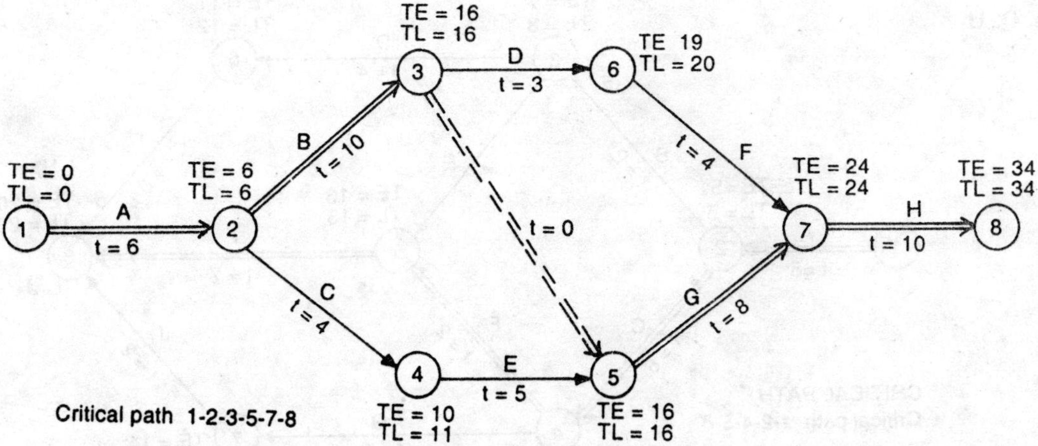

Critical path 1-2-3-5-7-8

Fig. 8.27.

Ans. Q. 9.

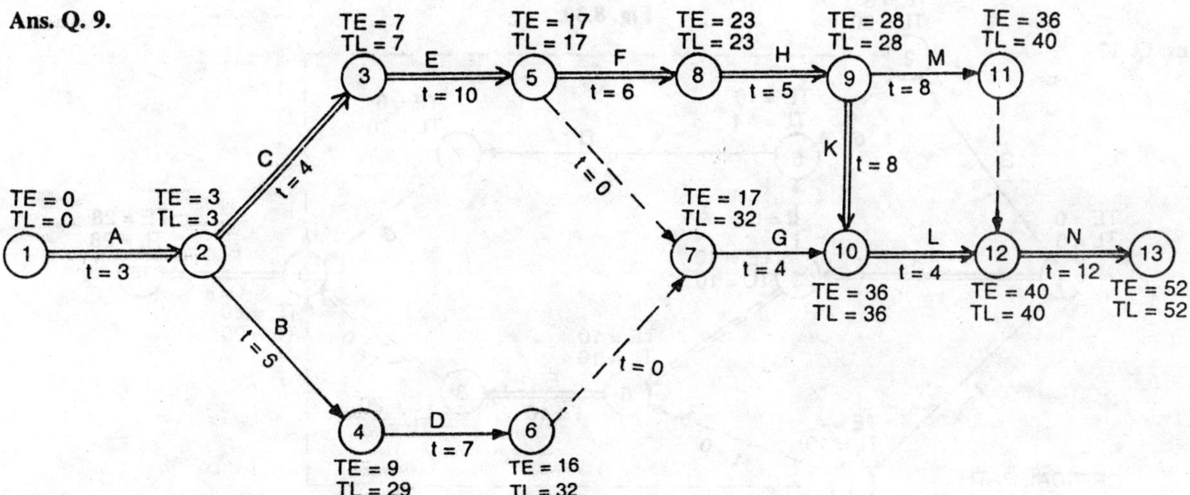

Critical path 1-2-3 5-8-9-10-12-13

Fig. 8.28.

Ans. Q. 10.

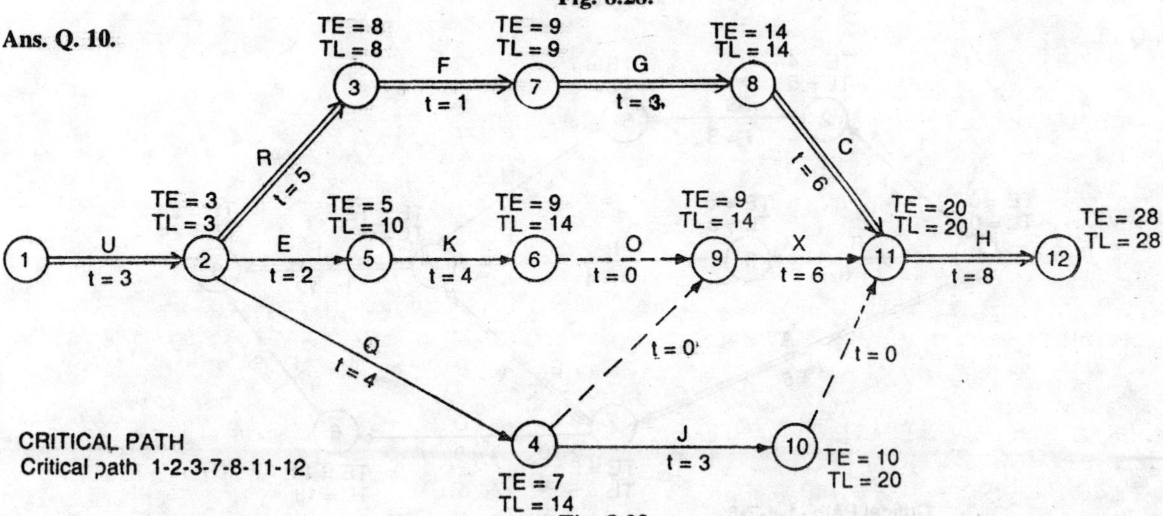

CRITICAL PATH
Critical path 1-2-3-7-8-11-12

Fig. 8.29.

Ans. Q. 11.

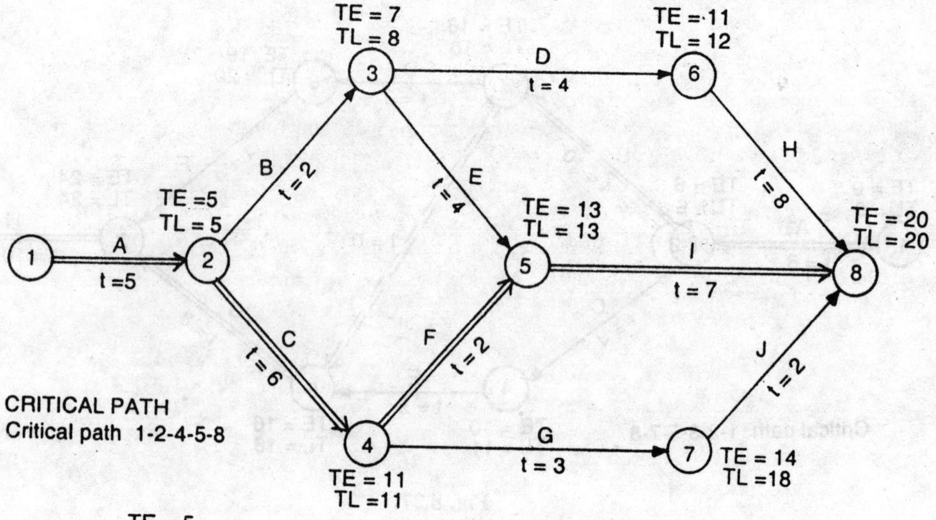

Fig. 8.30.

Ans. Q. 12.

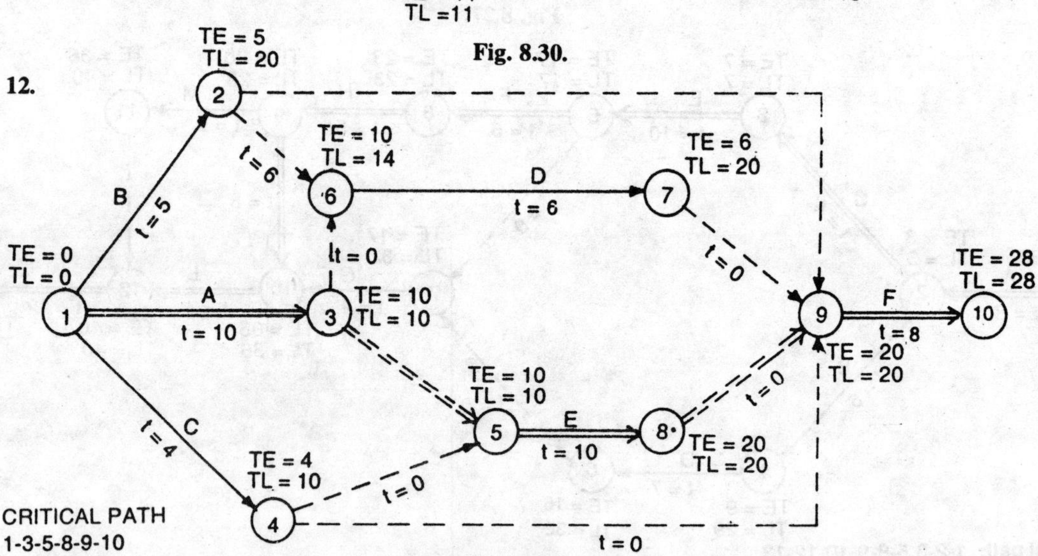

Fig. 8.31.

Ans. Q 13.

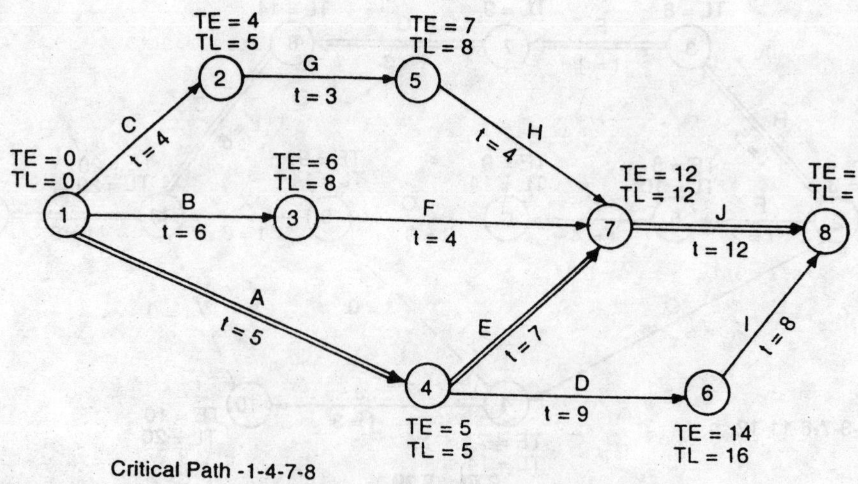

Fig. 8.32.

Ans. Q. 14.

(*a*) All times shown on the Fig. itself.
(*b*) Critical path is along 1-2-4-6-8. Hence activities A, C, F and I are critical.
(*c*) No Effect.

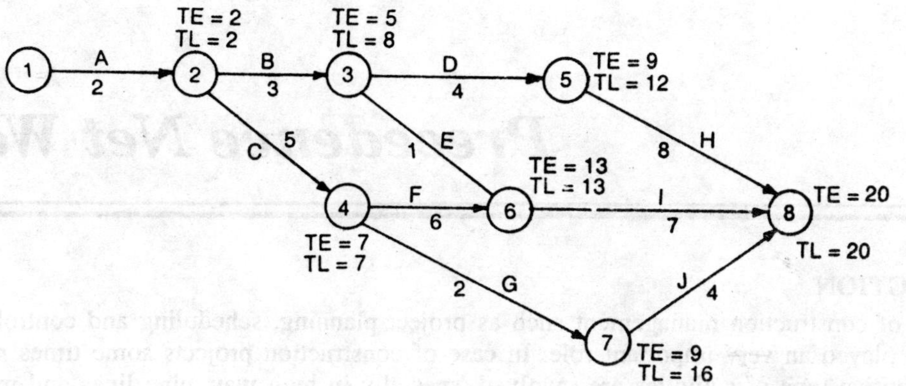

Fig. 8.33.

Ans. Q. 15.

Activity	*Duration* t_{ij}	T_E^j	*EST* (T_E^i)	*EFT*	*LST*	*LFT*	*Total float*	*Free float*	*Independent float*	*Inter firing float*	*Remark*
(1-2) A	3	0	0	3	8	11	8	0	0	8	
(1-3) B	4	0	0	4	6	10	6	0	0	6	
(1-4) C	14	0	0	14	10	14	0	0	0	0	Critical
(2-6) E	5	3	5	8	11	16	8	0	– 8	8	
(3-4) D	2	4	2	6	12	14	8	8	2	0	
(3-5) G	4	4	4	8	11	15	7	7	1	0	
(3-6) F	6	4	4	10	10	16	6	6	0	0	
(4-5) H	1	14	14	15	14	15	0	0	0	0	Critical
(5-6) I	1	15	16	15	15	16	0	0	0	0	Critical

Critical path = 1-4-5-6.
Duration of project = 16 days.

9

Precedence Net Works

9.1. INTRODUCTION

In the field of construction management such as project planning, scheduling and control, net work techniques have played an very important role. In case of construction projects some times many over-lapping and repetitive type of activities are involved, specially in high way, pipe lines and multistoryed building projects. In such cases a careful study need to be made before preparing a schedule.

The CPM net work has two systems of net works as follows:

1. A-O-A system *i.e.* Activity on Arrow network system.
2. A-O-N system *i.e.* Activity on the Node network system.

A-O-N system is also called precedence net work. In this system nodes represent the activities and the arrows show their inter dependence. The A-O-N system or precedence system net works represent the logical and sequential interrelationships between various activities required to be performed to achieve the scheduled completion of the project in the same way as in the case of A-O-A system.

In projects having repetitive type and over lapping activities, C.P.M net works have been found more realistic and useful. Now a days A-O-A system of net work is gaining popularity and in majority of cases has been adopted. But to acquaint the reader with the precedence net work it is discussed in this chapter in brief.

9.2. REPRESENTATION OF NODES IN A-O-N NET WORKS

In this system the activities are represented by nodes and the arrows represent their interdependence or precedence relationship. Nodes are usually represented by square or rectangles, but circles and other conventional geometrical shapes may also be used. One of the most common type of node representation is shown in Fig. 9.1.

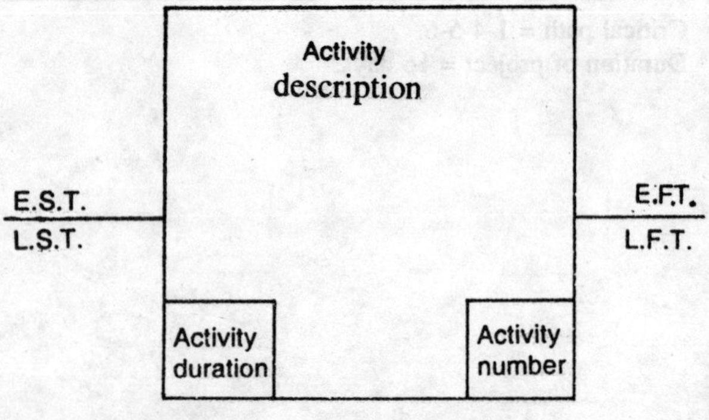

Fig. 9.1. Representation of node

When the squares and rectangles are used to represent the nodes, one of the ways is to write the activity description on the top half of the box, activity number at the bottom right corner and duration on the left hand corner of the box. The earliest start time (EST) and the latest start time LST are written just before the box on the left hand side above and below the connecting line, the earliest finish time EFT and latest finish time LFT are written on the right hand side of the box as shown in Fig. 9.1.

9.3. LOGIC OF PRECEDENCE DIAGRAM

Some of the basic relationship are given below:

1. **Finish to start.** In Fig. 9.2 (*a*) activities A and B are shown. In case activity B can only be started after finishing the activity A, the time lag between the completion of activity A and commencement of activity B can be defined or it can be zero. In some situations it may be negative *i.e.* the activity B may be started before the completion of activity A. The relation is shown in Fig. 9.2 (*a*).

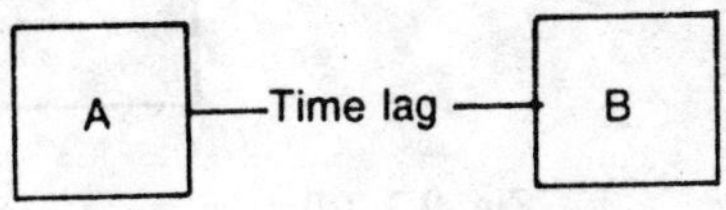

Fig. 9.2. (*a*)

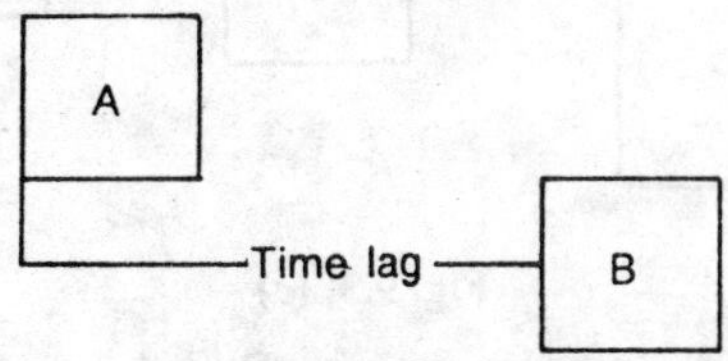

Fig. 9.2. (*b*)

2. **Start to start.** In case the activities A and B can be started at the same time, but activity B can not start before A. In case a time lag is defined then activity B can not be started until that interval is over *i.e.* activity B can only be started after the given interval. It is shown in Fig. 9.2 (*b*).
3. **Finish to finish.** In case activity B can not be finished until activity A finishes. If time lag is given then activity B can not be finished earlier than given time lag after finishing the activity A. How ever it can be finished later than the given time lag. It is shown in Fig. 9.2 (*c*)
4. **Start to start combined with finish to finish.** Activity B neither cannot be started nor finished

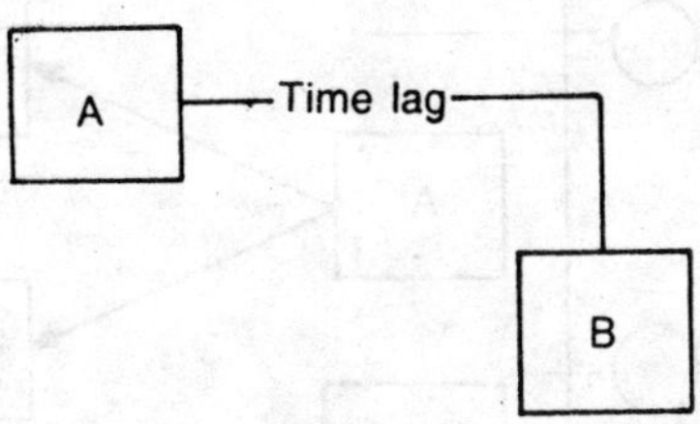

Fig. 9.2. (*c*)

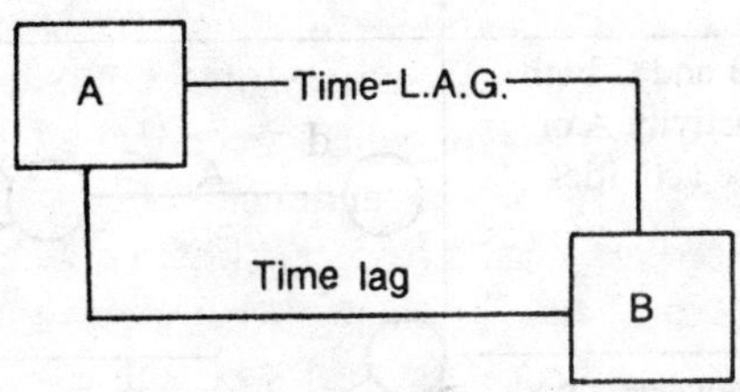

Fig. 9.2. (*d*)

earlier than the given time lag after the start and finish of activity A. This sequence is used to define overlapping independent activities. Fig. 9.2 (*d*)

9.4. SOME EXAMPLES OF PRECEDENCE DIAGRAMS

1. Activity A precedes activity B or activity B succeeds activity A. This relationship is shown in Fig. 9.3 (*a*)

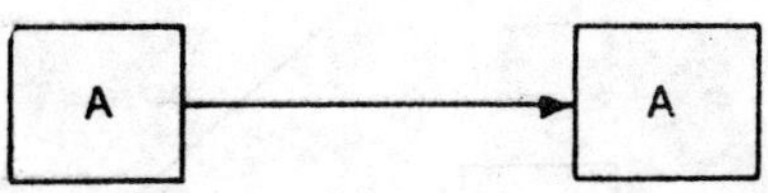

Fig. 9.3. (*a*)

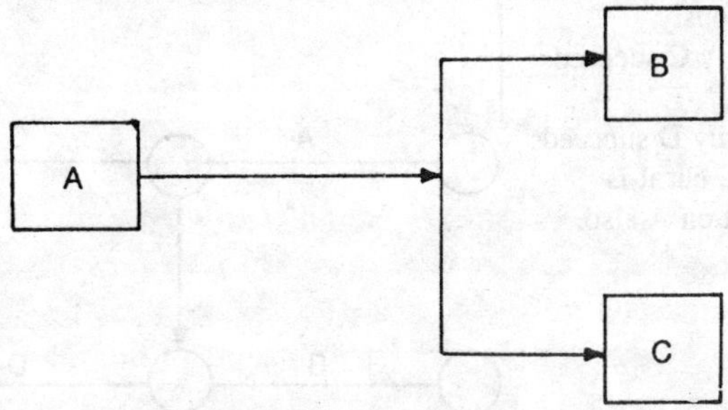

Fig. 9.3. (*b*)

2. Activities B and C succeed activity A or Activity A is preceded by both activities B and C. It is shown in Fig. 9.3 (*b*).

3. Activity N is dependent upon both the activities L and M and it cannot start untill both activities L and M are completed. It is shown in Fig. 9.3 (*c*)

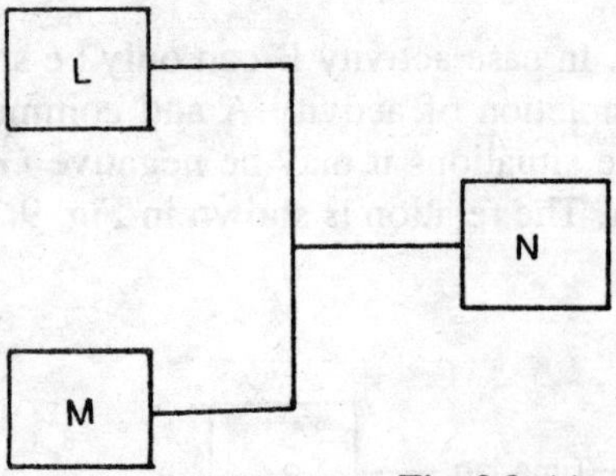

Fig. 9.3. (*c*)

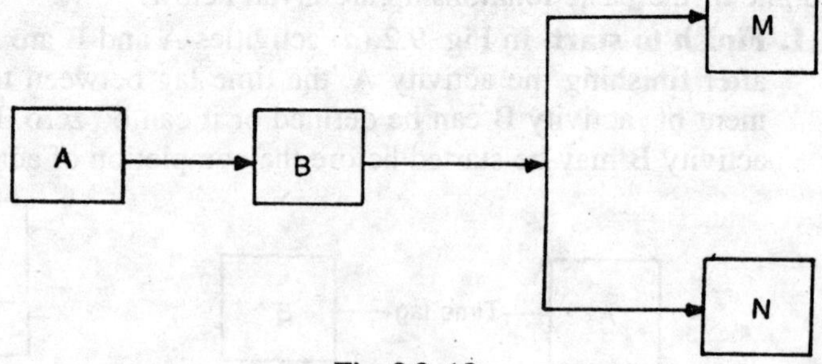

Fig. 9.3. (*d*)

4. Activity A precedes activity B and activities M and N are dependent upon activity B. Activities M and N succeed activity B. It is shown in Fig. 9.3 (*d*).

9.5. REPRESENTATION OF RELATIONSHIP IN A-O-A DIAGRAM AND A-O-N DIAGRAM

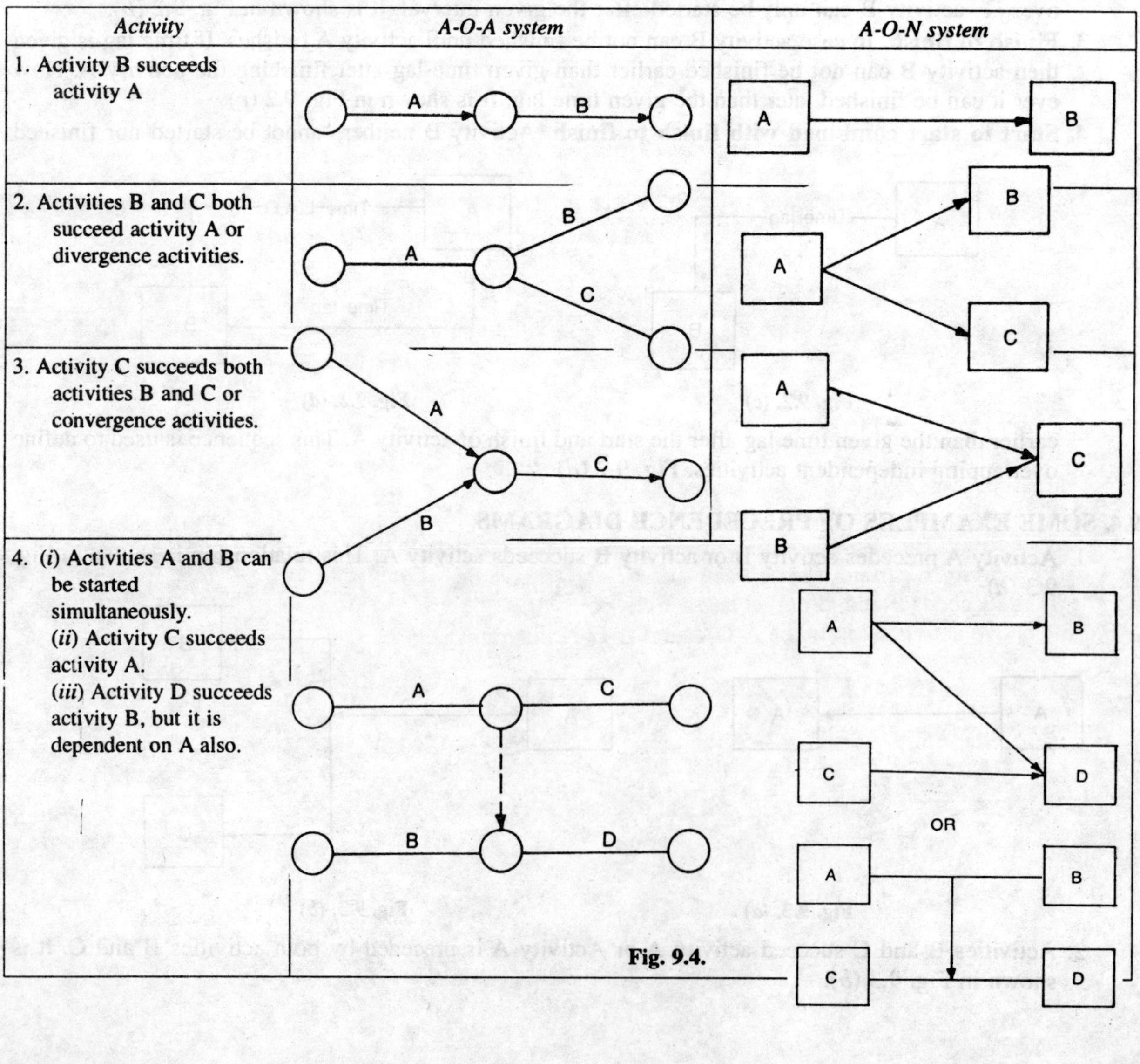

Fig. 9.4.

Activity	*A-O-A system*	*A-O-N system*
5. Activity A precedes activity B. Activities A and P can be started independently simultaneously. Activity C can not be started till the completion of activities B and Q. Activities R and S are dependent on Q and Q controls the start of activities R, S and C. Draw the A-O-A and A-O-N diagrams.	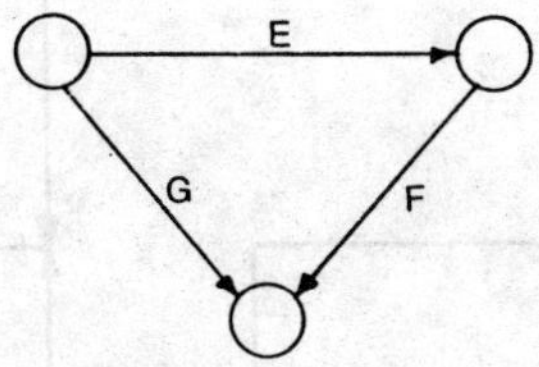 Fig. 9.5.	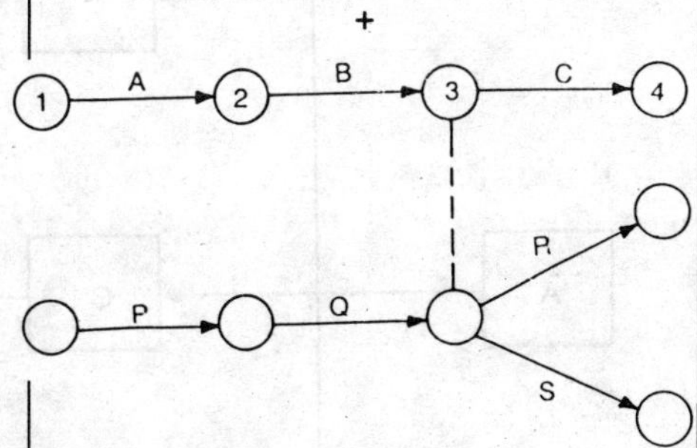
6.	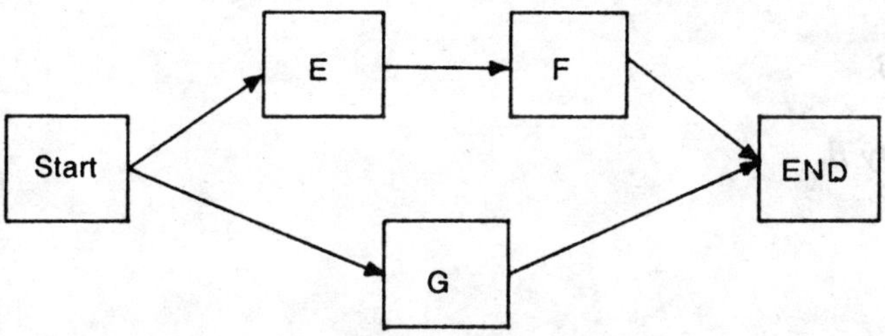 A-O-A diagram	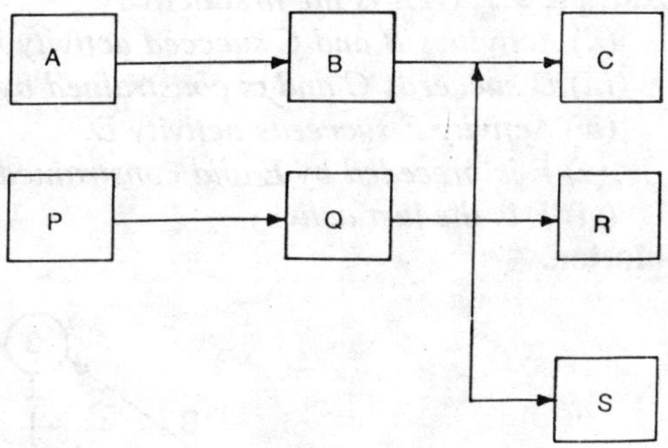 A-O-N diagram

Fig. 9.6

6. (*i*) A is the first activity.
   (*ii*) Activities B, C and D are dependent upon activity A.
   (*iii*) Activity G can not start till activity B has been completed.
   (*iv*) Activity E can not start till activity D has been completed.
   (*v*) Activity F can not start till activities C and E have been completed.
   (*vi*) H succeeds F and G and is last activity.

For the above activities draw the A-O-A and A-O-N diagrams.

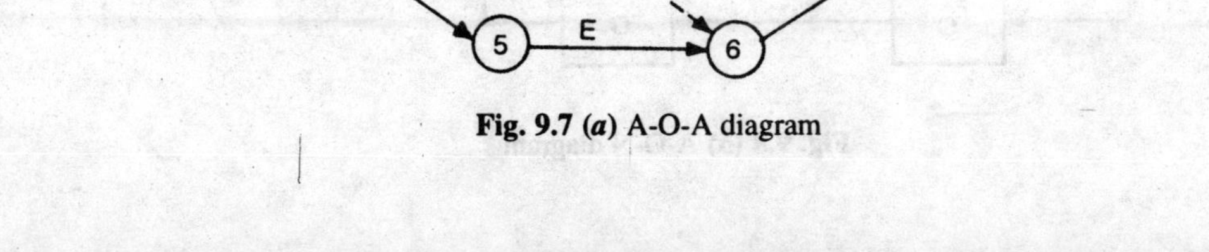

Fig. 9.7 (*a*) A-O-A diagram

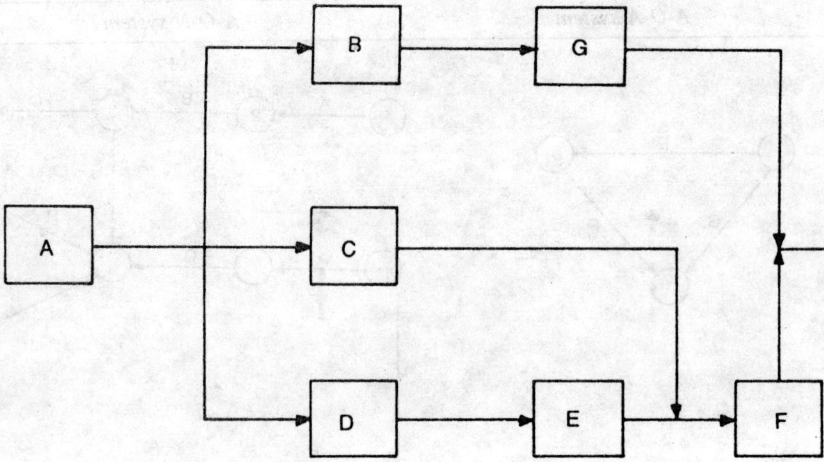

Fig. 9.7 (*b*) A-O-N diagram

Example 9.7. (*i*) *A is the first activity.*

(*ii*) *Activities B and C succeed activity A.*

(*iii*) *D succeeds C and is constrained by B.*

(*iv*) *Activity E succeeds activity D.*

(*v*) *F is preceded by E and constrained by B.*

(*vi*) *F is the last activity.*

Solution.

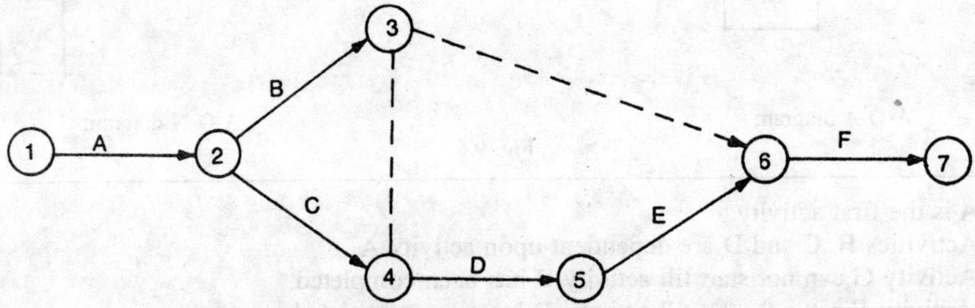

Fig. 9.8 (*a*) A-O-A diagram

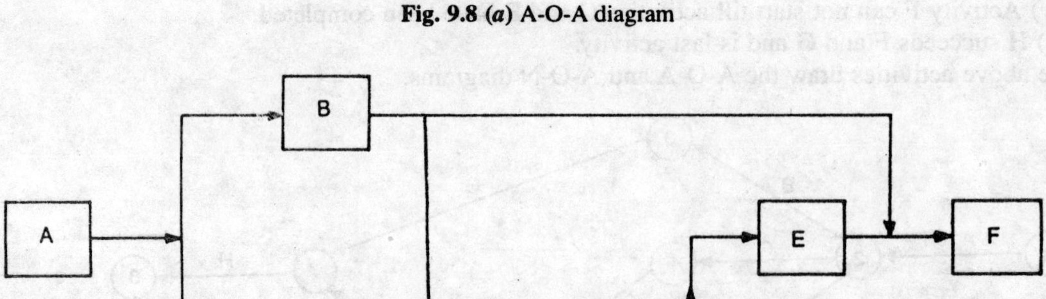

Fig. 9.8 (*b*) A-O-N diagram

9.6. POINTS TO BE KEPT IN MIND WHILE DRAWING A A-O-N OR PRECEDENCE DIAGRAM

While drawing a precedence net work diagram following points must be kept in mind:

1. Events have no duration, while activities have their durations. Numbering of activities are same as in A-O-A net work.
2. Start of an activity must be linked to the end of all activities, which must the completed before that start *i.e.* the start under consideration may take place. Activities which may take place simultaneously are not linked in any way.
3. The connecting lines generally run in the left-right direction. A few vertical lines drawn to connect the appropriate nodes, should preferably join on the left hand side of the box and as close to it as possible. This helps to have the diagram clear, easily understandable and manageable in size.
4. When a number of activities start simultaneously, one activity is provided as the first activity, though such an activity may not exist in the list. This activity is known as debut activity and denoted by letter (Do). Debut activities have zero duration. Similarly a finish activity (F) is provided to indicate the last activity. It also has zero duration. The A-O-N diagram of A-O-A diagram of Fig. 9.9 (*a*) is shown in Fig. 9.9 (*b*).

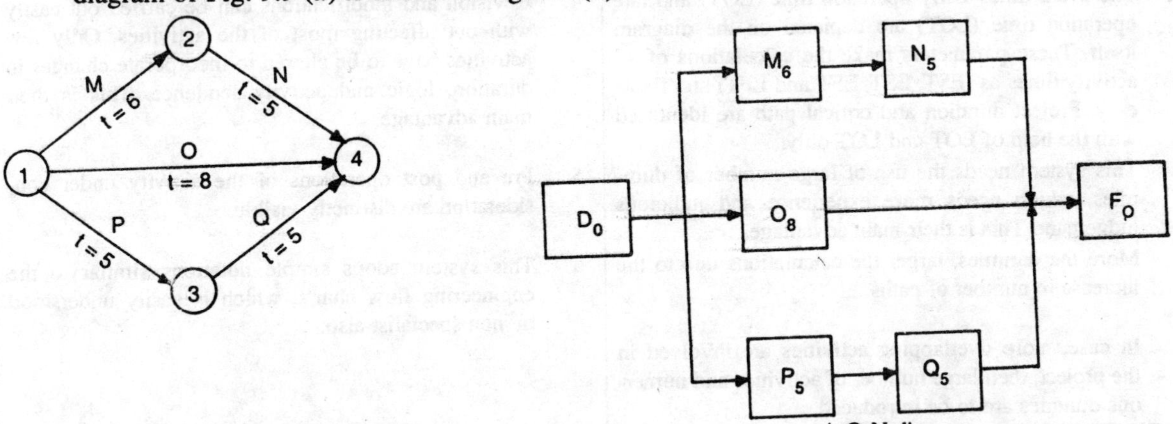

A-O-A diagram A-O-N diagram

Fig. 9.9.

5. During execution of work, delays always occur. The reasons for delays may be many as seasonal, technical or resource constraints etc. In such cases the lag or delay is indicated over the connecting line, joining the concerned activities and is denoted by the letter '*d*'

In addition to representing the lag and start of succeeding or overlapping activities, it is necessary to indicate the restraint imposed on the completion of the succeeding activity by the preceding activity. This is shown by drawing a second connecting line from right hand side of the first box and joining the top of the next box. If the "time lag" of start and finish are different, these may be written over both the connecting lines as shown in Fig. 9.10.

Activity M is the 1st activity.

Activity N has lag of 3 days in start and 3 days in finish.

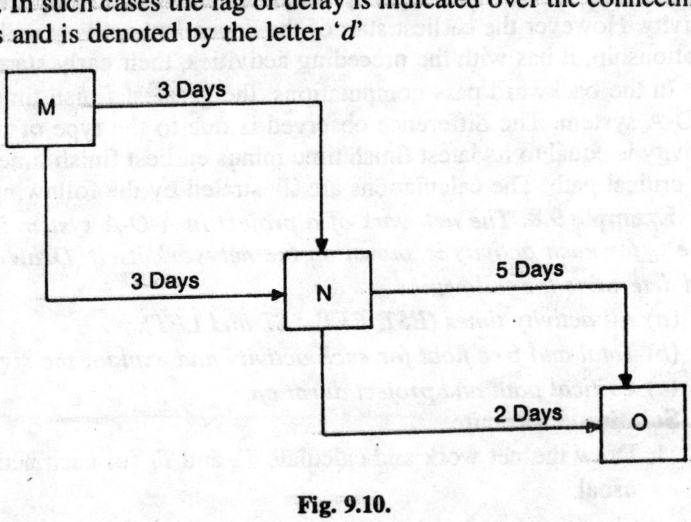

Fig. 9.10.

Activity O has lag of 2 days in start and 5 days in finish.

9.7. SALIENT FEATURES OF A-O-A SYSTEM AND A-O-N SYSTEM

The salient features of A-O-A system and A-O-N system are shown in tabular form below in table 9.1.

Table 9.1. Salient features of A-O-A system and A-O-N system

A-O-A System	*A-O-N System*
1. This system was the first method of CPM network introduced and developed. At present this is the most popular method.	1. This system eliminates the use of dunmy activities completely.
2. It can be conviently used for very complex projects having large number of activities and dunmies. In this system writing of computer programme is easy.	2. This system can distinguish the activities which should be allowed to overlap each other or must be separated by a time delay.
3. It is easier to associate with the time flow of activities.	3. This system is self sufficient as it contains all activity times as (EST, EFT, LST and LFT) written on the diagram it self. This facilitates the efficient scheduling and controlling.
4. The event times Early operation time (EOT) and late operation time (LOT) are depicted on the diagram itself. These parameters make the calculations of all activity times as (EST, LST, EFT and LFT) and floats easy. Project duration and critical path are identified with the help of EOT and LOT only.	4. Revision and modifications can be carried out easily with out affecting most of the activities. Only few activities have to be altered to incorporate changes in duration, logic and activity sequence. This is their main advantage.
5. This system needs the use of large number of dummies, which needs more experience and judicious judgemant. This is their main advantage.	5. Pre and post operations of the activity under consideration are distinctly visible.
6. More the dunmies, larger the calculations due to the increase in number of paths.	6. This system adops simple notations similar to the engineering flow charts, which is easily understood by non specialist also.
7. In case, more overlapping activities are involved in the project, then large number of activities and numerous dunmies are to be introduced.	

9.8. CALCULATIONS IN A-O-N SYSTEM

Computations in A-O-N system are similar to those of A-O-A net works. In the forward pass, the earliest start time of each activity is calculated by following the longest path influencing the start of each activity. However the earliest start of the dependent activity will be governed by the type of the precedence relationship, it has with the preceding activities, their early start and time lags.

In the backward pass computations, the greatest finish times are computed in the same manner as in A-O-A system. The difference observed is due to the type of precedence relationship. Total float for any activity is equal to its latest finish time minus earliest finish time. The activities having zero total float form the critical path. The calculations are illustrated by the following solved examples.

Example 9.8. *The net work of a project in A-O-A system is shown in Fig. 9.11 below. The estimated time t_E for each activity is shown on the net work itself. Draw the corresponding A-O-N system net work and determine the followings.*

(*a*) *All activity times (EST, EFT, LST and LFT).*

(*b*) *Total and free float for each activity and explain the significance of each of them.*

(*c*) *Critical path and project duration.*

Solution. Procedure

1. Draw the net work and calculate T_E and T_L for each activity as usual and write near each event as usual.

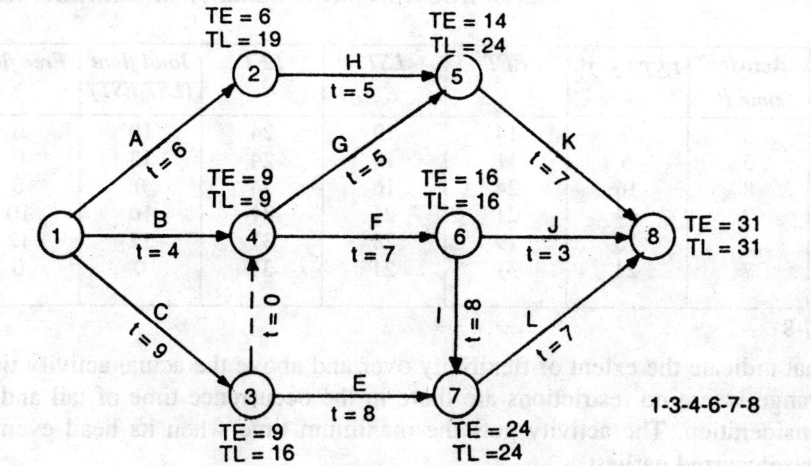

Fig. 9.11 (*a*)

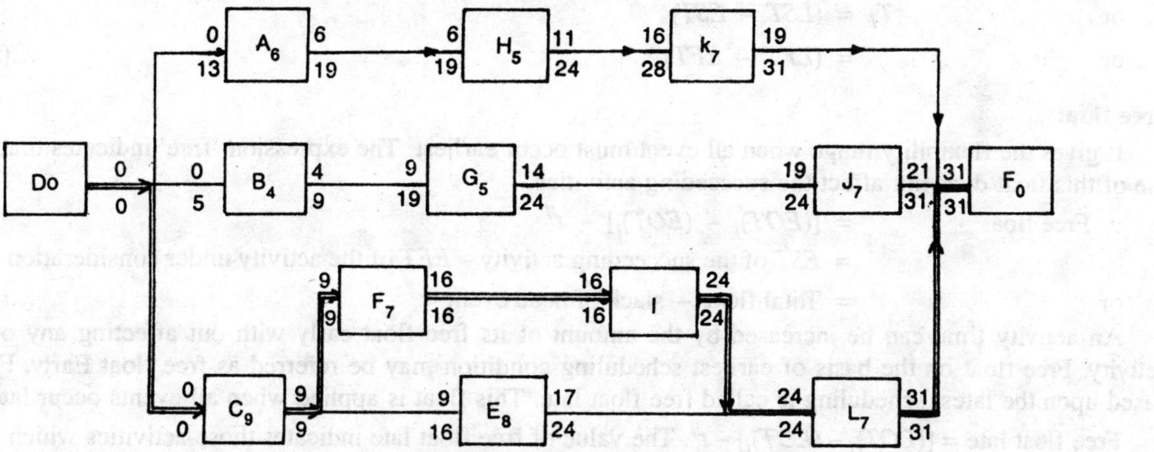

Fig. 9.11 (*b*) A-O-N diagram

2. Calculate activity times as EST, EFT, LST and EFT.

$$EST = T_E^{\,i}$$

$$EFT = T_E i + t^{ij}$$

$$LFT = T_L^{i}$$

$$EFT = LFT - t^{ij}$$

3. Tabulate these values in a tabular form as shown in table 9.2.

Table 9.2.

Activity name	*Activity No i-j*	*Activity time t^{ij}*	*EST i.e. T_E^i*	*EFT*	*LST*	*LFT*	*Total float (LST-EST)*	*Free float*	*Remark*
Do	0	0	0	0	0	0	0	0	
A	1 – 2	6	0	6	13	19	13	0	Critical
B	1 – 4	4	0	4	5	9	5	5	
C	1 – 3	9	0	9	0	9	0	0	Critical
D	3 – 4	0	9	9	9	9	0	0	Critical
E	3 – 7	8	9	17	16	24	7	7	
F	4 – 6	7	9	16	9	16	0	0	Critical

Activity name	*Activity No i-j*	*Activity time t^{ij}*	*EST i.e. T_E^i*	*EFT*	*LST*	*LFT*	*Total float (LST-EST)*	*Free float*	*Remark*
G	4 – 5	5	9	14	19	24	10	0	
H	2 – 5	5	6	11	19	24	13	0	
I	6 – 7	8	16	24	16	24	0	0	Critical
J	5 – 8	7	14	21	24	31	10	10	
K	6 – 8	3	16	19	28	31	12	12	
L	7 – 8	7	24	31	24	31	0	0	Critical
Fo		–							

Critical path is 1-3-4-6-7-8

Total and free float indicate the extent of flexibility over and above the actual activity time. Total float gives the flexibility range where no restrictions are there in the occurrence time of tail and head event of the activity under consideration. The activity gets the maximum time when its head event has occurred latest and tail event has occurred earliest.

Thus total float $= [(LOT)_j - (EOT)_i]$

or $T_F = (LST - EST)$

or $= (LFT - EFT)$ ...(9.1)

Free float

It gives the flexibility range when all event must occur earliest. The expression 'free' indicates that the use of this float does not affect the succeeding activities.

$\therefore$ Free float $= [(EOT)_j - (EOT)_i] - t^{ij}$

= *EST* of the succeeding activity – *EFT* of the activity under consideration

or = Total float – slack of head event ...(9.2)

An activity time can be increased by the amount of its free float early with out affecting any other activity. Free float on the basis of earliest scheduling condition may be referred as free float Early. Float based upon the latest scheduling is called free float late. This float is applied when all events occur latest.

Free float late = $[(LOT)_j - (LOT)_i] - t^{ij}$. The value of free float late indicates those activities which will have spare time under the latest scheduling condition. This float is used when part of the project is scheduled towards its possible dates.

Example 9.9. *The A-O-A net work of a project is shown in Fig. 9.12 (a) For the given net work draw A-O-N net work and determine:*

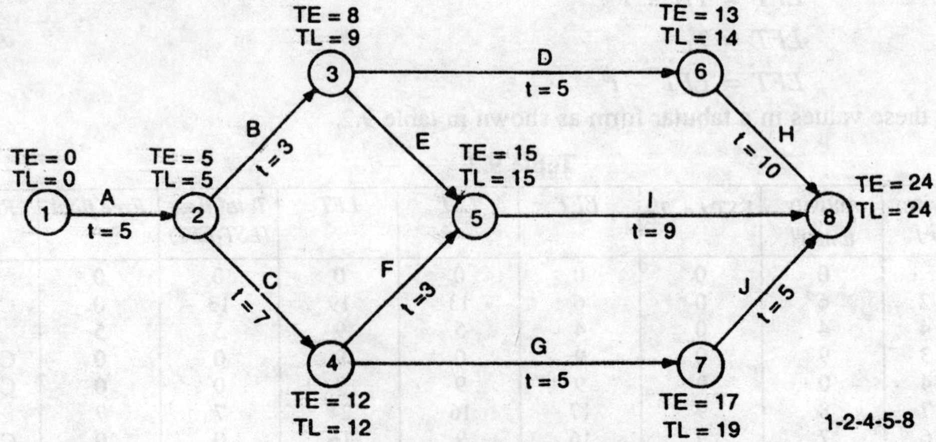

Fig. 9.12 (*a*) A-O-A diagram

(a) All activity times as EST, EFT, LST and LFT for each activity.
(b) Total float of each activity.
(c) Critical path and project duration.

Solution. First T_E and T_L of the activities are calculated and marked on the net work diagram

Table 9.3.

Activity name	*Activity i-j*	*Activity duration t^{ij}*	*EST*	*EFT*	*LST*	*LFT*	*Total float T_F*	*Remark*
Do	–	0	0	0	0	0	0	
A	1 – 2	5	0	5	0	5	0	Critical
B	2 – 3	3	5	8	6	9	1	
C	2 – 4	7	5	12	5	12	0	Critical
D	3 – 6	5	8	13	9	14	1	
E	3 – 5	5	8	13	10	15	2	
F	4 – 5	3	12	15	12	15	0	Critical
G	4 – 7	5	12	17	14	19	2	
H	6 – 8	10	13	23	14	24	1	
I	5 – 8	9	15	24	15	24	0	Critical
J	7 – 8	5	17	22	19	24	2	
Fo		0	24	24	24	24	0	

Critical path 1-2-4-5-8

Total duration of project = 24 dyas.

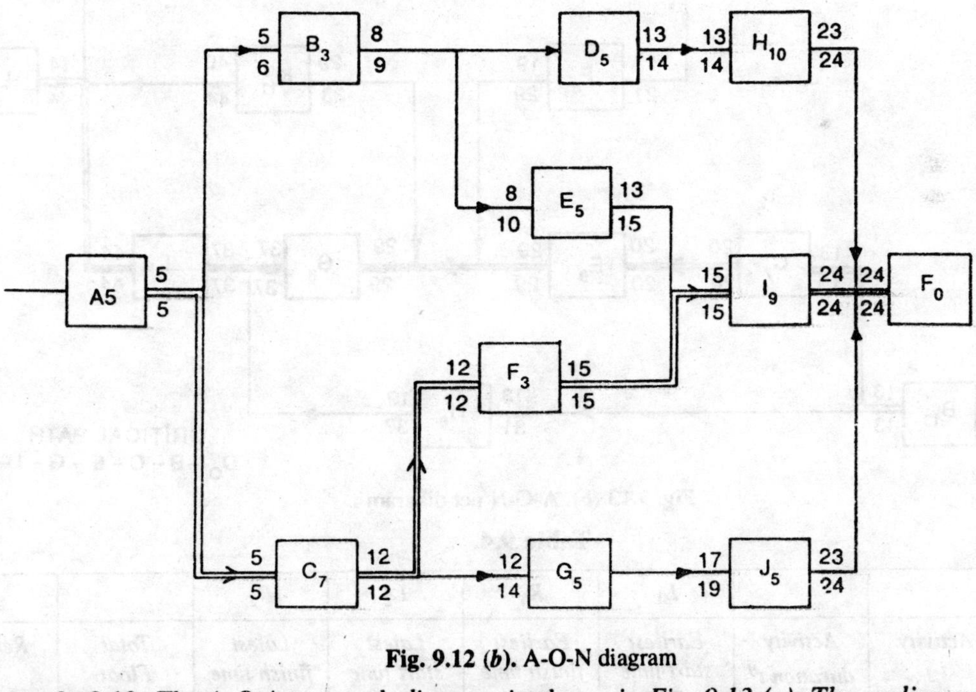

Fig. 9.12 (*b*). A-O-N diagram

Example 9.10. *The A-O-A net work diagram is shown in Fig. 9.13 (a). The earlier expected time in days or activity duration t_E^{ij} is shown on the net work it self. For this net work draw A-O-N net work diagram and determine the followings:*

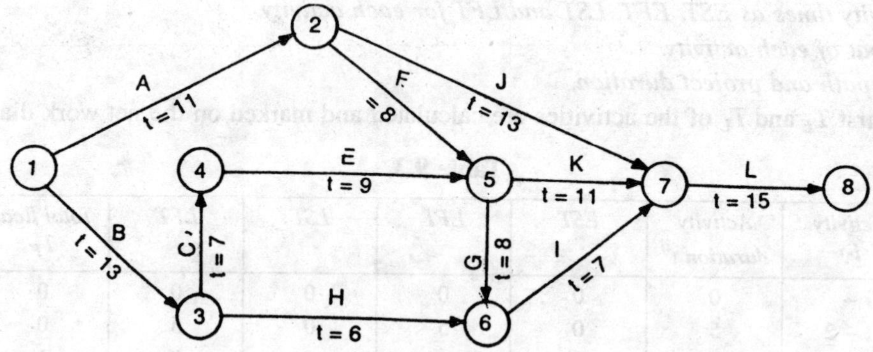

Fig. 9.13. (*a*)

(i) All activity time i.e. earliest start time EST, Latest start time LST, earlier finish time EFT and latest finish time LFT.

(ii) Total float for all activities.

(iii) Critical path and duration of the project.

Solution.

1. First calculate T_E and T_L of the given net work and mark them on the net work near events.
2. The calculations are shown in the tabular form below.

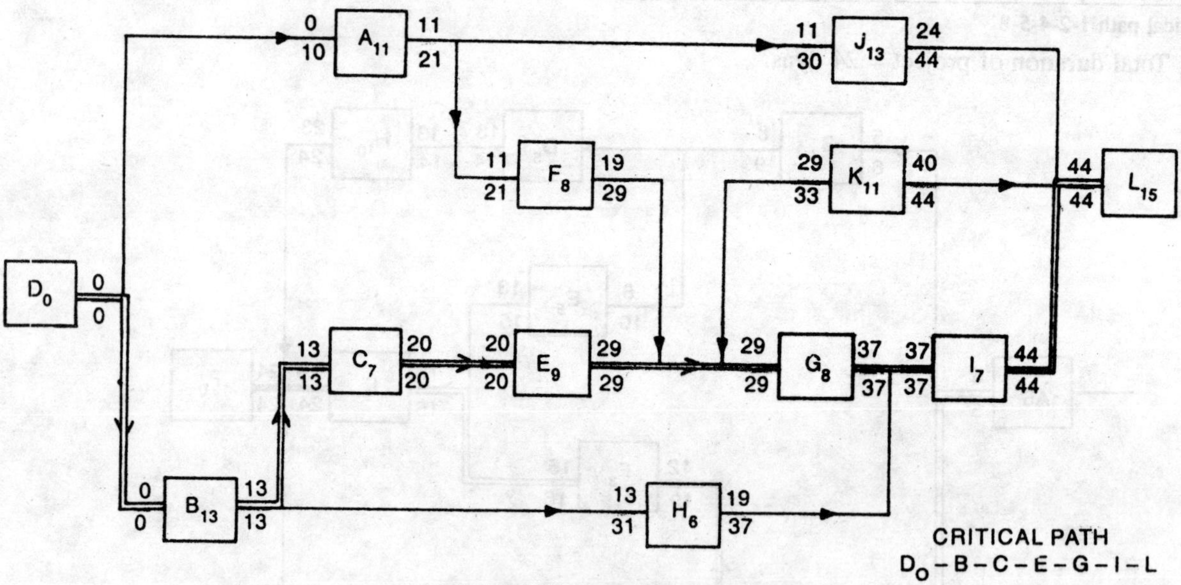

Fig. 9.13 (*b*). A-O-N net diagram

Table 9.4.

			L_1	R_1	L_2	R_2		
Activity name	*Activity i-j*	*Activity duration t^{ij}*	*Earliest start time EST*	*Earliest finish time EFT*	*Latest start time LST*	*Latest finish time LFT*	*Total Float*	*Remark*
Do								
A	1 – 2	11	0	11	10	21	10	

			L_1	R_1	L_2	R_2		
Activity name	*Activity i-j*	*Activity duration t^{ij}*	*Earliest start time EST*	*Earliest finish time EFT*	*Latest start time LST*	*Latest finish time LFT*	*Total Float*	*Remark*
B	1 – 3	13	0	13	0	13	0	Critical
C	3 – 4	7	13	20	13	20	0	Critical
E	4 – 5	9	20	29	20	29	0	Critical
F	2 – 5	8	11	19	21	29	10	
G	5 – 6	8	29	37	29	37	0	Critical
H	3 – 6	6	13	19	31	37	18	
I	6 – 7	7	37	44	37	44	0	Critical
J	2 – 7	13	11	24	30	44	19	
K	5 – 7	11	29	40	33	44	4	
L	7 – 8	15	44	59	44	59	0	Critical
Fo			59	59	59			

Critical path is 1-3-4-5-6-7-8

Critical path is along B-C-E-G-I-L

Total duration of project = 59 days, A-O-N Net work shown in Fig. 9.13 (*b*)

Example 9.11. 1. *An precedence diagram is shown in Fig. 9.14 (a). For the diagram find out the activity times i.e. EST, EFT, LST and LFT.*

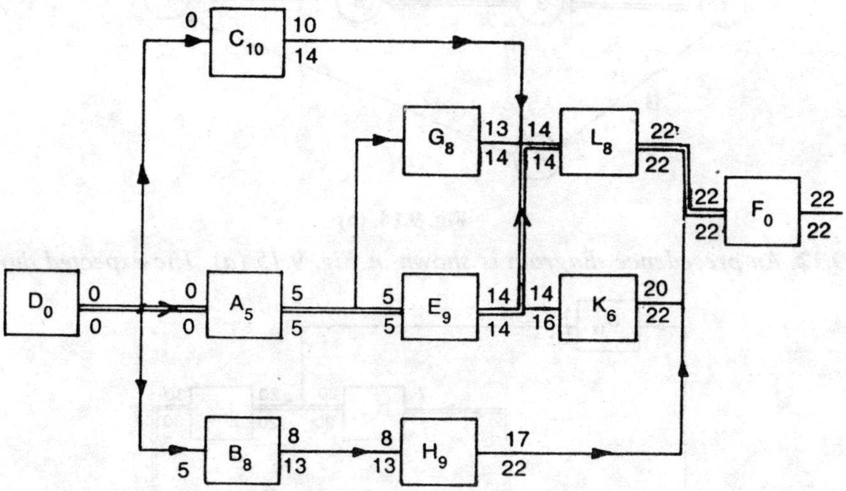

Fig. 9.14. (*a*)

2. *Critical path and project duration.*

3. *Draw the A-O-A diagram for the given A-O-N diagram.*

Solution. The activity times EST, EFT, LST and LFT and total float for each activity for the above net work are tabulated in the table 9.5. below.

Table 9.5.

			L_1	R_1	L_2	R_2		
Activity name	*Activity i-j*	*Activity duration* t^{ij}	*Earliest start time EST*	*Earliest Finish time EFT*	*Latest start time LST*	*Latest finish time LFT*	*Total Float*	*Remark*
Do	0	0	0	0	0	0	0	Critical
A	1 – 3	5	0	5	5	5	0	Critical
B	1 – 4	8	0	8	4	13	5	
C	1 – 2	10	0	10	5	14	4	
E	3 – 5	9	5	14	6	14	0	Critical
G	3 – 6	8	5	13	13	14	1	
H	4 – 7	9	8	17	16	22	5	
K	5 – 7	6	14	20	14	22	2	
L	6 – 7	8	14	22	22	22	0	Critical
Fo		0	22	22		22	0	Critical

Do-A-E-L-Fo are critical

Hence critical path is along Do-A-E-L-Fo

Total duration of project = 22 days.

The net work in A-O-A system will be as shown in Fig. 9.14 (*b*)

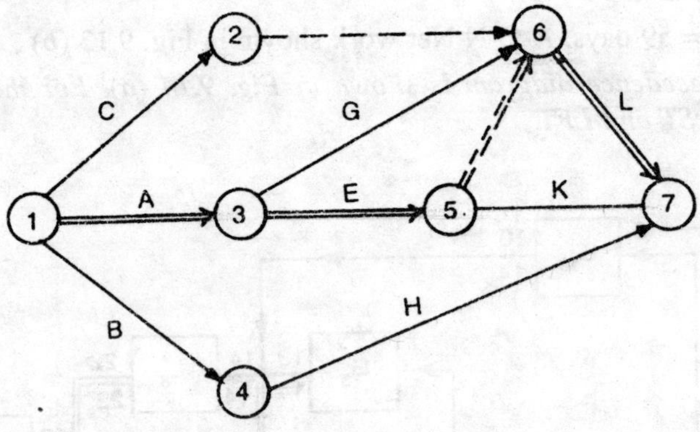

Fig. 9.14. (*b*)

Example 9.12. *An precedence diagram is shown in Fig. 9.15 (a). The expected duration is shown on*

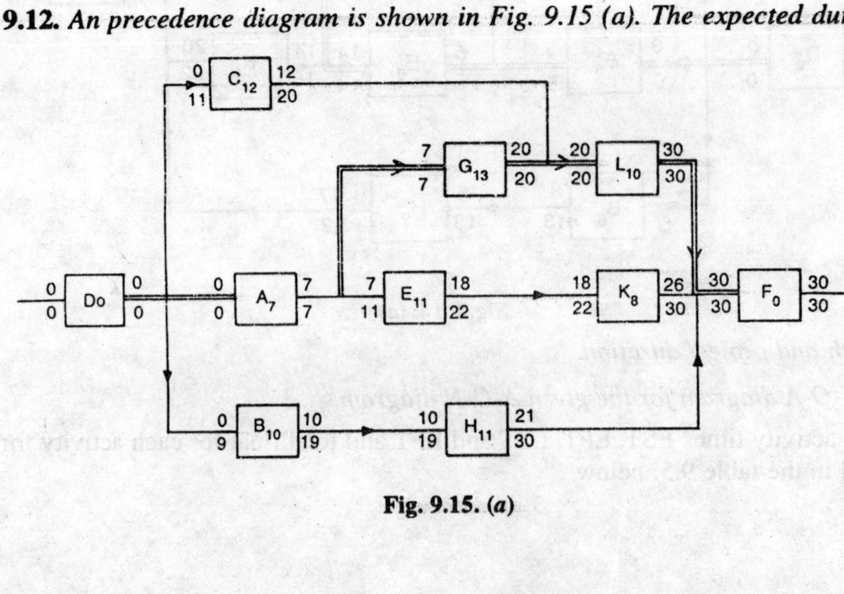

Fig. 9.15. (*a*)

the diagram. From this diagram determine the followings:

(i) Activity times i.e. EST, EFT, LST and LFT and total float.

(ii) Critical path and project duration.

(iii) Draw the A-O-A diagram of the given precedence diagram.

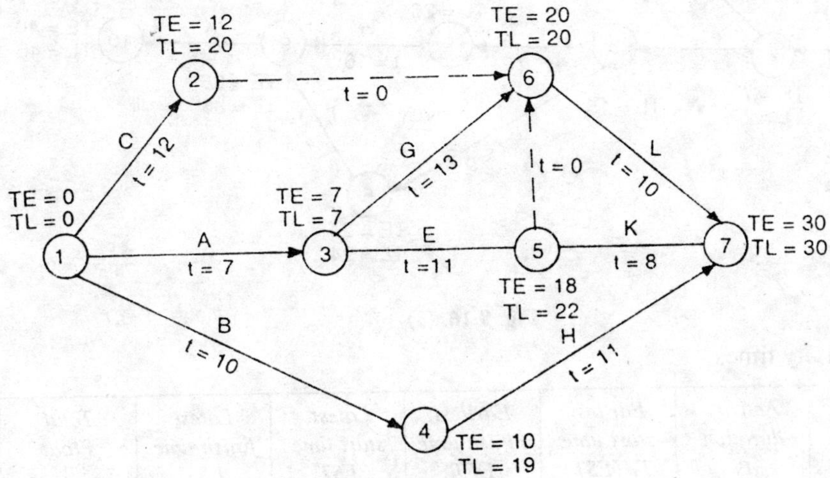

Fig. 9.15. (*b*)

Solution. The activity times and total float are shown in tabular from below in Table 9.6.

Table 9.6.

			L_1	R_1	L_2	R_2		
Activity name	*Activity i-j No.*	*Activity time t^{ij}*	*Earliest start time EST (T_E^i)*	*Earliest Finish time EFT ($T_E^i + t^{ij}$)*	*Latest start time LST*	*Latest finish time LFT (T_L of head event)*	*Total Float*	*Remark*
Do	–	–	0	0	0	0	–	
A	1 – 3	7	0	7	0	7	0	Critical
B	1 – 4	10	0	10	9	19	9	
C	1 – 2	12	0	12	8	20	8	
E	3 – 5	11	7	18	11	22	4	
G	3 – 6	13	7	20	7	20	0	Critical
H	4 – 7	11	10	21	19	30	9	
K	5 – 7	8	18	26	22	30	4	
L	6 – 7	10	20	30	20	30	0	Critical
Fo								

Critical path is 1-3-6-7- or A-G-L. Fig. 9.15 (*b*)

Project duration = 30 days.

Example 9.13. *The net work of a project is shown in Fig. 9.16. The estimated duration of each activity is shown on the Fig. itself. Determine the following and also draw the A-O-N diagram.*

1. *Earliest and latest activity time.*
2. *Total float for each activity.*
3. *Critical path for the net work.*

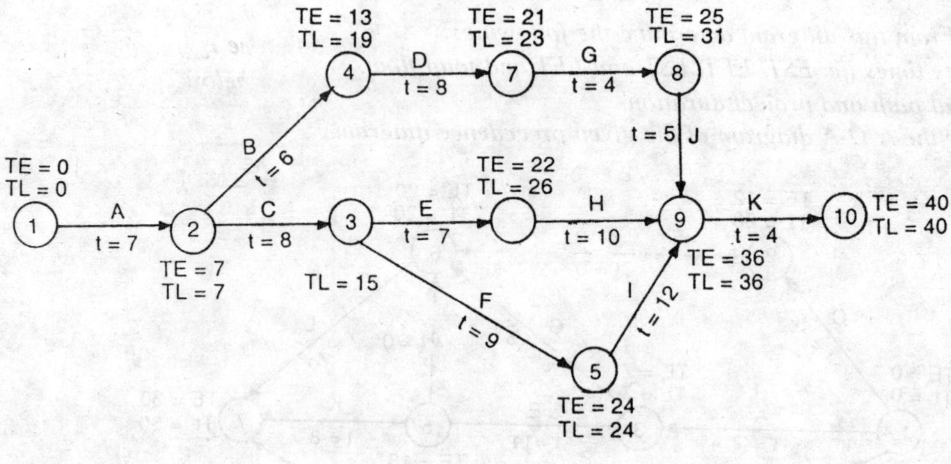

Fig. 9.16. (*a*)

Solution. (*a*) Activity times

Activity Name	*Activity i-j*	*Activity duration* t_E	*Earliest start time* T_E *(EST)*	*Earliest Finish time EFT*	*Latest start time LST*	*Latest finish time LFT*	*Total Float*	*Remark*
A	1 – 2	7	0	7	0	7	0	Critical
B	2 – 4	6	7	13	13	19	6	
C	2 – 3	8	7	15	7	15	0	Critical
D	4 – 7	8	13	21	19	27	6	
E	3 – 6	7	15	22	19	26	4	
F	3 – 5	9	15	24	15	24	0	Critical
G	7 – 8	4	21	25	28	32	7	
H	6 – 9	10	22	32	26	36	4	
I	5 – 9	12	24	36	24	36	0	Critical
J	8 – 9	5	25	30	31	36	6	
K	9 – 10	4	36	40	36	40	0	Critical

Critical path 1-2-3-5-9-10 or A-C-F-I-K

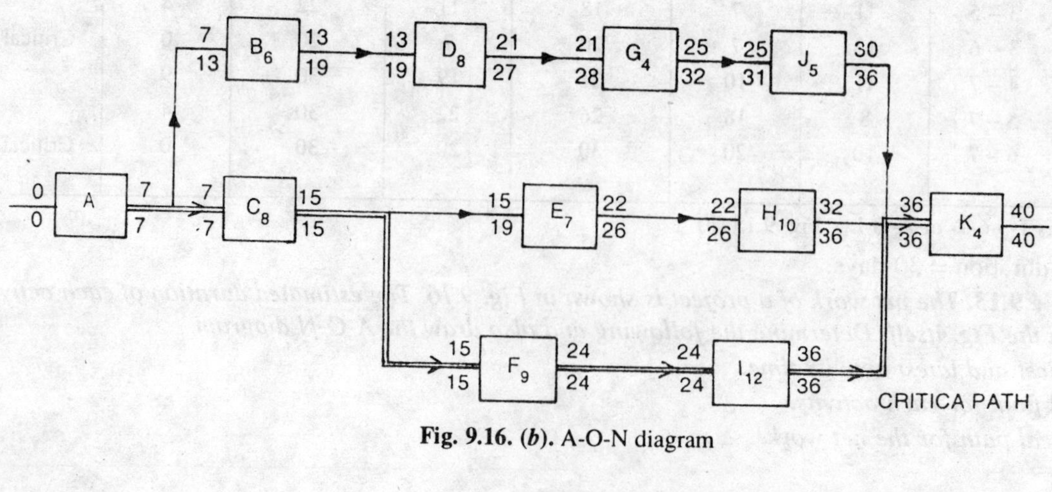

Fig. 9.16. (*b*). A-O-N diagram

Example 14. *The three time estimates optimistic time t_o, most likely time t_L and pessimistic time t_p of each activity together with the predecessors of a building project are given below:*

Job description		*Predecessor*	*Three time estimates*		
			t_o	t_l	t_p
A	Foundation	–	5	6	11
B	Frame and roof	A	5	7	15
C	Brick work including window frame.	B	6	8	12
D	Door frames	B	1	2	3
E	Plumbing and wiring	C	4	5	7
F	Plastering	E	4	6	11
G	Doors and window panes	C, D	3	4	6
H	Flooring	C, D	2	3	5
I	Finishing	F, G, H	5	7	10
J	Land scaping	I	2	3	5

(*i*) Draw the diagram and determine the expected duration, variance and standard deviation of the project.

(*ii*) Draw the A-O-N diagram also. [UPSC, Civil Services, 1985]

Solution. The net work of the project is drawn as shown in Fig.9.17.

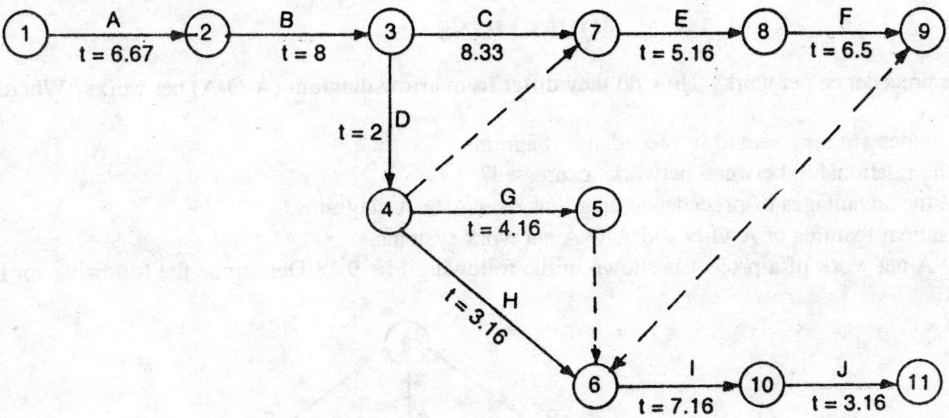

Fig. 9.17 (*a*).

Table

Activity	*Optimistic time t_o*	*Most likely time t_L*	*Pessimistic time t_p*	*Expected time* $t_E = \frac{t_o + 4t_e + t_p}{6}$	*Variance* $\sigma^2 = \left(\frac{t_p - t_o}{6}\right)^2$	*Standard deviation* $\sigma = \left(\frac{t_p - t_o}{6}\right)$
A	5	6	11	6.67	1	1
B	5	7	15	8	2.78	1.66
C	6	8	12	8.33	1.0	1.0
D	1	2	3	2	0.111	0.33
E	4	5	7	5.16	0.25	0.5
F	4	6	11	6.5	1.36	1.16
G	3	4	6	4.16	0.25	0.5
H	2	3	5	3.16	0.25	0.5
I	5	7	10	7.16	0.70	0.833
J	2	3	5	3.16	0.25	0.5

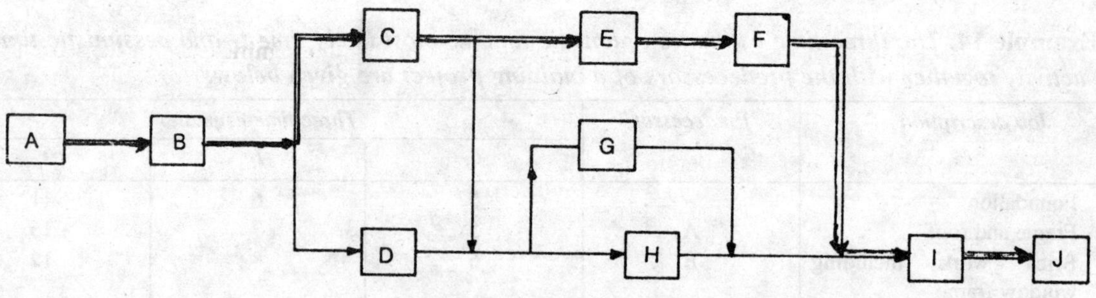

Fig. 9.17 (*b*). A-O-N diagram

Critical path is A-B-C-E, F, I-J.

Critical path is A-B-C-E, F, I-J.

Total variation of the project along the critical path = $\Sigma \sigma^2$

$$= 1.0 + 2.78 + 1.0 + 0.25 + 1.36 + 0.95 = 7.34$$

$\therefore$ Standard deviation $\sigma = \sqrt{7.34} = 2.7$

The expected time of project = 45 days

Variance of the project along critical path = 7.34
Standard deviation of the project = 2.7
Duration of the project = 45 Days. **Ans.**

QUESTIONS

1. What are precedence net works. How do they differ from arrow diagram (A-O-A) net works? Where they are used?
2. How the nodes are represented in precedence diagrams.
3. How is the relationship between networks expressed?
4. What are the advantages of precedence diagrams over A-O-A diagrams.
5. Discuss salient features of A-O-N and A-O-A net work systems.
6. The A-O-A net work of a project is shown in the following Fig. 9.18 Determine the following for the given net work.

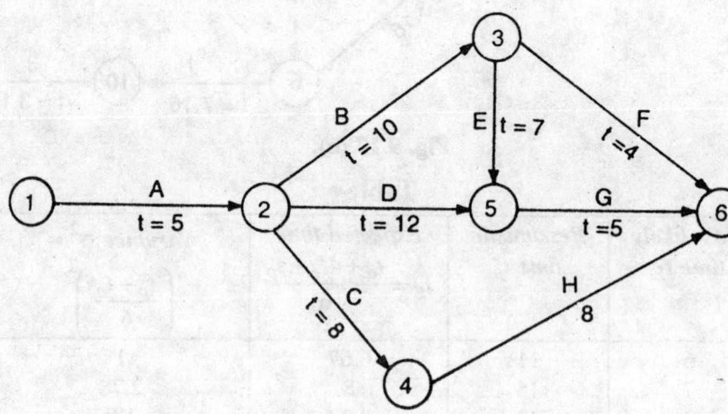

Fig. 9.18.

(*a*) Earliest and latest activities times *i.e.* EST, EFT, LST and LFT.
(*b*) Total float for each activity.
(*c*) Critical path and duration of the project. Also draw the A-O-N diagram of the given net work.

7. (*a*) With the help of suitable diagram compare and contrast activity on the arrow net works with the activity on the node (A-O-N) net works.

(*b*) What are the main advantages of activity on the node net works over activity on the arrow net works?
(*c*) What is the difference between total float and free float? Explain the significance of each term.
[UPSE Engg. Services 1999]

OBJECTIVE TYPE QUESTIONS

1. Precedence net works are best suited in the situations when:
   (*a*) Arrow based (A-O-A) net works are to be avoided
   (*b*) There are large number of overlapping activities in the project
   (*c*) The project is to be executed efficiently
   (*d*) There are many critical activities
2. Float calculations in A-O-N net work system is
   (*a*) Same as that in A-O-A system (*b*) Different that of A-O-A system
   (*c*) Involves complicated procedure (*d*) Dependent on backward pass computations
3. Identify the correct statement of the following:
   (*a*) A precedence net-work does not contain any dummy activity
   (*b*) A precedence net-work contains many dummy activities
   (*c*) It contains many parallel activities
   (*d*) It contains many serial activities
4. Identify the correct statement of the followings
   (*a*) All activity times such EST, EFT, LST and LFT are written on the diagram itself in A-O-N net diagram.
   (*b*) No activity times are written on the A-O-N net works
   (*c*) All activity times are written on the A-O-A system of net works
   (*d*) All of the above are correct
5. Identify the incorrect statement of the followings:
   (*a*) Precedence net works are self sufficient and useful for projects having large over lapping activities
   (*b*) A-O-A system of net work was the first in CPM system and is most popular method
   (*c*) It is easy to write a computer program of A-O-A net work. Hence it is easy to use for very complex projects
   (*d*) Precedence net work system is very efficient and used for the projects having large number of dummy activities.
6. Identify the correct statement/statements of the followings
   (*a*) Total float is the difference of latest finish time and earliest finish time of a activity
   (*b*) Total float is the difference of earliest finish time and latest start time
   (*c*) Total float is the difference of earliest finish time and latest finish time
   (*d*) All are correct

ANSWERS

1. (*b*)	3. (*a*)	5. (*d*)
2. (*a*)	4. (*a*)	6. (*a*)

Ans. Q. 6.

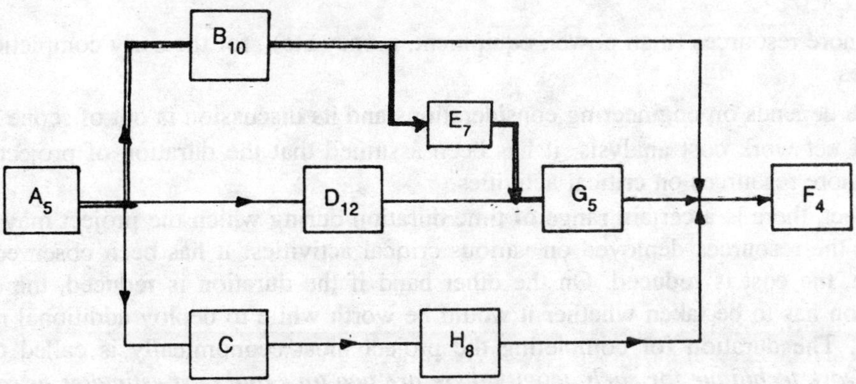

Critical Path is
A-B-E-G-F. (1-2-3-5-6)
Duration = 27 Days

Fig. 9.19.

10
Cost Control

10.1. INTRODUCTION

Since the introduction of net work analysis around 1957, the net work planning and critical path analysis has provided powerful tool to project managers. The ultimate object of the net work technique is not only to bring improvement in planning, scheduling and control of the project or to estimation of project duration or to determine the critical duration of the project, but to explore the possibility of establishing feasible and desirable relationship between the duration and cost of the project. In the execution of projects, some times situation arises to reduce the total duration, such as in war time repair of air field road work needs earliest repair and cost is no criteria. As a matter of fact the policy of every organisation is to reduce the target time, so that the time saved may be utilised some where else to get additional production. The reduction in time will require additional deployment of resources such as additional manpower, equipment and money etc., which will increase the project cost. The overall project duration can be reduced by reducing the duration of only critical activities in the project net work by C.P.M. analysis.

Thus the object of CPM net work analysis is to develop an optimum time-cost-relationship. As stated above many a times it becomes necessary to complete the project earlier than the normal time duration. In such cases the cost of expediting the activities has to be taken into account. Thus CPM net work analysis makes use of the cost estimate along with the time estimate and provides a schedule for completing the activities at the total minimum cost.

10.2. METHODS OF REDUCING DURATION OF ACTIVITIES

The duration of activities can be reduced by the following two methods:

1. By relaxing the technical specifications for critical activities which control the duration of the project.
2. By deploying more resources (man power, equipment, money etc)., for the early completion of the critical activities.

The first alternative depends on engineering considerations and its discussion is out of scope here.

In the whole CPM net work cost analysis, it has been assumed that the duration of project may be reduced by deploying more resources on critical activities.

For any given project, there is a certain range of time duration during which the project may be completed depending upon the resources deployed on various critical activities. It has been observed that by increasing the duration, the cost is reduced. On the other hand if the duration is reduced, the cost will increase. Thus a decision has to be taken whether it would be worth while to deploy additional resources to reduce the duration. The duration for completing the project most economically is called *Optimum duration. In CPM net work technique for each activity there are two time and cost estimates as follows:*

(*a*) *Normal estimate.* In this estimate emphasis is laid on cost, time being associated with minimum cost.

(*b*) *Crash estimate.* In this estimate the emphasis is given to absolute minimum time required to complete the job. The necessary cost to complete the project with in the minimum time is provided. Here the emphasis is on time. The cost is secondary as in the case of repair of air field run ways during war time.

10.3. PROJECT COST

For any project total expenditure incurred in terms of man power, equipment, machinery and materials and time to achieve a particular goal is known as total cost of the project. The total cost of a project is the sum of two distinct costs.

1. Direct cost 2. Indirect cost

The components of the total cost are as shown below

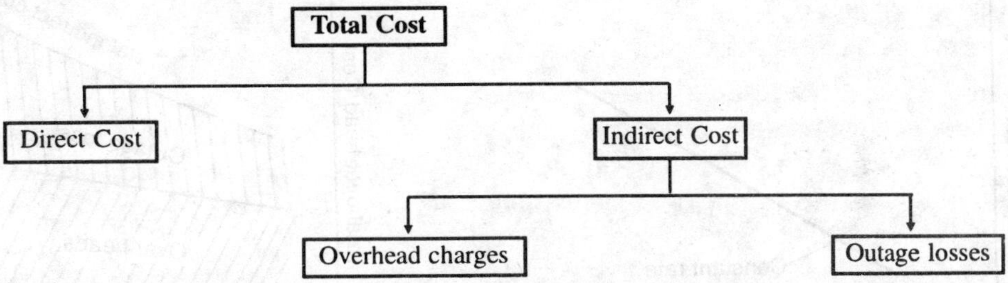

10.3.1. Direct cost

The cost of materials, equipment and money spent on man power form the direct cost. The direct costs of project are of major concern and the behaviour pattern of direct costs with time is of importance.

The direct costs of a project depend on the completion time of the project, but the variation is not linear. Normally for any project there is an optimum duration for which the direct cost is minimum. During this time duration the resources are used optimally. Usually this duration is called *normal duration.*

If needed, the duration of a project can be reduced below the normal duration, but it needs to deploy additional resources. The deployment of additional resources increases the direct cost of the project. A typical curve between direct cost and time duration is shown in Fig. 10.1. It can be seen from the figure that the direct cost increases if either the time is decreased or increased beyond the normal duration. The curve has the following characteristics.

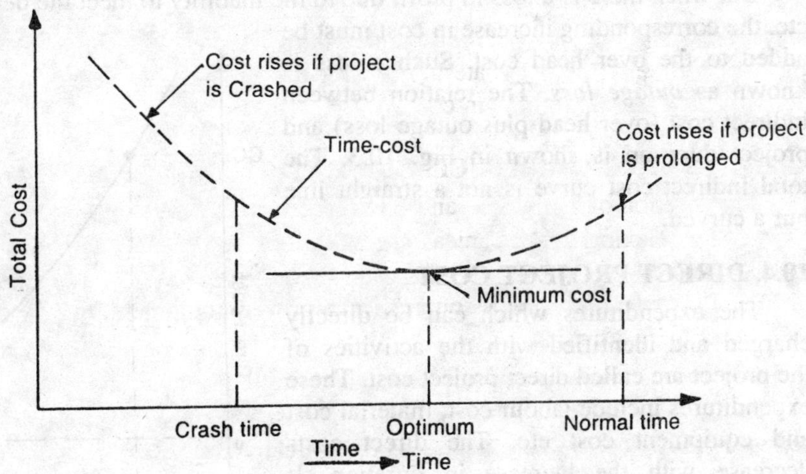

Fig. 10.1. Variation of total cost with time

1. The direct cost of the project is minimum at some optimum project duration (normal duration).
2. The direct cost increases on either side of the optimum (normal) duration, but at a steady rate on the higher side of the normal duration.

3. There is a point beyond which the project duration can not be reduced irrespective of the increase in direct cost. This duration is known as *crash duration* and the corresponding cost is known as *crash cost.*

10.3.2. Indirect Cost

The expenditures which can not be allotted clearly to the individual activities of the project, but are assessed as a whole are called indirect costs. The indirect cost includes over head charges, administrative and establishment charges, supervision charges, expenditure on a central store organisation, loss of revenue, loss in profit and penalty etc.

The indirect cost is directly proportional to the increase in duration. For any project the relation between the indirect cost and duration of the project is shown in Fig. 10.2.

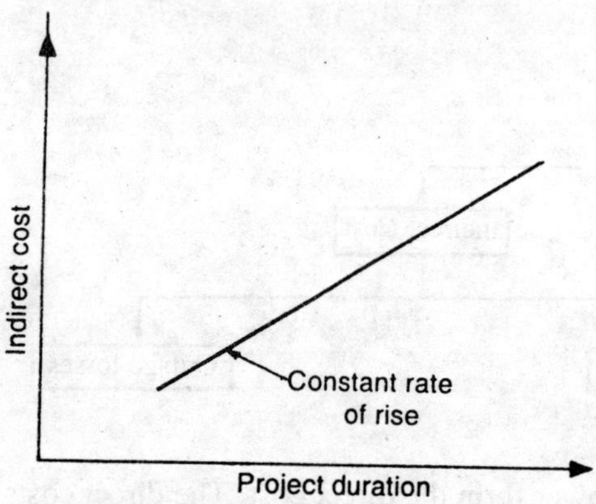

Fig. 10.2. Indirect cost (Supervisory and over head charges)

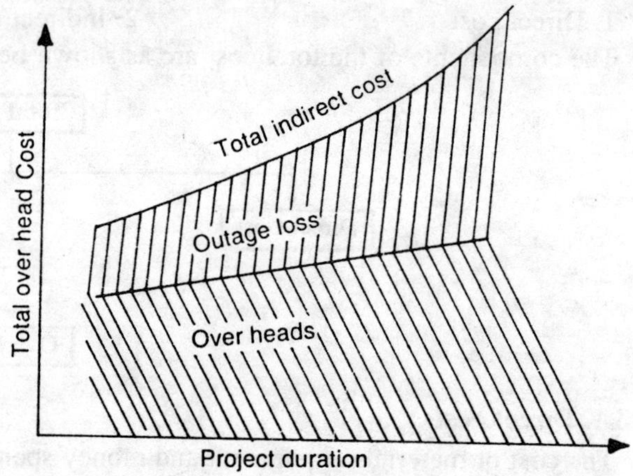

Fig. 10.3 Variation in indirect cost with duration

But when there is a loss in profit due to the inability to meet the demand or due to penalty due to delay etc. the corresponding increase in cost must be added to the over head cost. Such a loss is known as *ouage loss*. The relation between indirect cost (over head plus outage loss) and project duration is shown in Fig. 10.3. The total indirect cost curve is not a straight line but a curved.

10.4. DIRECT PROJECT COST

The expenditures which can be directly charged and identified with the activities of the project are called direct project cost. These expenditures include labour cost, material cost and equipment cost etc. The direct costs decrease with the increase in duration. It means that direct costs of a project are inversely proportional with duration, where as total indirect cost curve rises with the increase in duration. A generalised curve between the cost and duration of a project is shown in Fig. 10.4.

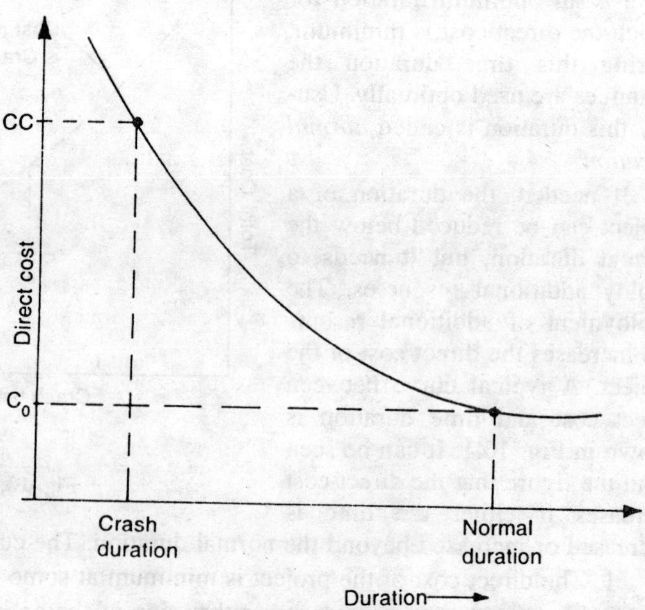

Fig. 10.4. Generalised direct cost time curve

10.5. DEFINITIONS

1. **Normal time.** The time usually allowed for an activity by the estimator is known as normal time. It is the standard time for that activity and is denoted by (t_n).
2. **Crash time.** The minimum possible time in which an activity can be completed by deploying extra resources is known as *crash time.* Beyond the crash time the duration of any activity can not be reduced or shortened by any amount of increase in the resources mobilisation. It is denoted by (t_c).
3. **Normal cost.** The direct cost required to complete the activity in the normal duration is called *Normal cost.* It is denoted by (c_n).
4. **Crash cost.** The direct cost corresponding to the crash time of completing an activity is known as *crash cost.* It is denoted (c_c).
5. **Cost slope.** The direct cost curve generally is a curve as shown in Fig. 10.4. But this curve can be approximated by a straight line or more than one straight lines depending upon the flatness of the curve. Thus the slope of this straight line is known as *Cost slope*. The cost slope is very helpful in carrying out the cost analysis. In mathematical terms it is defined as follows:

$$\text{Cost slope} = \frac{\text{crash cost} - \text{normal cost}}{\text{normal time} - \text{crash time}}$$

or

$$CS = \frac{C_c - C_n}{t_n - t_c} \quad \ldots(10.1)$$

where C_S = Cost slope.

The single or multiple cost slope will depend upon the non linearlity of the direct cost curve. Though multiple cost slope is more accurate but complicated in calculations. Thus usually single cost slope is assumed.

6. **Minimum Duration.** The duration obtained after crasning all activities is known as *minimum duration.*

10.6. TOTAL COST OF THE PROJECT

The sum of direct costs and indirect costs is known as total cost of the project. The relationship between indirect costs, direct costs and total cost with duration is shown in Fig. 10.5. From Fig. 10.5 it will be seen that the curve of direct costs does not have a linear relationship with time. Thus the combination of direct and indirect costs gives a curvilinear relationship with time as shown in Fig. 10.5.

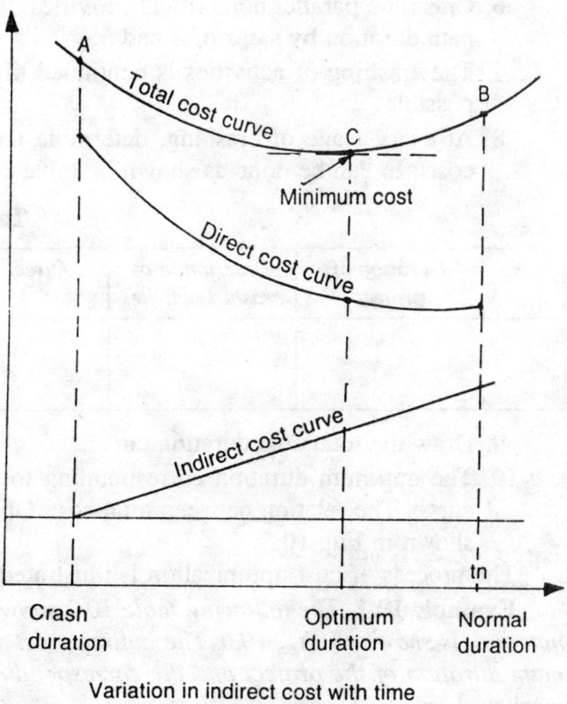

Fig. 10.5. Total cost curve

From the total cost curve ACB, it can be seen that the total cost of the project is minimum for a certain time duration. This duration is known as optimum duration for the minimum cost. Further if the project duration is increased, the total cost will also increase. On the other hand if the project duration is decreased to the crash value, the project cost will be the highest. The optimum duration is less than the normal duration corresponding to the direct costs. This is due to the fact that both direct and indirect costs increase beyond the normal duration, where as below the normal duration the indirect cost decrease, but the direct cost increases.

10.7. COST OPTIMIZATION THROUGH NET-WORK

For cost optimizing, after establishing the critical path corresponding to the given duration of activities, the optimum duration and minimum cost necessary for the completion of the project is determined. For determining the optimum duration and minimum cost, it is necessary to know the normal direct cost for the activity to be completed in normal duration and the crashed direct cost if that activity is to be expedited. From this data the cost slope for each activity is determined, assuming the straight line approximation for the cost slope. Further to know the total cost of the project, the indirect cot of the project incurred per unit time should be known.

The normal duration of completion of a project will be the sum of normal time duration of each critical activity. Similarly the crash time of completion of project will be the sum of crash time duration of all critical activities. Crashing of all activities will lead to a very high cost with out any advantage that can be obtained by crashing only the critical activities. Hence non critical activities should not be crashed.

10.8. STEPS IN OPTIMIZATION OF COST

1. Analyse the past record and establish a direct cost and time relationship for various activities of the project *i.e.* draw a graph between the cost and time for different activities of the project.
2. Determine the cost slope for various activities and arrange them in ascending order of cost slope.
3. Compute the direct cost for the net work with normal duration of activities.
4. Crash the activities in the critical path, starting with the critical activity having least cost slope.
5. Continue the crashing of critical activities in the ascending order of the cost slope.
6. Crash the parallel non critical activities which have become critical due to the reduction of critical path duration by steps of 4 and 5.
7. The crashing of activities is continued till a stage is reached beyond which no further crashing is possible.
8. At every stage of crashing, determine the total cost of the project by adding indirect and direct costs. In can be done as shown in Table 10.1 shown below.

Table 10.1.

S. No.	*Duration of project*	*Description of crashed activites*	*Direct cost*	*Indirect cost*	*Total cost*	*Remark*

9. Draw the total cost duration curve.
10. The optimum duration corresponding to the minimum total cost of project is obtained from the curve. The relation between total cost. Optimum cost, optimum duration, direct and indirect cost is shown in Fig. 10.5.

The process of cost optimization is illustrated with the help of the following examples.

Example 10.1. *The following table 10.2 shows the costs and duration of each activity of a project. The net work is shown in Fig. 10.6. The indirect cost may be taken as Rs. 3150/- per week. Determine the optimum duration of the project and the corresponding minimum cost. Draw the time scale version of the net work.*

Table 10.2.

Activity	*Normal duration*	*Normal cost*	*Crash duration*	*Crash cost*
A (1 – 2)	7	8000	4	15,500
B (1 – 3)	9	5000	6	9,500

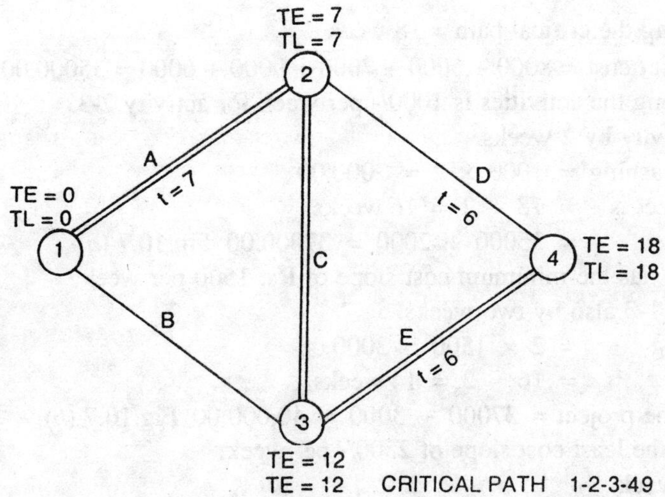

Fig. 10.6.

Activity	*Normal duration*	*Normal cost*	*Crash duration*	*Crash cost*
C (2 – 3)	5	7000	2	10,000
D (2 – 4)	6	9000	4	16,000
E (3 – 4)	6	6000	4	12,000

Time Scaled version shown in Fig. 10.7.

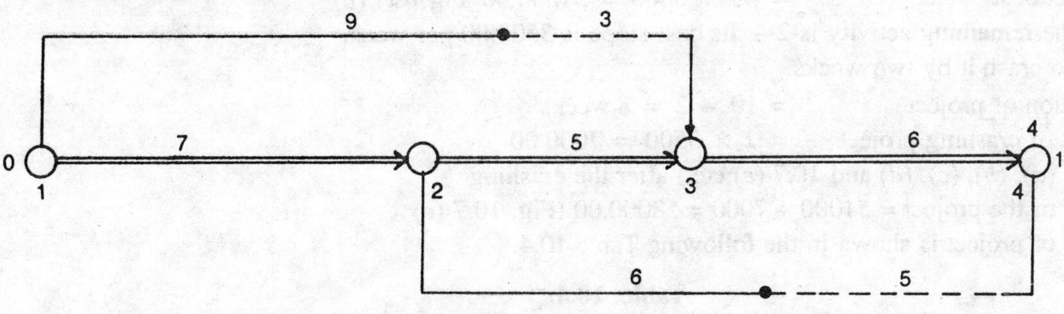

Fig. 10.7. Time version of project

Critical path is 1-2-3-4
Duration of project = 18 weeks.
Solution.

Table 10.3. Cost slope

S. No.	*Activity*	*Difference in crash and normal cost* Δ_c	*Difference in crash and normal duration* Δ_t	*Cost slpoe per week*
1.	1 – 2	15,500 – 8,000 = 7,500	7 – 4 = 3	2,500
2.	1 – 3	9,500 – 5,000 = 4,500	9 – 6 = 3	15,000
3.	2 – 3	10,000 – 7,000 = 3,000	5 – 2 = 3	1,000
4.	2 – 4	16,000 – 9,000 = 7,000	6 – 4 = 2	3,500
5.	3 – 4	12,000 – 6,000 = 6,000	6 – 4 = 2	3,000

Normal duration along the critical path = 18 week.

Normal duration direct cost = 8000 + 5000 + 7000 + 9000 + 6000 = 35000.00

Least cost slope among the activities is 1000/- per week for activity 2-3.

Let us crash this activity by 2 weeks.

Then extra cost of crashing = 1000 × 2 = 2000.00

The duration of project is = 18 − 2 = 16 weeks

Total direct cost = 35000 + 2000 = 37000.00 Fig.10.7 (*a*)

Next the activity 1-3 has the minimum cost slope of Rs. 1500 per week.

Let us crash activity 1-3 also by two weeks.

Extra cost of crashing = 2 × 1500 = 3000.00

Duration of project = 16 − 2 = 14 weeks

Total direct cost of the project = 37000 + 3000 = 40,000.00 Fig.10.7 (*b*)

Step 6. Activity 1-2 has the least cost slope of 2500/- per week.

Let crash it by two week.

Extra cost of crashing the project = 2 × 2500 = 5000.00

Duration of project = 14 − 2 = 12 weeks

Total direct cost of project = 40,000 + 5,000 = 45,000.00 Fig.10.7 (*c*)

Step 7. Activity 3-4 has the next lower cost slope of 3000/- per week

Let us crash it also by two weeks.

Extra cost of crashing the project = 3000 × 2 = 6000.00

Duration of project = 12 − 2 = 10

Total direct cost = 45 + 6000 = 51000.00 Fig.10.7 (*d*)

Step 8. Last the remaining activity is 2-4. Its cost slope is 3500.00 per week.

Let us also crash it by two weeks.

then duration of project = 10 − 2 = 8 weeks

Extra cost of crashing project = 2 × 3500 = 7000.00

(Fig. 10.7 (*a*), (*b*), (*c*), (*d*) and 10.7 (*e*) etc.) after the crashing

Total cost of the project = 51000 + 7000 = 58000.00 (Fig. 10.7 (*e*)

Total cost of project is shown in the following Table 10.4.

Table. 10.4.

Project duration weeks →	18	16	14	12	10	8
Direct cost	35000	37000	40000	45000	51000	58000
Indirect cost	47700	50400	44100	37800	31500	25200
Total cost	82700	87400	84100	82800	82500	83200

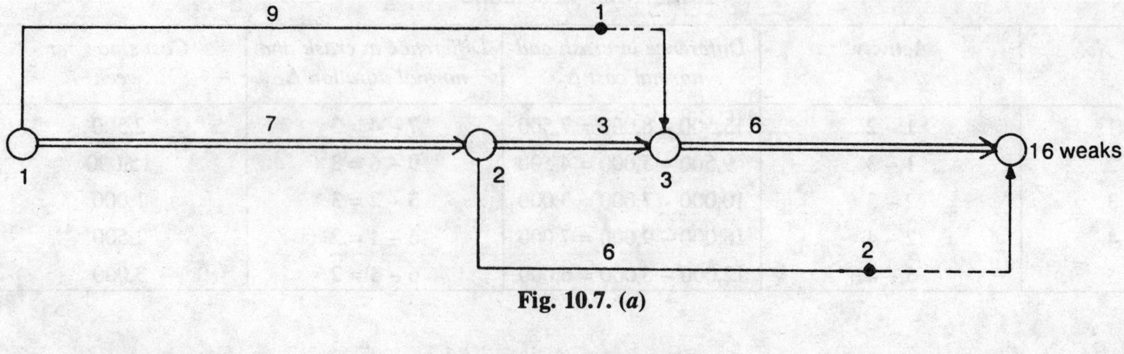

Fig. 10.7. (*a*)

After crashing beyond 10 weeks, the cost of project again increase.

Hence the optimum duration of the project is 10 weeks

The corresponding total cost of project = **Rs. 82500/-**

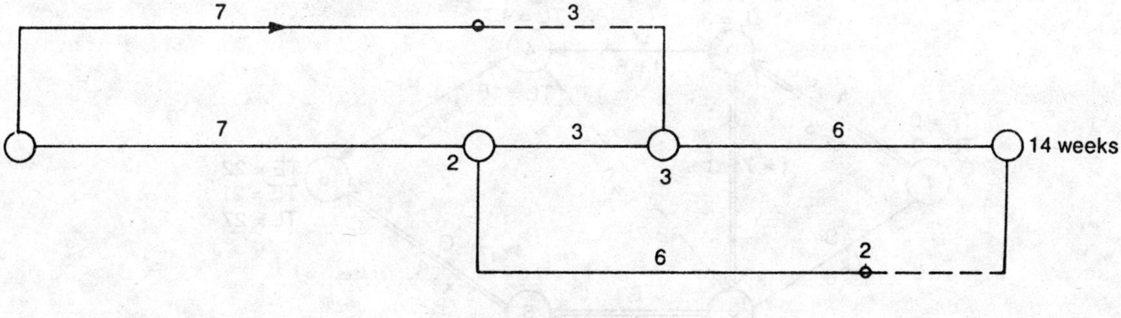

Fig. 10.7. (*b*)

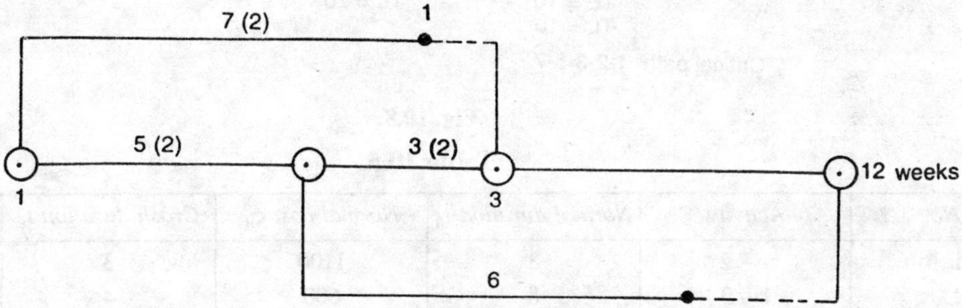

Fig. 10.7. (*c*)

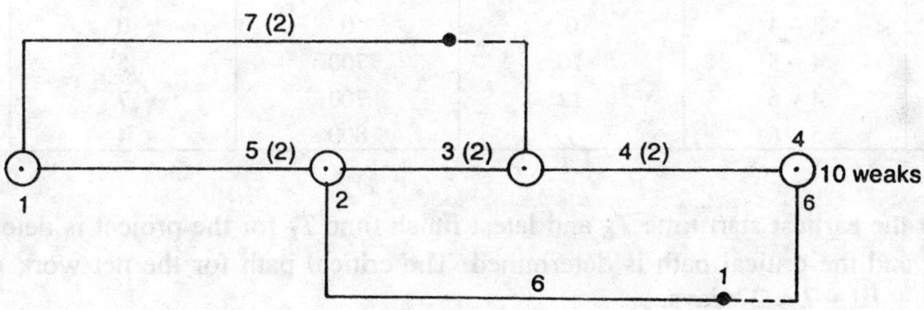

Fig. 10.7. (*d*)

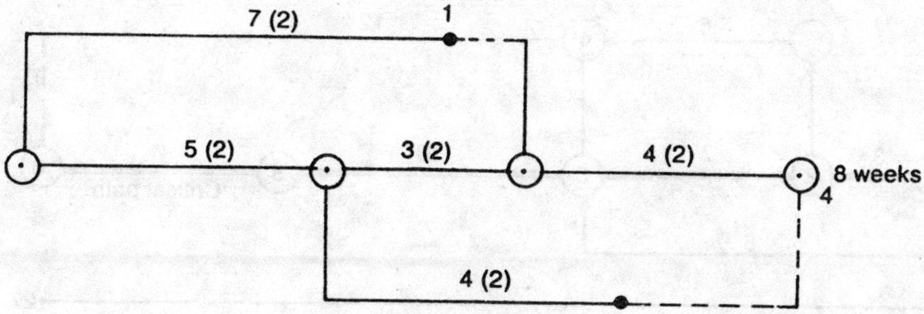

Fig. 10.7. (*e*)

Example 10.2. *The net work of a project is shown in Fig. 10.8. The data for the project is shown in the table 10.5. below. Determine the minimum cost and optimum duration for the project net work. Indirect cost is Rs. 100 per day.*

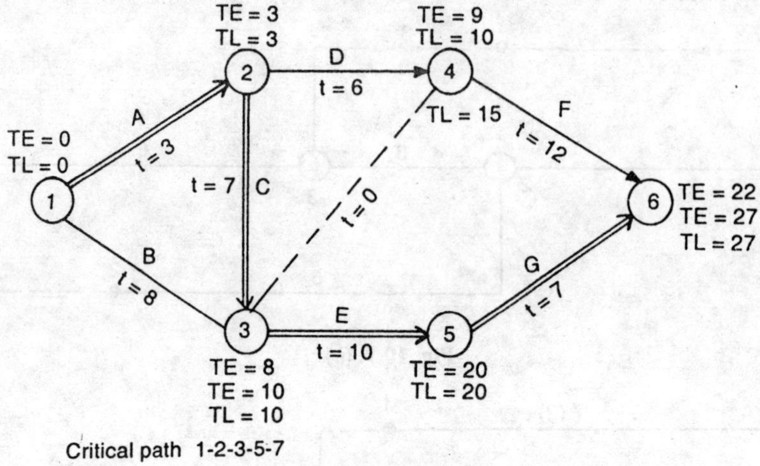

Fig. 10.8.

Table 10.5.

S. No.	*Activity*	*Normal duration t_n*	*Normal cost c_n*	*Crash duration t_c*	*Crash cost c_c*
1.	1 – 2	3	1100	3	1100
2.	1 – 3	8	600	4	1000
3.	2 – 3	7	400	4	580
4.	2 – 4	6	300	5	365
5.	3 – 4	0	0	0	0
6.	4 – 5	10	700	5	1050
7.	4 – 6	12	700	7	1100
8.	5 – 6	7	800	4	1055

Solution.

Step 1. First the earliest start time T_E and latest finish time T_L for the project is determined as shown on the net work and the critical path is determined. The critical path for the net work is 1-2-3-5-6. The duration is 3 + 7 + 10 + 7 = 27 days.

Step 2. The time scaled version of the net work is drawn, keeping the critical path horizontal. Fig. 18.9.

Step 3. Determine the cost slope as follows:

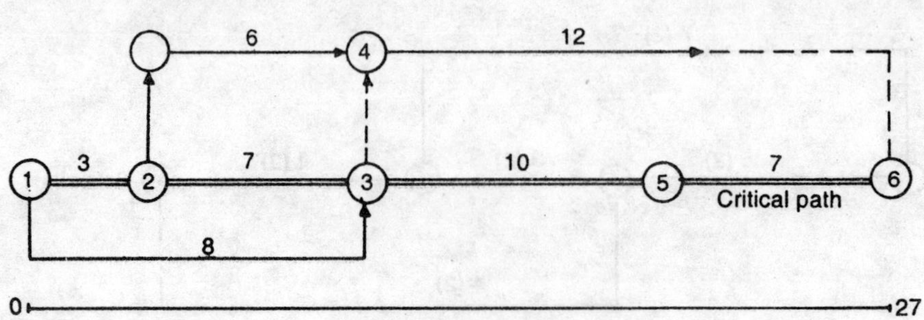

Fig. 10.9. Time scale version

Table 10.6. Cost slope

S. No.	*Activities*	*Difference in crash and normal cost as Δ_c (Rs.)*	*Difference in normal and crash duration Δ_t*	*Cost slope (Rs/days)*
1.	1 – 2	1100 – 1100 = 0	3 – 3 = 0	–
2.	1 – 3	1000 – 600 = 400	8 – 4 = 4	400/4 = 100
3.	2 – 3	580 – 400 = 180	7 – 4 = 3	180/3 = 60
4.	2 – 4	365 – 300 = 65	6 – 5 = 1	65/1 = 65
5.	3 – 4	0 – 0 = 0	0 – 0 = 0	0 = 0
6.	3 – 5	1050 – 700 = 350	10 – 5 = 5	350/5 = 70
7.	4 – 6	1100 – 700 = 400	12 – 7 = 5	400/5 = 80
8.	5 – 6	1055 – 800 = 255	7 – 4 = 3	255/3 = 85

Step 4. Determine the direct cost of normal duration of the project.

Normal duration of the project along the critical path = 3 + 7 + 10 + 7 = 27 days

Thus direct cost of project = 1100 + 400 + 700 + 800 = 3000.00

Step 5. First stage of crashing.

Choose the minimum cost slope and arrange them in ascending order. In this case minimum cost slope is of activity 2-3. Its value is 60. Let us crash it by 2 days in the 1st stage.

New duration of the project is 25 days.

Extra cost of crashing activity 2-3 for 2 days = 2 × 60 = 120

∴ Total direct cost = 3000 + 120 = 3120/–

The time scale version is shown below Fig. 10.9 (*a*)

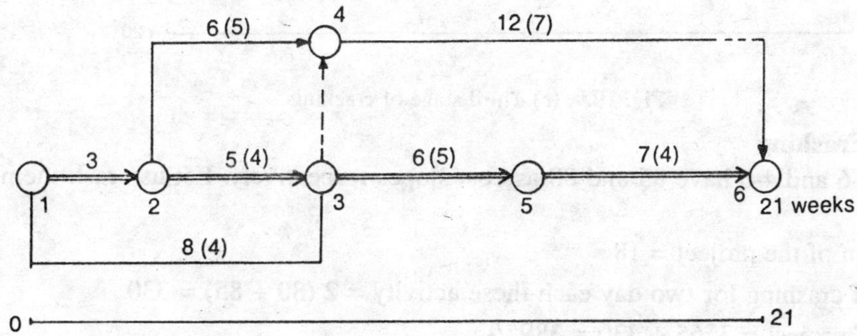

Fig. 10.9. (*a*) Second stage of crashing

Step 6. Second stage of crashing

After activity 2-3, the next lowest slope is for activity 3-5, which is equal to 70. Let us crash it by 4 days.

Now the duration of the project = 25 – 4 = 21 days

Extra cost of crashing activity 3-5 for 4 days = 4 × 70 = Rs. 280

Total direct cost = 3120 + 280 = 3400/–

The time scale version for 21 days is shown in Fig. 10.9 (*b*)

Step 7. Third stage of crashing. The activity 4-6 and 5-6 have cost slope as 80 and 85. Let us crash them by 1 day each.

Now the duration of project = 20 days

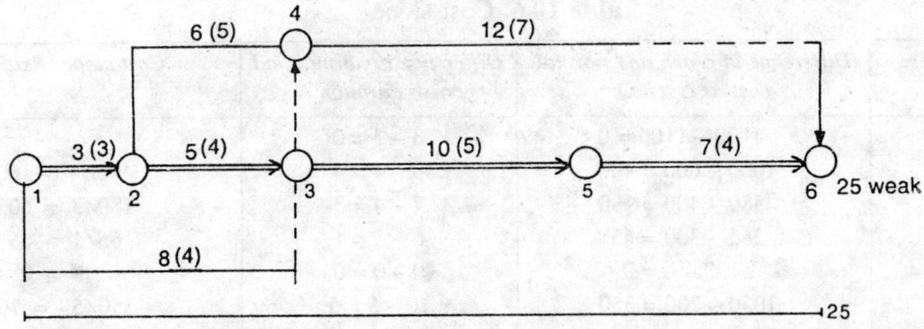

Fig. 10.9. (*b*) Stage of cracking

Extra cost of crashing activities 4-6 and 5-6 for 1 day = 1 × (80 + 85) = 165/–

Total direct cost of the project = 3400 + 165 = 3565/–

The time scale version of the project is shown in Fig. 10.9 (*c*).

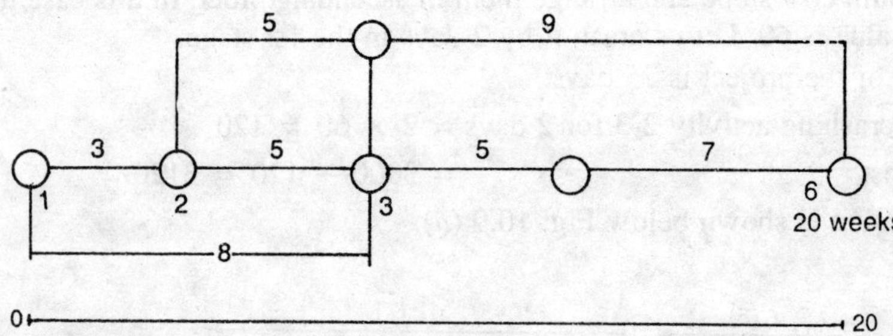

Fig. 10.9. (*c*) Third stage of cracking

Stage Four for crashing

Now activities 5-6 and 4-6 have 85 and 80 as cost slopes respectively. Let us crash them by two days each.

Now duration of the project = 18

Extra cost of crashing for two day each these activity = 2 (80 + 85) = 330

∴ Total cost of project = 3565 + 330 = 3895/-

The time scale version of project is shown in Fig. 10.9 (*d*)

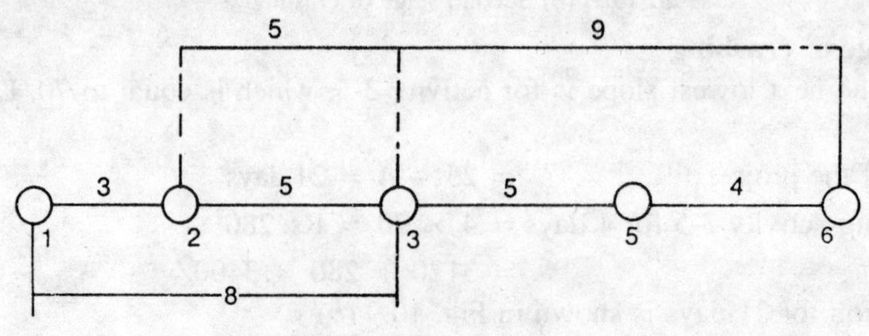

Fig. 10.9. (*d*) Four stage of cracking

Stage five for crashing

Activity 4-6 and 5-6 control the cost, let us crash them by 1 day further

Now duration of project = 17 days

Extra cost = 165/- days

Total cost of project = 3895 + 165 = 4060/-

Table 10.7.

Duration of project →	27	25	21	20	18	17
Direct cost	3000	3120	3400	3565	3895	4060
Indirect cost	2700	2500	2100	2000	1800	1700
Total cost	5700	5620	5500	5565	5695	5760

From the above table 10.7 the optimum project duration is 21 days.

Corresponding cost to the minimum duration is Rs. 5500/-

Further it will be seen that beyond optimum duration crashing further increases the cost.

10.9. LINEAR PROGRAMMING

Linear programming is a mathematical technique to determine the optional uses of an organization's resources. The word 'LINEAR' is used to describe the proportionate relationship of two or more variables. In other words linear refers to the assumption that the variables are linearly related to each other. The word 'PROGRAMMING' is used to specify a sort of planning that involves strategy from various alternative strategies or economic allocation to achieve the desired objective.

Linear programming deals with the maximising or minimising of an objective function subjected to some constraints in those situations where the objective functions and constraints can be described in terms of linear expressions.

10.10. CHARACTERISTICS OF A LINEAR PROGRAMMING PROBLEMS

The characteristics of a linear programming are as follows:

1. The activities are also known as decision variables such as $x_1, x_2, x_3 ... x_n$ etc. (All these variables are non negative).
2. There must be an objective function represented by a linear equation that is required to be maximised or minimised *i.e.*. A single objective optimization is an essential requirement.
3. There are always certain constraints (limitations) on the use of limited resources *i.e.* labour, machines, time and money etc.
4. There must be an alternative course of action represented by linear equations that the firm may decide to opt.

10.11. STANDARD FORM OF LINEAR PROGRAMMING

Let there be '*n*' decision variables and *m* constraints.

Let the decision variables be $x_1, x_2, x_3 \ldots x_n$ ...(10.2)

It is required to optimize (Maximize or minimize the values of $x_1, x_2 \ldots x_n$

i.e. Optimize $Z = c_1x_1 + c_2x_2 + c_3x_3 + \ldots c_n x_n$

where c_1, c_2, c_3 etc. are constraints subject to

$$a_{11}\, x_1 + a_{12}\, x_2 + a_{13}\, x_3 + \ldots a_{1n}x_n\ [\leq_r\ \approx\ r \geq]\ b_1$$

$$a_{21}\, x_1 + a_{22}\, x_2 + a_{23}\, x_3 + \ldots a_{2n}x_n\ [\leq_r\ \approx\ r \geq]\ b_2 \text{ constraints}$$

$$a_{m1}\, x_1 + a_{m2}\, x_2 + a_{m3}\, x_3 + \ldots a_{mm}x_n\ [\leq_r\ \approx\ r \geq]\ b_m$$

and $x_1, x_2, x_n > 0$ *i.e.* variables are non negative.

10.12. METHODS OF SOLVING LINEAR PROGRAMMING (L-P) PROBLEMS

Following methods may be used for solving the L-P problems:

1. Simplex method
2. Dual simplex method etc.

10.12.1. Simplex method

In the use of simplex method for solving L-P problems following two conditions must be satisfied.

1. The right hand side (RHS) of each constraint should be non negative.
2. Each of the decision variables as $x_1, x_2 \ldots x_n$ etc. should be non negative.

A simplex tableau shows an optimum solution, if all the entries in a row are zero or negative for maximization problems and zero or positive for minimization problems.

i.e.

$$\Delta_j = C_j - Z_j$$

where,

C_j = Contribution per unit from objective function.

Z_j = Each element of the column × corresponding coefficient of the solution variables appearing in the basic column.

10.12.2. Dual Simplex method

This method can be used to solve a linear programming problem (LPP) provided the LPP satisfies the optimality conditions. Actually simplex method moves towards optimality, maintaining feasibility. In dual simplex method the reverse happens. The starting basic solution is not feasible and optimability condition satisfied. The rules for entering and leaving the variables in dual simplex method are such that it moves towards feasibility, maintaining optimality.

10.13. RULES TO BE APPLIED TO DUAL SIMPLEX METHOD

Following rules are applied to the dual simplex method:

1. The linear programming problem (LPP) must be in the following format with out using artificial variables:
   (*a*) Either it is a maximization or minimization problem.
   (*b*) All the constraints must have '≈' (approximation) sign.
   (*c*) All decision variables are greater than zero *i.e.* positive.
   (*d*) All right hand side constraints are negative.
2. It is assumed that LPP satifies the optimality requirements and the procedure followed. The difference between the dual simplex and simplex method is that in dual simplex method all or some entries in solution column (not including row) are negative.
3. The variables having most negative values under solution column are known as leaving variables.
4. The entering variables are found as follows:
   In the row of leaving variable, pickup all the negative entries and take the absolute value of the ratios. The variable corresponding to the minimum of these ratios, enter in the basis column. If all values are positive, then the problem's solution is not possible.
5. When all the values of variables under solution column become negative, the repetition of the procedure is stopped. This is the optional stage of solution.

10.14. USE OF LINEAR PROGRAMMING

The use of linear programming is illustrated by a simple example involving only two variables as follows:

Example 10.3. *A factory owner can manufacture either roof truss or column/beams. The options and profit margin is shown in the table 10.8 below.*

Table 10.8. Options and profit margin

Operations	*Hours required for 1 ton of product*		*Total hours available*
Assembly	6	3	90
Welding	3	6	72
Profit per ton	Rs. 1200	Rs. 900	

The objective function can be stated as:

Maximize the equation $P = 1200\,T + 900\,C$ ...(10.2)

where,

P= Profit

T = No of trusses

C = No of columns

The costraints that can be derived from above table 10.8 are as follows:

Assembly $6\,T + 3\,C \leq 90$ ...(10.3)

Welding $3\,T + 6\,C \leq 72$ ...(10.4)

Limit $T \geq 0$ ...(10.5)

$C \geq 0$ ...(10.6)

The equations from 10.3 to 10.6 can be solved by graphical method. Though graphical approach is simple, but not really suitable for practical problems.

The solution of the above problem by simplex method is illustrated as follows:

Step 1. Prepare Table 10.9 from Table 10.8. Table 10.9 shows the equation involved in simplex method in tabular from.

Table 10.9. Simplex table

	ij	*Product*	*Quantity*	Rs 1200 T	Rs 900 C	0 S_A	0 S_W
Replaced row	0	S_A	90	6	3	1	0
	0	S_W	72	3	6	0	1
		Z_j	Rs 0	0	0	0	0
		$C_j - Z_j$		1200	Rs 900		

In Table 10.9 first row describes equation 10.2. and second row describes equation 10.3 respectively. The inequalities of equation 10.2 and 10.3 are made equal by introducing two variables called the slack variables, namely S_A for assembly and S_W for welding. Two additional rows namely Z_j describing the total profit and $C_j - Z_j$ describing the net profit is added in table 109. A positive number is net profit *i.e.* $C_j - Z_j$ row (Rs 1200 in case of truss) shows that the profit would be increased by Rs 1200 per unit of truss added. The column which has the largest positive number in $C_j - Z_j$ row is called the optimum column and is replaced as follows:

Ratio's to be determined

Following ratios are determined:

$$\frac{\text{quantity in each row}}{\text{No. in optimum column in the same row}}$$

The ratios in the example under consideration are as follows:

S_A row 90/6 *i.e.* 15:1

S_W row 72/3 *i.e.* 24:1

Since S_A has smaller positive ratio, hence this row is called replacing row and the number in the inter section of optimum column and replacing row is called *inter sectional element,* in the present case it is 6.

Step 2. From Table 10.9 an other simplex table 10.10 formed as follows:

The number of trusses (*t*) row of the new table is computed by dividing each number in the replaced row (the S_A row) by inter sectional element 6 as shown below.

$$\frac{90}{6} = 15,\ \frac{6}{6} = 1,\ \frac{3}{6} = 0.5,\ \frac{1}{6} = 0.16,\ \frac{0}{6} = 0$$

The remaining values in the table are computed as follows:

$$\text{New row} = \begin{bmatrix}\text{Eelment in}\\ \text{old row}\end{bmatrix} - \begin{bmatrix}\text{Inter section element}\\ \text{of old row}\end{bmatrix} \times \begin{bmatrix}\text{Corresponding element in}\\ \text{replacing row}\end{bmatrix}$$

Calculations for change in numbers of S_W row is represented below:

$$72 - (15 \times 3) = 27$$

$$3 - (3 \times 1) = 0$$

The second simplex table developed is shown as Table 10.10.

Table 10.10. Second simplex table

C_j	*Product mix*	*Quantity*	Rs 1200	Rs 900	0	0
			T	C	S_A	S_W
RS 1200	T	15	1	0.5	0.16	0
0	S_W	27	0	4.5	– 0.75	1
	Z_j	18000	1200	600	192	0
	$C_j - Z_j$		0	300	– 192	0

The total profit Z_j is estimated as

$$Z_j \text{ (total profit)} = 1200 \times 15 + 0 = 18000/-$$

Similarly Z_i for T is estimated as

$$1200 \times 1 + 0 \times 1 = 1200$$

Similarly for $C\,Z_j = 1200 \times 0.5 + 0 \times 1 = 600$

For $S_A = 1200 \times 0.06 + 0 \times 1 = 192$

In the second simplex table the column/beams *i.e.* C column is the optimum column and inter-sectional element will be 4.5 and the same procedure is repeated as above. The procedure should be repeated till no positive sign appears in the net profit row ($C_j - Z_j$).

Further it has been observed that linear programming is less efficient than conventional C.P.M. algorithm for obtaining the net work schedule and critical path data, but it provides access to extensively developed linear programming packages using the computer.

10.15. APPLICATION OF LINEAR PROGRAMMING IN CRITICAL PATH METHOD (CPM)

The technique of linear programming for the identification of critical path of an activity based or event based net work can be applied easily as follows:

Let the variable x_i be the eariy occurrence time of the node where $i \approx 1, 2, 3... m$, m being the number of nodes in the net work. The objective is to minimise the difference between x_1 and x_m, where, 1 refers to first node and m to the last node. The constraints are the time difference between any two adjacent nodes.

Thus the objective function is to minimise $x_o \approx x_n - x_i$ subject to $x_j - x_i > t^{ij}$ for all activities $i - j$.

$t^{ij} \approx$ duration of activity $i - j$

$x_1 \approx$ unconstrained in sign.

10.16. PROJECT COST FORMULATION

In the project cost formulation, each activity is associated with the following three quantities:

1. Crash duration $a\ (i, j)$
2. Normal duration $b\ (i - j)$
3. Cost slope $c\ (i, j)$

Let the cost of executing activity $(i - j)$ increases linearly with the decrease in time, while determining the cost slope. Hence $c\ (i, j)$ is the cost slope

i.e. Cost slope $\approx$ increase in cost per unit decrease in time.

Generally $a\ (i, j) \le b\ (i, j)$

Now let us calculate the cost of performing a job $(i - j)$ in 't' units of time. The value of t lies between a and b. In Fig. 10.10, the thick line represents the cost curve for job $(i - j)$ and the slope is equal to $c(i - j)$.

The cost slope $C = \tan \theta$

Here $S \approx$ Cost of the job in the normal duration $b\ (i - j)$

$R \approx$ Cost of the job in the crash duration $a\ (i - j)$

The time 't' lies between

$$a\ (i, j) \le t(i, j) \le b(i, j)$$

From Fig. 10.10, the cost of the job $(i - j)$ in time 't' is OP

or $OP = OR - RP \approx OR - (Ot - Oa) \tan \theta$

or $OP \approx OR - (Ot - Oa)\ C$, eliminating θ,

i.e. $P = R - (t - a)\ C$

or $P = R - tc + ac$

or $P = R + ac - t\,c$ (taking (R+ ac) a constant)

$P = K - t\,c$

i.e. $p\ (i, j) \approx K\ (i, j) - t\ (i, j)\ C\ (i, j)$

The total cost $Q(T) \approx$ sum of costs of all activities $(a - j)$

i.e. $Q(T) = \Sigma_{ij}\ p(i, j)$ for all (i, j)

$= \Sigma_{ij}\ K(i, j) - t(i, j)\ c(i, j)$

The project duration

$T =$ sum of all activities duration

i.e. $T = t(n)$

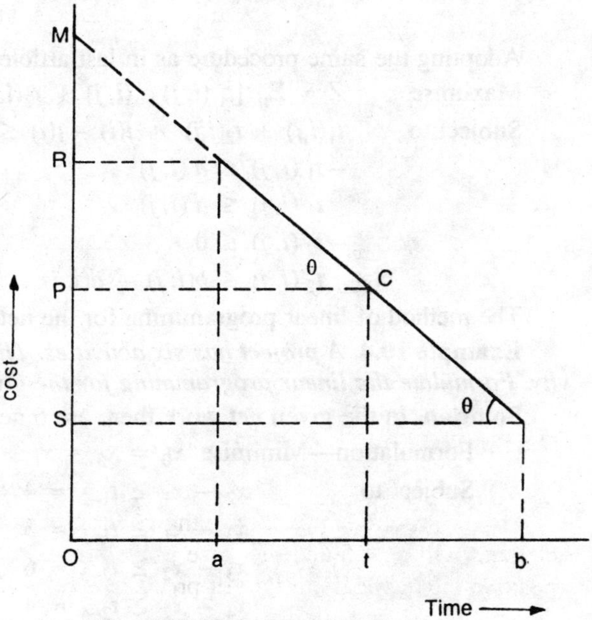

Fig. 10.10. Project cost formulation

The objective functions is

Minimise $Q(t) = \Sigma_{ij}\ [K(i, j) - t(i, j), c(i, j)]$ ...(*a*)

The cost of project $Q(t)$ can also be minimised by maximising the negative part of the above equation (*a*).

So maximise $\Sigma_{ij}\ t(i, j)\ c(i, j)$ where $t(i, j) > 0$

Subject to $t(i, j) + t(i) - t(j) \le 0$

$$- t(ij) \leq - a\,(i, j)$$
$$t(i\,j) \leq b(i, j)$$
$$t(m) \leq T$$

Where $t(n)$ is the earliest occurrence time of end event.

10.17. NON LINEAR COST TIME RELATION

Now let us consider an activity $(i - j)$ which does not have linear cost time relationship. The non linear curve can be replaced by two activities 1 and 2, each of them having a linear curve as shown in Fig. 10.11. The activity 1 has normal duration, crash duration and cost slope as 'a', 'd' and c, respectively. Activity 2 has crash duration as 'o', $(b - d)$ as normal duration and c_2 as cost slope.

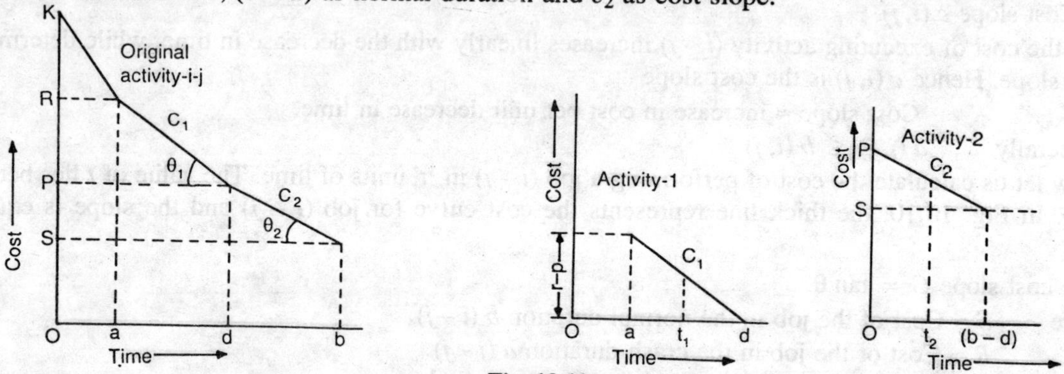

Fig. 10.11.

Adopting the same procedure as in last article 10.16, the objective function in this case will be

Maximise $\quad Z \approx \Sigma_{ij}\ [t_1\,(i, j)\, c_1(i, j) + t_2(i, j)\, c_2\,(ij)]$

Subject to $\quad t_1(i,j) + t_2(i,j) + t(i) - t(j) \leq 0$

$$- t_1\,(i, j) \leq a\,(i, j)$$
$$t_1\,(i, j) \leq d\,(i, j)$$
$$- t_2\,(i, j) \leq 0$$
$$t_2\,(i, j) \leq b(i, j) - d(i, j)$$

The method of linear programming for the net work problems is illustrated by the following examples.

Example 10.4. *A project has six activities. The duration of each activity is shown along with the activity. Formulate the linear programming for the given net work.*

Solution. In the given net work there are 6 activities

Formulation—Minimise $x_0 = x_5 - x_1$

Subject to

$$x_2 - x_1 \geq t_{1-2} \approx 4$$
$$x_3 - x_1 \geq t_{1-3} \approx 3$$
$$x_3 - x_2 \geq t_{2-3} \approx 6$$
$$x_4 - x_2 \geq t_{2-4} \approx 4$$
$$x_5 - x_3 > t_{3-5} \approx 7$$
$$x_5 - x_4 \geq t_{4-5} \approx 4$$

But $x_1 = 0$, being the early start time.

So minimize $\quad x_0 \approx x_5$

Subject to

$$x_2 \geq 4$$
$$x_3 - x_2 \geq 6$$
$$x_4 - x_2 \geq 4$$

$$x_5 - x_3 \geq 7$$
$$x_5 - x_4 \geq 4 \textbf{ Ans.}$$

Example 10.5. *The normal and crash cost and normal time and crash time of a project net work Fig. 10.12 are shown in the following table 10.11. The indirect cost of the project may be taken as Rs. 4500 per week.*

Table 10.11.

Activity	*Normal*		*Crash*	
	Duration (weeks)	*Cost in Rs.*	*Duration (weeks)*	*Cost in Rs.*
1 – 2	7	8000	4	15500
1 – 3	9	5000	6	9500
2 – 3	5	7000	2	10000
2 – 4	6	9000	4	16000
3 – 4	6	6000	4	12000

Determine the linear programming formulation for the project.

Solution.

Table 10.12.

Activity	*Normal*		*Crash*		*Cost-slope*
	Duration (weeks)	*Cost (Rs)*	*Duration (weeks)*	*Cost in (Rs)*	
1 – 2	7	8000	4	15500	2500
1 – 3	9	5000	6	9500	1500
2 – 3	5	7000	2	10000	1000
2 – 4	6	9000	4	16000	3500
3 – 4	6	6000	4	12000	3000

Let t_{1-2}, t_{1-3}, t_{2-3}, t_{2-4} and t_{3-4} be the optimum duration for each activity to be performed.

Let x_4 be the indirect cost of project.

The objective function—It is to be developed with the corresponding time and cost slope.

∴ From table 10.12 above

Objective function

Minimise $x_0 = 2500\, t_{1-2} + 1500\, t_{1-3} + 1000\, t_{2-3} + 3500\, t_{2-4} + 3000\, t_{3-4} + 4500\, x_4$

Constraints from the table 10.12

$x_2 - t_{1-2} \geq 0 \quad (\because x_1 = 0),\ t_{1-2} \leq 7,\ t_{1-2} \geq 4)$

$x_3 - t_{1-3} \geq 0,\ t_{1-3} \leq 9, t_{1-3} \geq 6$

$x_3\, x_2 - t_{2-} \geq 0,\ t_{2-3} \leq 5,\ t_{2-3} \geq 2$

$x_4 - x_2 - t_{2-4} \geq 0,\ t_{24} \leq 6, t_{2-4} \geq 4$

$x_4 - x_3 - t_{3-4} > 10,\ t_{3-4} \leq 6, t_{3-4} \geq 4$

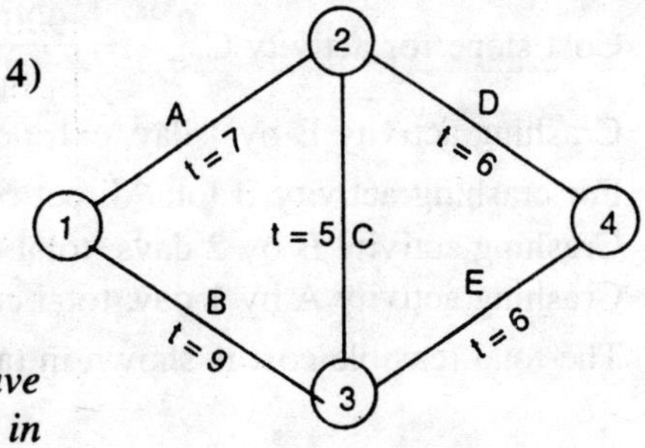

Fig. 10.12.

Example. 10.6. *Three activities implementable in parallel have the following time cost relation ship for direct cost component in each case.*

Activity	*Duration*	Cost
A	10 days (normal) 9 days 8 days	Rs. 800 Rs. 900 Rs. 1000

Activity	*Duration*	Cost
B	11 days (normal) 10 days 9 days	Rs. 1200 Rs. 1350 Rs. 1500
C	7 days (normal) 6 days 5 days	Rs. 500 Rs. 700 Rs. 900

What would be the feasible range of total direct cost component for the three activities together.

[UPSC Engg. Services, 1995]

Solution. The net work of given activities is shown below Fig. 10.13.

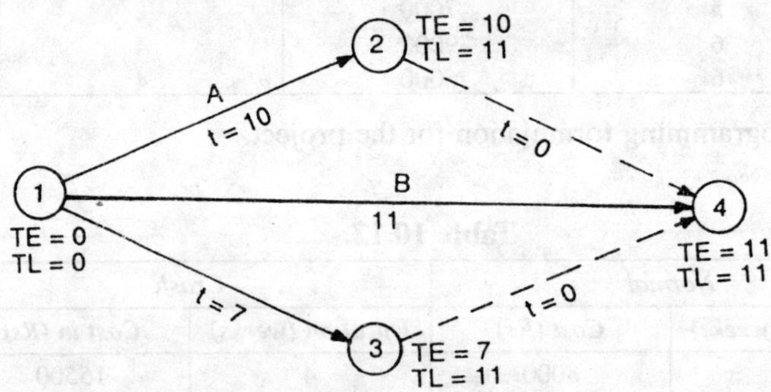

Fig. 10.13.

Critical path is along activity B *i.e.* 1-4 shown by thick line.

$$\text{Cost slope} = \frac{\text{crash cost} - \text{normal cost}}{\text{normal time} - \text{crash time}}$$

$$\text{Cost slope for activity A} = \frac{1000 - 800}{10 - 8} = \frac{200}{2}$$

$$= 100 \text{ per day}$$

$$\text{Cost slope for activity B} = \frac{1500 - 1200}{11 - 9} = \frac{300}{2} = \text{Rs. } 150 \text{ per day}$$

$$\text{Cost slope for activity C} = \frac{900 - 500}{7 - 5} = \frac{400}{2} = \text{Rs. } 200 \text{ per day}$$

Crashing activity B by 1 day, extra cost involved = Rs. 150/-

For crashing activity B total direct cost = 1200 + 150 = 1350/-

Crashing activity B by 2 days, total cost = 1200 + 2 × 150 = 1500/-

Crashing activity A by 1 day, total cost = 800 + 100 = 900.

The total feasible cost is shown in table below:

Table 10.13

Description	*Feasible range of activities time*	*Deriect cost component*	*Total direct cost*
All activities in normal time	A – B – C 10 days – 11 days – 7 days	800 + 1200 + 500	2500/-
Crashing B by 1 day	10 days – 10 days – 7 days	800 + 1350 + 500	2650/-
Crashing A & B together by 1 day	9 days – 9 days – 7 days	900 + 1500 + 500	2900/-

As one of the three parallel activities C is saturated, no more crashing will be allowed. The possible range of total direct. Cost will vary from Rs. 2500 to Rs. 2900. **Ans.**

Example 10.7. With the following data of a CPM project, find the normal duration, optimum duration and minimum duration of the project. Indirect cost is Rs. 90/- per day.

Table 10.14.

Activity	*I node*	*J mode*	*Normal*		*Crash*	
			Duration days	*Cost (Rs.)*	*Duration days*	*Cost (Rs.)*
A	1	2	5	60	4	90
B	1	3	7	150	5	250
C	2	3	3	30	2	60
D	3	5	6	150	4	250
E	2	4	3	100	3	100
F	1	5	9	115	7	305
G	4	5	4	100	2	440

Solution. The net work of the project is shown in Fig. 10.14.

The earliest occurrence time T_E and latest occurrence time T_L are calculated and marked on the net work.

The critical path is along 1-2-3-5 *i.e.* along A-C-D.

The normal duration of the project is the sum of duration of critical activities = 5 + 3 + 6 = 14 days.

Normal direct cost of the project = sum of cost of all activities in normal duration.

= 60 + 150 + 30 + 150 + 100 + 115 + 100 = 705/-

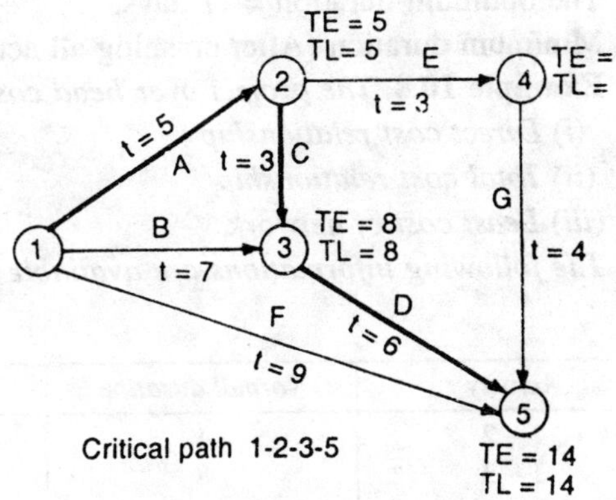

Fig. 10.14.

$$\text{Cost slope} = \frac{\text{crash cost} - \text{normal cost}}{\text{normal time} - \text{crash time}}$$

$$\text{Cost slope of A} = \frac{90 - 60}{5 - 4} = \text{Rs. 30 per day}$$

$$\text{Cost slope of B} = \frac{250 - 150}{7 - 5} = \text{Rs. 50 per day}$$

$$\text{Cost slope of C} = \frac{60 - 30}{3 - 2} = \text{Rs. 30 per day}$$

$$\text{Cost slope of D} = \frac{250 - 150}{6 - 4} = \text{Rs. 50 per day}$$

$$\text{Cost slope of F} = \frac{305 - 115}{9 - 7} = \frac{190}{2} = \text{Rs. 95 per day}$$

$$\text{Cost slope of G} = \frac{440 - 100}{4 - 2} = \frac{340}{2} = \text{Rs. 170 per day}$$

Activity (1-2) and (2-3) *i.e.* A and C have equal cost slope of Rs. 30/-

Hence crashing each activity by one day, the extra cost will be Rs. 30 + 30 = 60.

∴ Direct cost of project after crashing for 1 day A and C activity = 705 + 60 = 765/-

Duration of project = 14 – 1 = 13 days.

Now crashing activity D *i.e.* activity (3-5) for two days.

The Direct cost of project after crashing D for 2 days = 765 + 100 = 865/-

Duration of project = 13 – 2 = 11 days.
Now crashing activity F for 2 days, the direct cost increase = 190.
Total direct cost of project = 865 + 190 = 1055
Duration of project = 11 – 2 = 9 days.
After crashing G for for 2 days, increase in direct cost = 340/-
∴ Total direct cost = 1055 + 340 = 1335
Duration of project = 9 – 2 = 7 days.

Total cost computed by adding direct and indirect costs together are shown in tabular form as below.

Table 10.15.

Duration project	14	13	11	9	7
Direct cost	705	765	865	1055	1335
Indirect cost	1260	1170	990	810	630
Total	1965	1935	1855	1865	1965

From the data of the project the normal duration of the project is 14 days.
The optimum duration = 11 days.
Minimum duration (After crashing all activities) = 7 days.

Example 10.8. *The project over head costs are Rs. 2000/- per week. Determine*

(i) Direct cost relationship
(ii) Total cost relationship
(iii) Least cost of network.

The following informations are available about the various activities of the net work.

Table 10.16.

Activity	*Normal duration*	*Normal cost*	*Crash duration*	*Crash costs*
1 – 2	4	4000/-	3	7000/-
1 – 3	8	5000/-	7	8000/-
2 – 3	5	8000/-	3	10,000/-

[UPSC, Engg Services, 1988]

Solution.

Table 10.17. Data of the project

Activity	*Normal duration (weeks)*	*Normal cost (b)*	*Crash duration weeks*	*Crash cost (b)*	*Over head charges per week*
1 – 2	4	4,000	3	7000	2000
1 – 3	8	5000	7	8000	
2 – 3	5	8000	3	10,000	

(*ii*) Net work of the problem is shown in Fig. 10.15

The normal duration of the project on critical path = 9 weeks

Normal duration = 17 weeks

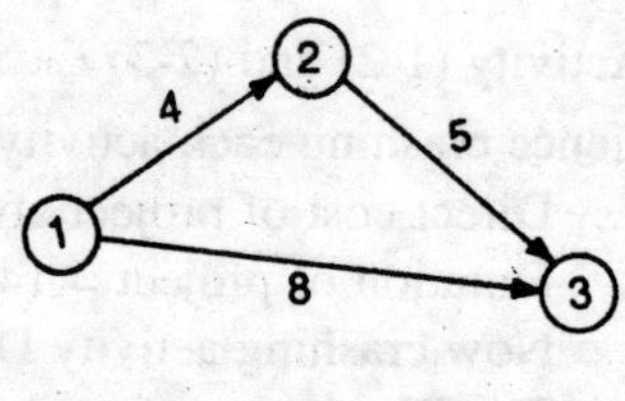

Fig. 10.15.

$$\text{Cost slope for activity 1-2} = \frac{\text{crash cost} - \text{normal cost}}{\text{normal time} - \text{crash time}}$$

$$= \frac{7000 - 4000}{4 - 3} = \frac{3000}{1}$$

Cost slope for activity 1-2 = 3000/– per week

Cost slope for activity 1-3 = $\dfrac{8000 - 5000}{8 - 7}$ = 3000/– per week

Cost slope for activity 2-3 = $\dfrac{10{,}000 - 8000}{5 - 3} = \dfrac{2000}{2}$ = 1000/– per week

Step 3. Direct cost of normal duration = Direct cost of project will be the sum of the normal cost of all activities

Direct cost = 4000 + 5000 + 8000 = 17000/-

Step 4. First stage of crashing

In the first instance, select that activity for crashing, which has minimum cost slope. In this case activity 2-3 has minimum cost slope of Rs. 1000/- per week.

Let us crash it fully *i.e.* for 2 weeks.

Extra cost of crashing activity 2-3 for 2 weeks = 2 × 1000 = 2000

Direct cost of project of 7 week duration = 17000 + 2000 = 19000

Step 5. Crashing activity 1-2 by 1 week,

Extra cost of project = 3000/- per week.

Total direct cost of the project of 6 week duration = 19000 + 3000 = 22000.

Step 6. Crashing activity 1-3 by 1 week,

Extra cost of project = 3000/- per week.

∴ Total direct cost of project of 5 week duration = 22000 + 3000 = 25000/-

Table 10.18.

Project duration week	*9 (normal)*	7	6	5
Direct cost	17000	19000	22000	25000
Indirect cost	18000	14000	12000	10000
Total cost	35000	33000	34000	35000

Thus the minimum cost of project would be = 33000/-

Minimum duration = 7 weeks.

Thus crashing activity 1-3 for 2 weeks is sufficient. **Ans.**

Example 10.9. *A project consists of eight activities. The indirect cost of the project may be taken as Rs. 250/- per day. Determine the normal, optimum and minimum duration of the project from the data given below:*

Table 10.19.

Activity	*I node*	*J node*	*Duration*		*Cost*	
			Normal	*Crash*	*Normal*	*Crash*
A	1	2	9	6	2500	3130
B	2	5	9	5	3500	3700
C	5	6	10	9	5500	5680
D	2	3	8	7	2700	2800
E	3	6	8	6	5800	6040
F	2	4	10	5	3400	4250
G	4	6	5	3	6500	6860
H	6	7	2	1	7600	7900

Solution. The net work of the project drawn from the given data is shown in Fig. 10.16.

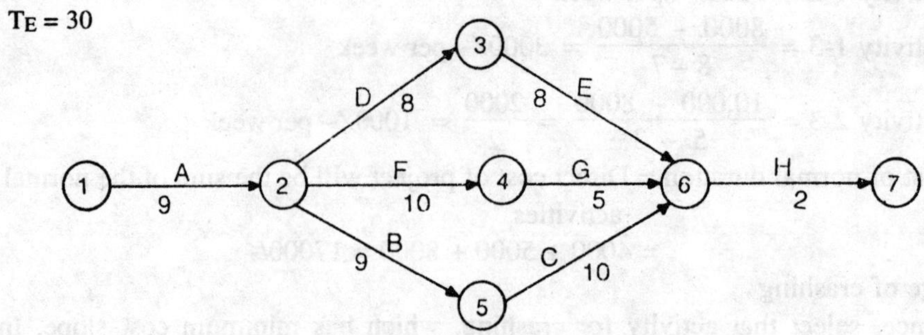

Fig. 10.16

Cost slope of A $= \dfrac{3130 - 2500}{9 - 6} = \dfrac{630}{3} = 210/\text{– perday}$

Cost slope of B $= \dfrac{3700 - 3500}{9 - 5} = \dfrac{200}{4} = 50/–$

Cost slope of C $= \dfrac{5680 - 5500}{10 - 9} = 180/–$

Cost slope of D $= \dfrac{2800 - 2700}{8 - 7} = 100/–$

Cost slope of E $= \dfrac{6040 - 5800}{8 - 6} = \dfrac{240}{2} = 120/–$

Cost slope of F $= \dfrac{3650 - 3400}{10 - 5} = \dfrac{250}{5} = 50/–$

Cost slope of G $= \dfrac{6860 - 6500}{5 - 3} = \dfrac{360}{2} = 180/–$

Cost slope of H $= \dfrac{7900 - 7600}{1} = \text{Rs. } 300/–$

Critical path is along 1-2-5-6-7

Duration of project = 30 days.

Now crashing the activity having lowest cost slope, thus crushing the activity B say for 3 days. Extra cost will increase by 50 × 3 = 150/-

Direct Normal cost of all activities

= 2500 + 3500 + 5500 + 2700 + 5800 + 3400 + 6500 + 7600 =/37500/-

Direct project cost after crashing activity B for 3 days = 37500 + 150 = 37650/-

Now the duration of project = 30 – 3 = 27 days.

Now B is left by 1 day to be crashed. Let us crash B and D by 1 day each having least cost slope.

Increase in direct cost of project due to crashing activity B and D by one day = (50 + 100) × 1 = 150/-

Duration of project left = 27 – 1 = 26.

After crashing A and D by one day, total direct cost = 37650 + 150 = 37800

Crashing A by 3 days, extra cost of crashing = 3 × 210 = 630

∴ Direct cost of project = 37800 + 630 = 38430/-

Duration of project = 26 – 3 = 23 days.

Now crashing E, F, C simultaneously by 1 day, extra cost of project, = 1 (50 + 120 + 180) = 350/-

Total direct cost of project = 38430 + 350 = 38780/-

Duration of project = 23 – 1 = 22 days.

Now crashing remaining activities G and H simultaneously by one day, the increase in direct cost of project = 180 + 300 = 480/-

Total direct cost of project = 38780 + 480 = 39260/-

Duration of project = 22 – 1 = 21 days.

The results are tabulated in below 10.20.

Table 10.20.

Duration of project	30	27	26	23	22	21
Direct cost	37500	37650	37800	38430	38780	39260
Indirect cost	7500	6750	6500	5750	5500	5250
Total cost	45000	44400	44300	44180	44280	44510

Normal time = **30 days**

Optimum time = **23 days**

Minimum time = **21 days Ans.**

(after crashing all activities)

QUESTIONS

1. Explain the method of time cost optimization of a project net work.
2. What is meant by cost slope? How is it determined?
3. Define the following terms, and draw a curve showing their relationship
   (*a*) Direct cost (*b*) Indirect cost
   (*c*) Outage cost
4. Define the following terms
   (*a*) Normal project time (*b*) Normal cost
   (*c*) Crash cost (*d*) Crash time
   (*e*) Optimum duration of the project (*f*) Mnimum duration of the project
5. Formulate the linear programming for the following data:

Activity	1 – 2	1 – 3	2 – 3	2 – 4	3 – 4
Duration (days)	4	5	7	11	9

6. Determine the minimum cost and optimum duration for the project of the net work. The data of each activity of net work is given in the following table. Indirect cost may be taken as Rs. 2500/- per week.

Activity	*Normal*		*Crash*	
	Normal time (weeks)	*Cost (Rs)*	*Crash time (weeks)*	*Cost (Rs.)*
0 – 1	3	5,000	2	5,500
1 – 3	14	10,000	11	13,000
1 – 2	7	6,000	4	9,000
2 – 3	9	11,000	6	18,000
3 – 4	4	9,000	3	12,000
4 – 5	3	6,000	2	7,800

[**Ans.** Normal duration = 26 days, Optimum duration = 20 days
Minimum cost = 107633, Minimum duration 17 days]

7. A project consists four activities as listed below. If the indirect cost is Rs. 190/- per day determine,
   (*a*) Minimum cost (*b*) Optimum duration
   (*c*) Minimum duration

Activity	*I node*	*J node*	*Duration*		*Cost*	
			Normal	*Crash*	*Normal*	*Crash*
A	1	2	7	6	250	350
B	1	3	10	8	350	500
C	2	3	5	3	300	400
D	3	4	9	8	700	950

[**Ans.** Minimum cost = 5259/-, Optimum duration = 18 days
Minimum duration = 17 days, Normal duration 21 days]

8. From the following data of a project, determine the optimum and minimum duration and minimum cost of the project corresponding to optimum duration.

Activity	*Duration*		*Cost*	
	Normal	*Crash*	*Normal*	*Crash*
(0 – 1) A	3	2	5000	5500
(1 – 3) C	14	11	10000	13000
(1 – 2) B	7	4	6000	9000
(2 – 3) D	9	6	11000	18000
(3 – 4) E	4	3	9000	12000
(4 – 5) F	3	2	6000	7800

[**Ans.** Normal duration = 26 days, Optimum duration = 25 days
Minimum duration = 19 days, Minimum cost = 85000/0]

OBJECTIVE TYPE QUESTIONS

1. Identify the correct statement:
   (*a*) Generally the direct cost decreases as the time decreases
   (*b*) Generally the direct cost increases as the time decreases
   (*c*) Generally the direct cost is independent of time
   (*d*) Generally the direct cost varies erratically with time.
2. The time corresponding to minimum total project cot is called:
   (*a*) Optimum time (*b*) Crash time
   (*c*) Normal time (*d*) Optimistic time
3. The cost slope is
   (*a*) $\dfrac{\text{crash cost} - \text{normal cost}}{\text{normal time} - \text{crash time}}$ (*b*) $\dfrac{\text{normal cost} - \text{crash cost}}{\text{normal time} - \text{crash time}}$
   (*c*) $\dfrac{\text{crash cost} - \text{normal cost}}{\text{crash time}}$ (*d*) $\dfrac{\text{crash cost} - \text{normal cost}}{\text{normal time}}$
4. The time beyond which the direct cost will not be reduced with increase in time is known as
   (*a*) Normal time (*b*) Crash time
   (*c*) Optimum time (*d*) Optimistic time
5. The direct cost of a project with respect to normal time is
   (*a*) Maximum (*b*) Minimum
   (*c*) Zero (*d*) Infinite
6. Identify the correct statement
   (*a*) The crash duration of a project is obtained by adding the crash durations of all activities

(*b*) The crash duration of a project is obtained by adding up the normal durations of all the activities
(*c*) The crash duration of a project is obtained by adding up the crash durations for all activities along the critical path obtained by taking into account the crash durations of all the activities
(*d*) The crash duration of a project is obtained by adding up crash durations for all the activities along the critical path obtained taking into account the normal durations of all the activities

7. Economic saving of project time would result by crashing
(*a*) Cheapest non critical activity
(*b*) Cheapest critical activity
(*c*) Costliest non critical activity
(*d*) Costliest critical activity

8. Identify the correct statement
(*a*) Reduction in project time normally increase the direct cost and decreases the indirect cost
(*b*) Reduction in project time normally decreases the direct cost and increases the indirect cost
(*c*) Reduction in project time normally increases both direct and indirect costs
(*d*) Reduction in project time normally decreases both direct and indirect costs

9. Identify the incorrect statement/statements
(*a*) The total cost curve is curvilinear
(*b*) The total cost curve is a straight line
(*c*) The direct costs of a project are inversely proportional with the duration
(*d*) The direct costs of a project are directly proportional with the duration
(*e*) The optimum duration is less than the normal duration corresponding to the direct costs
(*f*) Beyond the normal duration the direct as well as indirect costs increase
(*g*) Maximum advantage may be obtained by crashing all activities rather crashing critical activities only
(*h*) Crashing all activities will lead to a very high cost without any advantage that can be obtained by crashing critical activities only
(*i*) Crashing of non critical activities has been found advantageous

ANSWERS

1. (*b*)	4. (*a*)	7. (*d*)
2. (*a*)	5. (*b*)	8. (*a*)
3. (*a*)	6. (*c*)	9. (*b, d, g, i*)

11

Resources Allocation

11.1. INTRODUCTION

A resource is a Physical veriable such as man power, materials, money, machines and equipment, space and time etc. that is required to complete various activities of a project. While performing CPM and PERT net work analysis, it is assumed that sufficient resources are available to complete a project. But in actual practice or in reality all the necessary resources are not available in unlimited quantities *i.e.* resources are always limited and the limitations of resources significantly affect the initiation, performance and completion of activities in time or on schedule time, causing the delay in the completion of the project Thus the various activities of the project should be scheduled in such a manner that the available resources may be utilised in the best possible manner.

The availability of certain resources may fluctuate from time to time. If materials or unskilled labour is available as per need, then fluctuations in demand will not affect the cost of the project. But on the other hand if skilled technicians and specified equipment is restricted, then they have to be employed on a permanent or semi permanent basis and the equipment has to be hired in advance, resulting in increasing the project cost. The rise in project cost will be due to the high idle time in which the rare equipment and skilled technicians remained idle. Thus the fluctuations of resources should be utilised in an optimal manner.

The main objective of any organisation is to utilise the available resources to the optimum extent and not to waste it in any way. To carry out the project smoothly and to complete it on schedule, it is necessary that required resources be made available in the specified quantity at the desired moment. This can be done by shifting the activities on non critical path by making use of floats and generating an alternative schedule by comparing more important resources with a view of smoothing the demand on resources. The float time of an activity may be utilized to delay it for some time and use its resources to complete the urgent activities.

11.2. OBJECT OF RESOURCE PLANNING

At the time of preparing the net work of any project, usually it is assumed that all resources needed for its execution are available in plenty and no consideration of resource constraints is taken into account. But at the time of execution of the project some of the resources fall short of the requirement. In such situations the duration of the project may increase escalating the cost of the project.

The planning of resources should be done in such a manner that no increase or decrease in resource demand may occur. As the engagement of skilled labour all a sudden is difficult, similarly the lay off of the labour suddenly is more difficult than their employment. Thus for a good resource plan, it is essential that the project may be completed during the stipulated period. To achieve this objective some times it becomes essential to make changes in the earliest start time of some critical activities or the execution of some activities may be postponed for the time being.

While taking decision for postponing the execution of any activity or effecting changes in the earliest time of critical activities following points should be kept in mind.

1. Such activities should be started first, whose completion duration is minimum.
2. The activity having maximum time of completion should be postponed.
3. The activity having maximum float time should be chosen for postponement first.

11.3. METHODS OF RESOURCE ALLOCATION

Depending upon the situation, the resource allocation can be done by the following two methods.

1. Resource smoothing
2. Resource levelling

11.4. RESOURCE SMOOTHING

Resource smoothing is resorted or done when there is restriction on the duration of project completion time. The resource smoothing is applied in such a way that the total project duration remains the same *i.e.* there is no change in the total duration of the project. First the periods of minimum demand for resources are determined or located and the activities are shifted according to the availability of float and requirement of resources. Thus the intelligent use of floats can smoothen the demand to the maximum possible extent. This type of resource allocation is known as *resource smoothing.*

11.5. STEPS IN RESOURCE SMOOTHING

Following steps are involved in resource smoothing:

1. The list of resources required for the execution of different activities is prepared and the important activities are identified.
2. The resource profiles are prepared by resource aggregation and cumulative resource requirements for each unit are plotted in the form of histogram.
3. The time periods of peak and low demand are identified and the peaks are lowered and the troughs are filled up.
4. If there is no restraint on the availability of resources, the demand of resources should be made as uniform a possible. This can be done by changing the time of start and finish of non critical activities in the first instance. These activities have some float. Hence the available float can be used for doing adjustment in the start or finish of the concerned activities. Thus the peak demand may be lowered by staggering the resource requirements with out delaying the project duration.

Example 11.1. *The expected time and number of labour to finish each activity of a project are shown in the following table 11.1. Smoothen the requirement of the resource so that the project may be completed in schedule duration.*

Table 11.1.

S. No.	*Activity*	*Expected time t^{ij}*	*No of the labour required*
1.	(1 – 2) A	3	4
2.	(1 – 3) B	2	5
3.	(1 – 4) C	5	7
4.	(2 – 7) D	6	6
5.	(3 – 5) E	4	2
6.	(4 – 5) F	3	4
7.	(4 – 6) G	1	2
8.	(5 – 7) H	4	5
9.	(6 – 7) I	2	3

Solution. The resource allocation is done by drawing the net work of the activities of the project.

Step 1. Draw the net work of the project with the given data. Let it be as shown in Fig. 11.1.

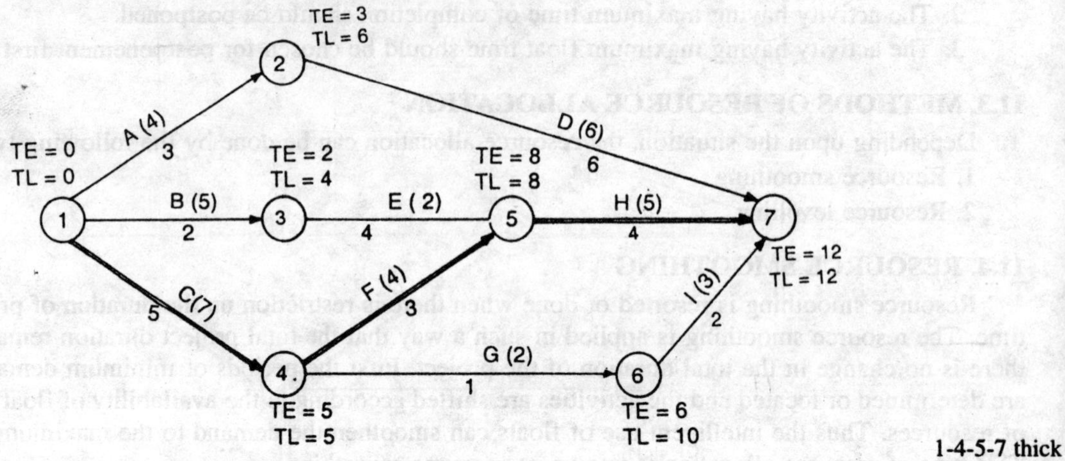

Fig. 11.1.

Step 2. From the diagram determine the earliest expected start time T_E^i and latest finish time T_L.

Step 3. From the value of T_E^i and T_L determine the earliest and latest time values of activities as EST, EFT, LST and LFT. Also determine the total float for each activity.

Step 4. From the float, determine the critical path and project duration for the critical path.

Step 5. Show the earliest start time of each activity on a bar chart and determine the value of total resource required each day.

Step 6. The values of T_E^i and T_L determined are shown on the diagram neatly near the each node as shown on the Fig. 11.1.

Table 11.2.

Activity	*Activity duration*	*Earliest start time (EST) (T_E^i)*	*Earliest finish time LFT*	*Latest start time LST*	*Latest finish time LFT*	*Float*	*Remark*
(1 – 2)	3	0	3	3	6	3	
(1 – 3)	2	0	2	2	4	2	
(1 – 4)	5	0	5	0	5	0	Critical
(2 – 7)	6	3	9	6	12	3	
(3 – 5)	4	2	6	4	8	2	
(4 – 5)	3	5	8	5	8	0	Critical
(4 – 6)	1	5	6	9	10	4	
(5 – 7)	4	8	12	8	12	0	Critical
(6 – 7)	2	6	8	10	12	4	

The critical path is along 1-4-5-7 as shown on the diagram with thick line.

The duration of project along the critical path = 12 days.

Step 7. The chart of activities and resource requirement is prepared and resource demand determined as follows:

Table 11.3.

Duration → *Activity ↓*	1	2	3	4	5	6	7	8	9	10	11	12
1 – 2	4	4	4									
1 – 3	5	5										
1 – 4	7	7	7	7	7							
2 – 7				6	6	6	6	6	6			
3 – 5			2	2	2	2						
4 – 5						4	4	4				
4 – 6						2						
5 – 7									5	5	5	5
6 – 7							3	3				
	16	16	13	15	15	14	13	13	11	5	5	5

From the bar chart of Table 11.3 it will be seen that the demand of labour varies from 5 to 16. The maximum demand of 16 labours is for two days only. To smoothen the fluctuation let us adjust the activities having floats.

The activities are rewritten having floats in descending order as follows:

Table 11.4.

Activity	EST	EFT	LST	LFT	FLOAT	*Remark*
6 – 7	6	8	10	12	4	Non critical activity
4 – 6	5	6	9	10	4	"
2 – 7	3	9	6	12	3	"
1 – 2	0	3	3	6	3	"
1 – 3	0	2	2	4	2	"
3 – 5	2	6	4	8	2	"
1 – 4	0	5	0	5	0	Critical activity
4 – 5	5	8	5	8	0	"
5 – 7	8	12	8	12	0	"

The activities 6-7 and 4-6 have maximum float of 4 days each. Activators 2-7 and 1-2 have floats of 3 days each. The float is so adjusted that the requirement of resources may remain practically constant. The resource distribution is shown in table 11.5.

Table 11.5.

	1	2	3	4	5	6	7	8	9	10	11	12	
1 – 2			4	4	4								2 days shift
1 – 3	5	5											Same
1 – 4	7	7	7	7	7								Same
2 – 7						6	6	6	6	6	6		3 days shift
3 – 5			2	2	2	2							Same
4 – 5						4	4	4					Same
4 – 6									2				Same
5 – 7									5	5	5	5	Same
6 – 7							3	3					Same
	12	12	13	13	13	12	13	13	13	11	11	5	

By shifting the activity 1-2 by 2 days, activity 2-7 by 3 days the resource variation has come down to 5 to 13. The histograms of the problem are shown in Fig. 11.2 (*a*) and (*b*).

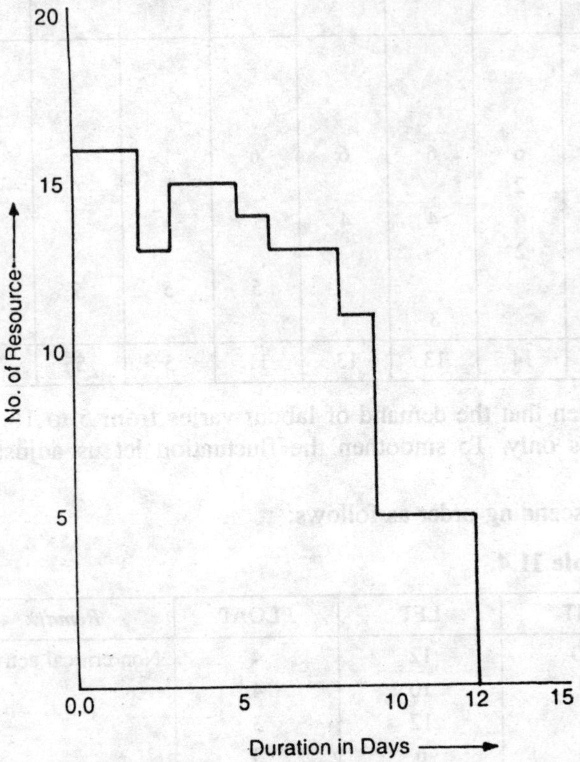

Fig. 11.2. (*a*) Original Histogram

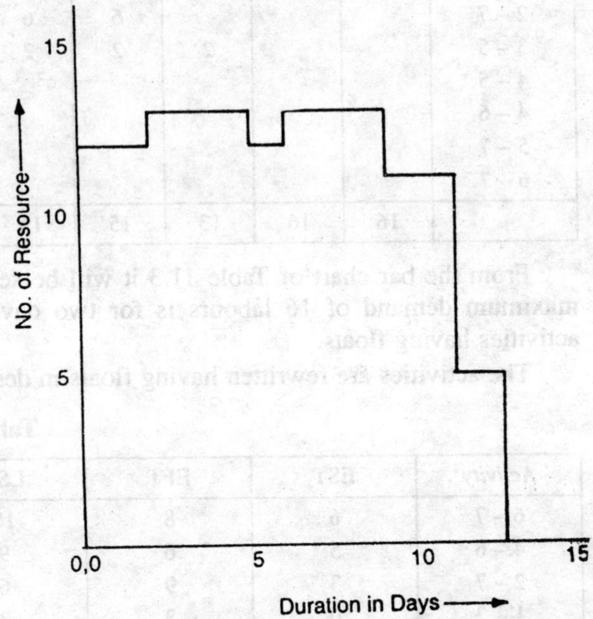

Fig. 11.2. (*b*) Modified Histogram

Example 11.2. *A project has 13 activities. The expected time of completion of each activity and different type of human resource required to complete the project are shown in the following table 11.6. Reallocate the human resource to maximise the use of human resource.*

Table 11.6.

S. No.	*Activity*	*Duration in days* t^{ij}	*No. of labour required*	*No. of carpenters required*
1.	A	3	2	0
2.	B	4	2	2
3.	C	4	2	4
4.	D	3	2	0
5.	E	5	0	6
6.	F	6	2	0
7.	G	2	0	4
8.	H	4	2	4
9.	I	3	0	2
10.	J	5	0	2
11.	K	2	2	0
12.	L	4	4	0
13.	M	2	4	0

Solution.

Step 1. Draw the net work of the project with the given activities. The net work is shown in Fig. 11.3.

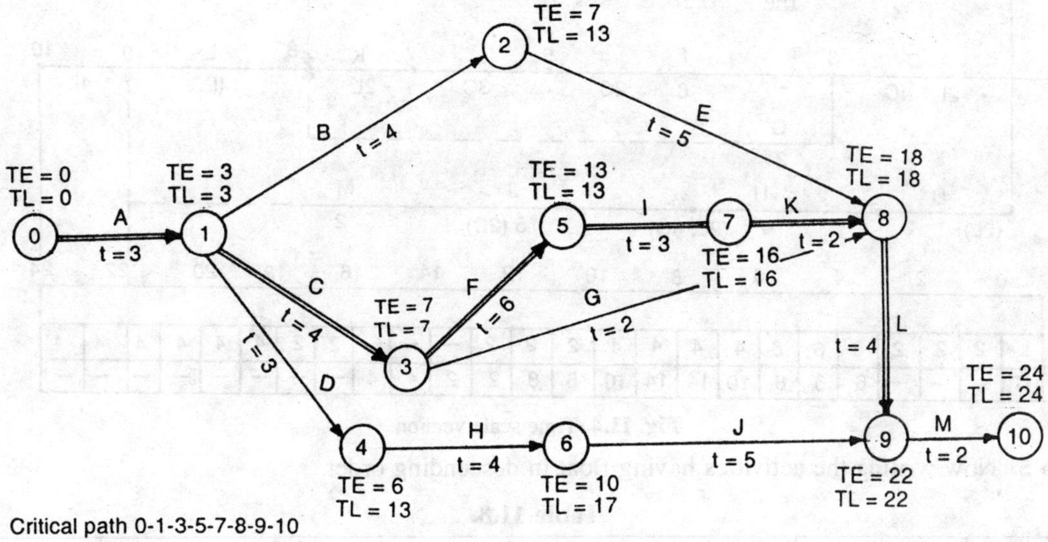

Fig. 11.3

Step 2. Determine the earliest expected time T_E^i and latest allowable time T_L and write on the net work as shown in Fig. 11.3

Step 3. To establish the critical path, determine earliest and latest activities times *i.e.* EST, EFT, LST and LFT. From these values find out the total float as shown in table 11.7.

Table 11.7

Activity	*Activity duration* t^{ij}	*Earliest start time EST* (T_E^i)	*Earliest finish time EFT* ($T_E^i + t^{ij}$)	*Latest start lime LST*	*Latest finish line LFT* (T_L^j)	*Float*	*Remark*
(0 – 1) A	3	0	3	0	3	0	Critical
(1 – 2) B	4	3	7	9	13	6	
(1 – 3) C	4	3	7	3	7	0	Critical
(1 – 4) D	3	3	6	10	13	7	
(2 – 8) E	5	7	12	13	18	6	
(3 – 5) F	6	7	13	7	13	0	Critical
(3 – 8) G	2	7	9	16	18	9	
(4 – 6) H	4	6	10	13	17	7	
(5 – 7) I	3	13	16	13	16	0	Critical
(6 – 9) J	5	10	15	17	22	5	
(7 – 8) K	2	16	18	16	18	0	Critical
(8 – 9) L	4	18	22	18	22	0	Critical
(9 – 10) M	2	22	24	22	24	0	Critical

Thus the critical path is along 0-1-3-5-7-8-9-10 and the duration of the project is 24 days.

Step 4. The demand of resource may be obtained by drawing the time scaled version of the project activities assuming the early start of each activity. The activities along the critical path have been arranged along the horizontal line. Float is shown by doted line. From the above, it will be seen that the fluctuation on 6, 7, 8 and 9th day is maximum.

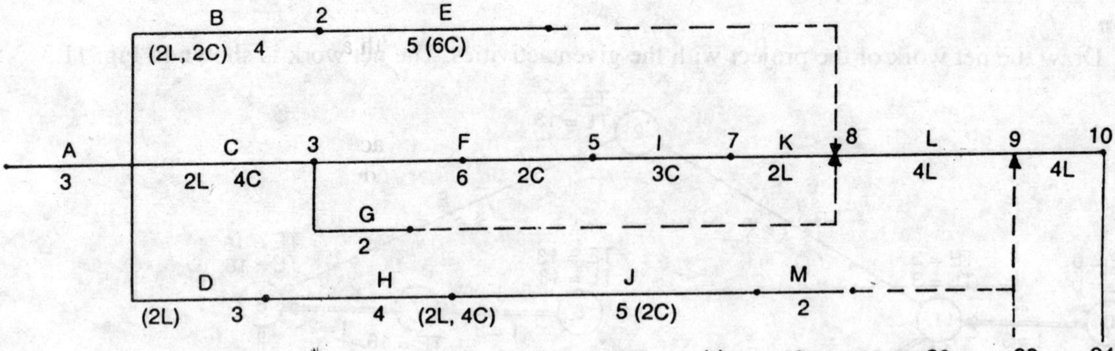

	0–2	2–4	4–6	6–8	8–10	10–12	12–14	14–16	16–18	18–20	20–22	22–24

L	2	2	2	6	6	6	4	4	4	4	2	2	2	–	–	–	2	2	4	4	4	4	4	4
C	–	–	–	6	6	6	10	14	14	10	8	8	2	2	4	4	–	–	–	–	–	–	–	–

Fig. 11.4. Time scale version

Step 5. Now writing the activities having float in descending order.

Table 11.8.

Activity	EST	EFT	LST	LFT	FLOAT	*Remark*
(3 – 8) G	7	9	16	18	9	Non critical
(4 – 6) H	6	10	13	17	7	"
(1 – 4) D	3	6	10	13	7	"
(1 – 2) B	3	7	9	13	6	"
(2 – 8) E	7	12	13	18	6	"
(6 – 9) J	10	15	17	22	5	"
(0 – 1) A	0	3	0	3	0	Critical
(1 – 3) C	3	7	3	7	0	Critical
(3 – 5) F	7	13	7	13	0	Critical
(5 – 7) I	13	16	13	16	0	Critical
(7 – 8) K	16	18	16	18	0	Critical
(8 – 9) L	18	22	18	22	0	Critical
(9 – 10) M	22	24	22	24	0	Critical

From table 11.8 it will be seen that the activity (3-8) has a float of 9 days. Let us shift this activity on

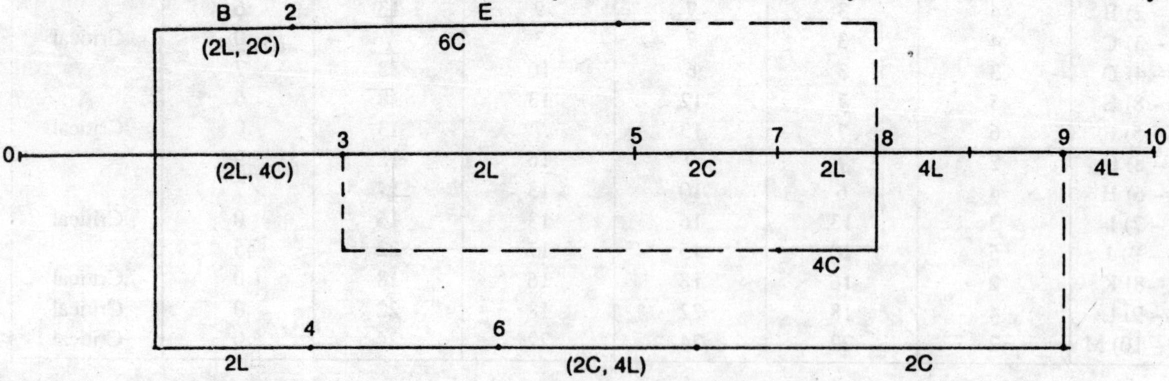

L	2	2	2	6	6	6	4	2	2	2	2	2	2	2	2	2	2	2	4	4	4	4	4	4
C	–	–	–	6	6	6	6	6	6	6	6	6		6	6	6	8	6	2	2	2	2	–	–

Fig. 11.5

16th day from 7th day. This change will reduce the demand of carpenters on 7th and 8th day from 14 to 10. This change has been shown in Fig. 11.5.

Step 6. For further smoothing, now let us take advantage of floats of activities (1-4), (4-6) and (6-9). Let he activity (4-6) be started from 13th day in stead of 7th day and activity (6-9) on 17th day. This shift is shown in Fig. 11.6. From this shift only 8 carpenter are needed on 17th day only. On the remaining days 4 labours and 6 carpenters are sufficient. By more trials further smoothing is possible. The resources may also be determined by bar chart as shown below in table 11.9.

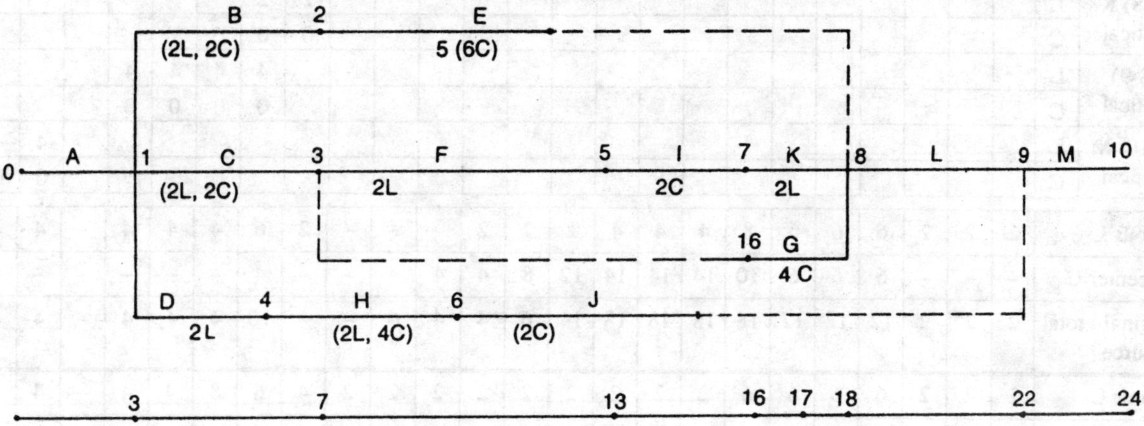

L	2	2	2	6	6	6	4	2	2	2	2	2	2	2	2	2	2	2	4	4	4	4	4	4
C					6	6	6	6	6	6	6	6	6		6	6	6	8	6	2	2	2		

Fig. 11.6.

Table 11.9.

Days →		1	2	3	4	5	6	7	8	9	10	11	12	13	14	15	16	17	18	19	20	21	22	23	24
(0-1) A	L	2	2	2																					
critical	C	0	0	0																					
(1-2) B	L				2	2	2	2																	
	C				2	2	2	2																	
(1-3) C	L				2	2	2	2																	
critical	C				4	4	4	4																	
(1-4) D	L				2	2	2	2																	
	C				0	0	0	0																	
(2-8) E	L								0	0	0	0	0												
	C								6	6	6	6	6												
(3-5) F	L								2	2	2	2	2	2											
critical	C								0	0	0	0	0	0											
(3-8) G	L								0	0	0	0					0	0	0	0					
	C								4	4	4	4					4	4	4	4					
(4-6) H	L							2	2	2	2			2	2	2	2								
	C							4	4	4	4			4	4	4	4								

Days →		1	2	3	4	5	6	7	8	9	10	11	12	13	14	15	16	17	18	19	20	21	22	23	24
(5-7) I critical	L													0	0	0									
	C													2	2	2									
(6-9) J	L											0	0	0	0	0		0	0	0	0	0			
	C											2	2	2	2	2		2	2	2	2	2			
(7-8) K critical	L																	2	2						
	C																	0	0						
(8-9) critical	L																		4	4	4	4			
	C																		0	0	0	0			
(9-10) M critical	L																							4	4
	C																							0	0
Labour L		2	2	2	6	6	6	8	4	4	4	2	2	2	–	–	–	2	6	4	4	4	–	4	4
Carpenter C		–	–	–	6	6	6	10	14	14	14	12	8	4	4	4	–	–	4	–	–	–	–	–	–
Original total resource		2	2	2	12	12	12	18	18	18	18	14	6	4	4	4	–	–	10	4	4	4	–	4	4
Labour L		2	2	2	6	6	6	6	2	2	2	2	2	2	2	2	2	4	6	8	4	4	–	4	4
Carpenter C		0	0	0	6	6	6	6	6	6	6	6	6	6	8	6	8	6	6	10	6	6	–	–	–
Modified total resource		2	2	2	12	12	12	12	8	8	8	8	8	8	10	8	10	10	12	18	10	10	–	4	4

Histogram of total resource are shown in Fig. 11.7 (*a*) and (*b*). Histogram of carpenters and labourers may also be shown separately. [ ] Shows shifted resource.

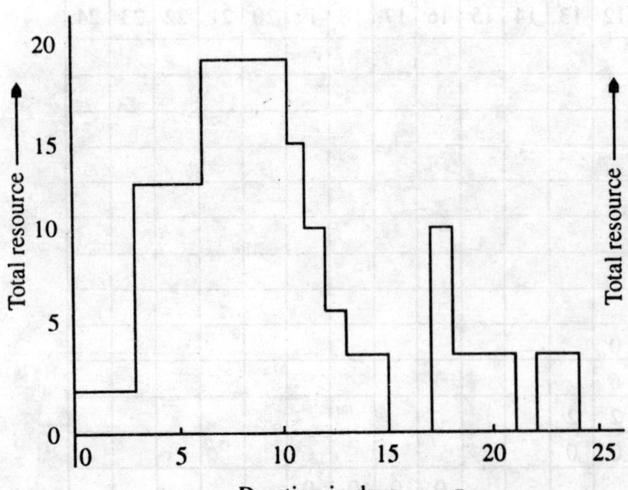

Fig. 11.7 (*a*). Original Histogram

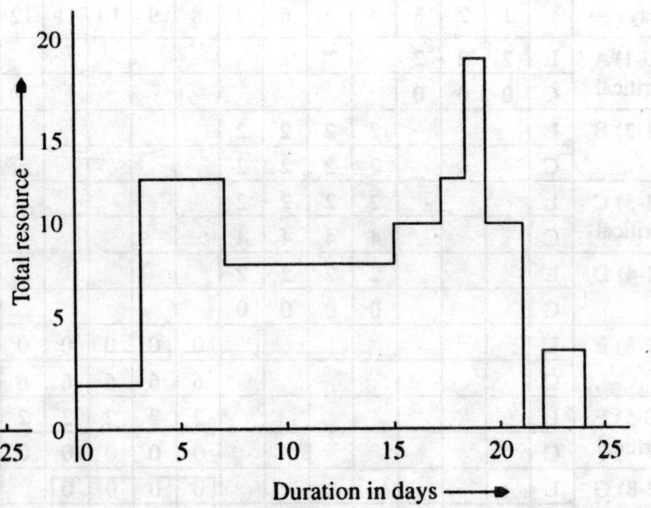

Fig. 11.7 (*b*). Modified Histogram

Example 11.3. *Determine the aggregate resource requirements period by period for the net work given below. The figures over the arrow show the requirement of brick layers and figures below the arrows are duration of the activities for the project. Smooth out the requirements and show the resulting revised schedule.*

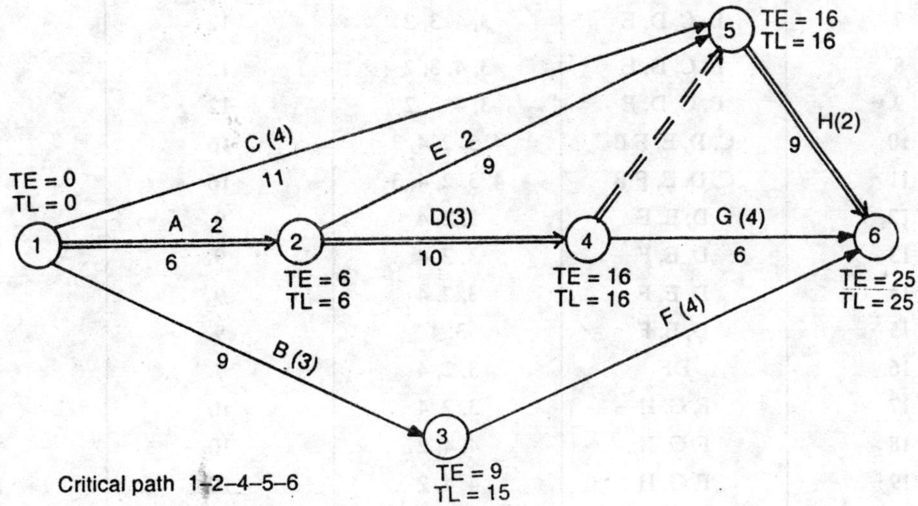

Fig. 11.8.

Solution. (*i*) First T_E^i and T_L of the activities are determined.

(*ii*) From the values of T_E^i and T_L, the activities times EST, EFT, LST and LFT and floats of all activities are determined as shown in the Table 11.10 below.

Table 11.10

Activity	*Activity duration* t^{ij}	EST	EFT	LST	LFT	Float (LFT – EFT)	*Remark*
A (1 – 2)	6	0	6	0	6	0	critical
B (1 – 3)	9	0	9	6	15	6	
C (1 – 5)	11	0	11	5	16	5	
D (2 – 4)	10	6	16	6	16	0	critical
E (2 – 5)	9	6	15	7	16	1	
F (3 – 6)	10	9	19	15	25	6	
G (4 – 6)	6	16	22	19	25	3	
H (5 – 6)	9	16	25	16	25	0	critical

The critical path is along 1-2-4-5-6.

Now according to earliest start time, the cumulative resource (brick layers) is calculated for each day as follows Table 11.11.

Table 11.11

S. No.	*Duration in days*	*Activity*	*Resource in units*	*Total resource requirement per day*	*Revised schedule*
1.	1	A, B, C	2, 3, 4	9	9
2.	2	A, B, C	2, 3, 4	9	9
3.	3	A, B, C	2, 3, 4	9	9
4.	4	A, B, C	2, 3, 4	9	9
5.	5	A, B, C	2, 3, 4	9	9

S. No.	*Duration in days*	*Activity*	*Resource in units*	*Total resource requirement per day*	*Revised schedule*
6.	6	A, B, C	2, 3, 4	9	9
7.	7	B, C, D, E	3, 4, 3, 2	12	12
8.	8	B, C, D, E	3, 4, 3, 2	12	12
9.	9	B, C, D, E	3, 4, 3, 2	12	12
10.	10	C, D, E, F B	4, 3, 2, 4, 3	16	12
11.	11	C, D, E, F B	4, 3, 2, 4, 3	16	12
12.	12	D, E, F	3, 2, 4	9	5
13.	13	D, E, F	3, 2, 4	9	5
14.	14	D, E, F	3, 2, 4	9	5
15.	15	D, E, F	3, 4	9	5
16.	16	DF	3, 2, 4	7	3
17.	17	F, G, H	3, 2, 4	10	7
18.	18	F, G, H	4, 4, 2	10	14
19.	19	F, G, H	4, 4, 2	10	14
20.	20	G, H	4, 2	6	10
21.	21	G, H	4, 2	6	10
22.	22	G, H	4, 2	6	10
23.	23	H	2	2	2
24.	24	H	2	2	2
25.	25	H	2	2	2

From the table 11.11 it will be seen that the demand of mason will be higher from the seventh day to 19th day. The histogram is shown in Fig. 11.9 (*a*) and (*b*). From the net work or Table 11.11 it will be seen that the maximum float of 6 days occurs in activities 1-3 (B) and (3-6) F. Hence the start time of activity F can be shifted by 6 days so that it can start on 16th day instead of 10th days. The revised histogram after

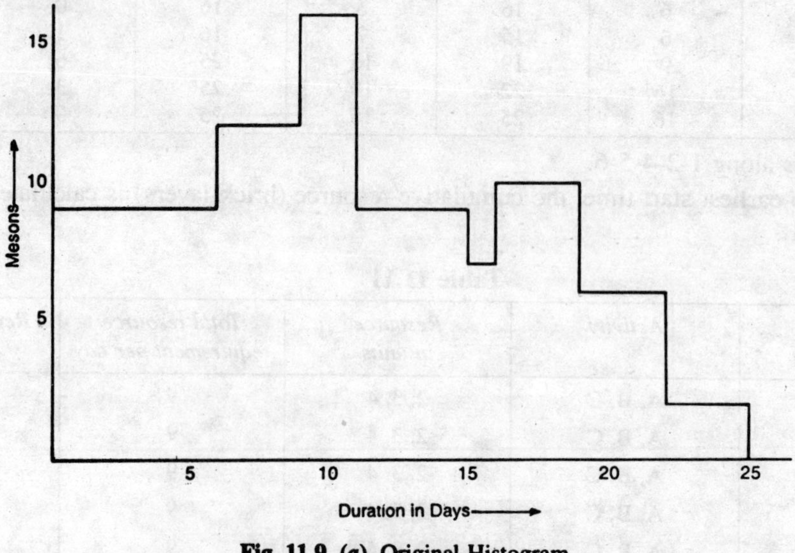

Fig. 11.9. (*a*). Original Histogram

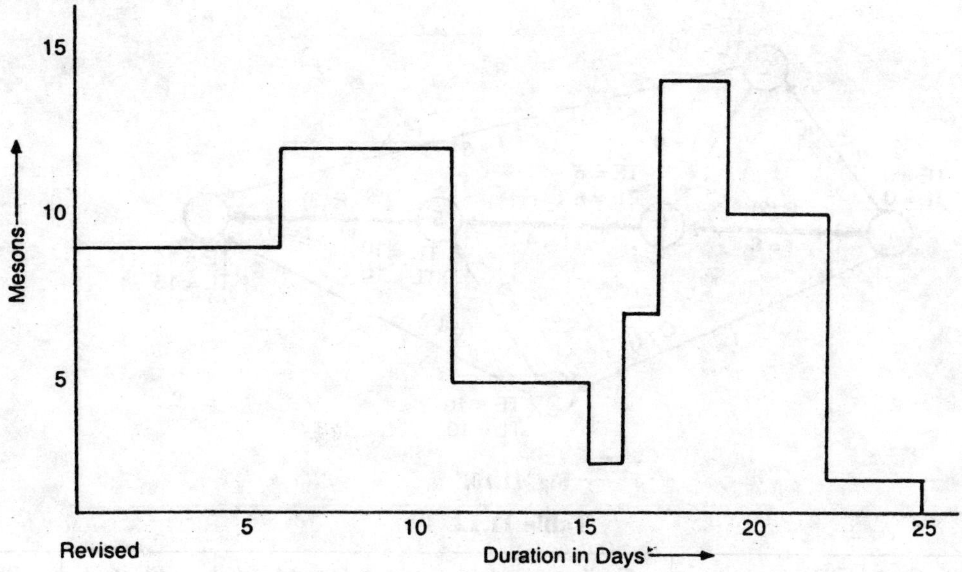

Fig. 11.9. (*b*) Modified Histogram

smoothening the original histogram is shown in Fig. 11.9 (*b*). Hence following this procedure it is always possible to smoothen the resource requirement with out affecting the total duration of the project.

11.6. RESOURCE LEVELLING

In a project there are many activities which need varying resources. The demand on specific resource should not increase beyond the prescribed limit. If the demand of a resource increases more than its availability, then the only alternative is to delay the activity having maximum float. This process is called resource levelling. If there are more than one activities requiring the same amount of resources, in that case activity having minimum duration is chosen for resource reallocation. Resource levelling is adopted in case there is restriction on the availability of resources.

11.7. STEPS IN RESOURCE LEVELLING

1. The peak requirement of the resources is lowered by staggering the resource input on non critical activities. If need be sub critical and critical activities may also be re scheduled to bring down the peak demand than specified limits. Thus the completion of project work may be delayed due to resource constraints.
2. Either some of the concurrent activities may be placed in series or the duration of critical activities may be increased to reduce the peak demands below the specified limits. This will increase the duration of the project.
3. Rearrange the activities having larger magnitude of positive float as resources can be diverted conveniently from the activities having large amount of float.

Following procedure may be adopted.

1. First the high peak of resource demand should be lowered utilizing the free floats of the activities.
2. Non critical activities may be rescheduled to the required extent utilizing the floats, starting with the activity having larger float. If necessary critical activities may also be tackled. The method has been illustrated by the following examples.

Example 11.4. *The net work of a project is shown below in Fig. 11.10. The requirement of masons of each activity is shown in bracket on the arrow and the duration below the arrow. Level out the requirement of resources, if the maximum number of masons on any day has to be limited to 7.*

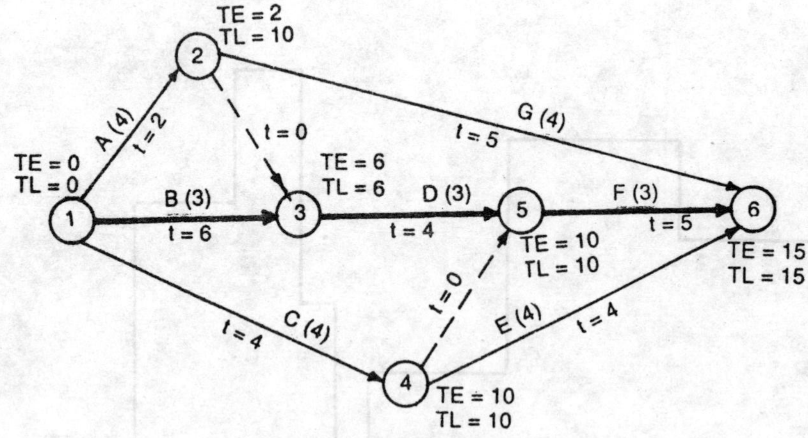

Fig. 11.10.

Table 11.12.

Activity	*Activity duration*	*Earliest start time (EST)* (T_E^i)	*Earliest finish time EFT*	*Latest start time LST*	*Latest finish time LFT*	*Float (LFT – EFT)*	*Remark*
(1 – 2) A	2	0	2	8	10	8	
(1 – 3) B	6	0	6	0	6	0	critical
(1 – 4) C	4	0	4	6	10	6	
(3 – 5) D	4	6	10	6	10	0	critical
(2 – 6) G	5	2	7	10	15	8	
(4 – 6) E	4	4	8	10	15	7	
(5 – 6) F	5	10	15	10	15	0	critical

The critical path is 1-3-5-6. The duration of the project along critical path is 15 days.

Now prepare the bar chart for determining the cumulative requirement of masons on each days.

Table 11.13

Duration → *Activiy ↓*	*Days*														
	1	2	3	4	5	6	7	8	9	10	11	12	13	14	15
(1 – 2) A	4	4							4	4					
(1 – 3) B	3	3	3	3	3	3									
(1 – 4) C	4	4	4	4											
(3 – 5) D							3	3	3	3					
(2 – 6) G			4	4	4	4	4				4	4	4	4	4
(4 – 6) E					4	4	4	4							
(5 – 6) F											3	3	3	3	3
	11	11	11	11	11	11	11	7	7	3	3	3	3	3	3

From the bar chart, of table 11.13 the histogram prepared is shown in Fig. 11.11. From the bar chart it will be seen that demand of mason varies from 11 to 3. The demand of 11 mason is during the first seven days. Now prepare the table of activities in descending order of their floats as follows:

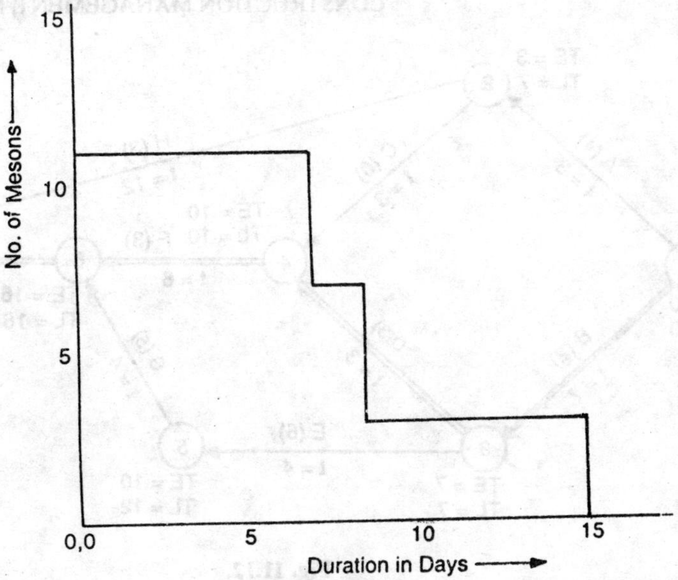

Fig. 11.11.

Table 11.14

Activity	EST	EFT	LST	LFT	FLOAT	*Remark*
(1 – 2) A	0	2	8	10	8	Non critical
(2 – 6) G	2	7	10	15	8	"
(4 – 6) E	4	8	10	15	7	"
(1 – 4) C	0	4	6	10	6	"
(1 – 3) B	0	6	0	6	0	critical
(3 – 5) D	6	10	6	10	0	"
(5 – 6) F	10	15	10	15	0	"

Activity 1-2 *i.e.* A has a float of 8 days, delay the start of this activity by 8 days and start it from 9th day instead of first day. Activity G has a float of 8 days. Shift it 8 days, start it on 11th day instead 3rd day. By this adjustment the demand on masons comes down to 7 as shown in Table 11.15.

Table 11.15

Duration →	*Days*														
Activity ↓	1	2	3	4	5	6	7	8	9	10	11	12	13	14	15
A									4	4					
B	3	3	3	3	3	3									
C	4	4	4	4											
D							3	3	3	3					
G											4	4	4	4	4
E					4	4	4	4							
F											3	3	3	3	3
	7	7	7	7	7	7	7	7	7	7	7	7	7	7	7

Example 5. The net work of a project is shown below in Fig. 11.12. The requirement of labour for each activity is shown on the top of arrow in bracket and the duration at the bottom. Level out the requirement of labour if the maximum number of labour not to exceed to 12 on any day.

Solution.

(*i*) First draw the net work and determine the earliest start time T_E^i and latest finish time T_L for the project.

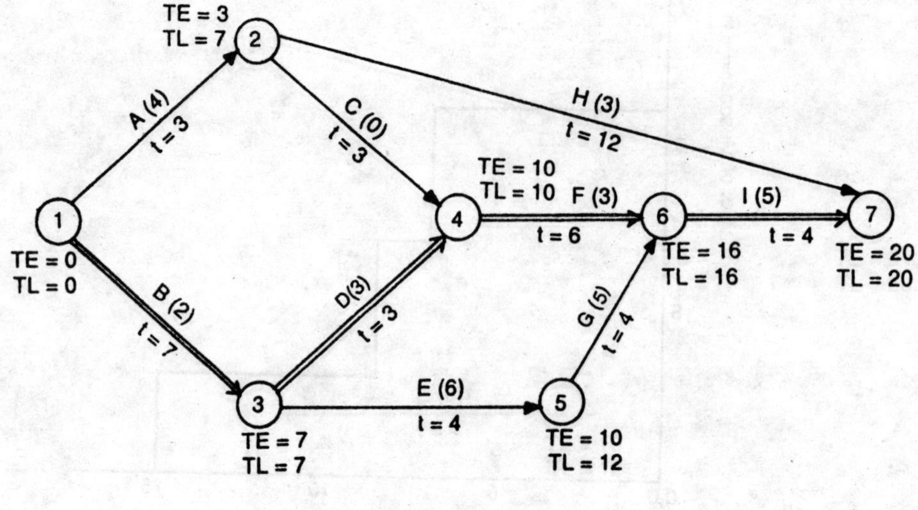

Fig. 11.12.

(*ii*) Find out the activities times as EST, EFT, LST, LFT and floats for each activity as shown in table 11.16.

Table 11.16

Activity	*Activity duration* (t^{ij})	*Earliest start time (EST)* (T_E)	*Earliest Finish time EFT* ($T_E^i + t_{ij}$)	*Latest start time LST*	*Latest finish time LFT*	*Float (LFT – EFT)*	*Remark*
(1 – 2) A	3	0	3	4	7	4	
(1 – 3) B	7	0	7	7	7	0	critical
(2 – 4) C	3	3	6	7	10	4	
(3 – 4) D	3	7	10	7	10	0	critical
(3 – 5) E	4	7	11	8	12	1	
(4 – 6) F	6	10	16	10	16	0	critical
(5 – 6) G	5	10	15	11	16	1	
(2 – 7) H	12	3	15	8	20	5	
(6 – 7) I	4	16	20	16	20	0	critical

The critical path is 1-3-4-6-7. The duration of project along the critical path is 20 days.

Now on the basis of earliest start time, determine the cumulative labour for each day either in the same way as in the last example or draw the bar chart for each activity as shown Table 11.17.

Table 11.17

Activity	1	2	3	4	5	6	7	8	9	10	11	12	13	14	15	16	17	18	19	20
A	4	4	4																	
B	2	2	2	2	2	2	2													
C	0	0	0	–	–	–	–	–												
D								3	3	3										
E								6	6	6	6									
F											3	3	3	3	3	3				
G											5	5	5	5						
H				3	3	3	3	3	3	3	3	3	3	3	3					
I																	5	5	5	5
	6	6	6	5	5	5	5	12	12	12	17	11	11	11	6	3	5	5	5	5

The resource requirements have been ploted with time in histogram of Fig. 11.13. From the histogram it will be seen that the labour requirement varies between 3 to 17. The fluctuation in resource requirement is quite high. Hence it needs levelling up.

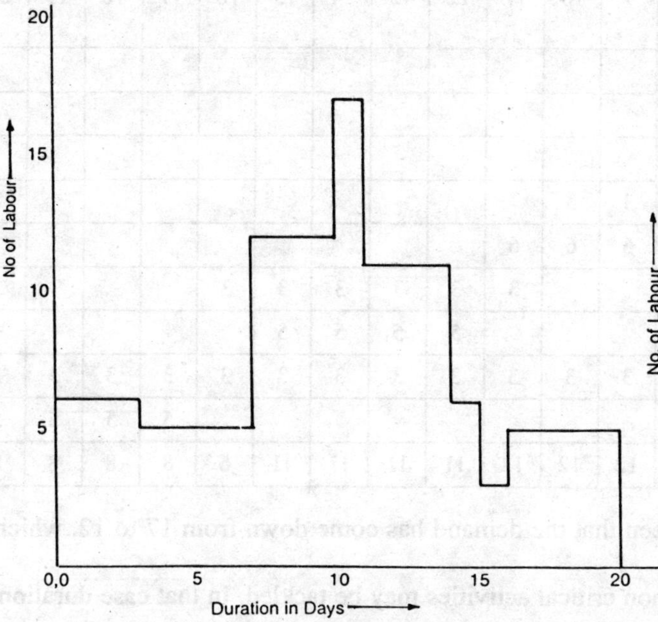

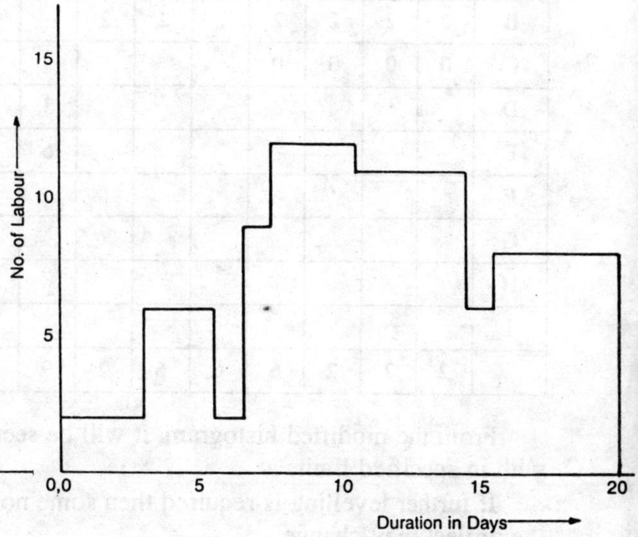

Fig. 11.13 (*a*) Original Histogram **Fig. 11.13 (*b*)** Revised Histogram

Now the activities are tabulated in descending order of their floats as shown in Table 11.18.

Table 11.18

Activity	*Activity duration*	*Earliest start time EST*	*Earliest finish time EFT*	*Latest start time LST*	*Latest finish time LFT*	*Float*	*Remark*
(2 – 7) H	12	3	15	8	20	5	Non critical
(1 – 2) A	3	0	3	4	7	4	"
(2 – 4) C	3	3	6	7	10	4	"
(3 – 5) E	4	7	11	8	12	1	"
(5 – 6) G	5	10	15	11	16	1	"
(1 – 3) B	7	0	7	7	7	0	critical
(3 – 4) D	3	7	10	7	10	0	"
(4 – 6) F	6	10	16	10	16	0	"
(6 – 7) I	4	16	20	16	20	0	"

Activity H has a float of 5 days. Let us delay its start by 5 days. Let it start on 9th day instead of 4th day and activity A is delayed for 3 days. Now it should start on 4th day instead of 1st day. Activity (5-6) G has one day float, delay it by one day and start it on 12th day instead of 11th day Histogram is shown in Fig. 11.13 (*b*). The calculations are shown in table 11.19.

Table 11.19.

Days →	1	2	3	4	5	6	7	8	9	10	11	12	13	14	15	16	17	18	19	20
A				4	4	4														
B	2	2	2	2	2	2	2													
C	0	0	0	0																
D								3	3	3										
E								6	6	6	6									
F											3	3	3	3	3	3				
G												5	5	5	5					
H									3	3	3	3	3	3	3	3	3	3	3	3
I																	5	5	5	5
	2	2	2	6	6	6	2	9	12	12	12	11	11	11	11	6	8	8	8	8

From the modified histogram, it will be seen that the demand has come down from 17 to 12, which is with in specified limit.

If further levelling is required then some non critical activities may be tackled. In that case duration of the project may change.

Example 11.6. *Smooth out the requirement of resources for the given net work shown in Fig. 11.14. The figure over the arrow indicate the requirement of carpenters per day and the figure below the arrow indicate the duration of completion of the activities.*

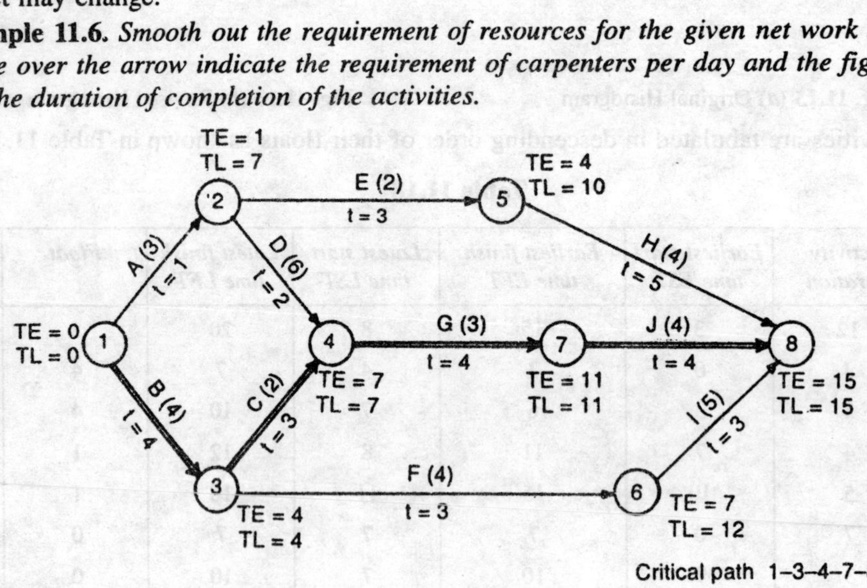

Fig. 11.14

Solution.

(*i*) Find T_E^i and T_L for the activities.

(*ii*) Find out the activities earliest and latest times EST, EFT, LST, LFT and float as shown in table 11.20.

Table 11.20.

Activity	*Activity duration*	EST (T_E^i)	EFT	LST	LFT	*Float*	*Remark*
(1 – 2) A	1	0	1	4	5	4	
(1 – 3) B	4	0	4	0	4	0	critical
(3 – 4) C	3	4	7	4	7	0	critical
(2 – 4) D	2	1	3	5	7	4	
(2 – 5) E	3	1	4	7	10	6	
(3 – 6) F	3	4	7	9	12	5	
(4 – 7) G	4	7	11	7	11	0	critical
(5 – 8) H	5	4	9	10	15	6	
(6 – 8) I	3	7	10	12	15	5	
(7 – 8) J	4	11	15	11	15	0	critical

The critical path is 1-3-4-7-8.

Duration along critical path = 15 days.

Now according to earliest start the cumulative resource carpenters may be determined for each day as follows:

Table 11.21

Duration →	*Days*														
Activity ↓	1	2	3	4	5	6	7	8	9	10	11	12	13	14	15
(1 – 2) A	3														
(1 – 3) B	4	4	4	4											
(3 – 4) C					2	2	2								
(2 – 4) D		6	6		6	6									
(2 – 5) E		2	2	2											
(3 – 6) F					3	3	3								
(4 – 7) G								4	4	4	4				
(5 – 8) H					4	4	4	4	4		4	4	4	4	4
(6 – 8) I								5	5	5					
(7 – 8) J											4	4	4	4	4
I	7	12	12	6	9	9	9	11	11	7	4	4	4	4	4
II	7	6	6	6	11	11	5	9	9	9	8	8	8	8	8

Originally carpenters demand varies from 4 to 12. The maximum demand is on 2nd 3rd day. The histogram is shown in Fig. 11.15. The requirement is maximum from 2nd, 3rd, 5th, 6th, 7th, 8th and 9th day. The float of activities is as follows:

Activity	*Float in days*
(2 – 5) E	6
(5 – 8) H	6
(3 – 6) F	5
(6 – 8) I	5
(1 – 2) A	4
(2 – 4) D	4

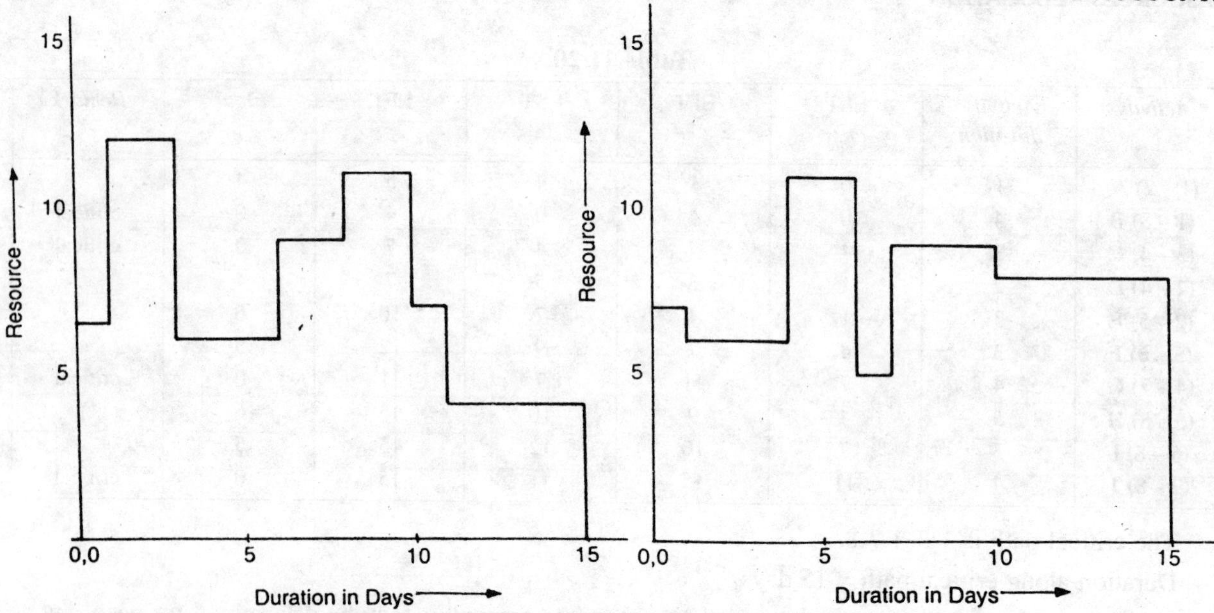

(a) Original (b) Modified

Fig. 11.15.

Shifting the activity D from 2nd to 5th days and activity H from 5th to 11day's requirement is shown in last row of table 10.20. ☐ shows activity shifted. Requirement varies from 5 to 11.

Example 11.7. *Smooth out the requirement of resource for the given net work. Fig. 11.16 figure over the arrow indicates the requirement of carpenters per day and the figure below the arrow indicates the duration of activities. Show the resulting revised schedule.*

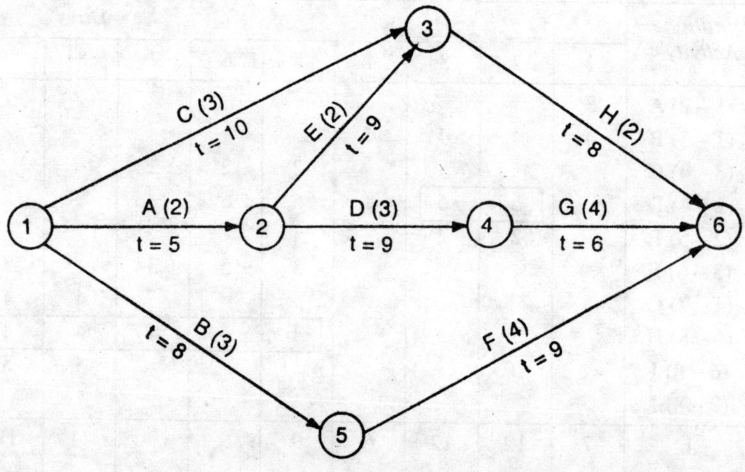

Fig. 11.16.

Solution. (*i*) Determine T_E^i and T_L of the activities.

(*ii*) Determine the activities times as EST, EFT, LST and LFT and floats of all activities as shown in Table 11.22.

Table 11.22.

Activity	*Activity duration*	*EST* (T_E^i)	*EFT* ($T_E^i + t_{ij}$)	*LST*	*LFT* T_L	*Float*	*Remark*
(1 – 2) A	5	0	5	0	5	0	critical
(1 – 3) B	8	0	8	5	13	5	
(1 – 5) C	10	0	10	4	14	4	
(2 – 4) D	9	5	14	7	16	2	
(2 – 5) E	9	5	14	5	14	0	critical

Activity	*Activity duration*	*EST* (T_E^i)	*EFT* $(T_E^i + t_{ij})$	*LST*	*LFT* T_L	*Float*	*Remark*
(3 – 6) F	9	8	17	13	22	5	
(4 – 6) G	6	14	20	16	22	2	
(5 – 6) H	8	14	22	14	22	0	critical

The critical path is along 1-2-5-6.
Critical duration = 22 days.

Table 11.23.

Activity	1	2	3	4	5	6	7	8	9	10	11	12	13	14	15	16	17	18	19	20	21	22
(1 – 2) A	2	2	2	2	2																	
(1 – 3) B	3	3	3	3	3	3	3	3														
(1 – 5) C	3	3	3	3	3	3	3	3	3	3												
(2 – 4) D						3	3	3	3	3	3	3	3	3								
(2 – 5) E						2	2	2	2	2	2	2	2	2								
(3 – 6) F									4	4	4	4	4	4	4	4	4	4	4	4	4	4
(4 – 6) G															4	4	4	4	4	4		
(5 – 6) H															2	2	2	2	2	2	2	2
Original total resource	8	8	8	8	8	11	11	11	12	12	9	9	9	9	10	10	10	6	6	6	2	2
Revised resource	8	8	8	8	8	11	11	11	8	8	5	5	5	9	10	10	10	10	10	10	6	6

The time estimates and floats are calculated as per table 11.22 The total requirement of labour is calculated by bar chart in table 11.23. The activities B and F have floats of 5 days each. Starting the activity F from 14th day instead of 9th day, the requirement is smoothened. The requirements are shown at the end of table 11.23. The histograms are shown in Fig. 11.17. The values in rectangle have been shifted.

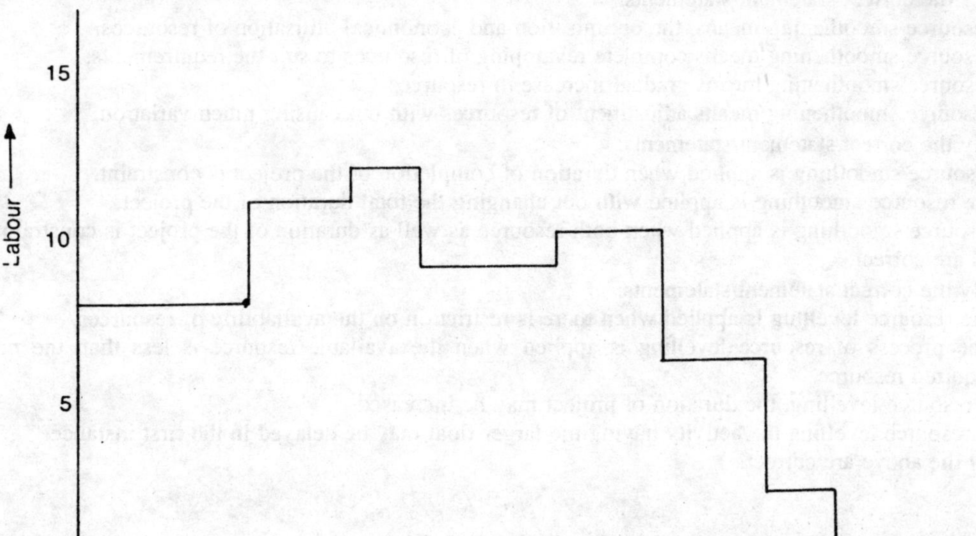

Fig. 11.17. (*a*) Original Histogram

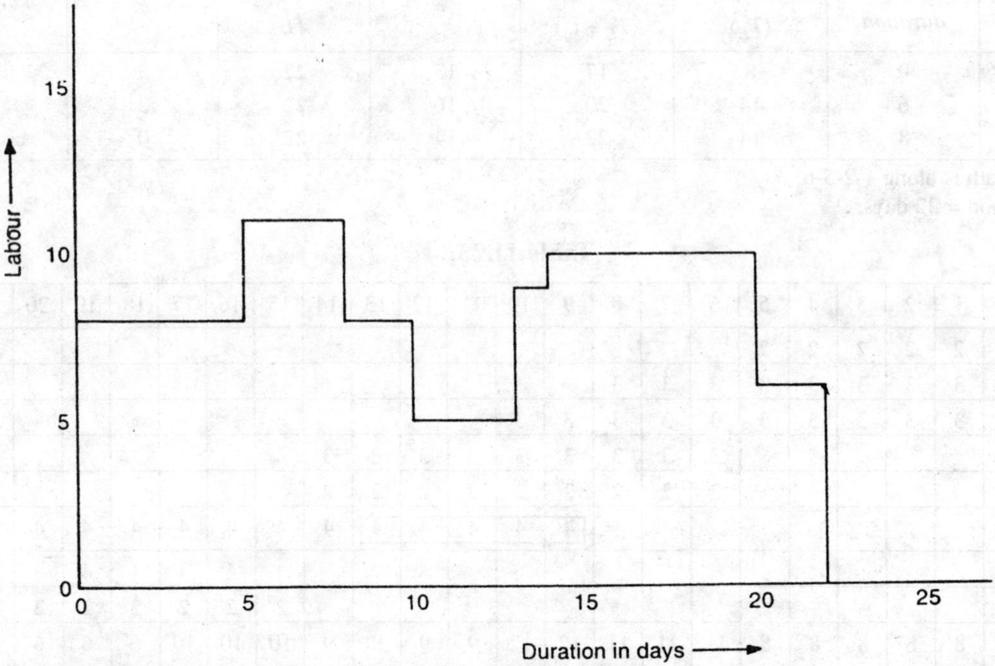

Fig. 11.17. (*b*) Modified Histogram

QUESTIONS

1. Discuss the objectives of resource allocation.
2. Discuss the resource smoothening and resource levelling step by step.
3. State the objectives of resource planning.
4. Identify the correct statement/statements.
   (*a*) Resource smoothening means, the optimisation and economical utilisation of resources.
   (*b*) Resource smoothening means complete revamping of resources to suit the requirements.
   (*c*) Resource smoothening means gradual increase in resources.
   (*d*) Resource smoothening means adjustment of resources with out causing much variation.
5. Identify the correct statement/statements:
   (*a*) Resource smoothing is applied when duration of completion of the project is constraint.
   (*b*) The resource smoothing is applied with out changing the total duration of the project.
   (*c*) Resource smoothing is applied when both resource as well as duration of the project is constraint.
   (*d*) All are correct.
6. Identify the correct statement/statements:
   (*a*) The resource levelling is applied when there is restriction on the availability of resources.
   (*b*) The process of resource levelling is applied when the available resource is less than the maximum required resource.
   (*c*) In resource levelling, the duration of project may be increased.
   (*d*) In resource levelling the activity having the larger float may be delayed in the first instance.
   (*e*) All the above are correct.

ANSWERS

4. (*d*) 5. (*a, b*) 6. (*e*)

12

Net Work And Control (Updating)

12.1. INTRODUCTION

For execution of any project, proper control is essential. With out proper control, it is not possible to get the desired results inspite of best planning and scheduling. Thus controlling is complementary to the planning. After the preparation of the proper schedule and commencement of the work, control over the progress of the work has to be exercised in order to get the work properly executed with in the schedule duration. The process of control involves comparing the actual progress of the work with the original plan at regular intervals, and taking necessary corrective measures to get the desired progress, if it is behind the schedule. The controlling requires an upward information through a suitable system. The information received is analysed and the project plan is brought upto date with the necessary changes if required to keep the progress as per schedule. The changes incorporated in the schedule of work is known as *updating* of the project. The conventional approach to updating is the complete recomputation of all data.

12.2. BASIC CHANGES THAT MAKE UPDATING NECESSARY

The following three basic changes make the updating necessary:

1. Changes in the project plan.
2. Rescheduling of activities.
3. Changes in the duration of an activities.

12.3. PROCESS OF UPDATING

During the process of implementation of the net work as per plan of the project following situations may be encountered.

1. Some or all the activities are progressing as per schedule.
2. Some or all the activities are behind the schedule.
3. Some or all the activities are ahead of the schedule.

If all the activities are progressing as per schedule, then there is no need for updating the net work, but this seldom happens. Thus based on the progress of the work, the activities behind their scheduled duration of completion are revised and the net work redrawn as per the revised duration. This process of revising the activity duration of completion and redrawing of net work is known as the *process of updating*.

12.4. REASONS FOR CHANGES IN PROJECT PLAN

Following are the major reasons for changes in the project plan:

1. Due to unforeseen reasons, such as natural calamities and changed conditions at the project site.
2. Based on additional knowledge of the jeb to develop better and more detailed plan.

12.5. REASONS FOR RESCHEDULING OF THE PROJECT

Following are the major reasons for rescheduling of the project:

1. To match the actual progress closely.
2. To expedite the job knowingly or to take advantage of the available float (extra time).

12.6. DATA REQUIRED FOR UPDATING

To update the plan at an intermediate stage of execution of the project, following information is necessary.

1. Original net work.
2. Progress report of the project at the updating stage.
3. Calculation charts based on the original net work.
4. Duration after which the updating is desired.
5. New information and knowledge which will affect the duration of the activity to be performed.

12.7. METHODS OF UPDATING

Following methods may be adopted for updating the project:

1. By describing the stage
2. By recording the progress
3. By summarising the work
4. By calculations

1. **By describing the stage.** In this case the stage of the work at which updating is desired according to original plan is described *i.e.* what period has elapsed before the updating is to be done according to the original plan.
2. **By recording the progress.** In this case, progress of completion of activities are recorded till the date of updating *i.e.* what actually has happened till the date of updating.
3. **By summarising the work.** Following information is to be collected:
   (*a*) What activities have been completed?
   (*b*) What activities are in progress? What portions of them have been completed?
   (*c*) What activities could not be started as yet.
   This information should be given in tabular form as shown in table 12.1.
4. The information contained in the updating table should be placed on the original net work in the following manner:
   (*a*) Assigning the time of update as the earliest occurrence time for the tail event of the project.
   (*b*) The activities already completed, allot them zero time.
   (*c*) Entering the remaining duration of those activities which are in progress.
   (*d*) Entering the estimated duration based on new knowledge of activities which are still to be completed.

4. **By calculations.** Calculate the earliest occurrence time T_E and latest occurrence time T_L. Mark these times on the net work known as updated net work.

Table 12.1.

Activity	*Whether completed or not*		*If in progress additional time required for completion*	*Completion required for activities yet to begin*
	Yes/no	*If yes, time taken for completion*		

12.8. UPDATING CYCLE OR FLOW CHART

It is shown in Fig. 12.1 below:

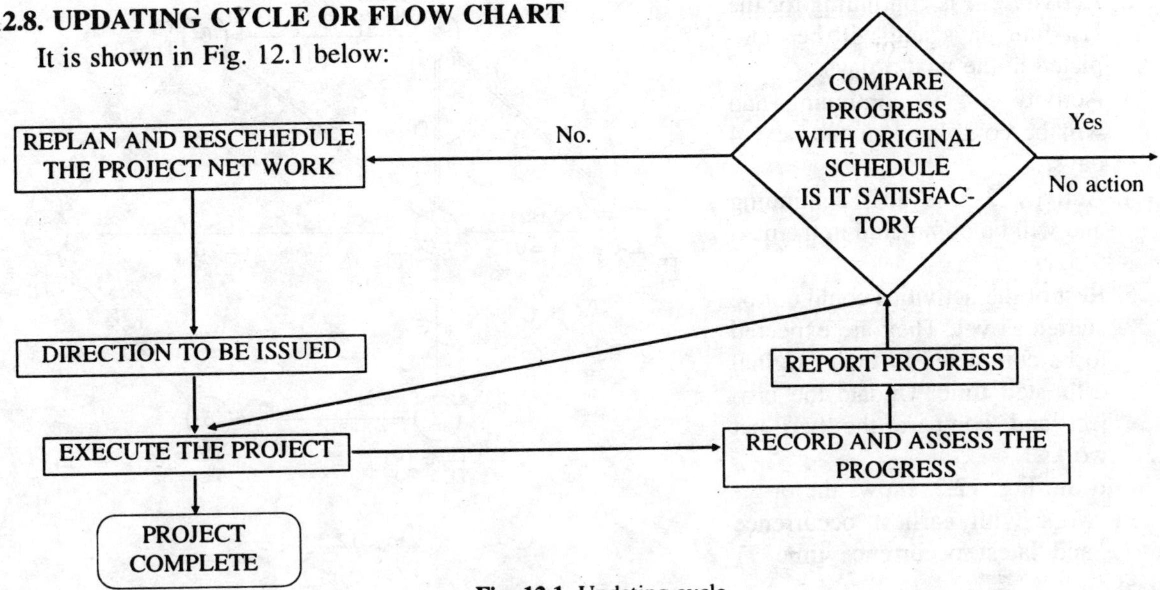

Fig. 12.1. Updating cycle

12.9. WHEN TO UPDATE

While deciding about the time of updating, following points must be kept in mind.

1. The updating should be done whenever there is a major change in the duration of any activity.
2. In case of short duration projects, updating must be done frequently by taking into account the latest position of completion of the project. It is essential for short duration projects as there are more chances of occurring delay in any activity. The delay in completion of one activity may affect the execution of the whole project. Thus updating from time to time is essential in short duration projects.
3. In case of larger duration projects, the duration of updating must be increased as the project progresses towards completion. In this case any delay in a small activity will not cause any significant effect on total execution duration of the project. Towards the end of the project; it should be treated as short duration project.
4. If there is any change in the estimated duration of any activity falling on the critical path, its updating is essential. If the duration of the critical activity increases, its remedial measures are essential. On the other hand if the duration on the critical activity decreases, this may allow changes in the project plan which were not possible previously.

After updating, it is possible that there are some changes in the completion duration of the project. In case duration of completion comes out more after updating then there are following two options.

1. The planner may ask the executing authority to increase the progress of activities falling on the critical path. This increased progress than originally estimated progress will need more resources.
2. The planner may redraw some portion of the net work containing those activities which have not yet commenced. Such alterations may lead to revised interdependence of operations.

Thus from the above it may be concluded that the critical path method (CPM) is not only useful in the planning stage of a project, but also helps the decision makers during the execution of the project and also to some extent in controlling the completion of the project on schedule. The method of up dating is illustrated with the help of following examples.

Example 12.1. Fig. *12.2 shows the net work of a project which is to be updated on the 15th day. Following conditions exist at the time of updating:*

1. Activities 1-2, 1-3 and 1-4 have been completed at the originally planned duration.

2. Activity 2-4 is continuing for the last four days and will be completed in the next 3 days.
3. Activity 3-4 is continuing and will be completed in the next 4 days.
4. Activity 3-5 is also continuing and will be completed in the next 5 days
5. Rest of the activities could not be started as yet. They are expected to be completed in their original estimated time. Update the project and compare the two net works.

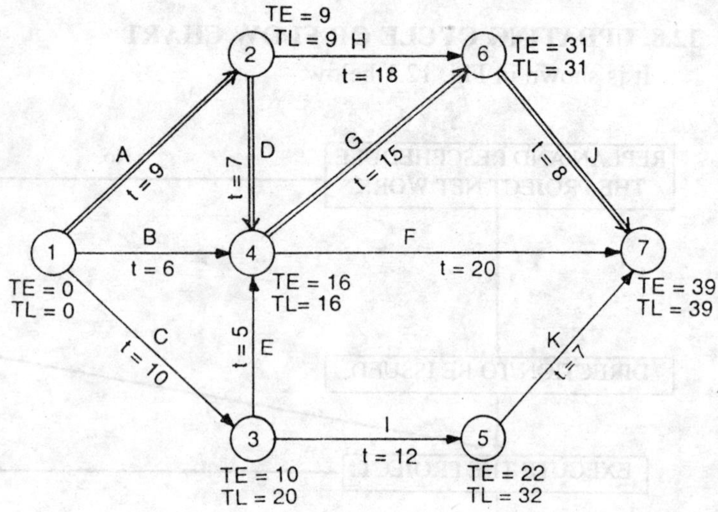

Fig. 12.2.

Solution. Fig. 12.2. shows the original net work with earliest occurrence time T_E and latest occurrence time T_L marked on it.

The critical path is 1-2-4-6-7 and is shown by thick lines.

The duration along the critical path is 39 days.

The details of execution of various activities are shown in table 12.2 below:

Table 12.2. Data for the net work to be redrawn

Activity	*Whether completed or not*		*Additional time required for activities in progress*	*Completion time required for activities yet to begin (days)*	*Remark*
	Yes/no	*If yes, timetaken in days*			
1	2	3	4	5	6
1 – 2	yes	9	–	–	
1 – 3	yes	10	–	–	
1 – 4	yes	6	–	–	
2 – 4	no		3	–	
2 – 6	no		–	18	
3 – 4	no		4	–	
3 – 5	no		5	–	
4 – 6	no		–	15	
4 – 7	no			20	
5 – 7	no			7	
6 – 7	no			8	

Now the net work of the project is redrawn with the data of column (1), (2), (4) and (5) of the table 12.2, while redrawing the net work following points should be kept in mind.

1. The activities which have been completed, they will not require time any more. Hence time for their completion should be assumed as zero.
2. The activities which are in progress their time for completion should be taken their original time minus the time for which they are in progress. For example activity (2-4) is in progress for the last 4 days. Thus the time for its completion is (7-4) = 3 as shown in column (4).

3. Now determine the earliest occurrence time T_E and latest occurrence time T_L for each event with reference to original starting time.
4. For event (1) the earliest occurrence time T_E may be assumed the day on which the updating is to be done. In the present case it may be taken 15.

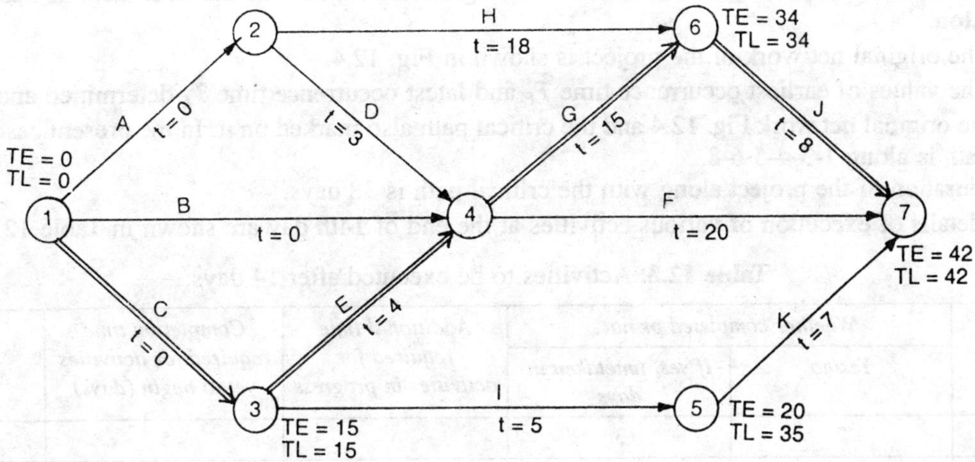

Fig. 12.3.

5. After computing T_E and T_L they should be marked on the net work, redrawn as shown in Fig. 12.3. The critical path for the redrawn net work is 1-3-4-6-7 while for the original net work, it was 1-2-4-6-7.

According to updated net work, the project will take 42 days to complete in stead of 39 days as originally planned. On the day of updating the remaining period of the completion of project = 42–15 = 27 days.

Note: Infact for updating a net work, the bar chart technique is easier than the net work technique.

Example 12.2. *The net work of a project is shown in Fig. 12.4. This net work is to be updated at the end of 14 days. Following conditions exist at the time of updating. Update the net work and draw the revised critical path.*

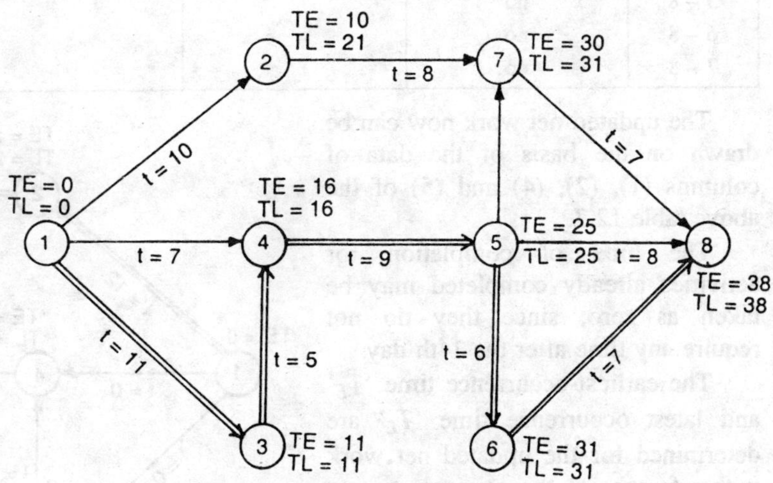

Fig. 12.4.

1. Activity 1-4 has been completed as originally planned.
2. Activity 1-3 executed earlier than expected time. it took 8 days for its completion.
3. Activity 3-4 commenced following the completion of activity 1-3 and was completed at th end of 14th.
4. Activity 4-5 was commenced after the completion of activity 3-4 (*i.e.* at the end of 14th day) and still require 8 days for its completion.
5. The completion of activity 1-2 was delayed very much and still require 12 more days for its completion.

6. Activity 2-7 will commence after the completion of activity 1-2 and will require 12 days for its completion in stead of 8 days.
7. The time required for the completion of activity 5-8 has been revised. It requires 13 days instead of 8 days.
8. No other activity has yet been started and original estimated time has been kept as such.

Solution.

1. The original net work of the project is shown in Fig. 12.4.
2. The values of earliest occurrence time T_E and latest occurrence time T_L determined and marked on the original net work Fig. 12.4 and the critical path also marked on it. In the present case the critical path is along 1-3-4-5-6-8.

The duration of the project along with the critical path is 38 days.

The details of execution of various activities at the end of 14th day are shown in Table 12.3 below.

Table 12.3. Activities to be executed after 14 days.

Activity	*Whether completed or not*		*Additional time required for activities in progress*	• *Completion time required for activities yet to begin (days)*	*Remark*
	Yes/no	*If yes, timetaken in days*			
1	2	3	4	5	6
1 – 2	no	–	12		
1 – 3	yes	8			
1 – 4	yes	7			
2 – 7	no			12	
3 – 4	yes	3			
4 – 5	no		8		
5 – 6	no			6	
5 – 7	no			5	
5 – 8	no			8	
6 – 8	no			7	
7 – 8	no			7	

The updated net work now can be drawn on the basis of the data of columns (1), (2), (4) and (5) of the above table 12.3.

The time of completion for activities already completed may be taken as zero, since they do not require any time after the 14th day.

The earliest-occurrence time 'T_E' and latest occurrence time 'T_L' are determined for the updated net work with-reference to the original starting date of the project and written on the net work. T_E' is assumed as (14) *i.e.* the day of updating.

The critical path is along the path 1-2-7-8 instead 1-3-4-5-6-8.

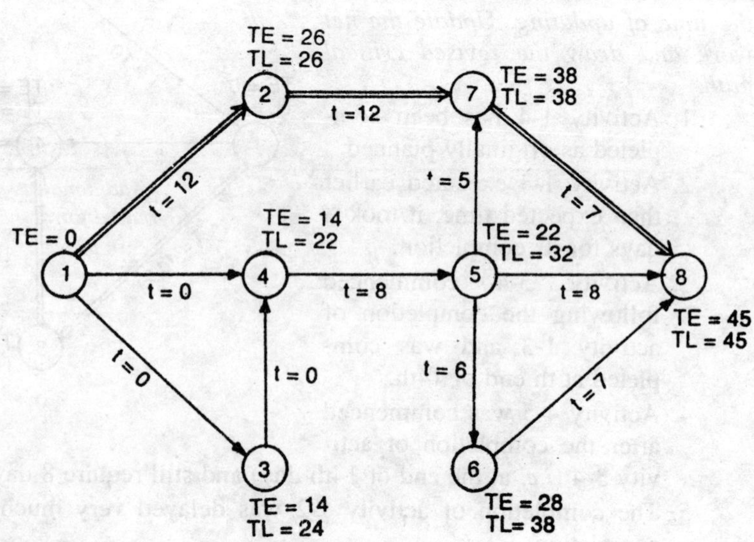

Fig. 12.5.

The duration of completion of the project along the critical path is 45 days instead of 38 days. On the updating, the remaining duration of the project is 45-14 = 31 days.

Example 12.3. *The net work of a project is shown in Fig. 12.6. The net work has been updated after 14 days of its commencement. At the time of updating following conditions existed.*

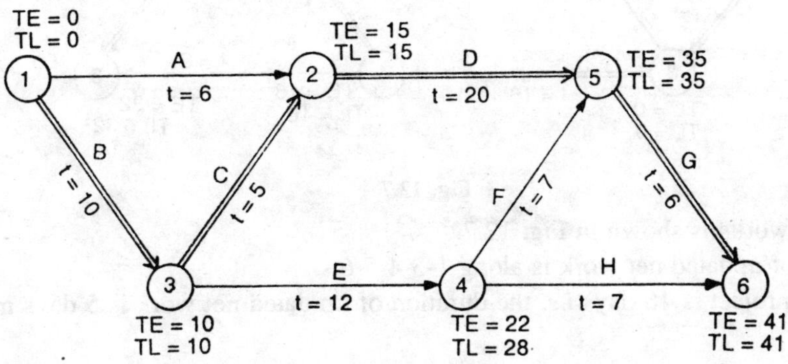

Fig. 12.6. Critical path 1-3-2-5-6

1. *Activities 1-2 and 1-3 have been completed as originally planned.*
2. *Activities 3-4 is in progress and will need 16 days for completion.*
3. *Activity 4-5 has some problem and is expected to be completed in 10 days.*
4. *Activity 4-6 can be completed in 5 days instead of 7 days.*

Update the net work and compare the critical path of the old and updated network.

Solution.

1. The earliest occurrence time T_E and latest occurrence time T_L are determined and noted on the net work.
2. The critical path is along 1-3-2-5-6 and duration of project is 41 days.
3. The details of execution of various activities are shown in Table 12.4.
   The updated net work can be drawn from the data of columns (1), (2), (4) and (5) of table 12.4.
4. The activities who have been completed, completion time is taken as zero.
5. The earliest occurrence time T_E and latest occurrence time T_L of each event is determined with reference to original starting date of the project.
6. For updating, T_E is taken as the date of updating. In this case it is 14.

Table 12.4. Revised table

Activity	*Whether completed or not*		*Additional time required for activities in progress*	*Completion time required for activities yet to begin (days)*	*Remark*
	Yes/no	*If yes, timetaken in days*			
1	2	3	4	5	6
1 – 2	yes	6			
1 – 3	yes	10			
3 – 4	no		16		
4 – 5	no			10	
4 – 6	no			5	
2 – 5	no			20	
5 – 6	no			6	
3 – 2	no			5	

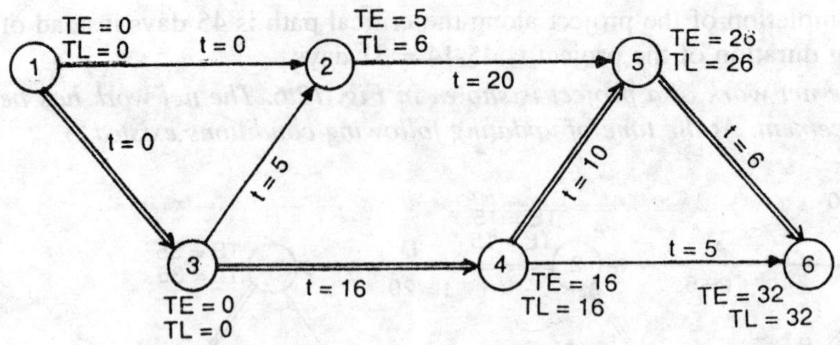

Fig. 12.7.

The up dated net works is shown in Fig. 12.7.

The critical path of updated net work is along 1-3-4-5-6.

Total duration of project is 46 days *i.e.* the duration of up dated net work is 5 days more than original net work.

QUESTIONS

1. Explain the term 'updating'. Why is it necessary?
2. What data is necessary for updating the network of a project?
3. When updating should be performed? Discuss fully.
4. The net work of a project is shown in Fig. 12.8. After 10 days of commencement of the work, the progress of the work is found as follows:
   (*a*) Activity 1-2, 1-3 and 1-4 have been completed during the expected time.
   (*b*) Activity 2-4 is in progress and will be completed after 1 day only.
   (*c*) Activity 3-4 is in progress and will be completed after 3 days.
   (*d*) Activity 3-5 is in in progress and will be completed after 1 days.
   (*e*) Rest of the activities could not be started as yet. They are expected to be completed in their original estimated duration.

   Redraw the net work and establish the critical path. Find out the increase in project duration.

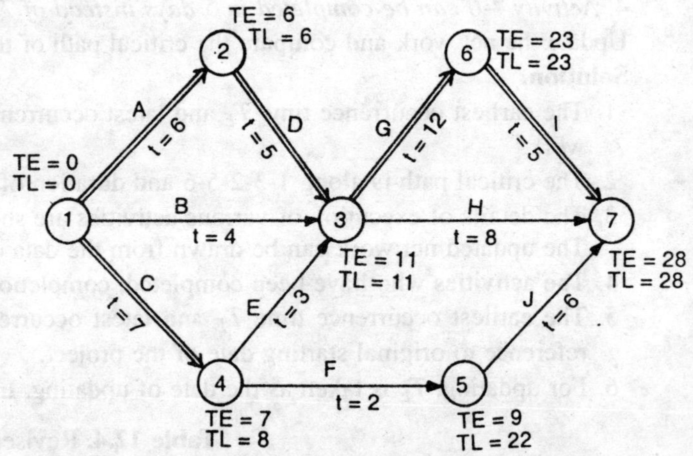

Fig. 12.8.

5. A net work of a project is shown in Fig. 12.9. The net work is to be updated after 10 days of its commencement. Following conditions existed at the end of 10 days.
   (*a*) Activities 1-2, 1-3 and 1-4 have been completed as per original schedule.
   (*b*) Activity 4-5 is in progress and will require 6 more days to complete.
   (*c*) Activity 4-6 is in progress and will be completed in 6 more days.
   (*d*) Activity 3-6 is in progress and will be completed in one day.
   (*e*) Activity 5-7 will be completed in only 3 days in stead of 5 days originally planned.
   (*f*) Rest of the activities have not yet been started. They are expected to be completed in their original schedule time.

   Update the net work and determine the critical path of the updated net work. What is the total increase in the

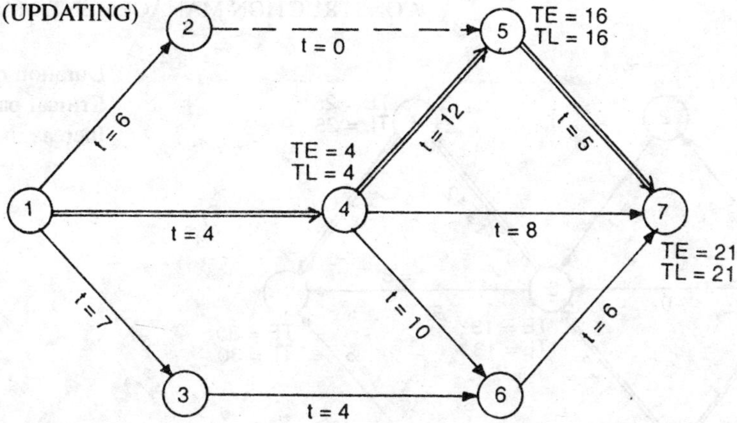

Fig. 12.9.

project duration?

Original critical path along 1-4-5-7 and duration is 21 days.

OBJECTIVE TYPE QUESTIONS

1. The process of incorporating changes in a net work by rescheduling and replanning is known as
   (*a*) Resource levelling (*b*) Resource smoothening
   (*c*) Scheduling the critical path (*d*) Up dating
2. Identify the correct statement/statements
   (*a*) Updating of a net work is done to decrease the project completion time.
   (*b*) Updating of a net work is done to increase the project completion time.
   (*c*) Updating of a net work is done to change the critical path of the net work.
   (*d*) Updating of a net work is done to change the critical path and to increase or decrease the project duration.
3. Identify the correct statement/statements
   (*a*) For updating a project net work, original net work of the project must be available.
   (*b*) For updating a project net work progress report of the execution of the project must be available.
   (*c*) For updating a project net work calculation charts based on original net work must be available.
   (*d*) for updating a project net work, the stage at which updating is to be done must be known.
   (*e*) All are correct
4. Identify the incorrect statement/statements
   (*a*) The updating is done when ever there is a major change in the duration of any activity.
   (*b*) The updating in case of larger duration projects should be done towards the completion of the project.
   (*c*) Updating of small duration projects is not necessary
   (*d*) In case of small duration projects updating must be done frequently.
5. Updating becomes necessary except in
   (*a*) Changes in the project plan (*b*) Rescheduling of activities
   (*c*) Change in the duration of any activity (*d*) Change in critical path
6. Identify the correct statements
   (*a*) The changes in the project plans are made to develop better and more detailed plans based on additional information gathered.
   (*b*) The changes in the project plans are made due to unforeseen difficulties such as natural calamities.
   (*c*) The changes in the duration of a project are done to expedite the job to take advantage of available float.
   (*d*) The changes in the duration of a project are done to match the actual performance closely.
   (*e*) All are correct.
7. Updating of projects should be done
   (*a*) When there is major change in duration of the activity
   (*b*) There is change in the estimated duration of the critical activities
   (*c*) Both are correct (*d*) None is correct

ANSWERS

1. (*d*)	3. (*e*)	5. (*d*)	7. (*c*)
2. (*d*)	4. (*c*)	6. (*e*)	

Ans. Q. 4.

Duration of project = 30 days
Critical path 1-4-3-6-7
Increas in duration = 2 days

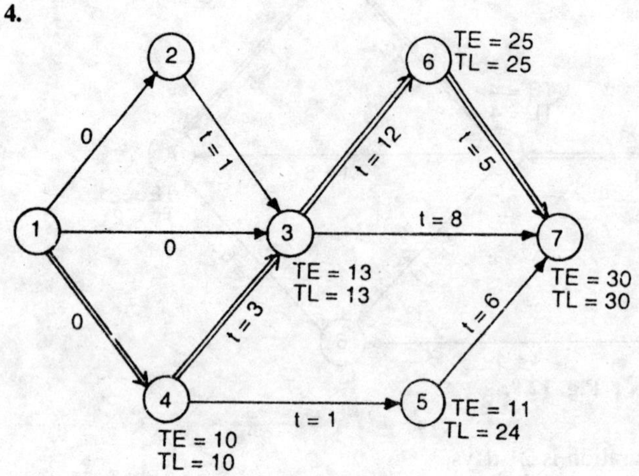

Fig. 12.10. Updated diagram

Ans. Q. 5.

Duration of project = 22 days
Critical path 1-4-6-7
Increas in duration = 1 days

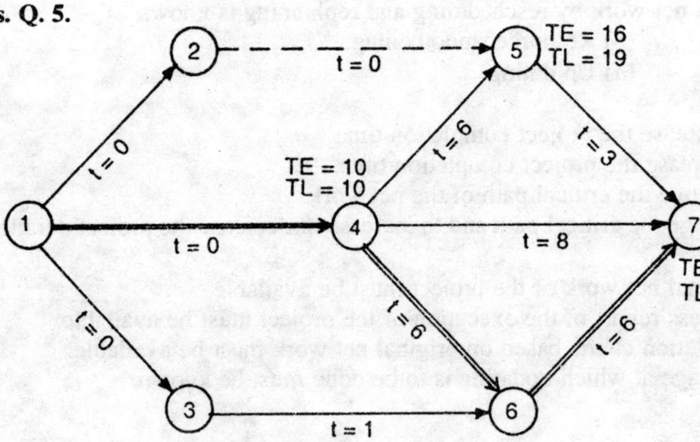

Fig. 12.11. Updated diagram

13

Cost Control In Construction

13.1. INTRODUCTION

Cost control is the process of controlling the expenditure on a construction project during all the stages of construction right from its inception till its execution and final payments are made. The main aim of planning, scheduling and supervising a project is to ensure the maximum benefits from the expenditure incurred on the project. To achieve this objective, it is necessary to have estimates of cost of the proposed works and reasonably make sure that it can be completed with in the available resources or funds. During construction stage measures should be taken to ensure that project cost is kept with in the estimated expenditure or cost.

Cost control is an important aspect of construction management, not only for the owner of the project, but for contractor also, who has to earn profit out of it. If he does not exercise sufficient control on cost he may not only loose profit margin, but could suffer heavy losses also. To have effective cost control, the trends of the cost must be established as early as possible. These trends should be compared with the planned and actual progress and remedial measures taken if found necessary. This is called the impor- tance of cost control.

13.2. AIMS OR OBJECTIVES OF COST CONTROL

Following are the main aim or objectives of the cost control.

1. To determine or estimate the profit.
2. To locate the areas of inefficient functioning.
3. To serve as a basis for estimating.

1. **To determine the estimated profit.** The cost control data provides the total expenditure incurred on the work at the regular interval or at any given duration. The contractor can determine his profit or loss by comparing the likely payments to him from the measurements of the completed portion of the work with the actual expenditure incurred by him. Thus the cost control provides an opportunity to the contractor to take corrective measures if found some deficiency somewhere.
2. **To locate areas of inefficient functioning.** Cost control data provides the day to day cost incurred on various items of works and gives warning to the site Engineer if the expenditure is higher than the estimated cost. The reasons for inefficient working can be investigated and remedial measures taken at the appropriate time.

   In case cost control methods are not adopted, the profit or loss from the work executed will be known at the end of completion of the work and it would be impossible to pin point the exact reason for the loss. Thus cost-control technique is a useful tool to find out the inefficiency in the execution of the work.
3. **To serve as a basis for estimating.** The cost control data of work provides feed back to the

estimator for updating the knowledge of out put data of men and machines. The unit rates of cost for various items of work can be worked out after the completion of a job, which would be helpful in preparing the realistic estimates for the future works for which the contractor may like to tender. How ever the cost depends upon the local conditions as well as on the rates of labours. Thus at the time of comparing costs of two similar works these factors also should be kept in mind. Thus the unit rates of costs should not always be applied to similar types of works without proper study.

The inefficiency in the use of labour and machinery is wide spread. Thus cost control on projects has been found very useful when applied to labour and machinery. Cost control of materials used at site of work also has been found very useful.

13.3. STAGES OF COST CONTROL

At the following stages, cost control has been found very useful

1. Pre contract stage or at the design stage.
2. Post contract stage or at the construction stage.

13.3.1. Pre contract or design stage

1. The cost of a project depends to a great extent upon its design and specifications. Hence at design stage various alternative designs should be considered and out of them the most economical as well as consistent with the requirements should be chosen.
2. The specifications should be decided judiceously based on requirements. The specifications which increase the cost with out producing commensurate benefits should be rejected.
3. As far as possible, local construction materials should be specified as their use will reduce the transportation and storage cost along with some other minor costs.
4. The estimates should be prepared accurately from the detailed drawings using standard specifications and approved rates.

13.3.2. Post Contract or Construction stage Cost Control

During construction stage, the cost consists of expenditure on the following items:

1. Labour	2. Construction materials
3. Machinery and equipment	4. Over head charges

Out of the above items the most likely wastage is found in items of labour and machinery and equipment.

1. Labour. In order to have proper cost control, there should be effective supervision of labour. The workmen to be engaged should be selected carefully to suit the job and should be appointed as per minimum requirement. Over staffing leads to inefficiency. The out put should be evaluated regularly. To increase the output, some incentive may be announced.

2. Construction materials. Construction material is one of the main component of any construction job. Thus the cost control must be exercised at its purchasing stage. About 5% more quantities than required of right quality materials should be purchased at the most competitive rates from proper sources. Surplus materials should not be purchased as it deteriorates in storage.

3. Machinery and equipment. Cost control over machinery and equipment can be exercised in the following ways:

(*a*) The right type of equipment as per requirement should be arranged well in advance of the commencement of the work.

(*b*) The equipment should not be allowed to remain idle either due to shortage of material or due to oiling or minor repair etc. Thus their servicing should be ensured timely and sufficient material must be available for the work as per requirement of the equipment.

(*c*) For carrying out repairs, workshop having proper equipment must be set up near the site of work, so that much time may not be wasted in cartage of equipment to the workshop.

(*d*) In order to safeguard against loss of work due to the frequent break downs, some extra equipment may be hired.

4. Over head Charges. The over head charges can be reduced to a minimum by reducing the duration of the completion of the work.

5. Safety and security measures. The safety measures reduce accidents resulting saving in time and money paid as compensation to workers. Security measures also check the pilferage of materials, resulting in over all saving. Thus for efficient and economical completion of any job proper safety and security measures are essential.

13.4. CLASSIFICATION OF COST CONTROL SYSTEMS

The cost control system to be used for a particular work depends upon the degree of details required to be exercised. The cost of operating a cost control system varies linearly with the details of works. In other words the cost of operating cost control measures increases with the increase in details of the various operations to be recorded. Thus due to the high cost of operation for detailed cost control system, it is desirable to use simpler and quick acting system. Commonly following methods of cost control are used.

1. Over all profit or loss method
2. Profit or loss with reference to partial payment
3. Unit costing
4. Comparison with standard costs
5. Combination with other functions

1. Over all profit or loss method. Though this method is simplest and cheapest involving least details, but is extremely risky. In this method the contractor has to wait till the work is completed. At this stage he compares the amount received by him for the completed work with the amount he spent on it. This comparison gives the idea of profit or loss. Such a system is useful for very small contracts of short duration. This system hardly has any control on the construction as the result is available at the completion of the work. However experience gained by this information can be utilised in future for the execution of similar works.

2. Profit or loss with reference to partial payment. In this method the contractor is paid on running bill basis at regular intervals for the portion of the work completed by him. By comparing the amount received by him with the expenditure incurred on the work completed by him, he knows his profit or loss.

Though this method is a bit better than the previous method but it has the following draw backs.

(*a*) While taking the measurement for preparing the running bills of the contractor all items of work done and materials lying unused at site-might not have been taken into account.

(*b*) In this system of comparision, there is no break up of the cost figures for different items of work. Thus it only indicates the losses which need attention, but does not pin point the area which needs attention.

3. Unit cost method. In this method, the rate of cost of each item of work is calculated by dividing the expenditure on the item by the quantity of work done. The comparision of the rate of cost with the rates of the cost estimates gives the idea of the efficiency of the work. This method gives a clear picture of the items which are going un economical and need attention. Though limited details of cost records will not provide clear picture whether the poor performance is due to labour, material or equipment, yet for most purposes, it is sufficient indication of the items which need attention to avoid losses. Hence it is a better method.

4. Comparision with standard costs. In this method the cost records of details of rates of cost of labour, materials, and machinery are prepared separately and compared with the rates of these items called as standard costs. The cost of stores is estimated at the time of estimating. This comparision of rates of costs gives an idea of the areas of inefficient works and the scope of improvement. Though this method is ideal, but it is laborious and costly as it requires great details to be maintained separately for each item of work pertaining to labour, material and equipment costs.

In construction works, detailed record of labour and equipment need to be kept, as in these two areas considerable inefficiency is likely to arise. On large works, control on materials is also necessary and it should be maintained in the form of material at site account. The consumption of materials may be compared with the theoritical consumption for the quantities of work executed. Any appreciable variation should be investigated for any pilfeeage. It should also be investigated whether the materials used are more or sub standard quality.

5. Combination with other administrative function. To effect economy some times cost control system is combined with some other necessary operations such as of an incentive or bonus scheme. In the profit sharing type of incentive schemes it is essential to know the cost of efficiency of the work before announcing the bonus.

13.5. ESTIMATING AND COST CONTROL

There is an close or intimate relationship between cost control and estimation as expenditure is regulated on the basis of the estimates of works. An abstract of the cost of a construction job indicates the quantities of work involved in various items of works, their rates, and the estimated cost. The cost control is effected on the basis of the estimated cost of each item of work as provided in the estimates.

An abstract of cost indicates item wise cost only. It does not provides details of cost of each operation. The details of costs separately for labour, material, and other items may also not be available. Thus cost estimates are not suitable as a basis of cost analysis.

If cost analysis is to be made from cost estimates, then it is necessary to separate all material and labour costs for ready reference. It is also essential to indicate the quantities of materials to be purchased with the unit price and its total cost. The cost analysis is also known as the *work estimates* and forms the basis for the purchase of materials, engaging labour and cost keeping.

Cost analysis can be divided into the following divisions.

1. **Labour division.** The labour division will be responsible for keeping and checking the labour costs.
2. **Materials division.** This division will be responsible for the purchase and checking the costs of all materials.
3. **General items.** Items which can neither be classified under the head 'materials. nor 'labour'. are classified under the head 'general items'.
4. **Sub contract head.** If due to economic consideration or due to the specialised nature of the work, contractor decides to get some part of the work done on sub contract basis, then the amount of each sub contract will be shown under this head.
5. **Over head charges.** Expenses for site supervision, maintaining a head office etc. are shown under the head 'over head charges'.

Apart from these expenses, the profit of the contractor also has to be kept in mind.

13.6. METHODS OF COST ANALYSIS

At the time of cost analysis, all the estimates are analysed first and afterwards labour and material costs are separated. All similar materials are grouped under one head. The expenditure under 'over heads' 'general items' and profits are also separated. The total expenditure obtained from cost analysis must be equal to the total of the abstract cost in the estimate. The cost analysis must cover every material necessary and every labour operation. While preparing estimates, temporary works, such as equipment and material sheds, labour huts, temporary office sheds etc. generally are not taken into account, often such works are very expensive and must be taken into account at the time of cost analysis. For example in the construction project of a dam, the diversion of main stream is often essential, but this is not included in the estimate of project, though it is a major item of expenditure. Thus such items must be included in the cost analysis, because all expenditure will be distributed against one or the other of the items.

Thus the estimates prepared in the form of cost analysis is quite suitable to form the basis for the cost control system and to compare the actual cost with the estimated cost. It can provide an indication whether the actual costs are more or less than the estimated costs. The form of abstract of cost is shown below.

Table 13.1. Farm of abstract of cost

S. No.	*Items*	*Quantity*	*Rates per unit*	*Cost*

13.7. CODES FOR COST CONTROL

In cost analysis, instead of writing full description of each item they are denoted by either certain symbols or codes by which they can be identified easily. To avoid labour and wastage of time, the codes are applied for labour operations. In actual practice there may be two types of cost control codes as follows:

1. Alphabetical classification
2. Decimal classification

1. Alphabetical Classification. In this classification the initial letter denotes the trade group to which the operation pertains and the second letter represents the operation carried out in that trade. A list of trade wise notation is given below:

1. Trade wise main code:

B-Brick laying
C-Concreting
D-Drain laying
E-Excavation
F-Form work
R-Road work
S-Structural work
O-Preliminaries

2. Code sub division.

B-Brick laying
Bl-Laying brick in lime mortar
Bc-Laying brick in cement mortar
Bf_{10}-Laying facing bricks in 10 cm wall
B_p-Brick pointing
C-Concreting
Cf-Concrete or cement finish
C_{fi}-Interior rubbed finish
C_{fr}-Roof finish
C_{fp}-Paving finish
C_{fo}-Concrete in foundation
C_b-Concrete in drain bed.

3. Decimal classification. In this system of classification first two numbers denote the functional division of the work as shown below.

01-Foundation
02 Sub structure
03-Super structure
04-Roofing
10-Work shop shed
20-Septic tank
30-Tube well and pump house
40-Office block
50-Electric sub station
60-Garage and out-house etc.

Further division of the work is based on the associated trade. Trade wise distribution may be as follows:

0.01-Clearing site
0.02-Excavation
0.03-Concreting
0.04-Brick work
0.05-Carpentry and joinery
0.06-Plumber
0.07-Plastering
0.08-Electrical fittings
0.09-Flooring
0.10-Polishing and painting

4. Third decimal place can be used for further division of work as follows:

0.021-Excavation by hand
0.022-Excavation by machines
0.031-Form work
0.032-Mixing and placing of concrete
0.033-Curing of concrete
0.034-Finishing
0.051-Door and window frame
0.052-Door and windows
0.053-Kitchen cabinet

For still further details, fourth decimal place can be used as follows:

0.0311-Form work for columns 0.0312-Form work for beams

0.0313-Form work for slabs 0.0314-Form work for lintel etc.

Though this classification can be used upto six digits of decimal, but it will be uneconomical and difficult to maintain. Generally for most of the works two or three digit cost code is sufficient.

13.8. COLLECTION OF SITE COST DATA

The site cost data should be collected every day. For collecting this data the incharge of labour in the field is the best source. Generally the incharge of labour in the field is the junior engineer, hence he is the best person to collect the site cost data. It will be better if the supervisor concerned provides the necessary data for the deployment of labour, materials and equipment. He should also specify the item of work at which these are being utilised. The sample of form used for collection of the site cost data is shown below.

Name of work...........

Name of supervisor..........

Table 13.1. Daily report

S. No.	*Work done*	*Quantity*	*Unit rate*	*Labour employed*							*Cost in (Rs.)*	*Allocation*
				super-visor	*Mason*	*Carpen-ters*	*Beldar*	*Coolie*	*Operator*	*Helper*		

QUESTIONS

1. What is meant by cost control? Why it is done in construction work? Explain its importance.
2. Discuss the objectives of cost control.
3. Discuss the various stages of work at which cost control is effected.
4. Give the classification of cost control system. Which of the methods is widely used.
5. Discuss the relation ship between estimating and cost control.
6. What are different stages of cost control methods?
7. Write a note on the collection of site cost data.
8. Discuss the various cost control codes.
9. Discuss the necessity for cost control codes in major construction jobs. Explain the system used for cost control codes.
10. During all the stages of a construction work, the process of controlling the expenditure is known as
    (*a*) Time control (*b*) Quality control
    (*c*) Cost control (*d*) Non of the above
11. In construction management, if cost control is neglected, it will result in
    (*a*) Reduced profit margins to the contractor (*b*) Increased profit margins to the contractor
    (*c*) Profit to the owner of the project (*d*) Non of the above
12. Identify the incorrect statement/statements
    (*a*) The objective of cost control is to locate the area of inefficient functioning
    (*b*) The objective of cost control is to serve as the basis for preparing estimates
    (*c*) The objective of cost control is the estimation of profit or loss.
    (*d*) None of the above is incorrect.
13. Identify the incorrect statement
    (*a*) The cost-control is effected at planning stage
    (*b*) The cost-control is effected at designing stage

(*c*) The cost-control is effected at construction stage
(*d*) The cost control is effected at all the above three stages

14. Construction cost consists of expenditure mainly on
(*a*) Plant and equipment (*b*) Labour
(*c*) Materials (*d*) Over head charges
(*e*) All the above

15. Identify the correct statement/statements
(*a*) Local construction materials are used to increase the transportation cost
(*b*) Local construction materials are used to decrease the transportation cost.
(*c*) Local construction materials will not change the cost of transportation
(*d*) All are correct

16. Identify the incorrect statement/statements
(*a*) The cost control can be best achieved in the area of labour
(*b*) The cost control can be best achieved in the area of equipment and machinery
(*c*) The cost control can be best achieved in the area of materials
(*d*) All are incorrect

17. The profit and loss system with reference to full payment is useful for
(*a*) Large contracts of small duration (*b*) Large contracts of large duration
(*c*) Small contracts for small duration (*d*) Small contracts of large duration

18. The six digit cost control codes are time consuming and laborious for
(*a*) Small works (*b*) Larger works
(*c*) Medium works (*d*) For all the above

19. The incharge for collecting site cost data collection is
(*a*) Executive Engineer (*b*) Assistant Engineer
(*c*) Junior engineer or supervisor (*d*) None of the above

20. The calculation of the rate of cost of each item of work can be obtained by
(*a*) Adding the expenditure on the item and the quantity of work done
(*b*) Subtracting the expenditure on the item from the quantity of work done
(*c*) Dividing the expenditure on the item of work by the quantity of work done
(*d*) Multiplying the expenditure on the item of work by the quantity of work done

21. Identify the correct statement
(*a*) The cost of operating a cost control system is inversely proportional to the details in which the costs of the various operations are recorded.
(*b*) The cost of operating a cost control system is linearcy proportional to the details in which the costs of various operations are recorded
(*c*) Both are correct
(*d*) Both are incorrect

ANSWERS

10. (*c*)	13. (*a*)	16. (*c*)	19. (*c*)
11. (*a*)	14. (*e*)	17. (*c*)	20. (*c*)
12. (*d*)	15. (*b*)	18. (*d*)	21. (*b*)

14

Job Layout

14.1. INTRODUCTION

The construction of a project is carried out in the form of a camp. It should be so designed that the work progresses efficiently with minimum interruption. Every project must be organised and executed in the most economical and safest way. The arrangements made for the smooth execution of the project is known as job layout. A job layout is a scaled drawing of the proposed construction site showing all relevant features such as entry and exit points to the site, storage areas for materials and other necessary aminities such as contractor's offices, space for keeping equipments, and labour housing etc. The basic input of a construction job, namely men, materials and machines must be controlled and placed at the site in such a way that.

(*a*) The materials are stored as near as possible to the place of their utilisation.

(*b*) The machines are positioned in such a way that they are fully utilised.

(*c*) Adequate storage and other accommodation must be available.

A job lay out that provides maximum efficiency is known as optimum job layout. Actually the activities at construction site go on changing with the progress of the work. Hence the job layout should be reviewed periodically and modified to suit the changed needs of the site activities.

Thus in order to prepare a job layout, an over all idea of the type, extent of work and the way in which it is to be carried out must be studied before hand from the construction plans, specifications and other contract documents. The knowledge of principles of storing and stacking of materials and placing of equipments is essential for preparing a good job layout.

14.2. OBJECTIVES OF PREPARING A JOB LAYOUT

Generally a job lay out is prepared for the following objectives:

1. To save time in delivering the construction material at the site of construction.
2. To safe guard construction material from damage and deterioration.
3. To keep the lead of cartage minimum, so that certage expenses may be minimum.
4. To adopt the best mode of working.
5. To complete the work with the minimum use of equipment and machinery.
6. To take maximum out put from labour and machines.
7. To provide safety to workers and passer by etc.
8. To avoid damage due to construction activities to the nearby properties.
9. The common use materials as fine and coarse aggregates should be stored near to each other.
10. To store construction materials as near the place of their utilisation as possible.

14.3. FACTORS AFFECTING THE JOB LAYOUT

Following factors have been found to affect the job layout:

1. **Nature and type of work.** Nature and type of work plays an important role in the preparation of job lay out. For example the job lay out for a Earthen dam or canal lining will be quite different from that of a multi-storeyed building as the nature and extent of requirements of supporting facilities are quite different in each case. In case of a multi storeyed building project, the job layout should be located centrally, where as in case of lining of canal or high way construction project a number of construction centres at suitable locations will be required. Availability of materials, labour also affect the site arrangements to a great extent.

2. **Access to site.** The access to the site of construction must be easy as it will facilitate the transportation of equipment and construction material at minimum cost. If the facilities for transportation of equipment and materials are not available, it will affect the job layout badly. Hence to complete any project economically and with in time schedule it is essential that the access to site must be easy.

   Site having different routes for entrance and exit is ideal. In case there is only one route for entrance and exit both, then near the main entrance, a sign post must be erected to indicate the position of the store. It will also help in avoiding accidents.

3. **Nature of the ground.** For the movement and fixing the machinery, strong and solid ground is essential. In case the site soil is soft, then for erecting heavy machinery, preparation of solid foundation will be essential. Pucca roads will also be required for the easy movement of heavy machines. Sites having high water table, some times require de-watering for lowering the water table of the site.

4. **Temporary roads.** If the soil is loose then to transport the heavy machinery and equipment, construction materials etc. from the main road or railway station pucca road is essential. In such situations road construction work should be completed before the start of the project.

5. **Construction methods.** The construction can be either cast in situ or pre cast elements. In case it is to be completed by pre cast elements, then the provision for casting yard should be included in the job layout.

6. **Availability of materials.** If the construction materials are available locally, then there storage problem will be less, other wise it will affect the job layout, as storage space for materials is to be included in job layout at suitable location. The location of material storage should be such that their cross movement is avoided and their lead time is minimum. Materials should be well protected from damage due to atmospheric and weathering effects. Pilferage of materials should never be tolerated.

7. **Miscellaneous factors.** Non availability of the following facilities will also affect the job layout.

1. Accommodation for administrative block and residences. To achieve a faster progress of work, it is essential that the administrative block and residences of officers and workers should be nearer to the site of work. During the full duration of the project, the residential accommodations should be permanent.

While selecting the site for accomadations following points should be kept in mind.

(*a*) The location of manager's, residence should have an easy approach. It should be easy to locate.

(*b*) To residential site should be away from work shop etc., where noise pollution should be minimum.

(*c*) As far as possible, the residential accommodation of all officers should be nearer to each other.

(*d*) The residential site should be such, that it may not be very use full for other works.

2. Medical facilities. The field medical facilities should be provided to workers and officers at site colony. There should also be following facilities.

3. Public health amenities

4. School facility for the children of the staff and workers.

5. Electricity, Telephone and water supply.

6. Daily necessity of life etc.

14.4. RECORD TO BE STUDIED BEFORE PREPARING A JOB LAYOUT

For preparing a good job layout following records should be studied carefully

1. Site plan 2. Working drawings
3. Specifications

1. Site plan. It is a scaled drawing indicating the orientation, shape, and dimensions of the site and relationship to the surrounding areas. The site plan shows the following details:

(*a*) The boundaries of the construction site.
(*b*) The boundaries of the adjacent area owned by the owner.
(*c*) The position of the site in relation to the adjacent road indicating name and width etc.
(*d*) The location and size of any built up work at site.
(*e*) The location and size of any existing building proposed to be demolished.
(*f*) The location of any service utility as existing water mains, sewers, electric lines etc.
(*g*) The presence of physical features such as natural drains, wells, river etc.
(*h*) The location of all proposed building works indicating their distances from the roads adjacent to buildings and boundaries with in 12 metres of the site and number of stories in each building.
(*i*) The location and width of all approach roads or passages from the existing roads or passages of all buildings to be constructed.
(*j*) North direction.
(*k*) Any other information considered necessary.

2. Working drawings. Working drawings include the plans of buildings and other works to be constructed at the site. Usually working drawings consist of the following items.

(*a*) Floor plans of the buildings and other works showing the position and dimensions of walls, structural members, openings such as doors and windows, size of the room, stair cases, lift if any and other essential services. The north direction and usage of all areas also is indicated.
(*b*) Elevations of all works from all open sides indicating the ground level, the height and depths of all salient features or points.
(*c*) Sections passing through walls, stair cases/lift wells etc., showing the details of structural members, such as foundations, walls, columns, floors, roofs, parapet etc.
(*d*) Tarrace plan showing the slope of the roof and drainage etc.
(*e*) Service plan showing the plans of water supply, sewage disposal, air conditioning or any other special services that have been planned to be provided.

3. Specifications. Specifications serve to guide the bidder at the time of tendering and the contractors to prepare job layout and executing the work.

14.5. CLASSIFICATION OF SPECIFICATIONS

Specifications can be classified based on use as follows:

(*a*) Standard specifications. These specifications are standardized for the general use of the trade. Indian standard Institution prepares standards for the general use. These standards are known as *Indian Standard Specifications.*

(*b*) Outline specifications. These are preliminary specifications and provide basic information. These are usefull at the time of bidding and are accompanied with the preliminary drawings of the work. These are further developed later at the planning stage of the project. They are also known as *guide specifications.*

(*c*) Project specifications. These are detailed specifications prepared taking into account the special requirements of the particular job.

(*d*) Manufacture's specifications. These are prepared by the manufacturers to indicate the quality of the products manufactured by them.

14.6. STORING AND STACKING OF MATERIALS AT SITE

Usually large quantities of construction materials have to be stored at the sites of construction. Thus to prepare a proper job layout at site, it is necessary to know the correct method of storing materials at site.

14.6.1. Points to be Considered while storing materials at site

Following points should be kept in mind while storing materials at site:

1. Materials should be stored in such a way that they are not affected by impurities or by atmospheric agencies such as sun, wind or moisture etc.
2. Cement should be stored in covered sheds. The plinth level of the shed should be at least one metre higher than the adjoining ground. The cement bags should be stacked on a raised platform of bricks or on planks about 15 to 20 cms above the shed floor. The space between the walls and cement bags alround should be at least 30 cms.
3. The inflammable materials must be stored separately from other combustible materials. This area should be specially protected from fire hazards. In such areas smoking should be prohibited.
4. Explosives should be stored in a safe place, away from combustible and inflammable materials under lock and key. The statutory requirements of explosives acts must be followed.
5. Materials of common use must be stored near the place of their use to minimise the handling.
6. As far as possible materials used for similar purposes must be stored close together.
7. Heavy items must be kept near the crane or hoist for ease in handling.
8. As far as possible, heavy items should be stored away from trenches, soft ground or improper support to prevent accidents and subsistances.
9. Materials which deteriorate with the passage of time such as cement and lime should not be stored for long. They should be used in such a way that the earliest supply is consumed first. To control the pilferage and theft of materials, they should be stored in secure place under watch and ward.

14.7. LOCATION OF MACHINERY AND EQUIPMENT

Now a days on construction projects a large variety of construction machinery and equipment is used. The use of equipment and machinery has been found economical both in cost and duration. The list of equipment commonly used is given below:

1. **Machinery for transportation of materials.** For this purpose different capacity of trucks, and wagons are employed for moving construction materials to the site and removing away overburden and surplus materials.
2. **Earth moving machinery.** For levelling and moving earth for short distances bulldozers, tractors, scrapers and grader etc. are employed.
3. **Excavating equipment.** For excavating the earth, shovels, drag lines and clam shells etc. are used.
4. **Lifting devices.** For lifting the materials cranes and winches are used.
5. **Conveyor system.** For moving or transporting materials such as concrete this system is used.
6. **Drilling equipment including air compressors.** This equipment is used for rock drilling.
7. **Rock blasting equipment.** For breaking rocks this equipment is used.
8. **Grouting equipment.** For making the rock more impervious, grouting equipment is used.
9. **Pile driving equipment.** For driving piles under under or on land pile driving equipment is used.
10. **Pump and well point equipment.** For draining out water this equipment is used.
11. **Equipment for concrete works.** For concrete works, concrete mixers, vibrators, polishing and grinding equipment is used. For transporting concrete dumpers and other equipment is also used.

14.8. STACK SIZE OF COMMON BUILDING MATERIALS

The stacking size of common building materials is shown in Table 14.1 below:

Table 14.1. Size of stacks

Name of material	*Method of stacking*	*Size of stack*
Cement	Cement bags should be placed on bricks or planks about 15 cm higher than the floor of the shed or store. There should be a minimum distance between the walls and cement bags of 30 cms alround.	In one stack not more than 12 bags should be placed one over the other
Lime	Hydraulic lime should be stored in such a way that it remains unaffected by moisture.	
Bricks	The bricks should be stacked at ground level. The height of the stack should not be more than 1.5 to 1.7 m.	
	The height of tiles stacks should not be more than 1 m, but the height of concrete block stacks may be upto 2 m.	
Aggregate	Different aggregates as coarse and fine aggregates must be stored separately on hard and clean ground.	The size of stack may be $2 \times 2 \times 0.5$ m
Timber	Timber should be stacked on concrete blocks or well seasoned timber planks at least 15 cms higher than the store floor. Timber of different lengths and size should be stacked separately. In two consecutive layers there should be a gap of about 2.5 cms for free circulation of air. There should be a minimum distance of 50 cms between two stacks.	Breadth of stack should be 1.5 m and height 2 m
Steel	The steel used for reinforcement should be stacked in such a way that it is not affected by moisture, oils and lubricants. For preventing it from rusting it should be given a cement paste coating.	

14.9. POINTS TO BE CONSIDERED AT THE TIME OF PREPARING LAYOUT OF EQUIPMENT

At the time of preparing equipment layout, following points should be kept in mind:

1. The equipment should be placed near the place of its use as well as near the place of materials it is supposed to utilise. For example a concrete mixer should be placed near the stack of aggregates and the mixed concrete may not have to be carried for long distances.
2. For costly equipment, temporary sheds should be provided to safe guard them from weather effects.
3. Arrangements for essential repairs, maintenance, oiling, lubricating and petrol filling should be made at the construction site.
4. The layout should be such that the safety of machinery can be ensured by the security staff.
5. Sufficient space should be available for erection of scaffolding and removal and shifting of equipment to places where it can be utilised fully.
6. For transport vehicles there should be adequate space for parking.
7. The main office of the establishment should be near the main entrance, so that visitors for bussiness need not to have to cross the work site.
8. Security check posts should be so located that no material could pass in or out with out proper check.
9. Adequate safety measures and fire prevention equipment should be provided in the layout.

14.10. PREPARATION OF JOB LAYOUT

To get the idea of the nature and extent of the work, the construction plans, specifications, contract documents and other available material describing the job should be studied carefully and a scaled drawing at a scale of 1 in 100 should be prepared showing the out lines of the work or job to be constructed. The entry and exit points as well as the areas of temporary facilities should be marked. From the above study following information should be collected.

1. Area needed for accommodation. This area includes the area required for office, stores and

residential accommodation for officers, staff and labour.

2. Area required for machines sheds, repair shops and workshop etc.
3. Area for miscellaneous amenities such as canteen, toilets, dispensary etc.
4. Areas for security and fire fighting facilities.
5. Area required for construction work.
6. For how much period the area may be available.

In deciding the location of each area, the principle of storage of materials and equipment as well as the factors which affect the job layout should be kept in mind. The problem of allocating the space for men, materials and machines has to be tackled separately for each site.

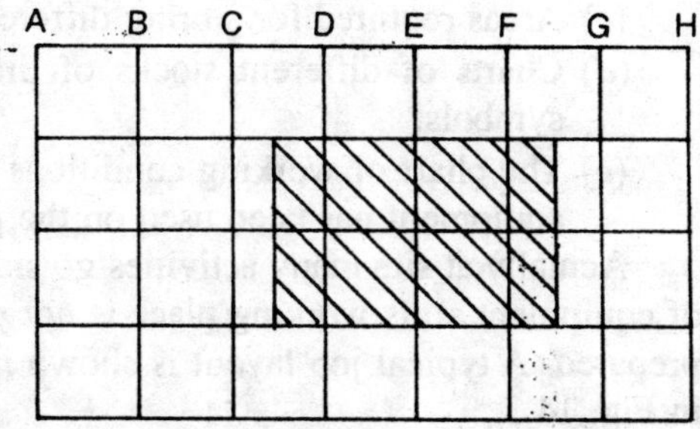

Fig. 14.1.

(*a*) From the data collected, a plan is prepared. On this plan natural features such as river, drainages, and other such obstacles should be marked.

(*b*) On the same plan different requirements of space as discussed above should be marked in the form of grid as shown in Fig. 14.1.

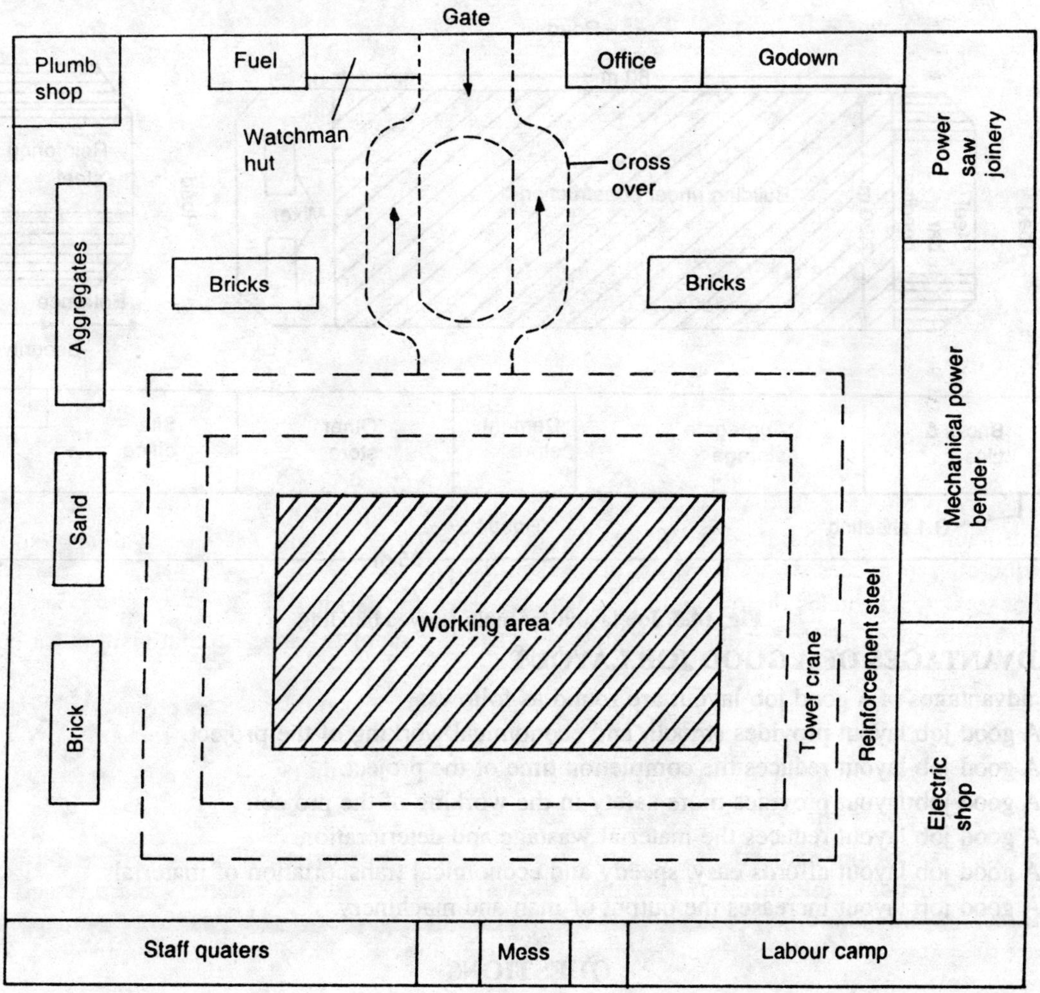

Fig. 14.2.

(*c*) Areas required for storing different materials are shown in a tabular form.

(*d*) Charts of different stocks of different materials and machines are prepared using the standard symbols.

(*e*) The chart of working conditions of different equipment and machines and duration for which the equipment has been used on the project are prepared.

Actually at site many activities go side by side. Hence the storage of materials at exact place and repair of equipment at its working place is not possible. Thus alternative most economical job lay outs should be prepared. A typical job layout is shown in Fig. 14.2. The job lay out of a multi-storyed Building is shown in Fig. 14.3.

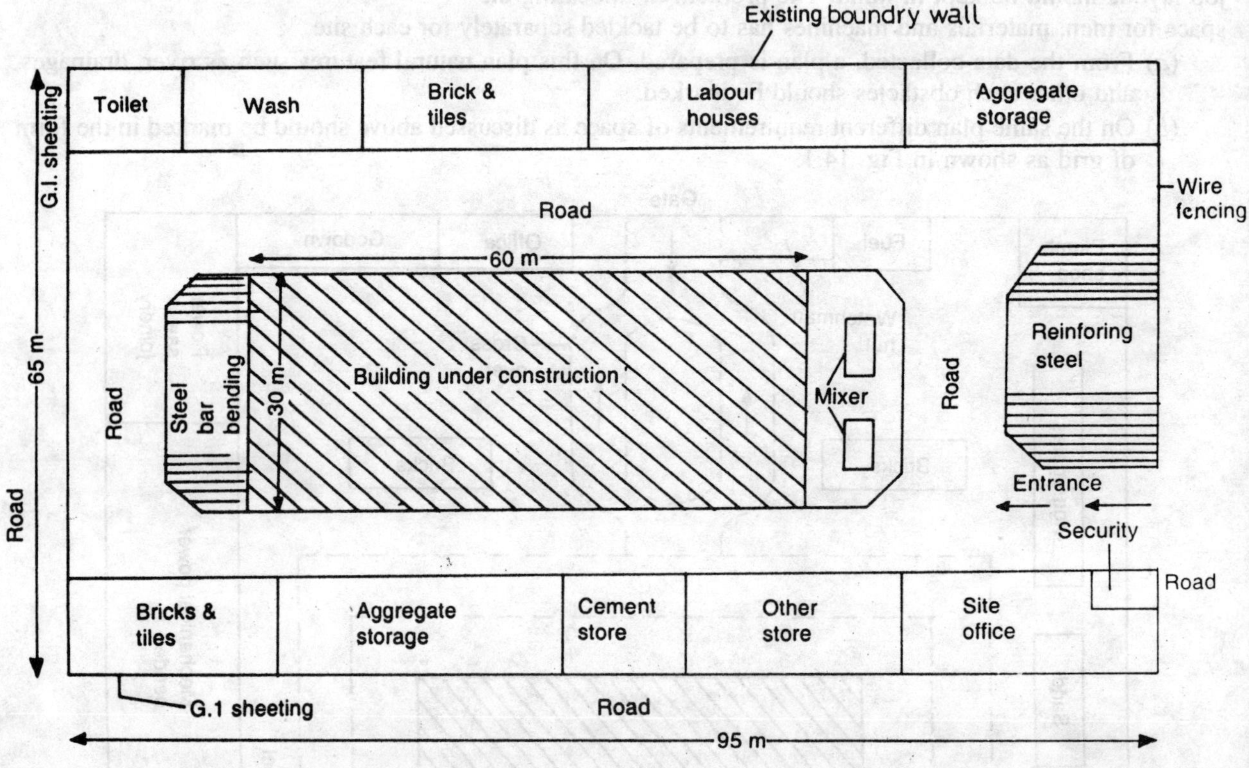

Fig. 14.3. Job layout for multi storyed building

14.11. ADVANTAGES OF A GOOD JOB LAYOUT

The advantages of a good job layout are found as follows:

1. A good job layout provides smooth and economical working of the project.
2. A good job layout reduces the completion time of the project.
3. A good job layout provides more safety in the working of the project.
4. A good job layout reduces the material wastage and deterioration.
5. A good job layout affords easy, speedy and economical transportation of materials.
6. A good job layout increases the output of man and machinery.

QUESTIONS

1. **What is a job layout. Explain its advantages.**

2. What are the factors which affect the job layout of a project.
3. What documents should be studied before preparing a job layout.
4. Describe the principles of storing and stacking of construction materials at the site.
5. Discuss the factors which influence the location of machinery at site.
6. Explain how good site management will result in the increased efficiency and economy.
7. Prepare a job layout for the construction of a multipurpose river valley project across a major river.

OBJECTIVE TYPE QUESTIONS

8. Job layout is
   (*a*) Detailed estimate of the cost of the project.
   (*b*) Demarcation of boundary on the ground of natural features.
   (*c*) It is a scaled drawing of the proposed construction site showing all relevant features.
   (*d*) All the above are true.
9. Identify the incorrect statement
   (*a*) The job layout produces hindrance in the smooth execution of a project.
   (*b*) The job layout helps in smooth execution of a project.
   (*c*) It is imperative to execute a project in the most economical and safest manner.
   (*d*) The job layout neither produces hindrance nor helps in the smooth execution of the project.
10. Identify the correct statement/statements
    (*a*) A good job layout-reduces the completion time of a project.
    (*b*) A good job layout provides more safety in the execution of the project.
    (*c*) A good job lay out reduces the wastage and deterioration of the construction materials at site
    (*d*) All the above are correct.
11. Identify the incorrect statement/statements
    (*a*) Nature of the project has a great influence on the preparation of a good job layout
    (*b*) Nature of project has no influence on the preparation of a good job layout.
    (*c*) A good job layout increases the output of men and machinery.
    (*d*) All are true.
12. The drawing of a job layout is prepared on a scale of
    (*a*) $\frac{1}{150}$ (*b*) $\frac{1}{200}$
    (*c*) $\frac{1}{100}$ (*d*) $\frac{1}{550}$
13. For a good job layout information should be collected
    (*a*) Area needed for residential accommodation
    (*b*) Area needed for construction
    (*c*) Area needed for machine sheds, work shops, repair shops etc.
    (*d*) Area required for material stacking, security and fire fighting equipment etc.
    (*e*) All the above
14. The job layout is influenced by
    (*a*) Nature and type of work (*b*) Nature of the ground
    (*c*) Availability of materials (*d*) Access to site
    (*e*) By all
15. Centrally located job layout is ideal for
    (*a*) Earth dam (*b*) Irrigation canal
    (*c*) Highway (*d*) Multi-stoyred buildings

ANSWERS

8. (*c*)	10. (*d*)	12. (*c*)	14. (*e*)
9. (*a, d*)	11. (*b*)	13. (*e*)	15. (*d*)

15
Progress Report

15.1. INTRODUCTION

Progress is the achievement in the concerned field and it can be assessed by comparing the achievements at regular intervals of time with the estimated work. All sorts of planning for any work will fail if progress of work is not checked at regular intervals.

Controlling is the managerial function of comparing the actual achievements with the planned achievements at every stage of construction and taking necessary action if required to ensure the attainment of the planned goal. Controlling of a construction work or job is necessary for the following three objectives.

(*a*) Control of progress. It shall be discussed in this chapter.

(*b*) Control of quality of the work. It shall be discussed in chapter 17.

(*c*) Control of cost. It has been discussed in chapter 10.

15.2. PURPOSE OF PROGRESS CONTROL

Construction works are full of uncertainties of many types and bottle necks due to which the progress will be less than planned. If the timely corrective action is not taken then the work will not be completed in scheduled duration and its over all cost will increase manifold than the estimated cost. Some times actual progress is observed more than the planned, which creates doubt about the quality of work. In such cases quality of work must be checked. The record of progress is also useful in case of dispute with the contractor. Sometimes contractor may demand extra time to complete a certain job on the plea that the work is delayed due to the reasons beyond his control such as delay in supply of materials by the department. In such cases factual progress data is useful to settle the dispute. The progress record also gives an idea of the payments to be made. Thus it can be summarised as follows.

1. The progress record gives idea of payments to be made.
2. It provides information to the planner, whether the work is going as per schedule or is behind the schedule.
3. It also gives an idea to the owner, whether he will get profit or loss.
4. It helps to take corrective steps well in time to bring back the work to the schedule if it is behind the planned schedule.

15.3. METHODS OF RECORDING PROGRESS

The methods of progress recording depend upon the size and type of the work as well as on manner in which it is executed. Generally following methods for progress recording are adopted.

1. By maintaining job diary
2. By maintaining the register of instructions

3. By maintaining progress report record.
4. By keeping construction record.
5. By keeping abstract of quantities and cost.

1. Job diary. This is a very important document for a construction job. In this diary everything of importance to the work is recorded. In this diary following details are recorded:

(*a*) Attendance of workers
(*b*) Details of payments
(*c*) Number of workers employed
(*d*) Receipt and issue of materials to the work
(*e*) Maintenance of log book
(*f*) Inspection record
(*g*) Progress of work
(*h*) Weather conditions
(*i*) Detailed note on break down at site, if any and its causes.

2. Register of instructions. Actually this register is the channel of communifications between the engineer incharge and the contractor. The site engineer records his observations regarding quality and progress of the work in this register. If any change in the design of the work is needed then the site engineer records the necessary changes in this register to be done to implement the work.

3. Progress report. The site engineer prepares the progress report and sends it to the owner and head office at regular interval as decided (weakly, monthly or daily). In public works department daily report is sent by junior engineer to his assistant engineer showing the number of labourer employed and quantity of work done.

4. Construction report. The position of materials used and progress of work is entered in a prescribed form daily. The test results of specimens tested in the field laboratory and inspection notes about the work are also recorded in this register daily. The aim of construction report is to record time, quality, quantity of work and general condition of work to ensure satisfactory progress as per specifications laid down.

5. Abstract of quantities. The quantities of various items of works executed are recorded in the measurement book. Payments to contractors are made on the basis of these measurements entered in the measurement book. From the quantities of work executed as entered in the measurement book (M.B.), the work abstract is prepared. This work abstract indicates the upto date physical progress of each item of work sub head wise. The work abstract also indicates the expenditure of work including the supplies of materials. If the record is to be kept sub head wise then, forms 33 and 34 are used.

15.4. ANALYSIS OF PROGRESS

For large works executed departmentally, analysis of progress of work is essential. This analysis is carried out by the works study cell, established for this purpose only. The study is carried out to ensure whether the work is executed as per schedule with in the estimated cost. To achieve this goal, the analysis of progress of work is done at different stages as follows:

1. Material account. In this account, it is ensured that proper accounts of the materials purchased and consumed on the works as per material schedule are maintained or not. In case of variation in the consumption of materials, its possible causes are investigated and corrective measures taken.

2. Labour record. In this record, the record of number of labourers employed, payment made to them and their out is maintained and compared with the labour schedule. In case any deviation is found, proper corrective measures are taken by the competent authority.

3. Equipment record. In this record the deployment of equipment and machinery is compared with the equipment schedule. The out put of the machinery and equipment deployed is worked out and compared with the given output of these machinery and equipment. For less progress or deviation between the two out puts, the possible causes must be investigated and corrective measures taken.

4. Execution of work. In this record the progress of construction is compared with the construction schedule. If the progress is found behind the schedule, the possible causes must be investigated. The possible causes may be:

(*a*) Late arrival of construction materials and equipment at site.

(*b*) Lack of supervision.

(*c*) In adequate arrangements of maintenance of equipment at site.

Thus to supplement the progress of work, proper corrective measures should be taken.

15.5. CORRECTIVE MEASURES

The analysis of progress of work pin points the important draw backs and causes for less progress. The engineer incharge should take the corrective measures immediately to improve the progress. Some of the corrective steps suggested are as follows:

1. **Procurement of materials well in advance.** Important construction materials should be procured well ahead of requirement, but not in such advance, that the quality of materials may deteriorate during this period and there may be much loss due to pilferage. If the materials are not received upto the stipulated date, then the firm should be given due reminder. If required, head office should also be informed with the action taken.
2. **Arrangements of equipment and machinery.** In case any required equipment is not received well in time due to any reason, its alternative arrangement should be done from alternative sources. Secondly no equipment whether defective or in working condition should be allowed to be idle due to any reason. For defective equipment, arrangements of its repair should be made at the earliest.
3. **Proper watch and ward arrangements.** To eliminate the chances of pilferage of constsuection materials and equipment, proper arrangements of watch and ward should be made.
4. **Provision of incentive.** To achieve a higher output and higher efficiency some incentive schemes for workers may be announced.

The above steps are as a guide only, the site engineer may take his own decisions as per site conditions.

15.6. PRODUCTIVITY

The term productivity denotes the out put of any productive work in relation to inputs. In other words productivity is the ratio of output to input. The maximum utilisation of the resources as men, machinery and equipment etc. increases the productivity.

Productivity should not be confused with production. Production in any production field denotes the output only with out any reference to inputs. Production can be increased by increasing the man power and machinery, but productivity can not be increased by simply increasing the resources as men and machinery. Productivity can only be increased by the optimum utilisation of resources as men power and equipment etc.

The techniques of achieving higher productivity has been successfully utilised in the production and industrial management, but these techniques could not be used in construction industry as yet fully. Thus it is very important that techniques to achieve higher productivity should be adopted in the construction industry expediously.

15.7. METHODS OF INCREASING PRODUCTIVITY

In construction industry, the productivity of men and machines is very important. Hence construction management should give proper attention to these two factors. In construction works, many items such as brick work, mixing and laying the concrete are amenable to improvement by modifications in the working methods, proper sequencing of operations, adopting rational methods of gauging labour and minimising the idleness of men and machinery. Similarly the optimum utilisation of equipment and machinery can be achieved by suitable modifications in the method of working. The cost of supervision can also be reduced to a great extent by giving proper training to the supervisory staff and workers, adopting systematic and rational work methods at the work site, adopting proper control system and fixing responsibility at various levels of supervisory staff.

Actually productivity is closely linked with psychological factors of human beings and plays a great role in their working capacity. Contented (satisfied) and happy workers are likely to give better results than dissatisfied and angry workers.

Thus the role of motivation is very important. Workers can be motivated to higher productivity by creating suitable conditions in which willing and sincere workers may be benefited. These conditions may be created either by recognising and appreciating their work or giving them some financial reward. The techniques of motivation have been discussed separately in chapter 16.

15.8. WORK STUDY

It is a major tool of productivity analysis. It consists of the following two parts:

1. Motion study or method study.
2. time study or work measurements

15.9. MOTION STUDY

The scientific study of motions of workers with a view to simplify and minimise the effort to be used to increase the productivity of workers is known as *motion study*. In other words it can be said that motion study essentially is concerned with finding better ways of doing things. Following steps are involved in the motion study.

1. **Selecting.** In this step the job which requires improvement is selected. After selection of the job the workers should be encouraged to adopt such techniques which may improve the productivity. This can be achieved by announcing some incentive schemes for workers.
2. **Recording.** In case of recording, all relevant informations about each operation in the existing system are recorded. For simplifying the work, man conducting the work study should put following questions:
   (*a*) What exactly is to be done?
   (*b*) What purpose will be achieved by doing this job?
   (*c*) Where it is to be done and why? And where else it could be done?
   (*d*) How it is to be done?
   (*e*) Where it is done? Where else it could be done?
   (*f*) When it is done? When could it else be done?
   After getting the answers of the above questions the researcher can go ahead and can improve the old project.
3. **Analysing.** Analyse all the facts recorded and decide whether each operation in the work is necessary and whether they can be operated by alternative methods more easily or completely eliminated and replaced by other operations or methods. The effect of alternative operations on all aspects of the work are to be studied.
4. **Developing.** From the study of existing methods and available alternatives, a new technique which may be simpler and easier to adopt should be developed, leading to higher productivity.
5. **Approving.** After the approval of the management, the new technique is adopted. Usually workers are found reluctant to accept changes in the techniques or methods they are using since long. Thus a consistent effort is necessary to ensure the adoption of new methods.
6. **Adhering.** In order to ensure that new methods have been accepted and adopted. Constant checking and inspection at site are necessary so that workers may not go back to old methods of working.

15.10. TIME STUDY

Besides motion study, time study of each operation also is important. Time studies are important and helpful in determining the least time consuming methods for performing a certain job, *i.e.* the most economical methods of performing a job. Time study is also helpful in establishing a standard time of an operation or completing a job. Standard time may be defined as the time in which an average worker can work continuously under standard conditions, with out adversely affecting his health.

Thus time study can be defined as a technique of observation and analysis of the modes of performance of an operation by measurement and evaluation of time required for the performance of an operation and afterwards to establish the reasonable standards. The efficiency of workers can be judged by comparing the actual time taken by them in completing the job with the standard time for the job. Following steps are involved in time study.

1. Selection of job which is to be studied and improved.
2. Recording the relevant information about each operation in the existing method and identifying the different elements in each operation.
3. Recording complete break up of the operation into various elements.
4. Recording the time taken to complete each element of the operation.
5. Comparing the observed time with the permissible time for each operation.
6. Finalising the time for each operation.
7. Finding the standard time for the job as a whole.

Thus each operation should be studied in detail and best method of performance be evolved and standard time for performance of the job should be determined.

15.11. MARROW'S QUESTIONARE

To improve the existing methods of work study. Marrow prepared questioniare which has been reproduced below:

1. Operation question are
   (*a*) What is the purpose of operation?
   (*b*) Is the operation necessary?
   (*c*) Can it be replaced by some other easier operation?
   (*d*) Can it be eliminated by the use of different materials?
2. Inspection question are
   (*a*) What is the finish required on the work?
   (*b*) Can a better finish be obtained at the same cost?
3. Material question are
   (*a*) What kind of material is being used?
   (*b*) Would a cheaper material be as good as the present one?
4. Miscellaneous questions are
   (*a*) Are materials and equipment properly placed?
   (*b*) How could better welfare schemes for workers be introduced?
   (*c*) What kind of handling apparatus is used?

After getting the answers of the above questions, improved methods may be evolved.

15.12. OPERATIONAL ANALYSIS

In a productive work, each operation can be done in a number of ways and the man incharge may feel that he is using the best method. Thus the purpose of operation analysis is to examine all the different ways of motion and time studies and to find out the best method of doing a work. Hence the study to find out the best method of doing a work is known as operational analysis.

15.13. OBJECTS OF OPERATIONAL ANALYSIS

The objects of operational analysis is to develop methods, which may eliminate the wastage of materials, delays in carrying out the operations, undesirable and inefficient ways of performing the construction activities, so that work can be performed in a systematic manner and high productivity may be achieved.

15.14. PROCESS CHART

The graphic representation of an operation analysis is called *process chart.* It shows various elements involved in an operation and their sequence of operation.

The various elements are represented by symbols.

15.15. FUNCTIONS OF PROCESS CHARTS

Following are the functions of a process chart:

(*a*) It helps to determine the elements, which can either be improved or eliminated altogether.

(*b*) It serves as a permanent record of the actual performance of the job or work.

(*c*) It is a quick and reliable method of furnishing informations, avoiding lengthy descriptions on the one hand and verbal information on the other.

(*d*) Improved methods would result faster progress of construction work. They will also result in over all saving.

15.16. SYMBOLS USED IN PROCESS CHARTS

Usually following symbols are used in a process charts:

S. No.	*Description*	*Symbol*	
1.	Operational element (Planning, Preparation, Collection Etc.)	Big Circle	○
2.	Transportation element	Small circle or arrow	○ →
3.	Storage	Triangle	Δ
4.	Delay	Letter D	D
5.	Levelling	Letter L	L
6.	Idle element	Dash line	------
7.	Inspection	Rectangle	▭
8.	Laying and compaction	Inverted triangle	∇

QUESTIONS

1. What is meant by the term progress control? Discuss the methods of recording the progress of work.
2. What is the purpose of recording the progress of work?
3. What is meant by productivity?
4. How motion and time studies are related with productivity.
5. Define motion and time study. How these studies are helpful for achieving higher rate of progress in construction work?
6. What is meant by operational analysis? Explain the use of operational analysis with the help of process chart for developing economical methods of handling work on the construction work site.
7. Explain different methods of recording progress of work.

OBJECTIVE TYPE QUESTIONS

8. Controlling of a construction job is necessary for

(*a*) Control of progress (*b*) Control of quality of work

(*c*) Control of cost (*d*) All are correct

9. Identify the correct statement/statements

(*a*) Achievement at regular interval of time in comparison with the estimated work is known as progress of work.

(*b*) The record of progress is useful in case of dispute with the contractor.

(*c*) The record of progress provides an idea of profit or loss to the owner.

(*d*) It helps to take corrective steps well in time to rectify the delay in work.
(*e*) All are correct.

10. Identify the incorrect statement
(*a*) Analysis of progress is essential for large works executed departmentally.
(*b*) The analysis of progress is essential for small works executed departmentally
(*c*) The analysis of work is carriedout by study cell, established for this purpose
(*d*) The study is carried out to ensure whether the work is executed as per schedule with in estimated sanctioned cost

11. Identify the incorrect statement
(*a*) Productivity denotes the output in any productive work in relation to input.
(*b*) Production denotes the output only in any productive work with out any reference to input
(*c*) Productivity and production convey the same meaning
(*d*) Production can be increased by increasing the resources, where as productivity can be increased by optimum utilisation of the resources.

12. Identify the incorrect statement
(*a*) The study to find out a best method for doing a work is called as operational analysis
(*b*) The operational analysis is adopted to develop methods to eliminate the wastage of materials and delays in carrying out operations
(*c*) The object of operational analysis is not to eliminate the undesirable and inefficient ways of performing constructional activities
(*d*) The object of operational analysis is to perform work systematically to achieve higher productivity

13. Identify the incorrect statement/statement
(*a*) Process charts serve as a temporary record of the actual performance of the job
(*b*) Process charts serve as a permanent record of the actual performance of the job
(*c*) Process charts help in identifying the elements which can either be eliminated altogether or can be improved
(*d*) All are correct

14. Productivity is
(*a*) $\dfrac{\text{Output}}{\text{Input}}$ (*b*) $\dfrac{\text{Input}}{\text{Output}}$
(*c*) Input × Output (*d*) All the above

15. Productivity can be increased by
(*a*) Increasing the resources (*b*) Decreasing the resources
(*c*) Optimum utilisation of resources (*d*) All are correct

ANSWERS

8. (*d*)	10. (*b*)	12. (*c*)	14. (*a*)
9. (*e*)	11. (*c*)	13. (*a*)	15. (*c*)

16

Motivation

16.1. INTRODUCTION

In any organisation it is the prime duty of the chief executive to get work done from the workers of the organisation to achieve its objectives. In order to achieve the desired goal, it is necessary to develop desire and will to work hard amongst the workers. Thus the art of developing desire to work hard amongst the workers or employees to achieve the desired goal is known as motivation. Hence the chief executive or key man in the organisation must have sound basic knowledge of motivation, so that he can motivate the workers to achieve the desired goal. Thus motivation removes frustration of the workers. It is equally helpful to industrialist, bussinessman and managers.

16.2. NEED FOR MOTIVATION

It has been observed that an motivated employee or worker takes his work more seriously and discharges it efficiently. The quality of work also improves and one feels happy and satisfied with his surroundings. A motivated person remains fully engaged in the activities of the organisation. Motivation also improves human relations in the organisation. Thus every action of workers depends how they are motivated.

16.3. OBJECTIVES OF MOTIVATION

Motivation serves the following objectives:

1. It stimulates the workers to improve their performance.
2. It inspires action by creating interest in the work.
3. It gives job satisfaction.
4. It removes frustration and improves industrial relations.
5. It develops sense of responsibility to achieve the desired goal with maximum efficiency and minimum wastage.
6. It reduces the tendency of remaining away from the work and reluctance on the part of the workers.

16.4. FUNDAMENTALS OF MOTIVATION

While considering the output, efficiency and adjustments in the profession of a person, the fundamental question arises is, why the person work? Every person works to satisfy his basic necessities for his existence and survival. For his survival, he requires fulfillment of his fundamental needs discussed below:

1. **Physiological needs.** Under this category of needs hunger, thrist, sleep, pain and sex etc. are placed. These needs are essential to maintain life. These needs must be satisfied as and when they arise. After the fulfillment of these needs one looks forward to other types of needs.
2. **Social needs.** Affection, respect, love, friendship etc. are placed under this category of needs.

Every individual wants these things in the society. If these needs are also satisfied, then one is motivated to work more.

3. **Security needs.** Every one wants to be secure against injury, disease etc. The safety needs also urge him to work more.
4. **Miscellaneous needs.** Apart from above needs, every person has a sense of ego and self respect. Thus he looks forward to fulfill these needs. Under this category of needs following two things, may be included:
   (*a*) *Reputation.* This includes the recognition of status and appreciation of one's feelings.
   (*b*) *Self esteem.* Self esteem means, self confidence, strength and independence.

Thus in any organisation, if the above mentioned needs of the workers are fulfilled, they will feel motivated and will work better with higher efficiency to achieve the desired goal of the organisation. On the other hand if they are deprived of these needs they will not only put the hurdles in the achievement of the goal, but may sabotage the whole system and put up unreasonable demands for economic benefits. An un-satisfied worker is more dangerous.

16.5. INCENTIVES

If the workers and employees are inspired to work more and to increase the production, they have to be paid something in return and this something is called *incentive*. This incentive works as a great motivating force to increase the output. Thus the incentive encourages the workers to put more effort voluntarily.

16.5.1. Categories of Incentives

Incentives may be divided into the following two categories:

1. Positive incentive. They may be financial and non financial.

(*a*) *Financial incentives.* Money is a great driving force. Provision of bonus scheme, increase in salary, financial awards, prize etc. for increased output are the financial incentives.

(*b*) *Non-financial incentives.* Financial and non financial incentives are complimentary to each other. For better results following non financial incentives may be awarded.

(*i*) Security of service
(*ii*) Social welfare facilities
(*iii*) Appreciation and prize for good work
(*iv*) Scope of promotion
(*v*) Good opportunities for training
(*vi*) Sympathetic attitude of management

2. Negative incentives. Negative incentives create fear in the mind of workers and some times help the management in correcting the attitude of workers. Followings may be some negative incentives:

(*i*) Punishment
(*ii*) Fine
(*iii*) Demotion in rank
(*iv*) Transfer to another job or place
(*v*) Stoppage of increments
(*vi*) Stoppage of bonus
(*vii*) Dismisal from service

As far as possible, negative incentive should be avoided as they create resentment and frustration among the workers. They should be resorted in extreme case of misconduct, inefficiency and careless ness etc.

16.6. HUMAN RELATIONS

Human being is a social creature and needs society, which may share his sorrows and joys of life. Thus the human behavior under different situations is known as *human relations*. The human relations means, relations between individuals, between individual and groups in the industry, bussiness, construction projects and society. Good relations give rise to pleasant atmosphere and makes life full of joy and happyness, while bad relations cause tension and bitterness. Thus it is very important that every body should have a sound knowledge of human relations.

16.7. NEED OF HUMAN RELATIONS

When ever two or more persons live together, problems of human relations arise. In construction industry or in other industrial enterprises, people are concerned with one another as employer and employees, supervisors and workers etc. If it is desired that workers work whole heartedly, they must be satified. To avoid strikes, lockouts, and to obtain increased output, it is essential that there should be good human relations between the management and workers. Workers should be treated as human beings and not as machines. Their feelings, emotions and thoughts must be understood properly. In this way the management will be in a better position to deal worker's problems more effectively. To maintain industrial peace is in the interest of both management as well as workers. In any industry, good human relations create healthy atmosphere for work and positive results. Hence it is essential to understand the various aspects of human behavior properly.

16.8. FACTORS AFFECTING THE HUMAN BEHAVIOUR

Human behaviour does not occur in a particular way, but is always caused. Human behaviour means, how a person reacts to a given situation. Some times a worker or employee behaves in a particular way which may not be liked by the management and management feels offended. The solution of undesirable behaviour is to find out the causes, and then possible ways and means to remove them. Following factors have been found affecting the human behaviour to a great extent.

1. Human needs. The whole human behaviour depends upon the satisfaction of his needs. Some of the basic human needs are as follows:

(*a*) *Economic need.* The fundamental needs of every human being are food, cloths and shelter. Thus every body struggles to meet these needs first. Hence every worker should get such emoluments with which he may meet his basic needs and save something for the rainy day. Thus for survival and to promote human relationship it is essential that workers are paid such wages, which may be sufficient to meet their basic needs.

(*b*) *Need of affection.* Every human being needs affection. Hence to develop good human relations, management should behave with them with affection. A word of affection will motivate a willing and sincere worker to work more.

(*c*) *Need of safety and security.* Every body wants that his job must be safe and secure. Hence schemes like state insurance, provident fund, pension and other benefits like medical and maternity leave etc. will help in the satisfaction of such needs.

(*d*) *Need of self respect.* Every human being has dignity and ego and wants that he should be treated with courtesy, respect, and dignity. Hence in order to promote good human behaviour, it is essential, that the workers are treated with courtesy, respect and dignity of labour should be respected.

(*e*) *Need of companionship.* Human being is a social animal and wants society. To promote this aspect, workers should be provided some place where they can meet together. Non provision of such facilities will lead to disappointment and loneliness in them.

2. Previous experience. A person having some experience of some events will behave differently than those who have no such experience. For example, a driver of a vehicle who has an experience of an fatal accident, will develop a better habit of safety than those who have no such experience.

16.9. TECHNIQUES FOR BEHAVIOUR MODIFICATION

The methods adopted to modify the behaviour of workers in a industry to attain good industrial relations and increased output are known as *Behaviour modification techniques.* In an industry some of the following techniques may be adopted to modify the behaviour of the workers.

(*a*) *Welfare facilities.* Education facilities for worker's children, state insurance, transport facilities, housing facilities, fair price shops, canteen, rest room, lunch room etc. can be grouped under welfare schemes. Such facilities will motivate workers to increase the output of the establishment.

(*b*) *Incentives.* Financial as well as non financial incentives as bonus, prizes, profit share schemes, certificates of appreciation etc. modify the human behaviour to a great extent and result in greater production.

(*c*) *Motivation.* As already discussed affects the human behaviour to a great extent.

(*d*) *Better environment.* A pleasant and happy atmosphere at the site of work has a marked improvement in the behaviour of the workers and results in increased output.

(*e*) *Removal of frustration.* If better output is desired from workers, there should be no cause of frustration for them. They must be satisfied with their jobs and should have opportunities for their improvement and promotion. They should be given equal remuneration for equal work. A frustrated worker will not only give less out put, but may also prove dangerous for the establishment.

(*f*) *Participation.* Workers should be made to feel responsible for the work they are doing. They should have a feeling that they have a say in the management and if something goes wrong they shall also be equally loser. Such feeling will make them more responsible and they will work whole heartedly.

By all these techniques workers may be made to feel that they are an integral part of the industry and any gain or loss in the industry is equally their gain or loss. If the above techniques applied properly, they shall prove a good tool to modify the behaviour of the workers.

16.10. GRIEVANCES AND THEIR CAUSES

Grievances in workers develop when they feel that injustice has been done to them or they have been not treated properly or other such complaints have developed. Generally grievances develop due to the feelings of dissatisfaction in the workers towards the policies of the management. An aggrieved worker will not work properly and will develop ill will towards the management. Such a attitude of workers is harmful to both management as well as to workers themselves. If the grievances are not handled at the earliest, they will go on multiplying and ultimately burst out in the shape of strike and unrest in the industry. Hence grievances should be handled at the earliest tactfully with care.

16.11. CAUSES OF GRIEVANCES

Some of the causes of grievances of employees are as follows:

1. **Discrimination.** Discrimination in salary, working hours, welfare facilities, granting leave and other such conditions of work etc. may cause grievances.
2. **Undue favouritism.** If favouritism is shown either by management or other officers of the management in the matter of promotion or in the distribution of work will cause grievances in the workers.
3. **Inhuman behaviour.** Inhuman behaviour by any body in the management towards worker will cause grievances in them.
4. **Lack of incentives.** Lack of incentive to good and willing workers will result grievances in them.
5. **Strict rules.** Too rigid rules and regulations also cause grievances.
6. **Victamisation.** Victamisation of trade union office bearers by way of transferring them from one place to an other place etc. may also cause grievances.
7. **Miscellaneous causes.** Under this category following causes may be grouped:

   (*a*) Bad working conditions

   (*b*) Long hours of work

   (*c*) Non implementation of bonus schemes etc.

   (*d*) Bad machinery and tools

   (*e*) Bad treatment and exploitation of workers

   (*f*) Taking action on old complaints by co workers etc.

16.12. GRIEVANCES HANDLING

Grievances should be handled promptly and whole heartedly. Improper handling of grievances will affect the production and efficiency of the organisation. While handling grievances following steps may be taken.

1. **Proper hearing.** The authority competent to hear the grievances should give patient hearing and then inquire the matter fully. No one should feel that he has not been fully heard. No one should be victamised for any kind of opinion expressed by him.
2. **Quick disposal.** To award justice and avoid frustation, the grievances of the employees should be disposed off quickly.
3. **Sympathetic attitude.** The complainant should be dealt with sympathetically. They should be taken into confidence and talked to the point.
4. **Nature of grievance.** The complaint should be understood clearly and realistic approach should be adopted to solve the problem. It is a very important point.
5. **Simple procedure.** Procedure to be adopted for redresal of grievances should be simple. It should be clear and well known to all. They should know it fully to whom they have to approach in case they have to make a complaint.

16.13. HUMAN RELATIONS

In a industry or project different categories of persons work together. Some of them are seniors to them and some of them juniors. One should have relations with his juniors as he wants from his seniors for himself. The best principle of human behaviour is, "Behave with others in the same way as you want to be behaved by others. This is the golden principle and is applicable in all walks of life. Following this principle one can understand easily what his subordinates expect from him. Some hints are given below about dealings with juniors, seniors and equals.

1. Dealing with subordinates. While dealing with subordinates, following points should be observed:

(*a*) *Punctuality and discipline.* Senior or superior persons should observe punctuality and discipline by themselves and set examples for their juniors of punctuality, discipline and courtesy.

(*b*) *Behaviour with subordinates.* The mistakes of subordinates should be pointed out in private gently. They should not be abused or scold publicly. Behave with them as you want to be behaved by your seniors.

(*c*) *Problem solving.* The problems of subordinates and workers should be solved expediously and sympathetically.

(*d*) *Encouragement for work.* Workers should be encouraged for their good work. Their good work should be appreciated. Defects if any should be pointed out in such a way that their feelings are not hurt in any way.

(*e*) *Disposal of grievances.* The grievances of subordinates should be removed expediously. If the solution of difficulties and grievances of subordinates is not in his powers, then they should be referred to the competent authority for speedy disposal.

(*f*) *Discrimination and favouritism.* In matters of promotions and allotment of work etc. discrimination and favouritism should not be shown.

(*g*) *Punishment.* While awarding punishment to an individual, one should be impartial and the punishment should be such to set examples for others.

(*h*) *Delegation of authority.* Where ever possible the authority may be delegated to the subordinate.

2. Relations withs equals

(*a*) *Interference.* Cooperate with your colleagues in their work. There should be no interference in their work. Do not criticise the work of others publicly unnecessarily.

(*b*) *Understanding the problems.* One should try to under stand the problems and difficulties of his equal colleagues and help in their solution.

(*c*) *Suggestions.* Give suggestions to your colleagues at the proper time and proper place to improve their working and also invite suggestions from others about your working.

(*d*) *Following good examples.* Follow good examples of work of others rather than being jealous of them.

(*e*) *Condemnation.* Do not condemn the work of your colleagues neither before your seniors nor before juniors. If possible praise it.

3. Relations with seniors.

(*a*) *Behaviour.* While talking to your seniors or discussing with them be polite. One must behave respectfully with his seniors. As far as possible do not criticise your senior's action.

(*b*) *Obedience.* One should be obedient to his seniors. Try to complete the assigned task well in time. If it is not possible, be frank in telling the reasons there of, rather than making excuses.

(*c*) *Criticism.* Do not criticise your superiors publicly. It may lead to unnecessary complications.

(*d*) *Carrying out orders.* The orders from superiors must be carried out with out much delay. If there is any ambiguity, it should be clarified immediately.

(*e*) *Feed back.* The superior should be informed from time to time about the progress of work and implementation of the orders.

(*f*) *Suggestions.* Offer suggestions to the superior, when asked for it.

In the light of the above points, it can be said at the end that one must keep a correct distance between the superiors and subordinates. Too much mixing with subordinates may spoil the decorum and respect. Similarly too closeness to the superior, his equals may feel jealous of him and may result in strained relations with them.

16.14. QUALITIES OF EFFICIENT CONSTRUCTION EXECUTIVES

An efficient and successful executive must have following qualities.

1. He should be an effective executive or manager.
2. He should be people oriented.
3. He should be a good communicator.
4. He should have sound knowledge of the work of the establishment.
5. He should be problem solver.
6. He should have patience and creativeness.

In addition to the above qualities, he should also have the following qualities:

(*a*) High standards of ethics and capabilities

(*b*) Motivational and leadership capabilities

(*c*) Good personal drive and mental toughness

(*d*) Good common sense

1. Personality. A construction executive should have a good personality. An construction executive has to handle resources like men, machines and material, hence he should have a good personality and out look. For an executive, good personality and out look is very important to provide leadership.

2. Ethics and integrity. Usually in a construction project a large sum of money is invested. For the successful and economical completion of the project, it is essential that money be spent properly in a effective manner so that good return may accrue to the contractor and the owner. Hence the high standards of ethics and integrity are important for a construction executive. To build a professional reputation in the construction business, it is essential to adhere to the standard set rules and procedures. A top executive should not show any undue favour to vendors, suppliers and sub contractors etc.

3. Personal drive. In the construction industry, management generates long working hours, extensive travelling and frequent family relocation. Problem solving and conflict resolution further adds stress on the management. Hence a person having a strong personal drive will be successful in the construction industry.

4. **Multi disciplinary capabilities.** In construction work people having experience in other disciplines are more suitable. Hence an top executive must have knowledge in the field of cost engineering, scheduling, procurement of materials and machinery and other areas of construction etc. Generally most of the top executives suffer from the weakness of lack of skills of running a project on bussiness lines. These skills may be obtained by getting formal training and undergoing a course on bussiness administration.

16.15. HUMAN RELATIONS FOR TOP EXECUTIVES

The top executive in a construction project is the top most boss. He is next to the owner. In construction management the area of human relations is very wide, due to the involvement of interpersonal contacts in a largely conflict oriented environment. For effective construction management following areas are most critical.

1. **Client-Contractor relationship.** This relation mainly depends upon the type of people and their nature. The client-contractor relations may break due to many reasons which ultimately affect the project completion schedule. To maintain the client-contractor relation, following two methods have been found very effective.
   (*a*) The contractor's opportunities for future work with the client.
   (*b*) Success of the present project.
   Thus it is important that both the client and the contractor try to keep good relations for the successful completion of the project.
2. **Contract administration.** Sometimes contract produces friction in the relationship of client and contractor. Event a best drafted contract has to be changed many a times. Thus to avoid any friction it is important that client and contractor take proactive stance on making contractual requirements.
3. **Relation with the project staff.** The top executive is fully responsible for keeping good relations between staff and also between client and contractor. This can be achieved by solving the problems in a amicable way (friendly way). Personality problems seem to be directly proportional to the size of the staff. Hence higher level people of the organisation must behave properly and set an example as role models for the subordinates.
4. **Internal relations.** For the successful completion of any project, it is important that team work relations are maintained between different people of the project. As the chief executive is the leader of the work, he is responsible to ensure the smooth running of the work. To attain this goal the chief executive should project himself as a knowledgeable person with a natural out look and respect for others.
5. **Labour relations.** In any industry, labour relation is the most critical and important human relation area. Labour relations have much effect on day to day site operations and ultimate success of the project. The chief executive must have basic knowledge of labour laws and labour relations. The main objective of the labour policy is to maintain high productivity and to minimise work stoppage, which hampers the progress of work and increases labour cost. Local labour practice and usage has a great influence on the labour relations and makes it difficult to develop new guide lines covering all situations.
6. **Public relations.** The chief executive usually acts as a public relation representative for the construction projects. He should establish contact with the local government and community officials before opening the site. He should inform them about the plan to handle problem areas such as production of dust, fumes, noise etc. which may adversely affect the area. He should also educate them about environmental effect due to the development of the project.

7. Leadership. This is an God gift quality of a person. This quality touches on most of the other human factors areas in construction management. Under this head following skills may be grouped:

(*a*) Skill to resource allocation
(*b*) Skill of leadership
(*c*) Skill of conflict resolution
(*d*) Skill in decision taking
(*e*) Skill of information processing
(*g*) Skill of introspection
(*h*) Entrepreneural skill etc.

8. Motivation skills. It has already been discussed above.

9. Negotiating ability. Negotiating situations arise almost in every aspect of executing the project. Negotiations are necessary in areas such as staffing, estimating and scheduling, purchasing and contract negatictions etc. Thus negatiction is one of the arts of the management. One learns this art through practice and training.

10. Common sense. It can be defined as sound practical judgement that is independent of specialized knowledge or training etc. Some persons have this skill by birth and some have to develop it.

11. Patience. Patience is the controlling power of one's temper in difficult situations. It increases as the person grows or gets matured. Patience is important in the client contractor relationship.

QUESTIONS

1. Define motivation. Why is it required?
2. Discuss the fundamentals of motivation.
3. What are the functions of motivation?
4. Discuss the factors which influence the human behaviour.
5. How the behaviour of human beings can be modified?
6. Discuss the causes of grievances. How they can be removed?
7. Discuss the relations with subordinates, equals and superiors.
8. Define incentive. Discuss different types of incentives and their importance.
9. Discuss the role of human factors in construction industry.
10. Write brief notes on the followings:
    (*a*) Labour relations
    (*b*) Client-contractor relationship
    (*c*) Neogociating ability
    (*d*) Contract administration

OBJECTIVE TYPE QUESTIONS

1. Motivation is
   (*a*) A technique to determine critical activities
   (*b*) A technique to increase the benefits from an project
   (*c*) It is an art to develop desire amongst workers to work more to achieve the goal of the project
   (*d*) None of the above
2. Identify the incorrect statement
   (*a*) A motivated worker takes his work seriously and discharges it efficiently
   (*b*) A motivated worker remains fully engaged in the activities of the organisation
   (*c*) A motivated worker does not take his work seriously and discharges it carelessly.
   (*d*) Motivation improves the human relations in the organisation
3. Identify the correct statements
   (*a*) Motivation stimulates the workers to improve their performance
   (*b*) Motivation gives job satisfaction
   (*c*) Motivation removes frustation and improves industrial relations
   (*d*) It inspires action by creating interest in the work
   (*e*) All are correct
4. Identify the incorrect statement/statements
   (*a*) Social needs are the fundamentals of motivation
   (*b*) Physical logical needs are the fundamentals of motivation

(*c*) Security needs and reputation etc. are the fundamentals of motivation
(*d*) Self esteem is the fundamentals of motivation
(*e*) None of the above

5. Human behaviour is affected by
(*a*) Economic needs
(*b*) Need of self respect
(*c*) Need of affection
(*d*) Need of safety and security
(*e*) By all the above

6. The human behaviour can be modified by adopting
(*a*) Welfare facilities
(*b*) By giving incentives
(*c*) By motivation
(*d*) By removing frustation
(*e*) By all the above

7. Grievances develop in workers due to
(*a*) Injustice done to them
(*b*) Dissatisfaction due to the policies of the management
(*c*) Inhuman behaviour
(*d*) Strict rules
(*e*) Undue favouritism
(*f*) All are correct

8. Grievances of workers can be removed by
(*a*) Quick disposal of their grievances
(*b*) By adopting sympathetical attitude to them
(*c*) By giving proper hearing to them
(*d*) By adopting simple procedure for removing their grievances
(*e*) By all

9. Motivation is
(*a*) The art of developing desire to work hard amongst workers to achieve the desired goal.
(*b*) Motivation is a technique to handle fire hazzards.
(*c*) Motivation is a technique to procure construction materials from out side sources.
(*d*) All are correct.

10. The objectives of motivation are except
(*a*) To develop sense of responsibility in workers
(*b*) To create interest for work in workers
(*c*) To develop tendency to be away from the work amongst workers
(*d*) To give job satisfaction.

ANSWERS

1. (*c*)	4. (*e*)	7. (*f*)	10. (*c*)
2. (*c*)	5. (*e*)	8. (*e*)	
3. (*e*)	6. (*e*)	9. (*a*)	

17

Inspection And Quality Control

17.1. INTRODUCTION

In all construction works or projects the proper inspection and quality control is very essential to ensure that the construction work has been carried out in accordance with the plans and specifications. The timely inspection and quality control will result in good quality construction at a reasonable cost. Many a times in construction projects a good and safe design is spoiled by careless execution. Thus inspection and quality control are as important as investigations and designs. Hence the objective of inspection and quality control is to provide a sound construction work resulting in a uniform and good quality structure at reasonable cost. Inspection is the most important and critical function during the execution of a project. Careful inspection and quality control is as important as good planning and design of the structure.

17.2. OBJECTIVES OF INSPECTION

Following are the objectives of inspection:

1. To find out the desired quality of work and materials through observation and testing.
2. To ensure the quality of work and materials as laid down in the specifications.
3. To determine the variation in the quality of work done and quality desired.
4. To have quality control at various stages of construction through inspection.

17.3. PRINCIPLES OF INSPECTION

The efficient and effective field inspection demands an understanding of the character of inspection procedure and appreciation of the statistical principles which must under lie any sampling and testing procedure. The fundamental laws of probability are so important in evaluating the validity of any checking, sampling and testing programme that some considerations should be given to them in setting up any inspection operations,

The probability concept under lies all quality control operations and explains, why the contractor and the field inspector are deeply interested in an orderly controlled procedure which will yield an acceptable end product every time. These laws also provide the theoretical basis for fairly detailed specifications concerning the step by step procedure to be followed in the construction process. Since the detailed requirements are nothing more than the design engineers device for establishing compliance with recognised methods of quality control.

The same laws of probability are important in setting up the inspection operations both in the discharge of the inspectors responsibility for following a procedure which will fairly and accurately develop truly representative check schedules and obtain truly representative material samples, equipment test specimens and carrying out the test procedures applied to the completed work and material samples. Many a times the critical decisions depend upon the results of inspection and tests carried out on relatively small samples, which represent more extensive items of work. Test Procedure must be followed with great care to ensure that they result in accurate determination of pertinent information.

When the inspection, sampling and tests are involved in a project, they are carefully set up in conformity with the principles out lined above. Carrying out day to day inspection becomes a matter of checking to ensure that proper procedures are followed.

17.4. FUNCTIONS OF INSPECTION

Following are the functions of inspection:

1. To adhere to the standards of material and craftmanship approved by the authorities in the final working drawings and specifications.
2. To avoid the extra construction cost beyond the approved construction contract.
3. To check the construction processes and evaluate the quality of material in conformity with the specifications.
4. To eliminate the unacceptable substitutes.
5. To have frequent meetings with the contractor to assist him in interpretation of contract document.
6. To eliminate the errors which result in unnecessary and costly maintenance and up keep costs.
7. To ensure the installation of guaranteed materials and workmanship at the time of their installation.
8. To coordinate the works of various crafts skillfully.
9. To discover the error left in the final drawings or specifications and their earliest removal.
10. Periodic reporting of the progress of the project for the information of higher authorities.
11. To protect the interests of owner, engineer, and contractor and to integrate their desired interests.
12. To prevent unfair practices and procedures to fulfil the contractual obligations.
13. to check the compliance of stipulated safety measures.

17.5. INSPECTION OF CONSTRUCTION WORK

Mainly following items of work need inspection:

1. **Sub soil.** To test and ensure bearing capacity of the sub soil, inspection is necessary.
2. **Materials of construction.** Materials supplied by the contractor for the construction work should be inspected to check their quality before they are paid and used. For this purpose tests at field and laboratory should be carried out as specified.
3. **Equipment.** After the receipt of equipment from any source and before entering them into the books, they must be inspected and checked fully to ensure their specifications and working as per the specifications supplied by the firm. Afterwards their regular inspection is necessary to ensure their serviceability and condition.
4. **Inspection of work.** At each stage of work completed should be inspected before the start of next stage. Any defect noticed must be got rectified before proceeding to the next stage.
5. **Process inspection.** To ensure the correct and systematic operation of the work, inspection is necessary. Inspection also ensures that work is completed with standard materials and set procedure and is free of defects.

17.6. GENERAL PRINCIPLES OF INSPECTION RELATED TO CONSTRUCTION WORK

Following are the general principles of inspection:

1. Usually the materials are inspected at the site of construction. In this case the supplier has to remove the rejected material from the site of work, in which he has to incur some expenditure. This is the main drawback of this method. To avoid expenditure and labour in removing the rejected material, he resorts to corrupt practices. In case the material is inspected at the supplier premises, then it is difficult to ensure that the actual supplies will be made of the same quality as the material is approved after inspection. Thus the site of inspection should be chosen very carefully.

2. For each material or item of work, it is necessary to lay down the exact nature of inspection required to be done. The defects and the importance of each defect and the limit of tolerance of defects should be fixed. Thus the limit of quality of each item that may be accepted should be fixed before hand.
3. In order to point out deficiencies quickly and to limit the loss in taking remedial measures, inspections should be made promptly. Delay in pointing out defects may increase the cost of defect removal.
4. The details and frequency of inspection should be such that it may result in the necessary degree of control on the quality of work.
5. In case the material inspected is just on the border line of acceptable limit of quality, then a definite procedure should be adopted.

In case payment is already made, then it should be used on inferior quality works.

17.7. INSPECTOR'S ROLE

The inspection agency has to play a very vital role in the execution of works. This agency has multiferous duties and responsibilities. The inspector essentially is a practical man with the knowledge of principles involved in the execution of works. He should know how a particular work is to be done and why it should be done in that manner. He should have the requisite knowledge to be able to get the work done according to the plans and specifications. The safety and stability of a large structure dependents upon his integrity, efficiency, technical skill and devotion to duty.

To start with, an inspector has to familiarise himself with plans and specifications of the work. He must understand fully the drawings and specifications and implication of each item of specifications with their back ground. He should also have good judgement of every thing he inspects. In general it can be said that an inspector should have a critical eye for every thing he inspects. Only then he will be able to make really useful contribution to his job.

An inspector is authorised to stop work which is not done according to the plan and specifications. However this step is taken as a last resort when it is clear that continuation of the operation will result in unsatisfactory work. He may get removed the faulty work or get it repaired before inspection.

Inspection should be done promptly when required. When ever it is anticipated that the prevailing conditions will lead to un satisfactory results, the construction authorities be told in advance of the actual operations. The inspector should suggest changes in the work, but before doing so he should make sure that his judgement is fair and sound.

17.8. TECHNICAL SERVICES REQUIRED FOR FIELD INSPECTION

The adequacy of construction work is accomplished by:

(*a*) Visual examination (*b*) By measurement

(*c*) By testing

The extent to which each of the above procedures are employed depends upon the local conditions, nature and importance of the work being inspected and on the skill of the inspector. During initial stages of construction the judgement of the inspector requires to be confirmed by test and measurement at frequent intervals, until his ability of visual examination is established.

17.9. RESOURCES REQUIRED FOR FIELD INSPECTION

Following resources are required for the effective field inspection:

1. **Properly trained personnel.** For a qualified inspector the foremost requirement is that he should not only be conversant with the nature and extent of inspections to be carried out, but should have sound knowledge of the methods and practices adopted in construction works.
2. **Equipment.** The type, nature, size and number of various equipments required for a laboratory

would depend upon the type of tests to be carried out and magnitude of the job. For the list of various equipments required for various laboratories, earth and concrete manuals (U.S.B.R.) and other standard references may be referred.

3. **Laboratories.** Depending on the nature of the job, during investigation stage of project various tests have to be carried out to establish the characteristics of various types of available materials. After tests the design is formulated using available materials.

17.10. LABORATORIES REQUIRED

Usually following laboratories are required:

1. **Soil testing laboratory.** To determine the properties of soil for its use in embankments and for other purposes, soil laboratory is required.
2. **Concrete laboratory.** To determine the properties of fine and coarse aggregate, the strength and other properties of concrete, concrete laboratory is required.
3. **Facilities for other measurements.** For setting out and other dimensional control survey equipment and other materials are necessary. Facilities for determining the size and quantity of sediment carried by water are also necessary.

17.11. QUALITY CONTROL

The aim of quality control is to ensure production of items for their intended use with out defects and variations from their prescribed standards within prescribed tolerance limits. Quality control also aims to avoid wastage of time, materials and money by highlighting the point at which a production process has become defective.

17.12. ELEMENTS OF QUALITY

The basic elements of quality are as follows:

1. **Quality characteristics.** The properties which define the nature of a product for quality control are strength, colour, dimension and temperature etc. are called quality characteristics. For example consider cement concrete which is a common construction material now a days, its compressive strength, size of aggregate, water-cement ratio, slump, surface finish etc. are important characteristics which should be checked frequently for structural purposes.
2. **Design quality.** No design can produce absolutely perfect results, what so ever good design it may be. Thus the desired standards for the characteristics such as strength, dimensions that define a product and also the tolerances for acceptable variations from the specified standards should be specified. The very high standards of quality and stiff tolerance limits will result in high cost of the project.
3. **Quality of conformance.** The degree of quality of the work found in actual construction work is known as the quality of conformance. As in the case of design quality, the degree to which the quality is to be enforced in the field has to be considered along with the cost necessary for quality control.

17.13. FACTORS AFFECTING THE QUALITY OF CONFORMANCE

The quality of conformance is affected by the following factors:

1. **Construction method in the field.** The quality of materials used, skill of workers and efficiency of machinery and equipment affect the quality of conformance.
2. **Field supervision.** The managerial control applied to direct the workers to conform to the plans and specifications and supervision enforced affects the quality of conformance.
3. The inspection and quality control procedures applied also affect the quality of conformance.

17.14. WORKS NEEDING QUALITY CONTROL

In construction works following works need quality control:

1. Concrete works	2. Steel works
3. Form works	4. Masonry works
5. Water proofing	6. Services etc.

1. **Concrete works.** In fact concrete is a very important construction material having a very high compressive strength. Its quality is influenced to a great extent by its constituent elements, water/cement ratio, size of aggregate and their grading, rate of loading, and curing conditions etc. Hence to obtain concrete of uniform quality, constant supervision on the different activities of its production is essential. The supervisor should be well versed with the properties of concrete. Thus to obtain a good quality concrete, the engineer incharge should be present through out the operations of mixing, placing, compaction and finishing etc.
2. **Steel.** It is a costly item and constitutes a major item of expenditure in most of the works. In R.C.C. works, it is used as reinforcement to take up tensile stresses. Before use, its tensile strength, its proper bending, binding and placing should be checked carefully. The reinforcing bars should be free from rust, scales, oil and grease and other harmful coatings. Care should be taken that reinforcement does not get displaced during concrete pouring and compaction operations.
3. **Form work.** The shape and finished surface of concrete depends upon the form work. Hence form work must have smooth surface, so that finished concrete may need minimum amount of rendering. In case finished surface is not required to be plastered, the pattern of surface left by the form work should be such that it gives a pleasant look. The form work should be strong enough to withstand the weight of green concrete. While removing the form work, care should be taken that concrete is not damaged while striking the form work.
4. **Masonry work.** Bricks to be used in masonry work should be of specified quality and grade, having requisite strength and water absorption capacity with in permissible limits. The bond in masonry should be properly maintained. The dimensions and verticality of masonry works are very important and care should be taken to maintain it.
5. **Water proofing**. Damp proof courses at plinth level and damp proofing of roof etc. are very important. Hence proper care should be taken to have them properly water proof.
6. **Joinery and timber work.** For timber work, timber of specified quality should be used. The workmanship of wood work should be properly checked and maintained as per specifications. These items are very important from the quality control point of view.
7. **Services.** Water supply, electric fittings, sanitary, air conditioning etc. are classified under this head. Proper control should be exercised on the execution of these works. These are very important items from the point of customer's comforts. Hence these works need special attention of quality control.

17.15. QUALITY CONTROL METHODS

Following are the major quality control methods:

1. **Inspection.** It has already been discussed in detail.
2. **Testing.** Testing is the examination of the material or product to check its conformance to the specified standards. Testing may be destructive or non destructive and can be performed at site or in the laboratory. For detailed testing the reader is advised to refer authors concrete technology book chapter 19 or any other standard work.
3. **Sampling.** The process of determining the quality of a large group by examining a part of the group that will be statistically representative to the whole group is called *sampling*. The reliability of the test results of the sample is determined by reliability number. It is given as the variation of results of individual test result from the mean value of the group. It is calculate in terms of standard

deviation and coefficient of variation. The reliability of information obtained increases with the size of the sample used.

1. Reliability number. The reliability number is taken as the reliability of the test results of the sample. It is expressed as:

$$\text{Reliability number} = 100 - \left[\frac{\text{no. of defective units}}{\text{no. of units tested}} \times 100\right] \quad ...(1)$$

2. Standard deviation. It is the root mean square of the deviation of all the results. It is denoted by σ or *S*. It is calculated as follows:

$$\sigma = \sqrt{\frac{\Sigma (x-\bar{x})^2}{N-1}} \quad ...(2)$$

where,

N = No of specimens tested.

x = Particular value of strength

$\bar{x}$ = Mean strength of specimens

3. Coefficient of variation. This is an alternative method of expressing variation of results. It is a non dimensional measure of variation. It is obtained by dividing the standard deviation by the arithmetic mean value. It is expressed as

$$V = \frac{\sigma}{\bar{x}} \times 100 \quad ...(3)$$

where,

(V) = Coefficient of variation.

In India the standard deviation is taken as the most reliable method of quality control. Standard deviation is an absolute measure of dispersion, where as coefficient of variation is a relative measure of dispersion. Lower values of standard deviation show a high degree of uniformity of observations and the homogeneity of quality of the concrete.

QUESTIONS

1. Discuss the importance of quality in construction projects.
2. Explain the basic elements of quality.
3. Discuss the necessity of testing materials and construction products.
4. Discuss the major items of construction work which require special attention with regard to quality control.
5. Discuss the principles of inspection. What are the main items of inspection in the construction work.
6. Describe the technical services required for the inspection.
7. Economy, Efficiency, Quality and Productivity of a project are dependent on effective inspection. Discuss in brief.

OBJECTIVE TYPE QUESTIONS

1. The reliability number is the measure of
   (*a*) Quality of a sample (*b*) Accuracy of a sample
   (*c*) Dimension of a product (*d*) None of the above
2. Sampling is the process of determining the quality of
   (*a*) Large group from a small part (*b*) Small part from a large group
   (*c*) Small group from a small part (*d*) None of the above
3. The basic elements of quality are
   (*a*) Quality and design (*b*) Design and structural quality
   (*c*) Design, structural quality and conformance (*d*) Design and conformance
4. The major quality control methods are
   (*a*) Inspection and testing (*b*) Testing and sampling

(*c*) Inspection and sampling (*d*) Inspection, testing and sampling

5. In a construction project the responsibility of enforcing quality in construction rests with the
   (*a*) Designer (*b*) Contractor
   (*c*) Resident enginéer and his is inspector (*d*) Architect
6. Quality control means
   (*a*) Adequate design at the minimum cost (*b*) Rational use of available resources
   (*c*) Completion of work at extra cost (*d*) None of the above
7. Quality control can be exercised by
   (*a*) Adequate compaction and curing
   (*b*) By resorting to acceptance test
   (*c*) By motivating the workers to carry everything from the first time
   (*d*) By inspection and testing at every stage
8. Standard deviation is the measure of
   (*a*) Variability of test results
   (*b*) Spread of compressive strength test
   (*c*) All the results falling out side or with in the certain range
   (*d*) All the above
9. For excellent control over the construction of a bridge, the value of standard deviation should be
   (*a*) More than 5.0 (*b*) Between 4 and 5
   (*c*) Between 3.5 and 4.0 (*d*) Less than 3.0
10. Identify the correct statement of the followings
    (*a*) Larger the value of standard deviation, poorer is the level of control
    (*b*) Larger the value of standard deviation, better is the level of control
    (*c*) Larger the value of standard deviation lower is the variability
    (*d*) All the above are correct
11. Identify the correct statement
    (*a*) Quality control of concrete can be defined by the conformity of specifications
    (*b*) The quality of concrete can be defined by the assurance that all aspects of materials, equipment and workmanship have been looked after well
    (*c*) The quality control of concrete can be defined by the assurance of serivicebility and safety of the structure
    (*d*) By all the above

ANSWERS

1. (*a*)	4. (*d*)	7. (*d*)	10. (*a*)
2. (*b*)	5. (*c*)	8. (*d*)	11. (*b*)
3. (*c*)	6. (*b*)	9. (*d*)	

18

Safety Measures In Construction Work

18.1. INTRODUCTION

After independence the construction industry has grown significantly. The construction industry in India to day is very large in size and complex in nature. In Civil Engineering projects many works big or small are executed. For the execution of these works skilled and unskilled labour along with machines and equipments are employed. With the introduction of machines for increasing the output of the work, the number of accidents also is increasing. It is a hard fact that where the safety ends, accidents start. Any work completed with out accidents results economical. No body wants to be injured, but it happens so sudden that one can not help. On the one hand accidents cause injury to the worker and agony to his family and on the other hand, they cause mental tension and financial burden to the owner.

Though the social concern of the safety of construction workers and their protection against injury is quite evident since long, but so far no tangible results have been observed. The survey of occupational injury and illness incidence carried out in 1982 shows that upto 14.5% workers suffer from these injuries. The break up of occupational injury in different industries is shown in Table 18.1.

Table 18.1. Occupational injury rate

S. No.	*Industry*	*% of total injury*
1.	Finance, Insurance etc.	2.0
2.	Services	4.9
3.	Whole sale and retail trade	7.2
4.	Agriculture, forestry	7.7
5.	Transportation utilities	8.5
6.	Manufacturing	10.2
7.	Mining	10.5
8.	Construction	14.5

18.2. DEFINITION OF ACCIDENT

An unplanned and unexpected occurrence which upsets the planned sequence of events and actions, resulting in the loss of production, injury to the person and damage to plants and equipment is known as *accident.*

18.3. IMPORTANCE OF SAFETY

In India the construction industry is labour oriented. It employees the largest labour force after agriculture. The injury rate is found about 10.0 to 14.5% of all the occupational injuries and about 20% deaths. The cost of accident is very expensive. The economic cost is not the only criteria for taking safety measures. Actually the reasons for safety considerations are as follows:

1. Humanitarian reasons. The sufferings and agony undergone by the injured worker and his family members is difficult to quantify in economic terms. Thus accidents should be prevented more on human considerations.

2. Economic reasons. The accidents have their own costs, which include direct and indirect cost. Direct cost includes.

(*a*) Medical expenses for the injured
(*b*) Compensation amount to the injured
(*c*) Legal charges
(*d*) Cost incurred in replacement of equipment and damaged materials etc.

Indirect Costs. These costs include:

(*a*) Slow down in progress of work
(*b*) Productive time lost by the injured worker and fallow workers
(*c*) Decrease in productivity due to moral decrease after injury
(*d*) Over time payment to make up the loss of time
(*e*) Loss of confidence by the client etc.
(*f*) Loss of administrative work due to accident.

3. Organisational image. Good safety measure record boosts the morals of the workers resulting in higher productivity and better loyalty of the workers to the organisation. Good safety measures will also enhance the public image of the organisation.

4. Laws and Regulation. The employer has to adhere to the laws and regulations laid down by the Government for the safety of the employees. The violation of these laws and regulation will attract punishment to the employer.

18.4. CAUSES OF ACCIDENTS

In construction industry there are many causes of accidents. Broadly the causes of accidents may be classified as follows:

A. Physical causes
B. Physiological causes
C. Phychological causes

A. Physical causes

Under the head physical causes following factors may be grouped:

1. Relating to machines
2. Relating to tools
3. Relating to materials
4. Relating to uniform
5. Relating to environment
6. Fixing unsuitable time table etc.

1. Causes Relating to machines. Under this head following causes may be classified:

(*a*) The working space for the machines may be inadequate. Due to obstruction free movement of man and material is not possible, which may cause accidents.
(*b*) The machines not being properly placed or adjusted
(*c*) Unsuitable machines being used for the job
(*d*) The machines not being properly guarded
(*e*) The electric motor of the machine not properly insulated

This may also be called as defective technical planning.

2. Causes relating to tools

(*a*) Due to constant use, the tools being blunt and worn out
(*b*) Tools employed on the job being too small for the job
(*c*) Tools used may be of brittle nature and break suddenly, for example blades of a circular saw

(*d*) The handle of the tool may be too short or loose
(*e*) Tools used may be unsuitable for the job

2. Causes relating to materials.

(*a*) Materials used may be poisonous and dangerous as acids and some salts etc.
(*b*) The materials may be too hot as tar or bitumen at the time of use of road construction and no proper precautions taken
(*c*) Explosives, petroleum products and brittle materials being handled carelessly.
(*d*) Not adopting proper precautions while cleaning sewer etc. which emit foul gases.

4. Causes relating to uniform.

(*a*) The uniform may be loose
(*b*) The shoes may be slippery and loose
(*c*) No protective device being used while working on welding job
(*d*) The sleeves of shirt being with out buttons

5. Causes relating to environment

(*a*) Poor lighting arrangement at the site of work
(*b*) Poor ventilation and unhygienic conditions at the site of work
(*c*) Uninsulated wires left carelessly
(*d*) Loose electric cables
(*e*) Obstacles in the working area
(*f*) Floor being sleepry
(*g*) Building used being unsafe
(*h*) Use of unsuitable *i.e.* weak or short ladder
(*i*) External disturbances as noise
(*j*) Loose discipline among workers

B. Physiological causes

This factor relates to the health conditions of the workers. Accidents due to this factor are grouped as follows:

(*a*) *Poor eye sight.* This a very important factor for every worker, especially for the workers handling machinery, automobiles and cranes etc. If a driver can not see an vehicle or obstacle ahead clearly especially in poor visibility conditions will result in accident.
(*b*) *Over work.* A tired worker due to over time, loses control over his limbs easily and may meet accident.
(*c*) *Poor health.* A worker due to poor health may not control his load of work and may meet an accident.
(*d*) *Old age.* Generally in old age eye sight becomes poor and also one becomes hard of hearing along with poor general health. These factors cause accidents easily.
(*e*) *Intoxication.* One loses control over his limbs and becomes prone to accident under the influence of intoxication.
(*f*) *Physical handicapness.* A physical handicap person is more prone to accidents.

C. Physchological factors

Under this head, the factors causing accidents are related to mental condition of a worker:

(*a*) *Mental tension and worry.* Under mental tension and worry one loses control over his mind and may meet an accident.
(*b*) *Emotional attitude.* An emotional person loses mental balance quickly.
(*c*) *Impulsiveness.* When a person acts under impulse, with out proper thinking, the chances of accidents are more.

(*d*) *Nervouness.* A nervous person loses control over his limbs quickly and has more chances of meeting an accident.

(*e*) *Over confidence.* Many a times over confidence results in accidents.

(*f*) *Carelessness.* A care less worker has more chances of meeting a accident than a conscious worker.

(*g*) *Fear*. Under fear also one loses control over his limbs quickly.

18.5. OBJECTIVES OF ACCIDENT PREVENTION

The main objective of prevention of accidents is to save human lives, equipment, and materials etc. Accident prevention results in:

1. Saving of human lives.
2. Prevention of temporary or permanent injury to workers
3. Prevention of damages to plants and equipment, and loss of materials.
4. Saving in the cost of compensation to workers.
5. Saving in loss of time due to injury.

18.6. CLASSIFICATION OF ACCIDENTS IN CONSTRUCTION INDUSTRY

The accidents in construction industry may be classified as follows:

1. According to the cause of occurrence
2. According to the nature of injury sustained as
   (*a*) Temporary disablement (*b*) Partial disablement
   (*c*) Total disablement (*d*) Death
3. According to the severity of injury as
   (*a*) Minor accident (*b*) Major accident (*c*) Accident hazard

18.7. SAFETY MEASURES

During the construction of a project, safety is also influenced to a great extent by the decisions taken during the planning and design processes. Some designs or construction plans are inherently difficult and dangerous to implement, where as others may considerably reduce the possibility of accidents. For example clear separation of traffic from construction zones can greatly reduce the possibility of accidental collisions. Besides design decisions, safety largely depends upon the education and training of workers, vigilance and cooperation during construction.

Choice of proper technology, and machines can also reduce the chances of accidents to a great extent. Proper choice of materials also influence the safety of construction.

Educating managers and workers about proper procedures and hazards has been found to have a impact on the safety at job site. The realization of the large costs involved in construction injuries and illness provides an motivation for safety.

18.8. SAFETY MEASURES REQUIRED IN CONSTRUCTION AREAS

Usually safety measures are required in the following areas of constructions

1. Excavation
2. Scaffolding, ladders and form work
3. Hot bitumen work
4. Demolition works
5. Drilling and blasting works

1. Safety measures in excavation work

In the construction of Civil Engineering works such as buildings, dams, bridges etc. excavation work for foundations etc. is one of the important activities. If during excavation operations proper safety measures are not adopted, it may cause serious accidents. Some basic principles of safety measures are discussed below:

(*a*) General guide lines:

(*i*) Before starting excavation work, complete information of under ground structures such as water pipe lines, sewers, gas lines, electric cables etc. is essential. All safety measures should be adopted to ensure the safety to the workers and the public.

(*ii*) The work should be entrusted to an experienced and competent supervisor. He should be made responsible for strict observance of safety precautions.

(*iii*) The excavated trenches should be given proper protection against slides and caving in during and after heavy rains and storms etc.

(*iv*) Workers should be asked to wear helmets, where there is danger of falling stones etc.

(*v*) Constant watch and supervision should be kept on new workers, while engaged on jobs involving risk or hazards.

(*b*) Precautions to be taken while working with machines:

In construction industry to increase the productivity, the use of machines and equipment is increasing day by day. Hence it is very important to take necessary precautions while using machinery and equipment. Following precautions should be adopted while working with machines.

(*i*) *Proper selection of machinery.* The excavating machinery should be selected properly depending upon the size of project and nature of soil to be excavated.

(*ii*) *Upkeep of the machinery.* The servicing and over hauling of the machinery should be carried out regularly by qualified persons. The maintenance and up keep of the machinery should be carried out regularly and the machines should be kept upto date.

(*iii*) *Operation of machinery.* For operating the machines only qualified persons should be appointed. Un qualified or unauthorized persons should never be allowed to handle the machinery as they are bound to have an accident.

(*iv*) Mentally and physically fit persons only be allowed to work on machinery.

(*v*) Faulty machines should not be pressed in operation.

(*vi*) Dangerous parts of the machines such as chain drive, belts etc. should be provided with proper cover.

(*vii*) While running the engine, replacement of oil, lubrication, or repair work should not be under taken.

(*viii*) While starting the machine, the operator should give a working signal and no body should be allowed to stand under the boom or raised part of the machine. Machine should not be left running.

(*ix*) After stopping a movable machinery, its driving wheels should be bracked.

(*x*) One should not jump into or from a moving vehicle or equipment.

(*xi*) While working in night, proper lighting arrangements must be ensured.

(*xii*) Work should not be executed partially by machines and partially by manual labour as it is likely to meet an accident.

(*c*) Shoring and timbering of excavated trenches:

(*i*) *Vertical cut trenches.* In medium soils the trenches more than 1.5 m deep should be securely shored and timbered. In case of hard soils, timbering is necessary if the depth of cutting exceeds more than 2.0 m. Sheathing is placed against the sides of the trench with planks held vertically. In loose soils the sheathing is firmly embedded into the bottom of the trench.

(*ii*) Loose boulders, lumps of earth etc. should be removed, so that they may not roll down into the trench and injure the workers.

(*iii*) The excavated material should be removed away back ward from the edge of the trench at least 1 m or more. Actually the excavated material should be removed to a distant place. If this is not practicable then boards should be provided to prevent the rolling down of the soil into the trench. Tools used in construction should also be kept away from the edge of the trench for similar reasons.

(*iv*) Vehicles should not be allowed to be driven close to the edges of the trench. While loading excavated soil into the trucks, care should be taken that loose soil does not roll down into the trench.

(*v*) The path ways and gang ways should be non slippery and of sufficient width. Planks used for gang ways should be provided with cleats to ensure safe walking.

(*vi*) If traffic passes near the trenches, strong fencing should be provided to prevent animals and public from falling into the trenches. To ensure safety of pedestrians and vehicles, the public walk sides should be lighted sufficiently. At both ends of the area under excavation red lights should be provided. Warning signals should also be placed.

(*vii*) Persons required to work under deep trenches or at high altitudes, safety ropes should be tied to their safety belts, so that they could be helped at the time of need. A single worker should never be allowed to work in a trench alone.

(*viii*) It should also be ensured that no harmful gases are present in the trenches. If they are present then appropriate mechanical ventilation should be provided to protect the life of the workers.

2. Scaffolding

(*i*) It is required for all types of structures constructed above ground level and maintenance of such works. The type of scaffolding to be used depends upon the nature of the work and its situation.

(*ii*) The vertical standards should be embedded into the ground sufficiently deep, so that they may withstand the loads coming on them. On pucca floors and streets these standards may be placed into the empty tar drums and packed with stones and bricks etc.

(*iii*) Various stages of construction may be erected at convenient heights.

(*iv*) While connecting ledgers to standards and putlogs to ledgers, lashing should be done securely. The rope used should be thick and stout.

(*v*) The sizes of different members should be properly designed according to the load they are supposed to carry.

(*vi*) To safeguard against over turning, inclined rakers are provided and lashed at the junctions of standards and ledgers at appropriate height and embedded into the ground at the bottom.

(*vii*) The boarding over which the mason sits, should be of sufficient width and strength to take up the load of workers and building materials needed for immediate use. Proper guide rails should be provided so that mason and workers may not fall.

(*viii*) To avoid the risk of its sliding, the putlog should be inserted sufficiently deep in the wall.

(*ix*) No body should be allowed to stand below the scaffolding, as stones or bricks may fall down from the scaffolding and injure the person standing below.

(*x*) As the scaffoldings are not designed to carry large quantity of building materials, only small quantity of materials should be put on the scaffolding.

(*xi*) When the work is over, the scaffolding should be dismantled step by step from upper side. Its members should be stacked on the hard ground. They should not be stacked against wall. This will avoid sagging and warping of the members. To avoid crack development they should not be exposed to direct sun rays.

(*xii*) Before using scaffolding members second time and subsequently, they should be tested for strength. Wooden members should be free from wet and dry rot.

(*xiii*) For repair work at high level of multistoyred buildings needle scaffolding is preferred as it will not obstruct traffic at the ground level.

(*xiv*) In sheds for ceiling works, suspended scaffolding is economical. It also does not occupy floor space, allowing workers to continue their work at ground level.

(*xv*) Workers should not be allowed to lit fire near the scaffolding.

2. B. Ladders

(*a*) **General.** In any construction activity, ladders constitute one of the essential part of construction equipment. If proper attention is not paid to this aspect, it may result in many accidents.

(*b*) **Causes of accidents.** The accidents may occur due to the following causes:

(*i*) Failure to secure properly ladder at top or bottom or at both places

(*ii*) Ascending or descending improperly

(*iii*) Structually failure of the ladder itself

(*iv*) Unsafe conditions of placing the ladder

(*v*) Carrying load carelessly while ascending or descending.

(*c*) **Construction of ladder**

(*i*) All ladders should be designed for the loads they are intended to carry.

(*ii*) Side rails for metal ladders should be of sufficient cross- section so that excessive deflection may not develop into them.

(*iii*) In bamboo ladders, the rungs should be fixed to the rails with spikes of proper design and strength. In other types of wooden ladders, the use of spikes or nails should not be allowed.

(*iv*) To avoid danger of slipping, safety shoes should be used.

(*d*) **Built-up ladders**

(*i*) In case of built-up ladders all surfaces of the ladder should be planed free from splinters, and the edges of hand rails should be bevelled.

(*ii*) The rungs should be spaced uniformly and should not be spaced more than 30 cms apart. They should be recessed at least 12mm into the rails.

(*iii*) Ladders used for heavy work, should not be more than 6 m long, where as for light work, the length may be upto 8 m.

(*e*) **Portable ladders**

(*i*) The over all length of stock ladders should not be more than 10 m. The minimum internal width of ladders should be 29 cms for ladders upto 3 m length. For longer ladders this width may be increased by 6 mm for every additional length of 0.3 m.

(*ii*) In case of metal, ladders, rungs must be made of steel pipe or solid round steel rods or angle sections, securely fastened to the side rails by bolting, riveting or welding. The metal treads should be flanged downwards not less than 50 mm at each end and secured to each side rail by two bolts or rivets. Dimension of the ladder should be adopted as per IS specifications.

(*f*) **Use of ladders**

1. Portable ladder. While using portable ladder following points should be kept in mind.

(*i*) Before use all ladders should be tested for the designed load. The ladder should be strong and rigid.

(*ii*) A defective ladder with missing rung, should never be used. Efforts should be made to repair it promptly.

(*iii*) The splicing of ladder should be avoided.

(*iv*) Ladder leading to lending should be extended at least one metre above the landing and secured at the upper end properly.

(*v*) Ladders should not be supported against window panes, sashes, or other unsafe or yielding objects. They should also not be placed infront of door opening towards it. When the ladders are used in public walk ways, suitable barricades should be provided.

(*vi*) While using ladder, one should not lean sideways more then 30 cms. It is safer to get down and shift the ladder to the new place.

(*vii*) While ascending or descending, the user should face the ladder. He should use his both hands and place his feet near the end of the rungs and not in the middle.

(*viii*) To prevent slipping, a ladder should be placed in such a way that it does not make an angle of more than 75 degree with the ground *i.e.* the distance between the vertical wall or face and the lower and of the ladder should not be more than one fourth of the length of ladder or ladder should be secured at the bottom properly.

(*ix*) Metal ladder should not be used around electric circuit or equipments.

(*x*) Extension ladders should be used up 10 m length. To ensure proper locking and full extension of the section, locks and guides should be checked properly.

(*xi*) The diameter of rope ladder should not be less than 25 mm and wooden steps should not be less than 38 mm thick.

(*f*) Inspection and storage of ladder

(*i*) If the ladder damaged or dropped while in use, it should be inspected carefully.

(*ii*) For damage or deterioration, wooden ladders should be inspected at least once a month.

(*iii*) The metal ladders should be inspected at least once in three months. All parts should be checked for structural failure and corrosion etc.

(*iv*) The wooden ladders should be treated with a clear preservative such as varnish.

(*v*) The ladders should be stored in covered space, where they may not be affected by direct sun rays, or rain. To avoid sagging in storage they should be supported adequately.

2. C. Form work

(*i*) Form work may be either of steel or timber. In case of timber form work, the timber used should be of coarse grained, so that nails may be driven easily with out causing damage to the timber. Timber should be free from knots and other defects.

(*ii*) The section of timber should be such that may be capable to bear the pressure of green concrete. The weight of green concrete may be taken as 2400 kg/m^3.

(*iii*) To make the timber form work water resistant, it should be provided G.I. sheet lining. The provision of sheet lining prevents the loss of water from the concrete and provides smooth surface to it.

(*iv*) The construction of form work should be such that it can be dismantled or removed easily, with out causing any harm to the concrete or form work it self, as it has to be used a number of times on future works.

(*v*) To provide smooth surface to concrete and to avoid damage to it as well as form work, the interior surface of form work should be given a thin coating of either grease, oil or such other material. To allow sags in beams the form work should be given a camber of 1 in 5.

Precautions to avoid shrinkage, bending and warping under loads

To avoid bending, warping and shrinkage under loads following precautions may be adopted:

(*i*) Partially seasoned timber should be used for form work. If dry timber is used for form work, allowance for bulging, and shrinking should be provided while preparing the surface.

(*ii*) Now a days for shuttering, water proof plywood is used. Plywood should conform to the Indian standard. It should be durable under alternate wetting and drying conditions. Its surface should be hard and sufficiently strong to take the load of concrete and impact during the placement of concrete and compaction.

(*iii*) To ensure economy, the sizes of members of the form work should be standardised, so that it could be used again and again. The design of structure and form work should be done simultaneously.

(*iv*) To provide facility at the time of removing and reusing of the form work, the use of clamps and screws is preferable.

(*v*) As the form work is to be used for a number of times, it should be removed very carefully with out causing any damage. It should be stacked in such a way that there is maximum circulation of air. The stacking should be done in such a way that bending, warping and cracks etc. are not developed in members. Members should not be kept inclined against walls, as this will cause bending in them. Wet members should not be exposed to hot sun.

(*vi*) Unauthorised persons or stray cattles should not be allowed near the form work as any damage to the form work may prove dangerous.

(*vii*) The reinforcement cage should not be laid in position with a jerk, but should be placed gently.

(*viii*) Concrete in the form work should not be thrown from a height of more than 1 m as it will damage the form work, displace the reinforcement from its position. It may also cause segregation in concrete.

(*ix*) Before the reuse of form work, its members should be checked carefully. Damaged members should not be reused. It should be free from dry rot and wet rot.

(*x*) Steel form work is more economical as it can be used for more number of times than timber form work. It is more safe and gives better concrete surface.

(*xi*) Concreting in the form work should be started after it has been inspected and checked by approved competent authority.

(*xii*) At the time of removing form work, no body except workers on the job should be allowed near the site of work as any falling member may cause injury.

(*xiii*) The form work should be removed with out any jerk or vibration as it may cause damage to the reinforced concrete. Before removing the bottom form work of the slab or beam, it should be ensured that the bottom surface has hardened sufficiently. Actually form work should be removed as per ISI recommendations.

3. Hot bitumen works

(*i*) The tar boilers should be equipped with suitable temperature recording device. The bitumen or tar should not be allowed to be over heated. By over heating the binding properties of tar are destroyed and with further heating it may catch fire. To keep constant temperature bitumen should be constantly stirred.

(*ii*) Only trained and experienced workers should be deputed for bitumen work.

(*iii*) Only physically fit and mentally alert workers should be engaged on the bitumen works.

(*iv*) The work should be planned in such a way that workers are given rest at suitable interval.

(*v*) The workers should be provided with protective wear. It should be ensured that every worker is wearing tarring outfit for his safety.

(*vi*) Workers should wear Goggles to avoid damage to eyes from funes of hot bitumen.

(*vii*) Work should be stopped during stormy weather. It will safeguard against fire hazards.

(*viii*) When the wind is blowing fast, bitumen spaying should be done carefully. It should not be done against the direction of the wind.

(*ix*) Warning signals such as sirens must be kept ready at the site of work and must be sounded promptly in case of fire hazards.

(*x*) Fire fighting equipment also be kept ready at the site of work.

(*xi*) First aid box and some trained persons in first aid also be available at site of work.

(*xii*) At both ends of the road under construction, sign boards indicating, "bitumen work is in progress" must be displayed.

(*xiii*) To check the entry of road users in the portion under construction, it should be protected from all sides by keeping empty drums and proper diversion should be provided.

(*xiv*) At a time only half width of the road should be constructed and the other half should be allowed to be used by road users.

(*xv*) To divert the traffic, proper barricades should be constructed at both ends of the stretch of road under construction. For the guidance of road users at night red lights should be provided at both ends. At night the area should be kept well lighted.

(*xvi*) At the time of actual bitumen spraying, a man with red flag should be posted at each end of the stretch of road under construction to divert the traffic.

4. Safety measures for demolishing the buildings

Demolishing of buildings structure is very hazardous work. Thus the demolition work should be properly planned and executed in different stages. In this way the injuries to workers and accidents can be reduced to a minimum. To ensure safety, cooperation between management, supervisors and workers is extremely important. Before starting the demolition work, the way in which the various parts of the building are supported and to what extent the adjoining structures will be affected by the step by step demolitioning work should be studied carefully. After careful study, the plans for systematic demolition work should be prepared and strictly followed while doing demolitioning work. Demolition operations should not endanger the adjoining structures. The workers should be guided by the foreman at each stage.

4. (*a*) Sequence of operations

The demolition operation should be started in such a way that damage to adjacent buildings and nuisance to public is caused minimum. To avoid accidents all safety requirements should be satisfied.

(*i*) Before starting the demolition work, all glazed doors, windows, and ventilators should be removed.

(*ii*) All exterior wall openings and floor openings, through which a worker may fall down should be provided with barricades and guide rails.

(*iii*) Demolition work should start from top and should be completed in upper most story before starting it in the story below it.

(*iv*) The demolished material should be thrown on ground only after taking all safety measures.

(*v*) Metallic chutes should be used for removing the debris. It is advisable to store the debris inside the building after it has been lowered to the ground.

(*vi*) If the floor below to receive the debris is strong enough to bear its impact then the debris may be dropped directly through holes made in the floor.

(*vii*) Opening in the intermediate floors should not be more than 25% of the area of that floor. These openings should remain covered when not in use and provided with guard rails. Unsafe intermediate floors and supporting walls should be properly shored before starting work.

(*viii*) Stairs and ladders should be kept intact as long as possible and kept safe till demolition work of the story above it is completed.

4. (*b*) Precautions to be taken while demolishing

During demolishing operations following precautions should be observed:

(*i*) Near all sides of the structure to be demolished and approach roads leading to it danger sign boards should be displayed at a distance of 30 m.

(*ii*) At night at important points near the site of demolition red signals should be provided.

(*iii*) If possible a watch man should be engaged to stop entry in dangerous situations.

(*iv*) To safe guard against any damage, the walls of adjoining buildings should be properly strengthened.

(*v*) The demolition work should not be done at night or during heavy rains, and stormy weather etc.

(*vi*) Before starting demolition work electric service lines, gas, water or steam service lines should be closed. The meters installed in the building should be removed or protected.

(*vii*) The passage to be used by workers should be well lighted and free from debris.

(*viii*) Projected nails in the wooden members should be removed.

(*ix*) While working at high levels, safety belt should be used by workers.

(*x*) At the time of demolishing operations, workers must use safety appliances such as goggles, leather gloves, cellolouid lens etc.

(*xi*) Warning system such as siren should be installed to warn the workers in case of any danger.

(*xii*) In case of demolishing multi-storeyed buildings, a strong shed should be provided over the side lanes, if it is with in 4.5 m from the building, so that people can use this side walk with out any danger. In other cases strong railing should be provided to keep the people away from the dangerous areas.

(*xiii*) All the main roads should be kept open to the public. There should be no obstruction to the traffic at any time.

4. (*c*) Demolition of walls

(*i*) The walls should be demolished in small heights, layer by layer so that falling debris may not damage or collapse the floor.

(*ii*) To avoid over loading, the debris should be removed constantly.

(*iii*) Weaker walls, whose height is more than 15 times of its thickness should be braced laterally.

(*iv*) Before starting the demolition work of walls in a story, the openings not required for use, should be covered with planks.

(*v*) In frame structures, steel frames may be left in place during demolishing the masonry work, provided the frame work is sufficiently strong to act as an independent structure.

(*vi*) At the close of work, walls should be supported against sudden falling.

(*vii*) The load supporting members should be demolished after the demolishing work in the story above this is completed.

(*viii*) Foundation walls should be demolished after under pinning the adjoining structures, till then they should be allowed to remain intact.

4. (*d*) Demolition of floors

(*i*) For demolishing floors, first of all a 30 cms wide slit is cut for the full length of the slab and 25 cms wide and 5 cms thick planks are placed at 40 cms spacing for workers to do demolishing work.

(*ii*) Demolished steel structural members should be lowered from the building. They should not be thrown or dropped from the building.

(*iii*) Beams should be cut only after ensuring all safety precautions to the workers.

(*iv*) While demolishing external walls of multistoreyed buildings of height more 20 metres, catch platforms of heavy planks should be provided to provide safety to workers as well as to public.

(*v*) While demolishing a R.C.C. beam, a supporting rope should be put around the beam. Afterwards the concrete is removed from both ends by pneumatic drills and reinforcement exposed.

(*vi*) The reinforcement should be cut in such a way that the beam could be lowered safety to the floor level.

5. Drilling and blasting

Safety measures while handling explosives. Following precautions should be taken while handling and storing explosives.

5. (*a*) Transportation

(*i*) During transportation, explosives and their caps should be kept separately.

(*ii*) While transporting explosives, the word "Explosives" should be marked or play carded on all sides of the vehicle in bold letters 10 cms in height in colour contrast with the back ground of the vehicle. It should also carry a red flag 60 cms square in size. On the flag word "Explosive" should be written clearly in bold letters.

(*iii*) Detonators or blasting caps should not be transported along with explosives. Metal tools, matches, oils, fire arms, acids, inflammable substances also should not be carried in the vehicle along with explosives.

(*iv*) Vehicles transporting explosives should not be over loaded. In no case explosives be piled in the container higher than the closed sides of the body.

(*v*) Open body vehicles carrying explosives should be covered with tarpaulin.

(*vi*) All vehicles carrying explosives should be inspected carefully for the followings.

(*a*) Brakes and steering mechanism of the vehicle should be in perfect condition.

(*b*) Electric fittings should be well insulated and firmly secured.

(*c*) Body and chassis should be clean and free from accumulation of oil and grease etc.

(*d*) Fuel tank and feed line should be well secured and have no leakage.

(*e*) Two fire extinguishers in working condition should be located near the driver's seat.

(*f*) General condition of the vehicle should be good.

(*vii*) The floor of the vehicle should be tight. Any exposed metal inside the body should be well covered, so that explosive may not come in its contact.

(*viii*) No trailer should be attached to the vehicle carrying explosives.

(*ix*) Unauthorised persons or passengers should not be allowed to ride in the vehicle carrying explosives.

(*x*) Packages of explosives should not be thrown while loading or unloading. Explosive packages should be handled and lifted carefully.

(*xi*) Before loading or un loading explosives the engine of the vehicle should be stopped.

5. (*b*) Precautions while handling explosives

(*i*) The packages containing explosives should be lifted or lowered carefully. They should never be dropped or slide from one level to another level.

(*ii*) Packages containing explosives should neither be opened in side a magazine nor with in 20 m of the magazine.

(*iii*) Non metallic or wooden tools should be used for opening or packing the boxes containing explosives.

(*iv*) Explosives and detonators should be placed in separate insulted and closed carriers.

(*v*) No unauthorised person should be allowed to ride the vehicle.

5. (*c*) Precautions while storing the explosives

(*i*) Explosives should be stored in dry, well ventilated, fire resistant and bullet proof building.

(*ii*) Primers or blasting caps should be stored separately.

(*iii*) Explosives, fuse lighters etc. should not be stored in damp places or near oil or near any source of heat.

(*iv*) No grass or leaves should be stored with in 8 m of a magazine.

(*v*) Smoking or lighting any flame should not be allowed near a magazine. Warning notice should be displayed.

5. (*d*) Safety measures while drilling and loading explosives

(*i*) Before planning the drilling operations, the nature of the strata should be examined carefully to avoid sliding after blasting.

(*ii*) Drilling should not be done where undetonated explosives are suspected.

(*iii*) Before loading the explosive in the hole, it should be ensured that the hole is bored in full length and is free from dust etc.

(*iv*) Excess explosive should not be left near the site while loading the hole.

(*v*) Before loading a hole it should be ensured that the hole is cool and has no burning material in it.

(*vi*) While inserting the explosive into a bore hole no force should be applied.

(*vii*) Force also should not be applied while inserting the blasting cap into the explosive.

(*viii*) While placing the explosive in the hole, tamping should be done with wooden tools. In no case metal tamping rod should be used for this purpose.

(*ix*) The explosive should be confined to the bore hole with stemming material as earth, clay, or sand etc.

(*x*) While tamping it should be ensured that fuse wire is not damaged.

(*xi*) Detonating fuse should be connected to the blasting cap or electric blasting cap according to the instructions issued by the manufacturers.

5. (*e*) Safety measures while using the explosives

(*i*) At the place where explosives are to be used smoking or lighting fire should not be allowed.

(*ii*) After taking out the required quantity of explosive from the container it should be covered properly.

(*iii*) Explosives should not be carried in the pockets of clothings.

(*iv*) No body should be allowed to remove or investigate the contents of a blasting cap.

(*v*) No unauthorised person should be allowed to go near the place of use of explosive.

(*vi*) Explosives should not be handled in electrical stores.

(*vii*) Deterioted explosives should not be used.

(*viii*) Hard set explosives should not be softened by heating over the fire or rolling it on the ground.

5. (*f*) Safety measures adopted while electrical short firing

(*i*) During stormy weather uncoiling of wires and opening out of bare leading wires of blasting caps should not be allowed.

(*ii*) Firing circuits should be fully insulted from pipes, rails or ground.

(*iii*) Electric line wires should not be kept near the blasting caps or other explosives except at the time of firing the blast.

(*iv*) Electric cap wires or leading wires should be kept short circuited till ready to fire.

(*v*) In case blasting is to be done from power circuit, then the voltage should not be more than 220 volts.

(*vi*) Blasting operations near the over head power lines, communication lines, or other structures should be done after obtaining the prior permission from the competent authority and after ensuring all necessary precautions.

(*vii*) For the size of wires, fuses, circuits etc. the instructions issued by the manufacturers should be followed.

(*viii*) For firing of a circuit of electric, blasting cap with less current than specified value by manufacturers should not be allowed.

(*ix*) All holes loaded on a shift should be fired on the same shift.

5. (*g*) Safety measures for short firing with safety fuse

(*i*) To safe guard against the damage of fuse cover, it should be handled carefully.

(*ii*) The length of fuse wire should not be less than 1.2 m.

(*iii*) The time of burning of the full length of the fuse should not be less than 2.0 minutes. The rate of burning of fuse should be such that the person igniting it reaches the place of safety before the blast.

(*iv*) The fuse should be ignited with a fuse lighter of proper design.

(*v*) Before igniting the fuse, sufficient stemming should be placed over the explosive.

(*vi*) At the time of lighting the fuse, spare explosive should not be held in hand.

(*vii*) Excessive quantities of explosives should not be taken under ground.

5. (*h*) Safety measures to be adopted before and after firing

(*i*) Before firing, sufficient warning time should be given to persons working at the site to go to safe place or away from the danger zone.

(*ii*) Flag men should be posted on all approaches to keep the vehicles and public at least 400 m away from the danger zone.

(*iii*) No tool or other articles should be placed on the rock to be blasted.

(*iv*) Blasting should be done as per schedule, during the fixed hours of the day. Wide publicity should be given of the programme. Daily blasting hours should be displayed on the notice boards on all roads leading to the blasting site. At the time of actual firing traffic should be stopped 400 m away with the help of barriers. At the beginning and at the end of firing loud sirens should be sounded.

(*v*) The person who fires the shot should not return to the blasting site untill at least 5 minute have passed from the time of lighting the fuse. In case of electric shot firing the shot holes should be examined after firing and in case of misfiring no one should be allowed to come near the blasting site at least for 3 minutes and in case of firing with safety fuse, the time for preventing entry of any one to blasting site is 30 minutes.

(*vi*) In case of misfire, the steming should be removed by the use of water jet or air jet, till the hole has been opened to with in 60 cms of the cartridge. The water is then pumped out and fresh new charge placed and detonated.

(*vii*) No explosive should be abandoned or thrown away. It should be disposed off after consulting the appropriate authority.

(*viii*) Material used in packing of the explosive should not be stored at a place where it could prove dangerous to the human life. Papers used for packing explosives should be destroyed. They should not be used any where else.

18.9. ROLE OF VARIOUS PARTIES IN SAFETY MANAGEMENT

1. Designer. At the planning stage, the architect, engineers and designers should give due consideration to the safety of the workers. They should take into account the safety problems associated with the subsequent maintenance of structures. The designer should avoid anything in design which would require the use of dangerous structural procedures and hazards. Special care should be taken in case of tall buildings for cleaning the windows on the outside.

2. Employer. The employer should provide and maintain plant and equipment well and organise the work in such a manner that workers are protected against the risks of accidents. The employer should also ensure proper supervision to workers to perform their work under the best conditions of safety. Workers should be supervised by a person who knows the safety requirements and is competent enough to handle them. Workers should be given proper instructions about safety requirements.

3. Workers. All workers should do everything with in their power to provide safety to themselves and to coworkers also. Before starting the day's work they should inspect the place of work and equipment they have to use and any defect observed by them should be reported to the supervisor or any other competent authority. They should use all safeguards and safety devices etc. Precautions to be observed have already been discussed.

18.10. APPROACH TO IMPROVE SAFETY IN CONSTRUCTION WORK

Many rules and recommendations have been laid on how to improve safety in the construction work based on the research carriedout by several organisations and societies. Recognising the importance of safety performance, the approach to the safety problems can be made as follows:

(*a*) **Organisational approach.** The management may setup a safety department to look after the safety aspects of workers and job site representatives. It should also record and analyse the safety and other accident prevention programmes. Safety representative on each site should not be hired by the project management as it may compromise in safety issues later.

(*b*) **Safety committee.** A safety committee may be set up to guide the operation of safety programme. In this committee people from all levels of workers and management should be included so that opinion on safety measures from all sections of the organisation may be gathered.

(*c*) **Development of a safety system.** A system should be developed to process the safety suggestions from workers and people who carry out the daily construction process as they are in best position to detect any accident.

(*d*) **Incentives.** For field management and supervisors incentives may be declared on the basis of safety record as well as productivity and cost.

2. Physical approach. Under this head, to improve the safety performance following guide lines may be used.

(*a*) New workers should be taught safety features. It has been observed that new workers suffer more accidents than experienced workers. Hence they should be given proper guidance in safety measures.

(*b*) In hazardous jobs, the use of safety devices should be made compulsory for the workers as use of helmet, safety belt, safety glasses, Goggles, gloves and hearing device etc.

(*c*) Periodic checking of equipment and tools should be done to ensure that they are well maintained.

(*d*) Periodic safety meetings may be held to provide safety education to the workers.

3. Behavioural approach. Studies carried out by several agencies have revealed that about 80% of all accident take place due to the unsafe acts of workers and only about 10% accidents occur due to failure of equipment or faulty procedures etc. Hence works acts are the most important for improving safety performance. In this regard following guide lines may be useful.

(*a*) The management during their meetings should give same stress to the safety as to the schedule of time and cost. This will make the lower staff understand that safety is as important as schedule and cost. Thus the importance of safety will not be ignored.

(*b*) Unnecessary pressure on foreman should not be put to meet the schedule or estimated cost. Usually pressures encourage the foreman to choose unacceptable methods that often lead to higher possibility of accidents.

(*c*) Craft foremen are in better position to detect the abnormal behaviour of workers as they have daily contact with them.

(*d*) There should be sweet and cordial relationship between the management and employees.

18.11. SAFETY CAMPAIGN

For each and every construction industry, safety campaign is very essential. It should be made compulsory to be conducted by law. It is the responsibility of the management to launch the campaign and contribute the continuing support to keep it operating effectively. For carrying out safety campaign following steps may be adopted.

(*a*) An capable and experienced person should be made incharge of the safety campaign. He should be fully supported by the management.

(*b*) The safety director must ensure that all new workers have been educated to observe safety measures and he should have the power to get safety measures adopted by the workers.

(*c*) Committees should be formed consisting representatives of management, supervisors, and workers to go round each job frequently and find out deficiencies and causes for the likelyhood of accidents and suggest remedial measures. They should be encouraged to suggest new measures to promote safety.

(*d*) Safety rules to be observed in each section, should be written on notice boards in the language which may be easily understood by workers.

(*e*) DO's and DONT's must be written on separate notice boards. The notice boards should be placed at such places, where the workers could see them daily easily.

(*f*) Safety material should be brought out by the management periodically and distributed freely to the workers.

(*g*) The accident record of each concerned department should be displayed. Efforts should be made to reduce the number of accidents by adopting suitable safety measures.

(*h*) Safety contests should be held from time to time to enlighten the workers about the bad effect of accidents. Awards should be given to those supervisors, who produce best safety records. The names of prize winners must be publicised.

(*i*) Suitable safety quotations should be displayed written in bold letters on sign boards. Following quotations may be displayed.

1. To save time at the cost of life is a bad bargain.
2. Accidents do not happen, they are caused.
3. Where caution end, accidents begin.
4. Machines are good servant only if handled carefully.
5. Safety first and speed after wards.
6. Safe driving is a pleasure.
7. Make safety a habit.
8. Safety first and luck after wards.
9. If married divorce speed.
10. Safety saves.

(*j*) Safety weeks must be observed. Workers and public should be educated during this week about safety measures.

18.12. MEASURING OF SAFETY

Some terms are defined below which indicate the measure of injury:

1. Injury frequency rate. It is the number of disabling injures per one lakh man hours worked. It denotes how frequently an accident occurred. It does not take into account the time lost due to an injury. It is expressed as

$$\text{Injury frequency rate} = \frac{\text{no. of disabling injuries} \times 10^5}{\text{total no. of man hours worked}}$$

2. Injury severity rate. It is the number of days lost per 1000 man hours worked. It is expressed as

$$\text{Injury severity rate} = \frac{\text{no. of days lost} \times 10^3}{\text{no. of man hours worked}}$$

3. Injury index. It is expressed as

$$\text{Injury index} = \frac{\text{injury frequency rate} \times \text{injury severity rate}}{1000}$$

18.13. PREVENTION OF FIRES AT CONSTRUCTION SITES

Construction activity provides many opportunities to the spread of fire at the construction site as many activities are carried out simultaneously which may cause fire and there are very limited means of controlling fire at the site of work. In case of a fire hazard in a construction project, it not only damages equipments and causes injuries to workers, but also delays the completion of the project resulting in escalation of cost. There is a general conception that fire hazard at construction projects is negligible, hence no pre planning is made to meet the fire hazards.

Now a days due to the increase in the use of plastic materials as building materials, the chances of spread of fire have increased very much. Secondly materials in large quantities are stored in open at project site which also add to the chances of fire hazards.

The climatic conditions, make shift arrangements for timber form work and scaffolding, use of temporary electric wiring and connections, lack of availability of resources to control fire hazard cause a great fire risk. Actually alteration and rehabilitation measures to a building present greater risk of fire hazard than construction as it is carried out with parts of building still in use.

From the study of fire hazards at construction site, it is observed that frequent causes of fire are due to electrical short circuits, un controlled welding etc. Poor house keeping and unsafe storage of materials also are responsible for fire hazards. It has been found that main reasons of fires are as below:

(*a*) Due to portable heating equipment	25%
(*b*) Due to welding and cutting operations	20%
(*c*) Smoking and matches etc.	15%
	60%

Hence proper planning for fire prevention should be done.

QUESTIONS

1. What is the importance of safety in a construction project? Discuss briefly.
2. What is an accident? Discuss different factors leading to accidents in construction projects.
3. Discuss the role of different parties in safety management.
4. What safety measures should be taken during the following works
   (*a*) Excavation work (*b*) Demolition work
   (*c*) During drilling and blasting
5. Discuss the safety measures adopted during the following operations
   (*a*) While dealing with hot bitumen (*b*) Use of ladders
   (*c*) Use of scaffolding (*d*) While demolishing a multi storeyed building
6. Discuss the safety measures adopted before and after firing a blasting hole.
7. What precautions should be adopted in electrical short circuit firing method.
8. Discuss the different approaches to improve the safety in construction work.
9. What are the main objectives of accident prevention.

OBJECTIVE TYPE QUESTIONS

1. Safety in construction is important due to
   (*a*) Humanitarian concerns (*b*) Medical expenses
   (*c*) Economic reasons (*d*) All the above
2. The safety measures should be strictly enforced due to
   (*a*) It is beneficial to employees (*b*) It is beneficial to management
   (*c*) It is beneficial to customers (*d*) All are correct
3. The responsibility of safety should be exercised
   (*a*) By the Employer or management (*b*) By the designer
   (*c*) By the workers (*d*) All of the above
4. Major fire hazards at construction sites are due to
   (*a*) Welding and cutting operations (*b*) Unsafe storage of materials
   (*c*) Portable heating equipment (*d*) Matches and smoking
5. Accidents cause
   (*a*) Injury to the worker (*b*) Agony to his family
   (*c*) Mental tension and financial burden to owner
   (*d*) All the above
6. The aim of accident prevention is except
   (*a*) To save human lives (*b*) To earn more profit
   (*c*) To save loss of time (*d*) To prevent loss of materials

ANSWERS

1. (*d*)	3. (*d*)	5. (*d*)
2. (*d*)	4. (*c*)	6. (*b*)

19

Construction Equipment

19.1. INTRODUCTION

The aim of the designer and the contractor is to create something that will improve the quality of life for mankind and serve the purpose for which it is built in a satisfactory manner. The ultimate aim of a design is its construction and machines make it possible to accomplish this objective.

All over the world about 11.45×10^5 business use heavy equipment while engaged in contract construction. The ability to win contracts and perform them at a profit is determined mainly by two major factors; man and equipment. To be economically competitive, the spread of equipment of a contractor must be competitive, mechanically and technically both. The worn out machines which require costly repairs can not compete successfully with new machines which need no repair or less repair and have higher production rates. The equipment spread means a group of equipments needed for a particular job. For example for a earth work, the excavator loads the earth in trucks which take or haul the earth to the site of work. At the site of work, the material is dumped. This material is spread by the dozer and compacted by the roller to the desired density. Thus to perform a work, the entire spread (a group of equipments) is required. Thus for this spread of equipment large investment on equipment is required even for a small job. In some cases the value of the equipment will be much greater than the contract value. Therefore not only the mechanically competitive equipment spread must be maintained, but the individual project must be planned and executed in such a way that each machine complements the production capabilities of all the other pieces of equipment. A successful contractor is the one, who accomplishes a continuing series of jobs and completes each individual job at the least possible cost.

19.2. MACHINERY REQUIRED ON A PROJECT

Though the nature of equipment requirement of each project is different, but practically earth moving machinery is required on all projects. In this section machinery required for different projects will be discussed in brief. In this section following machinery will be discussed in brief.

1. Dozers which push the materials at site
2. Scrapers
3. Excavators. These include dipper or power shovel, drag line, clamp shell and drag shovel
4. Earth compaction machines
5. Earth hauling equipment
6. Rock and earth drilling equipment
7. Concrete producing equipment
8. Asphalt mix production plants
9. Lifting devices
10. Miscellaneous equipment as pile driving and water pumping equipment etc.

19.3. EARTH MOVING EQUIPMENT

Actually a vide range of earth excavating equipments are commercially available in the market and the selection of the most suitable machine for a particular job is most difficult and needs a much greater thought and care in the right selection. A large number of factors affect the best performance of a machine. The lack in the understanding of some or all these factors may result in lower efficiency of production. It is a hard fact that no machine is designed to a particular set of conditions only. They are designed to suit varying conditions of work. Hence to get the same efficiency from a machine under different sets of conditions is seldom possible.

19.4. FACTORS INFLUENCING THE OUTPUT OF A MACHINE

Generally following factors affect the output of a machine

1. Physical site conditions
2. Type of soil
3. Condition of the machine
4. Specifications of the machine
5. Method of operation etc.

19.5. TRACTORS

A tractor is a versatile *i.e.* multipurpose machine. They convert engine energy into tractive energy. Their main purpose is to pull or push loads. They may also be used for other purposes. From the point of view of earth moving machinery they are used as clearing, excavating, hauling and conveying machinery.

19.5.1. Classification of tractors

Tractors may be classified into two categories as follows:

1. Wheel units. These units are generally employed for light but speedy jobs.

Fig. 19.1. Wheeled Tractor

Fig. 19.2. Crawler Tractor

2. Crawler units. These units are track laying units. The are generally employed for heavy duty work, where more tractive power is required and the speed of movement is required less than wheel type units. Track has been discussed in detail under dozers. Now a days practically wheeled tractors are in use for all earth moving machinery.

19.6. FACTORS AFFECTING THE SELECTION OF TRACTORS

While selecting a tractor following points should be kept in mind.

1. The size required for the given job.
2. The type or kind of job for which the tractor is to be used as pulling or bulldosing, scraper or ripper or as pulling a wagon etc.
3. The type of footing over which it will travel as wheeled or crawler unit *i.e.* low or high tractive power unit.

4. The smoothness and firmness of the haul road.
5. The slope of haul road and the length of haul.
6. The type of work to be done after the completion of this job.

19.7. COMPARATIVE STUDY OF WHEELED AND CRAWLER TRACTORS

Table 19.1

S. No.	*Wheeled tractor*	*Crawler tractor*
1.	Wheeled tractors can travel faster than crawler tractors. They are found advantageous for long distances and where high speeds are required.	1. Crawler tractors are more compact and powerful. They can handle heavier jobs of hauling and digging.
2.	They can handle light duty job of hauling and digging.	2. Crawler tractors need expensive track. They are more costly.
3.	Wheeled tractors are less costly.	3. The track of a crawler tractor has large number of parts. The wear and tear of these parts increase the operating cost of crawler tractors.
4.	Wheeled tractors have wheel steering control as in case of other automobile vehicles and can be maneoured easily.	4. crawler tractors have stick control for steering and need greater skill in operation.
5.	Wheeled tractors can move on tarred roads with speed with out any damage to the road.	5. The crawler tractor if moved on pavements and tarred roads will damage them unless lifted with special shoes or device.
6.	Wheeled tractors can be self driven over long distances.	6. Usually transportation of crawler tractors over long distances is done on trailers due to their low speed of travelling and to avoid excessive load over the tracks.
7.	The wheeled tractors are liable to slip over very smooth or loose spots when increased power is to be applied to the wheels.	7. A crawler tractor can pass over very smooth and loose spots as it moves on its own tracks and the grousers on the tracks have a better grip on the road.
8.	Wheeled tractors need less maintenance and repair. They need less skill to drive than crawler tractors.	8. Crawler tractors require more skill in operation. They also need more maintenance and repair.

Grousers are shall projecting pieces.

19.8. RATINGS OF TRACTORS

The rating of wheeled tractors specify the engine h.p at the fly wheel or belt, the rim pull at different speeds in the various gears, the total operating weight of the tractor, and number and size of tyres. In addition to above other informations supplied by the manufacturers include

(*a*) Turning radius
(*b*) Wheel base
(*c*) Ground clearance
(*d*) Capacities of fuel tanks
(*e*) Cooling system
(*f*) Crank and transmission cases etc.

19.9. RIM PULL

The rim pull of tractor at any speed is the force between the tyres of the driving wheels of the tractor and the surface on which the tractor travels is called *rim pull*. It can be calculated by the following relation

(*i*) In F.P.S. system, Rim pull $= \dfrac{375 \times \text{efficiency} \times \text{h.p of tractor}}{\text{Speed in miles per hour}}$

(*ii*) In M.K.S. system, Rim pull $= \dfrac{268.5 \times \text{efficiency} \times \text{metric h.p.}}{\text{Speed in Km p.h.}}$

The pull exerted on the trailing load = Rim pull – rolling resistance – grade resistance – trailing load
Thus the pull depends upon the traction of the surface of travel and the weight of the tractor.

In case of a crawler tractor, the equivalent pull rating is equal to the drawbar pull. This is the net hauling force which a crawler tractor can exert on a trailing load.

Draw bar h-p can be calculated from draw bar pull and speed as follows:

(*i*) For f.p.s. units drawbar $= \dfrac{p \times v}{1000}$

where p is the drawbar pull in lbs and, v = speed in feet per minute.

(*ii*) For M.K.S. units, Draw bar h-p= $\dfrac{p \times v}{75}$

where p is in kg and v in m/second.

19.10. CONSTRUCTION OF TRACTOR

The main components of a tractor are:

(*a*) Engine

(*b*) Engine Clutch

(*c*) Transmission system including power take off

(*d*) Ground drive and controls.

The main difference in the construction of wheeled and crawler tractors is in the manner of delivering power to the final drive which is a result of the different steering mechanism of the two types of tractors. However detailed discussion is out of scope of this text.

19.11. GRADABILITY

It is defined as the maximum slope expressed as a percent, up which a wheel type prime mover or a crawler may move at a uniform speed. It may be determined for a loaded or empty vehicle. Thus the gradability of a tractor only will be greater than for a tractor that is pulling a loaded vehicle. Gradability may be specified for any desired gear.

19.12. FACTORS AFFECTING THE FORWARD MOTION OF A PRIMEMOVER

Following factors affect the forward motion of a prime mover.

1. The power developed by the engine and available as drawn bar pull or rim pull.
2. The rolling resistance of the haul road.
3. The gross weight of the prime mover and its load.
4. The grade to be negotiated. Adverse grade adds to the resistance while the favourable grade substracts from the resistance.

The gradability of a crawler tractor is determined by subtracting from the available draw bar pull, the total pull required to over come the rolling resistance on the unit and any load that it will pull. The surplus draw bar pull is then available to negotiate a grade. To provide a reasonable factor of safety not more than 85% of the rated draw bar pull should be used in determining the gradability of the unit. In F.P.S. unit, gradability can be determined by the following formula.

$$K = \frac{972 \times T \times G}{R \times W} - \frac{N}{20}$$

where,

K = %, gradability.

T = Rated engine torque lbs. ft.

G = Total gear reduction for a particular gear selected.

R = Radius of the load driving wheel measured from centre of axle to the ground surface in inches.

W = Gross weight of complete unit in lbs.

N = Rolling resistance in lbs per ton.

Table 19.3. Coefficient of traction for various road surfaces

Surface	*Rubber tyres*	*Crawler tracks*
Dry, rough concrete	0.80 – 1.0	0.45
Dry clay loam	0.50 – 0.7	0.90
Wet clay loam	0.40 – 0.50	0.70
Wet sand and gravel	0.3 – 0.40	0.35
Loose dry sand	0.20 – 0.30	0.30
Dry snow	0 .2	0.15 – 0.35
Ice	0..1	0.10 – 0.25

19.13. DOZERS

Dozer primarily is a pushing unit. It is one of the most important machines on construction projects. A dozer is a tractive power unit which has a blade attached to the front of the machine. They are self contained units equipped with blades.

They are designed to provide tractive power for drawbar work. A dozer has no set volumetric capacity. The amount of material that a dozer can move depends on the quantity of material that will remain infront of the blade during the push. Crawler dozers are excellent machines for land clearance as special clearing blades are attached to them.

19.14. CLASSIFICATION OF DOZERS

Dozers may be classified either as track laying crawler or wheel type machine. Consistent with their purpose as a unit for draw bar work they are low centre of gravity machines. This is an prerequisite of an effective machine. If there is large difference between the line of force of transmission from the machine and the line of resisting force, it will result in less effective utilization of developed force. Dozers are classified on the basis of running gears.

1. Crawler Dozers 2. Wheel Dozers

19.15. CRAWLER DOZERS

Actually these dozers are track laying machines. They have a continuous track of linked shoes that moves in the horizontal plane across fixed rollers. At the rear of the mach- ine, the track passes over a vertically mounted sprocket drive wheel. (Sprocket wheel is a wheel having a row of teeth around it). As the sprocket turns it forces the track forward or backward imparting motion to the dozer. In the front of the machine, the track passes over a vertically mounted idler wheel that is connected to a recoil device having adjustable tension. The idler wheel maintains the proper tension in the track and enables it to absorb heavy shocks. The linked shoes are made of heat treated steel designed to resist the wear and abrasion. A photograph of crawler dozer is shown in Fig. 19.3.

Fig. 19.3. Crawler dozer

The low ground pressure (LPG) under carriage configuration is for soft ground conditions. The ground pressure exerted by a crawler dozer with an LPG under carriage is about 21 to 28 kilow pascals *i.e.* 21 to 28 × 10^3 pascal (Pa). Such machines should not be used in hard and rocky conditions as it will reduce the life of under carriage. A crawler dozer can operate on slopes upto 45°.

19.16. WHEEL MOUNTED DOZERS

It this case the dozer is mounted on wider tyres which provide greater contact area and increase flotation (movement). However the width of tyres should be as per requirements. It has been observed that larger tyres reduce the rim pull developed. The photograph of wheel dozer is shown in Fig. 19.4.

Fig. 19.4. Wheel dozer

19.17. COMPARATIVE ADVANTAGES OF CRAWLER AND WHEELED DOZERS

The comparative advantages of crawler and wheel mounted dozers are shown in tabular form in table 19.2.

Table 19.2. Comparative advantages of crawler mounted and wheel mounted dozers

S. No.	*Crawler mounted dozer*		*Wheel mounted dozer*
1.	It delivers greater tractive effort especially when operating in soft grounds as loose or muddy soil.	1.	It provides higher travel speed from 13 to 42 kmph on the job or from one job to another job.
2.	It has the capacity to travel over muddy surfaces. It can work on variety of soils.	2.	It eliminates the necessity of hauling equipment required to transport the dozer to the job.
3.	It has the ability to operate in rocky formation, where rubber tires might be damaged seriously.	3.	Greater out put, especially when considerable travel is necessary.
4.	It has the ability to travel on rough surface, which may reduce the cost of maintaining the hauling roads.	4.	Less fatigue to operator. It is good for long travel distances.
5.	Greater flotation due to the lower pressure under the track. It is good for short distance jobs.	5.	It can travel on paved highways with out damaging the surface.
6.	Greater use on versatility jobs *i.e.* greater use on different types of jobs.	6.	It is best for handling loose soils.
7.	Can push large blade loads.	7.	It can push moderate blade load.
8.	It's speed is slow about 8 to 16 kmph.		

19.18. USE OF DOZERS

Dozers can be used from the start to the finish of the following operations:

1. Spreading earth or rock fill
2. Back filling trenches
3. Clearing construction sites of debris
4. Maintaining haul roads
5. Clearing the land of timber and stumps
6. Helping load tractor pulled scrapers
7. Opening up pilot roads through mountains and rocky terrain
8. Moving earth for haul distances upto approximately 100 m.
9. Clearing the floor of borrow and quarry pits.

19.19. POWER TO DOZERS

To power most dozers, usually internal combustion engines are used. The diesel engines are the most common primary power units. In smaller machines gasoline may also be used. For tunnel work electric and air powered dozers are also available.

Usually the crank shaft rotation derived from engine is too fast and does not have sufficient force (torque). Hence the transmission of the machine reduces the rotational speed of the crank shaft and increases the force avaible to do work. Transmission provides the opportunity to operator to change the machine's speed-power ratio, so that it matches the work requirements. Though manufacturers provide dozers with a variety of transmission, but the basic options are as follows:

1. Direct drive
2. Torque convert and power shift transmission

Less than 100 h.p. dozers with hydrostatic power trains are available in the market. The smaller less than 300 h.p. diesel powered machines are commonly available with either direct or power shift type transmission. However large dozers are always equipped with power shift transmission.

1. Direct drive crawler dozers

In case of direct drive, the power is transmitted straight (direct) through the transmission as if there was a single shaft. Usually this happens when the transmission is in its highest gear. In all other gears mechanical elements match speed and torque.

The direct drive dozers are found superior in case of constant loading conditions. An appropriate application of a direct drive dozer would be when full blade loads are required to push a long distance.

The draw bar pulls may be of two types as follows:

(*a*) **Rated draw bar pull.** It is the draw bar pull that can be sustained for continuous operation. The rated pull should be used for continuous operation.

(*b*) **Maximum draw bar pull.** It is the pull that the dozer can exert for a short period while pulling the engine, as when passing over an soft spot in the ground requiring a higher tractive effort temporarily. Available draw bar pull is subject to the limitation imposed by the traction that can be developed between the tracts and the ground.

2. Crawler dozers with torque converter and power shift transmission

The transmission that can be shifted while transmitting full engine power is known as *power shift*. Such transmissions are provided with torque converters to absorb drive train shocks loads caused by changes in gear ratios. A power shift transmission provides an efficient flow of power from the engine to the tracks and gives superior performance in applications involving variable load conditions.

3. Crawler dozer with hydrostatic power train

Oil confined under pressure as an effective means of power transmission is known as hydrostatic power train. An hydrostatic power train offers an infinitely variable speed range with constant power to both the tracks. This type of power train improves the controllability of the machine and increases its operational efficiency. Such type of power trains are available on some small sized dozers.

4. Wheel dozers

Usually wheel dozers are provided with torque converters and power shift transmission. Wheel dozers comparatively exert high pressure on the ground of the order of 25 to 35 PSi (172 to 241 KPa).

19.20. COMPARISION OF PERFORMANCE OF CRAWLER AND WHEEL TYPE DOZERS

As stated earlier also the usable pull or rim pull depends on the weight and traction of a fully equipped dozer. Even though the engine can develop a certain draw bar pull, all of that pull may not be available to do work. The coefficient of traction factor for a dry clay loam for rubber tyres may be taken as 0.5 to 0.7 and for track as 0.9. Thus, though both machines have approximately the same operating weight (25255 kg) or 45560 lbs, and fly wheel power, yet the track dozer can supply about 1.5 times the usable power than wheel tire dozer due to the variation of coefficient of traction factors.

In most cases of soil conditions, the coefficient of traction for wheels is less than tracks. Thus a wheel type dozer must be approximately 50% heavier than a crawler dozer to develop the same amount of usable force. As the weight of wheel type dozer is increased, a larger engine will be needed to maintain the weight to horse power-ratio. There is a limit of increasing the weight of a wheel type dozer, but still it has a machine with advantage over track dozers in respect of speed and mobility. The coefficients of traction for various road surfaces are shown in table 19.3.

19.21. BLADES OF A DOZER

The blades of a dozer are made from mold boards (The board having some what concave profile is called mold board) with replaceable cutting edges and side bits. The blade is connected to the dozer with the help of push arms and tilt cylinders or a C frame. Based on work application, the blades vary in size and design. The hardened steel cutting edges and side bits are bolted as they are susceptable to most of the abrasion and get wear out rapidly.

The bolted connection enable easy replacement:

(*a*) In some machines either end of the blade can be raised or lowered in the vertical plane of the blade, called *tilt*.

(*b*) The top of the blade can be pitched forward or backward varying the angle of attack of the cutting edge. It is known as *pitch*.

(*c*) Blades mounted on a C frame can be turned from the direction of the travel. It is known as angling. These features are not applicable to all blades, but any two of these may be incorporated in a single mount.

Tilt. This movement takes place with in the vertical plane of the blade. Tilting enables the concentration of dozer driving power on a limited portion of the length of the blade.

Pitch. This a pivotal movement about the point of connection between the dozer and the blade. When the top of the blade pitched forward, the bottom edge moves back. This increases the angle of cutting edge attack.

Angling. Turning the blade in such a way that it is not perpendicular to the direction of travel of the dozer is known *angling*. Angling causes the pushed material to roll off the trailing end of the blade. This process of rolling material off one end of the blade is known as *side casting*.

19.22. PERFORMANCE OF BLADE

The performance of a blade is measured by the following two ratios:

1. Horse power per 30 cms (12 inch) of cutting edge.
2. Horse power per loose cubic yard of material retained in front of the blade.

1. Horse pow per 30 cm (foot) gives an indication of the ability of the blade to penetrate into the soil to obtain a load. Higher the ratio, more aggressive is the blad.
2. Horse power per loose cubic yards (0.786 m^3) gives the blades ability to push the load. A higher ratio indicates that the dozer can push a load with greater speed.

A positive downward force can be exerted by raising or lowering the blade by Hydrulic rams. Further the basic earth moving blades are curved in the vertical plane in the shape of a flattened letter C. On pushing down the blade, the edge cuts into the earth. As the dozer moves forward the cut material is pushed up the face of the blade. The upper part of the flattened C rolls this material forward. The total effect is to ''boil'' spill over the pushed material over and over infront of the blade. The flattened C shape provides the necessary cutting angle for the edge. At the beginning of the pass the weight of the cut material on the lower half of flattened C helps to achieve the edge penetration. As the push progresses the load in front of the blade passes the mid point of C and begins to exert upward force on the blade. This upward force 'floats' the blade reducing the penetration of the cutting edge. Different types of dozer blades are discussed below.

19.23. TYPES OF BLADES USED ON DOZERS

Basically following five types of blades are used on dozers engaged in earth work.

1. Straight blades. These blades are abbreviated by '*S*'. These blades have no curvature in their length and are mounted in a fixed position, perpendicular to the line of travel of the dozer. The straight blade is designed for short and medium distance passes such as grading, back filling and spreading fill material. Generally it is a heavy duty blade and normally it can be tilted with in a 10° arc, increasing the penetration

Fig. 19.5. Common earth moving dozer blades

for cutting or decreasing penetration for back dragging. It may be equipped or set to pitch *i.e.* the operator can set the cutting edge to dig hard material or to move the edge's plane of attack to ease the drifting of light materials.

2. Angle blades. These blades are abbreviated by 'A'. This type of blade *i.e.* angle blade is wider 30 to 60 cms than straight blades. It can be turned or angled upto a maximum angle of 25° left or right of the perpendicular to the dozer or used as a straight blade. A angle blade is attached to the dozer by a C frame mount. Hence it can not be pitched, but can be tilted. It is very effective for side casting material particularly for making hill side cuts and back filling.

3. Universal blades (U). This type of blade is wider than straight blade and the out side edges are canted (sloped) forward by about 25°. The canting of the edges reduces the spilling of loose material resulting in increased efficiency of *U* blades in moving large loads over long distances. The ratio of h.p and length of the blade is lower for *U* blades than *S* blades mounted on similar dozers. Penetration is not a prime objective of the *U* blade. This blade is best suited for lighter materials. Typically it is best suited as for stock piling, and drifting loose or non cohesive materials.

4. Semi universal blades (S-U). This type of blades have the characteristics of both straight and universal blades. By the addition of short wings, the capacity of this blade has increased.

5. Cushion blades (C). This class of blades are mounted on large dozers which primarily are used for push loading scrapers. This class of blade is shorter in length than *S* blade. The shorter length avoids pushing the blade into the rear tires and cutting it. The shorter length also facilitates the maneuvering of the dozer while pushing loading into position behind the scrapers. Rubber cushions and springs in the mounting enable the dozer to absorb the impact of contacting "pusher block" to push scraper. By using a cushion blade instead of push block to push scrapers the dozer can clean the cut area and the production of the total fleet is increased. This blade has limited utility in pushing the material. Hence it should not be used in production dozing. It can not be pitched, tilted or angled. The photographs of different angles are shown in Fig. 19.5.

19.24. USE OF DOZERS ON A PROJECT

As already discussed a dozer can be economically used on a project for the following purposes.

1. Stripping. The removal of a thin layer of top soil at the project site is known as *stripping*. Dozers have been found excellent machines for stripping. The stripping by dozers should be conducted in such a manner that the push distances are minimised. Large dozers have been found economical for moving the material upto about 100 m (300 ft.). The economical push distance decreases as the size of the dozer decreases. The economical push distance also depends on the nature of push material. A cohesive material such as clay is easier to push than a granular material as sand which tends to run in front of the blade. In case the material is to be pushed to more than 100 m distance then scraper should be used.

2. Side hill cut. It is very difficult to develop the initial table for excavations made on steep ground. The excavated material from such a cut usually is pushed over the side of the hill. The first pushes are made perpendicular to the long direction of the work. Starting from higher side, short passes are made to push the material across the central line and over the side. The perpendicular passes being short, the dozer usually is not able to develop a full blade load. Once a bench is developed the dozer starts pushing in the long direction of the work developing a full blade load. Pushing down hill is easier due to gravity.

3. Ditching. A dozer can be used for digging a trench. Ditching by dozer can be done in very rough sections. Large and deep ditches are cut either with the help of excavators or scrapers. Scrapers are used if the cut is made before water enters into the ditch. After ditching by the scraper the dozer may be used for final dressing of the slopes.

If a dozer is used to cut rough ditches, the machine pushes the material out of the cut by working perpendicular to the line of the ditch. Small shallow ditches usually are cut with a motor grader.

4. Back filling. A dozer can efficiently accomplish the work of back filling by drifting material side ways with an angle blade. This process enables the forward motion parallel to the excavation. No part of the track should hang over the edge of excavation.

5. To move rocks or frozen ground. By using proper technique, rocks or frozen ground can be moved by dozers. In both cases the blade must be worked under the material to be moved. This can be done by tilting the corner of the blade. To maximize the driving force of the blade, hook only the tilted end under the rock or ground. Once the blade is in contact under side or beneath the rock and the dozer is driving forward the operator should lift the blade to split or remove up the rock.

6. Spreading. Spreading the material dumped by trucks or scrapers is the common task of a dozer. Uniform spreading is accomplished by keeping the blade of the dozer straight and at the desired height above the previously fill surface. The dumped material is forced directly under the cutting edge of the blade. Fairly uniform spreading can be achieved in two passes of the dozer over the dumped area. The second pass should be made at right angle to the first pass.

7. Slot dozing. This is a technique where side walls from previous cuts are used to hold material in front of the dozer blade on subsequent passes. To increase the production this method can be employed. At the time of employing this method the cuts should be aligned parallel leaving a narrow uncut section between the slots. Then the uncut sections are removed by normal dozing. This technique increases the production by about 20% and prevents the spillage of material at each end of the blade. The increase in production depends on the slope of the push and the nature of the material to be pushed.

19.25. ESTIMATION OF DOZERS PRODUCTION

A dozer has no set volumetric capacity. There is no hopper or bowl to load it. The amount of material which a dozer moves depends on the quantity of material that will remain in front of the blade during the push. The output of a dozer is controlled by the following factors.

1. Type of blade of the dozer
2. Type and condition of the material
3. Cycle time

These conditions have already been discussed.

Blade load. The load that a blade can carry can be estimated by the following methods:

1. Manufacturers blade ratings
2. Previous experience
3. Field measurements

1. Manufacturer's blade rating. It is given as:

$$V_s = 0.8\ WH^2 \qquad \ldots(1)$$

$$V_u = V_s + ZH\,(W - Z) \tan x^\circ \qquad \ldots(2)$$

where,

V_s = Capacity of straight or angled blade under ideal conditions

V_u = Capacity of universal blade under ideal conditions

W = Effective blade height in yards

Z = Wing length measured parallel to the blade width in yards

x = Wing angle

H = Effective blade height in yards.

2. Field measurement. Blade load in loose cubic yards = 0.0139 HWL ...(3)

where,

H = Height of the pile at the inside edge of each track in feet

W = Width of the pile at the inside edge of each track in feet

L = Greatest length of the pile at the inside edge of each track in feet

Production formula in loose cubic yard per 60 minute is given below

Production in ideal conditions per hour (All times in minutes)

$$= \frac{60 \times \text{Blade load}}{\text{Push time + returntime + maneuver time}}$$

3. Production formula developed by equipment manufacturers. This is an empirical formula under ideal conditions. It is reproduced below in F.P.S. units.

$$\text{Production per 60 minutes} = \frac{330 \times \textit{net h.p.}}{(D + 50)}$$

where,

D = One way push distance in feet

$h.p.$ = Net horse power at fly wheel for power shift crawler dozer

19.26. LAND CLEARING OPERATIONS

On all projects usually land clearing of vegetation and trees is under taken before starting the earth moving operations. Trees, brushes (dead branch of trees) and even grass and weeds make the material handling very difficult. If these materials are allowed to remain in soil, they will decay over the time and will cause the settlement of the fill. For land clearing operation crawler dozers equipped with special clearing blades have been found excellent.

19.26.1. Operations involved in land clearance

For land clearance following operations are involved:

(*a*) Removing of all trees, stumps including roots.

(*b*) Removing of all vegetation above the surface of the ground and leaving the stumps and roots in the ground.

(*c*) Disposal of vegetation by stacking and burning.

(*d*) Knocking down all vegetation, then crushing it or chopping it and burning it later.

(*e*) Killing or retarding the growth of brush by cutting the roots below the surface of the ground.

19.27. TYPE OF EQUIPMENT USED

Following types of equipment may be used for clearing the land.

1. Crawler dozer with earth moving blades. In the past crawler dozers with earth moving blades were used extensively for land clearance work. Later their use was found to suffer with the following two main disadvantages.

(*a*) Before felling a large tree, excavation of earth around the tree and cutting its roots was necessary. This operation required considerable time and left objectionable holes in the ground.

(*b*) During the stacking of trees and vegetation, considerable amount of earth was transported to the piles, which made the burning of the debris difficult.

2. Crawler dozer with special clearing blades. To over come the objections of the use of crawler dozer with earth moving blades, special blades to fell trees are designed. These blades are of two types:

(*a*) Single angle blade with projecting stinger

(*b*) V blade

(*a*) Single angle clearing blade. It consists of a stinger web, cutting edge, and guide bar. The stinger is a protruding (penetrating) vertical knife. It is designed to work as a knife to cut and split

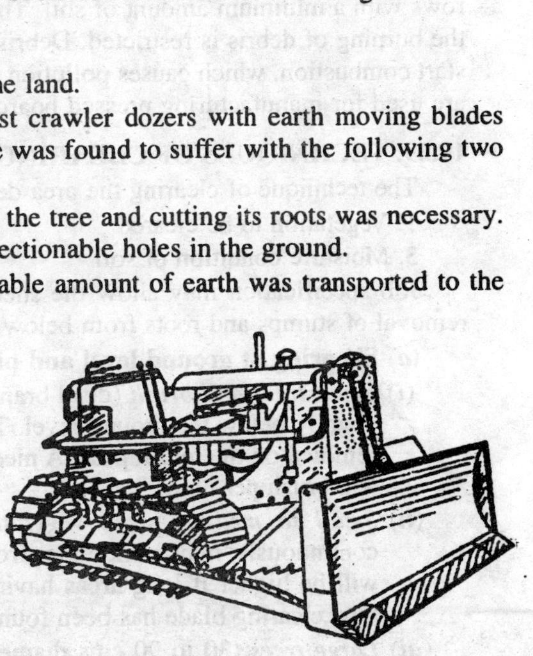

Fig. 19.6. Angle Dozer

trees, stumps, and roots. The stringer is sharp vertically, while the web is sharp horizontally. They both together cut the tree in both planes simultaneously.

The blade can be tilted and is mounted at 30° angle with the stinger forward. The guide bar guides the cut material forward and to the side of the tractor. A sketch of crawler angle dozer is shown in Fig. 19.6.

(*b*) **V-blades.** They are V shaped blades. The point of the V is to the front. It enables the debris to be cast off each side. There is a stinger also that penetrates from the lead point. The cutting edges down each side of the V are saw type. The design of the blade is such that the vegetation is sheared off at the ground level. Large trees are rammed (hit) in their middle and split by the stinger. Simultaneously the two halves are then sheared off at ground level by the cutting edges on each side of the stinger.

Both these blades are found most efficient in land clearing work if the ground is level and the cutting edges are able to maintain good contact with the ground surface. It is easier to work if the soil is able to hold the roots of the vegetation during the shearing off operation of the trunk. In large rocks progress of work will be less due to the damage to cutting edges.

(*c*) **Crawler with clearing rakes.** A rake is a frame with multiple vertical teeth's mounted in place of a solid faced blade. The clearing rakes are used to dig out trees and pile them after the clearing blades have done their work. The teeth of a rake are curved in the vertical plane in the shape of alphabet '*C*' to go under roots, rocks, and boulders etc. As the dozer moves forward, it forces the teeth of the rake below the ground surface. The teeth will catch roots under ground and surface brush left from the felling operation. The soil is allowed to pass through it. The size, weight and spacing of the rakes teeth depends on its intended use. Rakes are also used to push, shake, and turn piles of trees and vegetation before and burning duration. By shaking the dirt from piles is reduced which help in burning.

19.28. DISPOSAL OF TREES, BRUSH, STUMPS AND ROOT DEBRIS

The debris can be disposed off either burning it. If it is to be burnt, it should be piled into stacks or rows with a minimum amount of soil. The piled up or creating rows is also called '*windrows*]. Now a days the burning of debris is restricted. Debris containing high moisture contents need outside source of fuel to start combustion, which causes pollution of the atmosphere. The debris is converted into chips. Clean chips are used for manufacturing pressed boards, while mixed chip and bark etc. can be used as boiler fuel etc.

19.29. TECHNIQUES OF CLEARING THE GROUND

The technique of clearing the area depends upon the following factors:

1. Vegetation to be cleared
2. Type of ground soil
3. Moisture condition of soil
4. Job specifications

Job specification may allow the shearing of the vegetation and trees at ground level or may require removal of stumps and roots from below the ground.

(*a*) **Shearing at ground level and piling up.** For this job, following operations may be adopted:

(*i*) *Small trees and brush* (dead branches etc.) can be removed by advancing the dozer with the blade slightly below the ground level. The blade cuts or up roots most of the trees and bends the rest for removal on the return pass. A medium sized dozer can clear and pile up of 0.25 acres of small trees and brush per hour.

(*ii*) *Small to medium sized vegetation* (18 to 25 cms dia) through which the dozer can move continuously, may work either from outside or from the centre of the area. The production of work will be higher if long areas having width 60 to 120 m are worked. Under these conditions angle type clearing blade has been found very efficient.

(*iii*) *Large trees* (30 to 90 cms diameter). In this case first the trees are cut 60 to 120 cms above the ground level by holding the clearing blade in a raised position and driving the stinger into the tree.

The vertical edge of the stinger splits the tree vertically. After the tree is felled, the exposed stump at ground level is cut by the horizontal edge of the stinger. A medium sized dozer takes about 5 to 20 minute per tree to cut and pile it up. A tree dozer is shown in Fig. 19.7.

Fig. 19.7. Tree Dozer or Ripper or Rooter

(*iv*) *Steep slopes or large number of trees*. In case of steep slopes or a significant number of large trees, cutting and piling normally is accomplished in one operation only. Once a blade load material is obtained, the dozer is turned at right angle (90°) and the material is piled up. The cutting operation should be performed in the direction of the ground's contour and the pilling should be done on the down hill side. In this way the dozer has not to work against the natural grade.

19.30. REMOVAL OF TREE'S STUMPS

Stumps can be removed during clearing operation by the following techniques:

1. The stinger of the clearing blade is used to remove the stumps. First the roots of the stumps below the ground level are cut by the stinger and then they are pushed out of the ground with the edge of the blade. The stinger is designed to work as a knife or spear but not as a lever. The edge of the blade should be used for pushing.
2. Hard wood or extremely large trees do not split easily. These are removed first by cutting the lateral roots around the tree and then pushing the tree with the help of blade raised high to provide leverage. In case of very large trees, on one side of the tree an earth ramp may be built to get the greatest pushing leverage.

19.31. ROCK RIPPING

Rock can be ripped with the help of a ripper. Rocks have been ripped with the varying degree of success, for many years but in recent years, the knowledge and equipments for ripping the rocks have greatly increased. In the past ripping of rock was considered an very tedious job, but due to the development of new technology rocks are ripped with relative ease and at 50% cost compared with the cost of drilling, blasting, loading and hauling.

The ripper is a relatively narrow implement. It penetrates into the earth and is pulled to loosen and split the hard ground, week rocks, or old pavements etc. Heavy ripping is accomplished by crawler dozers equipped with rear mounted rippers. Power and tractive force is available from such machines. For light duty works motor graders can also be equipped with rippers.

The major developments responsible for increased ripping of rocks are as follows:

1. Availability of heavier and more powerful dozers.
2. Improvement in sizes and performance of rippers such as development of impact rippers.
3. Availability of better equipment for determining the rippability of rocks.
4. Availability of improved technique in using instruments and equipment.

19.31.1. Determining the rippability of rocks

It has been observed that the rippability of rocks depends on the type of rock and its density. To rip the igneous rocks is impossible as they have no cleavage planes and stratification. Basalt, granite etc. come in this category. On the other hand sedimentary rocks such as sand stone have layered structure due to their formation process. This characteristic of these rocks makes them easier to rip. The metephorbic rocks such as gneiss, quartzite slat etc. vary in rippability with their degree of cleavage. For determining the reppability refraction seismo graphic methods can be used with reasasonable accuracy.

19.32. PHYSICAL PROPERTIES THAT FAVOUR RIPPING

Following characteristics have been found to influence the ripping of the rocks:

1. Faults, fractures and joints, all these factors act as planes of weakness which help in ripping.
2. Brittleness and crystalline structures.
3. Weathering. Greater the degree of weathering, the more easily the rock can be ripped.
4. High degree of lamination or stratification offers good possibilities of ripping.
5. Large grain size, coarse grained rocks rip more easily than fine grained rocks.

It has been established that rippability of most types of rocks is related to the speed at which the wave travel through the rock. Further it has been found that rocks which propagate sound waves at low velocities less than 2100 m/s are rippable where as rocks that propagate sound waves at high velocities of 3000 m/s or more are not rippable. Rocks having intermediate velocities are classified as marginal.

19.33. RIPPER ATTACHMENTS

The ripper attachments for dozers generally are rear mounted. The mounting may be fixed radial, fixed parallelogram or parallelogram linkage with hydraulically variable pitch as shown in Fig. 19.8. The vertical piece that is forced down into the material is known as a SHANK. A ripper tip is fixed to the lower cutting end of the shank. For easy replacement, the tip is detachable. The tip is the high wear surface of the ripper. A tip can have a service life only 10 minutes to 1000 hours depending on the abrasive characteristics of the material to be ripped.

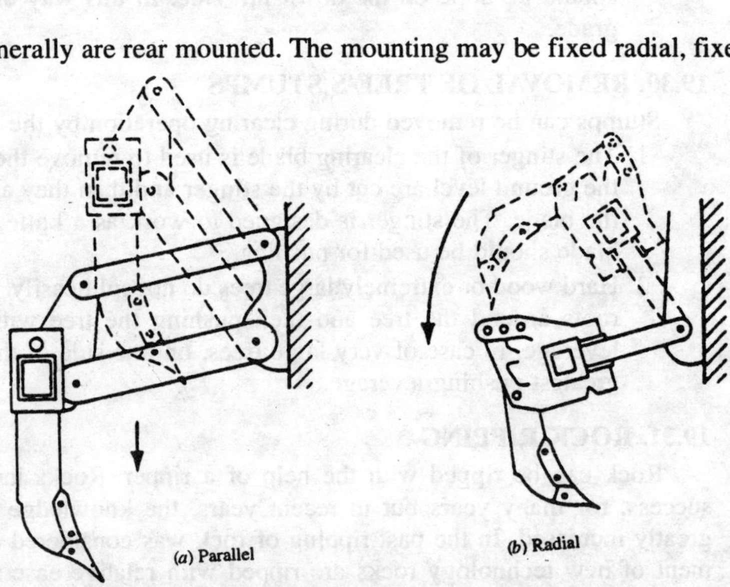
(*a*) Parallel (*b*) Radial

Fig. 19.8. Attachment of Ripper

Both straight and curved shanks are available. Straight shanks are used for massive formations where as curved shanks are use for laminated or bedded rocks or pavements, where a lifting action will help shattering the material.

The radial type ripper linkage has not found favour as the angle of tip attack varies with the depth of the shank depressed. This makes it difficult to achieve the penetration in hard materials.

The parallelogram type ripper maintains the shank in a vertical position and keeps the tip at a constant angle. The adjustable parallelogram type rippers enable the tip angle to be controlled by the operator.

Effectiveness of Ripper. The effectiveness of ripper depends upon the following factors:

1. *Properties of material to be ripped.* As weathered, faulted, laminated etc.
2. *Dozer's usable power to advance the tip.* It depends on dozers weight and coefficient of friction.
3. Down pressure at the ripper tip.

19.34. DETERMINATION OF SPEED OF SOUND WAVES IN ROCKS

For determining the thickness and degree of consolidation of rock layers at or near the ground surface a refraction seismograph can be used. The paths followed by sound waves generated from a wave generating sources through a formation are detected by the instruments shown in Fig. 19.9.

A geophone, a sound sensor is driven into the ground at known stations equally spaced along a line. The geophone driven stations may be 0, 1, 2, 3 etc. as shown in the Fig. 19.9. A wire from the geophone is connected to the seismic timer. From the seismic timer an other wire is connected to the sledge hammer or other impact producing device. In successive order, a steel plate is placed on the ground at the sensing stations. As the hammer strikes the steel plate, a switch closes immediately to send an electric signal to start

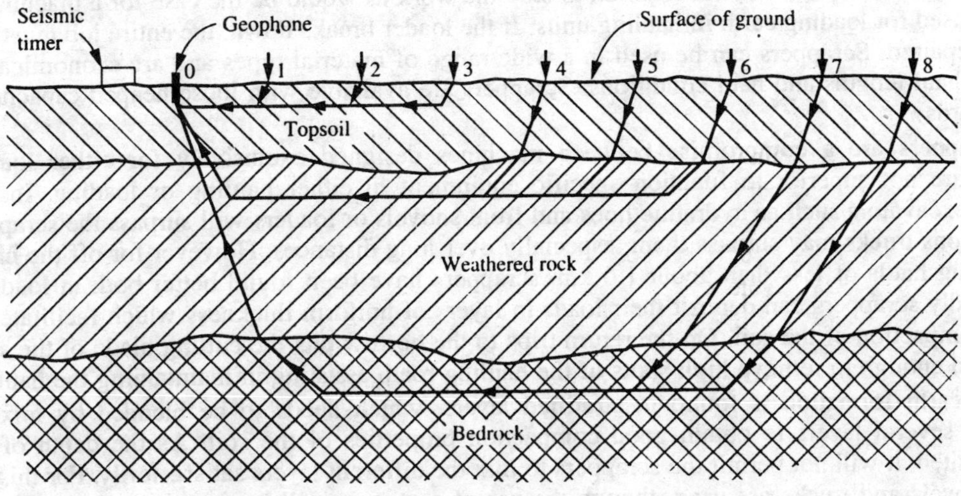

Fig. 19.9. Sound waves path through earth layers

the timer. At the same time, the blow from the hammer sends sound waves into the formation which travel to the geophone. On receipt of the first wave, the geophone signals the timer to stop recording the elapsed time. The times and distances of different waves are recorded. From the known time and distance the velocity of a wave through the formation may be determined. It has been observed that formations having sound velocity less than 2125 m/s are rippable *i.e.* they are soft enough, where as formations having sound waves velocities 3030 m/s or more are not rippable, *i.e.* they are sufficiently hard.

19.35. SCRAPPERS

A scraper is a digging and carrying device which picks up its own load through scrapping the ground, transports it to the required site and after discharging and spreading the load returns to the pit for picking up the next load. Scrapping means removing soil in layers of small thickness. The digging, hauling and finishing operations are accomplished with one machine. This machine has a great utility in hauling gravel and reclaiming coal. It is a unique machine for excavating and long distance hauling of plowable (ploughable) materials. This machine can not be used on small localized excavation jobs as its operation requires considerable area, particularly in length and reasonably a flat topography. The advantage of the scraper over the other machines is that the digging and loading are done simultaneously. If it is to be used on hard soils then prior use of rippers or rooters is required.

19.35.1. Type of Scrapers

Scrapers may be of two types:

1. Motorised
2. Towed

In the motorized units the scrapper is self powered being attached to a wheel tractor more or less permanently while the towed type, scrapper is like a trailer on two axels hauled by a separate tractor, usually a crawler tractor. Both types may require extra power during loading under difficult conditions. This power is provided by a pusher.

19.36. TRACTOR PULLED SCRAPERS

Tractor pulled scrappers have established an important position in the field of earth moving. They are designed to load, haul and dump the loose material. These scrapers are the result of a compromise between the best loading and best hauling machines. The greatest advantage of tractor scrapper is their ability to carry out many different activities *i.e.* their versatility. These machines are self operating to the extent that they can load, haul and discharge materials. They are not dependent on other equipments. If one of them suffers temporary breakdown, it is not required to stop the work as would be the case for a machine which is exclusively used for loading earth in hauling units. If the loader breaks down, the entire job must stop till the loader is repaired. Scrappers can be used in a wide range of material types and are economical over a wide range of haul lengths and haul conditions. Scrappers are available with loose heaped capacities upto 33.6 m^3 (44 yards).

Since scrappers are a compromise between machines designed exclusively for either loading or hauling, they are not superior to function specific equipment in either hauling or loading. In loading operation, the excavators such as hydraulic hoes and front shovels or loaders will surpass the scrappers. In hauling operations trucks may surpass them, especially over long distances. However for off the high way situations having hauls of less than about 1.6 km, scrappers have been found better both in loading and hauling. Secondly scrappers can deposit their loads in layers of uniform thickness which facilitates in the operation of compaction of the soil. On the return trips to the borrow pits the cutting blade of the scrapper may be lowered enough to remove high spots of the hauling road, assisting in maintaining the haul roads.

Generally earth formation is found in stratified layers, which needs to be blended by mixing the materials from several layers to obtain good compaction properties of the soil. As the depth of cut by scrappers is limited, it will not permit the scrappers to mix the different layers satisfactorily. For this reason some times shovels and trucks are used, though the use of scrappers will be more economical to handle earth than shovels and trucks.

19.37. CLASSIFICATION OF SCRAPPERS

Scrappers may be classified in many ways as according to number of powered axles and by the method of loading. All these are wheel tractor pulled machines.

1. According to running. In this category scrappers are classified as crawler tractor scrapper and wheel tractor scrapper.

2. According to the method of loading. In this category scrappers are classified as:

(*a*) Pusher loaded: (*i*) Single powered axle
(*ii*) Tandom powered axles

(*b*) Self loading: (*i*) Push-pull tandom powered axle
(*ii*) Elevating
(*iii*) Auger.

1. Crawler tractor scrappers

As already discussed, crawler is a track consisting of linked shoes that moves in the horizontal plane across the fixed rollers. At the rear of the machine the track passes over a vertically mounted sprocket drive wheel. As the sprocket turns, it forces the track forward or back ward, imparting motion to the machine. In the front of the machine the track passes over a vertically mounted idler wheel, that is connected to a recoil device having adjustable tension. The idler wheel maintains proper tension in the track and enables it to absorb heavy shocks. The linked shoes are made of heat treated steel and designed to resist wear and abrasion etc. of the surface.

For relatively short haul distances the crawler type tractor, pulling a rubber tyred self loading scrapper can move earth economically. The high draw bar pull in loading a scrapper, combined with good traction even on poor haul roads gives the crawler tractor an advantage for short hauls, but as the haul distance increases, the low speed crawler tractor scrapper is a disadvantage compared to a wheel tractor scrapper. Unless the loading operation is difficult, a crawler tractor can load a scraper with out the aid of a bulldozer.

2. Wheel tired tractor scrapper

For long haul distances the higher speed of a wheel type tractor pulled self loading scrapper will move earth more economically than with crawler type tractor. Although the wheel type tractor can not provide as great a tractive effort in loading a scraper as crawler tractor, but its higher speed about 50 kmph will offset the disadvantage of loading in case of long distance hauls.

The advantages and disadvantages discussed under the head dozers will also apply to tractor pulled scrappers. Actually now a days only wheel tired tractor pulled scrappers are used. A wheel tried tractor scraper is shown in Fig. 19.10.

Fig. 19.10. Wheel tired tractor scraper

3. Pusher-Loaded scrappers

These are wheel tractor pulled machines. They have potential to travel with high speed on favourable haul roads. Many modles of this category may attain speed upto about 54 kmph when fully loaded. The high speed haulage is their main advantage. However they can provide less tractive effort while loading on units, which makes their use uneconomical. In case of a single powered axle scrapper only 50 to 55% of the total loaded weight comes on driving wheels.

Secondly in most materials, the coefficient of traction for rubber tires is less than tracks. Hence to supplement the loading power of these scrappers is necessary. Usually the external loading power is a crawler tractor pusher. Both the scrapper and the pusher provide the total power required to obtain a full load, hence the loading costs are relatively low.

It has been observed that tendom powered units normally require help in loading resulting about 25% extra cost than single powered axle scrappers. For this reason tandom powered units are considered specialized units under the following situations.

1. For opening up a work or job
2. Working in extremely adverse grades
3. For working in soft soils

The single powered axle pusher loaded wheel tractor scrappers have been uneconomical under the following situations.

1. If haul grades are greater than 5%
2. If return grades are greater than 12%

. Push-pull scrappers

In this case two scrappers work together in loading operation. These machines are basically tendom powered axle units. They have the following features:

1. A cushioned push block bail mounted on the front.
2. A hook on the rear above the usual back push block.

These features enable the two scrappers (push and pull scrappers) to assist each other during loading operation by hooking together. The trailing scrapper pushes the lead or front scrapper as it loads. Then the front or lead scrapper pulls the trailing scrapper to assist it in loading. In this way the two scrappers work with out the assistance from a push tractor. They can also work individually with the help of a pusher. When these scrapers are used in abrasive materials or rocks they will suffer more tire wear due to more slippage than four wheel drive action. A pusher loaded scraper is shown in Fig. 19.11.

. Elevating scrappers

This is a totally self contained loading and hauling scrapper. In this scrapper a chain elevator serves as the loading mechanism. These scrapers are found economical in short haul situation, where the ratio of haul time to load time is low. These scrappers are used for utility work as dressing up behind high production

Fig. 19.11. Single-powered axle wheel-tractor scraper

spreads or shifting materials during fine grading operations. They are very good for small quantity works. As no pusher is required in these scrappers, problem of mismatch between the pusher and the number of scrappers does not arise.

Disadvantages

Following disadvantages are observed of these scrappers:

1. Due to the elevation mechanism, they can not be used to handle rocks or materials having rocks.
2. The weight of elevator loading assembly is a dead weight during the haul cycle of the scrapper.

6. Augur scrappers

This type of scrappers are also totally self contained in loading and hauling. These scrappers can self load in difficult conditions such as in granular materials or laminated or stratified rocks.

An independent hydrostatic system that powers the scrapper is located in the centre of the bowl. The rotating augur lifts the material off the scrapper's cutting edge and carries it to the top of the load, creating a void that allows the new material to enter into the bowl easily. This action reduces the resistance to the cutting edge, which enables the wheel tractor scrapper to continue moving through the cut. The auger also adds non load (dead weight) weight to the scrapper during the travel cycle. These scrappers are more costly to own and operate than conventional single or tendom powered scrappers.

19.38. FACTORS AFFECTING THE OUTPUT OF TRACTOR PULLED SCRAPERS

Following factors have been found to affect the output of a tractor pulled scraper.

1. Size of the tractor
2. Type of material
3. Size and condition of borrow pit or cut
4. Slope of loading zone
5. Extent of loosening of material before loading
6. Use of a helper tractor during loading
7. Haul distance
8. Slope and condition of haul road
9. Altitude of site.
10. Climatic conditions
11. Management conditions

19.39. OUTPUT OF A TRACTOR PULLED SCRAPER

App. output = Average net vol. per load × No. of loads per hour.

The number of loads depends on the time required to make a trip. It includes following times:

1. Travelling time between the pit and the fill.
2. Loading time
3. Dumping and turning time
4. Returning to the pit
5. Getting in position to load.

Items 2, 3, and 5 generally are constant for a given job. The variable times will be travelling times between the pit and the fill *i.e.* item 1 and 4.

19.40. FORMULAE FOR OUTPUT OF SOME MACHINES

The output of some machines may be calculated from the relations given below:

1. Output of scrapers $= \dfrac{100 \times C}{3.28\, D + 3}$

where,

D = distance of one way haul in metres.
C = struck capacity in loose soil in m^3.

2. Out put of dozers $= \dfrac{25.3 \times \text{draw bar h.p.}}{\text{Distance of haul in metres}}$

3. Vol. of earth or rock ripped in one pass of machine

$$= \frac{\text{Length of pass}}{\text{Speed of travelling}} \times \text{turned around time}$$

4. Output of motor grater = Effective width of blade × Average speed × Efficiency

5. Output of tractor. It depends upon the size of bucket, type of soil, type and grade of working surface, and type of machine.

QUESTIONS

1. Name different types of machinery required at a civil construction project.
2. Discuss the factors which influence the out put of earth moving machinery.
3. What is a tractor? For what purposes it is used?
4. Give comparative advantages and disadvantages of crawling and wheeled tractors.
5. What factors influence the selection of a tractor? Explain in brief.
6. What informations are received by the rating of a tractor?
7. Define Rim pull and write down the formula in M.K.S. units to determine it.
8. What are dozers? For what purpose they are used? Give their classification.
9. Enumerate the comparative advantages and disadvantages of wheeled mounted and crawler mounted dozers.
10. How the power is supplied to dozers?
11. Write a note on the blades of a dozzer.
12. For what uses a dozer can be put on a project.
13. How the trees and stumps etc. are disposed off?
14. Explain the methods of clearing ground at the site of work.
15. What is meant by rock ripping? How the rippability of rocks determined?
16. What is a scrapper? Discuss dozer pulled scrappers.
17. Give the classification of scrappers and discuss them in brief.
18. Explain ripper attachments with sketch.

OBJECTIVE TYPE QUESTIONS

1. Tractors mainly are used for
   (*a*) Lifting of loads (*b*) To pull or push the load

(*c*) For underground excavation (*d*) For all the above

2. The output of a earth moving machine is influenced by
   (*a*) Type of soil (*b*) Physical site conditions
   (*c*) Condition of the machine (*d*) Method of operation
   (*e*) All the above
3. The selection of a tractor is influenced by
   (*a*) Job requirements
   (*b*) Kind or type of work
   (*c*) Smoothness and firmness of the hauling road
   (*d*) Slope and length of haul road
   (*e*) All the above
4. A dozer mainly is used for
   (*a*) Pushing the material (*b*) Lifting the material
   (*c*) Digging the material (*d*) Pulling the material
   (*e*) For all the above
5. Dozers can be used for
   (*a*) Clearing construction site (*b*) Opening up pilot roads through mountains
   (*c*) Moving earth for about 100 m distance (*d*) Spreading and back filling the material
   (*e*) All the above
6. Type/Types of blades may be used for a dozer
   (*a*) Straight blade (*b*) Angle blade
   (*c*) Universal blade (*d*) Cushion blade
   (*e*) All the above (*f*) None of above
7. Tilting movement of a dozer blade takes place
   (*a*) In horizontal plane (*b*) In vertical plane
   (*c*) Inclined plane (*d*) In all the planes
8. Turning of blade of a dozer is called angling when the motion is
   (*a*) Perpendicular to the direction of travel of the dozer
   (*b*) Along the direction of travel of the dozer
   (*c*) When motion of blade is not perpendicular to the travel of the dozer.
   (*d*) All are true
9. Scrapers are capable to perform
   (*a*) For excavating (*b*) Hauling for long distances
   (*c*) Spreading the fill (*d*) All the operations simultaneously
10. The speed of pusher loaded scrapers is about
    (*a*) 35 kmph (*b*) 40 kmph
    (*c*) 55 kmph (*d*) 85 kmph
11. The velocity of sound waves in rippable rocks is less than
    (*a*) 100 kmph (*b*) 1500 kmph
    (*c*) 1750 kmph (*d*) 2125 kmph

ANSWERS:

1. (*b*)	4. (*a*)	7. (*b*)	10. (*c*)
2. (*e*)	5. (*e*)	8. (*c*)	11. (*d*)
3. (*e*)	6. (*e*)	9. (*d*)	

20

Earth Excavating Machinery

0.1. INTRODUCTION

For all Civil Engineering Projects excavation of earth is most important operation for the project as for arth dams much quantity of earth is required for its construction. Similarly for roads, railways and other ivil engineering works earth excavation is required. Excavation of earth is required on the surface of the round and below the ground surface also, for which different machines are used. The machines used for arth excavation are called excavators.

0.2. EXCAVATORS

In the category of excavating machines many machines are included as dipper or power shovel, drag ne, clamshell, hoes, drag shovels etc. Essentially all these machines belong to the shovel family. To onvert one type of machine into an other type, only the front end attachment is changed while the basic ructure of the machine remains the same. Though the name 'shovel' is often used for a particular type of xcavating machine fitted with a short length boom and working with forward strokes, but in fact the term hovel' refers to a class of machines which have a common type of operating and tracking mechanism. he shovel family of excavators constitute a major part of excavating machines and probably are most seful and lasting class of earth moving machinery.

0.3. POWER TO OPERATE EXCAVATORS

The excavators are operated by hydraulic power. Hydraulic power is the key to the advantages offered y these machines. The hydraulic control of machines provides the following advantages.

1. Outstanding control of attachments.
2. High overall efficiency.
3. Smoothness and ease in operation.
4. Faster cycle times.
5. Positive control that provides greater accuracy and precision.

.4. CLASSIFICATION OF EXCAVATORS

The hydraulically operating excavators are classified based on the digging motion of the hydraulically ntrolled boom and stick to which the dipper or bucket is attached. An upward motion unit is known as ont shovel' and the downward motion units are known as a 'Hoe'. It develops excavation breakout force pulling the dipper or bucket towards the machine and moving (curling) the bucket inward. A shovel velops breakout force by pushing material away from the machine.

.5. FRONT SHOVELS

These shovels mainly are used for digging hard earth above the track level and for loading haul units.

Loading of big boulders or shot rock would be a typical application. Shovels are capable of developing high break out force with their buckets, but the material excavated should be such that it can stand perpendicular to the ground. Mostly shovels are mounted on crawler tracks and have very slow travel speeds less than 5 kmph. The wide treads of the track produce very low pressure on the ground which allows them to operate on soft grounds. They can also be mounted on rubber tyred wheels. The single engine self propelled units are powered and operated from the excavator cab. The non self propelled units are mounted on the rear part of the truck and are known as truck mounted. They have separate engines for operating them. The rubber tyred wheel mounted shovels can travel with higher speeds than crawler mounted shovels. But they are useful for small jobs where considerable travelling is necessary and the road surfaces and ground are firm.

20.6. SIZE OF FRONT OR BASIC SHOVELS

The size of a shovel is indicated by the size of the bucket expressed in cubic yard (1 cubic yard = 0.765 m^3). In measuring the size of the bucket the earth is struck even with the contour of the bucket. This is called struck volume.

1. **Struck capacity.** The volume actually enclosed by the bucket with no allowance for bucket teeths is called struck capacity.
2. **Heaped capacity.** The rated heaped capacities represent a net section of bucket volume. Hence they should be corrected to average bucket pay load based on the characteristics of the material being handled. The angle of repose of the fill material may be taken as 45° or 1:1.
3. **Fill factor.** The amount of material actually in a bucket compared to its volume is called fill factor. It is an important factor for determining he shovel production. Fill factor is the percentage that, when multiplied by the rated heaped capacity adjusts the volume of the material loaded into the bucket. This factor varies from 0.85 to 1.15 depending upon the type of material. For rocks it varies from 1.0 to 1.15 and for soils from 0.85 to 1.0. Basic shovels are available in different capacities as 3/8, 1/2, 3/4, 1, $1\frac{1}{2}$, 2, $2\frac{1}{2}$ cubic yards. The basic crawler shovel is shown in Fig. 20.1.

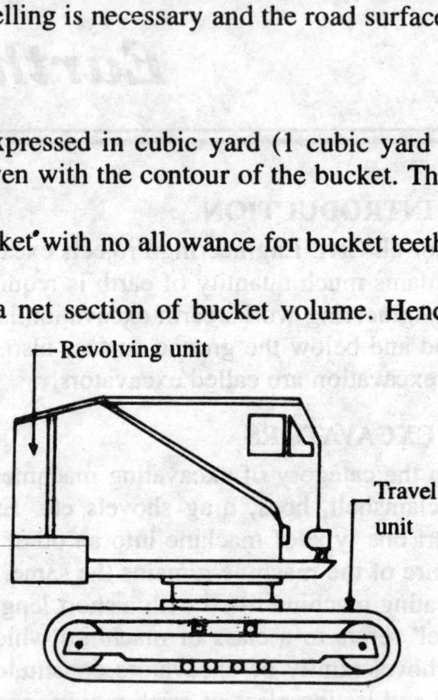

Fig. 20.1. Basic shovel (Crawler mounted)

20.7. BASIC PARTS AND OPERATION

The basic parts of a front or basic shovel include, the mounting, cab, boom, stick, bucket and hoist line. These parts are shown in Fig. 20.2.

Fig. 20.3 shows a dipper shovel attachment with a divided stick with rack on the under side.

Fig. 20.4 shows the bucket of a dipper shovel.

Fig. 20.5 shows the method of winding different cables over spools and shovels is known as reeving. The reeving for a crowd shovel is shown in Fig. 20.5.

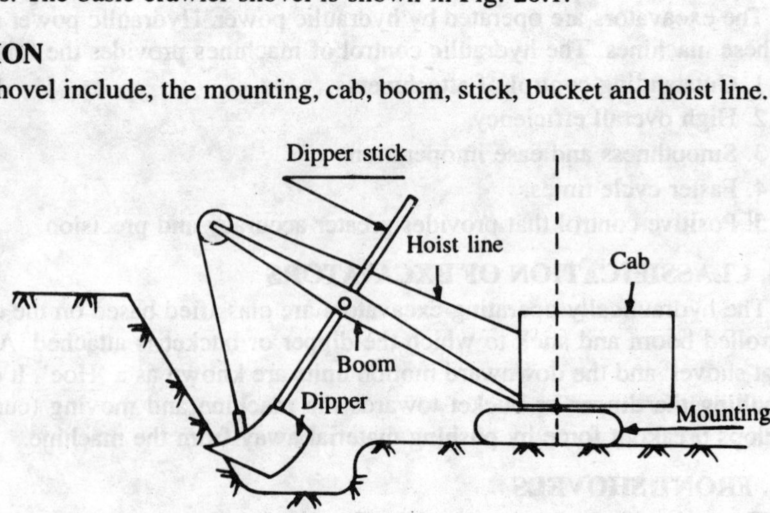

Fig. 20.2. Basic parts and operation of a power shovel

Operation of shovel

The shovel is placed in correct

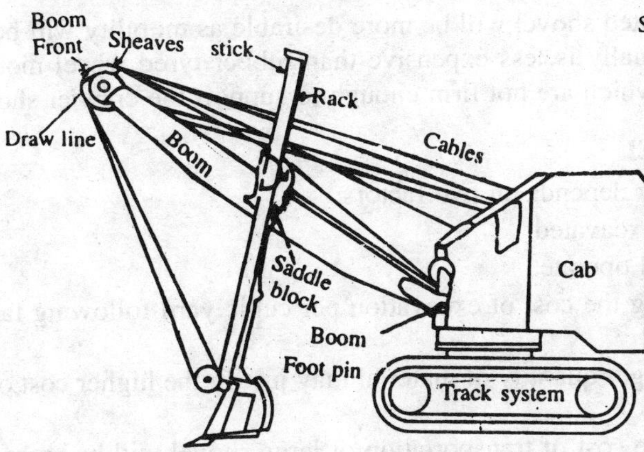

Fig. 20.3. Dipper shovel attachment with a divided stick with rack on the under side

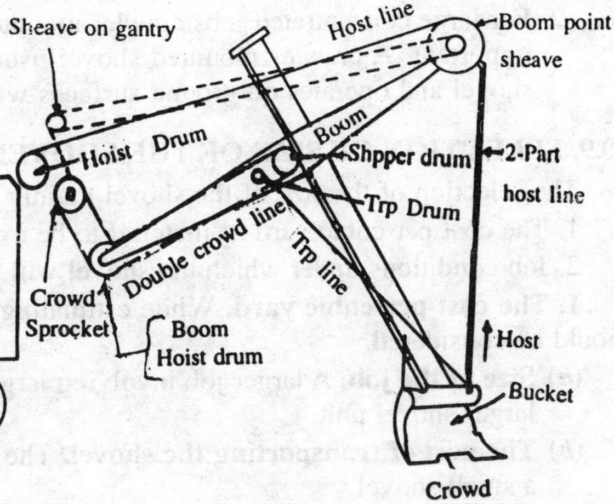

Fig. 20.4. Bucket of a dipper shovel

position, near the face of the earth to be excavated. The bucket of the shovel is lowered to the floor of the pit with the teeth pointing towards the face. A crowding force is applied by the hydraulic pressure to the stick cylinder and at the same time tension is applied to the hoisting line to pull the bucket up of the face of the pit. If the depth of the face is just right.

Considering the type of soil and size of the bucket, the bucket will be filled as it reach the top of the face or cut. If the depth of cut or face is too small or shallow it will not be possible to fill the bucket completely with out excessive crowding and hoisting tension. Possibly still it may not be filled fully. This puts excessive strains on the equipment and reduces it out put. On the other hand if the depth of the face is greater than the required depth to fill the bucket when operating under favourable crowd and hoist, reduction in depth of penetration of the bucket into the face will be necessary, if the full face is to be excavated or to start excavation above the floor of the pit. The material left near the floor of the pit will be excavated after the upper portion of the face is removed.

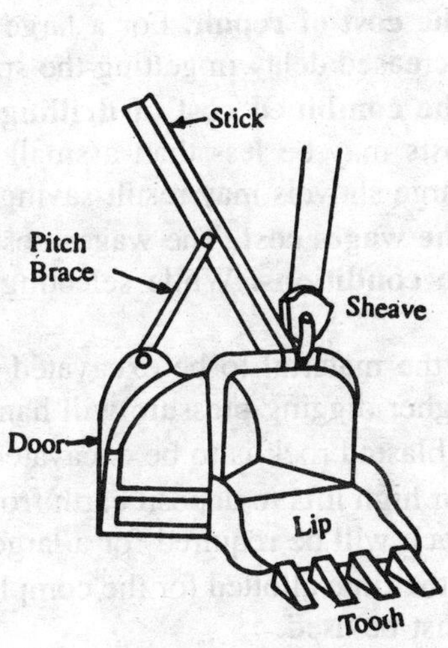

Fig. 20.5. Reeving for a cable crowed dipper shovel

Optimum depth of the pit or cut

The depth which produces the greatest out put, and at which the bucket of the shovel comes up with a full load with out undue crowding is known as the optimum depth of the pit. The optimum depth varies with the type of soil and the size of the bucket. (Refer page 320 also)

20.8. SELECTION OF TYPE OF SHOVEL

The selection of type of shovel depends on the concentration of the work or job to be performed.

1. For numerous small jobs in different locations rubber tyred wheel shovels will be advantageous as their mobility is more.

2. For large concentrated jobs crawler mounted shovel will be more desirable as mobility will be less important. A crawler mounted shovel usually is less expensive than rubber tyred wheel mounted shovel and operates on ground surfaces which are not firm enough to support the crawler shovel.

20.9. SELECTION OF SIZE OF THE SHOVEL

The selection of the size of the shovel mainly depends on two factors:

1. The cost per cubic yard of material to be excavated.
2. Job conditions under which the shovel will operate.

1. The cost per cubic yard. While estimating the cost of excavation per cubic yard following factors should be considered.

(*a*) **Size of the job.** A larger job involving larger quantity of material may justify the higher cost of the larger shovel unit.

(*b*) **The cost of transporting the shovel.** The cost of transportation of large shovel will be more than a small shovel.

(*c*) **Depreciation.** The rate of depreciation for a larger shovel may be higher than a small one especially if it is to be disposed off at the end of the job, probably due to higher cost of the large shovel unit it will be difficult to sell it.

(*d*) **The cost of repair.** For a large unit this cost may be considerably more than a small unit due to increased delay in getting the spare parts for a large unit.

(*e*) **The combined cost of drilling, blasting and excavation of rock.** For a large shovel unit these costs may be less than a small unit as large machine will handle bigger rocks than a small one Large shovels may result saving in drilling and blasting costs.

(*f*) **The wages cost.** The wages cost per cubic yard for large shovels will be less than for a small one

2. Job conditions. While selecting the size of a shovel following job conditions should be kept in mind.

(*a*) If the material to be excavated is hard and tough then the bucket of the large shovel that exerts higher digging pressure will handle the material more easily.

(*b*) If blasted rock is to be excavated, the large sized bucket will handle larger individual pieces.

(*c*) For high lifts to deposit earth from a basement or trench into the trucks at natural ground level, long reach will be required for a large shovel.

(*d*) If the time allotted for the completion of a project requires a high hourly output, then a large shovel must be used.

(*e*) In selecting the size of a shovel, the size of the available hauling units should be considered. If small hauling units are to be used then the size of the shovel should be small. In case large hauling units are available then a large shovel should be used.

(*f*) The weight restrictions imposed by states for hauling on a highway may restrict the size of the shovel, if it is hauled over a high way. The clearance of bridges and under passes also may restrict the size.

While considering the size of a shovel for a project the dimensions of the boom and dipper or bucket stick, the maximum cutting height, digging radius, dumping radius, and dumping height should also be considered. The maximum dumping height and radius are important while shovel in a pit is loading trucks at natural ground level. Representative dimensions and clearances for power shovel are shown in Table 20.1.

20.10. PRODUCTION OF A SHOVEL

The out put of a shovel is affected by many factors. Some of them are as follows:

1. Class of material
2. Height or depth of cut
3. Angle of swing
4. Operator's skill

Table 20.1. Dimensions and clearance for a power shovel for 45° angle of boom

Size of bucket m^3	*Length of boom m*	*Length of handle m*	*Max. cutting height m*	*Max. digging radius m*	*Max. dumping height m*	*Max. dumping radius m*	*Remark*
0.278 (3/8)	3.9 – 4.5	3.3 – 3.9	5.1 – 5.7	6.6	3.9 – 4.5	5.4 – 6.0	
0.383 (1/2)	4.5 – 4.8	3.6 – 3.9	5.7 – 7.2	6.3 – 7.2	4.2 – 4.8	5.7 – 6.0	
0.574 (3/4)	5.1 – 5.4	3.9 – 4.5	6.3 – 8.1	7.5 – 8.4	4.5 – 5.1	6.6 – 7.2	
0.765 (1.0)	6.0	4.8	6.9 – 8.1	9.3 – 9.6	4.5 5.4	6.9 – 7.5	
0.956	6.3	4.8	6.9 – 8.1	9.3 – 9.6	4.8 – 5.7	7.2 – 8.1	
1.148 ($1\frac{1}{2}$)	6.3 – 6.9	4.8 – 5.4	7.2 – 8.7	9.6 – 9.9	5.4 – 6.0	8.4 – 9.0	
1.34 (1 3/4)	6.6 – 7.2	4.8 – 5.4	7.8 – 9.0	9.6 – 9.9	5.4 – 6.0	8.4 – 9.0	
1.530 (2.0)	6.6 – 7.5	5.1 – 5.7	7.8 – 9.0	9.9 – 10.8	5.7 – 6.0	9.0 – 9.9	
1.913 (2.5)	7.5 – 7.8	5.4 – 5.7	8.4 – 10.5	10.5 – 11.4	5.7 – 6.3	9.6 – 10.2	

Note: Values in bracket are in cubic yards.

5. Management condition
6. Job condition
7. Size of hauling units
8. Physical condition of the shovel
9. Haul unit exchange
10. Clean up of loading area

The haul unit exchange means the total time required to move out a loaded truck from its loading position under the excavator and the next empty truck to be positioned for loading.

20.11. HANDLING OF SHOT ROCK

At the time of handling a shot rock, the amount of over sized material should be estimated carefully. A machine whose bite width and pocket are satisfactory for the average size pieces may require much more time in handling individual oversize prices. Thus where there is large percentage of over size material a large bucket or a large machine or change of blasting pattern should be considered.

The use of auxiliary equipment in the loading area such as a dozer may reduce the clean-up delays. The control of haul units and operator breaks are under the control of field management.

20.12. FACTORS AFFECTING THE OUTPUT OF A EXCAVATOR

Following factors affact the output of a excavator:

1. Effect of class of material. A loose, flowing material will fill a digging bucket in shorter sweep up the embankment than a thick and heavy material or material mixed with heavy pieces of rock called chunky material.

2. Effect of depth on out put of shovel.

(*a*) **Shallow depth.** If the depth or height of the face from which a shovel is excavating material is too shallow, it will be difficult or rather impossible to fill the bucket in one pass up the face. In such situations the operator has thé choice of making more than one pass to fill the bucket which will increase the time per cycle or may carry a partly filled bucket to the hauling unit. In either case the net effect will be the reduced out put of the shovel.

(*b*) **Greater height or depth than the minimum.** In case the height or depth of the face is greater than the minimum required to fill the bucket under favourable crowding (filling) and hoisting conditions. In this case operator has following options.

(*i*) In order to fill the bucket in one full stroke, he may reduce the depth of penetration of the bucket into face. This will increase the time for a cycle.

(*ii*) He may start digging above the base of the face. He may remove the lower portion of the face later.

(*iii*) The bucket may be run up for full height of the face and the excess material or earth is allowed to spill down to the base, which may be picked up later.

The choice of any of the three options will result in the loss of time compared to the time required to fill the bucket when it is digging at the optimum height.

The optimum height of a cut ranges from 30 to 50% of the maximum digging height. Lower percentage is applicable to materials which are easy to load such as loam, sand, or gravel. Materials hard to load are as sticky clay, blasted rock etc. need higher optimum height in the range of 50% of the maximum digging height value. Common earth usually required a slightly less than 40% of the maximum digging height.

3. Optimum depth. The optimum depth of a cut is equal to the vertical distance from the dipper stick pivot shaft to the ground level.

4. Angle of swing effect on the production of the shovel. The angle of swing of a shovel is the horizontal angle, expressed in degrees, between the position of the bucket when it is in excavating position and discharging load into a haul unit position. The total time in a cycle includes digging, swinging to the dumping position, dumping and returning to the digging position. The time of cycle is directly proportional to the angle of swing *i.e.* if the angle of swing is increased, the cycle time will also increase on the other hand, if the angle of swing is decreased, the cycle time will decrease. The reduction of 30° in angle of swing increases production of shovels by 15 to 20% and 10% in case of drag line.

The ideal production of a shovel is based on an operating angle of 90 degrees swing and optimum height of the cut. The effect of angle of swing on production of a shovel is shown in Table 20.2.

Table 20.2. Conversion factor for depth of cut for angle of swing for a power shovel

Percent of optimum depth	*Angle of swing in degrees*							*Remark*
	45	60	75	90	120	150	180	
40	0.93	0.89	0.85	0.80	0.72	0.65	0.50	
60	1.10	1.03	0.96	0.91	0.81	0.73	0.66	
80	1.22	1.12	1.04	0.98	0.86	0.77	0.69	
100	1.26	1.16	1.07	1.00	0.88	0.79	0.71	
120	1.20	1.11	1.03	0.97	0.86	0.77	0.70	
140	1.12	1.04	0.97	0.91	0.81	0.73	0.66	
160	1.03	0.96	0.90	0.85	0.75	0.67	0.62	

5. Effect of job conditions on the output of a shovel. A shovel has to work on different jobs and no two jobs have similar conditions. Job conditions may be classified as excellent, good, fair and poor. There is no uniform standard to define or classify the job condition. Each job planner has to use his own judgement and experience in deciding the job conditions.

(*a*) Excellent job conditions. A large enough job justifying the selection of balanced hauling units and having a large open pit with a firm and well drained floor on which the hauling units (trucks) can be placed on either side of shovel to eliminate the loss of time in waiting for hauling units. is called a excellent job condition.

The terrain of natural ground of uniform level with a optimum depth of cutting and the haul roads not affected by climatic conditions as rain are classified as excellent job condition.

6. Poor job conditions. The job on which the excavation has to be done through a hill. The depth of the cut may vary from zero to more than optimum depth. The cut may be very narrow so that no truck can move together in opposite sides *i.e.* the loaded truck moves out before the empty truck is placed in position of loading. The truck has to be placed behind the shovel, so the angle of swing will be approximately 180°. The hauling roads of the area and the floor of the cut may be muddy and slippery due to rains, which will delay the movement of the trucks. Even light rains may delay the operations for several days. Such a project site is classified as poor.

7. Effect of Management conditions on the output of shovel. The attitude of the owner in establishing the conditions under which a shovel is operated will affect its output. To improve the job conditions is not under the control of the owner, but he may improve the management conditions.

To improve the management conditions following actions may be taken:

1. Lubricating and greasing the shovel frequently.
2. Checking the shovel parts that are subjected to greater wear and tear. The worn out parts should be replaced during the ideal time of the shovel at the end of a shift.
3. Replacing the dull bucket teeths with sharp teeths as and when required.
4. Carrying out major overhauling of the shovel between two jobs if required.
5. Parts subjected to greatest wears, should be stocked at the site of the job to be replaced if required.
6. To reduce the angle of swing and provide better facility of placing the hauling units, the pit floor should be kept clean and smooth.
7. To eliminate the loss of time in loading and waiting for hauling units, adequate number of trucks of correct size should be provided.
8. The workers should be encouraged to work extra by giving them bonus.
9. Employing an experienced and competent supervisor to carry out the work smoothly. In short following factors should be given a careful consideration.
   (*a*) Maintenance of the equipment
   (*b*) haul road conditions
   (*c*) Layout of the loading area
   (*d*) Size and number of hauling units
   (*e*) Competency of field management.

20.13. ELEMENTS OF PRODUCTION CYCLE OF A SHOVEL

Following are the elements of the production cycle of a shovel:

1. Load bucket	2. Swing with load
3. Dump load	4. Return swing

A shovel does not move or travel during the digging and loading cycle. As the excavation work progresses, travel of shovel into or along the face is limited. During a study carried out on travel of shovel, it was found that on an average the shovel should be moved after about 20 bucket load. This movement during excavation took on average 36 seconds. The typical cycle element time taken for a 3 to 5 cubic yard capacity shovel is as follows: (1 cy. yd. = 0.765 m^3)

1. Load bucket	:	7 to 9 sec.
2. Swing with load	:	4 to 6 sec.
3. Dump load	:	2 to 4 sec.
4. Return swing	:	4 to 5 sec.

20.14. ATTACHMENT TO BASIC SHOVEL

To convert a basic shovel into different machines of the shovel family following attachments may be added as shown Fig. 20.6 to 20.10.

20.15. HOES (DRAGN OR PULL SHOVEL)

The term hoe applies to an excavating machine of the power shovel family. The machine derives its name from the resemblance of an ordinary garden implement used for digging called phawra. It has a long handle and one digging unit. It is known by several names as Hoe, back hoe, back shovel and pull shovel. The digging action results from the pull or drag of the bucket towards the machine unlike bucket shovel which makes outwards strokes while digging. A hoe is found more advantageous for digging below machine level as trenches, footings, basement pits and other general works which require precise control on depths. Their second advantage is that they can dump material at a higher level permitting hauling units

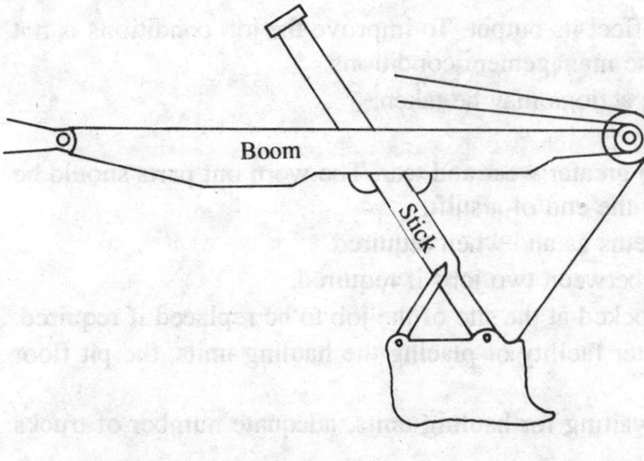

Fig. 20.6. Boom and Dipper Stick of a shovel

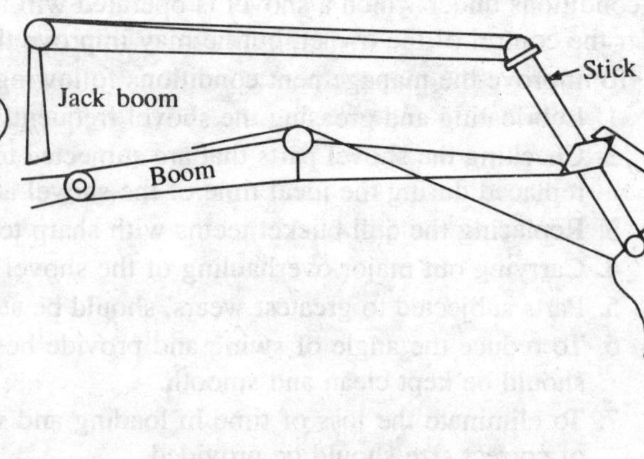

Fig. 20.7. Parts of a Drag shovel or hoe

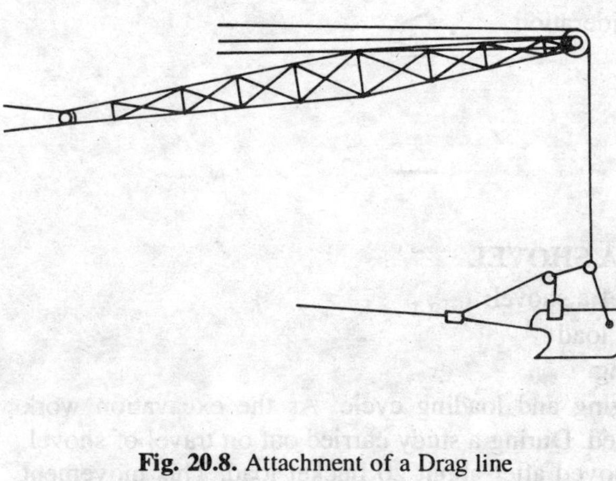

Fig. 20.8. Attachment of a Drag line

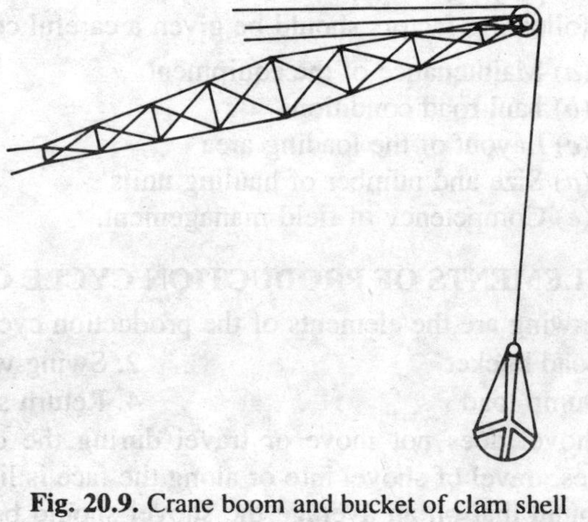

Fig. 20.9. Crane boom and bucket of clam shell

to stand at a higher level. Due to their rigidity they are superior to drag lines in operating on close range work and dumping into the trucks. Due to the direct pull on the bucket, hoes may exert greater tooth pressure on soil than power shovel. They can also dig hard material like power shovel due to positive control on the crowding (filling stroke) of the bucket into the soil.

A power shovel can be converted into a hoe by installing a bucket or dipper stick and a bucket (dipper) at the end of the shovel boom. A hoe usually is equipped with a goose neck boom to increase the depth of digging of the machine.

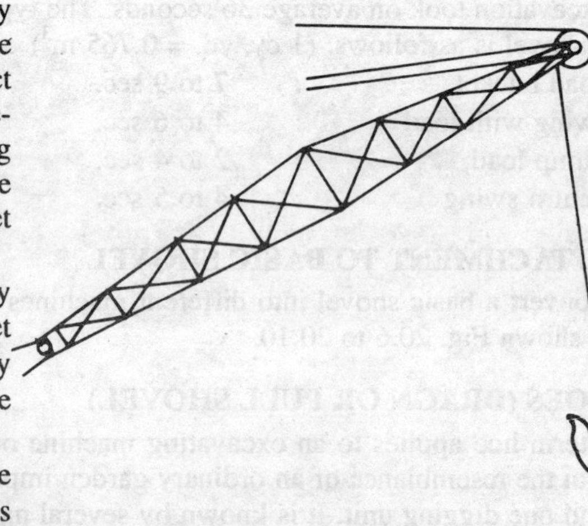

Fig. 20.10. Attachment of a crane

The maximum digging depth of a larger machine is about 8.0 m (25 ft.). The capacity of the bucket is available upto about 1.15 m^3 (1.5 cubic yards). The large machine can handle about 5 tonnes load at about 6.0 m radius. They are designed for mobility and general purpose works.

Advantages of Hoes

In some respects hoes have been found superior to trenching machines, especially in digging utility trenches whose banks are allowed to establish natural slopes and for which trench shoring is not to be used. Hoes can remove the earth as it caves in to establish natural slopes where as trenching machines are unable to do it easily. It can handle the trench excavation and the pipe, eliminating the use of second machine. The operation of the bucket can be managed to trim or dress the surface under digging and the manual operation of dressing excavated surface is reduced.

20.16. BASIC PARTS AND OPERATION OF A HOE

The basic parts of this machine are a boom, stick, a jack boom and the bucket attached at the end of the stick. The hoe stick is pin hinged with the boom point at an intermediate point of its length. Thus the stick of the hoe is capable of turning over the pin to take any desired direction suitable for digging or dumping. It is not possible in dipper shovel. To the lower end of the stick, the bucket is attached while the upper end carries a sheave bearing the hoist cable which is supported by the jack boom at the other end and passes on to the hoist drum. The boom as a whole including the stick is capable of upward and down ward movement through the reaction at the stick hinge when a pull is applied to the hoist cable. Fig. 20.11.

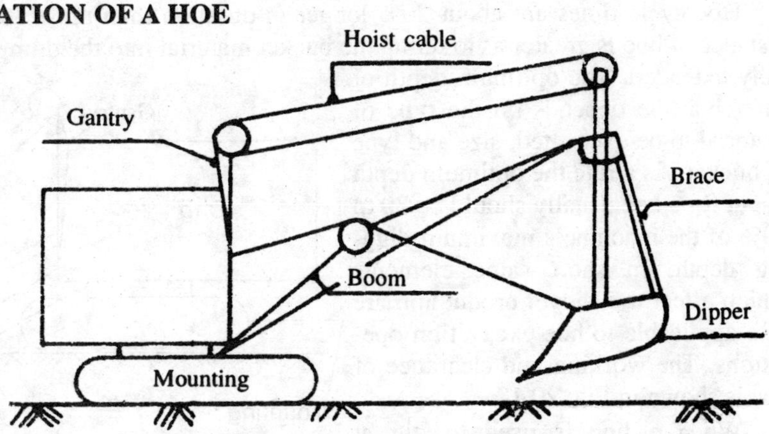

Fig. 20.11. Basic parts of a hoe

Operation. The machine is placed in operation position by setting the boom at the desired angle. The bucket is placed in the desired position by applying a pull in hoist cable and releasing the drag cable. The free end of the boom is lowered by releasing tension in the hoist cable till the bucket teeth engage the material to be excavated. To fill the bucket, the drag cable is pulled in. The bucket is lifted by raising the boom and then swinging it to the dumping truck or over the spoil bank.

20.17. SELECTION OF HOE

While selecting a hoe following points should be considered:

1. Maximum excavation depth required.
2. Maximum working radius required for digging and dumping.
3. Maximum dumping height required.
4. Hoisting capability required.

20.18. RATED HOIST LOAD

The hoist load may be established with the help of the following guide lines.

1. The rated hoist load should not exceed 75% of the tip load.
2. The rated hoist load should not exceed 87% of the excavator's hydraulic capacity.
3. The rated hoist load should not exceed the machine's structural capabilities.

20.19. DEMERITS OF A HOE

A hoe has the following demerits:

1. It is not as efficient as a power shovel.

2. It is slower in working especially when dumping into hauling units.
3. The extra weight of the boom to which the stick is hinged has to be lifted in each cycle.
4. The material is liable to fall off, while hoisting unless the bucket is pulled quite close to the boom before hoisting.

The best operation results are obtained when digging is done close to the track level and high dumping is not required.

20.20. HOE PRODUCTION

Hoe cycle times are about 20% longer in duration than those for similar sized shovel as the hoisting distance of hoe is greater as to dump the bucket material into the dumping unit, the boom and stick has to be fully extended. The optimum depth of cut for a hoe depends on the type of material to be excavated, size and type of bucket. As a rule the optimum depth of cut for a hoe usually should be 30 to 60% of the machine's maximum digging depth. In short same elements which affect the shovel production are also applicable to hoe excavation operations. The working and clearance of hoe is shown in Fig. 20.12.

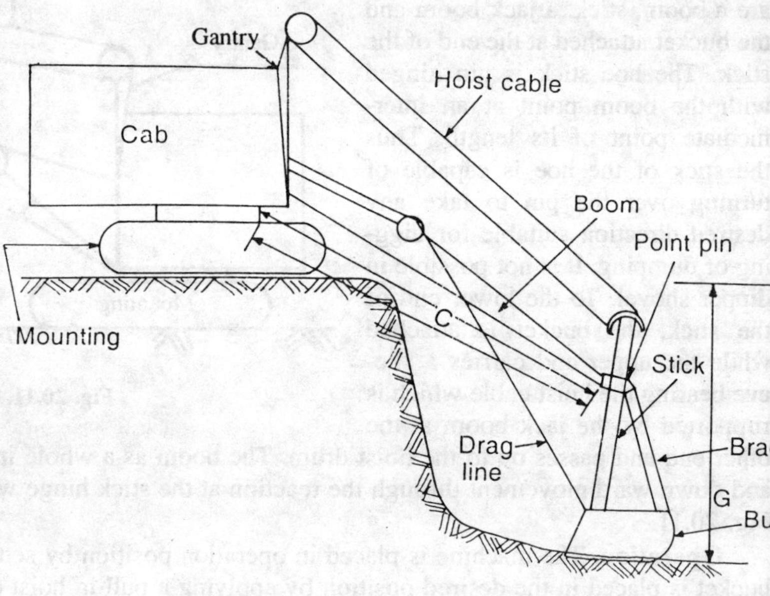

Fig. 20.12. Hoe clearance diagram

When a hoe is used to dig at moderate depth, the output is about the same that of a power shovel of comparable size and digging in the same class of material.

However as the depth is increased, the output of the hoe will decrease considerably. The most effective digging action takes place when the dipper stick and boom are at right angles. The greatest output is obtained when the digging is done near the machine. The dimensions and clearances for hoes are shown in Table 20.3.

Table 20.3. Dimension and clearance for hoes

Size of dipper or bucket in m^3/lit.	*Length of boom m*	*Length of stick m*	*Max. digging radius m*	*Max. digging depth m*	*Radius at in m*		*Clearance under dipper in m*	
					Beginning of dump	*End of dump*	*Beginning of dump*	*End of dump*
0.287 m^3 (3/8 cu.yds.)	4.2 – 4.5	1.8 – 2.4	6.9 – 7.5	3.3 – 3.6	2.4 – 3.0	5.1 – 5.4	2.7 – 3.0	4.5 – 5.1
0.383 m^3 (1/2 cu. yds)	4.8 – 5.1	1.8 – 2.4	7.8 – 8.1	4.5 – 5.4	2.4 – 3.0	5.7 – 6.6	2.7 – 3.3	4.5 – 5.4
0.574 m^3 (3/4 cu. yds.)	4.8 – 6.0	2.1 – 2.7	8.4 – 10.0	5.1 – 6.6	2.4 – 3.9	6.0 – 8.1	3.0 – 3.6	4.8 – 6.6
1 m^3 (0.765 cu. yds.)	5.4 – 6.3	2.4 – 3.0	9.0 – 10.2	6.0 – 6.9	2.7 – 4.2	6.6 – 8.7	3.6 – 4.2	5.4 – 7.8
1.148 m^3 (1½cu. yds.)	6.6 – 7.8	2.7 – 3.3	10.8 – 12.6	7.5 – 8.4	3.9 – 4.5	8.4 – 9.6	4.2 – 4.8	8.1 – 9.0
1.34 m^3 (1¾ cu. yds.)	7.2 – 8.1	2.7 – 3.6	11.4 – 12.9	7.8 – 8.7	4.2 – 4.8	8.7 – 10.0	4.5 – 5.1	8.4 – 9.3

20.21. TRENCHING MACHINES

These machines are designed strictly for one work application such as trench digging. These machines are known as trencher. These machines are designed for excavating trenches or ditches of considerable length and varying depths and widths. These machines are satisfactory for digging utility trenches for water, gas and oil pipe lines, telephone cables, drainage ditches and sewers where the soil and job conditions permit their use. These machines provide relatively fast digging with positive control on depths and widths of the trenches which reduce the expensive hand finishing to a minimum. These machines are capable of digging in any type of soil except rocks. These machines are available in various sizes for digging trenches of varying depths and widths. Usually they are crawler mounted which increases their stability and distribute its weight over a greater area.

Most of the work is not wider than 60 cms and about 2.0 m deep. The horse power of 95% of trenchers vary from 40 to 150 h.p. These machines are also satisfactory for digging shoulder drains on highways in addition to utility trenches. Larger machines may be used for laying large diameter cross country pipe lines for water and sewage system, main distribution lines. Larger machines have h.p over 340. These machines are fully hydrostatic having self leveling tracks. A vertical trench can be maintained on an un even terrain having slope upto 18.5%.

20.22. TYPES OF TRENCHING MACHINES

Trenching machines may be classified into two categories as follows:

1. Wheel type trenching machine. These machines are available with maximum cutting depth exceeding 2.4m (8 ft.) and trench width varying from 30 cms to 150 cms. Many of the available machines have 25 or more than 25 digging speeds to allow selection of the most suitable speed for almost all job conditions.

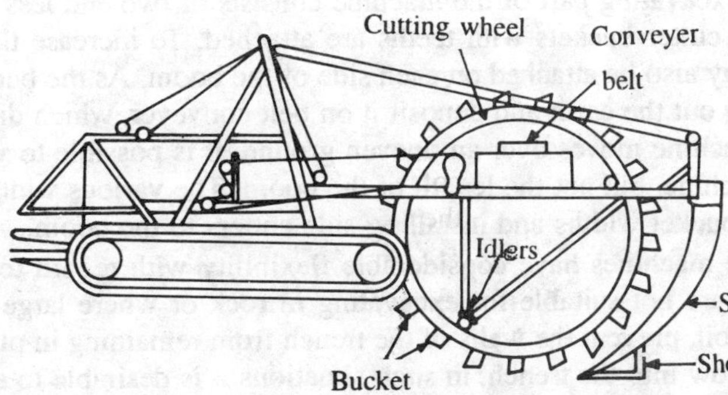

Fig. 20.13. Wheel Type Ditcher or Trencher

The excavating part of the machine consists of a power driven wheel on which a number of removable buckets equipped with cutter teeths are attached. The buckets are available in varying widths. When it is necessary to increase the width of the trench, the side cutters may be attached to the width of the bucket. The machine is operated by lowering the rotating wheel to the desired depth, while the unit moves forward slowly. The earth is picked up by the buckets and deposited on an end less belt conveyer that can be adjusted to discharge the earth on either side of the trench.

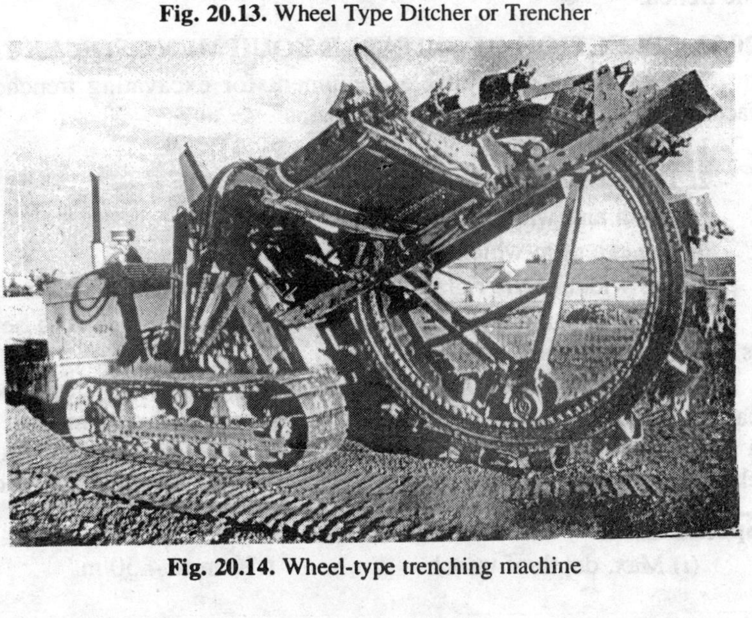

Fig. 20.14. Wheel-type trenching machine

Wheel type machines are especially suitable for excavating trenches for water, gas and oil pipe lines, burried telephone cables and pipe drains placed in relatively shallow trenches. They can also be used for excavating trenches for sewer pipes upto the maximum depth of digging of the machine. A diagram of a wheel trencher is shown in Fig. 20.13 and photograph in Fig. 20.14.

Specifications

(*i*) Maximum depth of trench	:	1.65 m to 2.55 m (1.65, 1.80 and 2.55 m)
(*ii*) Trench width	:	37.5 cms to 198 cms [37.5, 45, 62.0, 70, 75, 100, 129]
(*iii*) Engine horse power	:	55 hp to 110 hp or 41 to 82 kw (41, 50, 82 kw)
(*iv*) Weight of machine	:	6.820 metric tonnes to 28.2 tonnes
(*v*) Wheel speed	:	0.18 to 1.23 m/sec
(*vi*) Travel speed	:	0.8 to 3.1 km/hour
(*vii*) Digging speed	:	0.06 to 0.42 m per minute

2. Ladder type trenching machine

The boom or ladder length of these machines may be extended by installing extensions to them. Further by adding more buckets and chain links, it is possible to dig trenches more than 9.0 m (30 ft.) deep and more than 3.6 m in width with large machines. The boom length of most of these machines may be varied, permitting a single machine to be used on trenches varying considerably in depth. This eliminates the need of having large number of machines for each depth range. A machine may have 30 or more digging speeds to suit the needs of a given job.

The excavating part of the machine consists of two end less chains that travel along the boom. To this boom the cutter buckets with teeths are attached. To increase the width of the trench shaft mounted side cutters may also be attached on each side of the boom. As the buckets travel up the under side of the boom, they bring out the earth and deposit it on belt conveyer, which discharges it along either side of the trench. As the machine moves over an uneven ground, it is possible to vary the depth of cut by adjusting position of the machine, but not the length of the boom. The various widths of the trench may be obtained by using different bucket widths and installing side cutters to the boom.

These machines have considerable flexibility with regard to trench width and depths. However these machines are not suitable for excavating in rock or where large quantity of ground water combined with unstable soil, prevent the walls of the trench from remaining in place. If the soil, such as loose sand or mud, tends to flow into the trench, in such situations it is desirable to adopt some other method of excavation of the trench.

20.23. SELECTION OF SUITABLE EQUIPMENT FOR EXCAVATING TRENCHES

The choice of the suitable equipment for excavating trenches will be influenced by the following factors:

1. The job condition
2. The class of soil
3. Depth and width of the trench
4. The extent to which the ground water is present
5. The width of the right of way for disposal of excavated material.

If in a firm soil a relatively shallow and narrow trench is to be excavated then the wheel type machine is the most suitable.

If the soil is rocky, that requires blasting, then hoe will be the most suitable excavating machine. In case the soil is unstable and water saturated, a hoe or a clam shell may be used and let the walls establish a stable slope. If it is necessary to install the solid sheeting to hold the walls in place then either a hoe or clam shell may be selected, which can excavate in between the trench braces that hold the sheeting in place.

Specifications

(*i*) Max. depth of trench : 1.20 m to 4.50 m

(*ii*) Trench width : 0.15 m to 1.37 m
(*iii*) Power of the engine : 47 to 90 h.p.
(*iv*) Bucket speed : 1.24 to 2.72 m/sec.
(*v*) Travel speed : 1.1 to 2.7 kmph
(*vi*) Digging speed : 0.67 to 4.75 m/min.
(*vii*) Weight of the machine : 2.7 metric tonne to 18.2 tonnes

20.24. DRAG LINES

The drag line is a multipurpose (versatile) machine, capable of a wide range of operations. It can handle a wide range of materials from soft to medium hard material. It has derived its name from its prominent operation of dragging the bucket against the material to be excavated or dug. A drag line has a long light crane boom. The digging bucket with the teeths is attached loosely to the boom through cable as shown in Fig. 20.15. Due to its construction a drag line can dig and dump the excavated material over long distances, which is known as its long reach of digging and dumping. As it has long reach due to its long boom, it is not necessary to place the machine near the pit or to go into the pit to be excavated. Due to its long boom it can handle digging of wet material or under water digging standing on the firm soil from the pit. Secondly a drag line digs below its track level and can handle soft material only for best performance. A drag line does not have the positive digging force of power shovel or hoe. The bucket's filling force or (break out) force is derived from is own weight. Thus it bounce, tip over or drift side ways when it encounters a hard material. These shortcomings have been noticed particularly in smaller machines and light weight buckets.

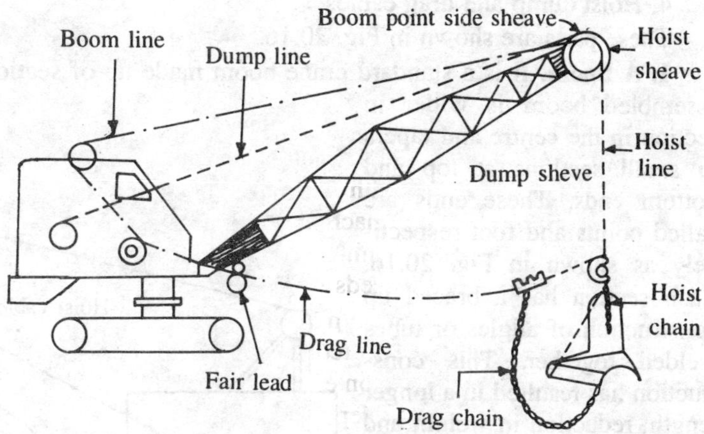

Fig. 20.15. Line Diagram of Dragline

Drag lines are used to excavate material and dump it into hauling units as trucks, or tractor pulled trollies or deposit it near the pit of excavation. A drag line usually not required to go into the pit or hole to excavate, it can operate on natural ground adjacent to the pit while excavating the material from the pit. This is very advantageous when earth is to be removed from a canal, ditch, or pit containing water. If the material is hauled by trucks, then these trucks need not to go into the pit and maneuver through the mud. If possible, it is better to position the haul units in the pit, positioning the haul units below the drag line will reduce the hoist time of the machine which will result in increased production. Due to the long boom of a drag line, it is possible to dispose off the excavated material in one operation if the material can be deposited along the canal or near the pit. This will eliminate the requirements of hauling units, reducing the cost of handling material. The greatest advange of a drag line over the other machines of the shovel family is its long reach for digging and dumping.

20.25. CLASSIFICATION OF DRAG LINES

Drag lines may be classified into the following categories:

1. Crawler mounted drag lines
2. Wheel mounted drag lines
3. Truck mounted drag lines
4. Walking drag lines

1. Crawler mounted drag lines. Crawler mounted drag lines can operate on surfaces which are very soft for wheel or truck mounted machines, but their speed of travel is very slow, usually less than 1.5 kmph.

The less speed nececiates the use of auxiliary hauling equipment to transport these machines from one job to an other job, especially when the distance is great. Wheel and truck mounted units may travel at a speed of about 50 kmph. Walking drag line has been discussed in next article.

20.26. BASIC PARTS OF DRAG LINE

The front end of the drag line consists of the following parts:

1. A boom
2. A bucket
3. A fair lead
4. Hoist dump and drag cables

These parts are shown in Fig. 20.16.

1. A Boom. It is a standard crane boom made up of sections of suitable lengths bolted together. The assembled boom is wider in section in the centre and tapers to small sections at top and bottom ends. These ends are called points and foot respectively as shown in Fig. 20.16. Each section has a braced up construction of angles or tubes welded together. This construction has resulted in a longer length, reduction in weight and maintaining sufficient structural strength.

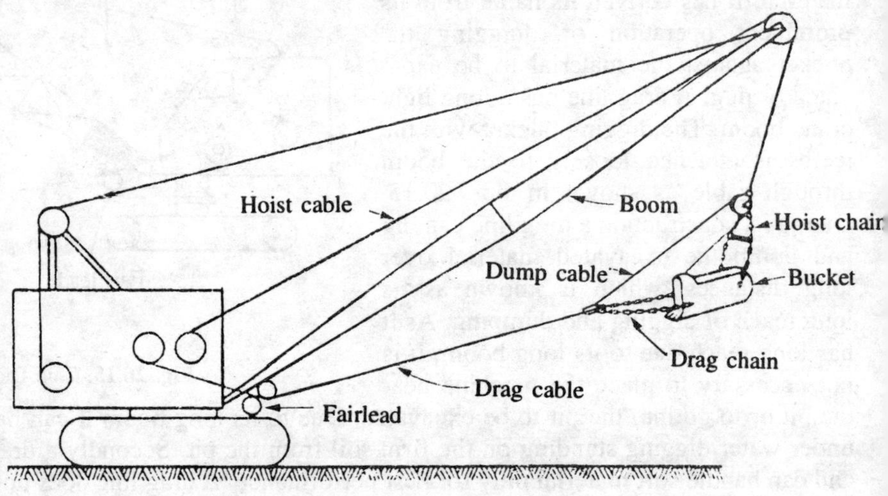

Fig. 20.16. Basic parts of a dragline.

For some models, particularly for the walking drag line, the top sections of the boom have been made of aluminum to reduce the total boom weight and enable a longer boom construction or enable to increase the bucket size. It is attached to the deck with pins at the foot and supported at the point through the boom hoist cable passing over a pair of sheaves placed one on each side. A central sheave at the boom point carries the bucket hoist cable. The boom is generally set at an angle of 30° to 40° to the vertical while working.

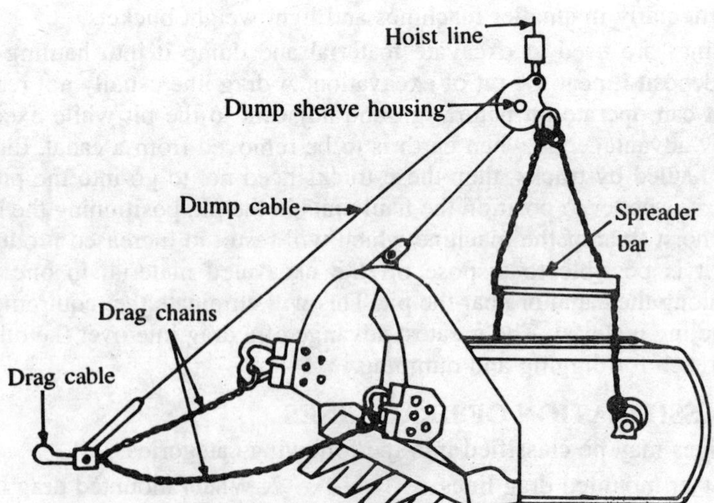

Fig. 20.17. Dragline Bucket

2. Bucket. As shown in Fig. 20.17, it is a steel box, open at top and front. The cutting teeths are fifted to the lower front edge pointing towards the machine. Two sets of chains are attached to the bucket. One set of chains known as drag chains is attached to the front and the second set of chains called hoist chains is attached to the rear. The drag chains terminate in a drag yoke to which a drag cable is anchored. The hoist chains end at the hoist line socket which takes the hoist cable. A dump cable is stretched between the bucket front and the drag yoke passing over a dump sheave which is supported by the hoist lines through a socket attached to the sheave case. Thus bucket is controlled in three ways by (*i*) the hoist, (*ii*) the drag, (*iii*) the dump. The dump is used to turn the bucket up side down, teeths pointing downwards, for dumping excavated material or for making impact with the ground. The digging range can be extended beyond the true swing radius by skillful operation of the bucket.

20.27. OPERATION OF A DRAG LINE

The drag line is operated for excavation work by swinging the empty bucket to the digging position by releasing both the hoist and drag cables, till it rests on the ground with teeth digging into the earth. By adjusting the pull on the two cables, it is possible to make use of momentum to drop the bucket beyond the true radius of the boom. For both hoist and drag cables, separate drums on the basic crane unit are available, so that they can be coordinated into a smooth operation. To fill the earth in the bucket while in horizontal position the hoist cable is slackened slightly and the drag pull is applied. It is then hoisted. The pull in hoist and the drag cables is so adjusted that the bucket has no tendency to dump during the hoist and swing operation. When the required dumping height is attained, the boom is swung to the position of dumping and drag brake is released. In this way the excavated material from the bucket is dumped into a hauling unit. The boom is then swung back to the digging position and the same cycle of operation is repeated.

It is more difficult to control the accuracy of dumping of a drag line compared to a power shovel. Hence to reduce the spillage of dumping material from a drag line, it is desirable to use larger hauling units in case of drag lines. The capacity of the hauling unit may be five to six times the capacity of the drag line bucket.

20.28. OUTPUT OF A DRAG LINE

The output of a drag line is found to vary with the following factors:

1. Type of material to be excavated
2. Depth of cut
3. Angle of swing of the drag line (the swing angle may be 45°, 90°, 135° and 180°).
4. Size and type of bucket
5. Length of boom
6. Method of disposal or loading haul units
7. Size of the haul units used
8. Skill of the operator
9. Physical condition of the machine
10. Job conditions.

20.29. SIZE OF A DRAG LINE

The size of a drag line is indicated by the size of the bucket, generally expressed in cubic yards. It is same as the size of dipper shovel bucket. How ever most drag lines may handle more than one size bucket, depending on the length of the boom and the material to be excavated. As the maximum lifting capacity of a drag line is limited by the force which will tilt the machine over. it is necessary to reduce the size of the bucket when a long boom is used or the material has a high specific gravity. In practice the combined weight of the bucket and the load should produce a tilting force not greater than 75% of the force required to tilt the machine. When it is necessary to increase the digging reach or the dumping radius a longer boom with small bucket should be used. In case the material is difficult to excavate, then smaller buckets should be used. When operating a drag line boom may be angled relatively low, but an angle less than 35 degree from horizontal is not advisable. Usually bucket capacity may range from 0.95 to 1.912 m^3.

20.30. OPTIMUM DEPTH OF CUT

The output of a drag line is maximum when it is allowed to work at the optimum depth. The ideal out put of short boom draglines working at optimum depth and 90° swing are shown in Table 20.4.

Table 20.4. Optimum depth of cut and ideal output of short boom dragline at 90° swing

S. No.	*Size of Bucket →* *Class of material ↓*	*0.29 m^3 (3/8 cu yd)*	*0.38 m^3 (1/2 cu yd)*	*0.57 m^3 (3/4 cu yd)*	*0.765 m^3 (1 cu yd)*	*0.956 m^3 ($1\frac{1}{4}$ cu yd)*	*1.15 m^3 ($1\frac{1}{2}$ cu yd)*	*1.34 m^3 ($1\frac{3}{4}$ cu yd)*	*1.53 m^3 (2.0 cu yd)*	*1.93 m^3 ($1\frac{1}{2}$ cu yd)*
1.	Moist Loam of Light sandy clay	1.5 53	1.7 72	1.8 99	2.0 122	2.1 149	2.2 168	2.4 187	2.5 202	2.6 233
2.	Sand and Graval	1.5 49	1.7 69	1.8 95	2.0 118	2.1 141	2.2 160	2.4 180	2.5 195	2.6 225
3.	Good common earth	1.8 42	2.0 57	2.4 81	2.5 104	2.6 127	2.7 147	2.8 162	3.0 177	32 204
4.	Hard tough clay	2.2 27	2.7 42	2.7 69	2.8 85	3.1 104	3.3 123	3.5 139	3.6 150	3.8 172
5.	Wet sticky clay	2.2 15	2.5 23	2.7 42	2.8 58	3.1 73	3.3 85	3.5 100	3.6 112	3.8 135

Note. 1st row shows values of optimum depth in metres.
2nd row shows ideal output in cubic metres.

20.31. WALKING DRAG LINES

These machines are used to handle more load. The capacity of the bucket of a walking drag line is 3 m^3 and more. If the capacity of crawler drag lines is increased more than 3 m^3, then the weight of the machine increases and the crawler tractor system becomes expensive to construct and maintain the pressure on the ground under the track with in limits. Thus to use the large machines on softer grounds, the crawler system has been replaced by a walking mechanism.

20.31.1. Walking mechanism

The walking mechanism consists of a turn table mounted on a flat round cylinder called the 'tub'.

The hub is flanked on two sides by the two walking shoes. These shoes are lifted above or brought in contact with the ground with the help of a pair of rotating lugs on the sides of the machine and worked with a common rotating shaft. The centre of gravity of the machine is kept slightly forward of the driving shaft, so that when the shoes come in contact with the ground and take up the load of the machine, the rear portion of the machine only be lifted clear off the ground. Normally the shoes remain in lifted position while the machine is working. As the movement of the lugs is continued, the front is dragged and a step is taken. The movement of

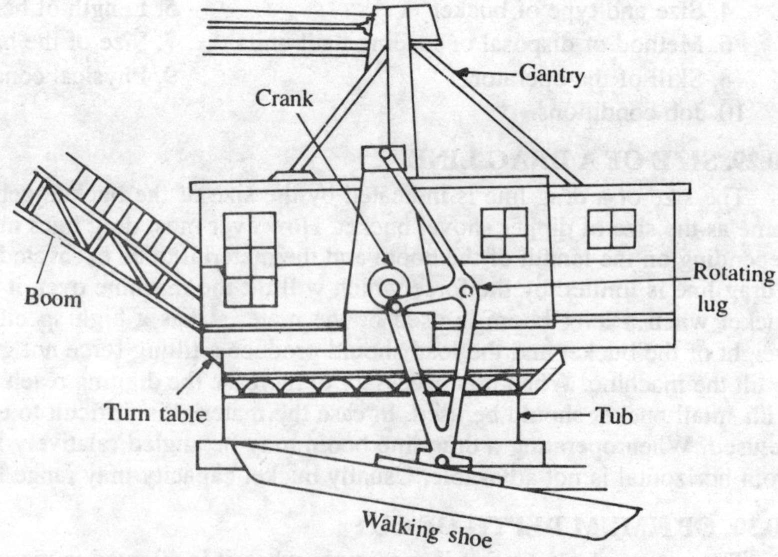

Fig. 20.18. Structure of a Walking Dragline Taking a step

the machine is very similar to that of a man walking on a pair of crutches. That is why it is called a walking drag line. The machine always moves opposite to the direction pointed by the boom. Steering being effected by revolving the body to a position opposite to the desired direction of the movement. A walking drag line diagram is shown in Fig. 20.18.

The walking operation of this machines is very simple. When it is desired to move the machine to a new location, the boom is rotated to a position opposite the direction of movement. The two shoes on each side of the revolving frame are lowered by an eccentric cam until most of the weight of the machine is supported by the shoes, and the base is lifted off the ground. As the cam continues to rotate, the machine is dragged backward several metres and the operation is repeated till the machine reaches its new location.

20.31.2. Specifications

Length of the boom in m	:	45 to 58 m
Maximum allowable load in kg	:	1660 to 12050 kg
Size of the bucket in m^3	:	5.4 m^3 to 3.83 m^3
Angle of boom in deg	:	25 to 35 deg
Dumping height in m	:	15.5 to 32 m
Dumping reach in m	:	38 to 58 m
digging reach under boom point	:	42.5 to 58.25 m
Digging depth in favourable condition	:	23.7 to 40.0 m

20.31.3. Advantages

Walking drag line has several advantages over crawler type drag line. The size of walking drag lines is large. It has long booms and large working ranges. Its design also is simple, and simple maneurverability, low soil pressures under the base. As its boom is large, it can be used for stripping over burden to permit open pit coal mining, for the construction of canals and levees, removal of materials from rivers, striping of over burden etc. Excavation and its disposal frequently be achieved in one operation, eliminating the need of hauling units. The soil pressure under the base of a walking machine varies from 0.3 kg/cm^2 to 0.75 kg/cm^2 (4 to 10 PSi). Hence it gives good stability, when operating on soft materials. A 7.65 m^3 machine fitted with a 49 m long boom is capable of giving 382 m^3 excavation per hour in ordinary soil. An increase of 10% in boom length and in bucket capacity by 15% may be possible if upper sections of boom are made of lighter material as that of aluminium instead of steel.

20.32. CLAM SHELLS

The name of this machine is derived from the shape of its bucket. The shape of the bucket is that of a shell fish with a hinged double shell, which can be opened into two parts. The front end of the machine essentially is that of crane. The bucket is hung from a lattice boom crane through cables as in the case of a drag line. The bucket consists of two shells or halves which are hinged at the top as shown in Fig. 20.19 At the bottom the bucket is provided with sharp edge or teeth. The clam shell can not be operated away from a jib boom. Clam shell drum leggings may be the same as that of a crane or may be changed as per requirement of the speed and pull of the clam shell.

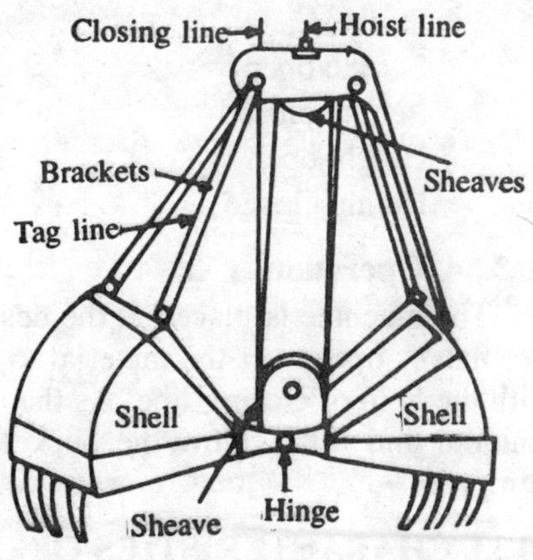

Fig. 20.19. Bucket of clamshell

The long boom of the clam shell is supported by the boom cables passing over two side sheaves at the point as in the case of a drag line. There are two central sheaves also at the point over which the bucket hoist line and the closing lines pass. The two shells of the bucket are hinged together at the top inner ends while the outer ends are joined together through brackets terminating at the bucket hoist line connection. Between these two connections the digging or closing cable is reeved over the sheaves. Finally this cable emerges at the hoist connection and passes over the boom point sheave. A tag line runs from the boom to the bucket and helps to keep the bucket steady so that it does not spin and twist.

20.32.1. Bucket

The bucket is shown in Fig. 20.19. The selection of the bucket of a clamshell depends largely on the requirement of the job as in the case of a drag line. It consists of two shells or halves which are hinged at the top and provided with sharp edge or teeth at the lower end. Clam shell buckets are available in various sizes *i.e.* heavy duty types for digging, in hard soils, medium weight for general purpose work, and light weight type for handling the light materials.

A heavy bucket with sharp cutting edge may be used for digging hard soils, while a light bucket with comparatively plane edges may be used for handling light materials. The clam shell bucket often is useful for lifting heavy rock pieces due to the effective grip of the jaws. Some times the shape of clam shell bucket is made as a set of tongs with more than two jaws for lifting large sized pieces of rock.

20.32.2. Capa city

The capacity of a clam shell bucket usually is given in cubic yards (1 cubic yard = 0.765 m^3). A more accurate capacity is given as follows:

(*a*) **Water level capacity.** Generally it is given in cubic feet. This capacity is defined as the capacity of the bucket, if it were hung level and filled with water.

(*b*) **Plate line capacity.** It indicates the capacity of the bucket following a line along the tops of the clams.

(*c*) **Heaped capacity.** It is the capacity of the bucket when it is filled to the maximum angle of repose for the given material. For specifying the heaped capacity usually the value of angle of repose is taken as 45°.

Deck area. The area in square feet covered by the bucket when it is fully open is known as deck area of bucket.

20.32.3. Specification of the buckets

(*a*) Capacity of bucket: 0.288 m^3 (3/8 cu. yards) to 1.9125 m^3 (2.5 cu. yards)

(*i*) Water line. It varies from 0.2265 m^3 (8 cft) to 1.472 (52 cubic feet)

(*ii*) Plate line. It varies from 0.331 m^3 (11 cft) to 2.1345 m^3 (75.4 cft)

(*iii*) Heaped. It varies from 0.368 m^3 (13 cf) to 2.55 m^3 (90 cft)

Weight	:	755.5 kg to 3534 kg
Deck area	:	1.3 m^2 to 4.38 m^2
Length open	:	172.5 cm to 300 cms
Length closed	:	144.0 cms to 279.4 cms
Height open	:	214.0 cms to 392.6 cms
Height closed	:	173.5 cms to 312.0 cms

20.32.4. Operation

The machine is placed at the desired level. For digging or filling operation the bucket is lowered with two halves open over the material to be dug till a good contact is made with the material. Now it is closed with the help of closing line. As the two halves close in, the weight of the bucket enables it to dig into the material and fill it. Now the bucket is hoisted and swung to the position of dumping and the material dumped.

20.33. CHARACTERISTICS OF CLAM SHELL

A clam shell has most of the characteristics of a drag line and some of the crane. It can be used for digging loose, soft and medium hard materials only such as sand, gravel, crushed stone, coal etc. It can also be used for removing materials from inside the coffer dams, pier foundations, sewers, manholes, sheet lined trenches etc.

A clam shell is a very useful machine when the operation is required in a vertical plane and placement of material needs precision such a loading and hauling unit or filling material into a bin, digging pits, building stock piles, and foundations etc. It can dig at, above or below its level. If it is used as a grapple (holding unit). it can lift large sized rocks and boulders and no chaining is required.

In short it can be said that a clam shell can be used for most of the jobs where other shovel family machines can be used. However in some applications it is not found very efficient due to its slower operation.

20.34. EFFECTIVE USE OF CLAM SHELL

For the efficient use of a clam shell unit, following points should be observed.

1. The unit should be placed on level ground.
2. The distance of unit from digging and dumping places should be equal. It will avoid wastage of time in lowering or raising the boom.
3. While working in soft materials the teeth of the bucket should be removed.

20.35. COMPARATIVE STUDY OF DIFFERENT TYPE OF EXCAVATING MACHINES

The comparative advantages of different type of excavating machines are shown in tabular form in Table 20.5 below.

Table 20.5. Comparision of different excavating machines

S. No.	*Items or point of comparision*	*Shovel family excavators*			
		Dipper shovel	*Drag line*	*Hoe*	*Clam shell*
1.	Operation in hard soil or rocks	Good	Not good	Good	Poor
2.	Operation in wet soil or mud	Poor	Moderately good	Poor	Moderately good
3.	Distance between digging and footing	Small	Long	Small	Long
4.	Efficiency in loading hauling units	Very good	Moderately good	Good	Precise but slow
5.	Digging level	Digs at or above footing level	Digs below footing level	Digs below footing level	Digs at, above or below footing level
6.	Cycle time	Short	More than shovel	Slightly more than shovel	More than other machines

20.36. LOADERS

A loader is a versatile machine designed to excavate at or above track or wheel level. It consists of a frame mounted on crawler tracks, a cutting blade, molboard plow, conveyor chute, conveyer belt and an engine to operate the belt. It is pulled by one or two crawler tractors depending on the class of material loaded. The over all width of cutting edge is about 3000 cms and the maximum cutting depth is 120 cms. The best cutting results are obtained when the cutting section has an area of about 0.36 m^2. It is used extensively in construction work to handle and transport bulk material, such as earth and rock, to excavate earth and load it into hauling units, to charge aggregate bins at concrete plant etc. The performance of this machine is best when working in long and relatively level barrow pits or cuts such as on high way projects. A loader can make an 180° turn in about 12.0 m (37 ft.) distance. The hydraulic activated lifting system exerts maximum break out force with an upward motion of the bucket. It does not need any other equipment to level or cleanup the area in which it has been working.

A tractor pusher can be converted into a tractor loader by providing a slightly longer pushing arms running between the front wheels or between the tracks suitably crossed braced as shown in Fig. 20.20. A bucket is attached to the arms at the front ends. The bucket can be raised, lowered and dumped by mechanical or hydraulic controls. Front attachment of a tractor loader is shown in Fig. 20.20.

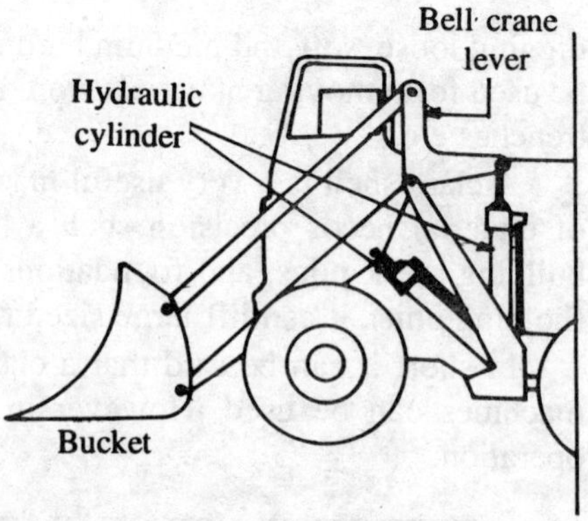

Fig. 20.20. Front Attachment of a tractor loader

20.37. CLASSIFICATION OF LOADERS

The loaders can be classified into two categories as follows:

1. Wheel tractor mounted loader. Wheel loaders are excellent machines for soft to medium hard materials, but their production decreases rapidly when used in medium to hard materials. For high efficiency a loader should be able to reach over the side of the hauling unit or truck's dump bed. A wheel loader attains its highest production rate when working in flat and smooth surfaced areas with enough space for maneuvering. In poor underfoot conditions or situations with little space to maneuver its use is not advisable.

Wheel loaders work in repetitive cycles, constantly reversing direction, loading, turning and dumping. The production rate of a wheel loader depends upon the following factors.

1. Time required to load the bucket, maneuver with four reversals of direction and dump the load.
2. Time required to travel from the loading to the dumping position.
3. Time required to return to the loading position.
4. The actual volume of material hauled during each trip.

20.37.1. Operating specifications of a wheel loader

Engine flywheel h.p.	:	119 at 2300 rpm
Speed forward and reverse Low	:	0 to 6.25 kmph
Intermediate	:	0 to 17.8 kmph
High	:	0 to 47.2 kmph
Operating load	:	3091 kg
Tipping load (straight ahead)	:	7909 kg
Tipping load full turn	:	7636.4 kg
Lifting capacity	:	8455 kg
Break out force Maximum	:	13636.5 kg

20.37. 2. Crawler tractor mounted loader

The speed of crawler loaders is less, but they can be used on soft spots as well as on hard spots. To increase the stability of the loader during load lifting, the tracks of crawler loader usually are provided longer and wider than tractors.

20.38. BUCKETS FOR LOADERS/ATTACHMENTS

The most common attachments of a loader are a shovel type bucket and a fork lift. The hydraulic system of the loader provides necessary control for operating these attachments.

20.38.1. Types of buckets

The loader buckets may be classified into the following three categories.

1. General purpose bucket. It is the most common type of bucket made of one piece of all welded steel. It is a heavy duty bucket. The replaceable cutting edge or teeth are bolted on the bucket itself. These replaceable teeth or cutting edge are provided for excavation for medium type materials.

2. Multipurpose bucket. It is a segmented (two piece) hinged jawed bucket made of heavy duty all welded steel. It is also provided with replaceable bolted cutting edges. These replaceable edges are provided for excavation of medium hard materials. The two piece bucket provides capabilities not available in one piece bucket. This bucket enables the loader to be used as dozer and to grab material.

3. Rock bucket. This bucket is a heavy duty bucked made of one piece. It has a hung or protruding V shaped cutting edge. This edge can be used to penetrate beneath the rock and loosening shot rock.

4. Fork lift. It is attached to the loader in place of a bucket. It is made of steel with two movable parts as those of a fork. It is designed for handling materials.

5. Others type of buckets. Followings are the other types of buckets and attachments:

(*a*) Side dump buckets. These buckets are found useful in cramped situations, where working space is very limited.

(*b*) Plow blades for removal of snow etc.

(*c*) Brush rakes for clearing applications.

(*d*) Heavy duty sweepers, demolition buckets, front booms etc.

QUESTIONS

1. Explain the term shovel.
2. Discuss the advantages of hydraulically operated power shovels.
3. Discuss the basic parts of a power shovel.
4. What factors govern the size of a power shovel.
5. Write the factors which affect the production of a shovel.
6. What is a hoe? Discuss its basic parts and operation.
7. Discuss the merits and demerits of a hoe.
8. What are trenching machines? Discuss ladder type trenching machine.
9. What is a drag line? Give its basic parts.
10. Discuss the operation of a drag line.
11. Give the mechanism of a waling drag line.
12. Discuss the characteristics of a clam shell.
13. Describe the construction and working of a clam shell bucket.
14. Write a note on the clam shell.
15. Give the comparative advantages and disadvantages of various excavating machines.

OBJECTIVE TYPE QUESTIONS

1. Power shovel can be used for excavation of all types of soils except...

(*a*) Loose soil (*b*) Clay

(*c*) Loam (*d*) Solid Rocks

(*e*) Gravel

2. Identify the incorrect statement/statements

(*a*) Shovels can be mounted on crawler track as well as on wheel tyres

(*b*) Wheel tyred mounted shovels have high travel speeds and are useful for small jobs

(*c*) Wheel tyred mounted shovels can be used on soft patches of low bearing capacity roads.

(*d*) Wheel tyred mounted shovels can be used where high speed of traveling is necessary and the road surface and ground are firm.

(*e*) The crawler mounted shovels exert low soil pressures on ground

3. The basic parts of a shovel are

(*a*) Mounting (*b*) Cab

(*c*) Boom (*d*) Bucket

(*e*) Hoist line (*f*) All of the above

4. The production of power shovel depends except
   (*a*) Nature of the soil (*b*) Depth of cut
   (*c*) Speed of machine (*d*) Angle of swing
   (*e*) Efficiency of operation
5. Power shovels can be used for
   (*a*) Stripping over burden (*b*) Digging cuts on road works
   (*c*) Below ground level (*d*) Digging for road side berms
   (*e*) Coal mining (*f*) All the above
6. A HOE is known by the names except
   (*a*) Back hoe (*b*) Push shovel
   (*c*) Pull shovel (*d*) Back shovel
   (*e*) Crane
7. Hoes are superior for dinging in the situations except
   (*a*) Below machine base level trenches (*b*) Footings
   (*c*) Basement trenches (*d*) Above machine level
8. Identify the correct statements
   (*a*) A hoe exerts greater tooth pressure on soil than power shovel due to direct pull on the bucket
   (*b*) A hoe can dump material at higher level permitting the hauling units to stand at higher level
   (*c*) A Hoe is superior to a drag line in operating on close range works due to their rigidity
   (*d*) Hoe can also dig hard materials due to positive control on the crowding
   (*e*) All are correct
9. The basics part of a hoe are
   (*a*) A jack boom (*b*) Bucket
   (*c*) Boom (*d*) Stick
   (*e*) All the above
10. Trenchers are used for digging in soils except
    (*a*) Loams (*b*) Clays
    (*c*) Rocks (*d*) Loose soils
11. Trenchers are used for
    (*a*) Digging utility trenches for water, telephone cables, oil pipe lines etc.
    (*b*) Drainage and sewer trenches
    (*c*) Trenches of considerable length and varying depths and widths
    (*d*) For relatively fast digging
    (*e*) All are correct
12. Identify the incorrect statement/statements
    (*a*) A drag line derived its name from its mode of operation of dragging the bucket against the material to be excavated
    (*b*) A drag line has a very short and heavy crane boom
    (*c*) A drag line has a very long and light crane boom
    (*d*) The digging bucket is attached loosely to the boom through cables
    (*e*) The drag line should be placed near the pit to be excavated
    (*f*) A drag line can handle digging under water or wet material standing on the firm soil
    (*g*) A drag line can not dig below its track level and it can not handle soft materials
    (*h*) A drag line can dig below its track level and can handle soft material for best performance
13. Drag lines may be classified as
    (*a*) Crawler mounted drag lines (*b*) Wheel mounted drag lines
    (*c*) Truck mounted drag lines (*d*) Walking drag lines
    (*e*) All are correct
14. The out put of a drag line depends except
    (*a*) Type of material to be excavated (*b*) Depth of cut
    (*c*) Angle of swing (*d*) Speed of the machine

(*e*) Length of boom (*f*) Skill of the operator

15. Identify the incorrect statement/statements
    (*a*) Size and method of loading of haul units have no effect on the out put of a drag line
    (*b*) The capacity of the bucket of a walking drag line is more than ordinary drag line
    (*c*) The centre of gravity of the walking machine is kept slightly backward of the driving shaft
    (*d*) Normally the shoes of the walking drag line remain lifted from the ground
16. While moving a walking drag line, its boom is rotated to
    (*a*) In the direction of the motion (*b*) In the opposite direction of the motion
    (*c*) To the right direction of the motion (*d*) To the left direction of motion
17. Identify the incorrect statement/statements
    (*a*) A walking drag line has long booms and ranges than crawler mounted drag lines
    (*b*) The design and maneuvariability of walking drag lines are complicated than crawler mounted drag lines
    (*c*) Walking drag lines can be used for stripping over burden and open pit coal mining
    (*d*) Very high pressure develops under the base of a walking drag line
18. Identify the correct statements
    (*a*) The name of a clam shell machine is derived by the shape of its bucket
    (*b*) The shape of a clam shell is that of a shell fish, which can be opened into two parts
    (*c*) The front of a clam shell is essentially that of a crane
    (*d*) The bucket of a clam shell is hung from a lattice boom crane through cables
    (*e*) The two halves of the clam shell bucket are hinged at the top
    (*f*) All are correct
19. Identify the incorrect statement/statements
    (*a*) A clam shell can only be used for digging very hard rocks
    (*b*) A clam shell has some characteristics of a drag line and some that of a crane
    (*c*) Clam shell can be used for removing materials from inside of coffer dams, sever man holes, pier foundations and sheet line trenches etc.
    (*d*) A clam shall can not dig above and below its base level
    (*e*) It can be used as a grapple
    (*f*) While working in soft materials, the teeths of the bucket should be removed
20. Identify the correct statements
    (*a*) A clam shell is very useful machine when operation is required in vertical plane
    (*b*) A clam shell is very useful when the placement of material needs precision loading
    (*c*) In some applications clam shell in not found very efficient due to its slower operations
    (*d*) The weight of clam shell bucket varies from 755 kg to 353 4 kg
    (*e* All are correct
21. Identify the incorrect statement/statements
    (*a*) A loader can be used extensively in construction work to handle and transport bulk materials as earth and rock
    (*b*) The performance of a loader has been found better while working in long and relatively level borrow pits
    (*c*) A loader can make an 180° turn in about 12 m distance
    (*d*) A loader can not excavate above its wheel level
22. Identify the correct statements
    (*a*) Wheeled loaders are the excellent machines to be used to handle soft to medium hard materials
    (*b*) The production of wheeled loader increases while working in flat and smoothed surface areas with enough space for maneuvering
    (*c*) The stability of crawler loaders can be increased during load lifting by providing longer and wider treads than tractors
    (*d*) More than one type of buckets may be provided in a loader
    (*e*) All are correct
23. Identify the incorrect statement/statements
    (*a*) The digging action in a Hoe results from the drag of the bucket away from the machine
    (*b*) The digging action in a Hoe results from the drag or pull of the bucket towards the machine
    (*c*) The Hoe is found more advantageous for digging above the machine level

(*d*) The Hoe is found more advantageous for digging below the machine level

24. Identify the correct statement/statements
    (*a*) A Hoe has a goose neck boom which increases the depth of digging of the machine
    (*b*) A Hoe can be obtained by installing a bucket at the end of a shovel boom
    (*c*) The maximum depth of cutting of a hoe is 8.0 m
    (*d*) Hoes are designed for mobility and general purpose works
    (*e*) In some respects Hoes are found superior than trenching machines
    (*f*) All are correct
25. A Hoe can handle load in about ... radius
    (*a*) 4 m (*b*) 10 m
    (*c*) 15 m (*d*) 6 m
26. The over all width of cutting edge of a loader is about
    (*a*) 30.0 m (*b*) 42.0 m
    (*c*) 18.0 m (*d*) 45 m
27. The maximum cutting depth of a loader is
    (*a*) 0.75 m (*b*) 1.20 m
    (*c*) 2.5 m (*d*) 3.6 m
29. Identify the correct statement/statements
    (*a*) For effective use clam shell should be placed on level ground
    (*b*) Walking drag line can perform excavation and disposal of material in one operation
    (*c*) To control the accuracy of dumping of a drag line is more difficult than power shovel
    (*d*) The angle of swing of a shovel has marked influence on its production
    (*e*) All are correct

ANSWERS:

1. (*d*)	8. (*e*)	15. (*a, c*)	22. (*e*)
2. (*c*)	9. (*e*)	16. (*b*)	23. (*a, c*)
3. (*f*)	10. (*c*)	17. (*d*)	24. (*f*)
4. (*c*)	11. (*e*)	18. (*f*)	25. (*d*)
5. (*f*)	12. (*b, e, g*)	19. (*a, d*)	26. (*a*)
6. (*e*)	13. (*e*)	20. (*e*)	27. (*b*)
7. (*d*)	14. (*d*)	21. (*d*)	28. (*e*)

21

Earth Compaction Equipment

21.1. INTRODUCTION

Soil compaction is the process of removing entrapped air from the soil mass to make it more dense. The device used to remove air from soil mass is called compaction equipment. Though soil will compact itself naturally, but the process is very slow and it may take years together to reach a desired density. The object of compaction artificially is to achieve the required density quickly. The earliest recorded use of compaction can be found in the Roman Empire records of their road construction projects. They realized that compaction would improve the engineering properties of soil. Thus they used large cylindrical stone rollers to achieve mechanical densification of their road bases.

The main objective of compaction is not only to get the greater unit weight, but to improve the following properties of soil also.

1. To reduce or prevent settlement.
2. To increase the strength of the soil.
3. To improve the bearing capacity of the soil.
4. To control volume changes of soil.
5. To lower permeability of soil.

Though there are many methods of achieving desired properties of soil but the most widely used method is the compaction of soil at optimum water content.

21.2. TYPES OF COMPACTING EQUIPMENTS

The compaction of soil can be achieved by applying energy to the soil by any of the following methods.

1. By impact-sharp blows
2. By pressure-static weight
3. By vibration-shaking
4. By kneading-Rearranging soil particles

The effectiveness of different compaction methods depends on the type of soil being compacted. Appropriate compaction methods based on soil type are shown in Table 21.1.

Table 21.1. Showing appropriate compaction methods of soil Compaction

Material	*Impact*	*Pressure*	*Vibration*	*Kneading*
Gravel	Poor	No	Good	Very good
Sand	Poor	No	Excellent	Good
Silt	Good	Good	Poor	Excellent
Clay	Excellent with confinement	Very good	No	Good

21.3. TYPES OF AVAILABLE COMPACTING ROLLERS

1. Smooth wheeled rollers
2. Sheep foot rollers
3. Grid rollers
4. Tamping rollers
5. Smooth drum vibrating soil compactors
6. Pad drum vibrating soil compactors
7. Pneumatic-tired rollers

The principal method of compaction for various types of compactors is shown below in Table 21.2.

Table 21.2.

S. No.	*Type of compactor*	*Impact*	*Pressure*	*Vibration*	*Kneading*
1.	Sheep foot roller	√	×	√	√
2.	Tamping foot	×	×	√	√
3.	Vibrating smooth	×	√	×	√
4.	Vibrating pad foot	×	√	×	√
5.	Pneumatic	√	×	√	×

21.4. SELECTION OF COMPACTING EQUIPMENT BASED ON THE NATURE OF MATERIAL

The selection of compacting soil depends on the type of soil to be compacted. The type of compactor, number of passes and thickness of soil layer etc. are shown in the following Table 21.3.

Table 21.3. Compaction Equipment based on soil type

S. No.	*Material*	*Type of equipment*	*Thickness of lift in cms*	*No. of passes*	*Remark*
1.	Gravel	Vibratory pad foot	20 – 30	3 – 5	Foot pressure 10.5 to 14.0 kg/cm^2
		Vibratory smooth			—
		Pneumatic			Tyre pressure 2.45 to 9.1 kg/cm^2
		Sheep foot roller			Foot pressure 10.5 to 14.0 kg/cm^2
2.	Sand	Vibratory pad foot	20 – 25	3 – 5	—
		Vibratory smooth			—
		Pneumatic			Tyre pressure 2.45 to 4.55 kg/cm^2
		Smooth static			Tendom pressure 14 to 28 kg/cm^2
3.	Silt	Vibratory pad foot	15 – 20	4 – 8	Foot pressure 14 to 28 kg/cm^2
		Tamping foot			—
		Pneumatic			Tyre pressure 2.45 to 3.5 kgcm^2
		Sheep foot			Foot pressure 14 to 28 kg/cm^2
4.	Clay	Vibratory pad foot	10 – 15	4 – 6	Foot pressure 17.5 to 35 kg/cm^2
		Tamping foot			
		Sheep foot			Foot pressure 17.5 to 35 kg/cm^2

21.5. BRIEF DESCRIPTION OF DIFFERENT TYPES OF ROLLERS

1. Smooth wheel rollers. This type of rollers are useful for compaction of cohesive soils. These rollers usually contain three rollers. One in the front and two in the rear. The weight of such rollers varies from 5.5 tonnes to 24.0 tones. The rear wheel exerts an pressure of the order of 30 to 80 kg/cm^2 per cms of its length. This type of roller can be used to compact silt, sandy soil, sandy matiyar, low plastic soils etc. 10 cms to 15 cms thick layers of the above soils at optimum moisture content can be rolled easily. Standard proctor density of the soil can be obtained in 8 to 10 passes of the roller Fig. 21.1.

2. Sheep foot roller. This roller consists of a hollow drum. On the periphery of the drum, pads or projections of the shape of sheep's foot are attached. Due to the shape of these projections the roller is called sheep foot roller. To obtain the desired weight of the drum, it is filled with moist sand or stones.

Fig. 21.1. Smooth drum steel wheel roller compacting asphalt

Specifications of the sheep foot roller

For a medium roller, the specifications are as follows:

(*i*) Diameter of the drum	1.5 m
(*ii*) Length of the drum	1.5 m
(*iii*) Length of pad or projection	15 cms to 35 cms
(*iv*) Area of pad which comes in contact with soil	45 to 80 cm^2

Fig. 21.2. Sheepsfoot roller

(*v*) No. of projections — One projection per 265 cm^2 area of the surface
(*vi*) Pressure of pad or projection on soil — 0.15 to 0.3 kg/cm^2
(*vii*) Weight of the roller — About 35 tonnes
(*viii*) Speed of the roller — The speed of roller may be 6.4 to 9.6 kmph

This roller can be used to compact following soils:
(*a*) Silty sand and sandy clay (*b*) Clayey soils
(*c*) Medium and heavy clays

For satisfactory compaction by this roller the thickness of the soil layer should be kept upto 30 cms or length of the projection or pad plus 5 cms. For compacting 30 cms thick soil layer, 12 passes of the roller are sufficient. For 20 cms clay layer compaction, 6 to 10 passes have been found satisfactory.

As this roller tends to aerate the soil as it compacts it, it has been found ideally suitable for compacting soil which have moisture content above the acceptable moisture range. However this roller does not compact adequately the upper 5 to 8 cms thickness of the layer. Thus to compact this layer a lighter pneumatic tired or steel wheeled roller should follow the sheep foot roller if no further layer is to be placed or if it is the last layer to be compacted. (Fig. 21.2)

3. Grid rollers. This roller also works on the principle of sheep foot roller. In this roller an iron grid made of 4.0 cms diameter rods and having an effective area of 9 cm^2 which comes in contact of the soil to be compacted. Two roller are attached at the axle of the machine. In these rollers concrete blocks or rock pieces etc. can be put to increase the weight of the equipment. The total weight of the equipment is about 15.5 tonnes. This roller can be drawn by a tractor at a speed of 16 kmph.

4. Tamping rollers. The tamping or pressing foot rollers or compactors are high speed, self propelled and non vibrating rollers. Usually these rollers have four steel padded (with steel layers) wheels. Some times it is also equipped with a small block to level the layer of the soil. The pads are tappered with an oval or rectangular face. The pads are smaller at their face than at their base at the drum. As the tamping roller moves over the surface of the soil, the pads or feet penetrate into the soil and produce a kneading or pressing action and a pressure to mix the soil from bottom to top of the layer and compact it. With the repeated passes of the roller over the surface, the depth of penetration of the feet decreases till the roller walk out or pulls out of the fill. As the pads are tappered, a tamping foot roller may come out or walk out the fill with out spreading the soil. If the roller does not come out, in that ease either roller is too heavy or the soil is too wet and the roller is shearing the soil.

Generally 20 to 30 cms thick layer of soil can be compacted to the desired density in two to three passes of this roller. However the number of passes depends on the size of the roller. For poorly graded plastic silt or very fine clays four passes of the roller are needed for the desired density. The working speed of these rollers vary from 13 kmph to 19 kmph. This class of rollers has been found very effective to compact all types of soils except clean sands.

Similar to sheet foot rollers these rollers are also found not to compact effectively top 5 to 7.5 cms thick layer of soil. Hence to attain the desired density

Fig. 21.3. Self-propelled tamping roller with blade

an other device as smooth drum roller or pneumatic tired roller has to be used, if no other layer is to be added to it. Fig. 21.3. To get their true economical compaction potential they require long un interrupted passess so that the roller can build up its speed, which generates high production.

Vibrating Compactors. Vibrations create impact forces, which result in greater compacting power than an equivalent static load. Thus due to this fact, vibratory compactors are more economical than static load rollers. The impact forces are higher than static forces as the vibrating drum converts potential energy into kinetic energy. Vibrating compactors may have one or more drums. Single drum models usually have two rubber tire driving wheels.

Non cohesive soils such as sand, gravel, blasted rock etc. have been found compacted quite well with a combination of pressure and vibration. When these materials are vibrated, the particles shift their position and settle or rest more closely with the adjacent particles to increase the density of the mass.

The vibrating drum rollers are actuated by an eccentric shaft that produces the vibrating action. The eccentric shaft is a body that rotates about an axis other than the axis which passes through the centre of the mass. The vibrating mass (drum) is always isolated from the main frame of the roller. Normally vibrations vary from 1000 to 5000 per minute.

Vibration has two components. One amplitude, which measures the movement or throw and second is the frequency which indicates the rate of the movement or number of vibrations per second or per minute. The amplitude controls the effective area or depth to which the vibration is transmitted into the soil, where as frequency determines the number of blows that are transmitted in a period of time.

The impacts imparted by the vibrations produce pressure waves that set the soil particles in motion producing compaction in the soil. In compacting granular materials, usually frequency is a critical parameter in comparision to amplitude.

Compaction is a function of the frequency of the blows, force of the blows and the time period over which the blows are applied. Working speed of a frequency vibrating compactor is important as it indicates the time for which a particular part of fill is compacted. A working speed of 3.2 to 6.4 kmph of a vibratory compactor gives the best results.

Smooth Drum vibratory compactors

These compactors whether single or double drum models generate following three compactive forces.

1. Pressure
2. Impact
3. Vibrations

These rollers are most effective to compact granular materials with particle size ranging from fine sand to large rocks Fig. 21.4.

They can also be used to compact semi cohesive soils having upto about 10% material whose plastic index (PI) is 5 or more. Large steel drum vibrating rollers can be effective on rock layers or lifts upto 90 cms thickness.

Padded drum vibratory compactors

Soils having upto 50% material whose plastic index (PI) is 5 or more can be compacted with the help of padded drum vibrating compactors. These units can compact cohesive soil layers ranging from 30 to 45 cms thickness. These pads

Fig. 21.4. Smooth drum vibratory soil compactor

are capable to come out of the layer with out spreading the soil. Some times these units are equipped with a levelling blade also. (Fig. 21.5)

Small vibratory rollers having width varying from 60 cms to 95 cms are also available, which are specially suitable for working in confined areas or trench work. The drums of these rollers extend beyond the sides of the roller body, which help to compact area adjacent to the trench walls.

Fig. 21.5. Padded drum vibratory soil compactor with a leveling blade

Pneumatic tired rollers

These are surface rollers and work on the principle of kneading action to produce compaction in the soil below the surface. These rollers may be self propelled or towed. Fig. 21.6. Shows a self propelled pneumatic roller.

Usually small tired units have two tandem axles with four to five wheels on each axle. The wheels oscillate, enabling them to follow the surface contour and reach into low areas for uniform compaction. The rear tires are spaced in such a way that they travel over the surface between the front tires, resulting in complete coverage of the surface. The wheels may be mounted slightly out of line with the axle, giving them a weaving action to increase the kneading action on the soil. The weight of a unit can be increased to suit the material being compacted by adding ballast.

Fig. 21.6. Self-propelled pneumatic roller

Small units are not suitable for high production and thick lift embankments compaction of a project. They are used for small to medium size soil compaction works.

Large tired rollers varying in size from 7 to about 100 metric tonne gross weight are available. In these rollers two or more big earth moving tires on a single axle are attached. In these tires the air pressure may vary from 6 to 11 kg/cm^2. These rollers are capable to compact all types of soils to greater depths due to their heavy load and high tire pressure. These units are used for precision work as to roll high way subgrade and air field bases and earth fill dams. To determine the compacting ability of pneumatic rolles following four parameters must be known

1. Wheel load
2. Tire size
3. Tire ply
4. Tire inflation pressure

21.6. VIBRO COMPACTION METHODS

There are two distinct techniques of vibro compaction as follows:

1. **Vibrating pile method**. This method utilizes a top mounted vibrator to create vibration in a vertical mode.

2. **Vibro flotation method.** This method develops horizontal motion in the penetrator.

Both these methods are applicable to densify the saturated cohesion less soils having upto 20% fines.

1. Vibrating pile method

In this method the compaction is achieved by the use of a vibratory pile driving apparatus along with an open end tubular pile. Usually in this method square spacing in used. Usually the spacing pattern is determined on the basis of project specific test panel construction. Using a square spacing pattern, the pile is driven into and extracted from the soil. During the driving and extracting phases of the pile, the densification of the soil takes place both inside and out side the pile. Extreme densification takes place in side the pile due to the concentration of vibratory energy which causes extreme densification in side the pile. The densification out side the pile decreases with the distance from the pile. (Fig. 21.7)

Fig. 21.7. Vibratory pile in position to densify the soil

Configuration of the pile

The best configuration of the pile is as follows:

1. A 76 cms diameter open end pipe with a 10 mm wall thickness.
2. Steel bands 10 to 15 cms wide made of 13 mm thick plate. These bends are fixed at 1.5 to 3.0 m apart on the out side of the pipe together with wider driving and clamping bands at top and bottom of the pile.

The 76 cms diameter pile has produced best results. It has been observed that smaller diameters than the above resulted in less densification in side the pipe, while larger diameters required more vibratory energy and a thicker and heavier pile, resulting uneconomic. Usually piles are made 3 to 4.6 m longer than the maximum penetration depth due to bending and spreading out of the pile or flexing particularly when the piles more than 15 to 17 m lengths are used. This extra length allows for any cut off requirements during driving and pulling operations.

The pile is attached to a vibrator with the help of a hydraulic clamp. The pile, hydraulic clamping head and transmission case act as a unit. The assembly of pile and the vibrator enables the vertical vibrating energy produced to travel to the pile material undiminished.

To handle the vibrating unit and the pile length during driving and extracting operations a mobile crane of sufficient size and capacity is required. To compensate the settling of the material due to compaction an extra material known as over burden is collected before beginning the operations. In most of the cases about 12% shrinkage allowance has been found satisfactory, but in case of hydraulic fill with a relatively low density, the shrinkage allowance of 15% may be sufficient.

The dimension of the spacing pattern of pile depends upon the required relative density of the soil. Square pattern with varying spacing from 0.9 to 2.4 m (3 to 8 ft.) has been found most satisfactory to give the desired density.

Compaction by this method in hydraulically placed cohesion less materials and saturated sands is very expeditious. An average rate of penetration of 15 piles of length 15.0 to 16.5 m per hour can be achieved. In loose soils with smaller piles, the rate of penetration may be more where as in denser soils with deeper piles the rate of penetration will be less.

2. Vibroflotation

In this method a vibrator penetrator having water jets at both its top and bottom has been used. At the time of lowering the penetrator extension tubes are attached to it. To handle the vibratory penetrator and extensions a crane of sufficient size and capacity is required. Actually the penetrator, penetrates into the soil by its own weight as the lower water jet creates a "quick sand condition" there. The typical penetration rate of 90 cms to 180 cms per minute has been observed. Fine granular formations can be densified either by vibration or saturating it with water, which is extremely difficult to arrange.

Process of compaction

For starting the compaction, the lower jets are closed and the water is directed to the upper jets at a reduced pressure. The penetrator is then withdrawn at a rate of 30 cms per minute and cohesion less material as sand is continuously fed as backfill to compensate the depression formed. The lifts method of raising or pulling out the penetrator ensures compaction for the entire depth. The soil will be compacted in a radial zone varying from 1.5 m to about 4.0 m from the vibratory penetrator. This method is more efficient for compaction finer granular formation. This method also has been found more effective than vibrating pile method in compacting with greater spacing patterns.

21.7. DYNAMIC COMPACTION

Densification of soil obtained by repeatedly dropping heavy weight from a height on the ground surfaces is known as *dynamic compaction.* This process is also known as heavy tamping, impact densification, dynamic consolidation and dynamic pre compression. This method of dynamic compaction has been found effective to compact either natural soil deposit or a placed fill upto a depth of about 10.5m. Usually a weight of 2.72 metric tonnes to 13.625 metric tonnes has been used on most projects with a drop height of 9.0 m to 22.5 m or so.

For dropping weights upto 9.1 metric tonne from heights of about 30 m, usually conventional cranes have been used. The weight is attached to a single hoist line. During the dropping, the hoist drum to which the line is attached, is allowed free movement releasing the line. For heavier weights, specially designed machines are required. By this method the strata is compacted at their prevailing water contents. This method has been found usefull for compaction upto about 2.0 m (6.5 ft.) above the ground water table. Compaction of saturated impervious deposits by this method has not been found satisfactory. The depth of improvement depends on the weight dropped and the height of drop.

$$\therefore \quad \text{Depth of improvement } D = n\,(W \times H)^{1/2}$$

where,

n = a coefficient, which is less than 1.0. For most of the soils its value may be taken as 0.5.
W = Weight of tamper in metric tonnes.
H = Height of drop in metres.
D = Depth of improvement in metres.

Disadvantages

The main disadvantage of this method is that it produces vibrations in the ground that travel upto signifact distances from the point of impact. These vibrations may damage the near by structures.

QUESTIONS

1. What are the objectives of compaction of soil.
2. Give the names of methods by which soil can be compacted.
3. Describe the sheep foot roller for compaction of soil. Give specification of a typical sheep foot roller.
4. Describe fully tamping roller.
5. Give the principle of vibratory compactor. Explain drum vibratory compactors.
6. Describe the vibroflotation method of compaction of soil fully.
7. Discuss dynamic compaction in detail.

8. Describe in detail the method of soil compaction by vibrating pile method.
9. Write a note on pneumatic tired roller.

OBJECTIVE TYPE QUESTIONS

1. The main objective of soil compaction is except
   (*a*) To remove air from the soil
   (*b*) To reduce the settlement of the soil
   (*c*) To increase the strength of the soil
   (*d*) To improve the bearing capacity of the soil
   (*e*) To remove the moisture from the soil
   (*f*) To lower the permeability of soil
   (*g*) To control volume changes of the soil
2. The soil can be compacted by
   (*a*) Impact
   (*b*) Pressure
   (*c*) Vibration
   (*d*) Kneading
   (*e*) Any of the above
3. Sheep foot roller is useful to compact soils except
   (*a*) Silty sand and sandy clay
   (*b*) Clayey soils
   (*c*) Medium and heavy clays
   (*d*) Crushed rocks
4. For compacting a 30 cm thick layer of soil passes of sheep foot roller are sufficient
   (*a*) 6
   (*b*) 9
   (*c*) 12
   (*d*) 16
5. Sheep foot roller has not been found suitable to compact top layer thickness
   (*a*) 8-10 cm
   (*b*) 5-8 cm
   (*c*) 10-12 cm
   (*d*) 15-18 cm
6. The speed of sheep foot roller usually varies
   (*a*) 4-5 kmph
   (*b*) 6.5-10 kmph
   (*c*) 8-12 kmph
   (*d*) 12-15 kmph
7. The tamping rollers compact the soil by
   (*a*) Impact
   (*b*) Vibration
   (*c*) Pressure
   (*d*) Kneading
8. In a tamping roller generally 20 to 30 cm thick layer of soil is compacted in passes
   (*a*) 2-3
   (*b*) 5-6
   (*c*) 8-12
   (*d*) 12-15
9. Vibrating compactors compact soils except
   (*a*) Sand
   (*b*) Gravel
   (*c*) Clayey soils
   (*d*) Blasted rocks
10. The diameter of a sheep foot roller drum is
    (*a*) 0.5 m
    (*b*) 2.5 m
    (*c*) 1.5 m
    (*d*) 3.5 m
11. The weight of a sheep foot roller is about
    (*a*) 30 T
    (*b*) 35 T
    (*c*) 45 T
    (*d*) 55 T

ANSWERS:

1. (*e*)	4. (*c*)	7. (*d*)	10. (*c*)
2. (*e*)	5. (*b*)	8. (*a*)	11. (*b*)
3. (*d*)	6. (*b*)	9. (*c*)	

22

Finishing And Hauling Equipment

22.1. INTRODUCTION

The process of shaping the materials to the required line and grade is known as finishing or finish grading or fine grading. Finishing operations follow closely behind excavation operation or compaction of embankments. The finishing operation includes the smoothing and shaping slopes, and finishing the grade of sections supporting the structural members. Usually for finishing operations graders are used. On projects such as roads and airfields special trimming machines are used for finishing under the pavement sections.

22.2. GRADERS

Grader is a versatile (multipurpose) machine used for finishing or levelling earth work, shaping bank slopes and ditching. A grader may also be used for mixing, spreading, side casting, levelling and crowning, light stripping operations and dirt road maintenance. The main purpose of a grader is cutting and moving the material with the blade. This blade is also known as mold board. Some times a grader is also used as a scarifire for hard materials and snow plow. But they are restricted for making shallow cuts in medium hard materials and not used for heavy excavation. Due to its structural strength and the position of its blade a grader can move small amount of materials only and can not be used as a dozer.

Graders are capable of working on steep slopes upto 3:1, but graders should not be used to construct ditches running parallel to such steep slope as the grader has a comparatively high centre of gravity and the correct pressure at a critical point on the board may roll over the machine on the slope. A grader is capable of cutting ditches progressively upto 0.9 m depth.

22.2.1. Motor grader

A motor grader is the most popular machine of this class. It is a self propelled and fast moving machine. The horse power of most of the graders vary from 91 to 304 metric h.p. and their speeds vary from 16 to 40 kmph. The frame of the machine is arch shaped converging and raised at the front and low at the rear where the prime mover is mounted. The front of the frame is supported by a pair of front wheels and the rear on the heavier tandem wheels which are also the driving wheels. The blade is supported on a circle with inside gear teeth which can be turned through 360°. The circle is attached to a draw bar pivoted at the front on the main frame and supported at the rear by a pair of lift arms. Steering of the grader is done through front wheels. For projecting the blade out on any side a side toothed sector is provided.

The power to operate the controls is supplied through a quill (long hollow) shaft passing through hollow clutch and transmission shafts. The quill or long hollow shaft is rotated when ever the engine is running irrespective of the movement of the machine. The long hollow shaft drives a propeller shaft which, through bevel gear drives, transmits power to a vertical shaft under the controlling dash board. This vertical shaft through an arrangement of bevel and spur gears drives six horizontal reversing shafts which power the different operations such as blade lift of left and right ends, scarifier, circle reverse, centre shift and front wheel lean etc. All these devices are controlled through levers at the dash. The steering is controlled through a wheel and a long shaft connecting the wheel to the steering box mounted on the front of the frame. To facilitate turning, the front wheel can be made to lean towards the direction of the turn. A motor grader is shown in Fig. 22.1. Fig. 22.2 shows a grader with rear ripper leveling a building site.

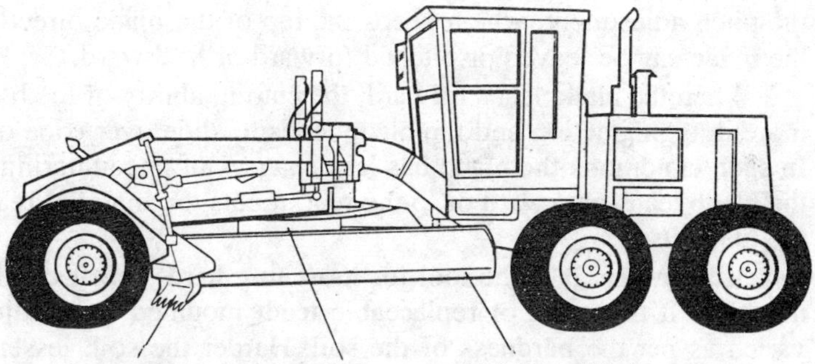

Fig. 22.1. The components of a grader

Fig. 22.2. Grader with rear ripper levelling a building site

22.3. GRADER ATTACHMENTS

The attachments of a grader are as follows:

1. Blade (also known as mold board)
2. Scarifire
3. Snow plow or bull dozer
4. Elevator
5. Roller etc.

These tools add the versatility to the grader to a great extent.

1. Blade. The blade of the grader is similar to that of a dozer. It is curved having heavy back reinforcement. It is fitted with replaceable edges on sides and bottom. It can swing or swivel through 360° and can be angled and tilted to suit the soil conditions. It can be side shifted and even can be extended beyond the base of the grader by fixing extension pieces on either side. The extended blade can be positioned vertically or at an angle for bank sloping. The ends of the blade can be raised or lowered together or independently of one another. The toe of the blade is the fore most end of the blade in the direction of travel and the heel is the discharge end.

2. Pitch of the blade (Leaning of the blade). For normal works the blade is kept near the centre of the pitch adjustment, which keeps the top of the blade directly over the cutting edge. However the top of the blade can be leaved or pitehed forward or backward.

When the blade leans forward, the cutting ability of the blade decreases. In this condition the blade has more dragging action and the blade tends to slide over (ride over) the material rather than cut and push it. In such conditions the blade has less chances of encountering solid obstractions. On the other hand, when the blade leans backward or to the rear, it cuts the material readily but tends to spill back the material over the blade itself.

3. Scarifire. It is the tool for loosening hard soil. It can be mounted in the front or in the rear of the machine. It has a set of replaceable teeth mounted on a adjustable shank. The number of teeth may be varied as per the hardness of the soil. Harder the soil, lesser the number of teeth. Before grading a soil having vegetation and brush, it can be scarified to remove vegetation or to loosen it. This operation saves the blade encountering a adverse surface. The teeths may be adjusted to cut upto a depth of 30 cm.

4. The snowplow and bulldozer are V shaped blades. They are the pushing attachments and are fitted in the front of the machine. When the top of the scarifier is pitched to the rear, the teeths are lifted and tear the material being loosened.

5. The elevator attachment enables the grader to pick up the material cut by the blade and drop it over an inclined belt conveyer which transmit it into a hauling unit to deposit at the desired place.

6. Rollers can be attached to the rear part of the grader to smoothen or compact the graded surface.

22.4. OPERATIONS OF THE GRADER

When the blade is set at an angle, the material being pushed tends to move slowly towards the rear end of the blade. The rolling action caused by blade curve helps this side movement. The side movement of the material increases with the increase in the tilt of the blade. In such conditions the material is not taken far enough and deeper cuts are made. To maintain and shape most roads the angle of tilt of the blade should be kept between 25° to 30°. For spreading medium height loose soil mounds, the angle should be decreased to less than 25° and for ditching and hard cuts the angle should be kept more than 25°.

1. Planing surfaces

To plane off the irregular surfaces and use the resulting material to fill the low spots, the blade can be set at an angle. To have some material in front of the blade enough material should be cut. To distribute the cut material evenly, the loosened material should be moved forward and side ways. On the next pass, pick up the material left of windrows at the trailing edge of the blade. (wind row is a continuous row of medium height of soil mounds). On the final pass, the lighter cut should be made and the rear or trailing edge of the blade should be lifted enough to allow the surplus material to go under rather than around the blade. This will avoid remaining a ridge on the surface. The windrows should not be piled up in front of the ridge. They should also not be piled in front of rear wheels as they will affect the grader's traction and efficiency to a great extent.

2. Ditch cuts

Normally for ditch cutting, the grader is brought in second gear at full speed or throttle. For getting more straight ditches and better control on the grader, 7.5 cms to 10 cms deep marking should be cut at the outer edge of the bank slope during the first pass. The toe of the blade should be in line with the out side edge of the lead tire. The marking cut provides a guide for subsequent operations. Each ditch cut should be made as deep as possible with out losing control of the grader. Each successive cut should be brought in from the edge of the bank slope so that the toe of the blade may remain in line with the bottom of the ditch on the final cut.

3. Creating a bank slope

Sloping the bank on a road cut prevents the slope failure as well as excessive erosion of the bank that could fill the road side ditch. To prevent to make additional passes, the cuts should be made as close to the design slope as possible. The material cut from the outer slope initially can be collected into the bottom of the ditch and latter must be removed.

4. Cleaning ditches

To remove the unwanted material collected into the ditch during the operation of the bank slope, the blade should be placed in the same position as used for the ditching cut. The material should be collected on the shoulder of the road.

5. Moving windrows

The side thrust is the force at the blade that tries to pull the front of the grader to one side. During the operation of making a cut by the grader a windrow is formed between the heal of the blade and the left rear wheel. This windrow will impart a side thrust. The front wheels of a grader can be leaned or sloped both left and right. Slope (lean) the wheels of the grader against the direction of the side thrust and shift the windrow across the grade (slope) with successive cuts. Some times cuts produce excess material than needed for road bed and shoulders. This excess material may be used as a fill at other places through out the project.

6. Maintenance of haul road

To increase the efficiency of scrapers, it is essential to maintain haul road in good condition. In case of large earth moving operations good haul roads increase the efficiency of trucks also. Graders are the best machines for maintaining the haul roads.

The most efficient method of road maintenance is to use sufficient number of graders to complete one side of a road with one pass of each grader. In this method one side of road is complete while the other side is left open to traffic.

Ordinarily levelling and maintaining is done by pushing the material across the road from one side to the other. It is easier to maintain the road if it is damp. Hence surface maintenance work should be taken in hand after rains. A too dry material may be made damp by sprinkling water from a spray tanker.

7. Smoothing pitted surfaces

If the fine material called binder is present and moisture content in the surface is appropriate, then the rough or badly pitted surfaces may be cut smooth. The cut material may be re spread over the smooth base surface. To re shape the earth or gravel roads, the best season or time is after a rain. Dry roads should be watered by using water sprinkler. Sprinkling of water will ensure the re compaction of the material.

22.5. HAULING EQUIPMENT

1. Trucks. Trucks are the hauling units that provide facility in transporting excavated material, aggregates and other construction material and equipment from one place to an other place. They provide relatively low hauling costs due to their high travel speeds. The weight capacity may limit the volume of the load that a unit may haul. The productive capacity of a truck depends on the size of its load, and number of trips it can make per hour. The number of trips completed per hour is a function of cycle time

(*a*) Load time (*b*) Haul time

(*c*) Dump time (*d*) Return time

The use of trucks as the primary hauling unit provides a high degree of flexibility. The number of trucks employed on a job can be increased or decreased easily to permit modification in the total hauling capacity of the fleet. Mostly the trucks may be operated over any haul road for which the surface is sufficiently firm and smooth and the grades are not excessively steep.

22.5.1. Classification of trucks

Trucks may be classified as follows:

1. The method of dumping the load as rear dump, bottom dump or side dump.
2. The type of frame as rigid framed or articulated.
3. The size and type of engine as diesel, gasoline, butane or propane etc.

4. The kind of drive as two wheel, four wheel or six wheel.
5. The number of wheels and excels and the arrangement of driving wheels.
6. The class of material hauled, earth, coal, rock and ore etc.
7. The capacity-Gravimetric (weight/or volumetric (volume))
8. Number of gears.

22.6. BRIEF DESCRIPTION OF DIFFERENT TYPES OF TRUCKS

1. Rigid frame rear dump trucks. This class of trucks are suitable for hauling many types of materials (Fig. 22.3). The shape of the truck body such as the extent of sharp angles and corners, and the

Fig. 22.3. Highway rigid-frame rear-dump truck

contour of the rear, through which materials will flow during dumping will affect the ease or difficulty of loading and dumping. The bodies of trucks to be used for hauling wet clay and similar materials should be free of sharp angles and corners. Gravel and dry sand can flow easily from almost any shape of the body. For hauling rock, the bodies of the truck should be shallow with sloping side boards. When hauling rock the impact of loading on the body of the truck is extremely severe. For continuous use of rock hauling, the body of the truck should be made of high tensile steel. Even with special body, care should be taken while placing the load in the truck. Usually the length of the truck body is 4.755 m, and width 2.5 m and about 1.0 m depth, having a capacity of about 11.5 m^3.

Off, high way dump trucks do not have tail gates, hence the body floor slopes forward at an small angle of the order of 15°. The floor shape perpendicular to the length of the body for some modules is flat and in others V shaped floor is provided which reduces the loading shocks. It also helps in keeping the load centrally. For excavator buckets the body having low sides and longer length and wider width have been found useful. This configuration of the body is found quicker for loading cycles.

2. Articulated rear dump trucks. This type of trucks are designed to operate over rough or soft grounds and in confined conditions where a rigid frame truck would be difficult to operate. An articulated joint and oscillating ring between the tractor and dump body allow all wheels to maintain contact with the ground at all times. The combined effect of articulation, all wheel drive, high clearance and low pressure and radial tires make a truck capable of moving through soft or sticky ground. (Fig. 22.4)

When the grades of the haul roads are an operating factor, articulated trucks have been found most

Fig. 22.4. An articulated dump truck

suitable, as they can climb steeper grades than rigid frame trucks. Articulated trucks can climb on grades upto about 35% where as rigid frame trucks can climb upto about 20% grades for short distances. For rigid frame trucks for continuous grades 8 to 10% limit is more reasonable.

Articulated dump trucks usually have high hydraulic dumping pressures *i.e.* they can hoist their beds faster. The bed also achieves a steeper dump angle. One model can attain 72° dump angle in 15 seconds. The combination of hoist speed and steep angle results in quick discharge of the material, resulting saving

Fig. 22.5. An articulated dump truck moving through soft ground

in time. The problem of unloading sticky materials can be solved by equipping the trucks with ejectors. Fig. 22.4 shows a articulated dump truck while Fig. 22.5 shows an articulated dump truck moving through soft ground.

The rear dump trucks whether of rigid frame or articulated should be used under the following conditions.

(*a*) When the material to be hauled is free flowing *i.e.* it may move itself or has bulky components.

(*b*) The haul material is to be dumped into restricted locations or over the edge of a bank or fill.

(*c*) Maximum maneuverability in loading and dumping area is required.

3. Bottom dump wagons or Tractors with bottom dump trailers. These units are economic haulers if the material to be moved is free flowing *i.e.* which moves easily such as gravel, sand, coal, reasonably dry earth. The use of bottom dump wagons or trailers will reduce the time required to unload the material. To take full advantage of time saving, the area where the load is to be dumped should be large enough so that the material can be spread easily into windrows. Actually these haulers have been found suitable for use specially where the material is to be distributed in layers on a fill or is discharged through restricted width holes into hoppers. When discharging the load on the fills, the haul unit, wagon or trailer can dump its load while moving, where as while discharging its load through restricted width hole it has to stop for few seconds. The rapid rate of discharging the load gives these units a time advantage over rear dump trucks.

The doors through which these units discharge their loads have a limited opening width. Difficulties may be experienced in discharging materials such as wet and sticky clay, specially if the material has large lumps in it.

The wagons or tractor towing bottom dump trailers are found satisfactory as hauling units on projects as earth dams, levees, high ways, and airports etc. where large quantities of materials are to be transported and haul roads can be kept in reasonably good condition. These units can have a single axle, tandem axles or even triaxles. These units can be loaded by hydraulic excavators as power shovel, drag lines, loaders, or belt loaders. They have maximum speed of approximately 50 kmph and hauling capacity more than 19 m^3 (25 cu yds). The use of these units should be considered under the following conditions.

1. At sites having unrestricted areas for loading and unloading or dumping the materials.
2. The material to be moved is free flowing *i.e.* easy to move.
3. The haul route grades are less than 5% as these units have limited ability to pull on steep grades.

22.7. CAPACITIES OF TRUCKS AND HAULING UNITS

The capacities of trucks and hauling units can be determined by the following methods:

1. **By Gravimetric method.** The load which it will carry, expressed as a weight.
2. **By struck volume.** The volumetric amount it will carry, filled upto the top of the sides, with no material above the sides.
3. **By Heaped volume.** The volumetric amount it will carry, if the load heaped on 2:1 slope above the body.

The gravimetric rating is expressed in pounds or kilograms and the other two in cubic yards or cubic metres.

The struck capacity of a truck is the volume of the material which will be carried by it, when it is filled level upto the top of the body side with no material above the body sides. The heaped capacity is the volume of the material that the unit will carry when the load is heaped above the sides. The standard heaped is takens 2:1. The actual heaped capacity will vary with the material being hauled. Wet earth or sandy clay may be hauled at a slope of about 1:1, where as dry sand and gravel may not permit a slope greater than 3:1. To determine the actual heaped capacity of a unit, it is necessary to know the struck capacity, length and width of the body and slope at which the material will remain stable while the unit is moving. The smooth haul roads will permit an higher heaped capacity than a rough haul road.

When a unit is used to haul a high unit weight material such as iron or even wet sand, the weight capacity will limit the volume of the material. In case the unit weight of the material is such that the safe load is not exceeded, the truck or haul unit may be filled to its heaped capacity. Always ensure that the volumetric load does not create a condition where the load weight excees the gravimetric capacity of the hauling unit. Over loading will flex the tier of the unit too much. The flexing of the tier produces excessive internal temperature causing permanent damage to the tire. The tier failure may cause considerable wastage of time. Hence excessive loading always should be avoided for the safety of tires and accidents.

22.8. EFFECTS OF TRUCK SIZE

The productive capacity of a truck depends on the size of its load it hauled and the number of trips it can make per hour. The number of trips completed per hour is a function of the cycle time. The truck cycle time has four components as follows:

1. Load time
2. Haul time
3. Dump time
4. Return time

The load time and the size of the load depends on the size of the truck body and the excavators bucket size. The haul and return cycle time depends on the weight of the vehicle, horse power of the engine, haul and return distances and condition of the haul road. Dumping time is a function of the type of the equipment and the condition of the dump area.

While loading the hauling units, it is desirable to struck balance between the capacities of excavating unit and hauling units. If it is not done, operating difficulties will develop and the combined cost of excavating and hauling the material may be higher than when balanced units are used.

When an excavator is used to load earth into the hauling units or trucks, the size of the truck may introduce several factors which will affect the production rate and the cost of handling earth.

22.9. COMPARATIVE STUDY OF TRUCKS

The advantages, disadvantages of small and large trucks are discussed in tabular form in Table 22.1 and 22.2.

Table 22.1. Advantages and disadvantages of small trucks compared to large trucks

S. No.	*Advantages of small trucks*	*Disadvantages of small trucks*
1.	They are more flexible in maneuvering which is an advantage on restricted work sites.	1. A small truck is more difficult for the excevator to load due to small target for depositing the bucket load or material.
2.	They can attain higher haul and return speeds.	2. More total time is lost in spotting the truck due to large number of trucks required.
3.	The loss in production in less when one truck in the fleet breaks down.	3. More number of drivers are required to haul a given out put of the material.
4.	It is easier to balence the number of trucks with the out put of the excavator, which will reduce the time lost by trucks or by the excavator.	4. The greater number of trucks may increase the danger of bunching of units at the pit, along the haul road, or at the dump.
		5. The greater number of trucks required may increase the total investment in hauling units, with more expensive maintenance and repairs and more parts to stock.

Table 22.2. Advantages and disadvantages of large units with small units

S. No.	*Advantages of large trucks compared with small trucks*	*Disdvantages of large trucks compared with small trucks*
1.	Fewer hauling units (trucks) of larger size are required, which will reduce the total amount of investment for hauling units, cost of maintanance and repair will also be less.	1. The cost of truck time at loading is greater, especially with small excavators
2.	Fewer drivers are required.	2. The heavier loads may cause more damage to the haul roads resulting in increased cost of maintenance of the haul roads. It will require more equipment for the repair of haul roads resulting in more invest- ment.

S. No.	*Advantages of large trucks compared with small trucks*	*Disdvantages of large trucks compared with small trucks*
3.	The smaller number of large trucks facilitates synchronizing of the equipment and reduces the danger of bunching the trucks. It is especially true for long hauls.	3. It is more difficult to balance the number of trucks with the output of the excavator.
4.	They give a larger target for the excavator during loading.	4. Repair parts may be more difficult to obtain.
5.	The frequency of spotting the trucks under the excavator is reduced.	5. The largest sizes may not be allowed to haul on highways.
6.	Fewer trucks are required to maintain and repair. Hence fewer parts have to be stocked.	

In selecting the size of the trucks usually following thumb role is applied.

The minimum capacity of the trucks selected to haul the material should be four to five times the capacity of the excavator bucket or dipper, when loading with a drag line or shovel.

QUESTIONS

1. What is a grader. Discuss its working.
2. Name the attachments of a motor grader and explain the functions of its blade fully.
3. Discuss the operations of a grader in brief.
4. What is a truck? For what purpose it is used.
5. Give the classification of trucks.
6. Explain in brief the following types of trucks.
   (*a*) Rigid frame type trucks (*b*) Articulated rear dump trucks
   (*c*) Bottom dump wagons.

OBJECTIVE TYPE QUESTIONS

1. A grader may be used, except for
   (*a*) Levelling earth work (*b*) Shaping bank slopes
   (*c*) Heavy excavation (*d*) Light stripping operations
   (*e*) Dirt road maintenance
2. Identify the incorrect statement/statements
   (*a*) A grader can be used with advantage to construct ditches running parallel to slopes as steep as 3:1.
   (*b*) A grader is capable of cutting ditches upto a depth of 90 cms
   (*c*) Graders are capable of working on slopes upto 3:1.
   (*d*) A grader can be used as snow plow.
3. Identify the correct statement/statements
   (*a*) A grader blade can swing through 360° (*b*) It can be angled at any position or angle
   (*c*) It is fitted with replaceable edges on sides and bottom
   (*d*) The ends of blade can be raised or lowered indepently or together
   (*e*) All are correct
4. Identify the incorrect statement/statements
   (*a*) For normal works the blade is kept near the centre of the pitch adjustments
   (*b*) The blade of a grader can not be leaned forward or backward
   (*c*) When the blade leans forward the cutting capacity of the blade decreases and it has a more dragging action than cut or push it
   (*d*) When the blade leans backward it cuts the material readily but tends to spill back the material over the blade itself
5. Identify the correct statement
   (*a*) To plane off the irregular surfaces the blade can be set at an angle
   (*b*) For spreading medium height of loose soil mounds the angle of the blade should be kept at less than 25°

(*c*) For ditching and hard cuts the angle of blade should be kept at more than 25°
(*d*) For getting better control and more straight ditches about 10 cms deep marking should be cut at the outer edge of the bank slope during the 1st-pass
(*e*) All are correct

6. The hauling units can be classified based on
(*a*) Method of dumping
(*b*) Type of frame
(*c*) Size and type of engine
(*d*) Class of material to be hauled
(*e*) Capacity
(*f*) All of the above

7. Identify the correct statement
(*a*) For hauling wet clays and similar materials the body of the hauling unit should be free from sharp angles and corners
(*b*) Dry sand and gravel can flow easily from any type of hauling unit
(*c*) For hauling rocks, the body of the hauling unit should be shallow with sloping boards
(*d*) For continuously hauling rocks, the body of the hauling unit should be made of high tensile steel due to severe impact of the rock on the body
(*e*) All are correct

8. Identify the incorrect statement/statements
(*a*) Articulated trucks are designed to be operated on rough or soft patches
(*b*) Articulated trucks are designed to be operated on hard and smooth surface only
(*c*) Articulated trucks can be used where rigid frame trucks can not be used
(*d*) Bottom dump wagons are more economic haulers for free flowing materials

9. Bottom dump hauling units have been found more useful under the following situations
(*a*) For hauling free flowing materials
(*b*) Sites having un restricted areas for loading and un loading the materials
(*c*) The haul routes grades are less than 5%
(*d*) All are correct

10. Identify the incorrect statements/statements
(*a*) Articulated haul units can climb on grades upto 35% only
(*b*) Articulated units can climb on grades up 45%
(*c*) Rigid frame hauling units can climb on grades upto 20% only
(*d*) For rigid frame units for continuous grades 8 to 10% limit is reasonable
(*e*) Articulated dumping units have high hydraulic dumping pressure

11. The maximum speed of bottom pump units is
(*a*) 30 kmph
(*b*) 35 kmph
(*c*) 50 kmph
(*d*) 65 kmph

12. Identify the correct statement
(*a*) While planing surface with a grader the wind rows may be piled up infront of the ridge
(*b*) A grader may be used for heay excavation with advantage
(*c*) A grader can also be used as a dozer
(*d*) Depth of cutting with a grader is limited to 90 cm

ANSWERS:

1. (*c*)	4. (*b*)	7. (*e*)	10. (*b*)
2. (*a*)	5. (*e*)	8. (*b*)	11. (*c*)
3. (*e*)	6. (*f*)	9. (*d*)	12. (*d*)

23

Rock Drilling Equipment

23.1. INTRODUCTION

The method of drilling a hole in hard materials did not change from the ancient times to the middle of the 19th century. The first practical mechanical drilling machine was employed in Alps for mount cenis tunnel work in 1861. Later in 1966 the first pneumatic drill was employed in U.S.A. at the eastern header of the Hoosac tunnel in western massachsetts. In this chapter different types of drilling equipment for rocks will be discussed.

23.2. DEFINITIONS

Before discussing the different equipment and procedures for drilling, following terms are explained as a guide to the reader.

Bit. The portion of the drill which comes in contact with the rock and disintegrates it, is called a bit. Bits may be of the following types:

1. **Carbide insert bit.** It is a detachable bit, whose cutting edges consist of tungsten carbide and embedded in a softer steel base.
2. **Detachable bit.** A bit that can be removed from the drill stem or attached to it, is called a detachable bit.
3. **Diamond bit.** A detachable bit whose cutting elements are made of metal called diamonds and embedded in a metal matrix are known as diamond bits.
4. **Forged bit.** The bit that is forged (shaped) on the drill steel is called forget bit.

Burden. The horizontal distance from a rock face to the first row of drill holes or the distance between rows of drill holes is called burden.

Cuttings. The disintegrated rock particles removed from a drill hole are called cuttings.

Coupling. A short hollow steel pipe having interior threads is called coupling. It is used to hold drill steel pieces together.

Depth per bit. The depth of a hole that can be drilled by a bit before it is replaced is known as depth per bit.

Drifter. An air operated percussion type drill similar to jack hammer is called a drifter. It is so large that it requires a mechanical mounting.

Abrasion drill. The drill that grinds rock into small pieces by the abrasive effect of the bit that rotates in the hole is called abrasion drill.

Blast hole drill. Arotary drill consisting of a steel pipe drill stem having a roller bit on its bottom is called a blast hole drill. As the bit rotates, it disintegrates the rock. The cuttings are removed by the stream of compressed air.

Churn drill. It is a percussion type drill consisting of a long steel bit that is mechanically lifted and dropped to disintegrate the rock. This drill is used to drill deep holes, usually 15 cms in diameter or more.

Core drill. This drill is used for taking samples of rock from a hole. Usually it is used for exploratory purposes. Shot and diamond drills are used as core drill.

Diamond drill. It is a rotary abrasive type drill, whose bit consists of a metal metrix in which large number of diamonds are embedded. As the drill rotates, the diamonds disintegrate the rock. This drill extensively is used for taking core samples.

Down hole drill or down hole bit. In this drill the bit and the power system are one unit, suspended at the bottom of the drill steel. This unit provides rotation and percussion to the drill.

Dry drill. The drill that uses compressed air to remove the cuttings from the hole is called dry drill.

Wet drill. The drill that uses water to remove the cuttings from the hole is known as wet drill.

Percussion drill. The drill that breaks the rock into small pieces by the impact from repeated blows is known as percussion drill. Hydraulic fluids or compressed air can power this drill.

Shot drill. A rotary abrasive type drill whose bit is consisted of a section of steel pipe with a roughened surface at the bottom is known as shot drill. As the bit is rotated under pressure chilled steel shots are supplied under the bit to accomplish the disintegration of the rock. The cuttings are removed from the hole by water.

Drilling rate. The number of centimetres of the hole drilled per hour per bit is called drilling rate.

Drill rods or drill steel. The steel rods that transmit the below energy and drill rotation from the shank to the bit are called drill rods. Drill steel or rods are threaded on both ends and usually are available in 3.0, 3.6 and 6.0 m lengths.

Face. Approximately a vertical surface extending upward from the floor of a pit to the level at which drilling is accomplished is called a face.

Jack hammer or sinker. An air operated percussion type drill is known as a Jack hammer. This machine is small enough to be handled by one worker.

Stopper. An air operated percussion type drill, similar to drifter is called a stopper. This machine is used for overhead drilling as in a tunnel.

Shank or striker bar. A short piece of steel attached to the percussion drill piston for receiving the blows and transferring the energy to the drill steel is called shank or striker bar.

Sub drilling. The depth to which a blast hole will be drilled below the final grade is called as sub drilling. This extra depth is necessary to ensure that the breakage will occur completely to the required elevation.

Bits. A bit is the essential part of a drill. The bit of the drill engages the rock and disintegrates it. The success of a drilling operation depends on the ability of the bit to remain sharp under the impact of the drill. Now a days many types and sizes of bits are available. Most of the bits are units that can be screwed to the drill steel. They are easily replaceable and can be resharpened. Bits are available in various sizes, shapes and hardness.

Steel bits for drifters and jack hammers are available in sizes from 25 mm to 113 mm. The depth of the hole that can be drilled with a steel bit varies from few centimetres to about 12 m (40 ft.) depending upon the type of rock.

Carbide insert bits. Some rocks are so abrasive that steel bits have to be replaced after they have drilled only a few

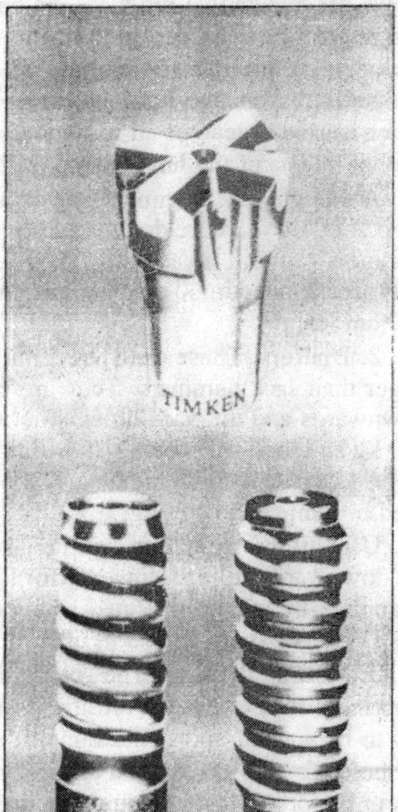

Fig. 23.1 Carbide-insert rock bit

centimetres of the hole. The cost of bit and time loss in changing the bit is so great that the use of carbide insert bit will prove economical. Fig. 23.1. The actual drilling edges consist of a very hard metal, tongsten carbide, embaded in steel. The size of the bit varies from 34.5 mm to 125 mm. These bits are available in four grades in the order of increasing hardness. The susceptibility to breakage increases with hardness.

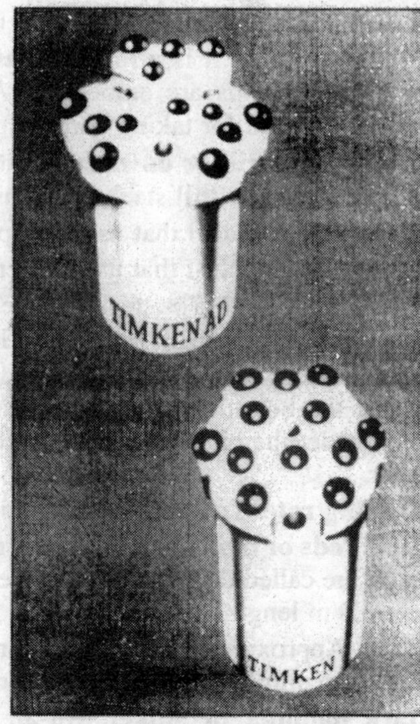

Fig. 23.2. Button bits

Bottom bits. These bits are available in numerous sizes and in different cutting face designs with a choice of insert grades. These bits require no grinding or sharpening. These buttons yield faster penetration rates in a wide range of drilling applications. They are used till destruction and never reconditioned. (Fig. 23.2)

23.3. DESCRIPTION OF DIFFERENT TYPES OF DRILLS

Following drills are discussed in brief in this chapter.

1. Jack hammers. These are hand held air operated percussion type drills. Primarily these drills are used for drilling holes in down ward direction. For this reason frequently they are known as "sinkers". They are classified according to their weight, such as 20kg, 25kg (45 to 55). A complete drilling unit consists of a hammer, drill steel, and bit. The flowing air through a hammer causes the piston to reciprocate at a speed upto 2200 blows per minute that produces the hammer effect. The energy of this piston is transmitted to a bit through the drill steel. Some of the air flows through a hole in the drill steel and the bit to remove the cuttings from the hole and to cool the bit. For wet drilling, water is used instead of air to remove the cuttings. The drill steel is rotated slightly following each blow so that the points of the bits may not strike at the same spot each time.

Although jack hammers are capable to drill holes more than 6.0 m (20 ft.) deep, but they are seldom used to drill holes more than 3.0 m deep. Heavier hammers can drill holes upto 7.5 to 8.0 cms in diameter. Usually drill steel or drill rods are supplied in 60 cms lengths, but longer lengths are also available (120, 180, 200 cm length).

2. Drifters. These drills are similar to Jack hammers in operation but they are larger than Jack hammers. They are used as mounted tools for drilling horizontal, downwards and up ward holes. The weight of drifters varies from 34 kg to about 140 kg and they are capable of drilling holes upto 113 mm in diameter. These holes are used extensively in rock excavation, mining, and tunneling. Water or air can be used to remove the cuttings.

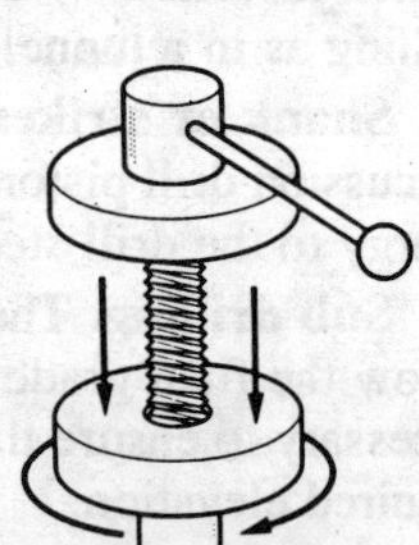
Fig. 23.3. Rotary drilling mechanism

Usually the weight of a drifter is sufficient to supply necessary feed pressure for downward drilling. However for horizontal or upward drilling the feed pressure is applied by a hand operated screw or a hydraulic piston or a pneumatic piston. Steel changes are available in 60, 75, 90, 120 and 150 centimetres.

3. Rotary drilling. The rotary drills are also called blast hole drills. While working a rotary drill for drilling a rock a down pressure on the drill steel and bit has to be applied and at the same time the bit has to be kept constantly rotated in the hole. To cool the bit and remove the cuttings from the hole the compressed air has to be forced down through the drill pipe and the bit constantly. These drills are self propelled drills that can be mounted on a truck or on crawler track. These drills are suitable for drilling in soft to medium hard rocks as dolomite and lime stone. However these drills are not suitable for drilling in hard rocks as igneous rocks. The rigs are available to drill holes of different diameters and depths upto 90 metres. The speed in dolomite has been found varing from 45 cms per hour in hard domite to 15 m per hour. Fig. 23.3 shows the mechanism of a rotary drill. Fig. 23.4 shows two rotary blast hole drill working on a highway project.

Fig. 23.4. Two rotary (blast hole) drill working on a highway project

4. Rotary percussion drilling. As the name suggests it is a combination of the hard hitting reciprocal action of the percussion drill and the turning action under pressure of the rotary drill. As we know that a percussion drill has only a rotary action to reposition the bits cutting edges. The rotation of this combined drill, whose bit remains under constant pressure has provided the ability to drill much faster than the regular percussion drill. The rotary percussion drills need special carbide insert bits. The carbide insert bits can be set and drill at different angles than those used with standard carbide bits. On one project rotary percussion drill was found to have drilled blast holes three times faster than regular percussion machine. (Fig. 23.5)

5. Down hole drilling. These units are usually air operated hammers. When drilling deep holes, often it has been found more efficient to place the driving mechanism in the hole with the bit. It eliminates sending the rotation and percussion forces through the drill steel. These hammers can be operated under water by

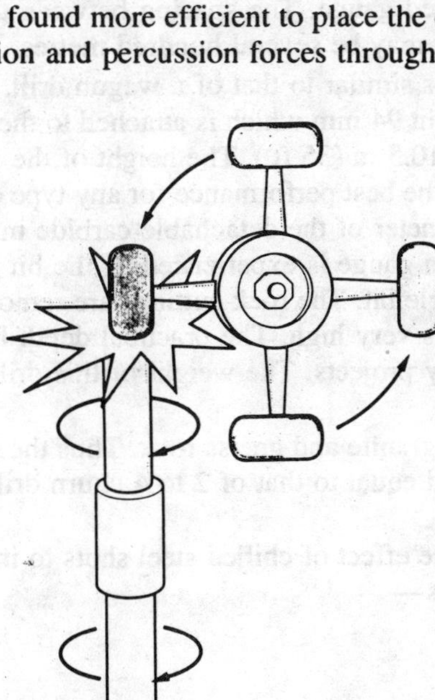

Fig. 23.5. Rotary-percussion drilling mechanism

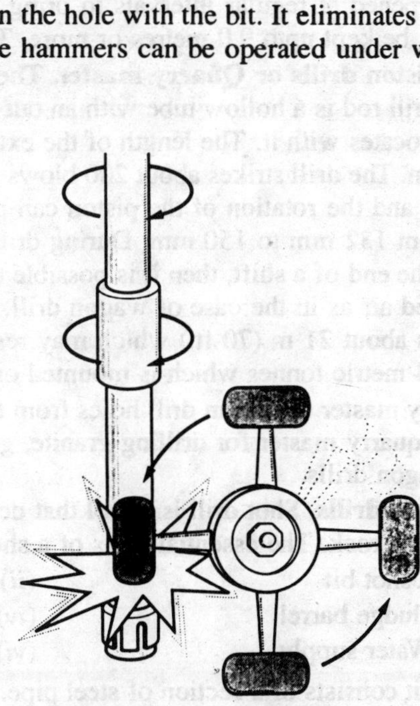

Fig. 23.6. Downhole drilling mechanism

maintaining a higher air pressure in the hammer than the out side pressure. Water or air can be used to clear the cuttings from the hole. Standard sizes are available from 102 mm to 762 mm. 864 mm down hole bits have been used to construct a cut off wall in dike at BEAVER DAM IN ARKANSAS. (Fig. 23.6)

6. Track mounted drills. These drills are used usually on construction projects. Often they are known as 'air track' drills. The production of these drills is very high due to their ability to move quickly between locations. Secondly the hydraulically operated boom enables easy positioning of the drill. Holes from these drills can be drilled at any angle from less than 15° back from the vertical to above the horizontal, ahead or on either side of the unit. All operations including travel can be powered by compressed air. Though there are also hydraulic powered units available, but compressed air is still used for cleaning the hole.

7. Drills mounted on excavators. These drills are similar in sizes and capacities to the track mounted drills. How ever to operate effectively these drills need a nearly level ground.

8. Wagon drills. These drills consist of drifters mounted on tall posts (masts) which in turn are mounted on wheels to provide them speed for mobility. These drills are used extensively to drill holes upto 113 mm (4.5 in) diameter and upto about 10 m (30 ft.) or more depth. The performance of wagon drills is better than jack hammers. These drills may be used to drill at any angle from down to slightly above the horizontal. The length of the drill steel may vary from 1.8 m to 3.0 m and 4.5 m or more depending on the length of feed of the particular wagon drill.

9. Churn drills. A churn drill is consisted of a steel bit attached to a heavy steel drill stem. This drill is lifted and dropped repeatedly in the hole being drilled with the help of a wire rope. The bits of the drill are available in diameters varying approximately from 15 cms to 30 cms. This drill can be used to drill holes in any kind of hard rock.

The hole is filled with water upto the desired depth. Then the bit weighing about 2275 kg (5000 lbs) is lifted several metres and dropped. This action is repeated many times. This action is repeated till a heavy slurry is formed in the hole from rock cuttings with water. Now the bit is removed from the hole and a bailer with a foot value is lowered into the hole to remove the cuttings in the form of slurry. The bit must be re sharpened at regular intervals to bring it back to the required gauge. The spacing between the two holes may be kept upto 9.0 metres or more. The depth of the hole may be several hundred metres.

10. Piston drills or Quarry master. The action of this drill is similar to that of a wagon drill. In this case the drill rod is a hollow tube with an out side diameter of about 94 mm which is attached to the piston and reciprocates with it. The length of the extension rod is about 10.5 m (35 ft.). The height of the mast is about 15 m. The drill strikes about 200 blows per minute. To give the best performance for any type of rock the stroke and the rotation of the piston can be adjusted. The diameter of the detachable carbide insert bit ranges from 132 mm to 150 mm. During drilling, very less loss in gauge is experienced. If the bit resharpened at the end of a shift, then it is possible to operate with a single bit. The rock cuttings are removed by compressed air as in the case of wagon drill. The cost of the bit is very high. The practical depth limit of the drill is about 21 m (70 ft.) which may restrict its use on many projects. The weight of this drill rig is about 16.4 metric tonnes which is mounted on crawler track.

Quarry master drills can drill holes from 6 m to 12 m deep in granite and gneiss rock. Thus the performance of quarry master for drilling granite, gneiss rock was found equal to that of 2 to 4 churn drills or 4 to 6 m wagon drills.

11. Shot drills. Shot drill is a tool that depends on the abrasive effect of chilled steel shots to insert or penetrate the rock. The essential parts of a shot drill are as follows—

(*i*) A shot bit	(*ii*) Core barrel
(*iii*) Sludge barrel	(*iv*) Drill rod
(*v*) Water supply	(*vi*) Power driven rotation unit

The bit consists of a section of steel pipe. At the lower end of this pipe there are a number of points as in a saw. Such a end is called serrated end. This end extends through drill rod. As the bit is rotated the cutting medium, the chilled steel shots are fed to the lower end through the drill rod. Under the pressure of the bit these shots erode the rock and develop cracks (kerf) around the rock *i.e.* these shots lodge themselves around the core and partially in a coring bit of slot steel. Water supplied through the drill rod forces the rock cuttings up around the out side of the drill, where they settle in a sludge barrel to be removed when the entire unit is pulled out from the hole. The flow of water should be regulated carefully, so that it removes rock cuttings only, but not the chilled shot along the cutting. Periodically, it is necessary to break the core off and remove it from the hole so that drilling may proceed uninterruptedly.

Standard shot drills can be used for drilling holes in diameters varying from 6.5 cms to 50 cms and upto a depth of about 180 m (600 ft.). This drill can be used with special arrangements for drilling of 2.0 m diameter and exceeding 300 m in depth in any rocks of any hardness.

Though bigger diameter holes are expensive, but they permit a man to be lowered into them for a thorough examination of formation in place. For this purpose 50 cms to 75 cms diameter holes are necessary. The smaller holes provide continuous cores for examination for essential structural information as rock of any hardness can be drilled.

Shot drilling can be used in nearly all types of rock, but it has been found most effective in medium hard and uniform rock. In soft rock, the shots instead of grinding may become embedded in the rock. In seamy rock the shots are often lost. In hard rock the progress of work is slow. The shot drilling can be used for down ward boring and is best suited for vertical holes. However it can be used for boring with an inclination upto 30°. The rate of drilling with shot drill is slow. Sometimes it has been found less than 30 cms per hour depending upon the size of the drill and the hardness of the rock.

Some authors have suggested that shot to be effective must be crushed during coring. In relatively soft rocks pre crushed shot called calyxite is often used.

12. Diamond drills. Primarily the diamond drills are used for exploration drilling, where cores are desired for the purpose of studying the structure of the rock. The diamond drills are available in four standard sizes 37.5 mm (1½″), 47 mm (1⅞″) 60 mm (2 ⅜″) and 75 mm (3″)). Larger sizes are also available, but they are very costly. For larger diameter holes shot drills are more economical than diamond drills.

A diamond drilling rig consists of the following components:

1. A diamond bit
2. A core barrel
3. A jointed driving tube
4. A rotary head to supply driving torque

To remove the cuttings from the hole, water is pumped through the driving tube. The pressure on the bit is regulated through a screw or hydraulic feed swivel head. Core barrels are available in lengths varying from 1.5 m to 4.5 m. When the bit advances to a depth equal to the length of the core barrel, the core is broken off and the drill is removed from the hole. These drills can drill in any desired direction from vertically down ward to upward.

The selection of the size of the diameters depends on the nature of the formation to be drilled. Large sized cores are preferred for the softer formations and small sized cores for fine grained hard and solid formations.

The diamond drills are capable of drilling upto depths more than 300 m. The bit speed can be varied between 200 to 1200 rpm. The drilling rate may vary from less than 30 centimetres to several metres per hour depending on the type of rock.

23.4. SELECTION OF DRILLING METHOD AND EQUIPMENT

Holes in rocks are drilled for many purposes such as for exploration, for ground modification by the injection of grout or to receive charges of explosives etc. The equipment that will produce with in practical limits, the greatest over all economy for the particular project is the most satisfactory. The selection of the equipment depends upon the following factors.

1. Nature of the terrain. For rough surfaces the jack hammers are best regard less of other factors.
2. The required depth of holes.

3. The hardness of the rock.
4. The size of the project.
5. The extent to which the formation is fractured or broken.
6. The purpose of the hole, such as blasting, exploration or grout injections.
7. The availability of water for drilling purposes. Lack of water favours dry drilling.
8. The extent to which the rock to be broken for handling or crushing.
9. The core size required for exploration. For small size cores the use of diamond drills has been found best where as for large size cores shot drills will be suitable.

On rough surfaces, where large drills can not be operated for small diameter, shallow blasted holes usually jack hammers or track mounted drills are used though their production rates will be low and cost of operation will be higher.

For blast holes upto about 15 cms in diameter and upto about 15 m depth where machines can be used the choice will be between rotary percussion, piston drills and track mounted drills.

For drilling holes from 15 cms to 30 cms in diameter and from 15 m to 90 m depth, usually the rotary or blast hole drill is the best choice. However the type of rock effects the choice.

For cores upto 7.5 cms diameter the diamond drill is the most satisfactory.

For cores from 7.5 cms to 20 cms in diameter the choice will be between a diamond drill and a shot drill. Usually a diamond drill will drill faster than a shot drill. Also a diamond drill can drill holes in any direction, where as shot drill can drill holes vertically down or so.

23.5. RATE OF DRILLING ROCK

The rate of drilling rock will be affected by many factors as follows:

1. Hardness of rock
2. Type of drill and bit size
3. Depth of holes
4. Drilling pattern
5. Type of terrain
6. Pressure of air in case pneumatic drills are used.

The rate at which a drill will penetrate the rock is a function of the rock, the drilling method and the type and size of the bit.

The critical properties of rock which affect the penetration rate are:

(*a*) Hardness of rock
(*b*) Texture of rock
(*c*) Formation of rock
(*d*) Breaking characteristics of rock.

QUESTIONS

1. Why rocks are drilled? Discuss.
2. Name different types of drills used for drilling rocks.
3. Discuss in details following types of drills.
   (*a*) Jack hammer
   (*b*) Rotary percussion drill
   (*c*) Wagon drill
   (*d*) Quarry master drill
   (*e*) Shot drill
   (*f*) Diamond drill
4. What factors affect the selection of drilling equipment.
5. What factors affect the rate of rock drilling? Discuss.

OBJECTIVE TYPE QUESTIONS

1. The holes in rocks are drilled for
   (*a*) Exploration
   (*b*) For grouting
   (*c*) To fill charges of explosives
   (*d*) All the above
2. The selection of the equipment for drilling depends on
   (*a*) Nature of the terrain
   (*b*) Required depth of holes
   (*c*) Hardness of rock
   (*d*) Purpose of the hole

(*e*) Extent of fracture of rock (*f*) All the above

3. Identify the correct statement/statements
   (*a*) For drilling on rough surfaces jack hammer is the best choice
   (*b*) For small size cores diamond drills are the best
   (*c*) For large size cores shot drills are found best
   (*d*) For holes about 15 cm in diameter and upto about 15 m depth rotary percussion drill is the best choice
   (*e*) All are correct
4. The rate of drilling is affected by
   (*a*) Hardness of rock (*b*) Type of drill and bit size
   (*c*) Depth of holes (*d*) Drilling patteren
   (*e*) Type of terrain (*f*) All are correct
5. Identify the incorrect statements
   (*a*) Jack hammers are hand held air operated percussion type drill
   (*b*) Jack hammers can be used for drilling holes in any direction
   (*c*) Jack hammers can drill holes only in down ward direction
   (*d*) Jack hammers usually are used for drilling holes upto 3.0 m depth
   (*e*) Drifters are smaller than Jack hammers
   (*f*) Drifter can drill holes upto 113 mm in diameter used extensively in rock excavation, mining and tunnelling
6. Identify the incorrect statement/statements
   (*a*) While working with a rotary drill downward pressure on the drill steel and bit has to be applied
   (*b*) The bit-need not be kept constantly rotated in the hole
   (*c*) To remove the cuttings from the hole and cool the bit, the compressed air is forced down through the drill pipe and bit constantly
   (*d*) These drills are suitable for drilling hard rocks only
   (*e*) These drills are suitable for drilling in soft, medium hard rocks
7. Identify the correct statements
   (*a*) A rotary percussion drill is a combination of percussion drill and turning action under pressure
   (*b*) Track mounted drills are usually used on construction projects
   (*c*) The performance of wagon drills is better than Jack hammers and can be used to drill at any angle from down slightly above the horizontal
   (*d*) Churn drills can be used to drill holes in any kind of hard rock
   (*e*) Churn drills are capable to drill holes upto a depth of several hundred meters
   (*f*) All are correct
8. Identify the incorrect statement/statements
   (*a*) Quarry master or piston drills can not be used for drilling holes in hard rocks as granite and geniss rocks
   (*b*) Quarry mater drills can be used to drill holes from 6 to 12 m depth in granite and geniss rocks
   (*c*) Quarry master drill strikes about 200 blows per minute
   (*d*) Shot drills can drill holes from 6.5 cms to 50 cms in diameter
9. To drill holes in rocks of any hardness, the most suitable drill is
   (*a*) Diamond drills (*b*) Shot drills
   (*c*) Quarry master drills (*d*) Churn drills
10. For drilling exploration purposes, the most suitable drill is
    (*a*) Diamond drill (*b*) Piston drill
    (*c*) Wagon drill (*d*) Churn drill
11. For drilling holes at any angle the most suitable drill is
    (*a*) Churn drill (*b*) Wagon drill
    (*c*) Truak mounted drill (*d*) Quarry master drill

ANSWERS:

1. (*d*)	3. (*e*)	5. (*b, e*)	7. (*f*)	9. (*b*)	11. (*c*)
2. (*f*)	4. (*f*)	6. (*b, d*)	8. (*a*)	10. (*a*)	

24

Rock Crushing And Concrete Producing Equipments

24.1. INTRODUCTION

The production of crushed stone aggregate is required for many Civil Engineering projects. Crushed stone is used on railway tracks as ballast, for the construction of high ways and air field run ways and connected works as road metal and for concrete production etc. The size of crushed stone for railway ballast and road metal is much larger than crushed stone used for concrete work. For concrete the maximum size may vary from 20 mm to 40 mm. However it should be well graded.

The production of crushed stone aggregate involves drilling, blasting, loading, transporting, crushing, screening, handling and storing the aggregate. In this chapter crushing of rock, screening, handling and storing aggregate will be discussed in brief. For drilling, blasting, loading and transporting rock reader is advised to consult standard text books on tunneling.

To produce suitable aggregate materials for construction purposes the amount of processing depends on the nature of the raw materials available and the desired properties of the end product. To accomplish the desired results following four functions are required to be done.

1. Particle size reduction—Crushing.
2. Separation into particle size ranges—Screening
3. Elimination of un desirable materials—Washing
4. Handling and movement of the crushed material—Storage and transport

24.2. PARTICLE SIZE REDUCTION (Classification of crushers)

Some times crushers are classified according to the stage of crushing that they accomplish such as primary, secondary or tertiary etc. A primary crusher receives the stone directly from the excavation after blasting and produces first reduction in the size of the stone. The out put from the primary crusher is fed into the secondary crusher that further reduces the stone size. Some of the stones have to pass through four or five crushers before they are reduced to the desired size.

Crushing plants use step reduction as the amount of size reduction obtained or accomplished is directly related to the energy applied. In case there is a large difference between the size of the feed material and the size of the crushed material, a large amount of energy has to be applied. If this energy is applied during a single step process excessive fines will be generated. For fine materials normally market is limited and at many plants it is simply a waste material. Thus to control the product size and limit the waste material, the degree of breakage is spread over several stages.

As stone passes through a crusher, the reduction in size can be expressed as a reduction ratio. The reduction ratio is the ratio of crusher feed size to product size. Usually the sizes are defined as the 80%

passing size of the cumulative size distribution. For a jaw crusher, the ratio could be estimated as the gap, that is the distance between the fixed and moving faces at the top, divided this gap by the distance between open side setting at the bottom. Thus if the gap distance between the two faces at top is 24 cms and at the bottom open side setting is 6 cms, then the reduction ratio is 24/6 = 4.0.

For a roller crusher the reduction ratio can be estimated as the ratio of the dimension of the largest stone that can be caught by the rolls divided by the setting of the rolls, that is the distance between the faces of the rolls. A more accurate measurement of the reduction ratio is, to use the ratio of size corresponding to 80% passing for both the feed and the product.

24.3. CLASSIFICATION OF CRUSHERS

Crushers are classified by their methods of mechanically transmitted fracturing energy to the rock as:

1. Jaw crushers
2. Gyrating crushers
3. Roll crushers
4. Impact crushers

Crushers may also be classified as primary, secondary and tertiary crushers.

Though there is no rigid classification of crushers, but they can be classified as:

1. Primary crushers
   (*a*) Jaw crushers
   (*b*) Gyrating crushers
   (*c*) Hammer mills
2. Secondary crusher
   (*a*) Cone crusher
   (*b*) Roll crusher
   (*c*) Hammer mills
3. Tertiary crushers
   (*a*) Roll crushers
   (*b*) Rod mill
   (*c*) Ball mill

24.4. JAW CRUSHERS

This crusher is very popular and employed as a primary unit as it has a very large energy storing flywheel and high mechanical advantage. It operates by allowing stone to flow into the space between two jaws, one of which is stationary, while the other is movable. The distance between the jaws dimishes as the stone travels downward under the effect of gravity and the movable jaw, until it ultimately passes through the lower opening. The movable jaw is capable of exerting a pressure sufficiently high to crush the hardest rock. Usually jaw crushers are designed with a tapper-ing piece known as toggle as the weakest part. The toggle will break if an unbreak-able material comes under the machine or the machine is subjected to overload. This limits damage to the crusher.

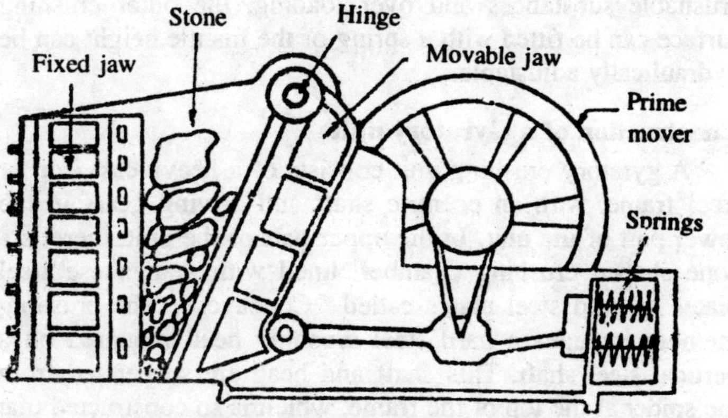

Fig. 24.1. Blake double-toggle jaw crusher

The line diagram of a double toggle BLAKE TYPE crusher is shown in Fig. 24.1 and its photograph has been shown in Fig. 24.2. The movable jaw is suspen-ded from a shaft mounted on bearings on the crusher frame. The crushing opera-tion is effected by rotating an eccentric shaft that raises and lowers the pitman and activates the two toggles. As the two toggles are raised by the pitman, a high pressure is exerted near the bottom of the swing jaw, which partially closes the opening between the bottoms of the two jaws. This operation is repeated as the eccentric shaft is rotated.

The jaw plates which are made of manganese steel may be removed, replaced or in some cases reversed. The jaws may be smooth or in case the stone tends to break into slabs, corrugated jaws may be used to reduce the slabbing. The swing jaw may be straight or curved to reduce the danger of chocking.

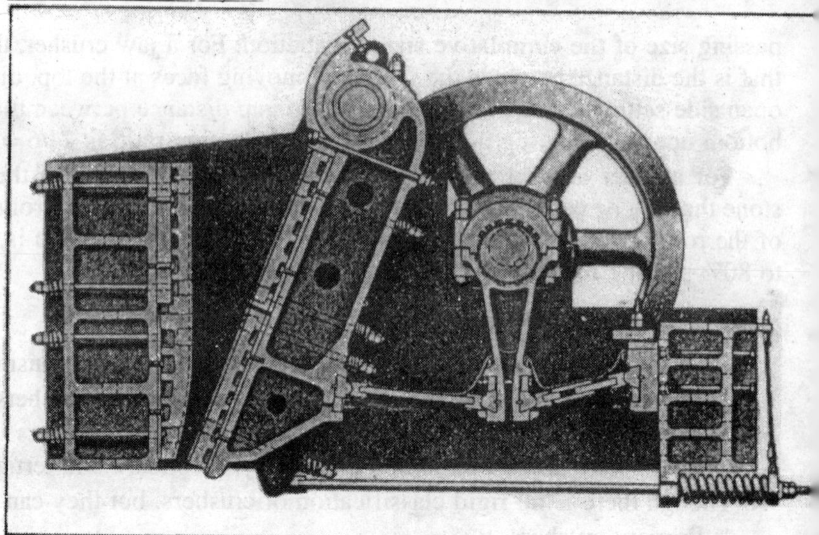

Fig. 24.2. Jaw Crusher

The movable jaw operates at a fairly slow speed, but has a large stroke at its bottom. This large stroke and conservative nip angle allows BLAKE TYPE crusher to handle hard, tough and abrasive rocks and still having good capacity. While selecting a jaw crusher the size of the feed rock should be kept in mind. The top opening of the jaw should be at least 5 cms wider than the largest stone to be fed into it.

When the eccentric shaft of a single toggle crusher is rotated, it gives the movable jaw a vertical and horizontal motion. Usually this type of crusher is used for portable rock crushing plants due to its compact size, light weight, and reasonably sturdy construction. The capacity of a single toggle crusher usually is less than that of a Blake type unit. The capacity is given in tonnes per hour based on standard material, for stones weighing 4767 kg/m^3.

24.5. GYRATORY CRUSHERS

Gyratory crushers are the most efficient of primary crushers. In this crusher a moving part (Gyrating mantle), is mounted with in a deep bowl. This gyrating mantle characterises these crushers. They provide continuous crushing action. These crushers are used for both primary and secondary crushing of hard, tough and abrasive rocks. To protect the crusher from un crushable substances and over loading, the outer crushing surface can be fitted with a spring or the mantle height can be hydraulically adjustable.

Construction of a Gyratory unit

A gyratory crushing unit consists of a heavy cast iron or steel frame, with an ecentric shaft and driving gears in the lower part of the unit. In the upper part of the unit, there is a cone shaped crushing chamber, lined with manganese steel plates or hard steel plates called "Concaves". The crushing member includes a hard steel crushing head mounted on a vertical steel shaft. This shaft and head are suspended from the spider at the top of the frame, which is so constructed that some vertical adjustment of the shaft is possible. The ecentric support at the bottom causes the shaft and the crushing head to move around or gyrate as the shaft rotates, there by varying the width of the space between the concaves and the head. As the rock fed at the top of the crushing chamber moves down ward, and under goes a reduction in size, till finally it passes through the opening at

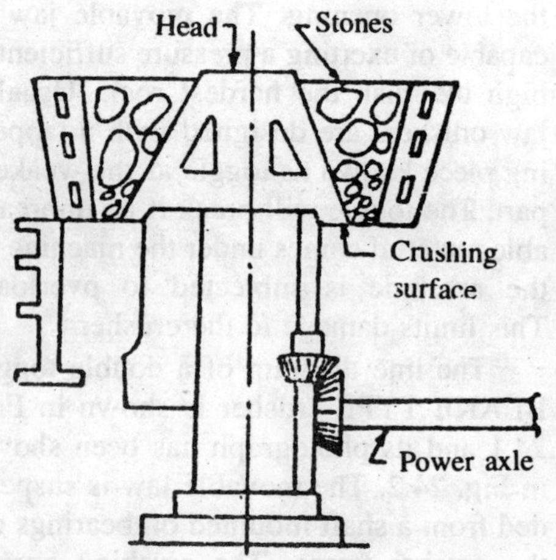

Fig. 24.3. Gyratory crusher

the bottom of the chamber. A line diagram of the gyratory crusher has been shown in Fig. 24.3 and its photograph in Fig. 24.4.

The size of a gyrating crusher is the width of the receiving opening measured between the concaves and the crusher head.

Fig. 24.4. Section through a gyratory crusher

Setting

The setting is the width of the bottom opening. It may be closed or open dimension. When a setting is given, it should be specified whether it is open or closed dimension. Normally the capacity of a gyratory crusher is based on an open side setting. The ratio of reduction for a gyratory crusher usually varies from 3:1 to 10:1, with an average value of 8:1.

If a gyrating crusher is used as a primary crusher, the size to be selected is dictated by the size of the rock from the quarry or blasting operation or by the desired capacity. When this crusher is used as a secondary crusher, then capacity usually governs the size to be selected. The capacity of a gyratory crusher may be increased by increasing the speed of the machine with in a reasonable limit.

24.6. CONE CRUSHERS

Cone or reduction crushers are used as secondary or tertiary crushers. They are capable of producing large quantities of uniformly finely crushed stone. The difference between a cone crusher and a gyratory crusher is as follows:

1. The cone crusher has a shorter cone.
2. The receiving opening of the cone crusher is smaller.
3. The cone crusher rotates at a higher speed about twice that of a gyratory speed. Its speed may be taken from 430 to 580 rpm.
4. The cone crusher produces more uniformly sized stone with the maximum size equal to the width of the closed side setting.

Fig. 24.5 shows the difference between a gyratory and a standard cone crusher. The conical head of the cone crusher usually is made of manganese steel. It is mounted on a vertical shaft and serves as one of the crushing surfaces. The other surface is the concave, which is attached to the upper part of the crusher frame. The bottom of the shaft is set in an eccentric bushing to produce the gyratory effect as the shaft rotates.

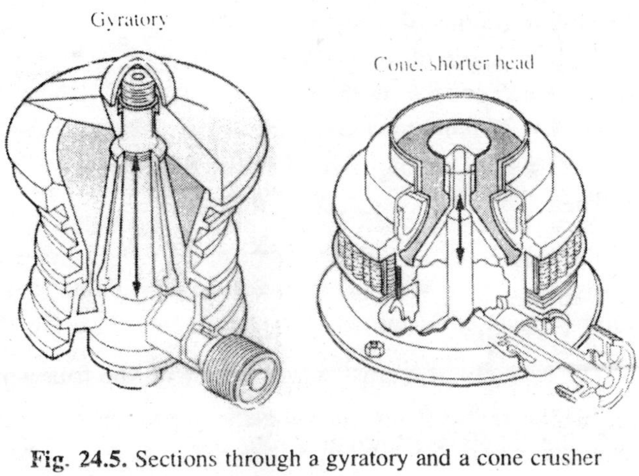

Fig. 24.5. Sections through a gyratory and a cone crusher

To designate the size of a cone crusher, the maximum diameter of the crusher head may be used. But it is the size of the feed opening (width of the opening at the crushing chamber) that limits the size of the rock that can be fed to the crusher. The magnitude of the ecentric throw and the setting of the discharge opening can be varied with in reasonable limits. Due to high speed of rotation, all particles passing through a crusher will be reduced to sizes not longer than the closed size setting, which should be used to designate the size of the discharge opening.

24.7. ROLL CRUSHERS

These crushers are used for producing additional reduction in the sizes of the stone after the output of the blasting operation has been subjected to one or more stages of prior crushing. A roll crusher consists of a heavy cast iron frame equipped with either one or more hard steel rolls, each mounted on a separate horizontal shaft. Most crushers are so constructed that each roll is driven independently on a slide frame, to permit an adjustment in the width of the discharge opening between the two rolls. The movable roll is spring loaded to provide safety against damage to the roll when the non crushable material passes through the machine.

(*a*) **Single roll crusher.** In a single roll crusher, the material is forced between a large diameter roller and an adjustable liner. These crushers have not been found economical for crushing highly abrasive materials as the material is dragged against the liner. However these crushers may handle sticky materials.

(*b*) **Double roll crushers.** The double roll crushers are so constructed that each roll is driven independently by a flat belt pull or V belt sheave. One of the rolls is mounted on a slide frame to permit an adjustment in the width of the discharge opening between the two rolls. The movable roll is spring loaded to provide safety against damage to the roll when non crushable material passes through the machine.

24.7.1. Feed size

The maximum size of material that can be fed into the roll crusher is directly proportional to the diameter of the roll. If the size of the feed stones is too large, the rolls will not catch or grip the stones or material and pull it through the crusher. The angle of grip or nip $\angle \beta$ is constant. For smooth rolls its value has been found to be 16.75° or 16°45′ (Fig. 24.6). The maximum size that can be crushed can be determined as follows. Refer Fig. 24.6.

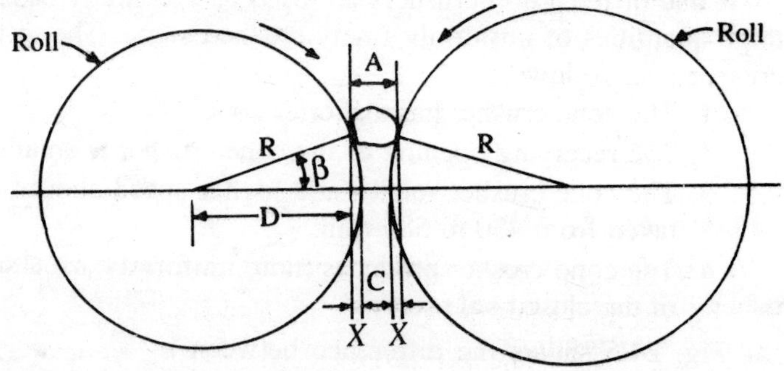

Fig. 24.6. Crushing rock between two rolls

R = Radius of rolls.

β = Angle of nip (16°45′).

$D = R \cos \beta = 0.9575\ R$

A = Maximum size of feed

C = Roll setting (size of finished product)

Then

$$X = R - D$$

$$= R - 0.9575\ R = 0.0425\ R$$

$$A = 2X + C = 0.085\ R + C$$

24.7.2. Capacity

The capacity of a crusher will vary with the following factors:

1. Type of stone
2. Size of feed
3. Size of finished product
4. Width of rolls

5. The speed at which the rolls rotate
6. The extent to which the stone is fed uniformly into the crusher.

In FPS units

$$Q = \frac{\pi C W R N}{864} \text{ tons per hour}$$

where,

C = Distance between the rolls in inches
W = Widths of rolls in inches
N = Speed of rolls in rpm
R = Radius of rolls in inches.

24.8. IMPACT CRUSHER

In these crushers the stones are broken by the application of high speed impact forces. In these crushers to use the initial impect energy fully, the advantage of rebound between the individual stones against machine surfaces is utilized. The design of some units additionally seeks to shear and compress the stones between the revolving and stationary parts. For the effective operation of these crushers, speed is important, as the energy available for impact varies as the square of the rotational speed.

24.9. CLASSIFICATION OF IMPACT CRUSHERS

The impact crushers may be classified as

1. **Single Rotor Crusher.** The single rotor type impact crusher breaks the stone by the impact action of the impellers striking the feed material and the impact which results when the impeller driven material strikes against the aprons with in the crusher unit. These units produce a cubical product. These units are economical for low abrasion feeds only. The production rate of the unit is affected by the speed of the rotor. Further speed also affects the reduction ratio. Thus the speed adjustment should be done after due consideration to the production and the final product.
2. **Double rotor.** These units are similar to single rotor units and accomplish the aggregate size reduction by the same mechanical mechanism. They produce higher proportion of fines. In both type of impact crushers, the impacted material flows freely to the bottom of the units with out any further size reduction.

24.10. HAMMER MILLS

A hammer mill most widely is used as a impact crusher. It may be used as a primary or secondary crusher. The basic parts of a hammer mill are as follows:

1. A housing frame
2. A horizontal shaft extending through the housing
3. Number of arms and hammers attached to a spool, which is mounted on a shaft
4. One or more manganese steel or other hard steel breaker plate
5. A series of grate bars whose spacing may be adjusted to regulate the width of openings through which the crushed stone flows. These parts are shown in Fig. 24.7.

As the stone to be crushed is fed into the mill, the hammers which move at a high speed (rpm), strike the particles. By the strike of the hammers the particles are broken and drived against the breaker plates, which further reduce their sizes. The final size reduction is accomplished by grinding the material against the bottom grate bars.

The size of a hammer mill may be designated by the size of the feed opening. The capacity of the hammer mill is affected by the following factors:

1. Size of the unit

2. Kind of stone crushed
3. Size of the feed material
4. Speed of the shaft etc.

Hammer mills produce a high proportion of fines and cannot handle wet or sticky material.

24.11. SELECTION OF CRUSHING EQUIPMENT

Before selection of a particular equipment at least following information should be collected:

1. The kind of stone to be crushed
2. The required capacity of the plant
3. Maximum size of feed stones
4. Method of feeding the crushers
5. The required specified size ranges of the product.

Fig. 24.7. Cutaway of hammer mill rock crusher showing breaking action

24.12. CONCRETE EQUIPMENT

Concrete is a mixture of a binding material as lime or cement, inert filler material as sand and coarse aggregate and water. Lime concrete is in use since 690 B.C. and cement concrete since 1824. Now portland cement concrete is one of the most widely used structural materials in the world for Civil Engineering projects. Its versatility, economy, adaptability and availability in all corners of the world and its low maintenance requirements have made it an excellent building material.

Cement concrete is a mixture of cement, sand, coarse aggregate and water. Now a days an ingredient known as admixture is also added to it to a have a specific property of the cement concrete. The fresh concrete can be moulded into any desired shape in the control plant and at site as well. This is the greatest advantage of the cement concrete. Now a days with the advancement in the cement technology the concrete may be produced of varying strengths from 10 kg/cm^2 to 800 kg/cm^2.

24.13. PRODUCTION OF CONCRETE

The operations in the production of cement concrete will vary with its end use. However in general following operations are involved in the production of cement concrete.

1. **Proportioning.** It is also called as mix design.
2. **Batching the material.** The correct measurement of the ingredients of the concrete is known as batching.
3. **Mixing.** The ingradients are properly mixed before use.
4. **Transporting.**
5. **Placing.**
6. **Compacting.**
7. **Finishing.**
8. **Curing.**

24.13.1. Proportioning

Proportioning of Concrete ingradients is one of the most important factor. Indian standard specifications and American Concrete Institute etc. have recommended many excellent methods of proportioning or mix design.

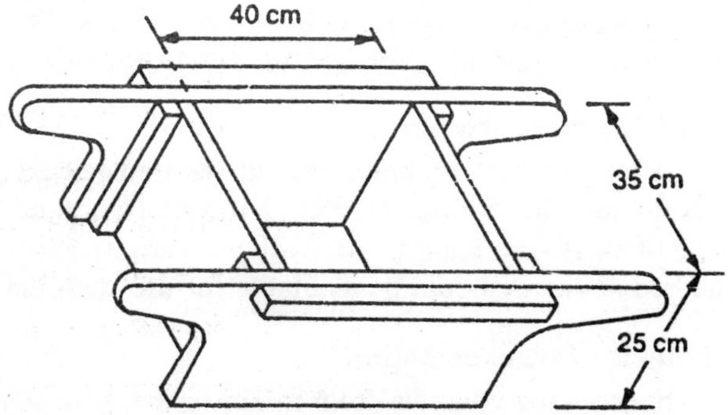

Fig. 24.8. Ferma

24.13.2. Batching

(*a*) Batching of material can be done either by volume or weight batching. For volume batching. Concrete association of Indian has recommended the dimensions of formas as 40 cm long 35 cms wide and 25 cm deep (Fig. 24.8).

(*b*) Weight batching. Now a days for the production of good quality concrete all materials are measured by weight Fig. 24.9 shows a concrete mixer with built in weight batching mechanism.

Fig. 24.9. Batching Mixer

24.13.3. Mixing

The object of mixing of concrete is to coat the surface of all aggregate particles with cement paste and to blend all ingredients of concrete into a uniform mass. Mixing of concrete can be done either by hand or by machines.

(*a*) **Hand mixing.** Hand mixing of concrete usually is done for un important and very small works. For good works this method is not used.

(*b*) **Machine mixing.** For mixing concrete many types of mixers are available as follows:

1. Batch mixer
2. Continuous mixers

1. Batch mixers. These mixers can further be divided as follows:

(*a*) **Tilting type mixers**. This class of mixers have a conical or bowl shaped drum with inside vanes. These vanes revolve on an inclined axis. It is charged by means of a loading skip and discharged by tilting the drum. On tilting the drum, all the mix can be tipped out rapidly in an unsegregated condition. For this reason tilting mixers are preferable for mixes of low workability and having large size aggregate.

(*b*) **Non tilting type mixers.** The drum of this class of mixers is cylindrical and always rotates about a horizontal axis. In this case the material is charged by means of a cable operated loading skip. The discharge of concrete is obtained either by inserting a chute into the drum or by reversing the direction of rotation of the drum. Due to slow rate of discharge, concrete is liable to segregate.

(*c*) **Pan mixers.** This type of mixer is not mobile. Thus it can be used either at a central mixing plant or at large concrete project or in a concrete laboratory or precast laboratory.

Capacity of mixers. Usually the capacity of mixers varies from 1.89 m^3 to 7.56 m^3 per hour. However for central plants mixers, the capacity may vary from 6.12 m^3 to 11.3 m^3.

Mixing time. During study at Central Building Research Institute Roorkee during 1954-1960 author observed that a mixing time of 90 seconds to 120 seconds is most satisfactory.

24.13.4. Transportation

After mixing, concrete should be transported and placed at site as quickly as possible with out segregation and drying etc. Hence transportation of fresh concrete is very important. Depending upon the type of work and equipment available various methods of transporting of concrete can be employed. The method selected should be available for use with the consistency of concrete employed.

Methods of transportation

For moving concrete from mixer to the form work following methods may be employed:

1. Pan method
2. Wheel barrows
3. Dumpers
4. Lorries
5. Mono rails
6. Hoists
7. Cranes
8. Skips and buckets
9. Pressure equipment

Here some of the above methods have been discussed.

1. Pan method. This method of concrete transportation can be employed for small jobs, where quantity of concrete required is small and labour is available at cheap rates.

2. Transportation by Dumpers and trucks. These are special types of trucks. These dumpers have been found suitable to transport concrete from mixer upto a distance of 350 m with out segregation and setting. These dumpers have been found more suitable on loose and un even grounds. The capacity of a dumper is 2 to 3 m^3 while that of a truck is $4m^3$.

4. Transportation by tipping lorries. Tipping lorries can be used to transport concrete upto 5 km. Concrete to be transported to a distance more than 350 m should contain less amount of water to avoid segregation in the transition due to shaking and bad condition of the road. The effect of segregation can be minimised by keeping the thicker layers of concrete in the lorry. The thickness of a layer of concrete should not be less than 40 cms. These lorries have arrangements for receiving, loading and discharging concrete. These lorries are used to transport concrete for the construction of roads, air fields, dams, tunnels and canal lining etc.

4. Transportation by Monorail and jubblee trucks. Monorail trucks are very convient for use with small and medium size mixing plants. Their main advantage is that they can be used across difficult and narrow sites with out requiring much space. The rail is readily fixed and can be moved to new positions as the job procceds. Their main disadvantage is the requirement of a special type of rail which is very costly. However they can be used in all types of terrains.

Jubblee tracks are special type of trucks which can be used to transport concrete through soft and difficult terrain with out much difficulty.

Transport by belt conveyer

Belt conveyers are available in convenient forms which allow the movement of concrete easily to different parts at the site. This method is used in situations where concrete is required continuously. This method of transpiration is most suitable for concreting in hot climate at a distance of 250 m to 500 m from the mixing site. This method can also be used to carry concrete up slopes less than 30°. This method has proved very useful at places where other modes of transportation of concrete are not feasible. The slump of concrete to be transported by belt conveyer should not be more than 9.0 cms. However 6.0 cms slump is quite sufficient.

The belt used has a rubber covering of 60 cms width. The seed of conveyer should not be more than 1 m per second. The inclination of the conveyer should not be more than 30°. Flat belts are used only upto

20 m distance. For larger distances trough shaped belts are used. While unloading or transferring from one part to the other, precautions to avoid segregation should be taken.

Transport by hoist

Now a days at multistory building sites upto a height of about 150 m hoists are used more frequently. The capacity of hoist may vary from 200 lit to 510 lit. These hoists work at a speed of 75 m per minute.

Transport by crane

To transport concrete by crane, a suitable bucket is required. It is also called skip. One of the type of bucket is known as *Lay back skip.* It is designed to fall on its back when lowered to the ground and it can be filled from a low level mixer discharge. When it is raised, it is pulled up right and can discharge its contents through a gate at its lower end. For larger batches dump buckets are used. Usually these buckets are cylindrical. The capacity of such buckets is 115 lit. While concrete is transported by crane, care should be taken that concrete is not thrown from an excessive height, so that form work may not be damaged.

Transportation of Concrete by elevating tower and chute

This system of concrete transportation is suitable for large dams. In this case the concrete is filled at the head of deep chutes by buckets in a central tower. From this point concrete reaches at the required place through these chutes. The height of the tower should not be higher than 170 m and the capacity of the bucket should not be more than 1.3 m^3. Concrete to be transported by this method should be sufficiently fluid. The slump of the concrete should be more than 5.0 cms. This method of concrete transportation has proved very useful when the strength of concrete is not important. For less fluid concrete, vibrators should be used on chutes to move the concrete.

Transportation of concrete by chutes

Usually chutes are employed for concrete transportation from ground level to a low level. The chute section should be lined with metal sheet and the slope for full length should be the same. it should not be flatter than 1 vertical and 2.5 horizontal. The layout of the chute should be such that concrete will be able to slide with out segregation as a compact mass.

Though this method is not good for concrete transportation, yet it is adopted when the movement of labour can not be allowed due to lack of space or due to fear of disturbance to the reinforcement.

24.14. READY MIXED CONCRETE

Concrete available for placing from a central plant is known as *ready mixed concrete or pre mixed concrete.*

24.14.1. Advantages of ready made concrete

The ready made concrete has the following advantages

1. This type of concrete specially is useful on congested sites.
2. It is useful for road construction where little space is available for mixing plant and for stacking aggregate and other materials.
3. Ready mixed concrete is made under better control than on site. Actually a factory type control on all operations is possible on the control mixing plant. This is the greatest advantage of the ready mixed concrete.
4. Ready made concrete can be considered as a factory made product almost comparable with steel. Hence a great deal of uncertainty and variability associated with the production of concrete on many sites is removed.
5. The use of ready made concrete is advantageous when only small quantities of concrete is required or concrete is to be placed at intervals.

Disadvantages

The ready made concrete has been found 10 to 15 times costlier than concrete mixed at site. This is its main disadvantage.

24.15. CLASSIFICATION OF READY MADE CONCRETE

The ready made concrete may be classified into the following two categories:

1. Central mixed concrete
2. Transit mixed or truck mixed concrete

1. Central mixed concrete

In this case the mixing of the concrete is done at a central plant and the mixed concrete is transported in a special type of truck known as agitator truck. The truck revolves slowly while moving. The agitating

Fig. 24.10. Central-mixed concrete plant, mixer drum is on the far right end of the plant

container is conical in shape having smaller blades than the mixer (Fig. 24.10). The capacity of the container varies from 1.25 m^3 to 3.0 m^3. However the height of this containers is more than a mixer. The container is put upright in the truck and an air tight stopper is placed on its top to check the evaporation of water from the concrete. The segregation and stiffening of the concrete is checked by revolving the container. The revolving of the container is also done by the engine of the truck. The rate of revolving of the container depends upon the speed of the truck varying from 2 to 6 revolution per minute. However 2 to 3 revolutions per minute are quite satisfactory.

Advantages of agitating trucks

Following advantages of agitating trucks have been observed:

1. To revolve the container, very less amount of energy is required.
2. During even one hour journey no ill effect on the properties of concrete has been observed.

Disadvantage

These agitating trucks can not be used for any other purpose. Hence they are un economical.

2. Transit mixed concrete

In this case, the materials are batched at a central plant and the dry mix is put in mixers kept in trucks. The mix is mixed either during the transit to the site or immediately prior to the concrete being discharged at the site. The speed of rotation varies from 4 to 16 revolutions per minute. The transsit mix truck transporting concrete is shown in Fig. 24.11.

Fig. 24.11. Transit-mix truck transporting ready-mixed concrete

ASTM has laid down the limit of 300 revolutions or $1\frac{1}{2}$ hour for both agitating and mixing duration between mixing water and placement of concrete. Thus concrete must be laid with in 90 minutes of mixing. The capacity of the mixer may vary from 0.75 m^3 to 4.5 m^3.

Advantages

Following advantages have been observed of this method:

1. Transit mixing permits a longer haul and is vulnerable in case of delay.
2. Dislocation of the work does not take place as water is added to the mix near the site of work.
3. The discharge of the concrete is done by reversing the direction of the revolving mixer rather than tipping the truck.
4. These mixers have a small revolving tubing, which can spread the concrete on a sufficient wide area. This operation makes the concrete spreading operation economical.

Disadvantages

1. The method of transportation is limited to an area with in a distance of 9 to 15 km.
2. These trucks can be used only for this purpose.
3. The moist aggregate should not remain in contact with cement for more than 90 minutes.

Note. It may be noted carefully, that the speed of mixing affects the rate of stiffening while the total number of revolution controls the uniformity of mixing.

24.16. TYPE OF READY MIXED CONCRETE AVAILABLE

Ready mixed concrete can be obtained in several ways as follows:

1. Recipe batch. (recipe means a set of conditions). From ready mixed units concrete can be obtained with the conditions imposed by the purchaser. In this case the purchaser may take the responsibility for proportioning the concrete mixture. He can specify the cement content, maximum w/c ratio, percentage of air and type of admixture required, type of aggregate etc. In short under this approach, the purchaser assumes full responsibility for the resulting strength and quality of the mixtures, provided the stipulated quantities are furnished as specified.

2. Performance batch. In this case, purchaser specifies the strength requirements of the concrete and the supplier assumes full responsibility for the proportion of various ingredients to be added into the batch.

3. Part recipe and part performance. In this case the purchaser generally specifies a minimum cement content, required strength and admixture to be added. Rest of the operations are left to the supplier with in the frame work of conditions imposed.

24.17. CONCRETE TRANSPORTED BY PUMPS

German made concrete pumps were used for the first time in India in 1930. This is an extremely simple machine. The concrete can be moved through a pipe by applying a suitable pressure to a column of fresh concrete in a pipe. For proper working of the pump, the concrete mixture should be properly proportioned and the outer layer of concrete in pipe is made lubricating. Further the concrete should be of uniform workability and consistency.

24.18. TYPE OF PUMPS

At present usually three types of concrete pumps are in use:

1. Piston pumps. A piston pump is shown in Fig. 24.12. After mixing the concrete, it is filled into a hopper and pump started. During the suction stroke, the inlet valve is opened as shown in Fig. 24.12 (*a*) and the delivery valve remains closed Fig. 24.12 (*b*). The diameter of the piston is some what less than the

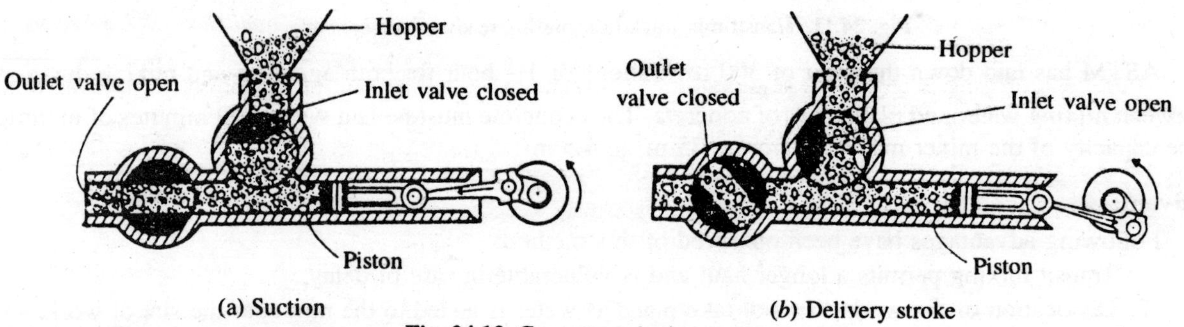

Fig. 24.12. Concrete pumping system

diameter of the cylinder. At the working end of the piston, rubber cups are attached, which check the wastage in the cylinder. At the other end, this piston woks in bushes. These bushes are lubricated by the water flowing through empty space between the cylinder and the piston. This water also dissolves the cement paste leaching through rubber cups, reducing the danger of setting the cement paste. In this way the pump is kept safe from damage. The whole assembly is set in such a way that every part of it can be opened, inspected, and repaired as per need.

Capacity

Usually concrete can be pumped along a straight and level pipe line for a distance of 300 to 450 m and upto 40 m vertical height using a single pump. Any rise of 30 cm is equivalent to 2.4 m on the level ground and a right angled bend is equivalent to about 12 m length. Hence for a $22\frac{1}{2}^{\circ}$ bend 3 m and for a 90° bend 12 m horizontal line should be reduced. No sharp bends should be attached in a concrete pipe line. In between bends straight pipe should be attached. The size of pipe may vary from 11.25 to 20 cms inside diameter.

2. Squeeze type concrete pump. This pump was developed in U.S.A. in 1963. In this pump, concrete placed in a collecting hopper is fed into the flexible pipe by the rotating blades. The flexible pipe is connected to the pumping chamber. In the pumping chamber a vaccum of about 600 mm of mercury is created. This vaccum ensures the shape of pipe cylindrical except when squeezed by the roller. This condition ensures the continuous flow of concrete. Two rotating rollers progressively squeeze the flexible pipe and move the concrete into the delivery pipe. The action of squeeze pump is shown in Fig. 24.13. These pumps are lorry mounted and the concrete is delivered through a folding boom.

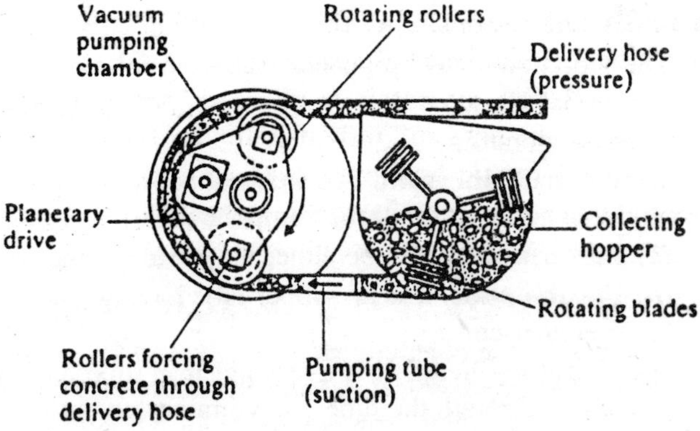

Fig. 24.13. Squeeze type pump

24.19. ADVANTAGE OF CONCRETE PUMP TRANSPORTATION

Concrete transportation by concrete pumps has been found very advantageous under the following conditions:

1. At congested sites where mixing plant can not be taken close to the point of placing the concrete.
2. At sites where stacking of aggregate is not possible due to non availability of space.
3. By this method concrete can be delivered to points over a wide area, otherwise not easily accessible.
4. This method of concrete transportation has been found very useful for tunnel lining, large mass concrete structures and densly reinforced concrete structures etc.
5. This method of concrete transport is more economical where large quantities of concrete are required.

Pumped concrete is free from segregation. In this method concrete can be put directly from the mixer to the form work, avoiding the double handling.

24.20. PROPERTIES OF CONCRETE TO BE PUMPED

Concrete to be pumped should satisfy the following specifications:

1. The concrete should neither be too wet nor too dry. The slump may vary from 5.7 cms to 10 cms.
2. Cement aggregate ratio should not be more than 1:6.
3. Water cement ratio may vary from 0.5 to 0.65.
4. A mix proportion of 1:2:4 has been found ideal for this concrete.
5. Well graded aggregate should be used for pumped concrete.
6. Light weight aggregate should not be used for this concrete.
7. Maximum size of aggregate for this concrete should be 20 mm. The optimum amount of fine aggregate should be between 35 to 40% and the material finer than 300 micron should be between 15 to 20%. 3.0% material should pass the 150 micron sieve.
8. The quantity of fine particles (cement and sand) passing through 300 micron should be 350 to 400 kg/m^3.
9. The slump of pumpable concrete should be 7.5 cms and the diameter of the pipe line should be 3 to 4 times the size of the maximum aggregate.

24.21. COMPACTION OF CONCRETE

Concrete is a heterogeneous mixture of cement, aggregate and water in a stiff state containing large voids and entrapped air. The aim of consolidation is to remove these air voids. The process of compaction or consolidation of concrete essentially consists of the elimination of entrapped air in the concrete. It has been observed that each one percent less compaction reduces the strength of the concrete by 5%. Consolidation normally is achieved by the use of mechanical vibrations.

24.22. TYPES OF VIBRATORS

The vibrations may be generated by the following three types of vibrators:

1. Internal vibrators
2. Surface vibrators
3. Form vibrators

1. Internal vibrators. An internal vibrator is also known as needle vibrator. A internal vibrator essentially consists of the three components.

(*a*) **Power unit.** It can be either an patrol engine or electric supply unit.

(*b*) **Flexible tube.** It is an rubber tube having power connecting device at one end and vibrator head on the other end.

(*c*) **Vibratory head.** It is a straight iron tube having eccentric weight fitted in side it. As the current passes through the tube, the vibratory action is caused by the rotation of the eccentrically weighted shaft at high speed usually over 7000 r.p.m. which are transmitted to the concrete particles.

The diameter of the needle varies from 2.0 cms to 17.5 cms and length from 25 cms to 90 cms. The frequency of vibration may vary from 10,000 to 15,000 cycles per minute. The bigger diameter needle is used in the construction of mass concrete work. The vibrating head should be immersed vertically in the concrete and should be kept in side the concrete. While running the vibrator, its bearings should be kept cool to avoid break-down. As the concrete consolidates, its surface level falls and surface becomes smooth. Air bubbles may be seen breaking at the surface. When these bubbles cease to appear on the surface, the concrete may be assumed as compacted sufficiently.

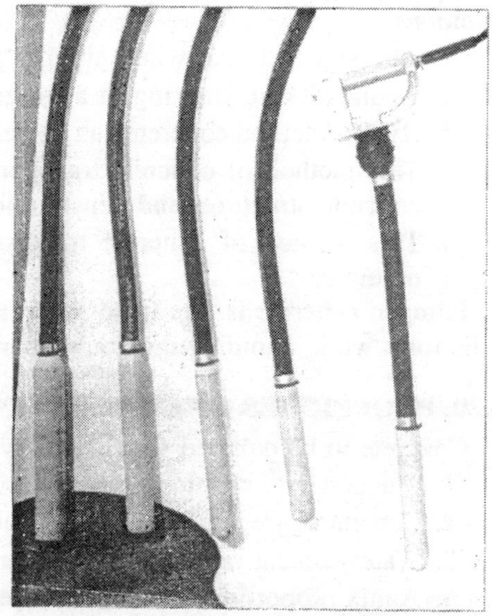

Fig. 24.14. Internal Vibrator

The vibrator should be lowered vertically in the concrete and when the concrete is compacted it should be withdrawn vertically slowly at the rate of about 8.0 cms/sec. At this speed the withdrawal hole caused will fill itself with out entrapping air in the concrete. Now the vibrator is inserted at another point at a distance of 50 cms to 100 cms. However this distance depends on the shape of form work and amount of reinforcement. How ever the distance should be kept uniform.

When the concrete is filled in layers, the vibrator should be immersed through the entire depth of the freshly laid layer and into the layers below it about 5 to 6 cms thickness. For layers more than 50 cms thick, the vibrator may not be fully effective in expelling the air.

24.23. TIME OF VIBRATION

The time of compaction by the internal vibrator depends on the consistency of the mix. Usually from 5 to 30 seconds compaction is sufficient depending on the consistency of the mix.

2. Surface vibrators. These vibrators are used to compact horizontal concrete surfaces are roads. They impart vibration at the surface of the concrete. The frequency of these vibrators vary from 3000 to 6000 cycles per minute. There are four general class of these vibrators as:

(*a*) Vibrating screed
(*b*) Pan type vibrator
(*c*) Plate type tamper and
(*d*) Vibratory rolling screed

Form vibrators. These vibrators are external vibrators and are attached to the out side of the concrete form work. They vibrate the form work and inturn form work vibrates the concrete. This class of vibrators generally are used in large precast concrete plants.

24.24. FINISHING OF CONCRETE

After the completion of the compaction, the concrete surface is finished by trawling, floating or by belts etc.

24.25. CURING

It is the last operation in concrete production. Curing is the process of checking the evaporation of water from the body of the concrete so that sufficient amount of water may be available in the body of the concrete for full hydration. There are several methods of curing as follows:

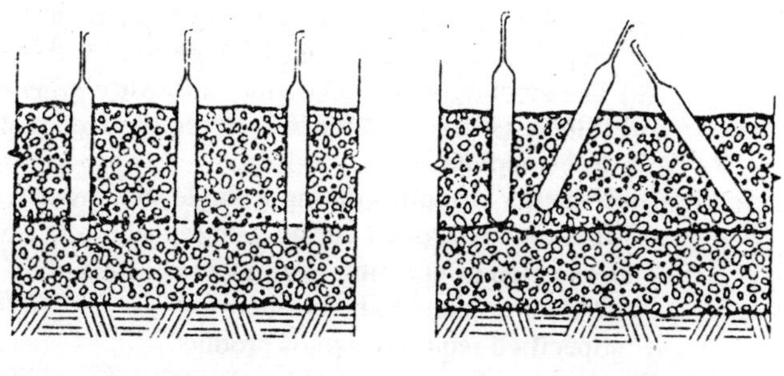

Fig. 24.15. Position of vibrator

1. Shading of concrete
2. Covering of concrete surface from gunny bags, burlaps, etc.
3. Sprinkling water on the concrete surface.
4. Ponding of concrete surface. This method of curing has been found to give more strength than other methods.
5. Membrane curing
6. Steam curing etc.

QUESTIONS

1. Why crushing of rock is required?
2. Give the classification of rock crushers. Also mention the field of application of each type.
3. Name different types of screens used in the manufacture of crushed aggregate. Describe their characteristics.
4. Compare the tilting and non tilting type concrete mixers.
5. Describe the working of concrete pumps.
6. Give the characteristics of the pumpable concrete.
7. Describe different types of concrete vibrators.
8. Describe the working of truck mixers.
9. Give the advantages of ready mixed concrete.
10. Discuss the transportation of central mixed concrete, giving advantages of each method.
11. Give the advantages of pump transportation of concrete.
12. Write a detailed note on the internal vibrator of concrete.
13. Write a note on curing of concrete.

OBJECTIVE TYPE QUESTIONS

1. Rock crushing is required to use smaller pieces as
   (*a*) Balast for railway track
   (*b*) Road material for the construction of high ways and air field run ways
   (*c*) Aggregate for the production of concrete
   (*d*) All the above
2. To produce suitable aggregate the amount of processing depends upon
   (*a*) Nature of raw material (*b*) Desired properties of the end product
   (*c*) Both are correct (*d*) Both are incorrect
3. To obtain the suitable aggregate following functions are done
   (*a*) Crushing of rock (*b*) Screening of particles
   (*c*) Washing (*d*) Storage and transport
   (*e*) Al the above
4. Identify the incorrect statement/statements

(*a*) Crushing plants use step reduction to obtain the desired sized stones
(*b*) Some stones have to pass through four to five crushes before they are reduced to the desired size
(*c*) The amount of size reduction is directly proportional to the energy applied
(*d*) If there is large difference between the feed material and the size of the crushed material large energy has to be applied
(*e*) If energy is applied during a single step process best crushed product is obtained which has a good market
(*f*) If energy is applied during a single step process excessive fines are generated, which have little market

5. The selection of crushing equipment is affected except
(*a*) Nature of stone to be crushed (*b*) Size of feed stone
(*c*) Specified required size of product (*d*) Size of the equipment

6. Concrete can be transported by tipping lorries without segregation upto a distance of
(*a*) 2 km (*b*) 3.5 km
(*c*) 5 km (*d*) 7.5 km

7. By dumpers and trucks concrete can be transported with out segregation for a distance of
(*a*) 200 m (*b*) 350 m
(*c*) 450 m (*d*) 800 m

8. Identify the incorrect statement/statements
(*a*) To transport concrete across different terrains and narrow sites mono rail is most convent
(*b*) To transport concrete through soft and difficult terrain jubilee trucks are most convient
(*c*) Mono rail is difficult to fix and to move to new positions as the work proceeds
(*d*) The mono rail is a special type rail which is very costly

9. Concrete to be pumped should have properties
(*a*) Slump from 5.7 to 10 cm (*b*) Cement aggregate ratio 1:6
(*c*) Mix proportion 1:2:4 (*d*) Water-cement ratio 0.5 to 0.65
(*e*) Maximum size of aggregate 20 mm (*f*) All are correct

10. The best mix proportion for pumpable concrete is
(*a*) $1:1\frac{1}{2}:3$ (*b*) 1:2:4
(*c*) $1:2\frac{1}{2}:5$ (*d*) 1:3:6

11. The diameter of the pipe line for pumpable concrete should be times larger the maximum size of aggregate used
(*a*) 1 to 2 (*b*) 2 to 3
(*c*) 3 to 4 (*d*) 5 to 6

12. The maximum length of the internal vibrator may be
(*a*) 150 cms (*b*) 250 cms
(*c*) 175 cms (*d*) 90 cms

13. The time of compaction by internal vibrator depends on
(*a*) Consistency of the mix (*b*) Size of the coarse eggregate
(*c*) Amount of fine aggregate (*d*) Length of the vibrator needle

ANSWERS:

1. (*d*)	4. (*e*)	7. (*b*)	10. (*b*)	13. (*a*)
2. (*c*)	5. (*d*)	8. (*c*)	11. (*c*)	
3. (*e*)	6. (*c*)	9. (*f*)	12. (*d*)	

25

Hoisting Equipment (Cranes)

25.1. INTRODUCTION

In our every day life we need weight lifting and moving. Hoisting is the operation of lifting a load from one location, transporting it to an other location situated at a reasonable distance and landing it down. Present day construction involves handling of heavy loads with fast speed, safety and economy. Hoisting equipment includes rope pully blocks, chain hoists, jacks, winches and cranes.

Crane is a versatile and most useful machine. It is the only single machine capable of providing three dimensional movement to a load virtually in one continuous operation. It is able to perform the operations with speed, safety and precision. It is necessary to know the lifting capacity and working range of a crane to be selected to perform a given job. Thus it is an unavoidable piece of equipment on a construction project. In this chapter only cranes have been discussed.

25.2. CLASSIFICATION OF CRANES

Broadly cranes may be divided into four categories as:

1. Stationary cranes
2. Over head or gantry crane
3. Mobile cranes
4. Traveller crane

25.3. STATIONARY CRANE

It is also called derrick crane. These cranes give an exceptionally large working radius and can be designed to give almost any lifting capacity. They may be steam, electric-diesel or electrically driven.

Constituents of a derrick crane. A derrick crane consists of:

(*a*) A mast

(*b*) A boom

(*b*) A bull wheel on which the boom rotates about a vertical axis

(*d*) Supporting members called guys.

The derrick cranes may be used on a wide range of works, from large civil works to industrial building construction, erection of plants, handling of timber, hoisting works at ship yards, loading and unloading cargoes at ports etc.

25.4. CLASSIFICATION OF A DERRICK CRANE

A derrick crane can be classified into two types as follows:

(*a*) Guy derrick type (*b*) Stiff leg derrick type

(*a*) **Guy derrick.** A guy derrick crane has small boom supported by a number of members called guys. The boom is pivoted at the lower end of the mast. The boom can revolve through 360° with in a radius which can pass inside the guys. A bull wheel is attached to the mast at its lower end. The bull wheel can be moved by a cable on reversible drum. The boom support cable passes over the top of the mast and winds over to the boom drum. The load line passes over boom point sheave and winds over an other drum for load hoist. The power for operation usually is supplied by a diesel engine or by an electric motor. The prime mover may be mounted on a platform attached to the mast and may swing with the derrick or it may be mounted on land near the derrick. A typical guy derrick crane is shown in Fig. 25.1. The capacity of a guy derrick crane may be upto 182 metric tonnes.

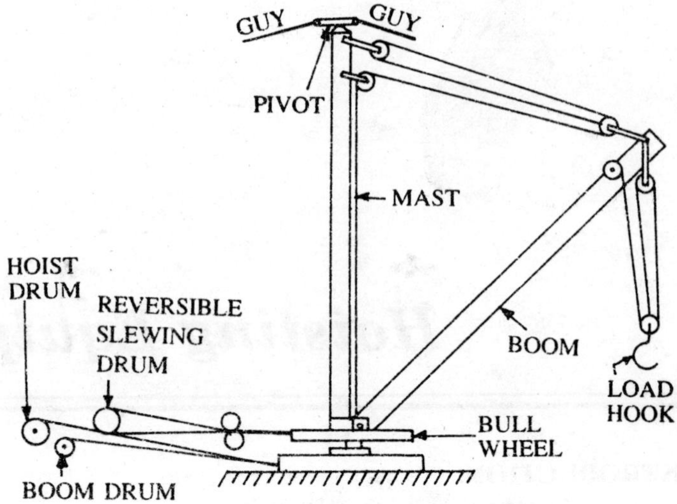

Fig. 25.1. Parts of Derrick Crane

(*b*) **Stiff leg derrick.** When the guy ropes are replaced by trussed structure the crane is called stiff leg derrick crane. The stiff leg derrick consists of a revolving mast and boom. The mast is supported at its top or upper end by two braced stiff legs, which have a horizontal angle of 60° to 90°. Thus the boom rotates through angle of 270° to 290°. This type of crane or stiff leg derrick is used in situations where a light and compact derrick crane is required or for the same boom length and working radius greater load capacity is required. Usually a stiff leg derrick may be used for loads from 9.1 to 45.4 metric tones (10 to 50 F.P.S. system tons). (Fig. 25.2)

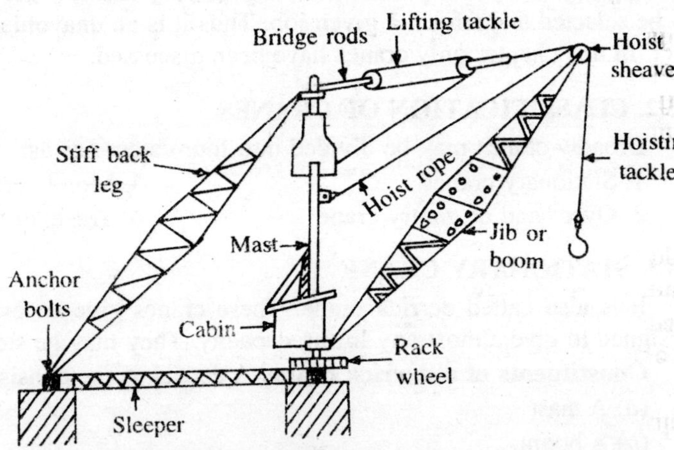

Fig. 25.2. Stiff leg derrick crane

25.5. OVERHEAD OR GANTRY CRANES

These cranes are used for handling loads over a long rectangular area such as in factories and work shops to move machines and other loads in any direction. These cranes consist of a hoisting mechanism mounted on a carriage or crab capable travelling laterally across a girder which spans the gantries. The girder resting on wheels travels longitudinally on rails on a over head gantry. The capacity of these cranes vary from 0.9 to 455 metric tonnes. Fig. 25.3 shows an electric over head crane.

25.6. MOBILE CRANES

These cranes are mounted on mobile units as a pneumatic tyred truck or a crawler chassis. Usually a

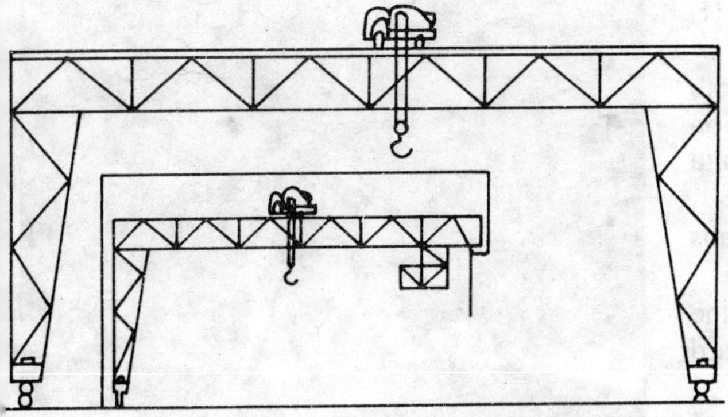

Fig. 25.3. Gantry Crane

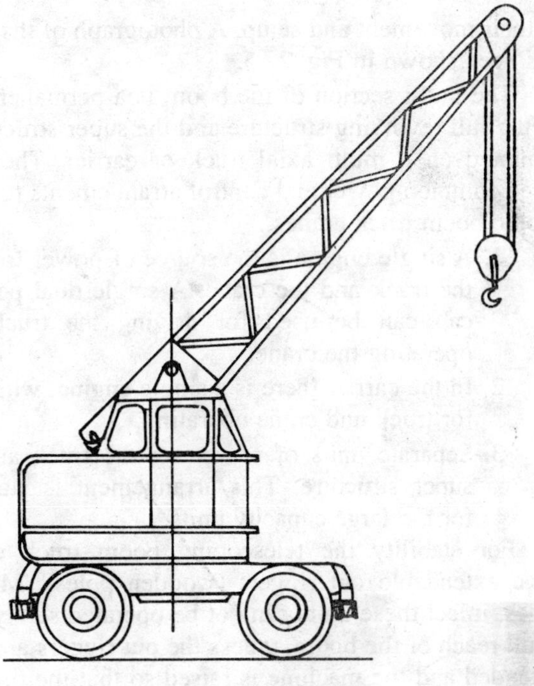

Fig. 25.4. Mobile Crane

single prime mover provides power for propulsion as well as for rig operation. Truck cranes have high mobility, where as crawler mounted cranes move slowly.

25.7. CLASSIFICATION OF MOBILE CRANES

Mobile cranes may be of the following types:

1. Crawler
2. Telescopic boom truck mounted cranes
3. Lattice boom truck mounted cranes
4. Rough terrain
5. All terrain
6. Heavy lift cranes etc.

1. Crawler cranes. A full revolving super structure type of unit is mounted on a pair of continuous parallel crawler track. The crawlers are capable of moving on rough terrains. The crawlers also provide the capability to the crane to travel around the job site. These crawler tracks provide a large ground contact area where soil failure under these machines is only a problem, when operating on soils having a low bearing capacity. Before lifting or hoisting a load the machine must be levelled and ground settlement considered. If there is a possibility of ground settlement the crane may be positioned and levelled on mats.

Most crawler cranes have a fixed length-lattice boom. A lattice boom is cable suspended and acts as a compressive member where as the telescoping hydraulic boom acts as a bending member. The capacity of load lifting of these cranes is about 90 metric tones. These units move slowly and need transportation facilities to the other job site. They have to be dismantled and carried to the new site. For the movement of one unit of such a crane 15 or more truck trailer units are required. Again to assemble it on the new job site it need time. Hence such units should be used where they can be used for a sufficient long period at one location. Frequent movement of these units is very costly and uneconomical. However their initial cost is lower. (See Fig. 26.6)

2. Telescopic Boom truck mounted crane. These are truck mounted cranes and have a self contained telescopic boom. Most of these units can travel on public highways under their own power with a minimum dismantling. Once this crane is leveled at the new work site, it is ready to work with out set up delays. These cranes have been found handy when required to work from few hours to a couple of days due to ease in their movement and setup. A photograph of the crane has been shown in Fig. 22.5.

The multi-section of the boom is a permanent part of the full revolving structure and the super structure is mounted on a multi axial truck or carrier. There are three common power and control arrangements for telescopic boom truck cranes.

1. A single engine is the source of power for both the truck and the crane. A single dual position cab can be used for driving the truck and operating the crane.
2. In the carrier there is a single engine, with cabs for truck and crane operating.
3. Separate units of power for the truck and the super structure. This arrangement is standard for the large capacity units.

For stability the telescoping boom truck cranes have extendable out riggers (wooden poles). Many a times, infact these units can not be operated safely with a full reach of the boom, unless the out riggers are fully extended and the machine is raised so that the tires are clear of the ground. Some times the width of out riggered vehicle may be 13 m (40 ft.), which needs careful planning of the operational area. These heavy machines transfer extremely high loads to the ground through out riggers. These machines need more width, which is their main disadvantage.

Fig. 25.5. Telescoping truck crane on a building site

3. Lattice Boom truck mounted cranes. Lattice boom truck cranes also have a full revolving structure mounted on a multi axial carrier as in the case of telescopic boom truck cranes. The advantage of this crane is the *lattice boom.*

The lattice boom structure is light weight, which adds to its lift capacity, as the machine predominately handles hoist load and less weight of boom. The lattice boom does not take longer time to assemble it. The light boom provides a less expensive lattice machine with the same hoisting capacity as that of larger telescoping boom unit. To move these machines from one site to an other site much time and efforts are to be wasted which is their main disadvantage.

Fig. 25.6. Rough-terrain crane

4. Rough terrain cranes. To improve the maneuverability at the job site these units are equipped with unusually large wheels and closely spaced axles. They have high ground clearance and have the ability to move on slopes of upto 50% to 70% depending upon their make. These units may move on high ways with a speed of about 50 kmph. For transportation from one site to another they need transportation. The usual capacity of these cranes vary from 17 to 45.5 metric tonnes. Primarily they are lift machines, but they are capable of light intermittent duty cycle work. In many machines the cab is located on the carrier. Some times these units are known as Cherry pickers. These units have lower cost.

5. All terrain cranes. An all terrain crane is designed with an under carriage capable of long distance high way travel. The carrier has all axle drive and all wheel steer, crab steering, large tires and high ground clearance. It has dual cabs, a lower cab for fast high way travel and a super structure cab has both drive and crane controls. This machine is a combination of job site mobility and transit capability, It can be used for limited pick and carry work. This machine is also useful for sites where multiple lifts are required at scattered project sites or at multiple work locations on a project.

The cost of this machine is highest than an equivalent capacity telescoping truck crane or rough terrain crane. This machine can be positioned on the project site with out the necessity of having other construction equipment to prepare a smooth travel way as in the case of truck cranes. They also do not need any device to haul them between distant project sites as in the case of rough terrain cranes.

6. Whirler Crane. This carne is a combination of a derrick and mobile crane as shown in Fig 25.7. In this crane the advantage of long boom of derrick crane and the mobility advantage of mobile cranes are combined. These cranes are mounted on high towers and are capable of longitudinal travel on rails. The rotating structure consists of an outer frame work. At the front end of this frame the boom is attached and at the rear end a counter weight is attached. All necessary operating and control gears are mounted inside the rotating structure. The centre of gravity of the machine is always inside the path of swinging and the machine is quite stable in any position of swing. The movement of the tower usually is obtained through separate motors mounted on two diagonally opposite corners of the base and connected to the track wheel axle through spur gear reductions. The capacity of a whirler crane with 24 m (80 ft.) boom length and 15 m (50 ft.) working radius may be about 40.7 metric tonnes (45 tones).

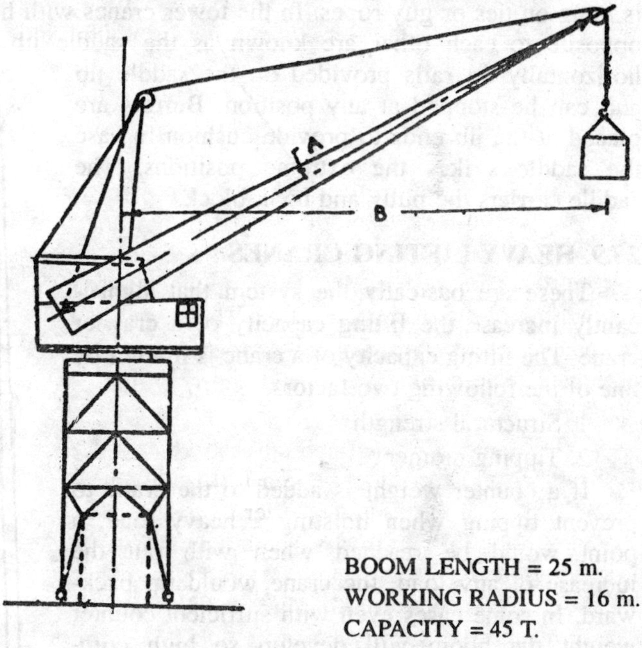

Fig. 25.7. Whirler Crane

25.8. TOWER CRANE

Usually this crane is used in the construction of industrial and multi-storyed residential buildings. It is also used in assembling of high industrial plants with elements of steel structure. It also can be used for loading and unloading heavy structural pieces.

25.8.1. Components of tower crane

The principal components of this crane are as follows:

1. Under carriage
2. Slewing platform
3. Tower with operators cabin
4. Jibs and operating mechanism

1. Under carriage. It is welded together and mounted on four travelling bogies. These bogies run on rails and get their drive from electric motors through clutch and gear box. The supply is made through a cable wound on a cable drum placed on the under carriage. The cable ends in a switch board, which is also mounted on the undercarriage. From this switch board power is supplied to the central cabinet placed on the slewing plateform through a central ring collector. From the central cabinet power is supplied to all mechanism through the contactor case. The conductors run along the tower and jib are passed through steel conduits. The chassis also supports the ballast or counter weight for providing stability.

The slewing platform may be placed on the under carriage, or in case of high towers on an upper section of the tower, the lower section being on slewing. Power for slewing is transferred from electric motor through a clutch and gear box. A double shoe brake weight placed on the brake drum of the clutch provides the braking system. An electromagnetic brake usually holds the jib from turning during working.

The tower has a truss structure made of welded angles bars and channels. Tower extension pieces are generally provided which are bolted to the main tower. To reach the top of the tower and the cabin, inside ladders are provided along the tower through out its height. The last tower section is provided with a support to which the jib is attached. The jib is also a welded steel structure, but may be made in sections bolted together. The foot of the jib is joined to the support of the highest tower section. The top of the jib is hung on ties or guy ropes. In the tower cranes with horizontal cantilever boom, two sections of the jib, opposite to each other are known as the saddle jib and the counter weight jib. The saddle moves horizontally on rails provided on the saddle jib and can be stopped at any position. Buffers are placed at the jib ends to provide cushion in case the saddle strikes the extreme positions. The saddle carriers the pully and hook block.

25.9. HEAVY LIFTING CRANES

These are basically the system that significantly increase the lifting capacity of a crawler crane. The lifting capacity of a crane is limited by one of the following two factors.

1. Structural strength
2. Tipping moment

If a counter weight is added to the crane to prevent tipping when hoisting a heavy load, a point would be reached when with out the increase of any load, the crane would tip backward. In some cases even with sufficient counter weight the boom will develop so high compressive stresses that it will break at the butt. Hence to over come these difficulties following four systems have been developed which provide the capability of hoisting heavy loads, while maintaining the integrity of the machine. These systems are as follows:

1. Trailing counter weight
2. Extendible counter weight
3. Ring system
4. Guy derrick

1. Trailing counter weight. The counter weight is not an integral part of the base crane. It is an additional weight mount on a wheeled platform behind the crane and connected to the crane as shown in Fig. 25.8. The system utilizes the mast positioned behind the boom. The boom suspension lines are mounted at the top of the mast. This arrangement

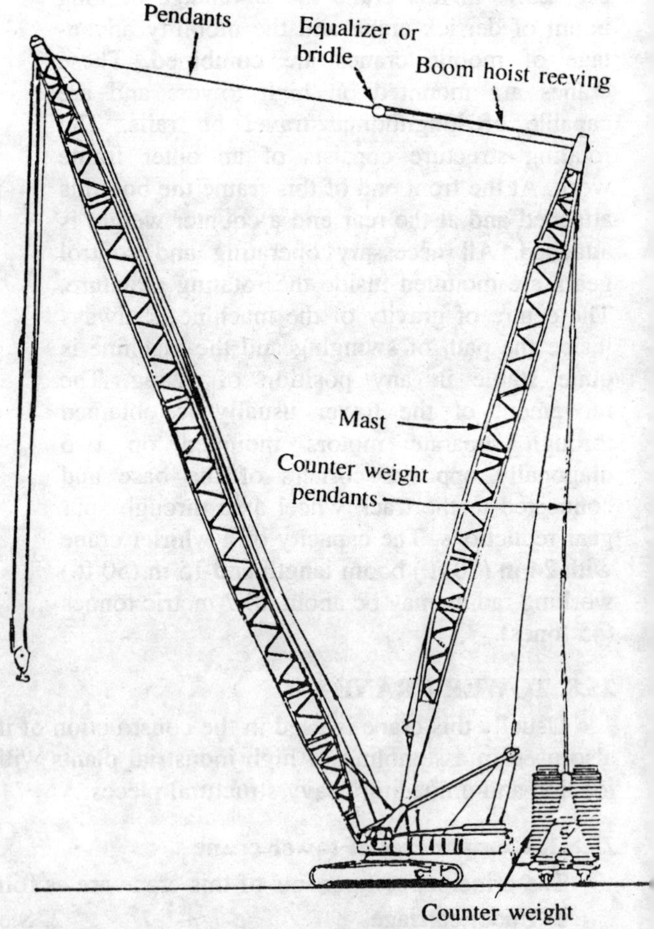

Fig. 25.8. Trailin counter weight crane modification for heavy lifting

increases the angle between the boom and suspension lines resulting decrease in compressive forces on the boom.

2. Extendible counter weight. In this model of crane the counter weight system is extended away from the rear of the machine to match the leverage with the requirement of the lift.

3. Ring system. In this system a larg^e turn table ring is created out side the base of the machine. The heavy weight system is supported on this ring. At the front and rear of the base of the machine, there are auxiliary pin connected frames. With the help of these frames the boom/mast foot and the counter weight can be moved away from the base of the machine. These ausiliary frames can ride the ring by using rollers or wheels. The base crane really is only a power and control source.

4. Guy derrick. It has already been discussed on page 383-384.

The lifting capacities of a crawler 180 metric (200 tone) tone weight crane with 54 m (180 ft.) of boom** are given in the following Table 25.1.

Table 25.1.

Radius m	*Capacity metric* tone	*Radius* m	*Capacity metric* tone
9.6 (32 ft.)	65.84	31.5	11.69
10.8	55.31	33.0	10.76
12.0	47.48	34.5	10.0
13.5	40.14	36.0	9.27
15.0	34.61	37.5	8.64
16.5	30.24	39.0	8.10
18.0	26.73	40.5	7.52
19.5	23.85	42.0	7.00
21.0	21.42	43.5	6.53
22.5	19.40	45.0	6.12
24.0	17.64	46.5	5.72
25.5	16.11	48.0	5.31
27.0	14.76	49.5	5.0
28.5	13.59	51.0	4.64
30.0	12.56	52.5	4.32

** The capacity is based on 75% tipping load.

Tipping load. It is that load which produces a tipping condition at a specified radius. Tipping is that condition of the machine when a balance is reached between the over turning moment of the load and the stabilizing moment of the machine, the crane being on a firm and level supporting surface in calm air. The tipping load includes the weight of the item being lifted plus the weight of hook, hook block, slings and other items used in hoisting the load including the weight of hoist rope located between the boom point sheave and the item being lifted.

Radius. The radius of the load is the horizontal distance from the axis of the rotation of the crane to the centre of the vertical hoise line or tackle with the load applied.

Rated load. It is the load that the machine is capable to lift safely. The rated load of a crane should not exceed the following percentages of tipping load at specified radii.

1. Crawler mounted machines : 75%.
2. Rubber tyre mounted machines : 85%.
3. Machines on out riggers : 85%.

QUESTIONS

1. Why cranes are necessary in our life. Give the classification of cranes.
2. Give the constituents of a derrick crane and explain its working.
3. Describe a stiff leg derrick crane.
4. Give the classification of mobile crane. Discuss fully the crawler crane.
5. Discuss the telescopic boom truck mounted crane.
6. What is a whirler crane? Explain with sketch.

OBJECTIVE TYPE QUESTIONS

1. A crane is used for
   (*a*) Boring holes in rocks
   (*b*) Transporting heavy loads
   (*c*) Lifting and placing loads at desired place
   (*d*) Compacting earth fills
2. Cranes may be classified as
   (*a*) Stationary
   (*b*) Over head or Gantry
   (*c*) Mobile crane
   (*d*) Traveler crane
   (*e*) All are correct
3. Derrick cranes can be used except
   (*a*) For industrial building construction
   (*b*) For consolidation of soil
   (*c*) Erection of plants
   (*d*) Hoisting loads at ship yards
   (*e*) Loading and unloading cargoes at ports
4. The width of out riggers on vehicles may be
   (*a*) 5 m
   (*b*) 7.5 m
   (*c*) 13 m
   (*d*) 25 m
5. The tipping condition in a crane develops when over turning moment is
   (*a*) Less than stabilizing moment
   (*b*) More than stabilizing moment
   (*c*) Equal to stabilizing moment
   (*d*) All are correct
   (*e*) None of the is correct
6. The maximum radius of a crawler crane may be upto
   (*a*) 20 m
   (*b*) 35 m
   (*c*) 40 m
   (*d*) 52 m

ANSWERS:

1. (*c*)
2. (*e*)
3. (*b*)
4. (*c*)
5. (*c*)
6. (*d*)

26

Piles And Pile Driving Equipment

26.1. INTRODUCTION

Pile is a structural member driven into the ground for the following purposes:

1. Transmitting the surface loads to the suitable stratum below the ground surface or to the soil mass around the pile.
2. To effect cut off of seepage of water or movement of soil.
3. To consolidate soft soil as sand.

26.2. CLASSIFICATION OF PILES

Piles may be classified as:

1. On the basis of their functions
2. On the basis of material of their construction

1. Classification based on the function of pile. On the basis of their functions piles may be classified as:

(*a*) Sheet piles. Sheet piles are installed under hydraulic structures to resist the seepage of underground water or loose soil or both.

(*b*) Load bearing piles. The piles driven underground to transfer the load of the super structure to the suitable stratum.

2. According to the material of construction. According to the material of construction piles may be of the following types:

(*a*) Wooden piles
(*b*) Steel piles
(*c*) Concrete piles
(*d*) Composite piles

The piles are manufactured in specified lengths.

26.3. FACTORS AFFECTING THE CHOICE OF THE TYPE OF PILE

Following factors have been found to influence the choice of the type of pile:

1. Size, type and weight of structure to be supported.
2. Physical properties of the soil stratum at the site.
3. Depth of stratum capable to support the pile.
4. Availability of material for the construction of piles.
5. Number of piles required.
6. Driving equipment for piles available.
7. comparative cost.
8. Durability required.

9. Type of structures adjacent to the project.
10. Depth of water and its salinity above ground into which piles will be driven.

26.4. BRIEF DESCRIPTION OF DIFFERENT TYPES OF PILES

1. Timber piles. These piles are made from the track of trees such as pine and douglas, fer etc. Timber piles are available in 20 to 33 m length. However now a days their use is restricted due to non availability of timber due to depletion of forests. The advantages sand disadvantages of timber piles are as follows.

Table 26.1.

S. No.	*Advantages*		*Disadvantages*
1.	They are economical in cost	1.	It is difficult or rather impossible to drive them in hard formations
2.	They can be handled easily with little danger of breakage	2.	It is difficult to splice them to increase their lengths
3.	They can be cut off to any desired length after they are driven	3.	They are not suitable for use as end bearing piles undr heavy loads. However they can be used as friction piles
4.	They can be pulled out easily if required	4.	The life of un treated piles is very short.

2. Concrete piles. To over come the disadvantages of timber piles, concrete piles have been invented. Concrete piles may be of the following types:

(*a*) Precast reinforced concrete piles
(*b*) Cost in situ concrete piles
(*c*) Pre-stressed pre tensioned concrete piles

(*a*) Precast reinforced concrete piles

With the exception of short lengths, concrete piles are reinforced with sufficient reinforcement to prevent the damage while being handled from the bed to the driving positions. The reinforcement should be provided as per design calculations. As a thumb rule, the main or longitudinal reinforcement should not be less than 2% of the volume of the pile. The lateral reinforced of 6.0 mm diameter should not be spaced more than 30 cms apart. In the top and bottom portion of pile for a distance of 90 cms, the spacing of lateral reinforcement should not be more than 7.5 cms. The concrete cover to the main steel bars should not be less than 5 cms.

Square and octagonal piles are cast in horizontal forms, while circular piles are cast in vertical form. Usually the precast piles are cast in central plants or factories. After casting the piles they should be moist cured at least for 21 days or as decided by the designer.

To avoid damage during handling and to effect economy in transportation, they should be cast near the

Table 26.2. Advantages and Disadvantages of precast piles over timber piles

S. No.	*Advantages of precast conc. piles*		*Disadvantages of precast conc. piles*
1.	They can resist high chemical and boilogical reactions or attacks	1.	It is dificult to increase or reduce its length.
2.	They have high strength	2.	They are liable to break during handling or driving
3.	To facilitate jetting a pipe may be installed along the centre of the pile.	3.	Large sized piles are difficult to handle. They require heavy and expensive handling and driving equipment
		4.	Non avoidability of desired size piles may delay the start of the project.

site of the work. To minimize the damage during handling, they should be picked up at several points instead of two points only. The length of such piles may vary from 13 to 20 m and it section may be 20 × 20 cms. In some cases the length of such piles may be upto about 33 m. The size of the pile to be used on a project is determined by the economy. Advantages and disadvantages of precat piles over timber piles are given in Table 26.2.

(*b*) Cast in place or cast in situ concrete piles

In this case a hole of desired depth and section is prepared and the freshly mixed concrete is filled in the ground and allowed to cure there. There are two principal methods of constructing such piles as follows:

1. Driving a metallic shell in the ground and leaving it there and filling it with concrete.
2. Driving a metallic shell in the ground upto the desired length and pouring concrete while pulling the shell from the ground. The piles obtained by these two methods are known as Raymond concrete piles and Franky concrete piles.

Advantages of cast in place piles

The advantages and disadvantages are shown in Table 26.3 below.

Table 26.3.

S. No.	*Advantages of cast in situ piles*		*Disadvantages of cast in situ piles*
1.	The light weight shells may be handled and driven easily	1.	Slight movement of earth around the un reinforced concrete may damage it
2.	Variations in length presents no serious problems	2.	An uplift force acting on the shaft of the un cased and un reinforced pile may cause its failure in tension
3.	The shells may be transported in short lengths and assembled at the site	3.	The bottom of the pedestal pile may not be symmetrical.
4.	Reinforcement required for handling stresses is eliminated, resulting in economy		
5.	Risk of breakage of piles during driving operations is eliminated		
6.	If needed, additional piles may be provided easily		

(*c*) Augured cast in place concrete piles

In this case a hollow shaft auger along with a minimum inside diameter of about 6.25 cms is rotated into the ground upto the desired depth. After the penetration upto the desired depth, the augur is withdrawn slowly by giving it slow rotation, a cement grout is injected under pressure through a hollow shaft. Then concrete is filled in the hole. The diameter of such piles may be upto 50 cms and length upto about 37.5 m.

(*d*) Under reamed piles

This is a patented pile by Central Building Research Institute Roorkee. This pile has been found very useful for the house construction in expansive soils. It is similar to auger bored pile, but it has a bulb at its bottom which increases its bearing capacity.

Advantages and disadvantages of augured cast piles

The advantages and disadvantages of auger cast piles are shown in Table 26.4.

26.5. SHEET PILES

Sheet piles primarily are used to retain or support earth. They are also used to check erosion of soil blow the hydraulic structures. Sheet piles may be made of steel, concrete or timber. Sheet piling sections are available in more than 200 types.

Table 26.4.

S. No.	*Advantages of Auger bored piles*	*Disadvantages of Auger bored piles*
1.	It does not require to drive a casing	1. To ensure an structurally sound shaft, concrete has to be placed very carefully.
2.	The noise level is very low during construction stages	2. Cost and time of instalation may be greatly affected by the soil and ground water condition
3.	During construction there is very little adverse effect on the adjacent structures due to vibrations	3. Horizontal or vertical ground movement from adjacent pile construction can damage the completed piles
4.	It does not require a casing	4. No penetration resistance correlation can be made about the capacity of the pile due to construction technique
5.	They can be installed in areas having low over head restrictions	5. In situations where uplift forces can be encountered require placement of reinforcement which is difficult to provide.
6.	Practically there is no displacement of soil	6. Under seismic loading conditions pile behaviour can not be predicated correctly due to insufficient available data.
7.	They can be installed in areas having minimum clearance along side the existing structures	
8.	Pile splicing is eliminated	

Flat sections are designed for inter locking strength that makes them suitable for the construction of cellular structures. The *Z* sections are designed for bending, which makes them more suitable for use in the construction of retaining walls, coffer dams and for use as excavation support.

Sheet piles are driven individually or in pairs, usually with the help of vibratory hammer and a guide frame. Where ever possible it is best to drive the sheet piles in pairs. The height of guide frame should be at least half of the sheet pile. The pile should remain in plumb in both direction. It is very difficult to work with damaged sheet piles. They should be avoided if possible. To remove dirt trapped in the interlocks, sheet piles should be struck with sledge hammer. When using a vibrating hammer, it should be brought to speed before starting the driving.

26.5.1. Points to be kept in mind while driving sheet piles

1. The sheet pile must be straight and undamaged. A damaged pile will be difficult to drive.
2. The interlocks must always be free of any dirt, sand or other debris.
3. While driving a sheet pile, a guide frame should be used. This guide frame will keep the sheet pile in plumb when an obstruction is encountered or excessive driving conditions exist.
4. When ever possible piles should be driven in pairs.
5. The length of the boom of the crane should be long. Normally the length of the boom of the crane should be twice the length of the pile plus few metres.
6. Sheet piles never be over drived. Bending, bouncing or vibrating with no penetration is the indication of over driving.

26.5.2. Resistance of piles to penetration

Total resistance of a pile to penetration = skin friction + end bearing

The relative portions of resistance contributed by either of the skin friction and end bearing may vary from 0 to 100% depending upon the soil condition and type of pile. Soil condition is more important than type of pile. A steel H shaped pile driven to refusal in stiff clay may be classified as skin friction, where as the same pile driven through mud deposit to rest on solid rock is classified as on end bearing pile.

The value of skin friction is a function of the coefficient of friction between the soil and the pile and the pressure of the soil normal to the surface of the pile. However for soils as some clays the value of the skin friction may be limited to the shear strength of the soil immediately adjacent to the pile. Taking coefficient of friction as 0.25 and normal pressure on the vertical surface of the pile as 7 kg/cm^2, the value of skin friction will be $0.25 \times 7 \times 100 \times 100 = 1.75 \times 10^4$ kg/m^2 (17500 kg per metre square of surface)

Based on experiments, the values of skin friction are shown in Table 26.5 below. These values are a guide and should not be used as such in any or all cases.

Table 26.5. Allowable values of skin friction on piles in kg/cm^2

S. No.	*Material*	*Skin friction in kg/m^2* *Approximate depth*		
		6.1 m (20 ft.)	*18.3 m (60 ft.)*	*30.5 m (100 ft.)*
1.	Soft silt and dense muck	244 – 488 (50 – 100)	244 – 586 (50 – 120)	273 – 738 (60 – 150)
2.	Silt (wet and confined)	488 – 976 (100 – 200)	610 – 1220 (125 – 250)	738 – 1476 (150 – 300)
3.	Soft clay	976 – 1464 (200 – 300)	1220 – 1710 (250 – 350)	1476 – 1952 (300 – 400)
4.	Stiff clay	1464 – 2440 (300 – 500)	1710 – 2685 (350 – 550)	1952 – 2928 (400 – 600)
5.	Clay and sand mixed	1464 – 2440 (300 – 500)	1952 – 2928 (400 – 600)	2440 – 3416 (500 – 700)
6.	Fine sand (wet and confined)	1464 – 1952 (300 – 400)	1710 – 2440 (350 – 500)	1952 – 2928 (400 – 600)
7.	Medium sand and small gravel	2440 – 3416 (500 – 700)	2928 – 3904 (600 – 800)	2928 – 3904 (600 – 800)

The values in bracket are pound square feet.

26.6. SELECTION OF PILE DRIVING HAMMER

Following factors have been found to affect the selection of a pile driving hammer:

(*a*) Size and type of pile
(*b*) Character of the soil
(*c*) No of piles
(*d*) Location of the project
(*e*) Topography of the site
(*f*) Type of rig available
(*g*) Whether piles to be driven on land or under water

In general, largest available hammer that can be used with out damaging the pile should be selected. It has been observed that in case of large hammers, greater portion of the energy is effective in pile driving producing higher operating efficiency.

26.7. PILE DRIVING EQUIPMENT

The equipment for pile driving consists of the followings:

1. Skid mounted driving rig called pile frame or shovel crane unit equipped with necessary winches.
2. Power unit
3. Guide leads
4. Pile hammer with accessories
5. Additional aids such as arrangements for pre boring or jetting.

1. Pile driving rigs. The basic operations in pile driving are:

(*a*) Lifting and holding pile in position.

(*b*) Hammering the pile into the ground or pulling it out of the ground.

(*c*) Guiding the pile accurately in the desired direction of movement.

All these functions are performed by the mechanism provided on the driving rig. The rig supports the boom and winch mechanism for driving hammer, the guide leads and a platform for mounting the auxiliary equipment such as jet pump, drilling auger, steam boiler or air compressor etc.

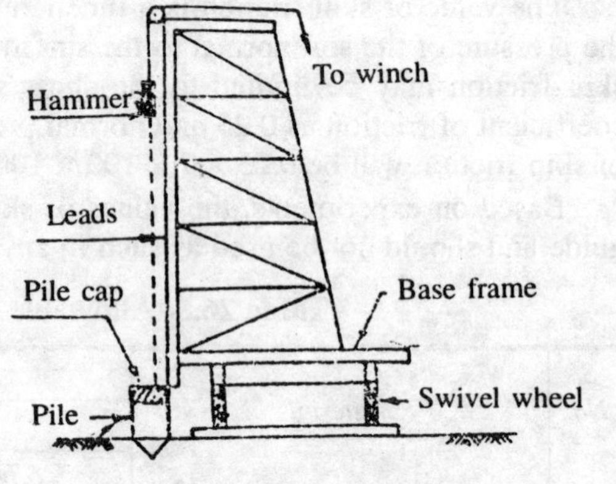

Fig. 26.1. Leeds and Pile Frame

The leads extend to the full height of the rig and guide the pile and hammer during the driving operation. The length of the leads should be sufficient to handle the longest pile on the job with space left over the pile top for locating the hammer and its rigging. The leads are constructed with a pair of channel section of 15 cms to 20 cms deep and a spacing of about 15 cms in between them. The lugs of standard size form an integral part of the hammer frame. These lugs slide in between the space of the leads when the hammer moves over the leads. Generally two sheaves are mounted above the leads. Over these sheaves winch ropes pass to lift the hammer and the pile. A lead is shown in Fig. 26.1.

26.8. TYPES OF PILE DRIVING HAMMERS

A pile driving hammer furnishes the energy required to drive the pile into the soil. Commonly used pile hammers work by hitting or pounding the pile on its head. Recently vibratory hammers and sonic hammers have been developed. These hammers drive piles by vibration and as well suited to drive and extract piles in granular non cohesive soils.

26.9. HAMMERS WORKING ON HITTING OR POUNDING PRINCIPLE

Following types of hammers work on pounding principle:

1. Drop hammers
2. Single acting steam or compressed air hammers
3. Double acting steam or compressed air hammers
4. Differential acting hammers
5. Diesel hammers
6. Hydraulic hammers

26.9.1. Drop hammers

The drop hammer is the oldest type of hammer, which is still in use. This type of hammer is the simplest form of driving hammers and does not use any source of power, such as steam, or compressed air for operation. A winch which lifts the hammer through a cable is the mechanism that is needed for the working of this hammer.

A drop hammer is a heavy metal weight, which is lifted by a winch line and then released and allowed to fall on the top of the pile. Due to high dynamic forces, a pile cap is positioned between the hammer and the pile head. The pile cap serves to distribute the blow to the pile head uniformly and also as shock absorber. The cap contains a cushion block usually made of wood.

Working. The hammer is lifted to the desired height of fall with the help of winch and then released to fall freely under the force of gravity. Two different systems of releasing the weight are in use. In one case the weight is tripped free of the hoisting rope each time a fall is made and re connected for the next lifting. In the other case the weight is allowed to fall with the hoist line still attached and the weight revolving freely in the unwind direction. Though the first arrangement gives 10 to 15% greater energy of blow, but it is slow in working. The rate of strike is 8 to 10 blows per minute. The second arrangement gives a little lesser energy per blow, due to friction loss but the rate of strike is higher being about 15 to 20 blows per minute.

The weight of the hammer is limited by the capacity of the winch. The weight of drop hammer varies from 0.68 to 2.75 metric tonnes. Drop hammers having weight more than 2.75 tonnes are also available.

The height of fall varies from 1.5 to 6.0 m depending upon the energy required per blow. The ratio of weights for hammer and pile are recommend as follows using the drop hammer. (Table 26.7)

Table 26.7. Ratio of weight of hammer and pile

S. No.	*Type of pile*	*Recommended weight of hammer*
1.	Timber piles	Recommended weight of hammer 1.0 to 1.5 times the weight of pile
2.	Steel bearing piles	Same as above.
3.	Concrete piles	At least 50% weight of pile.
4.	Steel sheet piles	(a) For easy conditions of driving it should be at least 50% of weight of pile.
		(b) For average conditions of driving it should be equal to the weight of pile.
		(c) For hard conditions of driving it should be upto 2.5 times the weight of pile.

Advantages and disadvantages of drop hammer

The advantages and disadvantages of drop hammer are shown in the following Table 26.8.

Table 26.8

Advantages of drop hammer	*Disadvantages of drop hammer*
1. Small investment in equipment	1. Rate of pile driving is slow.
2. Simplicity of operation (It is simple to operate)	2. Danger of damage to the pile due to lifting the hammer too high.
3. The energy per below can be varied by varying the height of fall.	3. Unable to be used directly for under water driving.
4. Handy when source of energy is not available.	4. Danger of damaging the adjacent buildings as a result of heavy vibrations caused by the hammer.
5. In can be used for a variety of driving conditions from light, short pile to long piles.	
6. These are suitable for driving piles on remote projects where few piles are to be driven	

26.9.2. Single acting hammer

The single acting hammer has a freely falling weight called a "ram". The difference between a single acing hammer and the drop hammer is only in the manner of lifting of the ram after each below. The drop hammer is raised by winding the hoist rope on the winch drum, where as single acting hammer utilizes the motive power of steam or compressed air for this purpose. The ram is connected to the pressure system of piston and cylinder. The ram is raised when the steam or compressed air works on the under side of the piston. The pressure of steam or compressed air is released when the ram reaches the top of the stroke, resulting the fall of the ram under the force of gravity. This fall of the ram gives an blow to the anvil block located at the top of the pile. A pile cap is used with a single acting hammer. This cap is mated to the case of the hammer and commonly known is "helmet" or "anvil".

The ram weights of single acting hammers are much higher than drop hammers, while the stroke is short generally limited to 1.2 m, resulting in a lower striking velocity of the ram. Thus the hammer energy is transmitted to the pile head with lesser losses. The danger of damaging the pile during driving is also reduced. The weights of ram range from 1.36 to 9.1 metric tonnes and the over all weight 1.8 to about 18.0 metric tones. The ram speed varies from 55 to 65 blows per minute, which is much higher than drop hammers. The striking energy ranges upto 24000 kg-m (18×10^4 ft. lbs).

The single acting hammers may be open or enclosed type. However these hammers are used in a pile

Fig. 26.2. Crawler crane driving 12-in concrete piles using a single-acting air hammer and hydraulic leads

lead, though they can be fitted to operate free hung. Enclosed type hammers can be used under water pile driving.

Advantages and disadvantages of a single acting hammers compared with drop hammers are given Table 26.9.

Fig. 26.2 shows a crawler crane driving a pile with a single acting air hammer and leads and Fig. 26.3 shows a steam single acting hammer driving a pile.

26.9.3. Double acting hammers

In the double acting hammers the motive fluid acts on both sides of the piston. The motive fluid may be steam or compressed air. First the pressure is applied to the under side of the piston to raise the ram to

Fig. 26.3. Raymond 60X steam hammer driving 54-in cylinder pile

the top of the driving stroke and then drives down in its down ward stroke assisting the force of gravity in striking the blow *i.e.* during down ward stroke the fluid pressure is applied on the top side of the ram, which increases the energy per blow. Thus with a given weight of ram, it is possible to attain a desired amount of energy per blow with a shorter stroke than with a longer single acting hammer. The number of blows per minute will be about twice as that for a single acting hammer with the same energy rating. Commonly these hammers deliver from 95 to 300 blows per minute. These hammers do not require cushion blocks. The ram strikes upon an alloy steel anvil that fits the pile head.

Table 26.9. Advantages and disadvantages of single acting hammers over drop hammer

S. No.	*Advantages of single acting hammers over drop hammers*	*Disadvantages of single acting hammers over drop hammers*
1.	Single acting hammers give higher number of blows per minute resulting in faster driving.	1. Single acting hammers require higher investment in equipment such as steam boilers or air compressors.
2.	Greater frequency of blows reduces the increase in the skin friction between the blows.	2. These hammers are more complicated and need more maintenance, resulting in higher maintenance cost.
3.	The heavier ram falling at lower velocity transmits a greater portion of the energy to the driving pile.	3. These hammers require more time to set up and take down.
4.	The reduction in the velocity of the ram decreases the danger of damage to piles during driving operation.	4. A large number of workers are required to operate the equipment.
5.	The enclosed type single acting hammers can be used for under water driving.	5. They require a crane of higher lifting capacity.
6.	They are capable to deliver heavy blows and can be used to drive heavy timber or RCC piles in most soils as stiff clays, dense cohesion less formations etc.	6. They are not suitable for jobs where very fast driving of lighter piles is required.

The lighter ram and higher velocity of double acting hammer has been found advantageous to drive light to medium weight piles into soils having normal frictional resistance. Further it is claimed that high frequency of blows keeps the pile moving down wards·continuously, reducing the development of static skin frictional resistance during driving. Thus resulting the elimination of energy loss from bouncing of ram and faster driving.

However when heavy piles are driven, specially into soils having high frictional resistance, the heavier weight and slower velocity of a single acting hammer will transmit a greater portion of the rated energy into the driving pile. The ratings of single acting and double acting hammers are given below in Table 26.10.

Table 26.10.

Item	*Single acting hammer*	*Double acting hammer*
1. Ram weight	2270 kg (5000 lbs)	2270 kg
2. Rated striking energy	2245 m-kg per blow (16250 ft. lbs/blow)	2645 m-kg per blow (19150 ft. lbs/blow
3. Boiler size	40.5 metric h.p. (40 B.H.P.)	60.6 metric h.p. (60 B.H.P.)
4. Air consumption	17 m^3/min (600 cfm)	25 m3/min. (900 cfm)
5. Pressure at hammer	5.6 kg/cm^2 (180 psi)	7.0 kg/cm^2 (100 psi)
6. Rated speed	60 blows/min.	95 blows/min.

The advantages of double acting hammer compared with single acting hammers are given in Table 26.11

Table 26.11.

S. No.	*Advantages of double acting hammer*	*Disadvantages of double acting hammer*
1.	The greater number of blows per minute reduces pile driving time.	1. The relative light weight and high velocity of ram is disadvantageous to drive heavy piles into soils having high frictional resistance.
2.	The greater number of blows per minute reduces the development of static skin friction during driving.	2. The hammer is more complicated.
3.	Piles can be driven more easily with out leads.	3. The actual performance of the hammer depends upon the soil conditions and the weight of the pile being driven.
4.	They deliver about 20% more energy per blow and 90% more energy per minute in comparision to single acting hammers.	

26.9.4. Differential acting hammer

The differential acting hammer is an combination of advantages of both single acting and double acting hammer with out having any disadvantage of any of the hammers. It provides a heavy ram weight, which is the characteristic of the single acting hammer and the high speed of operation of double acting hammer. Thus this hammer can be used under a wide range of pile driving conditions. This hammer requires a pile cap with cushioning material and a set of leads. It has been reported that this hammer can drive a given pile to a given depth in 50% of the time required for a single acting hammer of the same size. At the same time in doing so, the differential acting hammer will save from 25 to 35% steam or air. This class of hammers are available in open or closed type models. They can also be operated either with steam or air. Their lubrication system is similar to that of single acting hammers.

Specifications of the hammer

1. **Size.** The hammer is available in various sizes.
2. **Weight.** The ram weight of this hammer varies from 1350 to 1800 kg.
3. **Energy.** The rated strike energy varies from 970 m-kg to 15700 m kg per blow.
4. **Ram speed.** The ram speed for the largest size is about 100 blows per min. and for the smallest size about 130 blows per min.
5. **Fall of the ram.** The distance or fall of the ram varies from 30 cm for the smallest hammer and 40 cms for the largest hammer.
6. The over all weigh range of hammer varies from 3150 kg 36000 kg.

Table 26.12. Advantages and disadvantages of differential acting hammer over double acting hammer

S. No.	*Advantages of differential hammer*	*Disadvantages of differential hammer*
1.	The weight of its ram is much larger.	1. Its initial and maintenance cost is more.
2.	It has a higher striking rate.	2. The repair and part replacement is very costly. Thus this hammer is not used unless conditions of driving vary very widely.
3.	Due to rapidly applied blows, the pile remains in the state of vibration and much of the skin friction is eliminated.	
4.	A pile can be drived in any kind of soil by selecting a suitable model of hammer.	3. For effective operation it needs specified fluid pressure.

26.10. DIESEL HAMMER

A diesel pile driving hammer is a self contained driving unit, which does not need an external source of energy such as a steam boiler or an air compressor. In this respect it is simpler and more easily movable from one place to an other place. A complete unit consists of a vertical

Fig. 26.4. Diesel hammer driving sheet piling

cylinder, (*ii*) A piston or ram, (*iii*) An anvil, (*iv*) Fuel, and Lubricating oil tanks, (*v*) A fuel pump, (*vi*) Injectors, (*vii*) A mechanical lubricator.

Working. After placing the hammer on the top of a pile, the combined piston and ram are lifted to the upper end of the stroke and released to start the unit operating. Fig. 26.5 shows the operation of a diesel hammer. As the ram reaches near the end of the down stroke, it activates a fuel pump that injects the fuel into the combustion chamber between the ram and anvil. The continued down ward stroke of the ram compresses the air and the fuel to generate heat to ignite the fuel. The resulting explosion drives the pile downward and the ram upward to repeat its stroke. The energy developed by blows can be controlled by the operator. This energy varies over a wide range Fig. 26.4 shows a diesel hammer. The working principle of diesel hammer is shown in Fig. 26.5.

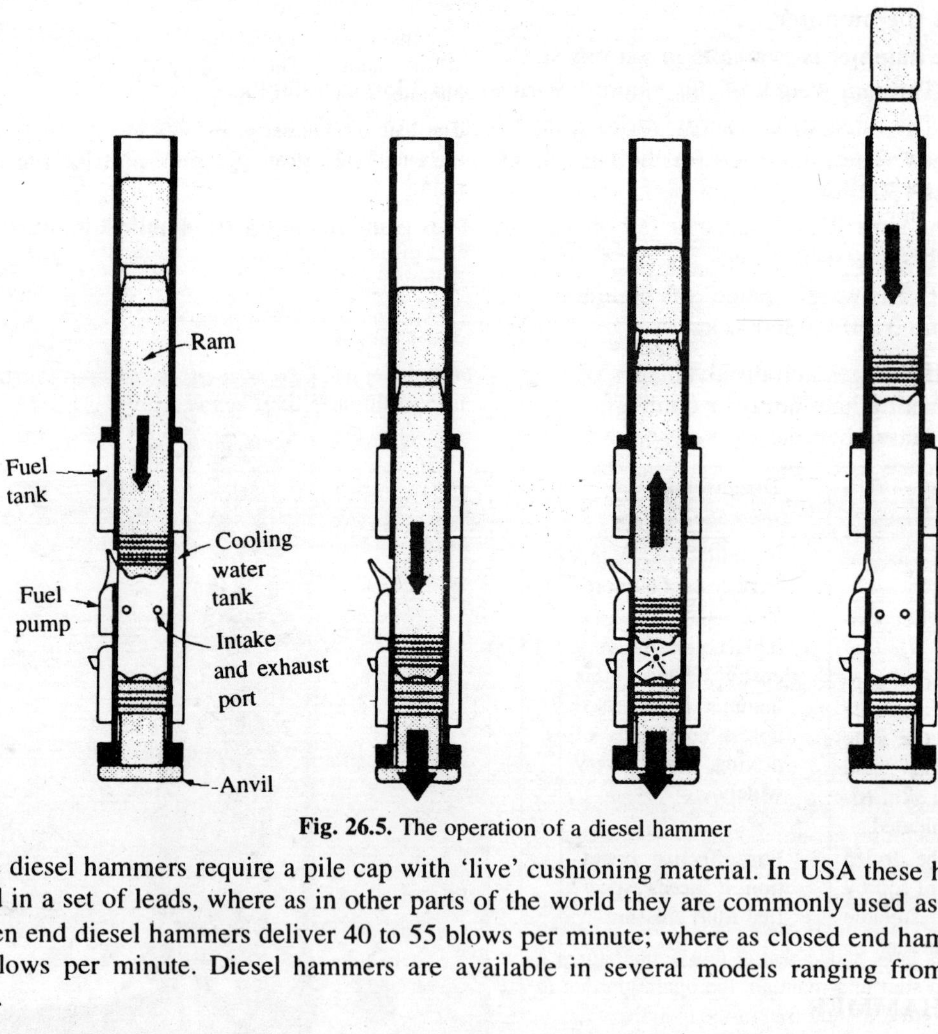

Fig. 26.5. The operation of a diesel hammer

The diesel hammers require a pile cap with 'live' cushioning material. In USA these hammers usually are used in a set of leads, where as in other parts of the world they are commonly used as free hanging.

Open end diesel hammers deliver 40 to 55 blows per minute; where as closed end hammers deliver 75 to 85 blows per minute. Diesel hammers are available in several models ranging from light to heavy weights.

Specifications of diesel hammers

1. **Weight of ram.** The weight of the ram varies from 450 to 15000 kg.
2. **Speed of ram.** The speed of the ram varies from 50 to 100 blows per minute.
3. **Rated energy.** The rated energy per blow of a diesel hammer is over 34500 kg-m.
4. **Fuel consumption.** The fuel consumption per hour of diesel hammers varies from 3.8 litres/hour

for smaller models to about 11.8 lit/hour for larger hammers.

5. Lubricating oil. The consumption of lubricating oil is found about 4.0 to 8.0 litres per day.

6. Total hammer weight. The total hammer weight ranges from 1350 kg to over 9000 kg.

7. Energy to weight ratio. It varies from 4.5 to 1 for air and 1.75 to 1 for steam models.

Table 26.13. Advantages of diesel hammers in comparision with other hammers

S. No.	*Advantages of diesel hammers*	*Disadvantages of diesel hammers*
1.	This hammer needs no external source of energy. Thus it is more mobile and requires less time to set up and start operation.	1. The diesel hammer may not operate well while driving pile into soft ground. The hammer will not operate unless the pile offers sufficient driving resistance to activate the ram.
2.	Its cost of operation is less. Its fuel consumption is 1/6 to 1/10th of an air operated hammers as its operation is not continuous, it needs less fuel.	2. The number of stroke of diesel hammer is less than a steam hammer. This is especially true for a diesel hammer with an open top or end.
3.	The use of this hammer is convenient in remote areas. This hammer needs only diesel for operation as a source of energy and it is not necessary to own a boiler, water and fuel tanks to generate steam.	3. The length of diesel hammer is slightly greater than the length of a steam hammer of comparable energy rating.
4.	Diesel hammer is light in weight in comparision of steam hammer of equal rating.	4. It is difficult to determine the energy per blow of this hammer. Hence there is uncertainty about the accuracy of applying the dynamic pile driving formula to diesel hammers.
5.	The maintenance and servicing of diesel hammer is simple and fast.	5. The diesel hammers have not been found suitable for heavy piles as precast concrete piles.
6.	The energy per blow of diesel hammer increases as the driving resistance of the pile increases.	
7.	If a pile breaks or falls out from under the hammer, the diesel hammer will not operate as for the continuous operation of the diesel hammer the continuous resistance of the pile during driving is necessary.	
8.	Due to the low striking velocity and as the piston reacts to the impact needed for each blow by rebounding up its cylinder, the diesel hammer is less likely to damage or batter a pile while driving.	
9.	For an existing condition to permit a diesel hammer to operate most effectively the energy per blow and the number of blows per minute can be varied easily.	
10.	Some authors have suggested that a diesel hammer can be used well below of where it would be difficult or impossible to provide steam, on the other hand some authors have stated that at low temperatures it is difficult to start and maintain the operation due to in adequate ignition condition in the cylinder.	
11.	US Navy during their tests found the performance of a diesel hammer under easy driving conditions is much better than the conventional hammers.	
12.	In India diesel hammers have been found very effective in driving steel sheet piles in sandy river beds.	

26.11. VIBRATORY PILE HAMMERS

The vibratory pile hammers have been found much effective in driving piles into coarse grained non cohessive soils as sand. In certain types of soil they have been found very speedy and economical. These hammers have been found most effective in driving piles into water saturated non cohesive soils. These hammers have been found to experience some difficulty in driving piles into dry sand or similar materials or cohesive soils that do not respond to the vibration.

The vibratory hammer sets the pile under vibrations so that it is constantly on the move, eliminating the surface frictional resistance. The pile sinks into the soil due to its own weight and the weight of the driver assembly. The driving is very fast and is accomplished with out much effort.

Hammer

The hammer comprises of a vibratory unit which produces vibrations to oscillate the pile along its vertical axis and, (*ii*) a clamping device, which transmits these vibrations to the pile. The vibrator units may be powered with electric motors or with internal combustion engine. The vibrations are generated by the rotation of counter rotating shafts to which eccentric weights are attached. The movement of the shaft is synchronized to eliminate the horizontal thrust and to give only the vertical oscillations. The upper end of the clamping unit is attached to the bottom of the vibrator unit and its lower end to the pile top. The pile is clamped in hardened steel, serrated blocks attached to hydraulically operated jaws (working at a pressure of 350 kg/cm^2) of the clamping unit.

This clamping arrangement is very tight and holds the pile effectively during operation of the hammer. The hammer is suspended from the pile frame through a sling and fitted with adequate spring shock absorbers to eliminate passage of oscillations to the pile frame. Some models also incorporate an anvil and striking pin assembly to furnish blows on the pile head to accentuate the effect of vibrations.

As the surface friction effects are eliminated due to rapid oscillations, a small hammer blow is capable of achieving considerable penetration with out deforming the pile. The advantages and disadvantages of vibratoty hammers are shown in Table 26.14.

Specifications

1. The weight of one model of the striking assembly is 435 kg.

2. Energy delivered. Energy delivered per blow is 55 m-kg.

3. Striking rate. The striking rate is as high as 900 blows/min.

Table 26.14. Advantages of vibratory hammer

S. No.	*Advantages of vibratory hammer*	*Disadvantages of vibratory hammer*
1.	In appropriate driving conditions this hammer or driver is much faster in completing a job than conventional hammer.	1. Heavier pile sections can be driven to shorter depths.
2.	The time taken in clamping and un clamping pile is very short due to light and compact design of the hammer.	2. These hammers are not suitable to drive piles in heavy and cohesive soils.
3.	Power requirement is small.	3. A lighter capacity crane is required to handle the hammer in operation.
4.	Its owning and operation costs are low.	
5.	This hammer operates silently and with less shocks to the adjacent ground. Thus it can be used in busy locations as near hospitals and in close proximity to buildings.	
6.	The models having anvil and striking arrangement save the pile foot from damage when hitting normal obstacles such as rocks, boulders etc. due to lack of impact.	

S. No.	*Advantages of vibratory hammer*	*Disadvantages of vibratory hammer*
7.	The vibratory hammer is best suited to drive thin, light pile sections in sandy non cohesive soils.	
8.	Steel sheet piles in pervious formations can be effectively driven or withdrawn by vibratory hammer.	
9.	Its driving speed may be about four times the speed of conventional double acting hammers.	

The capacity of the crane may be determined by the following relations:

1. Capacity of crane for driving = 1.2 times the weight of hammer + weight of (pile + grip)
2. Capacity of crane for extracting = 2.0 times the weight of hammer + weight of (pile + grip)

QUESTIONS

1. What is a pile? Give its classification.
2. What factors govern the choice of a pile?
3. Name the constituents of a pile driving rig.
4. Name different types of hammers used for pile driving and explain one of them fully.
5. Give the working of drop hammers with their advantages and disadvantages.
6. Compare and contrast the working and advantages of single acting and double acting pile driving hammers.
7. Write a detailed note on a differential acting pile driving hammer.
8. Discuss the working and advantages of diesel hammer.
9. Discuss the vibratory pile hammer fully.

OBJECTIVE TYPE QUESTIONS

1. Piles are used for
   (*a*) To consolidate soft soils as sand
   (*b*) To resist seepage of under ground water
   (*c*) To check erosion of soil under hydraulic structures
   (*d*) To transfer loads to suitable strata below the ground
   (*e*) All are correct
2. Sheet piles are used except
   (*a*) To resist water seepage under hydraulic structures
   (*b*) To check erosion of soil under hydraulic structures
   (*c*) To transfer loads to suitable strata below ground level
   (*d*) To check seepage and erosion of soil under hydraulic structures
3. Load bearing piles are driven for except
   (*a*) To transfer surface loads to the suitable strata below the ground level
   (*b*) To transfer surface loads to the soil mass around the pile
   (*c*) To resist the soil erosion under the hydraulic structures
   (*d*) To resist horizontal thrust of the soil mass on the pile
4. Piles transmit load to the soil through
   (*a*) Through skin friction between the surface of the pile and soil
   (*b*) Through the lower tip or end of the pile
   (*c*) Through skin friction and lower top
   (*d*) All are correct
5. The choice of type of pile is affected by
   (*a*) Size, type and weight of structure to be supported
   (*b*) Physical properties of soil strata at the site
   (*c*) Depth of strata capable to support the pile
   (*d*) Durability required

(*e*) Depth of water and its salinity above the ground into which piles are to be driven
(*f*) All are correct.

6. For pile driving hammers working on pounding principle are
   (*a*) Drop hammers, single and double acting hammers
   (*b*) Differential acting hammers
   (*c*) Diesel hammers
   (*d*) Hydraulic hammers
   (*e*) All the above
7. The selection of pile driving hammer is affected by
   (*a*) Size and type of pile (*b*) No of piles
   (*c*) Characteristics of the soil (*d*) Topography and location of the site
   (*e*) Whether pile driving is to be done on land or under water
   (*f*) Available pile driving rig (*g*) All are correct
8. Identify the incorrect statement/statements
   (*a*) Single acting hammers give higher number of blows per minute and greater percentage of energy to the pile to be driven
   (*b*) Single acting hammers can be used to drive heavy timber or concrete piles in stiff clays and dense cohesion less formations
   (*c*) Single acting hammers are simple in construction, hence cheaper in initial cost and maintenance cost
   (*d*) More persons are required to operate this equipment
9. Identify the correct statement/statements
   (*a*) The initial and maintenance cost of a differential hammer is less
   (*b*) The differential hammer has larger hammer and higher rate of striking
   (*c*) A diesel hammer can operate easily in soft soils offering little resistance to activate the ram
   (*d*) Precast concrete heavy piles may be driven economically and easily with diesel hammers
   (*e*) The diesel hammer does not need any external source of energy. Hence it is easy to set up and start operation and its cost of operation is less.
   (*f*) The maintenance and servicing of the diesel hammer is simple and fast. Hence it can be used in remote areas conveniently
10. Identify the incorrect statement/statements
   (*a*) Leads extend to the full height of the rig
   (*b*) Leads guide the pile and hammer during driving operation
   (*c*) The length of lead should not necessarily be equal to the longest pile to be driven
   (*d*) Generally largest available hammer that can be used with out damaging the pile should be selected
   (*e*) For driving concrete piles the weight of hammer should be atleast half of the pile
   (*f*) For driving a timber pile the weight of hammer should be 1.0 to 1.5 times the weight of pile

ANSWERS:

1. (*e*)	4. (*d*)	7. (*g*)	10. (*c*)
2. (*c*)	5. (*f*)	8. (*c*)	
3. (*c, d*)	6. (*e*)	9. (*b, e, f*)	

27

Water Pumping Equipment

27.1. INTRODUCTION

Almost all projects need water for one or the other purpose such as water supply for human consumption or for other process as for washing, curing, jetting etc. Thus pump is the basic tool in the operation of a water handling system on any project.

A pump is a device which transfers the mechanical energy supplied from an external source to the liquid flowing through the machine. In the construction work we are principally concerned with water as liquid. It may be pure water or dirty water with suspended matter. For some projects a pump may be the most critical item of construction equipment, even though it may not be a direct production machine.

27.2. SELECTION OF PUMP FOR CONSTRUCTION APPLICATION

While selecting a pump following factors should be kept in view:

1. Dependability
2. Availability of repair parts
3. Economical installation and operation
4. Simple and easy to repair
5. Operating power requirements

27.3. CLASSIFICATION OF PUMPS

On the basis of working principles all types of pumps can be classified into the following two classes:

1. Positive displacement pump
2. Rotodynamic pumps

1. The positive displacement pumps may be of reciprocating type or rotary type. In these pumps the operating force is applied directly to the liquid, increasing the energy of the liquid. In a reciprocating pump the pump chamber is alternately filled with and emptied of the liquid which is pumped.

(*b*) **Rotary type pump.** Though in appearance it resembles with the rotodynamic pump and embodies the rotation of the impeller as against the forward and back ward movement of the piston of the reciprocating type pump, but it is essentially a positive displacement pump. Its characteristics are in some respect mid way between those of reciprocating and centrifugal type pumps. The discharge of liquid of the rotary and reciprocating pumps depends almost on the speed of rotation and very little on the pressure developed These pumps have little direct application in pumping water on construction jobs. They are widely used for transfer of oils. Pressure lubrication, paint spraying, hydraulic power transmission and machine tool coolant circulation etc.

2. Rotodynamic pumps. In these pumps a rotor moves in the liquid in the casing of the pump. The movement of the rotor imparts high velocity to the liquid which is discharged due to its centrifugal force. The force applied to the liquid generates the acceleration in a direction perpendicular to the direction of flow. In this pump the flow of liquid is continuous unlike reciprocating pumps where the flow usually is pulsating or intermitent.

The above classification is based on the operating principles of the pumps and not on the service for which they are intended. Further the pumps may be sub divided depending on their construction features, material used and disposition of its axis. While selecting a pump it is essential to consider the following factors.

27.4. POINTS TO BE CONSIDERED WHILE SELECTING A PUMP

Following points should be considered while selected a pump:

1. The height of lift from the existing water surface to the point of discharge.
2. The rate at which the water is to be pumped.
3. The pressure head at discharge, if any.
4. The variation in water level at suction or discharge.
5. The altitude of the project.
6. The height of the pump above the surface of water to be pumped.
7. The size of the pipe to be used.
8. The type, sizes, number of fittings and values to be used in the pipe line.
9. Lowest cost of the pump and pipe line to be used.

27.5. RECIPROCATING PUMP

These pumps have not been found of use in the construction work except when designed for special jobs to handle impure water etc. The suction lift of a reciprocating pump depends on the nature of the liquid and the temperature. These pumps are self priming, the suction lift including friction head will not be more than 6.7 m (22 ft.) for clean water at 16°C (60°F). At sea level theoretically this value may go up to 10.4 m (34 ft.) At a temperature of about 71°C (160°F) the suction lift will reduce to 0 and a positive suction head would be required for the effective pump operation. At a temperature of 100°C a suction head of 3.7 m would be required. The head loss due to friction in the pipe line may be calculated by the following relation,

$$\text{head loss} = \frac{4flv^2}{2g}$$

where,

f = coefficient of friction
l = length of pipe in metres
v = velocity of flow in m/second
g = gravitational force taken as 9.81 in m.k.s. units.

27.5.1. Advantages of reciprocating pumps

1. The rate of discharge practically is constant, irrespective of the head and is limited by the power of the pump.
2. These pumps are well suited to handle thick and unclean liquids as molasses due to the slow speeds of liquids passing through them.
3. They are usually self priming.
4. They have reasonably high efficiency regardless of head and speed.

27.5.2. Disadvantages

1. They are heavy weight and large size for a given capacity and not so handy a. rotary pumps.
2. In case of rise in discharge pressure, there is likelyhood of damage to pump unit. Hence a relief valve should be attached out side the discharge side as close to pump as possible.
3. Possibility of valve trouble especially when pumping water contains abrasive solids.
4. The volume, pumped usually is small, but high discharge pressure may be attained.

27.6. CENTRIFUGAL PUMPS

A centrifugal pump is the most popular type of rotodynamic pump and is used for capacities upto 15.1 m^3/min. and head upto 34 m. Centrifugal pumps may be of the following two types.

1. **Volute type.** This type of pump is more popular. In this case the impeller discharges into a progressively expanding spiral casing which is proportioned to produce a gradual reduction of velocity of the liquid, thus changing the velocity head into pressure head. (Fig. 27.1.)

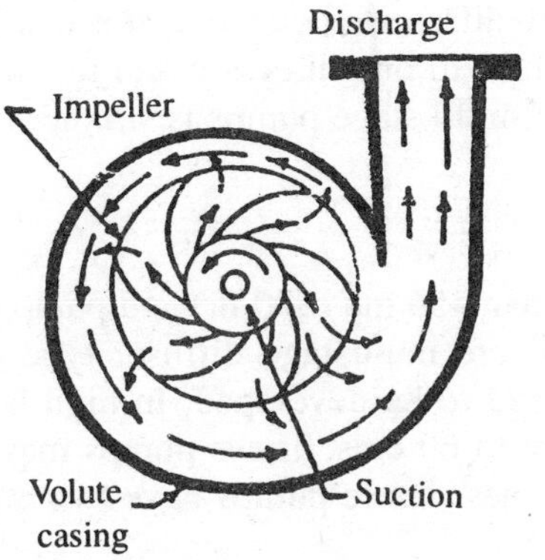

Fig. 27.1. Volute C.F. pump

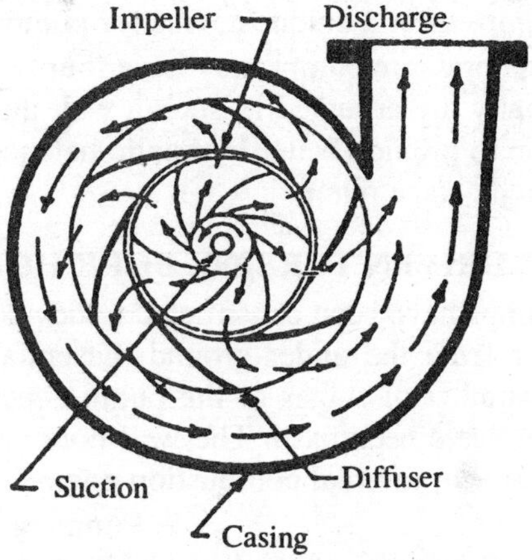

Fig. 27.2. Diffuser C.F. pump

2. **Diffuser type.** In this case the stationary guide vanes surround the runner, producing gradual expanding passage which changes the direction of liquid flow and converts the velocity energy into pressure head. This type of centrifugal pump is more efficient than volute type due to more completely conversion of velocity head into pressure head. But their construction is not simple and their cost is also high.

27.7. PRIMING OF CENTRIFUGAL PUMPS

A centrifugal pump installed below the level of water on the suction side does not need any priming as the pump casing and suction pipe always remain filled with water. On the other hand when the pump is installed above the suction level and works with a suction lift, the casing and the suction pipe would contain air instead of water. In such situations the differential pressure generated by pumping will not raise water level even by one cm. Thus in order to make the pump lift the liquid, the removal of air from the pump casing and the suction pipe line will be essential. This removal of air from casing of the pump and pipe line is called *priming i.e.* pump casing and pipe line would have to be filled with water instead of air.

Methods of priming

Priming can be done by the following two methods:

1. By pouring water in to the pump casing. By filling the pump casing and suction pipe with water will displace air from there. This method is used for small sized installations. In this system a foot value is attached at the end of the suction line and a funnel with a cock and an air vent is provided on the casing. This arrangement makes it possible to feed the liquid (water) into the casing through the funnel and air escapes though the vent. The value essentially is a non return valve fitted at the bottom of the suction line. This value does not allow the water to flow back.

2. By exhausting air from casing and pipe line. In this method of priming an ejector or an evacuating pump is used for removing air from the suction system. The ejector is mounted above the highest point of the pump casing. During the pumping operation the main delivery value of the pump is kept closed and opened when the evacuation is complete. This condition is indicated by the water gauge fitted on the pump. This method is used for medium and large installations.

27.8. MULTISTAGE PUMPS

In general these pumps are used upto a head of 122 m (400 ft.). A stage comprises of an impeller and its recuperating element *i.e.* the discharge of one stage is fed to the suction of the next stage until the liquid is finally discharged from the pump. The head developed by the pump is thus multiplied in each stage. Vertical multistage pumps offer a unique device for pumping water from hundreds of meters under the ground.

Large high pressure pumps may have four or more stages with diffuser type recupcrator in a barrel. The impellers usually are arranged in such a way that half of them face in one direction and the other half in other direction to provide better hydraulic balance. The design of multi stage pumps is simpler than that of equivalent single stage pump.

27.9. SHAFT DRIVEN TURBINE BORE HOLE PUMPS

These pumps have been constructed to develop heads more than 456 m (1500 ft.) and pump upto 113.5 m^3/min. water from the under ground. Essentially these pumps are multistage diffuser type centrifugal pumps. The number of stages of the pump depends upon the head to be developed. In high head pumps upto 20 stages have been used. The well bore varies from 15 cm to 60 cms. These pumps may be driven by electric motor or internal combustion engine or by steam turbines. These pumps have two main parts:

1. Head   2. Pumping unit

In case large content of sand is anticipated in the water, the closed line shaft is used. In this arrangement the entire driving shaft with its bearings is enclosed in an inner tube. Lubrication of the bearings is done through filtered water supplied through the upper end of the inner tube. When water is required free of oil, as for drinking purposes, oil can not be used for lubrication. In such situations lubrication is done by water.

27.10. SUBMERSIBLE TURBINE PUMP

In these pumps a small diameter motor is mounted below the turbine bowls and submerged in water of the well. Water entry into the motor is prevented by providing a seal through mercury filled in a rotating cup attached to the motor. The motor and the pump form a compact unit which is attached to the discharge pipe. Generally a squirred cage type induction motor is used in this pump. This motor is fitted at one end with a thrust bearing. An oil of high dielectric properties is circulated all the time through the motor windings. These pumps have been made for heads upto 3666 m (12000 ft.) and as many as 300 stages in all.

For a submersible pump there is no restriction on suction lifts and they do not need suction hose. Further they do not suffer from the problem of noise. Aluminum and iron are the best materials for their construction as other materials are more prone to damage when the pump is dropped. These pumps may have 1/4, 1/3 and 1/2 h.p. units for small works and 1 and more horse power units for moving large volumes or for high head conditions.

27.11. SLUDGE PUMPS

These pumps are used to handle the liquids (water) containing solid materials as encountered in excavation of foundations. These pumps are capable of passing solids and withstanding the abrasion, which might result from the gritty nature of suspended solids. Essentially they are low head pumps. The maximum head is limited to about 15 m.

27.12. POWER REQUIRED FOR A PUMP

The power required for a pump can be determined by the following relation.

$$\text{H.P. (metric)} = \frac{q \times h \times d}{4500 \times \eta}$$

where,

q = quantity of liquid flow in litres per minutes
h = total head on the pump in metres of liquid
d = sp. gravity of liquid
η = pump efficiency.

27.13. CHARACTERISTICS OF PUMPS

The characteristics of reciprocating, rotary and centrifugal pumps are given in the Table 27.1 below.

Table 27.1.

S. No.	*Characteristics*	*Type of pumps*		
		Reciprocating	*Rotary*	*Centrifugal*
1.	Maximum recommended suction	6.7 m	6.7 m	6. 1 m
2.	Nature of liquid handled	(*a*) Clean water with piston pumps (*b*) Dirty with solid suspended material with diaphram pumps	Generally viscous and non abrasive	From clean and clear to dirty and abrasive
3.	Discharge from pump	Pulsating *i.e.* intermitent	Steady	Steady
4.	Discharge pressure attained	Low to very high 420 kg/cm^2	Low to medium	Low to high
5.	Volume of liquid pumped	Generally small about 0.378 m^3/min.	Small to medium	Small to very large 15.1 m^3/min.
6.	Effect of pumping head on volume pumped	Practically no effect	Practically no effect	Volume decreases with the increase of head.
7.	Effect of pumping head on power consumed	Increases with increase of head	Increases with increase of head	Depends on specific speed. For same specific speed it increase with discharge.
8.	Convenience in handling	Bulky, heavy and difficult to handle.	Compact and easily handled.	Compact and easily handled.

27.14. WELL POINTS

A well point is a perforated tube or pipe of 3 to 6 cms diameter. The perforated tube is surrounded with a screen made of brass mesh to prevent the entry of solids into the well point. The size of the brass mesh is suitable to handle the predominant grain size of the soil. Generally the mesh size is kept not more than four times the 85% size of the finest surrounding material and not less than four times the 15% size of the corset surrounding material. A shoe is fitted at the lower end of the well point to facilitate its penetration into the ground. The length of the well point varies from 0.6 m to 1.2 m. Most well points are self jetting type and are equipped with a nozzle to send water under pressure which washes the material ahead of the well point bottom and assists in penetration. Jetting pump is used to install the well points into the ground.

27.15. WELL POINT FITTINGS

At the top, the well point is connected to a riser pipe of diameter 3.8 to 6.0 cms usually made of iron or steel. The length of this riser pipe is such that its upper end projects out of the ground. Each riser is joined to the header through a pair of swinging elbows, a union nut and a brass cock. The cock enables any well point to be disconnected with out interfering with the rest of the system during operation. The diameter of the header varies from 10 cms to 60 cms and have couplings welded at approximately 1 m intervals for connection with the riser pipes. The header leads to the dewatering well point pump. A suitable discharge pipe carries the water from the pump to the point of disposal.

27.16. WELL POINT DEWATERING PUMP

For efficient operation of the well point, it is essential that a steady high vaccum of the order of 46 to 74 cms of mercury should exist on the header lines and well points, other wise water will not be withdrawn upto the dewatering pump. Due to the long length of the header and rising piping system the chances of air leaks into the suction side are considerable. Thus the arrangements of extracting this air is essential. Fig. 27.3 shows a well point and Fig. 27.4 shows the withdrawal of water from soil.

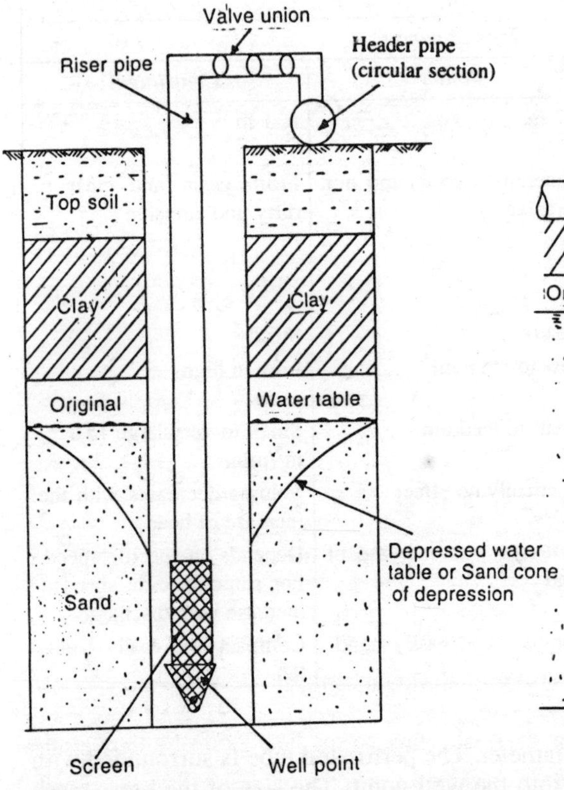

Fig. 27.3. Well point

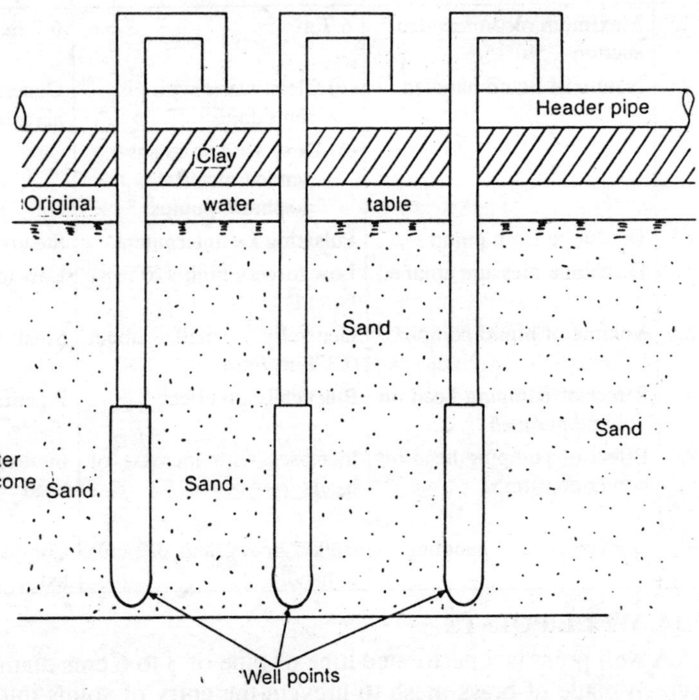

Fig. 27.4. Lowring water table by well points

The well points are made of much varied capacities for heads from 7.6 to 45.7 m. A common size of this pump has 15 cms suction and 15 cms delivery and delivers 2.84 m^3/min. against a head of 20 m. The power of the prime mover may be about 25.4 metric horse power.

27.17. CAPACITY OF WELL POINTS

The capacity of a well point system varies with the characteristics of water bearing strata as permeability of the soil and amount of water present. It also depends on the design of the screen.

The length of the screen usually varies from 90 cm to 120 cms and is limited by the thickness of the water bearing strata. The spacing between two well points depends on the probable quantity of water to be handled and the capacity of each well point. Generally spacing between two will points is kept from 0.6 m to 1.0 m.

The capacities of standard well points per unit length of the screen based on a velocity of 3 cm/sec and slot opening varying from 0.15 mm to 1.27 mm are given in Table 27.2.

Table 27.2. Capacities of well points based on velocity 3 cms/sec.

Size of the slot opening (mm)	*Open area as percent of total surface area (slot area %)*	*Capacity per 30 cms length of screen in litres per minute*
0.152	6.2%	4.9 lit/sec.
0.178	7.2%	5.7 "
0.203	8.0%	6.8 "
0.254	10.0%	8.0 "
0.305	11.0%	9.1 "
0.381	14.0%	11.4 "
0.507	18.0%	14.0 "
0.762	25.3%	19.0 "
1.015	31.3%	23.9 "
1.27	36.0%	27.3 "

QUESTIONS

1. What factors should be considered while selecting a water pump?
2. Give the classification of water pumps.
3. Discuss the working, and advantages of the following pumps.
   (*a*) Reciprocating pump
   (*b*) Centrifugal pump
4. What is a rotodynamic pump? Explain.
5. Write short notes on the following:
   (*a*) Multi stage pump
   (*b*) Submersible turbine pump
6. Define a well point and give factors which affect its capacity.

OBJECTIVE TYPE QUESTIONS

1. Pumps are a device to be used to handle except
   (*a*) Clean water (*b*) Water with solid gritty materials
   (*c*) Viscous liquids as molasses (*d*) Air and gases
2. Pumps are a device which transfer energy supplied from external source to the liquid flowing through the machine
   (*a*) Mechanical energy (*b*) Chemical energy
   (*c*) Kinetic energy (*d*) Static energy
3. In a reciprocating pump the movement of the piston is
   (*a*) Rotary type (*b*) To and fro
   (*c*) A combination of both (*d*) All are correct
   (*e*) None of the above
4. Rotary types pumps are mainly used for
   (*a*) Transfer of oils (*b*) Pressure lubrication
   (*c*) Paint spraying (*d*) Power transmission
   (*e*) Machine tool coolant circulation (*f*) All the above
5. Which of the pump can be used upto a head of 3650 m
   (*a*) Rotary (*b*) Centrifugal
   (*c*) Multistage pump (*d*) Submersible turbine pump
6. Shaft driven pump can be used upto a maximum head of
   (*a*) 650 m (*b*) 760 m
   (*c*) 456 m (*d*) 350 m

7. Multistage pumps can be used upto a maximum head of
   (*a*) 350 m (*b*) 275 m
   (*c*) 120 m (*d*) 95 m
8. Well points operate more satisfactorily if installed
   (*a*) In silty clays (*b*) Heavy clays
   (*c*) Permeable soils as sand and gravel (*d*) In rock formations
9. Identify the correct statement/statements
   (*a*) Removal of water from casing and pipe line of a centrifugal pump is called prining of pump
   (*b*) Pumping head has no effect on the volume of a centrifugal pump
   (*c*) The discharge of a centrifugal pump is pulsating
   (*d*) Reciprocating pump is a compact unit and can be handled easily
10. Identify the incorrect statement/statements
   (*a*) In case of a reciprocating pump, temperature has no effect on the suction lift
   (*b*) Reciprocating pumps are not suitable to handle thick and unclean liquids as molasses
   (*c*) These pumps may be used for any suction lift
   (*d*) Priming is essential for the use of reciprocating pumps
   (*e*) The rate of discharge of these pumps is not constant
   (*f*) They are handy to install and need less space
   (*g*) All the above are not correct
11. The capacity of a centrifugal pump is upto per minute
   (*a*) 10 m^3 (*b*) 15 m^3
   (*c*) 25 m^3 (*d*) 35 m^3
12. A centrifugal pump may work upto a head of
   (*a*) 34 m (*b*) 44 m
   (*c*) 24 m (*d*) 55 m
13. The well point tube is surrounded with fine screen mesh for
   (*a*) To give strength to the tube (*b*) To check the entry of soil particles in the tube
   (*c*) To increase the efficiency of well point (*d*) All the above
14. Identify the correct statement/statements
   (*a*) The discharge of liquid from rotary and reciprocating pumps mainly depends upon the speed of rotation
   (*b*) Pressure developed in rotary and reciprocal pumps has very little effect on discharge of liquid
   (*c*) These pumps have little direct application in pumping water on construction projects
   (*d*) All are correct

ANSWERS:

1. (*d*)	5. (*d*)	9. (*b*)	13. (*b*)
2. (*a*)	6. (*c*)	10. (*g*)	14. (*d*)
3. (*b*)	7. (*c*)	11. (*b*)	
4. (*f*)	8. (*c*)	12. (*a*)	

28

Asphalt Concrete Plants

28.1. INTRODUCTION

Asphalt concrete is most widely used material for the construction of high ways, air field pavements, and parking lots due to its ability to take the shape of desired section, to recycle the old pavements and the utilization of local material in the mix. design. An asphalt concrete is a mixture of asphalt and aggregate. Asphalt is a binding material as cement. Due to this reason some authors have given it the name as asphalt cement instead calling it simply as asphalt. In asphalt concrete about 10% binder either asphalt or asphalt cement is used by weight of the mix. The aggregate used should be of good quality and of proper gradation. The aggregate content varies from 90 to 95%.

28.2. CONSTITUENTS OF ASPHALT CONCRETE

There are mainly two constituents of asphalt concrete as follows:

1. Asphalt
2. Aggregate

1. Asphalt. Asphalt is a binding material produced by the distillation of petroleum crude oil. It is also available in nature. There are several sources of natural asphalt through out the world. Trinidad lake asphalt is the most famous natural asphalt. However the majority of asphalt is produced by the petroleum industry which is the waste product left after the extraction of different fuels as petrol etc. Due to the improvement in distillation of crude oil, the quality of asphalt also has changed. The quality of asphalt is also affected by the chemical composition of the crude oil. Crude oil obtained from different sources has different chemical composition. Thus the quality of asphalt is a function of the origin of the crude oil and the process of refining.

Asphalt is a visco elastic material. It behaves as a liquid at high temperature and as an elastic solid at low temperatures. At pavement operating temperatures asphalt has a semi solid consistency. Hence for preparing the asphalt concrete, the asphalt either can be heated to about 300°F to convert it into liquid state prior to mixing with aggregates or converted to a liquid product by dilution or emulsification. The quality of asphalt used for high way construction is controlled by the laid down specifications. Following four speci- fications have been suggested for the quality of the asphalt.

(*a*) **Penetration grades of asphalt.** This is the earliest codified specification for asphalt. According to this specification, the asphalt sample is heated upto a temperature of 77°F and a needle of 10 gram weight is placed in it for five seconds and its penetration in the asphalt is noted. The distance of penetration of the needle into the asphalt is the measure of the consistency of the asphalt. Soft asphalts have higher penetration than hard asphalts. On this basis asphalts may be graded as 40-50, 60-70, 85-100, 120-150 and 200-300 penetration.

(*b*) **Viscosity grades of asphalt.** This specification is based on the viscosity of the asphalt at a temperature of 140°F. Under this classification, two specifications have been specified as AC and AR.

In AC specification, the asphalt is tested at the "produced" state where as in AR, specifications, the sample is conditioned before testing *i.e.* the asphalt sample has been simulated to the condition of hardening during the construction process. The grades have been designated as AC grade-2. 5, 5, 10, 20 and 40 and in AR grade as 500, 1000, 2000, 4000, 8000 and 16000 etc.

Though the penetration and viscosity specification were found effective in controlling the quality of asphalt. But these test could not be used to correlate the quality of asphalt to the performance of the pavement. Hence other specifications were searched.

(*c*) **Performance grade.** In this case fixed test criteria is used and the temperatures for evaluating the asphalt are selected to reflect the local construction conditions. For the performance grade method the specifications are designated based on the temperature application range of the asphalt.

In this grade system the grade is designated as PG hh-II were PG indicates the performance specifications, and hh identifies the high temperature application for the asphalt while II identifies low temperature for the asphalt in degree celsius.

(*d*) **Liquid asphalt.** To use the asphalt on the construction with out heating it to 300°F, following two methods have been developed to reduce the asphalt to a liquid state.

(*i*) Cut back (*ii*) Emulsion

(*i*) **Cut back.** It is a mixture of asphalt and a fuel product, such as gasoline or naphtha, diesel, and kerosene oil. Rapid, medium, and slow cured cut backs can be formulated by diluting the asphalt with gasoline, or naphtha, diesel and kerosene oil respectively.

(*ii*) **Emulsions.** In this case the colloidal asphalt is treated into a mill to break the asphalt into very fine particles. These particles are added to the water which has been treated with an emulsifying agent. The emulsifying agent is a soap like material. The emulsifying agent allows the fine particles of asphalt to remain suspended state in the water. The empulsions being cheaper, safe, and environmently good are widely used and practically replaced cut backs. The primary applications of emulsion asphalt are tack coats and prime coats during pavement construction and as a binder for surface treatment, slurry seals and cold patch materials. As a binder asphalt is applied by spraying through a distributor truck.

2. Aggregates. The load applied to an asphalt pavement mainly is carried by the aggregate used in the mix. In the asphalt concrete portion of aggregates accounts 90 to 95% of the material by weight. For good performance of the pavement, good quality and proper gradation of the aggregates is most important Ideally the gradation of the aggregate should be such that the minimum amount of binder is needed in the mix. The binder fills most of the voids in between the aggregate particles as well as the voids in the surface of the particles. Generally 37.5, 25, 19.5, 12.5 and 9.5 mm size aggregates are used for pavement surfaces.

Besides good gradation, the other important properties of a pavement surface aggregate are, resistance to wear and abrasion, texture, porosity, resistance to debonding between asphalt and aggregates and cleanliness. The persence of foreign matter as soil or organic matter will reduce the load carrying capacity of the pavement.

The surface texture of the aggregate has a marked influence on the strength of the pavement structure and on the workability of the mix. The strength of the pavement is influenced by the interlocking of particles together. The interlocking ability of the aggregate is increased by the angular rough textured particles. However rough textured particles need a little more asphalt binder.

The porosity of the aggregate affects the amount of asphalt binder required in a mix. The porous aggregate absorbs more asphalt than a dense aggregate. Thus while using porous aggregates in a mix more binder asphalt will be needed to compensate the absorbed binder, which is not available to serve as a binder. Hence aggregate to be used in pavement asphalt concrete must be selected carefully.

28.3. ASPHALT-CONCRETE

In a asphalt concrete, asphalt is used as a binder. Hence some authorities have called it as asphalt cement. In a asphalt concrete the amount of asphalt by weight is about 10%, but it serves the following important functions in the concrete.

(*a*) It binds the aggregate particles together.

(*b*) It prevents the ingress of moisture into the surface

(*c*) It acts as a cushioning medium.

Though all asphalt concretes are a blend of asphalt and aggregate. However by using different aggregate gradation, different types of asphalt concrete can be obtained, such as dense graded, open graded and stone metrix mix. The most common type of asphalt concrete is dense graded mix.

The process of selection of asphalt, aggregate structure, and proportion of aggregate and asphalt to provide the optimum combination of materials for a given project is known as *mix design.* Though there are several methods of asphalt concrete design, but the common feature of all procedures is the laboratory evaluation and specifications. They include the grade of asphalt, specifications governing the quality of aggregate and quality control requirements for the asphalt concrete mixture.

Though different mix design procedures required different quality control parameters for construction, but the most common parameters are as follows:

(*a*) Aggregate gradation

(*b*) Asphalt content

(*c*) Density of the mix

(*d*) Volume of voids in the mineral aggregate

(*e*) Volume of air voids

(*f*) Dust to binder ratio

(*g*) Volume of voids filled with asphalt.

After estimating the aggregate gradation, different asphalt contents are taken and samples prepared. These samples are tested as per the appropriate method. Graphs are plotted of the prepared mix design parameters and asphalt content, and the optimum asphalt content is determined.

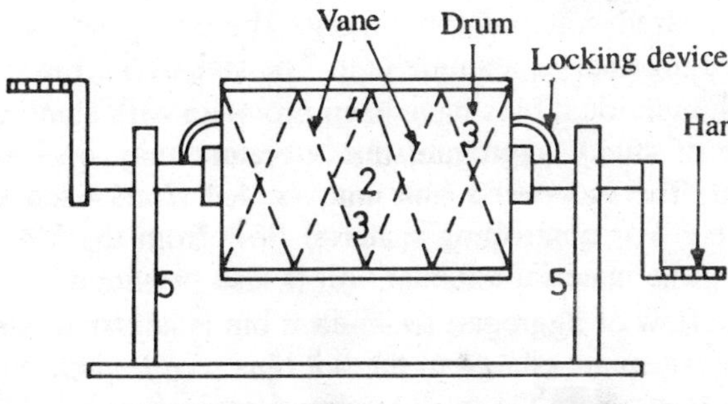

Fig. 28.1. Drum asphat mixer

28.4. PREPARATION OF ASPHALTIC CONCRETE

1. Drum mixer. For preparing asphaltic concrete usually asphalt is heated upto about 150°C (300°F). The equipment in which asphalt, and aggregate is heated and mixed is called asphalt concrete mixer. For small works drum mixer as shown in Fig. 28.1 was used. It is a cylindrical tube which rotates around a horizontal axis. In this mixer hot and cold both types of aggregate can be used. To mix the asphalt and aggregate the vanes are attached in side the mixer. First the aggregate is fed into the mixer and heated upto the desired temperature by burning wood etc. and then hot asphalt is poured into the aggregate and mixed by rotating it horizontally. The capacity of this mixer is 0.5 m^3.

2. Paddle mixer. It is a box made of thick steel sheets. It has a hinged bottom door and open at top as shown in Fig. 28.2.

In this mixer shafts are attached which rotate in opposite direction of each other as shown in the Fig. 28.2.

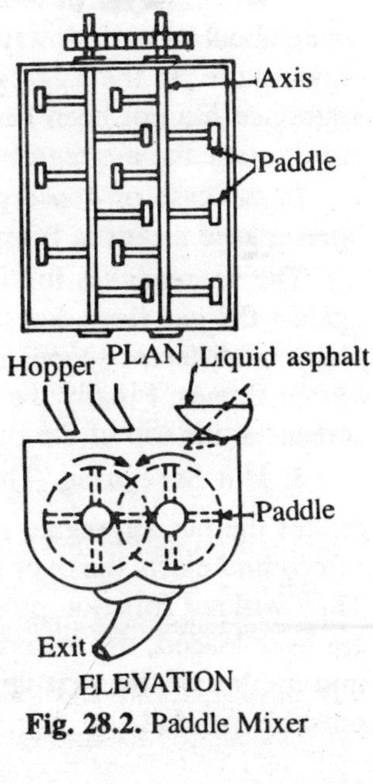

Fig. 28.2. Paddle Mixer

Working

In the mixer hot coarse and fine aggregate is fed through a hopper and the hot asphalt is added to it while the mixer is in rotating condition. The asphalt is added in a thin film. The asphalt and aggregate are mixed well in the mixer before taking out. The capacity of this type of mixer varies from 0.5 to 2.0 m^3.

28.5. MECHANICAL MIXERS

Due to the advent of technology, asphalt plants have come into existence. Now a days asphalt plants capable of uniformly blinding, heating and mixing the aggregate and asphalt are in use. The most common type of asphalt plants are drum type and batch type. The drum mix plants are based on newer technology than batch type plants. The drum mix plants have been found more economical than batch plants to operate. The drum plants were introduced in 1970 and about 95% of the new plants are of this type, but about 70% operational plants are batch plants. Hence here these types of plants have been discussed.

28.6. BATCH PLANTS

Batch plants are in use from the beginning of the asphalt industry. It has the following components:

1. Cold feed system
2. Drum dryer
3. Hot elevators
4. Hot screens
5. Hot bins
6. Asphalt handling system
7. Pug mill mixer
8. Dust collectors
9. Surge silo.

1. Cold feed system. The cold feed bins are provided to store and allow uniform and quick flow of properly sized material for mixing. The cold feed system consists usually of three to six open top bins mounted together as a single unit. The size of the bin is balanced with the operating capacity of the plant.

The individual bins have been provided with slanting or steep side walls to allow free flow of material. In case of sticky aggregate, the vibrators may be provided on walls for quick and free movement of material. The individual bins may be fed from sized aggregate stock piles by clam shell and front end loader etc. For controlling material flow from the bin, a gate is provided at the bottom of each bin. For metering the material a feeder unit is also provided.

The flow of aggregate from each bin is adjusted adequately to ensure the sufficient flow of material to keep the adequate charge in the hot bins. For transporting the aggregate from cold bins to the dryer drums the belt feeders are the most common equipment.

2. Drum dryer. It is a long cylindrical tube inclined to the horizontal from top towards bottom. It can rotate about its axis slowly. The purpose of this drum dryer is to heat and dry the aggregate upto the desired temperature. If the aggregate is heated excessively, the asphalt will harden during mixing. In case the aggregate has not been heated adequately, the aggregate will not be coated completely with asphalt. Thus at this stage the aggregate must be heated adequately to produce a final mix at the desired temperature.

In the case of dense graded mixes, all asphalts should be heated from 225°F to 350°. The range for open graded mixes is from 180°F to 250°F.

The aggregate is fed into the drum at the far end opposite to the burner and travel through the drum against the gas flow due to gravity as the drum is inclined towards bottom. As the drum rotates the steel plates of different shapes attached inside the drum, lift the aggregate and dump it through the hot gas and burner flames. Finally the heated aggregate is discharged into the elevator (bucket) which carries it to the screens at the top of the batch plant tower.

3. Hot Screening. The batch plant vibrating screen unit usually is a $3\frac{1}{2}$ deck arrangement. This unit grades the hot aggregate into four different sizes and sends each size into a bin meant for that size. The screen unit ejects the over sized material out of the production cycle. The screens provide gradation control. They will not function properly if the proportioning and flow from cold feed are not correct. If the screens are over loaded, the material which after passing through a screen should go into a hot bin, will be carried into the bin of the next larger size aggregate. Such a situation will destroy the concept of mix design and must be avoided.

Hot bins. These are temporary storage source or device for hot aggregate till the plant is ready to make a batch of asphaltic concrete. In operating a batch plant it is very important to ensure that the hot bins have sufficient material to feed the pugmill for the production of a batch of asphalt concrete.

Advantages of batch plant over drum plant

In case of batch plant, the batches are blended individually from the hot bins. This allows the aggregate blend of one batch to be different from the blend of the next batch. However it is dependent upon the availability of proper aggregate in the hot bins.

Disadvantages

Under high production rate conditions, the aggregate in hot bins will not be graded properly for gross changes in the gradation of the mix. Thus the flexibility of the batch plant is compromised. The large changes in the gradation of aggregate must be accomplished by altering the flow of aggregate from the cold bins so that the proper amount of material is stored in the hot bins.

Weight hopper

It weighs the hot aggregate. It is situated below the bins and above the pug mill. The aggregate is charged into the weight hopper from one hot bin at a time and weighed as per requirement of the gradation.

The weight hopper controls the gradation of the blended aggregate. The aggregate is weighed cumulatively in the hopper and the mineral filler is added at the end. After charging the weight hopper the bottom gates are opened to discharge the aggregate into the pug mill.

Asphalt handling system.

At site the asphalt is stored in a heated tank. The asphalt is pumped to the weight tank, ready for discharge into the pug mill. After adding the aggregate to the pug mill, the asphalt is pumped through spray bars into the pug mill to coat the aggregate.

Pug mill mixing

For mixing the batch mostly twin shaft pug mill is used. To achieve a uniform mixing, the live zone of the pug mill should be completely filled with the mix. The live zone consists from the bottom of the pug mill upto the top of the paddle arc. Normally mixing time is about 60 seconds. 15 seconds are needed for loading and drying the mix and 45 seconds for mixing asphalt and aggregate. Actually the mixing time depends on the extent of coating of the coarse aggregate. 90 to 95% of the coarse aggregate must be fully coated during the mixing time. Depending on aggregate size.

Capacity. The capacity of the plant is a function of the pug mill size and the mixing time. The capacity varies from 1.5 to 5.0 tones. A 5 ton capacity pug mill can produce 300 tons of mix per hour if continuous operations are maintained.

The plant is designed in such a way that the gates of the pug mill are sufficiently high to allow to pass a truck below it so that mixed concrete may be discharged directly into the truck from the pug mill or a hot elevator may be used to transport the mix to the silos, which allow the plant to operate independently of the availability of trucks for loading the asphalt concrete. These silos allow to store several batches of asphalt concrete to accommodate an uneven distribution of trucks arrivals at the plant.

Due to the influence of temperature on the quality of the mix, the temperature of the mix is specified. The temperature of the mix is taken just after the discharge from the pug mill and it varies with the type and grade of the asphalt. As stated above, for dense graded mixes the range varies from 225 to 350°F for all grades of asphalt and for open graded mixes the range varies from 180°F to 250°F. Mixing should be done at the lowest temperature as it will achieve complete asphalt coating of the aggregate and still allow for satisfactory workability.

28.7. RECYCLING IN A BATCH PLANT

To save money aggregate reclaimed from asphalt pavement is recycled. In reclaimed asphalt pavement, RAP can be added to the fresh aggregate in the batch plant. The reclaimed pavement may be added in one of the four locations of the plant:

1. Weight box
2. Separate weight hopper
3. Bucket elevator
4. Heat transfer chamber

In all the above four methods, the fresh aggregate has to be super heated to provide heat for drying the RAP. Usually RAP contains 3 to 5% moisture content. Thus on heating the RAP steam is released. This steam contains dust that needs to be filtered.

Adding RAP to weight box is the simplest method, but the time for heat transfer is limited and catching the dust laden steam requires additional equipment. Using separate hopper may reduce the time slightly and may improve accuracy also, but it has the same disadvantages as adding RAP directly to the hopper.

Fig. 28.3 shows a batch plant with truck below the pugmill.

Fig. 28.3. Batch plant with truck below pugmill mixer.

28.8. DRUM MIX PLANTS

The main components of a drum mix plant are as follows:

1. Cold feed system
2. Asphalt handling system
3. Drying and mixing drums
4. Elevator
5. Dust collector
6. Storage silo

1. Cold feed system. In a drum plant all the mixing of all sizes of the aggregate is done with in the drum itself and the final mix from the drum is discharged directly into the silos in a continuous manner. There is no facility of adjusting the blend in this case as was available in batch plant. Thus the aggregate from each of the cold feed bins must be weighed before feeding the material into the drum. As the aggregate is weighed before drying, the moisture content of the aggregate in the cold bins must be monitored and the weights adjusted to ensure the dry mass of the aggregate to be correct. To measure the weights of the aggregate, scales are mounted on the conveyer belts.

(*a*) **Mixing drum.** The mixing drum consists of a long tube fitted with metal plates of varying shapes placed longitudinally inside the drum known is 'flights'. These vanes or flights lift and allow to fall the aggregate and the mix *i.e.* they mix the aggregate well. The drum also contains a burner for heating the aggregate and a spray bar for applying asphalt.

The basic operation of the drum plant is that aggregate is fed into at one end of the drum. The aggregate remains in the drum from 3 to 4 minutes. During this duration the aggregate must be thoroughly dried and heated to the desired mixing temperature. Near the discharge end of the drum the asphalt is spread on the aggregate. Automatic control monitors the quantity of aggregate and measure the proper quantity of asphalt. The drum rotation and the inside vanes of the drum mix the aggregate properly.

(*b*) **Specifications of drum.** In a drum mix plant, drum usually has a slope of 4.2 cms to 8.4 cms per metre length of the drum (0.5 to 1 inch per foot length). The speed of rotation normally is 5 to 10 revolution per minute. The diameter of the drum varies from 0.9 to 3.6 m (3 to 12 ft.) and length from 4.5 to 18 m (15 to 60 ft.). The ratio of length to diameter varies from 4 to 6. Longer drum are used for recycling purposes. The drum specifications and the nature of the material control the mixing time.

(*c*) **Production.** The production rate of the plant is found inversely proportional to the moisture content of the aggregate. It has been observed that in a 2.4 m (8 ft.) diameter drum the increase in moisture from 3 to 8% reduced the production from 100 to 60% *i.e.* from 500 to 300 tons (450 to 270 metric tonnes).

Originally drum plants were designed as parallel flow operations in which aggregate and heated air travelled in the same direction down the drum. Subsequently it was observed that the flow of the hot gases in the opposite direction of the flow of the aggregate gave higher production of about 12%. Thus in the subsequent design the heated exhaust exits have been provided near the top of the drum from where the aggregate is introduced into the drum.

Recycling in a drum plant

Drum plants can also be used for the reclaimed asphaltic pavement (RAP) by placing a feed collar. The RAP is fed into this collar in the region of the drum that heats the aggregate and where the asphalt is introduced. For heating RAP heat is transferred from fresh aggregates as it can not be exposed to direct flames. For RAP treatment, the fresh aggregate is super heated to provide sufficient heat to raise the temperature of the RAP to the production temperature.

Storage Silos

As the drum plants produce a continuous flow of asphalt concrete, it must be stored in silos for subsequent dispatch into transport trucks. These silos have a bottom door or opening for discharging asphalt concrete directly into the haul trucks. To retain heat, these silos are typically insulated. To reduce the oxidation of asphalt during the storage period of asphalt mix, the sophisticated silos can be sealed completely and even filled with inert gas. The major problem of storage of asphalt concrete is the flow of

Fig. 28.4. Storage silo at a drum mix asphalt plant

asphalt from top to bottom of the silo. This results in poor quality paving mix. Fig. 28.4 shows storage silo at a drum mix asphalt plant.

Dust collectors

To control the air pollution, asphalt plants are equipped with dust control systems. There are two methods commonly employed for this purpose:

1. **Water venturi approach.** In this approach water is added at the point where dust ladden gas moves through the narrow throat of a venturi shaped chamber. The dust is entrapped in the water and thus separated from the exhaust gas. This approach needs the availability of adequate water supplies. The main disadvantage of this approach is that the collected material can not be reclaimed for use in the mix.
2. **Cloth filtration or dry bag house system.** This system allows mechanical collection and use of fine material from the aggregate. In this system the dust ladden gas is forced to pass through the fabric filter bags hung in a bag house. By mechanically shaking the bags or otherwise the collected dust is removed from the filter. The dust falls into hoppers in the bottom of the bag house and is removed by augers to a discharge vane feeder. The vane feeder is necessary to keep the bag house air tight. Filtre bags are made of fabric that can withstand temperature upto 450°F. An excessive temperature can melt the bags or cause fire.

Asphalt storage and heating

At the time of mixing asphalt with the aggregate the temperature of the asphalt should be in the range of 300°F in both systems.

Both systems, drum mix plant and batch plants have heating systems to keep the liquid asphalt at the required temperature. If the asphalt is delivered at a cooler temperature, the system must be capable of raising the temperature.

28.9. METHODS OF HEATING LIQUID ASPHALT

Commonly following two methods are used to raise the temperature of the liquid asphalt:

1. **Direct fire heater method.** The heater consists of a burner that fires into a tube in the asphalt storage tank. In such systems there must always be kept sufficient quantity of asphalt in the tank so that the burning tube always remains submerged in the asphalt. These systems have been found to have a higher thermal efficiency than the hot oil system.
2. **Hot oil system.** This system is a two stage approach. First the oil to be circulated through pipes with in asphalt tank is heated and then this oil is circulated through the pipes with in the asphalt tank.

The storage temperature of the asphalt varies according to the grade of asphalt. The viscosity of asphalt must be low enough to permit pumping. The storage temperature range for soft asphalts is 320°F and 350°F for hard asphalts as different asphalts have different temperature viscosity relationship.

28.10. PAVING EQUIPMENT

The paving of a high way needs following equipment:

1. *Dust remover or sweeper.* For removing dust from the surface to be paved dust remover or sweeper or brooms arc used.
2. *Hauling units.* To transport asphalt concrete from the plant to the construction site.
3. *Asphalt distributor trucks.* For applying the prime coat or seal coat.
4. Paver.
5. Rollers.
6. Material transfer vehicles (Optional)
7. Windrow elevators (Optional)

1. Dust remover or sweeper. To ensure the proper bonding between the existing pavement surface and the new asphalt concrete, the dust from the existing pavement must be removed prior to laying the new asphalt. When surfacing a prepared base course the dust layer should be removed either by sweeping with a broom or sweeper or by wetting the base course and recompacting.

Haul units

The hauling units used to transport asphalt concrete from the plant to the site are of the following three types:

1. Dump trucks
2. Live bottom trucks
3. Bottom dump trucks

Dump trucks and live bottom trucks transfer the mix directly into the hopper of the paver, where as bottom dump trucks are used to dump the concrete in heaps (windrows) directly on the pavement and only be used with pavers that have an elevator for lifting the mix from pavement and transferring it to the spreader box of the paver. As the heaped material loses temperature rapidly, this paving operation is feasible where the ambient or surrounding temperature is high.

Regard less of the type of truck used, the truck should be insulated and covered to reduce the heat loss during transportation. Before loading, the bed of the trucks should be coated with an approved release agent. In the past a heavy fuel oil as kerosene was used for this purpose, but it was found to contaminate the asphalt binder, and this practice was stopped.

Asphalt distributors

For applying an asphalt prime tack or seal coat, a specially designed distributor truck is used. An asphalt distributor truck requires constant attention to produce a uniform application. All measuring devices and gages such as pump techometer, measuring stick, thermometers and bitumeter must be properly calibrated. Nozzles and spray bars should be clean and set at the proper height above the surface receiving the application. To keep the asphalt heater and pump well maintained is essential.

Factors affecting the uniformity of application

Following factors have been found to affect the uniformity of application:

1. Asphalt spraying temperature
2. Liquid pressure across the spray bar length
3. Angle of the spray nozzles
4. Nozzle height above the surface
5. The speed of the distributor

For maintaining the temperature of the material, the asphalt distributors must have insulated tanks. They should also be provided with burners for heating the asphalt material to the proper application temperature. To maintain the continuous and uniform pressure for the full length of the spray bar the discharge pumps are used. To avoid interference of individual spray bars, the nozzles should be set at an angle of 15° to 30° from the horizontal axis of the spray bar. The height of the nozzle above the surface determines the width of an individual fan. To ensure the proper lap of the fans, the spray bar (nozzle) height must be set and maintained. To achieve a uniform application, the speed of the truck during the spraying should be kept constant. The relationship between application rate and truck configuration and surface area to be covered is given by the relation:

$$\text{In FPS system, } L = \frac{9 \times T}{W.R.}$$

where,

L = Length of covered surface in feet.
T = Total asphalt applied in gallons
W = Spray bar coverage width in feet.
R = Rate of application in gallons per square yard.

$$\text{In MKS system, } L = \frac{82\,T}{W.R.}$$

where,

L = Length of covered surface in metres.
T = Total asphalt applied in litres (Gallons = 3.785 lit.).
W = Spray bar coverage width in metres.
R = Rate of application in litres per squre metre.

The rate of application of prime coat varies from 1.0 to 3.0 lit. per m^2.

Tack coats are provided to create a good bond between the existing pavement and new asphalt overlays *i.e.* the new material. Tack coats are also applied between successive mats (layers) during new construction. The tack coat acts as an adhesive to prevent slippage of the two mats. The thickness of the tack coat is very thin. A tack coat is a very thin coat of uniform coating of asphalt.

Usually 0.23 to 0.7 litre per m^2 diluted emulsion is used for tack coat. The tack coat should become sticky with in a few hours of its laying. If the thickness of the tack coat is excessive, the layers will creep as the asphalt will work as a lubricant rather than as a tack. Hence the objective of providing tack coat will be defeated, Fig. 28.5 shows a distributer with hand spray

Seal coats consist of an application of asphalt followed by a light covering of fine aggregate which is rolled with pneumatic rollers. Normally 0.5 litre to 1.0 litre of asphalt per m^2 surface is used for this purpose.

Asphalt Pavers

An asphalt paver consists of a tractor and a screed. The tractor may be either a tracked or rubber tired.

Fig. 28.5. Using an asphalt distributor hand-sprayer attachment to apply a tack coat

The screed is a device which spreads the asphaltic concrete on the surface. The power unit of the tractor is provided with a receiving hopper in the front and a system of metallic thin pieces known as slat conveyors to move the mix through a tunnel under the power plant to the rear of the tractor unit. At the rear of the tractor unit, the mix is dumped on the surface to be paved and augers are used to spread it evenly across

Fig. 28.6. Track-mounted asphalt paver

the front of the trailing screed. The screed is drawn behind the tractor by two tow or pull arms which are pin connected to the tractor unit. The screed controls the asphalt concrete placement, its width and depth. It also imparts the initial finish and compaction to the material. Fig. 28.6 shows a track mounted paver, while Fig. 28.7 shows a paver having two screws for moving the mix through the tunnel. The use of the screw conveyors has been found to reduce the mix segregation.

Pavers can receive the mix directly into their front hoppers or can pick up dumped material placed in

Fig. 28.7. Asphalt paver having two twin screws for moving the mix through the tunnel

front of the paver. In the traditional method for directly loading the hopper, the truck directly dumps the asphalt concrete into the hopper of the paver. The push rollers mounted on the front frame of the Paver and extending beyond the hopper push the material against the wheels of the truck. The material is then transferred to the hopper by raising the truck bed or by activating the live bottom.

Loading the hopper with individual truck loads, usually requires the stopping of the paver intermittently, which may cause problems in constructing the smooth pavements.

Screed. The floating screed (not fixed in a particular direction) is free to pivot about its pin connections. The pin connected tow arm arrangement allows the screed to be self levelling and enables it to compensate for the irregularities of the base surface. The ability of the paver to level out the irregularities is controlled by wheel base length of the tractor and the length of the towing arms of the screed. The greater lengths of these two components provide smooth transition across the irregulaties resulting in smooth riding surface.

The mat (layer) thickness is controlled by the screed and can be maintained by using grade sensors tracing an external reference with a shoe. The screed can also be tied to a specified grade by using sensors tracing a string line. When all the forces acting on the screed are constant, it will ride at a constant elevation above the grade or follow the string line. However following factors may cause the variation in the sensor regulated screed height.

1. Screed angle of attack
2. The paver speed
3. The head of asphalt concrete in front of the screed

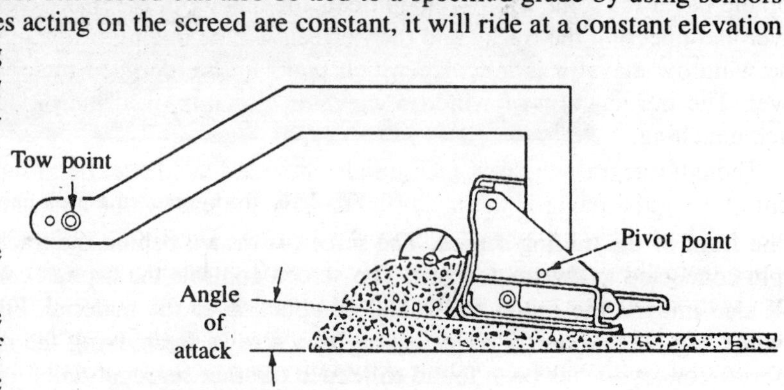

Fig. 28.8. Screed angle of attack.

1. Screed angle of attack. The angle subtended between the plane of the surface upon which the asphaltic concrete is placed and the plane of the bottom of the screed is known as the "screed angle of attack". as shown in Fig. 28.8. This angle is the principal mechanical factor which affects the variation in the thickness of the mat. It regulates the amount of material passing under the screed in a given distance.

The angle of attack changes, when either the screed or tow points are vertically displaced. The screed will immediately begin to move restoring the original angle. To accomplish this position requires about three tow arms length.

Asphalt material head

The asphaltic concrete directly infront of and across the length of the screed is known as *head of material*. When this material is not kept constant by the hopper drag conveyor and the auger feed, the screed angle of attack will be affected, resulting change in the thickness of the mat. If the head of the material becomes too high, the mat thickness will increase as the screed rides upon the excess material with the paver's forward progress. If the volume of the material decreases, the screed moves down, resulting in reduced thickness of the mat.

The sped of the paver is linked to the rate at which the asphalt concrete is delivered from the plant. To provide a smooth mat, the forward travel speed should be kept constant. Changes in the paver speed will affect the screed angle of attack. The increase in speed reduces the rise of the screed, where as decrease in speed causes increase in the ride of the screed. When the Paver is stopped, the screed tends to settle into the mat.

The initial compaction of the asphalt concrete or mix is achieved by the vibrations of the screed. To impart compaction to the mat, vibrators are mounted on the screed. The compaction of the mat is also influenced by mix design and temperature of the mix at the time of placement. In many pavers the speed of the vibrator can be adjusted to match the speed of the paver and the thickness of the mat.

The width of a screed can be changed by stopping the paver and adding fixed width extensions on one or both sides of the basic screed. Augur additions may also be required as screed width is increased to spread the material evenly across the entire screed and its extension width. Most of the screeds can be adjusted in the horizontal plane to create either a crown or super elevation. Some screeds can be extended hydraulically.

To prevent material from sticking to the screed at the beginning of a paving operation, it is necessary to heat the screed. To heat the bottom screed plates, built in diesel or propane burner heaters are used. The time of heating depends upon air temperature, type of the mix being placed. Normally 10 minutes time for heating is sufficient. Over heating will wrap the screed.

Windrow Elevators (Wind row is a line of dumped material).

In a paving operation the mix is filled in the paver hopper by trucks. The transfer of mix, requires to stop the paver for some time, which affects the quality of the mat. To eliminate the problem of stopping the paver and queering the tracks and their effects on the quality of the mat, windrow elevators are developed. The windrow elevator is a device which picks up the dumped material and fills it into the hopper of the paver. The introduction of windrow elevator also improved the production by eliminating the paver and truck matching.

Though integral windrow pick up elevators are available, but a separate elevator unit attachable to the front of a regular paver is the most popular. By the use of this attachment there is a flexibility of using the paver for both direct load and windrow situation. The flight system of the elevator lifts the mix into the hopper from the windrow continuously. For efficient operation the quantity of material in the windrow cross-section must be equal to the amount required for the cross-section of the mat. Minor variations in the quantity can be accommodated by the surge capacity of the paver hopper. Conventional windrow machines have limited widths and can handle only fairly narrow rows of material. How ever new designed machines have the capacity to handle wider windrow cross-sections.

Material transfer devices

A material transfer device is a device which can receive or hold multiple truck loads of asphalt concrete, remixes it and transfers it to the hopper of the paver. The use of material transfer unit has been found to improve the quality of the pavement.

Advantages of the use of material transfer devices

The use of material transfer devices have shown following advantages over the direct transfer from the haul truck to the paver hopper.

1. The material transfer device can hold several truck load of the asphalt concrete. Thus it reduces the surge loading of the paver. This allows the paver to operate continuously, while the haul trucks transfer the asphalt concrete to the transfer device. It can remix asphalt concrete and transfer to the paver hopper.
2. The material transfer device is self propelled. Hence the paver does not need to wait for a haul truck and push it.
3. The timing or arrival of the trucks to the job site is not critical as the paver can operate from the stock pile of material in the transfer device.
4. As the transfer device remixes the asphalt concrete before transferring it into the hopper of the paver, the thermal segregation of the concrete is reduced.

The thermal segregation occurs during the hauling operation as the asphalt concrete cools at the surface while the concrete at the centre of the load retains its heat. The self levelling screed of the paver is sensitive to the stiffness of the mix, which is largely a function of the temperature of the mix. By remixing the asphalt concrete, the stiffness of the asphalt concrete is more uniform, which allows smoother pavement construction.

28.11. COMPACTION EQUIPMENT

Due to the specific relationship between the air voids and stability, durability, water permeability, the asphalt pavements are designed on the basis of a specified compacted density having a specified percentage of voids. A properly designed pavement should have air voids between 3 and 5%. The compaction of the pavements is affected by the following factors:

1. Mix characteristics
2. Thickness of the layer to be compacted
3. Mix temperature at the time of compaction
4. Operational characteristics of the compacting equipment

28.12. TYPES OF ROLLERS USED

For the compaction of asphaltic pavements following types of rollers are used:

1. Smooth drum steel wheel rollers (Fig. 28.9)
2. Pneumatic tire rollers
3. Smooth drum steel wheel vibratory rollers
4. Vibratory rollers

Smooth drum steel wheel and pneumatic rollers have centre point articulation. The provision of the articulation allows the front and rear tires or wheels to maintain their overlap through out the turning range of the machine.

The contact surface area of a steel wheel roller is an arc of the cylindrical wheel surface and the roller width. This contact area decreases as the rolling progresses and the contact pressure attains a maximum value at the minimum contact area.

Fig. 28.9. Smoothed wheel roller

In case of pneumatic tire rollers the contact area is elliptical. This elliptical contact area is affected by (*i*) Wheel load, (*ii*) Tire inflation pressure and, (*iii*) Tire side wall flexure. The change in contact area of a pneumatic roller is less dramatic than in case of a steel wheel roller as the compaction progresses.

The compaction capability of pneumatic and vibratory steel wheel rollers can be altered to match the construction conditions. In case of pneumatic rollers the compaction effort can be altered by changing the ballast and the tire pressure. In case of vibratory steel wheel rollers the compaction effort can be changed by adjusting the vibrator frequency and amplitude. These capabilities enhences the operational flexibility of these rollers. (Details of Rolers are discussed in Chapter 21)

28.13. ROLLING TEMPERATURE

The compaction of the asphalt concrete is achieved by orienting the aggregates into a dense configuration. The hot asphalt acts as a lubricant and promotes the re orientation of the aggregates. On cooling the asphalt below the softening point to about 180°F the hot asphalt binder no longer provides the lubricating effect. Below the softening point, the asphalt begins to bind the aggregates into place making further compaction difficult. For determining the available time for compaction, the temperature of the mix at the time of placement is an important factor. The placing temperature is a function of the temperature during production and the heat loss during the haul. To check heat loss during hauling process the mix should be covered with tarpaulins. In extreme cases the trucks with insulated bodies should be used to transport the mix. On passing the mix through the paver, the rate of cooling of the mix is affected by the following factors:

1. Air temperature
2. Base temperature
3. Mix laying temperature
4. Layer thickness
5. Wind velocity.

1. Air temperature. Higher ambient air temperatures allows more time for compaction.

2. Base temperature. The base or surface upon which the mix is to be placed is of greater significance. There is a rapid heat transfer between the base surface and the mix surface.

3. Mix Laying temperature. The higher the temperature of the mix passing through the paver, more time will be available for compaction.

4. Layer thickness. Most probably this factor is the most significant which affects the cooling of the mix. As the thickness of layer increases, the time available for achieving the compaction will be more. But the thicker layers need more passes of the roller.

5. Wind velocity. Higher wind velocity will cool the mat very rapidly.

Thus rolling should begin at the maximum possible temperature. This maximum temperature is that point at which the mix will support the roller with out distorting the asphalt concrete horizontally. The increase in the diameter of the roller, increases the contact area reducing the contact pressure. Thus at higher temperature large diameter rollers can be used for compacting the mix.

28.14. CLASSIFICATION OF COMPACTION

Compaction of asphalt concrete can be categorised into the following categories:

1. Break down rolling. The aim of this type of rolling is to achieve the desired or required density with in the time frame defined by temperature constraints and consistent with the paver speed. For achieving the proper compaction there is an optimum mix temperature range. If the temperature of the mix is too high it will break off and will be spoiled. In case the temperature is too low, then it will be impossible to compact the mix due to the viscous resistance of the asphalt. These physical limits define the practical time duration available for the rolling portion.

2. Intermediate rolling. Some times density can not be achieved by a single roller with in the available time duration. In such cases an intermediate rolling is required to supplement the break down rolling to achieve the required density.

3. Finish rolling. It is the final rolling to remove any surface marks left by the previous rolling or by the paver.

For break down and intermediate rolling usually the vibratory steel wheel rollers are the best choice due to their adaptability to range of mixes and difference in mat thickness. In switched off condition of the vibrator they can also be used for finish rolling. Pneumatic rollers can also be used for break down and intermediate rolling. How ever if the temperature of the mix is high, the mix will stick to the tires of the wheel in case of break down rolling. Thus the pneumatic rollers should be used for intermediate rolling and steel wheel rollers for finish rolling. How ever vibratory rollers can be used for each type of compaction.

28.15. ROLLER SPECIFICATIONS

The paver speed and production depend on the asphalt plant capability. The number and type of rollers selected to be used on a project should match the placement capacity. Thus the speed of roller and the length of pavement is influenced by the following factors.

1. The gross speed of the roller
2. Number of passes of the roller
3. The number of laps
4. The non productive travel
5. The overlap between adjacent laps required to cover the mat width.
6. The extension overedge.
7. The extra passes for joints etc.

For a project the roller capability must match the net roller speed with average speed of the paver. The increase in the roller speed reduces the compactive effort. Thus sped alone can not be used to compensate for production needs. Typical acceptable roller speeds are suggested as follows:

1. Speed of roller for break down rolling. 3.2 kmph to 5.6 kmph.
2. Speed of roller for intermediate rolling. 4.0 to 6.4 kmph.
3. Speed of roller for finish rolling. 4.8 to 11.2 kmph.

QUESTIONS

1. What is the necessity of producing asphaltic concrete.
2. Describe drum and paddle mixers with sketches for preparing asphalt concrete for minor works.
3. Describe batch plant method for preparing asphalt concrete.
4. Describe the drum mix plant for preparing asphalt concrete.
5. Give the names of the paving equipment and describe rollers.
6. Write a note with sketch on the screed and a paver.

OBJECTIVE TYPE QUESTIONS

1. Which of the following is not correct
   (*a*) Asphalt is a bituminous material found naturally
   (*b*) Asphalt is the last product of distillation of crude oil
   (*c*) Asphalt is the first product of the distillation of crude oil
   (*d*) Asphalt is a visco-elastic material that behaves as liquid at high temperatures and as an elastic solid at low temperature
2. Identity the incorrect statement/statements
   (*a*) The quality of asphalt is a function of the original source of crude oil
   (*b*) The quality of asphalt is a function of the refining process
   (*c*) The quality of asphalt is a function of the method of storage of crude oil
   (*d*) Asphalt attains liquid condition at about 300°F temperature
3. Identify the correct statement/statements
   (*a*) Source of crude oil has no influence on the properties of asphalt
   (*b*) Temperature has no influence on the properties of the asphalt
   (*c*) There are no chemical tests to determine the characteristics of the asphalt

(*d*) Asphalt may be mixed with aggregate at any prevailing temperature

4. For carrying out the penetration test on asphalt it is heated upto
   (*a*) 36°F (*b*) 57°F
   (*c*) 77°F (*d*) 97°F
5. The amount of asphalt in asphalt concrete is about by weight
   (*a*) 5% to 10% (*b*) 10% to 15%
   (*c*) 15% to 25% (*d*) 25% to 35%
6. The amount of aggregate in asphalt concrete by weight is
   (*a*) 55-65% (*b*) 75-85%
   (*c*) 90-95% (*d*) 45-52%
7. The characteristics of the asphalt concrete are influenced by
   (*a*) Texture of aggregate (*b*) Porosity of aggregate
   (*c*) Grading of aggregate (*d*) Resistance to abrasion and to wear
   (*e*) All are correct
8. The asphalt concrete mix design is the process of
   (*a*) Selecting of suitable type of asphalt (*b*) Aggregate structure
   (*c*) Proportion of asphalt and aggregate (*d*) All are correct
9. A cut back is a blend of
   (*a*) Asphalt and water (*b*) Asphalt and aggregate
   (*c*) Asphalt and fuel product (*d*) Asphalt and air
10. Cut backs can be classified as
    (*a*) Rapid if blended with Naphtha or gasoline
    (*b*) Medium if blended with diesel
    (*c*) Slow if blended with fuel oil (Kerosene oil)
    (*d*) All are correct
11. Asphalt pavements should contain
    (*a*) No air voids (*b*) Some air voids
    (*c*) As many air voids as possible (*d*) All are correct
12. The capacity of rolling of a roller is mainly influenced by
    (*a*) The speed of roller (*b*) The number of passes
    (*c*) No of laps (*d*) Over lap between adjacent laps
    (*e*) All the above
13. Identify the correct statement/statements
    (*a*) The angle of attack of the screed is directly proportional to the speed of the paver
    (*b*) The angle of attack of the screed is inversely proportional to the speed of the paver
    (*c*) The speed of paver has no effect on the angle of attack of the screed
    (*d*) None is correct
14. Identify the incorrect statements
    (*a*) Twin screw pavers have been found to reduce the segregation of the asphalt concrete
    (*b*) The rate of production of a drum mix plant is inversely proportional to the moisture content of aggregate
    (*c*) The rate of production of a drum mix plant is directly proportional to the moisture content of the aggregate
    (*d*) Moisture content of aggregate has no effect on the production of the drum mix plant
15. The slope of drum of drum mix plant usually is
    (*a*) 0.083% (*b*) 0.05% (*c*) 0.9% (*d*) 1.1%
16. The amount of asphalt required for prime coat per m^2 varies
    (*a*) 0.5-0.9 lit. (*b*) 1.0-3.0 lit. (*c*) 4.5-6.5 lit. (*d*) 7.5-10 lit.

ANSWERS:

1. (*c*)	5. (*a*)	9. (*c*)	13. (*a*)
2. (*c*)	6. (*c*)	10. (*d*)	14. (*c, d*)
3. (*c*)	7. (*e*)	11. (*a*)	15. (*a*)
4. (*c*)	8. (*d*)	12. (*e*)	16. (*b*)

29

Organisation of Public Works Department

29.1. INTRODUCTION

Generally the construction of civil works of public utility is carried out by the Government, through public works departments of central and state Governments. The works of central Government are executed by central public works department. In addition to central public works department there are many major departments of Central Government such as Atomic Energy Commission, Central Water and Power Commission, Railways, Post and telegraph department. All India Radio department etc. Works related to defence ministry are executed by the Military Engineering Services. In recent times many construction corporations also have been formed for executing special types of works. The organisation and method of working of execution of the Civil Construction works of all government agencies, is more or less similar in nature. The works related to the state governments are executed by state public works department (P.W.D.).

States have separate departments for works relating to particular sphere such as irrigation and drainage, Highways, Flood Control, Power generation and distribution, Building and roads etc. In some states, power generation and distribution has been assigned to autonomous boards. Municipal boards, have their own Engineering departments for the execution of Municipal board works. State Governments also have set up some autonomous agencies for executing works of special nature as construction of bridges, dams and houses etc.

As stated above though the organisation and method of working of all Government agencies executing civil works is similar in nature, but differs in details from one organisation to the other depending upon the type of work and load factor.

29.2. ORGANISATIONAL SET UP OF PWD

The central and state public works departments work under one or more than one minister. All works are executed under his approval. The minister is assisted by an administrative officer called secretary in each department. He is responsible for all matters of administration in the department to the minister. On technical side one Chief Engineer is the over all incharge of each engineering department. The organisational set up of PWD is shown by line diagram on page 433.

The technical work of each engineering department is divided into circles. The number of circles usually varies from 3 to 4 as per need. Each circle is headed by a Superintending Engineer (S.E.). Further each circle is divided into divisions (usually from 4 to 6). Each division is headed by an Executive Engineer. He is also called Divisional Engineer (X.E.N.). Each division is further divided into sub divisions (usually 5 to 6). Each sub division is controlled by on Assistant Engineer. He is also known as sub divisional officer. The each sub division is further divided into sections (usually 5 to 6). Each section is headed by an Sectional officer or Overseer.

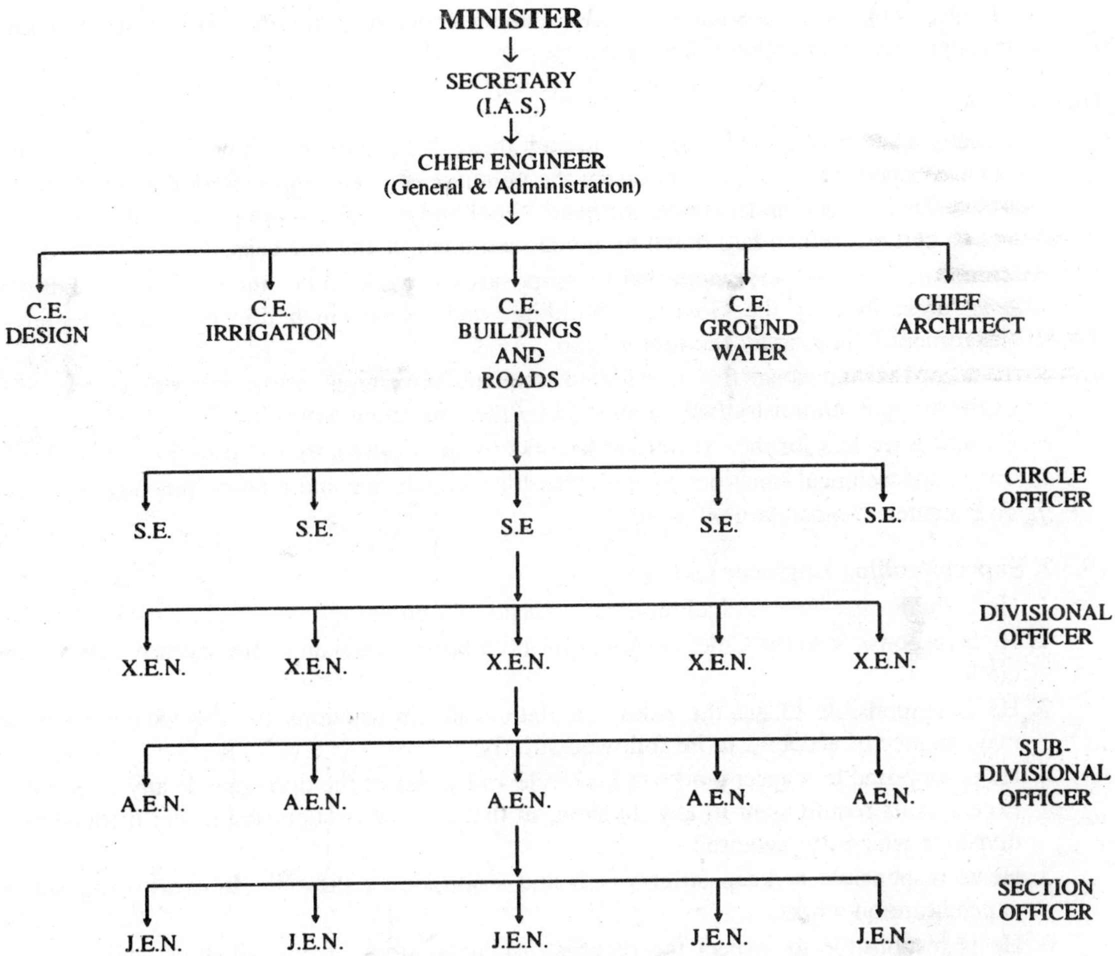

Fig. 29.1. Setup of P.W.D.

Similarly the architectural wing is headed by the chief architect (C.A.) with a town planning unit and senior architect unit attached to various zones.

29.3. RESPONSIBILITIES AND FUNCTIONS OF OFFICERS

29.3.1. Chief Engineer

1. He is the administrative as well as professional head of the concerned department and is responsible to the secretary to the Government for the performance of his branch.
2. He is responsible for formulating and framing the policies and programmes for the department. He gets prepared the annual budget estimates of works under his control. After the allotment of funds from the government, he has to ensure that the sanctioned amount for each work is utilised properly.
3. He is also responsible for maintaining proper accounts and to keep a close watch over the expenditure.
4. He also keeps liason with the Accountant General for maintaining accounts strictly according to laid rules.
5. Some times, if during the progress of work, more funds are required to complete the work, he has to apply to the Government for the same.

6. He also looks after the administrative matters concerning his department such as employment, transfers, leave and other related matters.

Jurisdiction

1. Usually all technical matters of that branch through out the state come under his jurisdiction.
2. He is competent to accord sanction for the purchase of live stock, purchase, manufacture and repair of articles included under the minor head "Tool and plant", except the purchase of motor vehicles upto a certain amount laid down by the Government in any one case.
3. To accord administrative approval to proposals for works other than residential buildings upto a limit prescribed by the Govt. for buildings and roads which do not pertain to any particular department falling under the minor head.
4. To accord technical sanction to detailed estimates of original works and repairs upto 5% in excess of the amount administratively approved by the competent authority.
5. To accept tenders for the execution of works by the contractors full powers.
6. To accord technical sanctions to estimates for maintenance and repairs, full powers.
7. To execute "Deposit works" no limit.

29.3.2. Superintending Engineer (S.E.)

1. He is the Professional and administrative head of a circle.
2. He is responsible to the Chief Engineer for both Professional and administrative performance of his circle.
3. He is responsible to get the rules, regulation and instructions for the execution of works and maintenance of accounts to be followed strictly.
4. He is supposed to inspect works in his circle and stores of the divisions. If any material is found in excess to its requirement in any division, in that case he is supposed to get it transferred to other divisions where it is required.
5. He is responsible to keep strict watch and control over the rates of works and sub head wise expenditure on works.
6. He is responsible to inspect the records, accounts, stock etc. of all divisional offices under his jurisdiction at least once a year. If any irregurality found it is reported to the Chief Engineer for further necessary action.

Jurisdiction

1. Depending upon the quantum of work four to five divisions remain under the control of a Superintending Engineer.
2. To accord technical sanction to detailed estimates of original works and repairs upto the limit decided by the state government.
3. To accord administrative approval to proposals of works other than residential buildings as per limit laid down by the government and roads which do not pertain to any particular department falling under minor head.
4. To accept tenders for the execution of work by contractors upto Rs. 5 lakh or limit decided by the government.
5. To accord technical sanction to estimates for the maintenance and repair upto Rs. 4 lakh in each case.
6. To execute deposit works upto the limit decided by the government.
7. To sanction estimates for the purchase or manufacture of materials to be used on works, for running and maintenance of jeeps, trucks and other machinery, full powers.

8. To sanction purely temporary increase of the reserve stock limit of the division upto 25% over the sanctioned permanent limit of any division. This increase should be adjusted with in one month.

29.3.3. Executive Engineer

1. As the name suggests, he is executive officer of the department and incharge of a division. He is responsible to the Superintending Engineer for the execution and management of works in his division.
2. He is responsible to ensure that no work is started unless proper sanction has been obtained and funds received.
3. After the commencement of the work he has to ensure that the work is carried out as per specifications and sanctioned design. Further he has to ensure that accounts are properly maintained and submitted to the Accountant General or other specified agency for this purpose.
4. After completion of the work, he has to ensure that accounts are closed and completion report prepared. In case of excess expenditure over the sanctioned estimate, he has to report to the S.E. for necessary approval.
5. Further, he has to ensure that existing works are properly maintained and no encroachment has been done on government land. As desired by the higher authorities, he gets estimates and drawings prepared for the new works along with detailed specifications and designs.
6. He is also responsible to ensure that original records of cash and stores are prepared regularly and posted.

An Executive Engineer is the drawing and disbursing officer of his division. He is authorised to draw money from the treasury and make payments on behalf of the government. Contractors are paid by cheques.

An Executive Engineer has to discharge following duties also:

1. To inspect each sub divisional office of his division at least once a year to submit the report to the S.E.
2. To ensure that measurement books are kept by sub divisional officer as per instructions of the department.
3. To check at least 30% measurements of the M.B. measured by the subordinates.
4. To ensure that machinery to be used on works or other wise is maintained properly and housed safely.
5. To ensure that plants and tools are kept in working order and the surplus items are kept well that they may not deteriorate.

Jurisdiction

1. According to quantum of work four to five sub divisions are under his control.
2. He is authorised to sanction purely temporarily increase of the reserve stock limit upto 10% over the sanctioned permanent limit of any division.
3. To issue work orders for works and repairs upto the limit laid down by the state government.
4. To accord technical sanction to detailed estimates of original works and repairs upto the limit laid down by the state government.
5. To accept tenders for execution of work by the contractor upto Rs. 50,000/- or limit laid down by the state government.

29.3.4. Assistant Engineer

An Assistant Engineer is responsible to the Executive Engineer for the execution and management of works. An Assistant Engineer is responsible for the following works.

1. To arrange and supervise the actual execution of all the works in his sub division in accordance

with the sanctioned estimates and specifications and drawings. For original works he should check all demarcations.

2. He is responsible for the up keep of all buildings and roads in proper condition in his charge.
3. To maintain all initial accounts of expenditure in respect of works in his charge and to submit them every month to the X.E.N.
4. To check the measurements of works, taken by sectional officer He should initial each cutting in measurement book with date.
5. To check muster roll in respect of labour employed.
6. To report to X.E.N. regarding any damage of work or accident.
7. To send progress report of work periodically and keep control on the expenditure.
8. To check all measurement books of overseers of his sub division at least once a year.
9. To check stores twice a year and tool and plants once a year.
10. To keep control over the safe custody of government cash.

Jurisdiction

Depending upon the quantum of work, there may be one or two sub divisional officer in one tehsil head quarter.

29.3.5. Sectional Officer

Under each sub divisional officer there are four to five overseers who are directly incharge of works at the field level and have to supervise the works in their day to day execution.

A sectional officer is responsible for the following works:

1. To give markings or dag bail for the works to be executed.
2. To carry out survey work for the works to be done in his section.
3. To supervise the actual execution of work carried out by the contractor or through daily labour.
4. To ensure that the work is carried out as per specifications and drawings.
5. To keep the progress record of works under his charge.
6. To arrange labour for works to be carried out through daily labour on reasonable rates.
7. To maintain accounts of all stocks, tools and plants etc.
8. To take measurements of all works and record them in measurement book.
9. To prepare running bills of all works and final bills for such works, where total cost is less than one lakh or limit laid by the government, and submit then to the Assistant Engineer.
10. To submit measurement book to A.E.N. for payment twice a month.
11. To superwise the work of daily labourers employed on daily wages and submit daily report to the A.E.N.
12. To check and supervise the regular labour of the department.
13. To prepare, maintain and submit the rolls of work charged establishment and make payment to work charge establishment as well as to regular gangs on behalf of the A.E.N.
14. To check visitor's register of rest houses in his charge at least once a month and the rent received is to be deposited in the A.E.N. office.
15. To ensure that no government land or property has been encroached by unauthorised persons. In case any encroachment is found it is to be reported to the A.E.N. in writing.
16. To check stores in his charge every six month and prepare half yearly distribution list of stock and yearly report of tools and plants incorporating the closing balances.
17. To check and measure all the road side materials every six months and record in his measurement book (M.B.).
18. To submit survey report of unserviceable stock, tools and plants.

19. To keep uptodate account of imprest money.
20. To carry out annual inspection of buildings under his charge and report to A.E.N. for entry in the register of building.
21. To prepare estimates for petty special repairs, additions and alternations.
22. To prepare estimates for petty works as per plan.

29.4. SET UP OF A DIVISIONAL OFFICE

In each divisional office there are following four branches:

1. Correspondence branch
2. Account branch
3. Drawing branch
4. Revenue branch

1. Correspondence branch. This branch is headed by a senior clerk, known as divisional head clerk. He is responsible to the Executive Engineer in general correspondence. His duties are as follows:

(*a*) To open all incoming dak promptly and dispose it off efficiently as per rules or as desired by the X.E.N.

(*b*) To deal all confidential work of the division personally and to ensure that office documents are not removed from the office.

(*c*) To maintain the register of measurement books.

(*d*) To deal correspondence concerning reservation of rest houses.

(*e*) To complete the register of contractors and black listed contractors.

(*f*) To deal with the cases relating to workmen's compensation act.

(*g*) To prepare returns other than those relating to budget or account matters.

(*h*) To write cash book. He is also responsible for handling all cash in the divisional office.

(*i*) To issue receipt for money received on behalf of the government.

(*j*) To prepare notice for inviting tender, contract agreements and also issue tender forms to the applicants after due entry.

(*k*) To deal with all matters concerning the establishment as checking and passing the T.A. bills.

In order to carry out the work smoothly and efficiently, he is assisted by assistants and other clerks as per need.

2. Account branch. This branch is headed by a divisional accountant. For the efficient working of the branch, he is assisted by senior accounts clerk, auditors and other clerks. His duties are as follows:

(*a*) To compile all accounts of the division as per rules.

(*b*) To carry out checks on the initial accounts, vouchers etc.

(*c*) To assist the X.E.N. in all matters relating to account and budget estimates.

(*d*) To advice the X.E.N. on financial aspects of all proposals for expenditure and keep control over the liabilities against the grants of the division as they incurred.

(*e*) If he feels that the expenditure has not been done as per rules, it is his duty to bring this fact to the notice of the X.E.N. in writing with reasons.

(*f*) To bring to the notice of X.E.N. all such cases where subordinate officers have exceed4d their financial limits.

(*g*) Before submitting the muster rolls, vouchers, store accounts etc. to the audit office he must him self carry out detailed audit.

(*h*) To check the expenditure with the estimates sub head wise, any deviation noticed, should be brought to the notice of the X.E.N.

(*i*) To check sub divisional accounts periodically as per laid down practice and to bring any discrepancy to the notice of the X.E.N.

(*j*) To ensure that the contract agreements conform to the conditions of the tender notice, inviting tenders and other relevant records.

(*k*) To prepare increment orders, leave accounts of the staff and to maintain post office pass books and register of securities, register of receipts and cheques books.

(*l*) To prepare the budget and accounts returns and to maintain the provident fund account.

(*m*) To check measurement books of sub divisional office from time to time as per rules.

(*n*) To prepare record for arbitration and for court cases.

(*o*) To check and pass T.A. bills etc. and deal other matters of establishment of account matters.

3. Drawing branch. This branch is headed by a senior draftsman known as head draftsman. He is assisted by junior draftsman, ferroman and tracer etc. His duties are as follows:

(*a*) To keep records of plans and other drawings, and maintenance of register of buildings, roads, bridges etc.

(*b*) To prepare and scrutinise the estimates and contract documents.

(*c*) To maintain the account of survey and drawing instruments of the division.

(*d*) To prepare drawings for new works to be taken in hand and other plans and sections as required by the department.

(*e*) To check the alignments and contour plans etc. drawn by the sub divisional officers before the final approval of the lay out is accorded.

4. Revenue branch. This branch is established in irrigation department only to realise the revenue for the utilisation of canal water. This branch is headed by a revenue officer. He marks those portions of land on the map in which canal water has been used for irrigation. A list is prepared and sent to the patwaries to inform the cultivators using canal water for the amount to be paid by them.

29.5. SET UP OF SUB DIVISIONAL OFFICE

The sub division office is headed by a clerk, known as sub divisional clerk (S.D.C.). There may be more than one clerk in the sub divisional office.

The duties of S.D.C. are as follows:

1. To write and maintain the cash book. He also keeps the keys of the locks of the chest. He sends fortnightly copy of main cash book to the divisional office.
2. To prepare running bills of all running accounts and first and final bills of account not exceeding Rs. 500/-.
3. To compile monthly accounts and send them to the divisional office on due dates.
4. To post and complete work abstracts and maintain account of materials at site.
5. To prepare and post, stock, tools and plants returns and submit them to divisional office on due date.
6. To prepare and complete the acquintance rolls of regular and contingent establishment attached to the sub division.
7. To check the rolls of workcharged establishment received from the sectional officer and compare with the sanction accorded by the competent authority in respect of each work.
8. To check the arithmetical calculations of the measurement book and initial in token of having checked it.
9. To prepare receipts of money received on behalf of the government in cash from any source.
10. To help the A.E.N. in disbursement of money and to maintain various registers.

29.6. ESTABLISHMENTS OF P.W.D.

For running the department, public works department has the following four establishments:

1. Regular establishment	2. Work charged establishment
3. Contingent establishment	4. Daily labour.

1. Regular establishment. This establishment may further be divided into two categories as follows:

(*a*) Permanent establishment (*b*) Temporary establishment

(*a*) Permanent establishment. Government sanctions a number of posts depending upon the quantum of work in each unit of the public works department. The persons working against these sanctioned posts constitute the permanent establishment. The strength of such establishment neither can be increased nor decreased due to temporary increase or decrease in the quantum of work. The salary of the permanent establishment is drawn on the regular pay bill from the treasury and charged to the head "Establishment". The service conditions of these employees are governed by the relevent service rules vol. 1, and vol. 2 in respect of pay, allowances, travelling allowances, leave, pension, general provident fund etc. In case of termination of services on the part of govern- ment or leaving the service by the incumbent a three months notice is essential on either side.

(*b*) Temporary establishment. At any time if quantum of work in the department increases to such an extent that it is beyond the capacity of the permanent establishment to cope with it, in such circumstances government may sanction additional temporary posts. Persons working against these temporary sanctioned posts is known as temporary establishment. These posts may be abolished when the work load is reduced and their existence is no longer is justified. The pay of this establishment also is drawn on pay bill from treasury. Their service conditions are also governed by civil service rules Vol. I, II and III. However the temporary establishment is not entitled for pension. Their services may be terminated with one month notice. On the other hand if the employee wants to resign his post, he may also can do so on one month's notice or surrendering one month's pay. How ever if government feels the necessity of these posts, the temporary posts may be converted into permanent one.

2. Work Charged Establishment. The staff employed to supervise the subordinate labour, stores or machinery used on certain works or for the actual execution of a specific work on a specific project is known as wok charged establishment. These persons are employed on monthly basis and their pay is charged directly to the work. Their services may be terminated at any time, but generally 10 days notice is given to them at the time of discharge. The service conditions of work charged establishment are quite different from permanent or temporary establishment. They are not entitled for pension and certain kind of leave etc.

29.7. CONDITIONS FOR THE EMPLOYMENT OF WORK CHARGED ESTABLISHMENT

The general conditions for the employment of work charged establishment are as follows:

1. In all cases of appointment of work charged establishment pre sanction of the competent authority is essential. In each sanction of appointment following things should be clearly mentioned.

(*a*) The consolidated rate of payment.

(*b*) The period of sanction of the appointment.

(*c*) Full name of the work as given in the estimate.

(*d*) The nature of duties on which a particular person would be engaged.

2. As stated above, persons employed on work charged basis are not entitled to pension, leave salary T.A. and certain other allowances, but they may be allowed certain benefits in certain conditions as follows:

(*a*) In case of injury, in extra ordinary conditions a worker may get pension and gratuity as per rules.

(*b*) Actual travelling expenses may be allowed by the X.E.N. in the following circumstances.

(*i*) In the interest of the work, to reach his place of work.

(*ii*) In the adjoining part of his division or in the state in the interest of work.

(*iii*) Food grain advance, if government has sanctioned to other establishment under fundamental rules framed.

3. Leave with full pay on sunday and other gazetted holidays may be allowed at the discretion of the X.E.N. or A.E.N. He may also grant short casual leave on full or reduced pay subject to rules.

29.8. PAY BILL OF WORK CHARGED ESTABLISHMENT

The pay bill of work charged employees is prepared on form no 29, whose specimen is shown below. In this form the bill is prepared monthly either for the whole division or sub division as may be convenient, but the names and claims of the entire establishment concerned including absentees should be shown in each bill. The names of employees of one trade should be written at one place and sanction of their employment should be quoted in each case.

1. Name of sub division/form no 29. Pay bill for work charged establishment
2. Name of voucher
3. Month of payment
4. Name of section

Form 29 Pay bill for work charged establishment.

Item No.	*Name of Employee*	*Designation*	*Period*	*Rate*	*Amount due*	*Amount paid*	*Dated acknowled gement of payee*	*Dated initials of the officer making payment*

29.9. DAILY WAGE LABOUR

This class of labour is employed for the execution of departmental work and includes all types of persons such as carpenters, welders, masons and labour etc. The payment to these workers is made on the basis of their attendance marked on the muster rolls and charged directly to the work. They are paid weekly or fortnightly or monthly. They are not entitled for pension, leave, T.A. G.P.F. and other privileges.

29.10. CONTINGENT ESTABLISHMENT

Some times, when certain categories of employees as water men or sweepers are not provided in the regular establishment; they are employed and paid from contingencies. Such employees are called as contingent establishment. This class of employees are employed on part time basis and are given adhoc monthly payment. If the contingent staff is employed on full day basis, then they are paid on daily wages basis. Benefits of leave, T.A. and other allowances may be allowed by X.E.N. as per rules.

QUESTIONS

1. Describe the organisational set up of public works department and explain its different parts.
2. Discuss the duties of the followings:
   (*a*) S.E. (*b*) X.E.N.
   (*c*) A.E.N (*d*) Overseer
   (*e*) Divisional accountant (*f*) Head clerk
   (*g*) Head draftsman.
3. Discuss the set up of divisional and sub divisional offices.
4. Describe the different establishments of P.W.D.
5. Differentiate between the following:
   (*a*) Permanent and temporary establishment.
   (*b*) Daily wage labour and work charged establishment.

OBJECTIVE TYPES QUESTIONS

1. Identify the correct statement/statements
   (*a*) Chief engineer is administrative as well as professional head of the concerned department

(*b*) He is responsible for framing the policies and programmes of the department
(*c*) He is responsible to ensure proper maintenance of departmental accounts
(*d*) He is also responsible for employment, transfers and other related matters.
(*e*) None of the above is correct
(*f*) All are correct

2. Identify the incorrect statement/statements.
(*a*) A chief engineer of the department is empowered to purchase motor vehicles
(*b*) He is competent to accord technical sanction upto 5% excess amount of the detailed estimates of original works and repairs
(*c*) He is competent to get executed works under "deposit head" of any amount
(*d*) He has full powers to accept the tenders for the execution of works from the contractors

3. Identify the incorrect statement/statements
(*a*) An Executive Engineer is not responsible to ensure that no work is started unless the proper sanction has been received
(*b*) An Executive Engineer is not responsible for the proper upkeep of existing works on government land
(*c*) An Superintending Engineer can sanction permanent increase of the reserve stock upto 40% over the sanctioned limit of any division
(*d*) An superintending engineer is not responsible to keep watch and control over the rate and sub head wise expenditure of works
(*e*) All are incorrect
(*f*) All are correct

4. Identify the correct statement/statements
(*a*) An Assistant Engineer is authorised to raise the purely temporary limit of the reserve stock upto 10%
(*b*) He is responsible for the up keep of all buildings and roads in his charge
(*c*) He is responsible for the safe custody of the government cash
(*d*) An sectional officer is responsible to ensure that the work is carried out as per laid specifications
(*e*) All are correct
(*f*) None is correct

5. What informations must be given in the sanction of appointment of work charged establishment:
(*a*) Period of sanction of the appointment
(*b*) Consolidated rate of payment
(*c*) Full name of work as in estimate
(*d*) Nature of duties
(*e*) All of the above
(*f*) Some of the above

6. Identify the incorrect statement/statements
(*a*) Daily wage labours are paid on the basis of attendance marked on muster rolls
(*b*) They are entitled for pension, T.A. and other privileges as well
(*c*) Contingent establishment is a permanent one
(*d*) The payment to work charged establishment is charged directly to the concerned work
(*e*) In the appointment of work charged establishment prior sanction of the competent authority is not essential
(*f*) The temporary establishment is entitled for pension.

ANSWERS:

1. (*f*)
2. (*a*)
3. (*e*)
4. (*e*)
5. (*e*)
6. (*b, c, e, f*)

30

General Outlines of P.W.D. System of Accounts

30.1. INTRODUCTION

Public work departments have to under take the execution of works of different kinds of buildings, roads, bridges, irrigation works, navigation works, drainage and embankment works etc. The annual cost of all these works all over the country runs into millions of rupees. These works are scattered all over the country and lakhs of people are engaged for their supervision, payments and maintenance of accounts. Thus it is essential that a systematic procedure should be followed to keep the accounts of all these works to have effective cheeks. It is essential to reduce the chances of occurring major losses. The systematic way of maintaining accounts of works is known a PWD system of accounts. This system is scientific and is in practice for more than a century.

30.2. SYSTEM OF ACCOUNTS

The accounts of an organisation are maintained in accordance with the laid down detailed procedures to be followed in different transactions involving financial matters and keeping the record of all such transactions. The system of accounts is devised to suit the requirements of the organisation for its smooth and efficient functioning.

30.3. PUBLIC ACCOUNTING SYSTEMS

For maintaining government accounts following three systems are followed;

1. Civil system of accounts
2. Forest system of accounts
3. P.W.D. system of accounts

1. Civil system of accounts. In this system of accounts, all government receipts are deposited into the treasuries/sub treasuries or Reserve Bank of India or its agencies. For payments, bills are prepared and presented to the treasury/sub treasury and the money is drawn from bank or treasury. The consolidated account of all receipts and payments is compiled monthly by the treasury officer and submitted to the Accountant General. This system is followed in those government departments, which do not deal with commercial or production work as a normal function.

2. Forest system of accounts. This system of accounts is similar to that of public works system of accounts. It is used in those government departments which deal with commercial or quasi commercial works as a normal function such as in forest and agriculture departments.

3. Public work department system of accounts. Following are the most important principles of this system:

(*a*) All transactions, whether income or expenditure have to pass through certain specified heads of accounts discussed later.

(*b*) A certain specified procedure has to be followed in entire accounting, which lays down the responsibility for receipt, drawing money, spending or depositing it and maintaining accounts according to rules.

30.4. MAIN FEATURES OF P.W.D. SYSTEM OF ACCOUNTS

Followings are the main features of this system.

The divisional officer is the primary disbursing officer of the department. He maintains the detailed account of the departmental receipts and payments. The accounts are kept by him and not at the treasury or pay and accounts office as in the case of civil accounting system. Thus:

1. The divisional officer obtains money required for disbursement in connection with the execution of works and contingent charges by cheques from the civil treasury or bank. He also collects departmental receipts and deposit them in the treasury or bank.
2. The account of all these transactions as well as transactions of subordinate officers acting on his behalf are compiled at the divisional office under the supervision of the divisional accountant and submitted to the pay and Accounts Officer/Accountant General.
3. The divisional officer also maintains accounts of the stores received by him and makes these accounts available to the Accountant General at the time of audit.
4. The accounts of expenditure for each project work or sub work is maintained separately under each major head of expenditure at divisional office.
5. For certain type of works as (*a*) irrigation, (*b*) quasi commercial undertakings like self supporting workshops, performa accounts are prepared either at divisional office or by Accountant general annually. The receipts for such types of works are also shown separately in the divisional accounts.
6. Claims of personal payments as pay and T.A. etc. of all government employees of the department are prepared on bill forms and presented to the treasury or pay and accounts officer. These expenditures are compiled either pay and accounts officer or by the A.G.
7. The accounts maintained by the divisional officer are audited by the A.G. Thus the Accountant. General has not only satisfy himself for the maintenance of accounts but about the audit also.

Thus the divisional officer should follow the following points carefully.

(*a*) He should ensure that a claim which has been accepted is valid, and the voucher is a complete proof of the payment which it supports and the account is correct in all respects.

(*b*) The details of all the accounts should be fully recorded and supported and kept in such a way that at the time of any inquiry they may be produced as evidence and they should show the propriety of the transaction.

(*c*) The record of all transactions should be so clear, explicit and self contained that they can form convincing evidence in a court of law if so required.

(*d*) Every transaction involving, giving and taking cash, stores, or any other properties, rights, privileges and concession, which have money value should be entered properly under proper heads.

30.5. PUBLIC FUNDS

The government funds raised through taxes, duties, levies and other receipts under the statutory or the rules are known as: **Public funds.** Government may also raise funds to finance expenditure for various projects and services from internal and external sources. Government funds may be grouped as follows:

1. **Consolidated fund.** This fund is composed of all receipts from taxes and other revenues. All government expenditure, both on capital side and revenue side is financed out of receipts in the consolidated fund.
2. **Contingencies fund.** This fund is created by the transfer of funds from the consolidated fund. This fund is used to meet the contingency expenditure.
3. **Public account.** This fund is composed of public savings as small savings, provident funds, reserve funds, deposits, advances and remittances.

30.6. GRANTS AND THEIR DISTRIBUTION

In the annual budgets of central as well as state governments estimate of all the anticipated income under the head 'Revenue' and expenditure on works of different categories as 'Grants' are made. A schedule of demands for grants for the ensuing financial year for each item of expenditure is also prepared, considering the existing liabilities and future programmes. Some part of the proposed expenditure may be for the developmental plans known as *plan expenditure*. The rest is non plan expenditure. The schedule of demand fully explains the variations from the current year's budget. In case of new items of expenditure full details and explanation in support of each item to be given.

The demands for grants by all departments and ministries are considered by the Finance Ministry in Consultation with departmental representatives and members of planning commission in case of plan expenditure. After this meeting, the final allotment is finalised and a statement showing the distribution of accepted provisions is sent to various budget authorities to enable them to take necessary action for implementing the programme, subject to the approval by the parliament.

After the approval of the parliament, the Finance Ministry forwards the statement of expenditure showing final allotment of budget grants for each major head to the concerned ministry. Then in turn the concerned ministry forwards the detailed statement showing the distribution of funds for each scheme or project to the budget authority for execution of works.

30.7. EXPENDITURE FROM GOVERNMENT FUNDS

The expenditure from government funds may be broadly grouped into the following two categories:

1. **Voted expenditure.** This expenditure can only be incurred against grants voted by parliament.
2. **Charged expenditure.** This expenditure can be incurred against the appropriation provided to meet the charged expenditure. The items pertaining to these expenditures are determined in accordance with the relevant provision of the constitution.

30.8. TYPES OF TRANSACTIONS OF THE PUBLIC WORKS DEPARTMENTS

In the public works department following transactions take place:

1. Revenue receipt. In public works department receipts may be due to the sale of tender forms, deposit of earnest money, building rents, sales proceeds of property, Irrigation revenue, realisations due to rights and privileges allowed by the government. These receipts are deposited in treasuries for final credit to the government account.

2. Expenditure. These transactions pertain to the expenditure incurred from government funds. This expenditure may further be divided into the following categories:

(*a*) **Revenue expenditure.** The expenditure which does not increase the assets of the government is known as *revenue expenditure*. Expenditures incurred on maintenance, establishment and other such services is classified under revenue expenditure.

(*b*) **Capital expenditure.** Expenditure incurred on items which increase the assets of the government is known as *capital expenditure.* Construction of new buildings, roads etc. are classified under capital expenditure.

(*c*) **Remittance.** The receipts from and to other divisions, departments or government is called Remittance.

(*d*) **Debt.** The receipts or payments which are held in suspense pending final clearance by payment or recovery is called debt.

30.9. CLASSIFICATION OF TRANSACTIONS

The functions of the government are varied and complex. Thus the financial transactions are also so large that it would neither be possible to maintain the accounts nor to control the expenditure unless there is a system to identify the various types of financial activities of the government. Basically the transactions of the government are of two types *i.e.* receipts and expenditure. Transactions of similar nature are grouped together under receipt and expenditure heads of account. The main units of classification of receipt or revenue and expenditure heads are known as *Major heads*. For account purposes, the receipts and expenditure are divided into a number of sectors. Each sector is further divided into major heads. Under each major head there are minor head, sub head and detailed head. For identification each sector has an alphabetical series. In the receipt section, there are following sectors.

(*a*) Tax revenue (*b*) Non tax revenue

(*c*) Grants in aid and contributions

In the revenue accounts sections, there are following sections:

(*a*) General services (*b*) Social and community services

(*c*) Economic services (*d*) Grants in aid and contributions

30.10. MAJOR HEADS

The major heads are assigned blocks of numbers as shown below:

1. Receipt 020 to 199
2. Expenditure on revenue account 211 to 399
3. Expenditure on capital account 411 to 599
4. Public debt 601 to 610
5. Loan and advances 611 to 799
6. Contingency funds 800
7. Public accounts 801 to 899

There is a difference of exactly 20 and 400 between receipt heads and expenditure revenue head and between receipt head and capital out lay head respectively. Some of the important expenditure major heads both in the receipt and expenditure sections are shown in Table 30.1 below.

Table 30.1.

S. No.	Description of the major head	Receipt section or head	Expenditure revenue side	Expenditure capital side
1.	Public works	059	259	459
2.	Education	077	277	477
3.	Art and Culture	078	278	478
4.	Medical	080	280	480
5.	Public health sanitary and water supply	082	282	482
6.	Housing	083	283	483
7.	Urban development	084	284	484
8.	Labour and Employment	087	287	487
9.	Agriculture	105	305	505
10.	Minor irrigation, soil conservation and tree development	106	306	506
11.	Forests	113	313	513
12.	Industjries	120	320	520
13.	Water and power development	131	331	531
14.	Multi purpose river projects	132	332	532
15.	Irrigation, drainage, navigation and flood control	133	333	533
16.	Power projects	134	334	534
17.	Roads and bridges	137	337	537

30.11. GENERAL PRINCIPLES OF CLASSIFICATION OF CIVIL WORKS

As a general rule, the classification of transactions in government accounts has a closer reference to the functions, programmes and activities of the government and the objects of revenue or expenditure rather than the department in which the revenue or expenditure has been incurred. Accordingly the expenditure on public works is classified in accordance with the following principles.

1. Expenditure on the construction of government non residential buildings, for administrative and office purposes, which is not specifically related to the construction of buildings for functional purposes such as schools, Hospitals etc. shall be charged to major head 259 public works/459 capital out lay on public works.
2. Expenditure on construction of purely functional buildings like colleges. Hospital etc. shall be charged to major heads closely connected with the functions such as 277 Education/477-capital out lay on education Art and culture etc.
3. Expenditure on the maintenance and repairs of government non residential buildings, whether for administrative office or functional purposes shall be charged to major head 259-public works.
4. Expenditure on government residential buildings is taken under sector "Social and community services" and shall be accounted under major head 283-Housing/483 capital out lay on Housing.
5. Expenditure on roads and bridges is taken under sub sector "Transport and Communication" of the sector economic services and expenditure accounted for under major head 337-Roads and bridges/ 537-capital out lay on Roads and Bridges.

30.12. CORRELATION BETWEEN THE WORKS AND ACCOUNT

There is a close relation ship between the works and accounts. Followings are some of the advantages of keeping accounts:

1. Better control can be exercised on the consumption of materials and labour employed.
2. The progress of the work can be judged from time to time and the work can be executed with in the scheduled time.
3. Cost control is possible.
4. Account of material at site gives the idea of the quality of work. If the material consumed is more than the estimated quantity, then either the material is misused or lost due to theft etc. and if less material is used than the estimated quantity, it indicates the possibility of inferior quality of work.
5. Expenditure incurred on materials used, labour employed and payments made to contractor when compared to estimated cost gives an idea of profit or loss.
6. Statistical data is available for future planning.

QUESTIONS

1. Describe the salient features of the public work department system of accounts.
2. Give different categories of public funds. Explain the procedure of expenditure from government funds.
3. Explain the following:
   (*a*) Civil system of accounts
   (*b*) Public works system of accounts
   (*c*) Forest system of account.
4. Explain the general principles of classification of civil works.
5. Explain the following terms:
   (*a*) Administrative approval
   (*b*) Technical sanction
   (*c*) Major and minor works
   (*d*) Voted and charged expenditure
6. Discuss the transactions of the public works departments.
7. Discuss the general principles of classification of civil works.

OBJECTIVE TYPE QUESTIONS

1. For maintaining government accounts system used is...
   (*a*) Civil system of accounts
   (*b*) Forest system of accounts
   (*c*) P.W.D. system of accounts
   (*d*) All the above systems
2. Identify the correct statement/statements
   (*a*) Civil system of accounts is followed in those government departments which donot deal with commercial or production work as their normal functions
   (*b*) In civil system of accounts bills are prepared and submitted to treasures for payment
   (*c*) Forest system of accounts is followed in those government departments which deal with commercial or quasi commercial works as their normal functions
   (*d*) In P.W.D. system mainly divisional officer is responsible for disbursing the payment of the department
   (*e*) All are correct
   (*f*) None of the above are correct
3. Identify the correct statement/statements
   (*a*) The expenditure which does not increase the assets of the government is known as revenue expenditure
   (*b*) The expenditure which increases the assets of the government is known as capital expenditure
   (*c*) The money received by the department from sale of tender forms, building rent, deposit of earnest many etc. is called as receipts.
   (*d*) 'Receipts obtained from other divisions or departments are called remittance.
   (*e*) All are correct.
4. Identify the incorrect statement/statements
   (*a*) There is no relation between the works and accounts
   (*b*) There is close relation between the works and accounts
   (*c*) The classification of transactions in government accounts has a closer reference to the functions, programmes and activities of the government.
   (*d*) By keeping accounts, better control can be exercised on the consumption of material and labour employed.
5. Keeping good account may lead to...
   (*a*) To control the cost
   (*b*) Progress of work can be judged from time to time
   (*c*) Profit or loss can be estimated
   (*d*) All the above
6. The expenditure which does not increase the assests of the government is called
   (*a*) Remittence
   (*b*) Capital expenditure
   (*c*) Revenue expenditure
   (*d*) Debt
7. The expenditure which can be incurred for grants volted in parliament is called
   (*a*) Charged expenditure
   (*b*) Revenue expenditure
   (*c*) Capital expenditure
   (*d*) Voted expenditure
8. The expenditure incurred which increases the assests of the government is called
   (*a*) Capital expenditure
   (*b*) Revenue expenditure
   (*c*) Debt
   (*d*) Remmittence

ANSWERS:

1. (*d*)
2. (*e*)
3. (*e*)
4. (*a*)
5. (*d*)
6. (*c*)
7. (*d*)
8. (*a*)

31

Works And Their Execution

31.1. INTRODUCTION

In public works department, the term works not only applies to the construction of new works or repair, but it also implies to other expenditures connected with the supply, carriage and repairs of tools and plants, manufacture or supply of other stores and operations of workshops etc.

31.2. CLASSIFICATION OF WORKS

The works in public work department may be classified depending upon the nature and cost of works as follows:

1. Classification depending upon the nature of the work. According of the nature of the works they can be divided into two categories as follows:

(*a*) **Original works.** These comprise of all new construction works and include:

(*i*) entirely new works

(*ii*) additions and alternations to the existing works that increase their value

(*iii*) repairs to newly purchased or Previously abandoned buildings to bring them to use.

The remodelling of an existing portion of a road, bridge, cause way, embankment, training works or protective works connected with roads are also treated as original works, if the change brings about a genuine increase in the value of the property.

(*b*) **Repairs.** These include operations undertaken to maintain the buildings and other works in proper condition and petty and miscellaneous items of works upto the limit laid down by the government. When they do not enhance the value of the property appreciably as discussed below, then they are called repairs.

(*i*) Ordinary maintenance including surface painting and necessary addition of stone chips, gravel or sand, but not including asphaltic concrete, premix asphaltic macadam, bitumen grout, cement concrete or cement macadam is called repair.

(*ii*) Periodical renewal and special repairs are also come under the head repair.

(*iii*) Petty and miscellaneous items of work are classified under the head repair.

2. Classification according to cost. Depending upon the cost of works they can be classified into the following categories:

(*a*) Major works

(*b*) Minor works

(*c*) Petty works

The limit of cost varies from state to state.

31.3. APPROVALS NEEDED FOR PUBLIC WORKS

For every public work following four approvals are needed:

1. Administrative approval
2. Expenditure approval or sanction
3. Technical sanction
4. Appropriation or re appropriation

1. Administrative approval. It can further be divided into two groups:

(*a*) Original (*b*) Revised

(*a*) **Original administrative approval.** For all works except for repair works or petty works whose cost is less than Rs. 25000/- it is necessary to obtain the concurrence of the competent authority of the administrative department requiring the work. Thus the formal acceptance of the proposal for the work by the competent authority of the administrative department is known as *administrative approval*. It is the duty of the local officers of the department, requiring the work to be done, to obtain the requisite approval on the basis of approximate estimate and necessary preliminary plans, prepared by the P.W. department. In respect of works which are required in the general interest of the public such as roads, irrigation works etc., the preliminary designs and estimates are prepared by the concerned department and administrative approval obtained. Various authorities of government are empowered to accord administrative approval to a work required to meet the needs of the departments upto a specified limit of expenditure.

(*b*) **Revised administrative approval.** When the expenditure on a work exceeds or likely to exceed the amount administratively approved for it by more than 10% or where there are material deviations from original proposal, revised administrative approval must be obtained from the competent authority to sanction the increased cost.

2. Expenditure sanction. In case of every original major work, for which funds have not been expressly allotted by provision in the grant, and for residential buildings in excess of the limit of the powers of the administrative department, the concurrence of the government to the proposed expenditure is essential. This concurrence is known as "*Expenditure sanction.*" Expenditure sanction by the government is implied in those cases where administrative approval for the work has been accorded by the government itself. The duty of obtaining expenditure sanction rests with the department for which the work is to be executed.

Revised expenditure sanction. If the expenditure on a work is likely to exceed 5% of the sanctioned amount, the revised sanction is essential to be obtained.

3. Technical sanction. For every work, after the receipt of the administrative approval and expenditure sanction, a detailed estimate of work is prepared for the sanction by the competent technical authority. This sanction is known as "technical sanction". Before the commencement of the work, it is necessary to obtain the technical sanction. As the name of the sanction suggests, it indicates that the proposals are structurally sound and the estimates are correctly calculated and based on adequate data. This sanction can be accorded by P.W.D. officers upto the authorised limits. Usually chief and additional chief engineers have full powers to accord technical sanction.

In case the expenditure is in excess of technical sanction by not more than 5%, the concerned officer may pass the excess amount with out framing a revised estimate upto the limit of the powers delegated to him to accord sanction to an original estimate. If the excess of expenditure is more than 5% of the sanctioned amount, then it is necessary to get a revised estimate prepared and to obtain the technical sanction afresh from the competent authority.

Appropriation of funds. For works likely to be executed during the financial year, funds are allotted at the commencement of financial year for different works. This allotment of funds to meet the expenditure on a specific work is called "*Appropriation.*"

Re-appropriation. If the funds for a particular work of essential nature are not allotted but necessary funds are transferred from one unit of appropriation to another sub unit, then this transfer of funds is known *re appropriation.* The appropriation is intended to cover all charges including the liabilities of previous years to be paid or adjusted in the account during the year. It is operative until the close of the financial year. Any unspent balance automatically lapses and is not available for utilisation in the following year, unless it is sanctioned again in the demand for the following year. The financial year closes on 31st March every year. All cash and stock transactions entered into after that date are treated as pertaining to the following year. However bonafide transfer entries are permissible upto 30th June or any date fixed by the government.

Watch over appropriation. Divisional officers are responsible to ensure that the appropriations placed at their disposal neither exceed nor left unspent and to take timely action to obtain additional funds or surrender the unspent funds if necessary. Appropriation for a sub head can be increased or reduced only by a formal order, "appropriation" by a competent authority, authorising the transfer of funds from one head to an other.

31.4. ESTIMATES

The papers that are submitted with the project of a work consist of a report, specifications and a detailed statement of measurement, quantities, rates, with an abstract of the total estimated cost for each item. These documents together form "Estimates" of work. In short an estimate is the probable cost of a work, calculated before the commencement of the work.

31.4.1. Types of estimates

An Estimate may be divided into the following categories:

1. Preliminary or rough estimate
2. Detailed estimate
3. Revised estimate
4. Supplementary estimate

1. **Preliminary or rough cost-estimate.** It is a brief estimate which indicates the cost of works approximately. It is prepared on the basis of preliminary drawings of works.
2. **Detailed estimate.** It is a precise estimate which is prepared on the basis of detailed drawings. The quantities of various sub heads of the work are calculated on the basis of detailed measurements. Their costs are worked out on the basis of approved schedule of rates. For no schedule 'items' analysis of rates is prepared. Actually no detailed estimate is prepared untill funds for the work are actually allotted or promised by the government.
3. **Revised estimate.** If during the execution of an work, the amount of the sanctioned estimate is likely to exceed by more than 5% due to rise in the cost of material or labour charges or due to any genuine reason, then the revised estimate of work is to be submitted. With the revised estimate a comparative statement showing items of original and revised estimates and the reason for the difference is also to be attached.
4. **Supplementary estimate.** When the work is in progress and it is felt that some additional item, which is not contingent on the proper execution of the work as initially sanctioned, it is necessary to obtain the sanction from the competent authority by submitting a supplementary estimate. This estimate should be accompanied with a full report of the circumstances leading to the addition of the item. The abstract of the supplementary estimate should show the amount of original estimate and the total amount of the sanction required, including the supplementry amount.
5. **Screening or order of magnitude estimate.** This estimate is prepared at the very early stage when the scope is clearly defined and the essential features of the facility are identified.

31.5. FORMALITIES TO BE OBSERVED BEFORE THE START OF WORK

Before the start of the work, following formalities have to be observed.

1. To obtain the administrative approval for the work from the competent authority.
2. To obtain the expenditure sanction from the competent authority.
3. After receiving the administrative approval and expenditure sanction a detailed estimate is got prepared by the Divisional Engineer and technical sanction accorded, if with in his competence. If it is not in his competence, then he will forward it to the competent authority to accord technical

sanction. In short after receiving the administrative approval and expenditure sanction, technical sanction is to be obtained.

4. *Allotment of funds or Appropriation.* In between the above period allotment of funds should be arranged. The Divisional Engineer should take the actual execution of the work in hand after the completion of all the above formalities.

31.6. EXECUTION OF WORK

No work should be commenced unless:

(*a*) Detailed design and estimate has been sanctined by the competent authority.

(*b*) Allotment of funds has been received.

(*c*) Orders for its commencement have been received from the competent authority.

Mere presence of an item in a budget estimate sanctioned by the government for the year is not sufficient authority for the commencement of expenditure. It is essential to obtain a specific sanction for each work except for petty works and repairs of buildings.

In case due to an real emergency, if an work is started in anticipation of specific orders for its commencement, an immediate report explaining the emergency should be submitted to the authorities competent to accord administrative approval and technical sanction. It must be kept in mind that the sanction of the design and estimate by the competent authority or government conveys no permission for the commencement of expenditure on the work, unless such expenditure has been provided in the budget estimate for that year or provision has been made for the expenditure with in the financial year either by appropriation or re-appropriation.

31.7. ACTION REQUIRED IF WORK STARTED WITH OUT COMPLETING FORMALITIES

In case an officer is required to carryout a work with out meeting the formalities as discussed above in compliance of written orders from the higher authorities, he should take the following action after the receipt of written orders for carrying out the work.

The officer executing the work should immediately intimate the A.G. that he is incurring liability with out provision in the budget. He should state the amount of liability likely to be incurred in compliance of written orders. A.G. will held all such expenditures under objection. The officer incurring the expenditure is responsible to obtain the necessary order for the expenditure from the competent authority.

31.8. CASES IN WHICH EXPENDITURE IS PERMISSIBLE WITH OUT SPECIFIC ALLOTMENT

Expenditure can be incurred from the commencement of a financial year in the following situations.

1. For all original works in progress at the end of the previous financial year which have not been stopped under any special orders.
2. For maintenance of tools and plants and liabilities arising from the previous year in respect of purchases.
3. Expenditure on repairs during the first three months of a financial year upto a fixed proportion of the total allotment in the previous year on the repairs.

31.9. ALTERNATION IN THE DESIGN DURING EXECUTION OF WORK

An Divisional Engineer is not authorized to carryout any material alterations in the sanctioned design, specially in case of standard designs with out the approval of Superintending Engineer. If any alteration is considered necessary a revised or supplementary estimate should be submitted for sanction. In case of material alterations Executive Engineer is responsible to obtain the sanction for such alterations from the competent authority. In case important structural alterations are needed, the orders from the original sanctioning authority should be obtained, even though these alterations may not involve any increased out lay. If the alterations involve substantial change in the cost of the work, revised estimate should be submitted for technical sanction.

31.10. MISCELLANEOUS RULES FOR THE EXECUTION OF WORKS

While executing a work, following points should also be kept in mind.

1. No work should be commenced on land, which has not been handed over by the competent authority.
2. No public building should be destroyed or damaged during the execution of a work without neither the full and free consent of persons interested in it nor with out the concurrence of the civil or political authority, except where government has given clear orders.
3. No religious building should be occupied as a dwelling house or for any other purpose.
4. All interruptions in the progress of work should be reported to S.E. for further action explaining the causes and duration of interruptions.
5. All unusual losses in the manufacture of materials should be reported to S.E. immediately on their occurrence.

31.11. CONTRIBUTION WORKS

The works executed by the P.W.D., but the cost is provided fully or partly from the following sources are called *contribution works*.

1. Fund of public nature, but not included in the public estimates and accounts of government.
2. Funds are provided from public or private individuals.

31.12. RULES FOR CONTRIBUTION WORKS

Contribution works are governed by the following rules:

1. The design and estimate is prepared by P.W.D. with information to the party, or parties depositing the funds.
2. The design and estimate is to be sent to the competent authority for technical sanction.
3. The provision of all charges such as the cost of establishment, tool and plant, audit etc. is made in the estimate.
4. Before starting the execution of the work, the written approval of the design and estimate is obtained from the authority depositing the funds. P.W.D. does not bind it self to complete the work with in the amount of estimate.
5. The necessary funds required for the work are realised and deposited on the treasury either in lump sum or in installments as decided by the government.
6. The officer incharge of the work is responsible to bring to the notice of his seniors and party concerned any anticipated excess over the estimate as well as to provide full information in connection with the progress of expenditure.
7. Government is not responsible for unavoidable and reasonable excess caused by any rise in price, losses by fires or theft or other unforeseen factors.
8. Where the work is of large magnitude, the agreement should be drawn under legal advice.
9. The contribution received for one work, under no circumstances be utilised on another work, the contribution of which may be in arrears.

31.13. DEPOSIT WORK

The works of construction or repairs, whose costs are met from non government sources are called *deposit works*. Works executed for Municipal Committees, Panchayats, Zila Parishad etc. come under this category. Funds are placed at the disposal of Executive Engineer as soon as the work has been sanctioned by the competent authority. The work is started only after the amount has been deposited in advance.

31.14. RULES FOR DEPOSIT WORKS

All rules which are applicable to contribution works are also applicable to deposit works. In addition to these rules, following rules are also observed.

1. The amount received for these works should be credited in the account of the head "public work deposits". All expenditure up to that amount of the deposit should be charged to this head. if any expenditure is incurred in excess of this deposit, then it is booked as "Miscellaneous P.W. Advances" till recovery of this amount is made from the authority for which this work is being done or from the office, who allowed this excess expenditure.

2. The amount of each deposit is divided into two parts:

(*a*) Pertaining to the expenditure of actual work and

(*b*) For charges on establishment, tools and plant, audit and account charges etc.

3. Consolidated account of all transactions of a month of all deposit works of the division should be prepared together.

Powers to accord sanction for deposit works of various officers vary from state to state. Usually Chief Engineers have full powers.

In estimates generally provision for establishment charges, tools and plant, audit and account establishment are made at 2%, 1.0% and 1.0% respectively. Further procedure is same as for contribution works.

QUESTION

1. Explain the following terms fully:
   (*a*) Administrative approval
   (*b*) Expenditure sanction
   (*c*) Technical sanction
   (*d*) Appropriation
2. Differentiate between the followings:
   (*a*) Administrative approval and technical sanction
   (*b*) Appropriation and Re-appropriation
   (*c*) Supplementary estimates and revised estimates
   (*d*) Original administrative approval and revised administrative approval
3. Explain the following terms:
   (*a*) Original work
   (*b*) Repairs
   (*c*) Major works
   (*d*) Minor works
   (*e*) Petty works
4. Write short notes on the following.
   (*a*) Deposit work
   (*b*) contribution work

OBJECTIVE TYPE QUESTIONS

1. In public works department works can be classified as
   (*a*) Original works
   (*b*) Repair works
   (*c*) Petty works
   (*d*) Miner works
   (*e*) All are correct
2. For executing a work by PWD approval needed are
   (*a*) Administrative approval
   (*b*) Expenditure sanction
   (*c*) Technical approval
   (*d*) Appropriation or re-appropriation approval
   (*e*) All the above
3. Estimate may be of the type
   (*a*) Preliminary
   (*b*) Detailed
   (*c*) Revised
   (*d*) Supplementary
   (*e*) All the above
4. Before starting an work formalities to be observed are
   (*a*) To obtain the administrative approval from the competent authority
   (*b*) To obtain the expenditure approval from the competent authority

(*c*) Preparation of detailed estimate (*d*) Allotment of funds
(*e*) All the above

5. Original works include except
   (*a*) Repair to previously abandoned buildings
   (*b*) Surface treatment of roads
   (*c*) Additions and alterations to the existing buildings
   (*d*) Remodelling of an existing bridge
6. Identify the incorrect statement/statements
   (*a*) For starting the execution of an work it is not necessary to obtain the expenditure sanction from any authority
   (*b*) For starting execution of an work administrative approval is not essential
   (*c*) To get prepared a detailed estimate is not the responsibility of Executive Engineer.
   (*d*) Work can be started with out the sanction of detailed design and estimate of that work from the competent authority
   (*e*) All the above
7. Expenditure can be incurred with out specific allotment except
   (*a*) For maintenance of tool, plants and liabilities from the previous financial year in respect of purchases
   (*b*) Expenditure in repairs during the first three months of the financial year
   (*c*) For all original works in progress at the end of a financial year
   (*d*) To start a new major work
8. Identify the incorrect statement/statements
   (*a*) A work can only be started after obtaining the sanction of the detailed design and estimate
   (*b*) A work can only be started after receiving the necessary funds
   (*c*) A work can be started only after the receipt of orders for commencement of work
   (*d*) The work can be started if it has been mentioned in the budget estimate
9. Identify the incorrect statement/statements
   (*a*) During the execution of a new work any public building can be destroyed with out any permission
   (*b*) Any religious building can be occupied for residential purposes
   (*c*) In case of contribution works, funds are allotted by the government
   (*d*) Deposit works can be started before the funds are deposited with P.W.D.
   (*e*) All the above are correct
   (*f*) All the above are incorrect
10. Identify the correct statement/statements
    (*a*) If the changes brought in existing road and bridges, which enhance the genuine value of the property, the works are called original works
    (*b*) When the operations carried out on existing works, without enhancing the value of the property, then these operations are called repairs
    (*c*) Divisional Engineer is not authorised to carry out material alterations in the sanctioned design
    (*d*) All are correct
    (*e*) None is correct

ANSWERS:

1. (*e*)	4. (*e*)	7. (*d*)	10. (*d*)
2. (*e*)	5. (*b*)	8. (*d*)	
3. (*e*)	6. (*e*)	9. (*f*)	

32

Methods of Execution of Works

32.1. INTRODUCTION

Public works department has to execute different types of works discussed in the last chapter. After completing all formalities as discussed in chapter 31, the works can be completed by any method considered economically and expeditious. Small works can be executed departmentally by engaging labour, where as big works are carried out through contractors.

32.2. METHODS OF EXECUTION OF WORKS

Different methods of execution of works in public works department are shown diagrametically in Fig. 32.1.

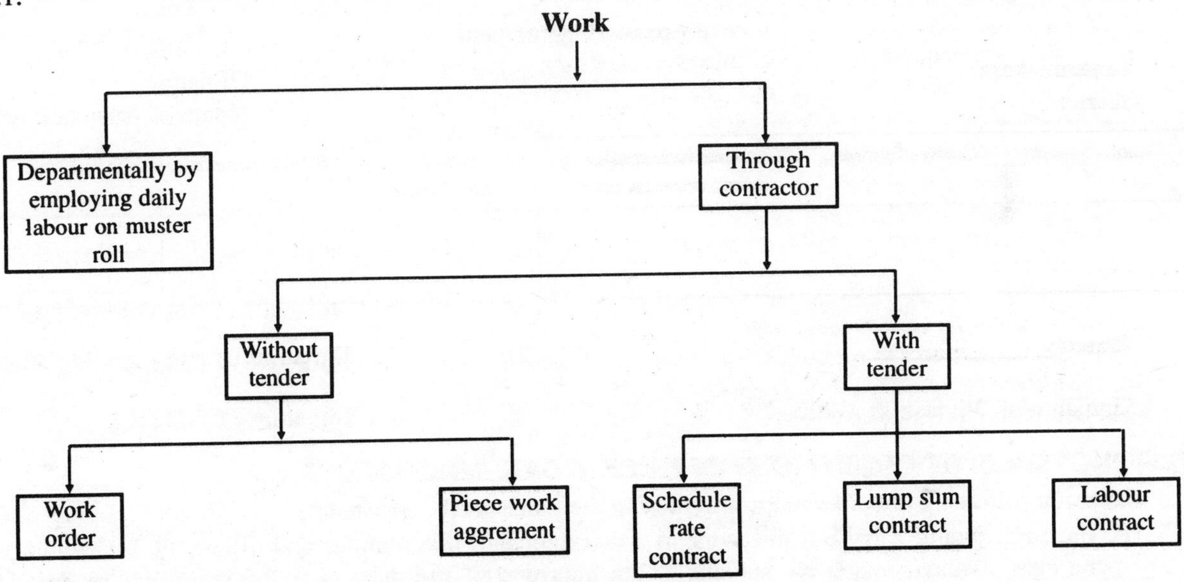

Fig. 32.1.

32.3. EXECUTION OF WORK DEPARTMENTALLY

By this method only small works are executed. In this method labourers are employed by the department on daily wages basis. Before taking the actual execution of the work in hand, sanction for engaging the labourers on daily wages basis has to be obtained from the Executive engineer. The attendance of the labourers is marked on muster roll. The payment to labourers is made weekly, fortnightly or monthly as agreed upon. After the payment, the muster roll is closed and a new muster roll is started.

The progress of the work is entered or recorded in the measurement book (M.B.) Abstract of quantities and cost of the work is entered in Part III of the muster roll giving reference to the number and page of M.B. where detailed measurements are entered. The amount of work done by labourers should not be less than the amount paid to them. Payment to labourers is made soon after the muster roll is passed for payment by the competent authority. Materials required for the work are arranged either from government stores or other sources if not available in government stores.

32.4. EXECUTION OF WORK THROUGH CONTRACTOR

Through contractor, work can be executed in the following ways:

1. On piece work basis
2. On contract agreement basis

1. On piece work basis. In this system of executing the work, only the rate is agreed upon without reference to the total quantity of work to be done in a given period. In this system generally small works costing about Rs. 15000/- or so as decided by the competent authority are given after calling quotations from approved contractors. The work is allotted on a simple form of agreement known as *work order form* as shown below. It is not a contract agreement. It should contain only description of the work to be done and the rates to be paid for each item of work with out any reference to the total quantity of work to be executed or the time limit with in which the work is to be completed. However specifications of the items of work to be done may be attached with the work order. A deduction of 5% may be done from the running bills of the contractor as security.

In case the contractor leaves the work incomplete, no penalty is imposed on the contractor. Similarly the officer incharge can ask the contractor to stop the work, if the progress of the work is not satisfactory or the quality of the work is not upto the mark.

Piece work agreement

Name of work
District

Division
Name of party tendering

Name of work	*Number of item*	*Class and description of work to be executed*	*Unit of calculations*	*Rate of payment*	*Remark*

Dated ______________

Signature of party making tender

Signature of Witness & Address

Signature of S.D.O.

32.5. PROVISION OF CONDITIONS IN PIECE WORK AGREEMENT

Generally following conditions are provided in the piece work agreement:

1. The party would carry out the work in a workmanship like manner and diligently. He would use the best available materials subject to the approval of the divisional Engineer, whose decision regarding the rate of progress and material would be final.
2. Payment would be made after the measurements of the work on its completion or termination of the agreement as the case may be. For long duration works payment may be made every month or as agreed upon.
3. The divisional or sub divisional engineer may terminate the work at any time.
4. In case of bad workmanship or use of inferior quality material, the divisional or sub divisional engineer may get it removed and replaced with good material or work. He may deduct the value of

the rejected work or materials removed or the cost of replacing them as the case may be, considered proper from the amount due or may become due.

5. In case any compensation has to be paid by the government to the labourer of the piece work gang under workman's compensation act, then this amount would be recovered from the party.
6. In case the agreement is terminated before the completion of the work, the divisional or sub divisional engineer would take over the materials required for its completion, if the party executing it accepts the valuation. If he does not agree, then he has to remove the materials from the site with in 14 days, other wise materials would be removed at his cost.

32.6. PROCEDURE TO TERMINATE THE PIECE WORK AGREEMENT

If the piece work agreement has to be terminated before the completion of the work, then a notice specifying the date of its termination has to be served on the party carrying out the piece work and its receipt is obtained. If materials at site are to be taken over, then under no circumstances these materials should be used until the valuation statement has been accepted in writing by the party carrying out the piece work.

32.7. DEFINITIONS

Tender. It is the contractors bid in writing offering to execute the specified work of construction or supply of material or equipment at the rates and amount offered in the bid and in the time limit and under conditions specified and agreed to.

Tendering. The process of inviting bids and accepting them is called tendering.

Tender documents. The set of other informations supplied to the contractor to enable him to offer his bid along with the tender notice is called tender document.

Tender notice. The information to be given to general public for getting the bid for executing a construction work or supply of material or equipment through news papers or putting notices on office notice board and pasting this information on public places is called tender notice.

Earnest money. At the time of submitting tender, the tenderer is required to deposit about 2% of the estimated cost of the contract value of the project with the department. This amount is known as Earnest money deposit (EMD). This money is collected in order to avoid the refusal from the contractor to accept the contract, once the contract is awarded to him. It is also collected to avoid unnecessary competition by avoiding the contractors, who may not have sound financial status. If the lowest quoted contractor refuses to take up the work, his E.M.D. will be forfeited. However the E.M.D. of unsuccessful contractors will be refunded to them.

Security money. After the acceptance of the tender of a contractor, the contractor has to deposit about 10% of the tender amount with the client. This amount is inclusive of the 2% amount already deposited by him. This deposit is called security deposit (S.D.). This deposit serves as a guarantee that the contractor will perform the work as per specifications and also will maintain satisfactory progress. This deposit usually is refunded to the contractor after 6 to 12 months from handing over the work to the client.

Specifications. Specifications are instructions which provide technical requirement of work and give details of the job to be carried out. Specifications supplement the drawings.

32.8. INFORMATION TO BE GIVEN IN THE TENDER NOTICE

Usually in a tender notice following informations should be given:

1. Name of the department calling tenders.
2. Name of work and location.
3. Designation of the officer inviting tenders.
4. Last date and time of receipt of tenders.
5. Period of availability of tender forms.

6. Cost of tender documents and estimated cost of work.
7. Time of completion and type of contract.
8. Earnest money deposit to be paid.
9. Date, time and place of opening tenders.
10. Designation of the officer opening the tenders.
11. Time and place from where tender documents may be obtained or inspected.

32.9. TENDER DOCUMENTS

Generally a tender document consists of the following informations:

1. General conditions of contract including time limit.
2. Special conditions of the contract.
3. Schedule of items of work with clear specifications.
4. Lay out plan or location of work.
5. Set of drawings including working drawings.
6. Detailed specifications.
7. Scheduled of stores to be supplied by the owner including the rates and place of handing over.
8. Amount of security money to be deposited.
9. Mode of payment for the work to be done.
10. Approximate quantity of work under each item.
11. Rate of supply of power and the point of supply.
12. Location of water supply.
13. Time of completion and the progress to be made.
14. Production of income tax and sales tax clearance certificates.
15. Penalty condition for slow progress and delay in completion.
16. Designation of the arbitration authority in case of disputes.
17. Weather conditions in the area and period of operation.

32.10. RULES FOR INVITING AND PROCESSING TENDERS

While inviting tenders following rules should be observed:

1. Tenders are invited in regard to work contracts except when any exemption has been granted by the government.

2. Tenders must be invited on the prescribed tender forms.

3. Tenders must be invited in sealed cover. In order to get more tenders wide publicity should be given. The publicity may be made through important daily news papers, government gazette and by pasting notices in public places and sending letters to the reputed contractors and dealers.

4. Tender notice should contain the following information:

(*a*) Name of place and time where the contract documents can be seen and blank tender forms obtained. The cost of tender form and mode of its deposit also should be given.

(*b*) Name of place, date and time, receipt and opening of tender should be given clearly.

(*c*) The amount and mode of deposit of earnest money should be written clearly. Whether the earnest money is to be deposited by bank draft, cash or cheque.

(*d*) In case, tender is accepted, amount of security and its mode of deposit also should be written.

(*e*) With whom the authority of acceptance of tenders will rest.

5. Reasonable time should be allowed to bidders to submit their tenders. Usually time period may vary from 7 days to 28 days depending upon the amount of work.

6. On the due date and advertised time and place all tenders received for the same contract should be

opened by the divisional officer or other competent authority in the presence of intending contractors or their representatives.

7. Every tender should be numbered serially, initialed and dated on the front page at the time of opening. Every page of the schedule or letter attached to the tender should also be initialed. Blank tenders should be cancelled under dated initials. Alterations in the tender made before submitting the tender should be initialed legibly by the officer opening the tender. If entries left blank, a line should be drawn across the blanks and initialed.

8. Under no circumstances any amendment in a tender be allowed after opening of the tender has commenced, even if a tenderer offers to reduce his rates. This offer should be taken in the form of a letter separately.

9. No tender should pass from one officer to the other in the open condition.

10. Tenders in which the quoted rates seem to be doubtful, under no circumstances should be accepted. Conditional tenders are liable to rejection.

11. No tender for the execution of work should be entertained unless it is accompanied or paid separately the earnest money as notified in the tender notice.

12. The earnest money of unsuccessful tenderers should be refunded as soon as possible after completion of tenders.

13. Usually the lowest tender is accepted, except in extra ordinary conditions. The acceptance or rejection of a tender is at the discretion of the authorised officer, but the reasons of its rejection should be sound and recorded fully and kept confidential.

14. Tenders received after due time and date should be rejected after recording "received after due date".

15. After opening the tenders, normally negociations with tenderers should not be carried out.

32.11. PUBLICITY AND SALE OF TENDERS

In order to get sufficient number of bids and most attractive offer, it is essential that the tender should be given wide publicity. In order to get good quality work, it is essential that the bids are obtained from the contractors, who have capability and capacity to execute the work. For this reason the departments such as P.W.D. and railways which regularly get work executed through contractors maintain a list of approved contractors.

Tenders are publicised by advertising in important news papers and also informing the approved contractors by post. The copies of tender notice are also pasted on the notice boards of various offices of big organisations.

32.12. TYPES OF TENDERS

Tenders may be classified in the following categories:

1. **Open tenders.** The tenders in which the bids are invited from contractors by open advertisement in the important news papers and Indian trade journal are known as *open tenders.*
2. **Limited tenders.** When only a selected number of contractors are invited to bid or quote the rates for the supply of articles or execute the work, then this type of tenders are called *limited tender.*
3. **Single tender.** When only a single firm or contractor is invited to provide the required service by quoting rates, then this tender is called as single tender. If it is felt that the quoted rates are high, then there may be negotiations prior to the agreement of the contract.
4. **Rate contract.** Normally rate contract system is used for the supply of stores of items. This system specifies the supply at a fixed rate during the period of contract. In this type of contract the quantities are not mentioned. The contractor is bound to accept any order placed on him.

32.13. SUBMISSION, OPENING AND SCRUTINY OF TENDERS

(*a*) **Submission.** In order to keep secrecy till the opening of the tender, they should be submitted under sealed cover latest by the closing time. For identity purpose, the name of work and its due date should be clearly written on the top of the envelop. Tender may be sent by post or can be put in the letter box kept for this purpose in the premises of the office. The closing time usually is kept upto 5.0, clock, *i.e.* the office hour or after the normal delivery time of delivery by post Tenders received after due time and date are rejected.

(*b*) **Opening of tenders.** The valid tenders are opened at the notified time in the presence of tenderer or their representatives. Each page of the tender has to be initialed with date by the opening officer.

(*c*) **Scrutiny.** Each tender is scrutinised carefully and any over writings or cuttings are initialed by the opening officer to ensure that tenders are not tempered with at a later stage. A note of any ambiguity or omission of words, figures, rates etc. also is made. A record of tenders received is also kept.

32.14. PREPARATION OF COMPARATIVE STATEMENT OF TENDERS AND THEIR ACCEPTANCE

The rates and amount quoted in all valid tenders are tabulated in the form of the comparative statement. In this statement, rates, specifications and terms and conditions of each bidder are noted correctly and their financial implications are worked out. This statement enables the comparasion of rates, terms and conditions to accept the most competitive bid. Generally comparative statement is made for stores of items.

Generally the lowest tender is accepted. The tenderer whose rates have been accepted is intimated in writing to sign the contract agreement with in a specified period of time. If he fails to do with out any valid reason and with out informing the tender accepting authority, his bid may be cancelled and his security money deposited may be forfeited. The work may be allotted to the next higher bidder.

After signing the agreement, the site of work is handed over formally to the contractor to start the work. The time of completion is counted from the day, the site is handed over to the contractor.

32.15. SPECIFICATIONS

The specification is the description in words of works to be done in a project along with details regarding the materials to be used and the workmanship to be done, the method of construction to be adopted, equipment and machinery to be used, the method of testing etc. The specifications along with detailed drawings completely define the structure and furnish full details physically as well as technically. Thus specifications are the instructions in words which supplement the drawings and provide technical requirement of work and give details of the job to be done.

32.16. TYPES OF SPECIFICATIONS

Specifications may be classified into the following categories:

1. **General specifications.** The specifications which may be applicable to more than one item in the schedule are called general specifications. These specifications also give the nature and type of materials which are to be used in different items of work. Thus the general specifications give brief and general idea about the whole work. These would be included while preparing the contract.
2. **Detailed specifications.** Detailed specifications give full information regarding quality, quantity and proportion of materials, tools, plant and machinery, method of execution and workmanship for a particular item of work, for example grade of concrete, its location, workability requirements and strength requirement etc. It specifies the general condition of contract, the quality of final product, inspection and tests etc. which should be carried out during the construction of the work. It also specifies the different standard provisions such as Indian standard and British standards etc. which will be used while writing the contract.
3. **Special specifications.** These specifications give the information about specialized works such as petroleum, gas, atomic and power projects. These specifications are required when General and detailed specifications fail to meet the requirements of specialized sector as noted above. It should be approved and included in the contract.

4. **Restricted specifications.** These specifications provide information regarding certain products which are accepted by the owner such as paints, water supply fixtures, sanitary wares and electrical products etc. These products are of approved quality and of approved brand.
5. **Manufacturer's specifications.** When standardized specifications of a product are not available, then the manufacturer has to develop the specifications for that particular product. The specifications developed by the manufacturer are known as manufacturers specifications. In this case the manufacturer provides the information about the physical and chemical properties of the product indicating strength, weight, thickness, volume and performance etc. required by the user.

32.17. IMPORTANCE OF SPECIFICATIONS

Following are the importance of the specifications:

1. Specifications enable the contractor to quote reasonable rates for the work. They clearly state the quality of material, workmanship of the work desired and the method of executing the work etc.
2. Specifications serve as a guide during the execution of work to the contractor and the supervising staff.
3. In case of dispute, specifications serve as a legal instrument and evidence.
4. Specifications give clear picture or detailed information regarding the quality of materials, tools and plant etc. to be used to complete the work. This information enables the agency excuting the work to procure them before hand in time to save time and money.
5. Specifications have a check on the quality of work involved in the project.
6. The cost of the work varies directly with its specifications. Thus specifications give correct idea about the estimated cost, which help in arranging the funds well in time.

32.18. CONTRACTS

A contract is an agreement, which will be valid by law or enforceable by law between or amongst the two or more parties for providing services or supplies against a consideration of monetary value, either in cash or in kind. The volume of work or supply, rates of payment, time limit for completion as well as penalties for default on the part of contractor form a part of the contract agreement. An offer to provide some services with out any consideration in its exchange will not constitute a contract.

32.19. ELEMENTS OF AN CONTRACT

A simple enforceable contract should consist of the following elements:

1. **An Agreement.** In any contract, there must be an agreement between the two parties consisting of firm offer and acceptance of the parties involved agreeing to all terms included in the contract.
2. **An consideration.** An consideration is some thing of value, generally the money to be paid after the goods or services have been delivered under the terms of the contract. With out an consideration, the agreement will not form contract.
3. **The intention to enter into legal relations.** With out the intention to enter into legal relations of the parties an agreement may exist with out necessarily being a contract.
4. **The capacity to contract.** In this respect both parties must be free to enter into the contract. This requirement may not be realised when the conditions of a contract are contravened (work done against law or rule) the existing regulations by one of the parties.
5. **Reality of the consent.** Under this part both parties must discharge their duties as per the terms of the contract.
6. The object of the contract must be lawful.

32.20. POINTS TO BE KEPT IN MIND WHILE CONTRACTING

As already stated, contracts essentially are communications which are legally binding on both parties.

Irrespective of form of communication, the principle should be clarity of expression so that the message is properly and accurately conveyed from one party to an other and understood. The legal documents, specifications, drawings which form the contract are the vehicles for transmitting and receiving the messages. As both parties are involved in a contract, are separate bodies the best strategy of contract should be as follows:

(*a*) The contract must be based on clear message which can be understood and agreed by each side before the acceptance of the contract.

(*b*) The contract should be fair to each side. It should take into account the nature of the work, the requirements and problems of both contractor and the user.

(*c*) The contract should utilise the common interests of each side to the best advantage. The party with better experience and resources should deal with the appropriate risks.

32.21. CONTRACT DOCUMENTS

Government departments, many industries and agencies have developed their own form and type of typical contracts and contract document. Contract documents for a construction project should be developed based on the joint effort by the designer, owner and manager. The bid package will vary depending on owner requirements and on designer and management procedures. A typical contract package may consist of the following items.

1. Invitation to bid. Generally this invitation gives the requirements and procedures for a responsive (quick) bid. It also gives additional information pertaining to the contract itself.

2. Bid form. The bid form is completed and signed by the bidder stating the terms of his offer. Usually following informations are submitted in the bid form.

(*a*) A statement, that the bidder has examined the plans, specifications and job site plan and location. The amount of compensation to be received for the work done by him. The liquidated damages if applicable. A statement that the bidder agrees to execute the contract if his bid is accepted.

(*b*) An agreement to submit a payment and performance bond, if required.

(*c*) Overhead and profit percentage applicable to extra work. Bid alternatives if applicable.

(*d*) Requirements for the completion of the contract or duration required for the completion of the work. There could be some special provisions applicable.

3. Bid break down. It gives the individual price components that will add up to the total contract price. It is to be filled in by the bidder. Later it may guide the progress payments.

4. Construction contract. A sample of contract is included in the contract document to inform the prospective bidder that he will be required to sign such a contract if his execution proposal form is accepted.

5. General conditions. Usually general conditions are the part of the specifications. These state the conditions applicable to all contracts to be awarded.

6. Special conditions. These conditions are also a part of specifications and state the specific conditions applicable to the particular contract or group of contracts to be awarded.

7. Work included in the contract. This section states the provisions of standard specifications applicable to a particular contract to be awarded.

8. Work not included in the contract. The provisions of standard specifications which are not applicable to the contract to be awarded are included in this section.

9. Specifications. and drawings etc. These are the technical requirements of the contract which fully define the scope, quality and extent of the work.

10. Supplementary provisions. This section may include additional items not included in the special conditions such as the definition of the status of the professional, construction manager and prevailing wage rates if applicable.

11. Owner furnished items. Certain items to be furnished by the owner to the contractor are included in this section. This section may include various items such as water and sanitation facilities, storage areas, equipment and materials, temporary utilities and survey control etc.

12. Construction schedule. This section shows the scheduled mile stones and over all completion requirements for the particular contract for which bids have been given. It also provides over all schedule showing general relationship between the work package and design activities.

32.22. TYPES OF CONTRACT

Depending upon the size and complex nature of the job following types of contracts may be adopted:

1. Lumpsum Contracts

This is the traditional method by which the construction of a project is implemented. The owner gets prepared a set of definitive documents consisting of design plans, specifications, and defining the scope of work. These documents must be complete in all details and project definition to make it possible for the owner to seek lumpsum bids and for contractor to know the situation.

In this contract a single lumpsum is quoted for the job and accepted as a fixed price. The lumpsum amount is arrived on the basis of detailed drawings and specifications provided by the owner as prepared. Some times a bill of quantities and schedule of rates are also presented to help the contractor for estimating the correct price. This contract is better suited for over ground works than under ground works as over ground works are always visible and the quantities could be measured at any time.

Situations where it is found very effective

This contract is found very effective under the following situations:

1. For comparatively small jobs
2. Where all details of the job are described exactly and precisely
3. When alterations in the job are kept to the minimum
4. Not much risk is attached to its execution.

Advantages of the lumpsum contract

Following are the advantages of this method:

1. Before the start of construction, the total cost of construction is defined and a definite contractual commitment between the owner and the contractor is established.
2. Contractual relations between the Owner, Contractor, Architect and Engineer are clearly defined.
3. The scope and limits of the project are defined before the start of the work.
4. Through competitive process, best price for the work is obtained.
5. It avoids a lot of detailing and accounting which makes the job easy.
6. It offers a fixed total price to the owner.
7. The contractor gets a chance to work without much hinderance.

Disadvantages

Following are the disadvantages of this method:

1. Due to the lack of time flexibility, it may result in delayed implementation of the project, which may further escalate the cost.
2. In this case all decisions regarding the materials and system are made during the design stage. Hence the Architect and Engineers must be highly proficient and competent in their work.
3. It becomes difficult to accommodate additions and alterations of design and specifications.
4. In case of unforeseen hazzards during the construction, the contractor is put to unlimited hardship.

2. Bill of Quantities

In this contract the provisional sum and prime cost of some of the items are quoted. The total cost is derived from the sum of the costs of the individual items as priced in the bill plus the lumpsum. The quantities are measured from the contract drawings supplied by the owner. The total quantities of work measured in the field may vary some what from the quantities measured from the design drawings. Hence it does not give a fixed total sum. Since the construction follows closely the design drawings, the total cost paid by the owner is more or less equal to the total sum tendered. Actually this contract comes under the fixed price contract as the unit rates quoted by the contractor for the individual items in the bill are fixed.

Advantages of bill of quantities contract

This contract has the following advantages:

1. Price quoted for individual items are fixed. Thus the total cost is more or less fixed as derived from the measurements of drawings.
2. Payment to contractor is made as per the work done.
3. Though deviations and alterations from the original drawings could be accepted during construction, but the unit price does not change, it remains as such.
4. Comparision of tenders become easier as the basis of tendering is the same for all the tenderers and the price quoted are much competitive.
5. The bill submitted gives a clear picture of the cost of construction, details of work done and the type of construction.

3. Schedule of rate contract

In situations where the visualisation of the quantities of work in advance is not possible, schedule of rate contract is used. In this case the contractor quotes only the price of the items. The special features of this contract are as follows:

1. In this case generally quantities are not inserted or noted. Even if some times inserted they are rounded off.
2. Generally in this case more items than the actually would be needed are quoted as it is difficult to fore tell the exact number of items required.
3. No guarantee is given that all the items of the work would be carried out. Thus the tenderer has to quote such rates so that each item carrys its own over head charges.
4. **Cost plus percentage contract.** In this contract the contractor is paid the actual expenditure he incurs in completing the work *i.e.* the cost of material, labour charges and expenditure in installing the plant and machinery. In addition of the actual expenditure, the contractor is also paid a certain amount to cover over head expenses and profit. This sum is fixed at the time of contract awarded. Generally the fixed amount is a certain percentage of the total cost incurred by the contractor to create the facility. This system is suitable for temporary use in case of emergency.
5. **Cost plus bid or fixed fee contract.** In this case also the contractor is paid the actual expenses incurred by him for creating the facility plus a fixed sum as fee unrelated to the amount of over heads and profits. The fixed fee may be decided on the basis of competition with other contractors at the time of accepting tender or the amount of fee may be negotiated between the owner and the contractor. In this contract there is full freedom to adopt any or best method of construction, change in specifications or the materials to be used in the construction with the consent of the owner. Efficient contractors work well with this contract.
6. **Unit price contract.** This contract is based on the estimated quantities of the items involved in the work. The estimated quantities of these items are provided by the owner and the contractor bids cost per unit of each item. These works are carried out in accordance with the contract documents. The payment to the contractor is made on the basis of the units of the work actually done and measured in the field. Thus the total cost of the construction can only be known by the owner after the completion of the work. The contractor has to perform the quantities of the work actually required in the field at his quoted unit prices, whether they are less or greater than the owners estimates.

32.23. QUOTATIONS

The rates quoted by suppliers for the supply of their goods in response to an invitation of a competent authority or department are known as *quotations*. Quotations are invited in sealed covers. In this case no earnest money is required with the quotation. Quotations are invited for piece work system of allotment of work.

QUESTIONS

1. Name various types of agreements for execution of works. Give special feature of each of them.
2. Discuss the important rules for inviting tenders.
3. What informations should be given in a tender notice.
4. Discuss the publicity procedure for inviting tender.
5. Discuss the conditions provided in piece work agreement.
6. Name different types of contracts and discuss lumpsum contract in detail.
7. What informations should be given in a contract document.
8. Define a contract giving its elements.
9. Differentiate between the following:
   (*a*) Unit price contract
   (*b*) Cost plus percentage contract
   (*c*) Schedule of rate contract

OBJECTIVE TYPES QUESTIONS

1. In public works department works can be executed
   (*a*) Departmentally
   (*b*) On contract agreement basis
   (*c*) On piece work basis
   (*d*) All are correct
   (*e*) Only a is correct
2. In a piece work agreement conditions provided are
   (*a*) Payment would be made after measurement
   (*b*) Best available material would be used
   (*c*) Divisional or sub divisional engineer is competent to terminate the work any time
   (*d*) All are correct
   (*e*) None of the above is correct
3. The amount of earnest money is about percent of the estimated cost of the work
   (*a*) 1.0%
   (*b*) 2.0%
   (*c*) 3.5%
   (*d*) 5.0%
4. The amount of security money to be deposited is about percent of the cost of work
   (*a*) 5.0%
   (*b*) 6.5%
   (*c*) 8%
   (*d*) 10%
5. Identify the correct statement/statements:
   (*a*) Tender is a contractor's bid in writing for the execution of an work
   (*b*) Tender document is the set of informations supplied to the contractor by the department to submit his bid
   (*c*) Specifications are the instructions which provide technical requirements of a work and give details of jobs to be carried out
   (*d*) Security money is deposited by the contractor as guarantee to execute the work as per specifications on the terms and conditions offered by him
   (*e*) All are correct
6. Tenders may be of the type
   (*a*) Open tender
   (*b*) Limited tender
   (*c*) Single tender
   (*d*) Rate contract
   (*e*) All are correct
7. Lumpsum contract is found very effective in situations except
   (*a*) For comparatively small jobs

(*b*) Where details are described exactly and precisely
(*c*) When the alterations in the job are expected very large
(*d*) In situations where there is no much risk is attached to the job

8. Identify the incorrect statement/statements
(*a*) In bill of quantities contract prices quoted for individual items are not fixed
(*b*) In the bill of quantities contract a fixed amount is paid to the contractor
(*c*) In case of bill of quantities contract, the comparision of tenders is most difficult
(*d*) The bill submitted by the contractor for the construction does not give clear picture of cost of construction and details of works done
(*e*) All are incorrect

9. Identify the correct statement/statements
(*a*) In case of schedule of rate contract usually quantities are not noted
(*b*) Unit price contract is based on the estimated quantities of the items involved in the work
(*c*) Quotations should always be invited in sealed covers
(*d*) No earnest money is required to be deposited in case of quotations
(*e*) All are correct

10. Identify the incorrect statement/statements
(*a*) The cost of work varies directly with the specifications
(*b*) Specifications have no relation with the cost of the work
(*c*) Specifications give detailed information regarding quality of materials and tools to be used in the construction work
(*d*) Specifications serve as a legal evidence in case of a dispute

11. Identify the incorrect statement/statements
(*a*) A contract for any service or supply or execution of work will be valid by law if carried out against a consideration of money value
(*b*) Money consideration has no role in the execution of a contract
(*c*) Specifications enable the contractor to quote reasonable rates
(*d*) The object of contract must be lawful

12. Identify the correct statement/statements
(*a*) Specifications are instructions in words which supplement the drawing and provide technical requirements of work
(*b*) A offer to execute a work without any consideration in its exchange will not form an contract
(*c*) Divisional and sub divisional engineers are competent to terminate piece work agreement any time
(*d*) All the above

ANSWERS:

1. (*d*)	4. (*d*)	7. (*c*)	10. (*b*)
2. (*d*)	5. (*e*)	8. (*e*)	11. (*b*)
3. (*b*)	6. (*e*)	9. (*e*)	12. (*d*)

33

Works Account

33.1. INTRODUCTION

The main object of keeping works accounts is to exhibit simply but accurately, the expenditure incurred on various works. However it is desirable to record the details of accounts for large works due to the following reasons.

1. To get information on various aspects of the work from statistical point of view, if necessary.
2. To analyse the cost of various items of works or class of works etc.
3. To facilitate the efficient control over transactions in large works, especially if the period of construction is prolonged.

The accounts of major works should be kept head wise, usually on the basis of the items sanctioned in the estimate. The abstract of the estimate should be framed to show separately (1) the quantity and cost of labour and (2) the cost of materials for each distinct item of work; if it is intended to purchase the materials and employ labour for construction either through a contractor or departmentally. However if it is intended to get the work executed by contract for completed items of work, the abstract of the estimate may only show the quantity and cost of each item.

33.2. GENERAL PRINCIPLES OF ACCOUNT

The accounts of works are based on the following two initial records:

1. Muster roll   2. Measurement book (M.B.)

1. Muster roll. A muster roll is a record in which the names, particulars, and attendance of daily labourers, amount payable to them and the work done by them are recorded. The advance for payment to labourers is issued on the basis of the muster roll. After the disbursement of wages, the necessary certificate on the muster roll is recorded and it is kept as a voucher. Muster rolls are prepared on form 21 of the department. This form consists of three parts. Part 1 is for a nominal roll meant for recording the attendance and absence of labourers and fine imposed on them. This part facilitates the calculations of net wages payable to the labourers and the classification of cost of labour on the basis of work and sub heads where necessary.

In part II of the muster roll, the details of unpaid items are recorded. The unpaid wages of the previous muster roll are also carried over. Payments made, out of the arrears are also recorded in this part. Particulars of all wages remained unpaid for a period of three months should be brought to the notice of Executive Engineer whose orders are necessary before they can be paid off.

The part III of the muster roll is used for recording the work done by the laborers employed as per the nominal roll of part I in cases where the work is susceptible to measurement. In case, the work is not susceptible to measurement it is certified that the work is not susceptible to measurement. To reproduce the details of measurements in part III are not necessary.

For preparing muster roll in Rajasthan and U.P. form no. 21 A is used instead of form 21. While central public works department muster roll has only part I and II. The details of unpaid wages are recorded in a register of unpaid wages of form 21 A maintained in the sub division.

33.3. NECESSARY INFORMATION TO BE GIVEN IN INITIAL ACCOUNTS AND VOUCHERS

Every entry of the initial accounts and vouchers connected with the payments relating to works provides the following informations:

1. Full name of the work as given in the estimate.
2. Name of sub heads, if the expenditure is booked under sub heads.
3. The charges if any, which are to be recovered from the contractor or any other person and names of persons from whom they are to be recovered.

33.4. RULES FOR PREPARING THE MUSTER ROLL

While preparing a muster roll, following rules should be observed:

1. For the same work more than one muster roll can be used.
2. For the same work muster roll should never be prepared in duplicate.
3. The presence of labour should be marked with a cross mark (×) and absence with letter A, just at the start of work or day on each day.
4. Labourers may be paid more than once a month depending upon local conditions. After each payment new muster roll has to be opened.
5. The daily record of attendance and fines should be recorded in such a way that:
   (*a*) The calculations of the net wages of each labourer for the purpose of payment become easy.
   (*b*) It may be difficult to tamper with the original entries.
   (*c*) It may be easy to classify the expenditure by sub heads of works.
6. After the muster roll has been passed, payment should be made as early as possible by sub divisional officer in the presence of concerned subordinate who should testify payment as "paid in my presence to the right person."
7. After the payment has been made, the S.D.O. should certify as "paid by me Rs.____________ on ________".
8. The unpaid items should be recorded in part II, the register of arrears.
9. Wages remained unpaid for three months, should be brought to the notice of the Executive Engineer, who will decide if these wages should continue to be borne in the accounts of the work.
10. If the work is susceptible to measurement, the progress of the work should be recorded in part III of the muster roll. In case the work is not susceptible to measurement, then it should be certified that "work is not susceptible to measurement."
11. Muster rolls are checked with reference to entires in the measurement books to the extent of 50% in the sub division and 50% in the division, when payments are made by the divisional office.

33.5. COMMON IRREGULARITIES FOUND IN THE MUSTER ROLLS

In the maintenance of muster rolls following irregularities are commonly noticed:

1. **The labourers employed on muster roll not grouped according to their class.** The description of labourers employed for the work should be given in the first column of the muster roll. Each category of labour such as carpenter, mason, black smith etc. should be grouped together separately.
2. **Muster rolls contain erasures and over writings.** To make changes in the entries already made, erasing them or over writing on them is highly objectionable. If any change is inevitable then entry already made should be crossed neatly under dated initials of the person making these changes and new entry made.

3. **Muster roll not signed daily.** Muster rolls should be signed daily by the person who marks the daily attendance.
4. **Attendance not marked daily.** The attendance of muster roll labourers should be marked daily.
5. **Discrepancy between daily report and muster roll.** The details of labourers given in daily labour report and muster roll should tally. Any difference between the two is highly objectionable.
6. **Corrections not attested.** Any correction made in the muster roll must be attested with the dated initials of the person who makes it.
7. **Delay in passing muster roll and its payment.** There are delays in passing and making payments of muster rolls. Very often delay in submission of muster roll to divisional office for adjustment has been observed. These delays are highly objectionable.
8. **Incorrect entry of the progress of work in part III of the muster roll.** Some times excess amount of progress is found in the muster roll. Thus the work done by the labour should be measured accurately and correct entries should be made in the muster roll. Any attempt to show exaggerated quantity of work is a serious irregularity.
9. **To show more work as not susceptible to measurement.** Large amount of work entered into muster roll as not susceptible to measurement creates suspicion. The work not susceptible to measurement must be reduced to the maximum possible limit and the cost of work should be calculated on the basis of the rates of measured work fixed by the competent authority.

33.6. CASES IN WHICH MUSTER ROLL CAN BE DISPENSED WITH

The use of muster roll can be dispensed with in case casual labour is employed on casual labour roll for urgent work of short duration as explained under casual labour roll.

33.7. LABOUR REPORT

For all large works or groups of works a labour report is submitted daily or periodically as directed by the divisional officer in the prescribed form. This report shows the number of each class of labourers employed on each work or sub head. When muster rolls are submitted, their entries are compared with the labour report. As a mater of fact there should be no difference between the two. If any difference is noted, it should be investigated. The report gives the following informations.

1. Category or class of labourers such as mason, carpenter etc.
2. Number of labourers engaged in each category.
3. Rate at which the labourers employed.
4. Name of work on which labourers employed.
5. Approximate amount of work done.

As these reports are prepared from muster rolls, there should be no variation between the two. When these reports are submitted daily, then they are known as daily reports.

33.8. CASUAL LABOUR ROLL

The record of labour employed for short duration in exceptional and urgent cases is known as casual labour. In this case the names of the labourers are not given on casual labour form. In this case only the number of labourers employed, period of employment. rate and amount is given. The attendance is marked by the section officer in his diary and daily report is sent to the sub divisional officer. At the end of the work, the casual labour roll is prepared and payment made on it only by a gazzetted officer. The circumstances under which the casual labour roll is permissible are as under:

1. In urgent cases when labour has to be engaged for a short duration on casual basis such as for closing a breach in a canal or silt clearance from a canal or clearing the road blocks etc.
2. In case of very petty works or repairs when there are only few entries of daily labour. Specimen of casual roll is shown below:

Casual labour roll

Division _________

Cash book voucher no. ___________

Sub division_________

Casual labour roll of labour employed

Date ________

No. of labourers employed	*Class of labour*	*Period*	*Rate*	*Amount*	*Dated initial and remarks of paying officer*	*Quantity of work done with reference to the recorded measurements*	*Work to which chargable*

Amount paid in words.

Sd- S.O.

Paid in my presence to the right person............ (Amount)

Sd.......... Section officer

33.9. LABOUR ENGAGED THROUGH A CONTRACTOR

Labour engaged through a contractor, the payment of wages is done on the basis of measurement of work done by the labour. The work can be measured after its completion or during its progress. The payment is done at suitable rates on the basis of the work actually done. In case the work is not susceptible to measurement, the contractor is paid on the basis labourers engaged every day. The commission or profit to the contractor is either included in the rates allowed or paid separately in lump sum or by percentage rate. When the work is got done by labour through contractor the daily report of labourers employed each day must be prepared by the section officer incharge of the work and sent to sub divisional or divisional officer. To avoid litigation signatures of the concerned contractor should also be obtained on this daily report. From this report check on expenditure can be exercised. In such cases M.B. or muster roll is not used.

33.10. MEASUREMENT BOOK (M.B.)

A measurement book is the initial record of all kinds of works which are susceptible to measurement. Thus measurement books are the basis for all accounts of quantities of work done by contract labour employed departmentally and the materials purchased for specific works. They should be kept and maintained in such a way that the transactions are readily traceable in the accounts of the department. Measurement books are very important record of the P.W.D. They should be kept in safe custody. They must be maintained accurately and kept carefully so that they may be produced in a court of law as evidence if required.

All measurement books belonging to a division should be numbered serially and a register should be maintained in the divisional office showing the serial number of each measurement book, the name of sub division to which issued, the date of issue and date of its return. A similar register should also be maintained in the sub division, showing the name of sub divisional officer and sectional officers to whom measurement books have been issued.

Books not in use must be withdrawn, when not in use, even though they may not have been completely written or used up.

33.11. General instructions about recording detailed measurements

Following points must be followed while recording the detailed measurements:

1. In the measurement book, the detailed measurements are recorded only by the person, who is incharge of the work, to whom the M.B. has been issued for this purpose as divisional, sub divisional or sectional officer.

2. All measurements should be entered in M.B. neatly, issued for this purpose and no where else.

3. Each set of measurements should begin with the following informations so that it is easily distinguished from other entries.

A. In case of bills for work done:

(*a*) Full name of the work as given in the estimate.
(*b*) Location of work.
(*c*) Name of contractor (who executed the work)
(*d*) No and date of execution of agreement.
(*e*) Date of written order for commencement of work.
(*f*) Date of completion of work.
(*g*) Date of measurement.
(*h*) Name of subordinate incharge of daily labour.
(*j*) Reference to previous measurement on account of same contract (No and page of M.B.) in case of running bills.

B. In case of bills for supply of materials

(*a*) Name of supplier.
(*b*) No and date of his agreement of supply order.
(*c*) Purpose of supply, which may be either of the following.
  (*i*) "Stock" when supplies are for stock purposes.
  (*ii*) Purchases for direct issues to the work (Full name of work as given in estimate)
  (*iii*) Purchases for issue to contractor.... (Full name of contractor as given in estimate)
(*d*) Date of written order to commence supplies.
(*e*) Date of actual completion of supplies.
(*f*) Date of measurement.

4. The person making the measurement must close each set of measurements with his dated initials.

5. All measurements should be recorded neatly in the M.B. at the site of work. It is not permissible to note the measurements else where and then copy them in the M.B. This practice is highly objectionable.

6. As far as possible all entries should be made in ink. When ever it is not possible, entries should be made with copying pencil, but later on they should not be inked. They must be left over as such. The entries in the last column "Contents" should be made in ink in the first instance itself.

7. No erasures and over writings should be allowed. If any mistake is made, it should be corrected by scoring out or crossing out the incorrect entry and inserting the correct one between the lines under initials. The pages of M.B. are machine numbered. Thus the entries should be recorded continuously and no blank pages should be left or torn out. If any line or page is left blank inadvertently, it should be cancelled by drawing a diagonal line under proper attestation with dated initials.

8. When any measurement is cancelled or disallowed, it must be supported by the dated initials of the officer ordering the cancellation or by a reference to his orders and initialed by the officer who has made the measurements. The reason for the cancellation also be recorded.

9. When a bill has been prepared for a work or supply, every page containing the related detailed measurements must be scored out by a diagonal line in red ink. At the time of payment an endorsement must be made in red ink giving a reference to the number and date of the voucher of the payment.

10. The description of various items of work as entered in the M.B. must tally with that given in the agreement and must be written in full.

11. The contractor should be given prior notice about the time and place of measurement. If he turns up, his signatures should be obtained at the bottom of the measurements in token of his acceptance of the measurements.

12. Each M.B. is provided with an index, which must be kept upto date.

13. At the end of each set of measurements an abstract of total quantities of each distinct item of work should be prepared, which provides the idea of the cost of work.

14. The loss of M.B. is a serious matter. It should be reported immediately to the higher authorities along with the statement explaining the circumstances under which it is lost. A report of loss of M.B. should also be lodged with the nearest police station.

33.12. COMMON IRREGULARITIES OBSERVED IN WRITING M.B.

Non compliance of the rules discussed above result in serious irregularities, which must be avoided. Following irregularities are of common occurrence.

1. Agreement number is not written on the top of the measurements. Other entries are also not entered as discussed in article 33.11.
2. Very often erasures and over writings on original entries has been observed, which is highly objectionable. If a mistake has been committed it should be corrected by crossing the incorrect entry and writing correct entry in between the lines and supported with dated initials of the officer making the correction.
3. Entries in the M.B. interpolated and corrected. Also changes in the amount of the bill made after the preparation of the original bill.
4. Blank spaces are left at the bottom of the pages and in between the lines of the M.B.
5. Measurements in the M.B. are shown on dates, on which he was not present there as per his T.A. bill.
6. Entries in M.B. not recorded at the site of work, but copied from some other record.
7. Originally entries are made in pencil and inked after wards.
8. Full particulars are not given of the work.
9. Name of the work does not tally with the sanctioned estimate.
10. Payments are made without the pay orders of the competent authority and check certificate from the clerk concerned.
11. Pages of M.B. are not crossed even though the bills for payments have been made.
12. Percentage check by senior officers is inadequate.
13. Corrections are not attested.
14. Voucher number and date are not indicated after making the payment.
15. Index of the M.B. has not been up dated.

At the time of inspection of S.E. or X.E.N. or at the time of audit inspection these irregularities are viewed very seriously.

33.13. PRACTICAL INSTRUCTIONS FOR TAKING MEASUREMENTS

Following points should be kept in view while taking measurements:

1. Before taking measurements, the junior engineer should make himself familiar with all the conditions and specifications given in the agreement of the work, whose measurements being taken. In Rajasthan and U.P. following rules have been prescribed for taking heights of some items.

(*a*) For kankar stacks of 32.5 cm height, the height of the stack should be noted as 30.0 cms.

(*b*) In case of earth work, certain deductions are made. The percentage varies from soil to soil and from state to state.

(*c*) The practice for the measurement of door frames differs from department to department. In some departments chaukats are measured separately on cubical content basis and door shutters on area basis, while in some departments entire door including frame is measured on area basis.

(*d*) While taking measurements of sand, provision of bulking of sand should be kept in mind. At the time of measurement sand should be completely dry.

2. The tape to be used for measurement should be calibrated with a good steel tape and it should not

increase in length when stretched to make it straight. Measurements of expensive items like R.C.C. must be taken with steel tapes.

3. To avoid any possibility of inaccuracy, the measurements of buildings should be taken with steel tapes as far as possible. It should be remembered that inaccuracy in measurements of a pucca work can be detected at any time during the life of the structure.

4. Following two things are very important for any measurement being taken:

(*a*) Records must clearly show that the man who takes the measurements was actually present at the site of work at the time of measurement. Some times it has been observed that the measurements are recorded as having been taken on a certain date, where as his T.A. bill record shows his presence some where else. Such instances are considered very serious and irregular.

(*b*) The item to be measured must be available to the person in such a form that the measurements may be taken easily. The lapse of this law is obvious from the following example.

(*i*) Petrol filled in the tank of a car which is constantly in use, is recorded after several days of the supply.

(*ii*) Measurements of stone metal recorded after its consolidation has started or a part of the metal has been consumed.

(*iii*) The profile measurements of earth work in a canal are recorded after the release of water in the canal and on a date when water is actually running in the canal as per regulation record.

(*iv*) Measurements of brick work are taken after plastering the walls. At this time it is not possible to judge the class of brick work.

(*v*) Measurements of foundations are taken after they have been covered.

4. If the work is found of inferior quality, the junior engineer must obtain the orders from sub divisional officer before measurement. With out the approval of acceptance of inferior work or supply of materials, measurements of such items should not be taken.

5. Measurements must be directly entered into the M.B. at the site. Under no circumstances the measurements be noted on separate note book etc. and copied after wards in the M.B.

6. While recording measurements, end of the tape should be held by departmental employee, who is intelligent and trust worthy and knows how and where the end of the tape is to be held.

7. The junior engineer taking the measurements should study the drawings and must ensure that the work has not been done in excess of the required.

33.14. METHOD OF PAYMENT AFTER MEASUREMENTS ARE RECORDED IN M.B.

After recording the measurements in the M.B., the quantities of items are worked out and filled in the last column "content or areas". After this, the abstract of cost is prepared with the help of rates already agreed upon. The abstract of cost along with M.B. is submitted to the paying officer (Divisional/sub divisional officer).

After being satisfied by scrutiny and thorough checking, the paying officer may modify the rates if he feels so as per condition of the agreement. In case, the paying officer is satisfied with the rates, he will ask the concerned clerk to check the calculations and prepare the bill under his initials. The clerk concerned will check the calculations and prepare the bill. He will write on the M.B. "checked and billed". and initial on it. The paying officer then will accord the pay order on the bill and the M.B.

After the payment is made for the work, each page of M.B. pertaining to the measurement of this work is crossed diagonally in red ink and on the relevant abstract of cost following endorsement is made

Paid vide voucher no. ....

Dated ....

Sub divisional officer's initials

After the payment, the bill is given voucher no and date entered in the account and kept as a voucher for record.

33.15. KINDS OF MEASUREMENT BOOKS

Measurement books may be of the following three types:

1. Ordinary measurement book
2. Standard measurement book
3. Check measurement book

1. Ordinary measurement book

As stated earlier, it is an initial record of all kinds of works which are susceptible to measurements In this book entries of work done and supplies made are recorded for making payments to the contractors. The specimen form of this book is shown below. Following item are written on the top of this form.

(*a*) Name of work
(*b*) Location of the work site
(*c*) Name of agency executing the work
(*d*) Date of written orders for the commencement of work
(*e*) Date of completion of work
(*f*) Date of measurement of work
(*g*) Date of agreement and its no.
(*h*) Name of subordinate officer incharge of labour
(*i*) Reference of previous measurements.

Measurement Book form

S. No.	*Description or particulars*	*No.*	*L*	*B*	*Depth or Height D*	*Contents or Area*
1. 2. 3.						

2. Standard Measurement Book

The measurement book in which the standard measurements are recorded is known as *standard measurement book.* If in the department there are some buildings which are repaired periodically and the quantities of various items of work remain unchanged from year to year. In such cases of repair work to save trouble of measuring them every time it is convenient to maintain standard measurement books for such buildings.

Advantages of standard M.B.

Followings are the advantages of standard M.B.:

1. It facilitates the preparation of estimates for repair work from time to time.
2. It simplifies the preparation of contractors bill as it is not necessary to take detailed measurements every time.

Precautions to be observed while using standard M.B.

While using standard M.B. following precautions should be observed:

1. To distinguish standard measurement books from ordinary books the standard Measurement books should be numbered in alphabetic series where as ordinary measurement books are numbered serially.

2. The entries in the standard measurement book should be recorded legibly in ink and be certified as correct by a responsible officer.

3. A certificate be obtained periodically from the divisional engineer that:

(*a*) All the standard measurement books of the division have been inspected by him.
(*b*) No entry has been tempered with.

(*c*) All corrections due to additions and alterations in the building have been made in the book.
(*d*) The books are reliable and upto date records.

4. When the payments are based on standard measurements, the gazetted officer or the subordinate preparing the bill for payment has to certify that.

(*a*) The whole of the work has been done as per standard measurements.
(*b*) It has not been billed any where previously.

3. Check measurement book

The check measurement book is used to check the measurements made by the sectional officer. It is used by sub divisional officer (A.E.N.). To avoid double payment no measurement is recorded in this measurement book for the purpose of payment. It is solely used for checking purposes. At the end of the measurement in the M.B. of the sectional officer following certificate is recorded by the sub divisional officer. "Check measurement was made by me in the check measurement book No. ________ on page ________. The sectional officer concerned was/was not present at the time of check measurements."

As a general rule following percentage of check measurements should be made by the sub divisional officer.

(*a*) The sub divisional officer must carry out check tests about 50% of the measurements made by the subordinates both in respect of measurements made for payments of running bill and final bill. The percentage is judged by their money value. Following percentage of measurements must be checked under all circumstances.
(*b*) 35% of the work costing more than Rs. 5000/-
(*c*) 25% of the work costing less than Rs. 5000/-

The divisional officer is expected to check about 20% of the measurements made by his subordinates in respect of final bills, but not less than 5% in any case.

(*a*) The test checks should preferably be carried out before the payment is made.
(*b*) The individual items checked must be attested by dated initials of the checking officer. He should also record the results of his checks.

If during the check measurements, the difference in the measurements made by the sectional officer is less than 2% in case of original work, 5% in case of repairs and 10% in the earth work, the sectional officer's entries may be corrected accordingly before the payment is made and the following note may be recorded.

Corrected in accordance with check measurement book no and page......

In case the difference found is more than the above limits, the whole work will have to be measured by the sub divisional officer and the matter has to be reported to the higher authorities for necessary action against the sectional officer.

33.16. REVIEW OF MEASUREMENT BOOK

All measurement books in use in the division once a year, usually in the month of september should be collected for review by the divisional accountant under the supervision of the divisional officer. The measurement books should be reviewed in the following respects.

1. To ensure that no erasures or over writing has been made or entry disfigured and all corrections have been duly initialed.
2. To ensure that no original sheet or page has been torn out of the M.B.
3. To ensure that entries in pencil have not been inked.
4. To ensure the accuracy of calculations in the M.B. a percent check must be made.
5. To ensure that the books have been initialed as per instructions issued.

33.17. LOSS OF M.B.

The safe custody of the M.B. is the personal responsibility of the officer to whom the M.B. has been issued for use. The loss of a M.B. is a very serious matter and it must be reported to the Chief Engineer at the earliest after the detection of the loss with explanation of all persons responsible for the loss for further necessary action. The Chief Engineer is empowered to write off the loss of M.B.

To avoid loss of M.B. in transaction when passed from one officer to an other officer they should be sent either through registered post or through messenger along with a challan. Three copies of challan should be prepared and II and III copies sent along with M.B. to consignee, who will return II copy to the consignor duly acknowledging the receipt of the M.B. and will retain the III copy with him for record.

33.18. CASES WHERE DETAILED MEASUREMENTS ARE NOT REQUIRED

In the following cases detailed measurements are not required:

1. In case of emergent works not susceptible to measurements such as clearance of silt from a canal. In such cases payments to the labourers are made on labour roll form for the period actually employed. The detailed measurements are not recorded in the M.B. and approximate quantity of work is recorded in the column prepared for the purpose.
2. **Advance payments.** In such cases payments are made to contractors for the work done or supplies made, but not measured. Only a certificate is given by the sub divisional officer that not less than the quantity of work done for which actually paid.
3. **Secured advances.** In this case also payments are made to contractors for supplies made, but no measurements recorded in the M.B., only a certificate is recorded by the sub divisional officer as above.
4. **Lump sum contract.** In this case also measurements are not recorded in M.B. A certificate has to be given as above.
5. **Works of periodical repairs.** In this case the detailed measurements are written in the standard M.B. Thus there is no need to enter measurements of repairs each time, but the standard M.B. must be maintained accurately.

QUESTIONS

1. Define a muster roll. For what type of establishment it is used?
2. What information is necessary in case of initial accounts and vouchers?
3. Define the labour report. What is its purpose?
4. What common irregularities are usually noticed in muster rolls?
5. What is a measurement book? What items are recorded in it?
6. What common irregularities are found in a measurement book?
7. Discuss general instructions for recording details in measurement books.
8. Explain precautions to be taken for taking measurements.
9. Discuss the method of payment after recording measurements.
10. Describe different kinds of measurement books.
11. What precautions should be observed while using standard M.B.
12. What is a check book. For what purpose it is used? What points should be kept in view while using a check book?

OBJECTIVE TYPES QUESTIONS

1. Muster roll is a record in which are recorded of the labourers
   (*a*) Name and particulars (*b*) Attendance
   (*c*) Amount payable to them (*d*) All the above
   (*e*) None of above
2. In the initial accounts information is necessary
   (*a*) Name of head/sub head
   (*b*) Full name of work as given in the estimate

(*c*) Charges to be recovered
(*d*) Nàme of person/persons from whom they are to be recovered
(*e*) All the above

3. The presence of labourer in the muster roll should be marked
   (*a*) By letter P (*b*) By letter A
   (*c*) By the cross mark (*d*) Any of the above
4. Identify the incorrect statement
   (*a*) Muster roll should never be prepared in dublicate for the same work
   (*b*) More than one muster roll can be used for the same work
   (*c*) Duplicate muster roll can be prepared for the same work if required
   (*d*) Labourers may be paid more than once in a month
5. Identify the correct statement/statements
   (*a*) Erasures and over writings are allowed in muster rolls
   (*b*) Labourers employed on muster rolls should be grouped according to their class as carpenter or mason etc.
   (*c*) To sign muster roll daily is not essential
   (*d*) Any correction made in muster roll must be attested
   (*e*) Delay in passing a muster roll and its payment is not considered objectionable
   (*f*) Any quantum of work as not susceptible to measurement can be shown on a muster roll
   (*g*) On a muster roll minimum possible amount of work should be shown which is not susceptible to measurements
6. Identify the correct statement/statements
   (*a*) A measurement book is the initial record of all kinds of works which are susceptible to measurement
   (*b*) Measurement books are very important records
   (*c*) All measurement books should be well maintained and kept in safe custody
   (*d*) All measurement books of a division should be numbered serially
   (*e*) All of the above are correct
   (*f*) None of the above is correct
7. Identify the incorrect statement/statements
   (*a*) In a measurement book (M.B.) detailed measurements should be entered by the incharge of work to whom M.B. has been given
   (*b*) All measurements in M.B. should be entered neatly
   (*c*) Measurements can be noted on separate piece of paper and after wards may be entered in M.B. neatly.
   (*d*) Over writings and erasures are allowed in writing measurements in M.B.
   (*e*) The index of the M.B. should be kept upto date
   (*f*) Loss of a M.B. is not a very serious matter
8. Identify the correct statement/statements
   (*a*) After the bill for a particular work or supply is prepared, the page of M.B. pertaining this bill should be crossed diagonally in red ink
   (*b*) Entries in M.B. should be recorded at site
   (*c*) Tempering of original record by erasing or over writing is highly objectionable
   (*d*) Blank space at the bottom of the pages and in between the lines of M.B. should never be left
   (*e*) All are correct
   (*f*) None of then is correct
9. Detailed measurements are required to be entered in the M.B. in case of
   (*a*) Advance payments (*b*) secured advance
   (*c*) Lump sum contract (*d*) Original work to be done by contract labour

ANSWERS:

1. (*d*)	3. (*c*)	5. (*b, d, g*)	7. (*c, d, f*)	9. (*d*)
2. (*e*)	4. (*c*)	6. (*e*)	8. (*e*)	

34
Payments

34.1. INTRODUCTION

Public works department requires various types of materials for the execution of works and also gets works done through contractors. The payments of supplies of materials or works executed by contractors or other services rendered are paid to them through bills. In this chapter bills, cash and its maintenance shall be discussed.

34.2. DEFINITIONS

1. **Bill.** Bill is an account containing full and clear particulars of the claim of the contractor or supplier either for the execution of work or supplies made or any other service rendered.
2. **Voucher.** A voucher is a written document which is kept on record as a proof of payment. After the payment of the bill to the contractor or supplier and duly acknowledged, the bill becomes voucher. Every bill becomes voucher after its payment. It is numbered and kept in safe custody. Thus bills passed and entered in the cash book are known as *vouchers.* They should be given serial number in a continuous series each month.
3. **Cash.** It includes legal tender coins, currency notes, cheques, drafts payable on demand and remittance transfer receipts.
4. **Running account.** This term is used for the account with a contractor, when the payment for supplies or work done is made to him at convenient intervals while the final settlement of the account is done either on the completion of work or termination of his contract. This account is known as *running account.*
5. **Running payment, on account payment or payment on account.** The Payment made on running account to a contractor in respect of supplies made or work executed by him and duly measured is known as running payment. Such a payment may or may not be for full value of supplies or work done.
6. **Intermediate payment.** Any payment of any kind made on running account not being the final payment is known as intermediate payment.
7. **Final payment.** The last payment on a running account made to a contractor on the completion or termination of his contract in full settlement of the account is called final payment. The bill on which final payment is made is known as *final bill.*
8. **First and final payment.** The single payment made for a work or contract on its completion is called *first and final* payment.
9. **Deposit agencies.** Any agency employed to execute a work at the cost of a contractor, who fails to complete or show satisfactory progress on a work contracted by him is known as *deposit agency.*

34.3. BILLS

The payments to the contractors are made by preparing bills. These bills are checked and passed by the sub divisional officer. The bills are only prepared for works done or supplies made by the contractor and simultaneously measured and recorded in the M.B. and its abstract prepared.

34.4. TYPES OF BILLS AND FORMS

Bills may be of the following types:

1. **First and final bill.** When a single payment is to be made to the contractor or supplier on the completion of the work or supplies as a final settlement of the claim, the bill prepared is known as *first and final* bill. This bill is prepared on form No. 24.
2. **Running account bill.** The bill prepared for the payment to be made on the running account basis to a contractor in respect of work done or supplies made by him and duly measured is known as running account bill. The payment may or may not be for full value of the work done by him. This bill is prepared on form no. 26.
3. **Final bill.** This bill is prepared for the payment to a contractor on the completion of the work or on termination of his contract in full settlement of the account on form no. 24.
4. **Lump sum contract account bill.** The bill prepared for the payment to the contractor for the final payment for the work completed by him on lump sum contract basis only. In this case form 27 B is used. This form is not used for any other type of contract.
5. **Hand receipts.** Hand receipts are used for all miscellaneous payments and advances.
6. **Accounts of secured advances.** If against a contractor several advances are outstanding or he is paid second advance, then form 26 A is to be attached with the bill prepared on form no 26. This practice is followed in C.P.W.D.
7. **Lump sum contract account bill.** When payments to contractor are to be paid for works on intermediate payment basis on lump sum contract including secured advance bill form 27 A is used. In this case no details of works are to be reproduced in the bill, but a reference of page and serial number of measurement entered in the M.B. should be made.

34.5. ADVANCES TO CONTRACTORS

Ordinarily no advances are permitted to be paid to contractors, how ever advances of the following types may be permitted with specific conditions.

34.5.1. Advance Payment for work actually executed

This kind of advance is made to a contractor on the running account for the work executed by him, but not measured. This advance is made on the basis of a certificate issued by a responsible officer not below the rank of a sub divisional officer. "The quantity of work actually executed by him is not less than that for which payment is made". The officer granting such a certificate is responsible for any over payment. Final payments under no circumstances can be made with out detailed measurements. Advance payments are recovered when on account payments are made through final bill.

34.5.2. Secured Advance

The advance made to an contractor on the security of materials brought to site of work is called *secured advance*, whose contract is for the completed items of works. Secured advance can be made subject to the following conditions:

1. The material brought to site of work is of an imperishable nature. In this category of materials included are bricks, rolled steel joists white lime, kankar, sand, cement, etc. Coal is excluded from both categories of advances and no advance is permissible on it.
2. The amount of advance on imperishable materials is limited upto 75% of the value of the material brought to the site. This amount can be sanctioned by the Divisional Engineer.

3. A formal agreement has to be made with the contractor, under which the government secures a lien on the materials and safe guards against losses due to the postponement of the execution of work by the contractor or due to shortage or misuse of materials and the expenses incurred on proper watch and safe custody of these materials.
4. An officer not below the rank of a sub divisional officer has to certify that the quantities of materials on which the advance has been made, have actually been brought to the site.
5. That the contractor has not previously received any advance on that security.
6. That all the materials are required by the contractor for use on items of work for which rates for finished items have been agreed upon.

The officer granting above certificate is responsible for any over payment which may occur due to his wrong certificate. The recoveries of secured advance should be made from his bills for work done in which these materials have been used. These recoveries should not be postponed till the completion of work.

The Divisional Engineer is also responsible to ensure that—

(*a*) The recoveries are made regularly from the very first payment made for those items of actual work, in which these materials have been used.

(*b*) No secured advance should be made for any materials unless they are to be used with in three months at the most.

(*c*) The materials are measured before making the secured advance on them and their value is based on actual rates for determining the percentage at which the secured advance on materials is to be made.

34.6. LUMP SUM ADVANCE PAYMENTS

The lump sum advance payment to a contractor can be made on receipt an application from him after the receipt of his "on account" bill in the divisional office and there is likelyhood of delay in the payment.

The payment should be made with the following conditions:

1. The bill in respect of which a lump sum advance is requested is under scrutiny in the divisional office.
2. The amount of advance should not exceed 75% of the net amount of the bill under check.
3. No advance payment should be made if the advance payable comes less than Rs. one thousand.
4. The reference number, date and amount of the bill against which the payment is made as well as the page number of M.B. should be recorded on the hand receipt on which payment is made. If previously any "on account". Payment has been made, the number, date, and amount of voucher should also be written on the hand receipt.
5. Also an undertaking from the contractor should be obtained that he will refund any amount paid in excess of the running bill against which the advance has been made.

34.6.1. Special advances

Advances sanctioned under exceptional conditions by the government are known as *special advances.*

34.6.2. Petty advances

The advance paid upto Rs. 50/- (Fifty) in the interest of the work is known as petty advance.

34.7. PREPARATION OF BILLS

1. Before preparing the bill of the contractor, the entries in the M.B. about quantities and description of work or supplies are scrutinised by sub divisional officer and the calculations of areas or contents are checked arithmetically. Then the bill is prepared on the appropriate form for the measurement entries in the M.B. The rates allowed are entered either in the bill itself or in the abstract of the measurement by sub divisional officer. If the quality of work done or supplies made are upto the stipulated specifications, then full rates as per agreement are allowed.

2. If the contract agreement does not specify the rates to be paid for work done or supply made, but merely states that the estimated rates or a certain percentage below or above them will be allowed. In such cases the standard rates to be adopted would be those of the sanctioned estimate, which was in force at the time of agreement was executed.
3. Extra ordinary payments such as bonus or compensation are not permissible to contractor. However these payments may be made if there are written orders from finance department of the concerned government.
4. As a general rules, payments for supplies is not permissible untill the stores have been received and examined properly except whereever government has permitted payment on production of Railway receipt. In such cases the payment is treated as an advance against final settlement on receipt of the stores.
5. In certain states as in Rajasthan and U.P. F.O.R contracts are permissible for the supply of coal, and payment can be made on receipt of Railway receipt, provided the consignments are checked for quality and quantity at the time of dispatch by an responsible officer of the government or supplies are made through the Mining Engineer of the Railway Board. The consignment may be booked under owner's risk or Railway risk, which ever economical. In such cases the payments to suppliers are accounted as final and debited to a suspence estimate "Coal in transit" to be cleared by debit to coal when actually received. Balance to "Coal" short received is cleared either by recovery or by written off to be sanctioned by the competent authority. If the shortage is with in 5% and the coal is booked at owner's risk, usually shortage is written off.
6. In certain states, the measurements are made by the subordinate incharge of the work and submitted to the concerned sub divisional officer. After scrutinizing the entries of the M.B. relating to the work concerned, the sub divisional officer issues pay order. The S.D.O. is authorised to check any measurement, he decides in case of any doubt. After the check, he writes the work "checked by me"

34.8. EXAMINATION OF THE BILLS BY S.D.O.

Before signing the bill, the sub divisional officer should see the following points:

1. He should compare the quantities of bill with the measurements of M.B.
2. He should ensure that the rates are entered correctly and calculations have been checked arithmetically.
3. When the bill is on a running account, then it should be compared with the previous bill.
4. After the check, the memorandum of payment is prepared and any recoveries which are to be made are shown in it.
5. In the bill, fraction less than half a rupee is left out and half or more than half is treated as full rupee.
6. In case the contract is for completed items of works and according to conditions of the agreement, the contractor is required to obtain certain materials of any description from the government, then it should be ensured that this condition is complied with and the necessary recoveries of the cost of materials supplied to him are made by deduction from the first bill.
7. Before signing the first and final bill or the first bill on a running account, the S.D.O. should ensure that the relevant measurement entries are marked as pertaining to such bill by the person taking the measurements.
8. All quantities entered into the documents from the M.B. on which the payments are to be made should be clearly traceable. The date of measurement, No of M.B. and its page number etc. should be clearly written in the document in space prescribed for it.
9. In states where S.D.O. is authorised for making payments, the fair copies of the bills are signed in accordance with instructions printed on the forms. In cases where divisional officer is required to take measurements himself, he signs the fair copy of the bill as officer preparing the bill.

34.9. PAYMENTS OF BILLS

Usually the divisional officer is the disbursing officer of the division. In case sub divisional officer is authorised for payment of bills, he records a formal pay order, specifying both in words and figures only the net amount, though the payee is required to acknowledge in his acquittance the gross amount payable, inclusive of the recoveries made from the bill. Before recording pay order S.D.O. should examine the bill carefully as explained above.

In case the S.D.O. is not authorised to make payment, then the bill is submitted to the divisional officer with or with out M.B. as prescribed. After due scrutiny the divisional officer authorises the payment.

2. When a bill is prepared for the work or supplies measured, every page containing the detailed measurements should be scored by drawing a diagonal line in red ink. At the time of payment the no of M.B. and its page no., date of voucher etc. should be entered in the abstract of measurement.

3. Payments for work done or supplies made on a running account, ordinarily is made every month. Quantities and amount of each distinct work or supply should be shown separately in the bill except in case of advance payment, in which case quantities need not to be specified. Such payments are treated as payment on account subject to adjustment in the final bill.

4. A separate running account should be maintained in respect of each account. Transactions relating to two or more separate wok estimates should not be brought on the same running account. Thus they are not covered by a single contract.

5. In case an advance payment has been made to a contractor, a printed certificate should be signed by the S.D.O. and the lump sum amount paid. On account of each item should be specified against the item of advance in part I of the bill.

6. In case secured advance is to be allowed by the Divisional Engineer, it should be done in accordance with rules of secured advance as discussed earlier. A detailed account of the advance should be kept in part II of the running account bill.

34.10. RULES FOR PREPARING VOUCHERS

As stated earlier, a voucher is a written document which is kept on record as a proof of payment. After payment and duly acknowledged every bill becomes a voucher. While preparing a voucher following points should be observed.

1. For every payment and repayment of money deposited with the government for any purpose, voucher should be prepared.
2. Printed form should be used for preparing a voucher. In case of non availability of printed form, manuscript prescribed for the form may be used.
3. When a voucher form in other language than the official language is used, a brief extract should be endorsed in the official language under the signature of government servant, stating the amount, name of the payee and nature of payment etc.
4. All vouchers should be filled in and signed in ink.
5. The amount of each voucher should be written both in words as well as in figures, ending with the word only.
6. Corrections, alterations and interpolations must be avoided, but in case it is not avoidable, then these must be attested under the full and dated signatures of the disbursing officer.
7. No document having erasures should be accepted.
8. If an amount has to be corrected, then previous entry should be scored out and the complete amount be re written.
9. No space should be left in between the pay order, so that it may not be misused by interpolation after wards.
10. Every voucher must give the following informations correctly in full.

    (*a*) Name of the work as given in the estimate.

(*b*) Name of the sub head of it. Separate account should be kept for the several component parts.

(*c*) The charges to be recovered and name of the contractor or other person from whom recoverable, the head indicating recoveries should be underlined with red ink.

(*d*) Charges against two major heads should not be included in one voucher.

34.11. CASH

34.11.1. Definitions

1. **Cash.** It includes the legal tender coins, currency notes, cheques and drafts payable on demand and remittance transfer receipts.
2. **Treasury challan.** It is a memorandum which is necessary to present to the treasury while depositing money in the treasury. It clearly shows the nature of payment, name of person depositing it and the government servant or person on whose account the payment is made.
3. **Subsidiary cash book.** It is the record of the division, in which the account of pay and allowances of regular establishment is maintained.
4. **Cash book.** It is one of the most important accounts record of the department. In this book the account of all transactions of every disbursing officer is maintained. The pages of cash book should be machine numbered.

34.12. ITEMS WHICH ARE NOT TREATED AS CASH

Following items are not treated as cash

(*a*) Government securities

(*b*) Postal and service stamps

(*c*) Deposit receipts of non schedule banks

(*d*) Cheques and demand drafts not in favour of self

(*e*) Debentures and bonds accepted as security money.

34.13. PRECAUTIONS DURING CUSTODY OF CASH

1. Every government officer is personally responsible for the public money which he deals and for prompt recording of the transactions of receipts and payments in the prescribed account as well as for the correctness of the account in all respects. Private cash or account in no case should be mixed up with public money or account. The rules should be followed strictly.
2. Public money in the custody of the department should always be kept in a strong treasure chest secured by two locks of different pattern. The keys of both locks of the chest should be kept in the custody of two persons, preferably one set should be kept with the officer incharge and one set with the person operating the chest. The duplicate keys must be kept in the treasury under a sealed cover.

34.14. MODES OF OBTAINING CASH

The drawing and disbursing officer of the department can obtain cash for disbursement in the following two ways.

1. Directly by presenting bill to the treasury. The amount of pay and allowances of government servants of regular establishment can be drawn on bills.
2. By cheques presenting them to the bank or treasury. Generally for all transactions except for drawing pay and allowances of regular establishment cheques are issued.

Generally all disbursements are made by the divisional officer. However sub divisional officer may also be authorised to make payments against expenditures on works etc.

No officer is authorised to draw cheques on treasures situated outside the limits of the state with out making pre-arrangements through A.G., eventhough his jurisdiction may extend beyond these limits.

Similarly a divisional officer is not authorised to draw cheques on any treasury situated out side the limits of his division except with the special sanction of the Accountant General.

34.15. SOURCES OF RECEIPT OF MONEY

Government money may be received from various sources. Some of them are as follows:

(*a*) Sale proceeds of dead and fallen trees

(*b*) sale proceeds of surplus stocks

(*c*) Sale proceeds of unserviceable tools and plants

(*d*) Rent and electric charges of inspection houses

(*e*) Sale proceeds of fruits crops of road side or canal trees or grass on channels etc.

On receipt of any government money by a government officer, it must be entered immediately in the cash book and kept in safe custody. A receipt should be issued to depositor. A revenue ticket should be affixed on the receipt for amounts more than Rs. Five hundred.

34.16. RECEIPTS NOT REQUIRING REVENUE STAMP

In the following cases revenue stamp is not required

(*a*) Receipts on postal money orders

(*b*) Receipts given by railways

(*c*) Receipt given by or on behalf of government

(*d*) Receipt for interest on government securities

(*e*) Receipts for payments made to schedule banks

(*f*) Receipts given by or on behalf of societies registered under the cooperative societies act.

34.17. CASH ACCOUNTS

The cash accounts are maintained in the following records:

1. Cash Book
2. Subsidiary cash book
3. Impress cash account
4. Temporary advance account

34.18. PROCEDURE FOR MAINTAINING CASH BOOK

As stated above, a cash book is the most important accounts record of the department and the account of all transactions of every disbursing officer is maintained in the cash book. Thus the cash book should be filled in very carefully. At the time of writing the cash book, following points must be kept in mind carefully.

1. Every entry must be concise. The number of voucher, date and name of work, should be entered against each item with brief description clearly to indicate the nature of transaction.
2. The amount debitable or creditable to each separate work, head of account, or contractor or other person should be entered separately. The amount required to be posted in the abstract book or schedule of accounts under each head of account should be distinctly indicated for classification for receipts and charges.
3. No payment or receipt other than cash as defined above should be entered in cash book. A deduction made at the time of payment, creditable to a head of account other than that to which the payment itself is debitable should however be entered on the receipt side.
4. Entries should be made continuously and no line should be left blank. If any line is left blank due to the fact that the other side of the folio has been written up, the space should be scored by drawing a diagonal line.
5. Erasures, cuttings, over writings, interpolation etc. must be avoided. If due to unavoidable circumstances cuttings are made, then these cuttings must be initialed with date by the disbursing officer. In no case any entry should be erased.
6. Transactions should be entered as soon as they occur in the order of the occurrence. In case the

officer is out of headquarter being on tour or due to any other official work, the entries should be made as soon as the officer returns to the head quarters and the date of issue of the cheques and date of entry both should be written in the cash book as the numerator and denominator respectively as

$$\frac{\text{date of issue of cheque ———}}{\text{date of entiry in the cash book or register ———}}$$

7. Earnest money received in cash from tenderers with tenders, if to be refunded the same day of the receipt, need not to be entered into the cash book.
8. If the transactions of private cheques are large enough, then these may be entered in a "Register of cheques received and adjusted", and only the totals of daily receipts and remittances should be entered in the cash book.
9. When a cheque is drawn to replenish the amount in the chest, the number of cheque and its amount should be entered on the payment side and the amount is entered on the receipt side as "cash received from treasury".
10. When a previously drawn cheque is required to be cancelled, the amount should be shown as minus entry and a cross reference is made in the cash book against the original entry of the cheque.
11. The validity of cheque expires after six months. If a cheque is not drawn with in six month's period, then a new cheque has to be issued in lieu of the time barred cheque. When a new cheque is to be issued in lieu of time barred or lost cheque, its entry should be made in the cash book in red ink on the date of issue of this cheque. A counter reference should also be made against the original entry in the cash book. New cheque should be issued after obtaining the "non payment" certificate from the bank.
12. When an imprest or temporary advance is given to a subordinate officer, it should be noted in the cash book with red ink.
13. While submitting the account of an imprest, an abstract of the total amount spent for each work or head of account should be prepared on the reverse of the imprest account and only these totals should be written in the cash book.
14. The amount of unpaid imprest received back is shown on the receipt side with red ink.
15. If any item of imprest account submitted, seems to be objectionable, the item should be entered in cash book as item awaiting adjustment in the imprest account under "miscellaneous work advance", and kept under watch till either objection is removed or the amount deposited by the imprest holder.
16. All payments should be debited immediately to the work or service on account of which they are made.
17. Money advanced to a subordinate for disbursement to labourers etc. should be noted in the cash book as temporary advance with red ink in the similar manner as for permanent imprest made for the first time. After the receipt of certified muster roll with unpaid amount if any, the amount actually paid should be debited to the work or services concerned and the unpaid amount returned is debited in the cash balance. A similar procedure is followed when the disbursing officer takes cash from his chest and takes with him for disbursement.
18. When an advance is made to a government servant from the cash for the journey accompanying the disbursing officer, this amount is not entered as a final transaction in the cash book, but is recorded as temporary advance. This amount forms a part of the cash balance for which the disbursing officer is responsible.

34.19. ACTION REQUIRED WHEN CASH IN CHEST IS FOUND DIFFERENT THAN CASH BOOK

In such situations the cash is recounted and the cash book is also checked thoroughly for any wrong entry or mistake in totals. If any mistake is detected it should be corrected. The cutting should be initialed with date.

In case no mistake is detected, the balance as per cash book should be taken as correct and the following certificates should be recorded in the cash book:

(*a*) In case the cash is found surplus, then a receipt entry is made in the cash book for the difference amount as "To cash found surplus in the chest". Under the head P.W. deposits.

(*b*) In case the cash is found deficient, then a payment entry is made for the difference of amount in the cash book as "cash found deficient in the chest" under head miscellaneous P.W. advances.

34.20. COMMON IRREGULARITIES FOUND IN CASH BOOKS

Generally following irregularities have been noticed in cash books:

1. Transactions are not entered in the cash book in order of their occurrence.
2. Blank spaces are left and not scored by drawing diagonal line with red ink.
3. Corrections or over writings and interpolations are not initialed with date by the disbursing officer.
4. Over writings and erasures are allowed in the cash book.
5. Entries are not verified by the disbursing officer and initialed in token of his having checked the entries.
6. Abnormal delay in the remittance of receipts of government money into the treasury.
7. Entries in the cash book for cash receipts are not compared with the counter foils of the receipt books and initialed in token of their having been verified.
8. Classification not recorded in respect of receipts and payments.
9. Red ink is not used for certain entries for which it is specified.
10. Temporary advance or imprest etc. are not shown in the opening balance.
11. Totals of cheque columns are not tallied with the progressive total of the amounts of cheques drawn during the month as given on the back of the counter foil of the last cheque.
12. Payments of Rs. one thousand are found to have been made in cash instead of cheque.

34.21. IMPREST ACCOUNT

Imprest is a standing advance of a fixed amount of money given to an individual to enable him to make certain petty payments entrusted to his charge by the divisional/sub divisional officer. The amount of imprest is fixed on the basis of actual requirement for current expenses with in a month. Ordinarily imprest account is not granted more than Rs. one thousand.

34.21.1. Payment made from imprest

Following types of payments can be made from imprest:

(*a*) Local or out station purchases not more than Rs. 25/-

(*b*) Petty repairs

(*c*) Payments of railway freight less than Rs. 50/-

(*d*) Miscellaneous petty expenses as cooli charges, cartage etc.

The government servants entrusted with an imprest of fixed amount have to maintain the account in the imprest account form and render it for reimbursement to the competent authority. The form is printed in two folios and bound in book form. The imprest account form is shown in table 34.1.

34.21.2. Procedure of compiling the imprest account

Following procedure is adopted for preparing the imprest account:

1. The amount with which the imprest cash account is opened should be entered in the book in specified column with red ink. If the imprest is received by cheque, then cheque no and its date of issue should be noted in the column specified for it.

Table 34.1. Imprest cash account

Imprest cash book of SHRI________.

Month and date	*Voucher no*	*Transactions*	*Amount of cash payment*	*Total*	*Head of account*

Abstract of charges ________.
Name of work ____________ .
Period _________ From __________ To _________.

2. Payments made from this imprest should be entered daily as and when they are made.
3. The account should be balanced from time to time as per convenience of the imprest holder. It should be balanced at least few days before the monthly closing of cash book of the disbursing officer from whom impress is obtained.
4. The right hand page of the form is cut and sent to the disbursing officer and the counter foil is retained by the imprest holder.
5. The account should be supported by voucher for each payment. The vouchers should be serially numbered.
6. The account should be submitted to the recouping officer. When ever it is to be recouped, increased, decreased or closed.
7. The imprest account contains neither any entry of receipt other than the opening entry of the fixed imprest and the subsequent recoupment of the expenditure, nor any entry of the expenditure other than those paid directly by the imprest holder himself from the imprest.
8. The money received by the imprest holder on behalf of the government is not to be mixed up with his imprest cash or brought into imprest cash book. It should be sent to the nearest superior officer having cash book with an intimation of full particulars of the receipt and date of realisation to enable him to make necessary entries.
9. In case any irregularity is found in the imprest account, the divisional officer is responsible for it.
10. The recouping officer should examine the imprest cash account and the supporting vouchers. He should initial the vouchers with date in token of his approval and record a formal pay order on the account authorising the recoupment.
11. The imprest holder is responsible for the safe custody of the imprest money.

34.22. TEMPORARY ADVANCE

The remittance made by an disbursing officer to his subordinate officer to make certain specific petty payments on a muster roll, or other voucher, pay bills of work charged establishment, which has already been passed for payment by the disbursing officer is called *temporary advance* or *imprest*. The account of temporary advance should be closed as soon as possible. The cash taken out of the chest by the disbursing officer himself to make payments out side head quarter is also treated as a temporary advance. The account of temporary advance is kept in the same way as that of imprest.

The difference between an imprest and temporary advance is shown in Table 34.2.

34.23. CUSTODY OF CHEQUE BOOK AND MODE OF DRAWING MONEY

1. Cheques are obtained directly by the drawing and disbursing officer from the treasury officer by sending a printed requition form duly signed. Only one cheque book can be obtained on a single requition form.

Table 34.2.

Imprest	*Temporary advance*
1. It is an standing or permanent advance of a fixed sum of money.	1. It is an advance given temporarily by the disbursing officer.
2. Payments can be made before obtaining pay orders from the disbursing and recouping officer.	2. Payments are made only after they have been duly passed for payments by the disturing officer.
3. The imprest is recouped from time to time.	3. Temporary advances are not recoupable.
4. The accounts are submitted from time to time and the amount recouped as required. The sanction of the imprest lapses at the close of financial year.	4. The account is tendered after making the payment as soon as possible.

2. On receipt of cheque book from treasury, it should be examined carefully and the leafs or forms are counted and a certificate of count should be recorded on the fly leaf.
3. For each head quarter treasury or sub treasury a separate check book is necessary.
4. Cheques drawn from books obtained from a particular treasury should not be drawn on other treasuries/sub treasuries of other districts.
5. Cheque books should be kept under lock and key in the personal custody of the drawing officer. On transfer, he should hand over these cheque books to his successor and should obtain an receipt for the correct number of unused cheque forms from the relieving officer.
6. Before a cheque book is brought into use, all its cheque forms should be marked by a distinguishing letter.
7. Cheques drawn by a disbursing officer on any treasury should be distinguished by a different letter from those drawn by other disbursing officers of the same division on that treasury and also from those drawn by himself on any other treasury.
8. The disbursing officer should inform the bank or treasury upon which he draws, the number of cheque book brought into use and the number of cheque forms it contains.
9. Every cheque should be written very carefully so that the amount may not be tampered with fraudulently. As per rules a cross entry of the sum, a little in excess of the amount of the cheque should be made.

34.24. PROCEDURES FOR TIME BARRED CHEQUES

Generally a cheque is valid for six months. If it could not be presented for payment with in this period then the cheque becomes *time barred.* A time barred cheque has to be sent back to the drawer, who can revalidate it or can draw a new cheque in lieu of this time barred cheque after destroying it. The facts of the destruction, number and date of the new cheque on the counter foil of the old cheque and number and date of the old cheque on the counter foil of the new cheque should be recorded.

34.25. PROCEDURE FOR CANCELLATION OF A CHEQUE

(*a*) **Cheque is in custody of the drawer.** In case it is required to cancel a cheque the drawer can do so after recording a certificate on the counter foil for its cancellation and the cheque can be destroyed.

(*b*) **Cheque not in custody of the drawer**. In this case the drawer has to request the treasury officer to stop the payment of the cheque. After ascertaining the stoppage of the cheque, the drawer has to make the entry of the amount of cash in his cash book showing this amount as a minus figure on the payment side in the treasury or bank column in the cash book. A cross reference is also to be given in the cash book against the original entry of the cheque.

34.26. ENTRIES TO BE MADE IN RED INK IN THE CASH BOOK

Usually following entries are made in red ink in the cash book:

1. Receipt side

(*a*) Corrections in an entry made in between the lines.
(*b*) Closure of temporary advance.
(*c*) Imprest withdrawn or decreased.

2. Payment side

(*a*) Correction in an entry made in between lines.
(*b*) Grant of an temporary advance or imprest including its enhancement.
(*c*) Issue of a new cheque in lieu of an old cheque.

QUESTIONS

1. Differentiate between the following:
   (*a*) Bill and voucher
   (*b*) Imprest and temporary advance
   (*c*) Standard measurement book and check measurement book
   (*d*) Muster roll and casual labour roll
   (*e*) Secured advance and lump sum advance
2. What points should be kept in mind while preparing a voucher?
3. What points should be checked by a sub divisional officer before signing the bill of a contractor?
4. Enumerate the different kinds of bills and their forms on which they are prepared.
5. Under what conditions an secured advance can be granted to a contractor?
6. Discuss the procedure of preparing a bill.
7. Discuss the rules for preparing voucher.
8. Define cash and discuss the procedure of maintaining a cash book.
9. Discuss the irregularities generally are found in a cash book.
10. Discuss the procedure while dealing with:
    (*a*) Time bared cheque (*b*) Cancelling a cheque
11. Discuss the procedure for compiling the imprest account.

OBJECTIVE TYPES QUESTIONS

1. Identify the correct statement/statements
   (*a*) The payment for supplies or work done by a contractor is made to him at convenient intervals while the final settlement account is done either on completion of work or termination his contract. This account is known as running account.
   (*b*) The last payment on a running account made to a contractor is called final payment.
   (*c*) The payment made on running account to a contractor for work done by him and duly measured is called running payment or payment on account.
   (*d*) Bills passed and entered into the cash book are called vouchers
   (*e*) All are incorrect.
2. Identify the incorrect statement/statements
   (*a*) Advance payment can only be made after the detailed measurements of the work or supplies
   (*b*) Secured advance may be made even with out bringing construction materials on site of work
   (*c*) The secured advance can be made upto 90% on all types of materials
   (*d*) Secured advance may be allowed even if the contractor has already taken such advance
   (*e*) All are correct
   (*f*) All are incorrect
3. The lump sum advance may be paid upto the net value of the bill
   (*a*) 50% (*b*) 65%
   (*c*) 75% (*d*) 90%
4. Identify the incorrect statement/statements
   (*a*) It is not essential to present the treasury challan at the time of depositing money in the treasury
   (*b*) The account of pay and allowances of regular establishment is kept in subsidiary cash book

(*c*) Accounts of all transactions of all disbursing officers of the department are maintained in the cash book
(*d*) It is essential to present the treasury challan at the time of depositing money in the treasury

5. Which of the following items are not treated as cash
   (*a*) Government securities
   (*b*) Postal and service stamps
   (*c*) Deposit receipts of non scheduled banks
   (*d*) Cheques and demand drafts not in favour of self
   (*e*) All of the above
6. Which of the following items do not require revenue stamps to be affixed
   (*a*) Receipt for payments made to scheduled banks
   (*b*) Receipts given by or on half of government
   (*c*) Receipts of postal money orders
   (*d*) Receipts given by railways
   (*e*) All the above
7. Identify the correct statement/statements
   (*a*) Impress is an permanent advance of a fixed amount while temporary advance is given temporarily by a disbursing officer to his subordinate officer
   (*b*) Payments from imprest can be made with out obtaining orders from the disbursing officer while in case of temporary advance prior sanction of payment is essential
   (*c*) Imprest is recoupable while temporary advance is not recoupable
   (*d*) The account of imprest is submitted from time to time while temporary advance account is submitted after making the payment at the earliest
   (*e*) All are correct.
8. The account of pay and allowances of the regular establishment is kept in
   (*a*) Cash book
   (*b*) Subsidiary cash book
   (*c*) Imprest account
   (*d*) Non is correct
9. Common irregularities found in cash book are except
   (*a*) Blank spaces left in between the lines
   (*b*) Red ink is not used for entries for which it is specified
   (*c*) Payments more the than Rs one thousand have been paid in cash instead of by cheque
   (*d*) Blank spaces are not scored by drawing diagonal line in red ink
   (*e*) Corrections and over writings and interpolations are not initialed with date by the disbursing officers
   (*f*) All the above
10. Cash accounts are maintain in the record of
    (*a*) Cash book
    (*b*) Subsidiary cash book
    (*c*) Ampress account
    (*d*) Temporary advance account
    (*e*) All the above
11. What entries are to be made in red ink in the cash book
    (*a*) Corrections in an entry
    (*b*) Closure of temporary advance
    (*c*) Imprest withdrawan or decreased
    (*d*) Issue of new cheque in liue of old cheque
    (*e*) Grant of temporary advance
    (*f*) All the above

ANSWERS:

1. (*e*)	4. (*a*)	7. (*e*)	10. (*e*)
2. (*f*)	5. (*e*)	8. (*b*)	11. (*f*)
3. (*c*)	6. (*e*)	9. (*f*)	

35

Stores

35.1. INTRODUCTION

A major part of expenditure for the execution of different kinds of works in P.W.D. is spent on materials and equipments. Thus to execute the works efficiently, it is essential to store the various types of construction materials and other articles at one or more places of the division. The materials of specified specifications should be arranged well in time before the start of the work.

The divisional officer of the department is responsible for the procurement, safe custody and proper distribution of the store articles. The stores should be protected from deterioration, fire damage and theft etc. Usually the charge of store remains with the sectional officer who is responsible for maintaining the initial records of all receipts and issues of various items of the store, but the ultimate responsibility rests with the divisional officer, who is responsible for proper up keep of all stores of his division.

In case stores are heavy, in that case an store keeper may be appointed by the competent authority. His duties are confined to the safe custody, preservation and issue of store and to maintain proper record of the store under his charge. The general administration of the stores of the division rests with the divisional officer, who is primarily responsible for (*i*) Procurement, (*ii*) Safe custody and distribution according to the requirement of work and, (*iii*) their disposal when rendered surplus or unserviceable.

35.2. CLASSIFICATION OF STORES

According to P.W.D. classification, stores may be classified into the following categories:

1. Stock
2. Tools and plants
3. Road metal
4. Materials charged direct to works

35.3. FUNDAMENTAL PRINCIPLES OF STORES ACCOUNTING

The accounts of stores are based on the fundamental principle that the cost of the acquition of stores is debited to the final head of account or the particular work for which they are required, if this is known. In case the work is not known the amount is debited to the suspense head of account, pending clearance as the material actually is issued. After the issue of material to a specific work, it is debited to the head of account of that particular work.

Thus as per above general rule the expenditure on the supply of all tools and plant for general use in the division is debited to the minor head "Machinery and Equipment" under the major head concerned. Special items of tools and plant which are not required for general use, but for a specific work are debited to that work. Similarly all road metal required for the maintenance of roads is debited to the sub head "maintenance and repairs" under the minor head 'Repairs' (communications), against the sanctioned estimate. However when the road metal is acquired for the construction of a certain road, its cost is debited to the estimate of that road construction.

In the case of other materials also, if purchases are made for general requirements, then the cost is debited to the suspense head "stock" other wise if the material is purchased specially for a particular work, it is debited to that work. Thus different class of stores can be categorised into the following two categories depending how the cost of their procurement is accounted for.

1. Stores debited to suspense head. Under this category stock is placed.

2. Stores debited to the concerned final heads. Under this category following stores are placed:

(*a*) Tools and plant (*b*) Road metal

(*c*) Material charged to work.

35.4. SUSPENSE HEADS

The heads for the temporary booking of transactions are known as *suspense heads*. In public works department any expenditure incurred either for the purchase of materials or for the execution of work is at once is charged to the final head of the expenditure. Some times the final head is not known and thus it is not possible to debit the expenditure to a final head. In such situations the expenditure incurred is charged to a minor head "suspense" under the main head "Expenditure" and kept the expenditure in it till the final head is known. On knowing the head, the amount of the quantity of stores issued or expenditure done on the execution of work is debited to the known head and an equal amount is credited to the suspense head, clearing the suspense head. The minor head 'stock' is a suspense head of account. The materials purchased for general use on works are kept in the stock and their value is charged to the suspense head 'stock' and as soon as materials issued for use on a particular work, their value is debited to the estimate of the work on which materials are used and the suspense head is cleared off by crediting an equal amount in the suspense head "stock".

35.5. SUSPENSE SUB HEADS

The minor head suspense has been divided into the following sub heads:

1. Purchases
2. Stock
3. Miscellaneous advance
4. Workshop suspense

Note: The above rules apply to all class of stores.

35.6. STOCK

For executing different kinds of works, items of common use in construction works as cement, bricks, aggregates, and steel etc. are kept in stores of the division and are issued as and when required for the execution of work. Thus such materials kept in stores are called as *stock*.

35.7. ADVANTAGES OF STOCK KEEPING

Following are the advantages of stock keeping:

1. The articles of general use are readily available and the execution of the work does not suffer.
2. The procedure of procurement of the same material is not repeated for different works.
3. The use of approved materials of specified quality and specifications is ensured.
4. The stock of consumable articles at convenient places in the division ensures smooth progress of the work.
5. A check on the use of inferior quality material in the work is exercised.
6. To purchase materials in bulk is economical than in piece meals. However it should be ensured that quantities of stores purchased should be utilised during a reasonable period of time.

35.7.1. Disadvantage of long storage of materials

Following disadvantages have been found of long storage of materials:

1. Deterioration in the quality of the materials has been observed. The storage of cement for more than 12 months reduces its compressive strength by 50%.

2. Long storage blocks the money which can be used on some other more important work.
3. Long storage results in increased cost of storage and handling.

35.8. RESERVE OF STOCK AND ITS LIMIT

The process of collecting materials in advance of the start of the work is known as *Reserve of stock*, but the materials should not be kept in stores for a unduly long period as it will deteriorate the quality of the material. The maximum limit of amount for the purchase of material and keeping them in the stock of division is fixed every year and is known as *Reserve stock limit.* However in special conditions of emergency the reserve stock limit can be exceeded by S.E. This increased limit is called temporary *Reserve limit.*

35.9. SUB HEADS OF STOCK

The stock is suspense head of account. When a item of stock is purchased, its cost is debited to the suspense head "stock". When the item is issued for use in the work, the cost of the item issued is credited to the suspense head "stock" and debited to the final head of the concerned work.

In order to facilitate the proper maintenance of stock accounts, the various items of similar nature are grouped to gether under different heads, "known as sub heads of stock". All fresh receipts should be posted under the appropriate sub head in the stock register. Following are the various sub heads:

Table 35.1.

S. No.	*Sub head of stock*	*Materials*
1.	Small stores	Screws, nails, bolts and nuts, hinges, handles, tower boths, glass panes etc.
2.	Building materials	Bricks, cement, aggregates, lime, sand
3.	Timber	Sal, deodar, teak, shisham, ply wood, hard boards, chir
4.	Metal	Metal steel bars, rolled steel sections, M.S. flats, iron angles, G.I. sheets expended metal, channel etc.
5.	Fuel	Coal, charcoal, fire wood, kerosine oil.
6.	Painter's store	Paints, Brushes, varnishes, linseed oil, red oxide, turpentine oil etc.
7.	House fittings	Wash basin, water closet, mirrors, pelmets etc.
8.	Miscellaneous stores	Empty bags and drums, bulbs, tree guards, road brushes, D.D. powder etc.
9.	Land, kilns	Coal chimney sheets, cost of hire of land for the manufacturing of bricks is booked under this head
10.	Manufacture	Cost of manufacture in government workshops is booked under this head
11.	Storage	Payment made to chokidar, rent of godown etc are booked under this head.

35.10. STOCK

Usually stock accounts are maintained by sub divisional officer incharge of godown. In the divisional office a separate account of each stock is maintained. These accounts can be classified as follows:

1. Quantity account. In this account number or quantity of materials is accounted.
2. Value accounts. In this account the value of each material is worked out.

35.11. RECEIPT OF STOCK

The stock materials may be received from the following sources:

1. From contractors and suppliers. Most of the supplies are procured from suppliers and contractors.
2. Transfer from other sub divisions, divisions or departments. Supplies from these sources are obtained when the availability of materials exceeds their requirements.
3. Direct from departmental manufacturers. Items like bricks, lime etc. may be manufactured departmentally.

4. Buildings and works. Some items may be obtained by recovery from buildings or works that are dismantled.

35.12. RECORD OF STOCK RECEIVED

All materials when received, must be examined carefully, counted or weighed or measured as the case may be and entered in the receipt register of goods made of specified forms. The authority to receive the materials is given by divisional or sub divisional officer. The pages of goods receipt register are machine numbered. The goods register is filled in triplicate with the help of carbon paper. One copy is retained by the store keeper and the other two copies are sent to sub divisional officer, who sends one copy to divisional officer for record and payment and keeps one copy in sub divisional office for record. The goods receipt sheets are very important accounts record as all payments of goods received are made on the basis of entries in these sheets. Therefore these sheets should b kept very carefully.

An entry of the receipt of goods should also be made in BIN CARD form no. 8 from the goods receipt sheets. The 'bin cards' are kept where materials are stored. The bin cards contain date wise record of the receipts, issues, and balance of each item of the stock. In some states a register of stock receipt and issue is maintained in place of good receipt sheets and bin cards system. The goods receipt sheets and bin cards or goods receipt register form the basic record of stock transaction. Hence should be maintained properly and their safe custody ensured.

35.13. PROCEDURE FOR FILLING STOCK RECEIPTS/ISSUES REGISTER

1. All transactions of receipts and issues are recorded strictly in order of their occurrence as soon as they take place.
2. The names of those articles should be shown for which the transactions have taken place during the month.
3. No space should be left between the lines. The reference of recorded measurements should always be filled against all receipts and issues in column 2. In case the materials are directly issued to works in that case letter D.I. should be written.
4. In case the transaction are light, then receipts and issues both can be shown on one page only. In case of heavy transations the receipts and issues should be shown on separate pages. All transactions of the stock should be closed on a fixed date every month except in March. In March they should be closed on 31st, and immediately after closing, a copy is submitted to the superior officer.
5. All particulars of transaction as to whom issued and head of account etc. should be entered very carefully and they should tally with entries on the indent in case of issues.
6. Articles found surplus in stock should immediately be shown as receipt. In case of shortage, they should be shown as issued by the officer incharge in the register of stock giving reference in column 2 of M.B., number and page on which the entries are recorded.
7. All issues to contractors and other stock holders should be supported by un stamped receipts.

35.14. ISSUE OF STOCK

Materials are issued from stock for the following purposes:

1. For use on works either departmentally or by the contractor.
2. For dispatch to other divisions or departments.
3. For sale to contractors, employees and other out side parties, local bodies etc.

35.14.1. Authority to issue

From stock any material can only be issued after the receipt of indent form No 7 signed by divisional or sub divisional officer. In case the junior engineer has to issue stock materials for the requirements of works under himself, the use of indent is not obligatory. For all other cases the issue of any material with out the proper authority from the competent authority is a serious irregularity.

35.15. RULES FOR PREPARING INDENT AND INVOICE

The indent is prepared on the prescribed form no 7 in triplicate with the help of carbon paper. The duplicate and triplicate copies are sent to the supplying officer. Following points should be kept in mind while filling an indent.

1. Full description, unit of supply and quantity of material indented should be written clearly.
2. The head of account to which the cost of the material is to be debited should be mentioned clearly.
3. When the material is to be issued for the work to be executed departmentally the name of the work as given in the sanctioned estimate should be written clearly. In all other cases, the name of the contractor together with number and date of his work order or contract should be given.
4. For issue materials to other departments or other division or for sale to any other person full details should be given.

35.16. PROCEDURE FOR ISSUE

1. On the receipt of two copies of indent, the supplying officer examines it carefully and signs as a token of approval. In case the indented item is in short supply, then he makes the necessary corrections in both copies of the indent and signs the corrections with date. He also signs at the place provided on the indent form. Then he gets approval by divisional/sub divisional officer as the case may be.
2. Then he prepares an invoice according to the supply to be actually made. He also makes an entry for the issue of materials in the stock register.
3. The two copies of indent are returned to the indenting officer, who makes correction in the original copy and returns the triplicate copy to the supplying officer after obtaining signatures of the receiving officer at the place provided on the indent. It is treated as voucher in support of issue or entry in the register.

The indenting officer makes detailed entries of materials in his M.B. and also records M.B. number and page no in the indent.

35.17. MONTHLY ABSTRACT OF RECEIPTS AND ISSUES

This abstract is prepared on the form of register of stock for receipt and issues. A copy of the transactions in respect of receipt, issues and balance in hand for each item is sent by the sectional officer every month on the last day of the month or on 22nd days of the month to the S.D.O. In this return only those items of the stock are shown which actually are issued or received. The S.D.O. sends the same to the divisional office for the record.

35.18. HALF YEARLY BALANCE RETURN OF STOCK

This return is prepared on form P.W. 9 and maintained in sub divisional office. This form has six sub columns under the head "Receipt" and "Issues". In these heads figures from monthly abstracts for receipts and issues are filled. These returns are prepared from October to March and April to September. These returns of each half year include the articles in stock. If there is no transactions in any particular month or even entire period of six months, then nil receipts and issues are shown. At the end of every six month this return is submitted to the divisional officer for comparision with the half yearly register of stock maintained in the divisional office. On the basis of these returns the storage rates are worked out. These returns give the clear picture of the stores in the division.

35.19. HALF YEARLY REGISTER OF STOCK

This register is maintained in the divisional office and all transaction are posted in it monthly from the stock accounts received from sub divisions for each sub division separately. At the end of six months *i.e.* in March and September every year the balances of this register are compared with the half yearly returns received from different sub divisions. The position of stock after due comparision is written in this register and a copy is sent to the A.G. for audit and scrutiny.

35.20. DEFINITIONS

1. **Invoice.** The list of articles giving price and particulars of the articles is known as invoice.
2. **Storage charges.** The expenditure incurred after the acquision of stores on worked charged establishment for handling and keeping the initial accounts, custody, up keep and maintenance of the stores and godown, yards, losses due to depreciation or wastage etc. is added on a percentage basis to issue rate at the beginning of the year, form a part of the issue price. The expenditure added on percentage basis is called *storage charges.*
3. **Supervision charges.** Charges levied in addition of the book value in respect of stock materials transferred or sold are known as supervision charges. These charges are levied to cover the expenses incurred on stores, which neither have been included in the book value nor in storage charges.
4. **Storage rate.** The percentage rate fixed for levy on all issues of stock to recover the storage charges is known as storage rate.
5. **Issue rate.** At the time of issue of certain quantity of store to the work, the cost fixed per unit of item of the stock of the department for the purpose of calculating the amount creditable to the sub head of work is called issue rate. This rate includes storage and handling charges, but does not include supervision charges.
6. **Market rates.** The cost per unit of an article at which it can be procured from the public market is known as *market rate.*

35.21. FIXING ISSUE RATES

The issue rate is fixed by the divisional officer on no profit no loss basis to the stock account. While fixing the issue rate following costs are taken into account:

1. Original price paid for the article
2. Cost of carriage
3. Storage charges

35.21.1. The issue rate is less than market rate

If the issue rate of an article is found less than the market rate, in such situations following precautions may be taken.

1. The sales and issues to contractors are made at market rates.
2. Issues to other divisions and departments may be made at a higher rate than the issue rate.
3. Restriction on sales or issues out side the division may be imposed by the divisional officer.
4. For the recovery of costs of issues in excess of actual requirement, punitive rates may be provided in the agreement. The excess of materials may be worked out by measurements.

35.22. SALE OF STORES

To recover the charges on account of supervision, storage and contingencies an addition of 10% of the cost of the material is made if the stock materials are sold to the public or other departments. Sales of any material from P.W.D. stores to any employee of the department or to any of his relative or dependent with out specific sanction of the government is irregular.

35.23. DISCREPANCIES OBSERVED IN THE STOCK

In case some discrepancies are observed during the checking of the stock, then junior engineer incharge of the stock should tally the book balances with actual balances. In case the quantity of the article is found is excess, it should at once be taken on stock and should be credited as "revenue receipt" and all shortages should be treated as losses. The losses can not be written off unless the causes of loss fully investigated and approval of the competent authority is obtained. In order to correct the balance, the article found short should be shown as issued and its cost is debited to suspense head "Miscellaneous P.W. advances". The suspense head is cleared off after investigation of the loss under orders from the competent authority.

35.24. LOSSES OF STOCK

In case of damages to the stock, the matter should at once be reported to the higher authorities. In case of theft the matter should be reported to the police in addition to departmental authorities as soon as the theft is detected "Loss of stock estimate" is prepared for all such losses and damages indicating the quantity of stock affected. In the estimate detailed report indicating the circumstances under which the loss occurred should be given. These estimates are sent to S.E. for sanction. Before sending the estimate to S.E. sub divisional and divisional officers should record their comments about the losses after investigating the matter fully. S.E. may sanction the estimate with his comments.

After receiving back the sanctioned estimate, the material is written off from the stock register with reference to the above sanctioned estimate. The cost is either recovered from the official found responsible for the losses or born by the department if losses found purely accidental.

35.25. STOCK TAKING

In order to detect shortages or surplus and to ensure that no stock may remain un utilised for long periods all stores of the division have to be checked regularly at least once a year.

35.26. RULES FOR CHECKING THE STORES

Following rules have been laid for checking the stores:

1. As far as possible checking should be a surprised one *i.e.* with out prior information.
2. Checking of stores means either counting the articles or weighing them or measuring them as the case may be. Mere inspection of stores does not constitute the checking.
3. The subordinate incharge of stores must check all stores every six month and record a certificate to this effect. He should also record the result of his check. He should prepare a half yearly distribution list of stock and yearly distribution list for tools and plants showing the closing balance. These lists should be submitted to sub divisional officer.
4. If the sub divisional officer has checked all stores personally, he should note on each distribution list. 'checked by me". In case he has not checked the stores, then he should write the name of sub divisional officer who did the checking during the previous year or half year.
5. The sub divisional officer must check all stores of his sub division once at least in two years.
6. It is not essential that all stores of a division or sub division are checked at one time only. But while checking the stores of a subordinate, the sub divisional officer must check entire stores under the charge of the subordinate. To detect any difference between the book balance and actual balance, the various stocks of articles should be checked at the same time.
7. If during the check, it is found that certain articles are not likely to be used during the next one year, the list of such articles should be sent to the divisional officer.

35.27. COMMON IRREGULARITIES FOUND IN THE MAINTENANCE OF STOCK ACCOUNT

Following irregularities have been observed in the maintenance of stock accounts:

1. The transactions of receipts or issues of stock are not posted in the register of stock strictly in the order of occurrence and the actual time of remaining in store.
2. The entries of stock receipts are not made in the M.B. and in the stock register at the same time.

3. Posting of materials is not done under the specified head of stock.
4. Names of works and heads of accounts are not entered according to the estimate of the work, which may result in wrong booking of the expenditure.
5. Names of contractors to whom materials have been issued are not shown properly along with the contract agreement number and rate of issue.
6. Accounts are not closed and submitted on due dates.
7. Physical verification of stock balances is not carried out as per laid rules.
8. Un stamped receipts of contractors for issue of stock are not submitted with the monthly abstracts.
9. The book balances do not tally with the actual balances. All surpluses and shortages are not adjusted suitably.
10. All materials received are not examined thoroughly for their quality and serviceability. Their quantity also not measured or weighed.
11. Issues of materials are not supported by correctly prepared indents and duly acknowledgment by the receiving officer.
12. Stocks issued to contractors as recoverable are not indicated distinctly as recoverable in the indent and the stock account.

35.28. TOOLS AND PLANT

For the execution of different kinds of works different types of machinery, equipment, vehicles, instruments and furniture etc. are required. The articles used are known as tools and plant.

35.28.1. Types of tools and plant

Tools and plant can be grouped in two categories as follows:

1. General or ordinary tools and plant. Tools and plant required in the division for the general use are classified in this category. The cost of these tools and plant is charged to the minor head "tools and plant".
2. Special machinery and equipment. Machinery and equipment required for special purposes is known as special machinery and equipment. These are procured for specific works. Cranes, tar boiler, compaction machines etc. come under this category. These are not required for general use in the division. Their cost is charged to the concerned work.

35.29. SUB HEADS OF TOOLS AND PLANT

In central public works department tools and plant are sub divided into the following sub heads:

1. Plant and machinery
2. Scientific instruments and drawing materials
3. Tools
4. Navigation plant
5. Camp equipment
6. Live stock
7. Furniture etc.

In some states tools and plant are grouped in sub heads as follows:

Table 35.2.

1. *Plant and machinery* (P)	*Example*
(*a*) Fixed	Batching plant, cooling plant, lathe, shaper, welding and milling machines etc.
(*b*) Movable	Crane, blower, pumps, vibrators, portable welding machine etc.
(*c*) Locomotive and rolling stock	Engine, wagons, coaches, trollies etc.
(*d*) Vehicles	Jeeps, trucks, tankers etc.
(*e*) Navigation and boat bridge equipemnt	Boats, cables, tugs etc.
(*f*) Road making equipment	Road roller, tar boiler, spraying plant, bitumen and bajri mixing plant etc.

2. *Tools* (T)	
(*a*) Fixed	Lathes, drills, saw etc.
(*b*) Movable	Jack hammer, shovel etc.
(*c*) Hand tools	Chisel, plier, wrench, pick axe etc.
3. *Scientific apporatus and instruments* (S)	
(*a*) Scintific apparatus	Thermometer, beakers, viscometer, pipette etc.
(*b*) Mathematical and drawing instruments	Pentagraph, planimeter, drawing borad, set square, compass, scales etc.
(*c*) Survey instruments	Compass, plane table, levels, theodolite, chain etc.
(*d*) Electric instruments	Electric motors.
(*e*) Meters	Water meters, Electric meters, strain meters etc.
(*f*) Other Engineering instruments	Stabilizers, voltmeters, current meters etc.
4. *Furniture* (F)	
(*a*) Office	Chairs, office tables, waste paper baskets etc.
(*b*) Residence and rest houses	Towel stand, wash basin stand, cots, chairs etc.
(*c*) Camp equipments	Tents, steel chairs, folding tables, tents etc.
5. *Hospital equipment* (H)	
(*a*) Furniture	Operation table, dentist chair etc.
(*b*) Plant (Equipment)	X-ray plant, forceps, stcthescope, syringe, measureing glass.
6. Live stock (L)	Horses, Elephants, Donkey, Camels.

35.30. ACCOUNT OF TOOLS AND PLANT

1. Of all types of tools and plant only the numerical account is kept in each sub division or division as a whole.
2. After the completion of a work, the accounts of tools and plant have to be maintained untill they are transferred or having become unserviceable are written off by the competent authority or they are actually sold out.
3. Tools and plant may be given on rent to contractors, local bodies or to sister departments. In such situations it has to be ensured that the articles are returned with out unnecessary delays and in good condition.
4. Same rules of numerical account is also applicable to imperishable articles such as type writers, furnitures and crockery etc. of rest and inspection houses, surgical instruments and furniture of hospitals etc., whether they have been charged to heads of accounts other than tools and plant or received free of cost.

35.31. RECEIPT AND ISSUE OF TOOLS AND PLANT

1. **Receipt of tools and plant.** On receipts of tools and plant they should be counted and examined carefully and their record is kept is prescribed form 13. The receipt is prepared in triplicate. One copy is retained by the store incharge and the two copies are sent to sub divisional officer, who retains one copy for his record and sends the other copy to the divisional officer for payment.
2. **Issue of tools and plant.** All tools and plant are issued on the receipt of requisition known as tools and plant indent on form 14. The indent should be signed by divisional or sub divisional officer. The indent should be prepared in triplicate by the indenting authority. The supplying authority or sub division makes appropriate entries as to the actual issues and sends one copy to the divisional officer and retains other copy for posting in the tool and plant ledger.

A consolidated account for twelve months ending september of all transactions of receipt, issues and balances in respect of tools and plant is maintained in sub divisional office in form no. 15. This form is known as tools and plant ledger form. The form has three parts, part one for articles in hand, pat two, for articles given on loan or sent out for short duration and part three for shortages awaiting adjustments.

35.32. PAYMENT FOR SUPPLY OF TOOLS AND PLANT

Payments for the supply of tools and plant are made on the similar basis as those for stock articles. The claim is verified in the divisional office on the basis of entries made in the tools and plant receipt sheets.

35.32.1. Physical Verification

The physical verification of tools and plant is done in the same way as for stock. However the articles found short are indicated in the tools and plant ledger by making a entry in red ink, but with out making any entry in the quantity column. The articles found short are continued to be recorded in the ledger till the loss is adjusted by way of recovery or written off.

35.33. DIFFERENCE BETWEEN THE ACCOUNTS OF STOCK AND TOOLS AND PLANT

Table 35.3.

S. No.	*Tools and Plant*		*Stock*
1.	There is no consumable articles.	1.	There are consumable articles.
2.	The value of article purchased is charged. (*a*) To tools and plant in case of ordinary tools and plant (*b*) To the work concerned in case of special equipment and machinery.	2.	The value is charged to the suspense head "stock".
3.	Only quantity accounts are maintained	3.	Both quantity and value accounts are maintained.
4.	The register is closed every year ending 30 th September	4.	The register is closed half yearly ending 30th September and 31st March.
5.	Articles found surplus continue to be there in part I of the register. The shortages are entered in part III and continued till recovered or written off. Loaned articles or articles sent for repair etc. are entered in part II.	5.	Articles found short are immediately issued to work from stock and the value of the article is debited to miscellaneous P.W. advances. The suspanse head is cleared under the orders of the competent authority.
6.	The articles found surplus are entered as receipt, but do not affect value of account.	6.	The articles found surplus are entered as receipt of stock and its value is credited to the head "revenue".
7.	For unserviceable articles, survey report is prepared.	7.	For damaged articles estimate of losses is prepared.

35.34. ROAD METAL

It is an important material for the construction and maintenance of roads. It is stacked along the road side. Its quantity account is maintained in the divisional and sub divisional offices in form no 16. This form is submitted monthly by the sectional officer. The registers of divisional and sub divisional officer are filled in on the basis of this form. This form indicates the details of issue of material and its balance per km length. The payment of road metal is made on the basis of measurement. The method of measurement, its entries in M.B. and related matters have been discussed in chapter 33 "works accounts".

35.35. RULES FOR UP KEEP OF ROAD METAL RETURN

Following rules should be followed for the up keep of road metal return:

1. The statement or return of road metal shows kilometer wise position of receipt, issue or disposal and balance of road metal of each kind as kankar, or stone metal.
2. All metal stacked along road side should be entered after measurement in the receipt column of this statement against the kilometer to which the transaction relates. To enter the material in this form,

it is not necessary that it should have been paid. It is immaterial whether the payment of the measured materials has been made or not. Even unpaid metal if measured should be entered.

3. In case the metal has been paid, then its voucher number and in case it has not been paid then M.B. number and its page number should always be quoted in support of all receipts and issues.
4. Usually all receipts and issues should be supported by measurements as recorded in the regular manner in the M.B. Some times a separate measurement may be kept for this purpose.
5. In each kilometer, the balance is shown irrespective of any transactions have been made during the month or not.
6. Book balances should be carried forward except where the actual balance exceeds the book balance. In case the actual balance exceeds the book balance, then the actual balance should be carried forward. In case of shortage, the book balance continues to be carried forward and a remark be made with red ink in the remark column about the shortage. After recovery of cost or receipt of sanction of written off after making a survey report, the shortage is adjusted as an issue and a entry with red ink is made in the remarks column giving a reference to the entry when the shortage was detected.
7. Sectional officer, sub-divisional/divisional officer enter the actual balances found by them in the statement. The sectional officer who checks the material first fills in the column for actuals, where as other officers fill measurements checked by them in remark column. All officers should initial the entries of their checks with date.
8. Generally separate statements are kept for metal collected for annual repair, petty repairs or renewals etc.

35.36. USE OF ROAD METAL RETURNS

Road metal returns have been found useful as follows:

1. It gives the idea of balance of road metal kilometer wise.
2. These balances are found useful for assessing the requirements for the next year.
3. This return also indicates the tendency of gangamen to work in a particular section near the inhabited area where they get better facilities.
4. In any particular section, nil balance for a long period indicates the negligence in the repair work of the gang and carelessness on the part of the sectional officer and sub divisional officer, *i.e.* no repair work has been done in that section since long. Senior officers should pay attention to these lapses.
5. This return also indicates the excess use of metal in any section. The use of large quantity of metal in petty repairs on a newly constructed road is objectionable and it should be checked.

35.36.1. Other materials accounted as road metal

Following materials are accounted in a similar way as road metal:

1. Coal tar
2. Pitch
3. Asphalt
4. Proprietary road surfacing materials stocked for maintenance estimates and for minor estimates for renewal of roads. Their returns are submitted on form no 16 along with the return of other road metals.

35.37. METHOD OF ROAD METAL CHECKING

The check measurements of road metal are recorded by Executive/Assistant Engineers in their note books, instead of their M.B. In public works department a note book is an official prescribed record book for general use. This is always carried by every officer when on duty and notes on works are recorded in this book. The pages of this note book are machine numbered. There are certain rules for its up keep.

The check measurements of road metal are noted in note book as no payments are made on the basis of these measurements. In case the measurements are entered in the M.B., for crossing the M.B. page the other adjustment or payment is necessary. In note book against the entry of actual, the reference of the note book, and its page number voucher no or M.B. number and its page no is always entered in the column. The note books are seen at the time of inspection of the divisional officer.

35.38. SCHEDULE OF RATES

It is a record kept in the divisional office in form no. 17. In this record book the lowest rates at which the road metal can be supplied to the road side through out the division are noted. These rates are revised from time to time.

35.39. MATERIALS ISSUED TO WORKS

For the execution of any work, materials at the site in sufficient quantities are provided either from stock or by purchase or transfer from other works etc. Thus the issue of materials to the works can be divided into two categories as follows:

35.40. MATERIALS ISSUED TO CONTRACTOR

Materials may be issued to the contractor under the following conditions:

1. When the supply of imported materials have to be arranged by the government. The cost of materials and the time taken in their arrangement by the government is comparatively less. In situations when materials are to be supplied by the government or department, the contractor arranges labour and other local materials needed.
2. When it is desired to utilize the existing stock of materials, the condition of supply of material by the department is inserted in the contract of work.
3. In situations of short supply of the construction material in the open market, the material will be available at higher rates in the black market or in case the material is not available easily in the market, department agrees to supply the construction material to the contractor.

35.40.1. Issued direct to work

When the works are executed departmently or the contractor has to supply the labour only materials are issued directly to the works.

35.41. CONDITIONS FOR ISSUE OF MATERIALS TO THE CONTRACTOR

Following points should be specified clearly at the time of issuing materials to the contractor:

1. Full description of the materials to be supplied by the government for use on works.
2. The place of delivery.
3. The rates including storage charges if any to be charged from the contractor for each item.
4. The contractor shall be responsible for obtaining from the government all materials needed for the work and for making payments there of at the rates specified by deduction from the bill.
5. The rates specified should be specific and clear. The use of vague language should be avoided as "at stock rates".
6. No accidental or carriage charges shall be borne by the government for moving the materials beyond the place of delivery agreed upon.
7. Contractor should not be allowed to take delivery of articles required for the work direct from the firm as it may lead to fraud.
8. The contractors should not be given stores in bulk long before they are actually required. In such cases there are chances of their misuse and pilferage. Thus the issue of stores should be regulated and restricted to the actual requirements over a reasonable period of time.

35.42. ISSUE OF MATERIALS WITHOUT PROVISION IN CONTRACT AGREEMENT

1. As a general rule no other material except for those agreed upon in the agreement of contract

should be supplied to the contractor for use on works. However sub divisional officer may waive this restriction in respect of petty materials and stocks not exceeding a fixed amount specified in any month for any contract may be issued. For such issues, full issue rates should be charged.

2. If after the execution of a contract, contractor desires to get material from government stocks which are not provided in the contract. In such situations the materials may be issued with the written permission of the Divisional Engineer. In this situation the Divisional Engineer specifies the rates to be charged for the materials at the place of delivery, where the materials are stored. These rates should be either prevailing rates at the time of issue or issue rates which ever is higher.
3. Issue of stock materials to the contractors for bonafide use on works are exempted from 10% surcharge.

35.43. SURPLUS MATERIALS

Materials remained unused after the completion of the work is known as surplus material. It is the property of the contractor. The materials procured by the contractor whether from the government department or from open market, government is not bound to take them back either after the completion of the work or termination of contract. However, if required for use on other works in progress, government may take back such materials by special arrangement at the prevailing market rates. If the materials were originally supplied by the government, the price allowed to the contractor can not exceed the cost charged from the contractor. Though the materials is the property of the contractor, but he is not at liberty to remove them from the site with out the written permission of the Executive Engineer.

35.43.1. Disposal of surplus materials

Surplus materials can be disposed off as follows:

1. Materials issued to work in excess of the requirement can be transferred to stock, provided they are serviceable and certain to be required for used.
2. If the surplus materials are not likely to be of any use with in a reasonable time, then no credit is allowed to a work on account of surplus materials.
3. A list of all surplus materials is maintained in the sub divisional and divisional offices as a supplement to the half yearly stock return unless S.E. considers it unnecessary.
4. Materials retired to stores or transferred to other works are priced at the current market rates. If there is any loss due to this valuation, it is borne on work, to which these materials were originally issued.
5. In case of works which have been completed or stopped, all surplus materials at their sites are transferred.
6. The above rules do not apply to those surplus materials which originally procured by the contractors themselves or were issued to them and charged to accounts. The disposal of such materials is governed as discussed under article 35.40 above.

35.44. MATERIALS ISSUED DIRECT TO WORKS

In all cases of materials issued direct to work, should be brought to book as soon as received as shown below in Table 35.4.

Table 35.4.

S. No.	*Source of receipt of material*	*Head of account to be credited*	*Value to be credited*	*Mode of adjustment of cost*
1.	Stock including manufacture	Stock	At issue rate.	Through stock account at the end of the month.
2.	Transfer from an other work	Work concenred	At valuation discussed under article 35.40.1.	By a special transfer entry prepared.

S. No.	Source of receipt of material	Head of account to be credited	Value to be credited	Mode of adjustment of cost
3.	Transfer from an other division or deparment	Purchase	At rates purchased by division or dept conconed.	– do –
4.	Supplier	– do –	At rates payable to the suppliers as per contract.	– do –

35.45. VERIFICATION OF UN USED BALANCES

The balances of un used materials charged direct to works should be verified as follows:

1. At least once a year as in the case of ordinary stores.
2. On the completion of work. On or before the completion of work when no more materials are required for the construction, steps should be taken to dispose off all the surplus materials by transfer or sale.
3. In case the gazetted officer or subordinate officer incharge of work is transferred before the accounts of the work are closed, then the relieving officer along with the relieved officer should check the unused materials at site.
4. In the following circumstances the verification of balances is not necessary at the close of the year.
   (*a*) If the work is not in progress for more than 3 months.
   (*b*) The accounts of work are expected to be closed with in 3 months.
   (*c*) The balances were verified during the year.

35.46. MATERIALS AT SITE ACCOUNT

In the case of minor works the cost of materials issued to works is treated as a final charge and no detailed account in form no 35 of the materials is necessary. The sub divisional officer is required to make suitable arrangements to exercise control on the use of material at the work site.

In case of major estimates, a detailed account of materials issued to work or returned from the work is kept under suspense head "Materials". The object of keeping a detailed account is to keep a watch on the total issue of each kind of material in comparision with the estimated requirements. The detailed account of material issued to work is known as the *material at site account*. The account is maintained in the register of material at site account. Form no 35 shows the following information separately for each material.

(*a*) The estimated requirement (*b*) Issue rate
(*c*) Receipts, issues, balances every month (*d*) Net issues at the end of each month

After the completion of the work, the theoretical calculations are made using authorised formula to know the quantities of materials used on each sub head for the quantity of work executed. The quantities are recorded in part I of the register showing the clearance of the suspence head "Materials" form no. 38. Part II of the form shows the surplus/deficit as per actual consumption and theoretical calculations. This also indicates the explanation of surplus/deficit of material consumption. If the difference is significant, the reasons should be inquired into and suitable action is taken as per rules. Part III of the form is a statement of disposal of un used material remained at site as per material at site accounts.

35.47. DISPOSAL OF UN USED MATERIAL

The un used materials may be disposed of as follows:

1. Materials may be transferred to stock, provided they are serviceable and are likely to be required for other works.
2. The materials may be transferred to other works in progress provided they are required.
3. Sale of items of materials that are no more required or are unfit for use.

35.48. DIFFERENCE BETWEEN STOCK, TOOLS AND PLANT, ROAD METAL AND MATERIAL AT SITE ACCOUNT

Table 35.5.

S. No.	*Stock account*	*Tools and plant account*	*Road metal account*	*Material at site account*
1.	Both quantity and value accounts are maintained.	Only quantity accounts are maintained	Only quantity accounts are maintained.	Only quantity accounts are maintained
2.	Cost charged to suspense head "stock".	Cost charged: 1. To tools and plant in case of ordinary tools and plant. 2. In case of special tools and equipment cost is charged to the work concerned.	Cost charged to repairs communications or to the estimate of road construction.	Cost charged to suspense account. "Materials" in the account of the work concerned.
3.	Accounts are closed yearly.	Accounts are closed yearly.	Monthly statements are submitted to the divisional officer.	Accounts are closed on completion of work.
4.	Losses are shown as issues in the quantity record and the value credited to stock account by debit to miscellaneous public works advances.	Losses continue to be borne on accounts till recovered or written off.	Losses continue to be borne on accounts till recovered or written off.	Losses are accounted for as losses of stock.
5.	Items found surplus are taken on stock and their value credited to "Revenue".	Items found surplus are shown as receipts, but do not affect value of accounts.	Items found surplus are treated as surplus in stock.	Items found surplus are treated as surplus in stock.

QUESTIONS

1. Give the classification of public works department stores.
2. Discuss the fundamental principles of stores accounting.
3. What is a suspense head? Give its classification.
4. Why is it essential to have a store in a division?
5. What is meant by stock? Discuss its sub heads.
6. Discuss the procedure for keeping records of receipts.
7. Discuss the method of stock taking.
8. Describe common irregularities found in the maintenance of stock account.
9. What action you would suggest in the following cases:
   (*a*) Some stock is found surplus and some stock short
   (*b*) Some materials are not likely to be used with in next one year.
   (*c*) Some cement bags have been found set
10. Explain the following terms:
    (*a*) Summary report
    (*b*) Reserve store limit
    (*c*) Unstamped receipt
    (*d*) Issue rate
    (*e*) Market rate
    (*f*) Supervision charges
11. How tools and plant classified? Explain with examples.
12. How the account of tools and plant maintained?
13. Discuss the receipt and issue procedure for tools and plant.
14. Explain the difference between the accounts of tools and plant and stock.

15. Define road metal and discuss rules for up keep of road metal return.
16. Under what conditions materials may be issued to the contractor?
17. Discuss the procedure of disposal of surplus materials.
18. Discuss the conditions under which it is necessary to maintain a material at site account.

OBJECTIVE TYPES QUESTIONS

1. For the safe custody and proper distribution of stores responsible is
   (*a*) Superintending Engineer (*b*) Executive/divisional Engineer
   (*c*) Sub divisional officer (*d*) Junior Engineer
2. Usually materials are not stored at
   (*a*) Circle head quarter (*b*) Divisional head quarter
   (*c*) Sub divisional head quarter (*d*) May be scattered at many places
3. Identify the incorrect statement/statements
   (*a*) Suspense head is used for temporary booking of transactions
   (*b*) Suspense head is used for permanent booking of transactions
   (*c*) In P.W.D. the receipt obtained from the contractor at the time of issue of stores is called unstamped receipt
   (*d*) Materials such as cement and bricks in the P.W.D. stores are known as stock
4. Identify the correct statement/statements
   (*a*) Stock can be issued for use on works to be executed departmentally or through contractor
   (*b*) Stock can be issued for dispatch to other departments or divisions
   (*c*) Stock can be issued for sale to contractors, local bodies and others
   (*d*) All are correct
5. The subordinate incharge of stores should check all stores every
   (*a*) 12 months (*b*) 9 months
   (*c*) 6 months (*d*) 3 months
6. Identify the correct statement/statements
   (*a*) In case of tools and plant only quantity accounts are maintained where as in case of stock both value and quantity accounts are kept
   (*b*) Tool and plant are non consumable articles, where as stock articles are consumable
   (*c*) In case of tools and plant the value of article is charged to tools and plant or to the concerned work where as in case of stock the value of article is charged to suspense head "stock".
   (*d*) All are correct
   (*e*) None of the above is correct
7. Identify the correct statement/statements
   (*a*) The check measurements of road metal are entered or recorded in note book
   (*b*) The check measurements of road metal are recorded in M.B.
   (*c*) The payment of road metal is made on these check measurements
   (*d*) Coal tar and asphalt etc. are not accounted as road metal
8. Identify the correct statement/statements
   (*a*) In case of minor works the cost of materials issued to work is treated as final charge and no detailed account is kept
   (*b*) In case of major works a detailed account of materials issued to work or returned from work is kept under suspense head "Materials".
   (*c*) The detailed account of material issued to the work is known as the material at the site account
   (*d*) All are correct
9. Identify the incorrect statement/statements
   (*a*) Standard measurement books are numbered serially
   (*b*) Standard measurement books are used for making payments of new works
   (*c*) Detailed measurements in respect of works and supplies are not recorded in ordinary M.B. but in check measurement book
   (*d*) All measurements books are reviewed every six month in September and March.
   (*e*) All are correct
   (*f*) All are incorrect.

10. Which of the material is not treated as road metal
    (*a*) Asphalt (*b*) Coal
    (*c*) Coal tar (*d*) Pitch
11. The issue rate of a article does not includes the costs
    (*a*) Cost of carriage (*b*) Supervision charges
    (*c*) Storage charges (*d*) Original price paid
12. Storage charges include
    (*a*) Original cost (*b*) Handling and upkeep charges
    (*c*) Maintenance charges (*d*) Cost of losses
    (*e*) All the above
13. The check measurements of road metal are recorded in
    (*a*) M.B. (*b*) Muster roll
    (*c*) Prescribed note book (*d*) Ordinary note book
    (*e*) Not necessary to note these measurements
14. In the maintenance of accounts irregularities found are
    (*a*) Posting of materials is not done under the specified head of stock
    (*b*) Accounts are not closed and submitted on due dates
    (*c*) Physical verification of stock balances is not carried out as per specified rules
    (*d*) Materials received are not properly examined for their quality and serviceability
    (*e*) All the above
15. Identify the correct statement/statements
    (*a*) The storage rates are worked out on the basis of half yearly returns
    (*b*) Half yearly returns indicate the clear picture of stores in the division
    (*c*) In storage charges an expenditure on percentage basis is added to the initial cost
    (*d*) The list giving the name, price, and particulars of the articles is known as invoice
    (*e*) All are correct
16. Identify the correct statement/statements
    (*a*) The materials purchased for general use on works are kept in stock and their value is charged to suspense head 'stock'
    (*b*) Materials of common use in construction are called as 'stock'
    (*c*) The process of collecting materials in advance of start of work is called reserve of stock
    (*d*) Materials from stock can only be issued after the receipt of indent
    (*e*) All are correct
17. Stores debited to their final heads are
    (*a*) Road metal (*b*) Tool and plant
    (*c*) Material charged to work (*d*) All the above

ANSWERS:

1. (*b*)	5. (*c*)	9. (*f*)	13. (*c*)	17. (*d*)
2. (*a*)	6. (*d*)	10. (*b*)	14. (*e*)	
3. (*b*)	7. (*a*)	11. (*b*)	15. (*e*)	
4. (*d*)	8. (*a*)	12. (*e*)	16. (*e*)	

36
Organisation

36.1. INTRODUCTION

A large group of persons or associations of persons united to achieve a common goal and defining the responsibilities and establishing relationship with each other is known as an *organisation.* For better performance every business needs an organisation. For every business three elements namely man, material and machinery are essential. Organisation is a coordination link between man, material and machinery in such a way that maximum output is achieved at ease and efficiently with total minimum cost. Hence organisation is a mechanism of clearly demarcating the authority, responsibility and coordination to achieve the common goal and to produce the cheapest products of better quality.

For executing a construction project the coordinated efforts of all the three wings namely administration, management and organisation are needed. Administration lays down the general policies. These policies are executed by the management with the help of the organisation. Thus organisation is the mechanism or machinery through which the coordination is brought out between the administration and the management.

The development of a sound organisational pattern should be such that the major responsibilities are born by the top management in any group of activities. The need of the organisation arises out of the fact that a manager at any level can manage functions of a limited number of persons efficiently. This limitation is known as the span of the management. This concept of span leads to a system of organisation, where each manager supervises and manages the work of a limited number of persons under his direct control.

36.2. STRUCTURE OF AN ORGANISATION

The organisational structure of an organisation is the network of relationship between the various positions of that organisation. It deals with the over all organisational arrangements in the enterprise. A clear understanding of an organisational structure will be helpful in making more frequent detailed adjustments in the organisational arrangements.

It is a common experience of the management consultants that majority of problems brought to them arose due to the defective organisational structure. Thus to remove the defects and make the organisation more effective a through and systematic study of its structure is essential. The efficient functioning of an organisation is possible only if each member of the organisation understands the following elements fully.

(*a*) The goal of the Organisation
(*b*) His duties and responsibilities
(*c*) Delegation of authority
(*d*) To whom one is responsible
(*e*) Who is to work with whom

36.3. GENERAL PRINCIPLES OF FORMING AN ORGANISATION

For any organisation to be effective, its has to follow certain principles. Scholars in the field of management have identified the following principles important for any organisation.

1. Span of management
2. Scalar principle
3. Delegation of authority and responsibility
4. Unity of command
5. Contact
6. Job definition
7. Increasing organisational relationship
8. Communication

36.3.1. Span of management

As already explained span of the management is the small number of workers which a manger has to supervise. Thus for a sound organisation the span of the management should be small so that a manager can supervise their work efficiently. Too small a number will lead to non utilization of full time and energy of the manager, on the other hand a large number will lead to difficulty to exercise proper control. The number of subordinates that can be supervised efficiently by a manager depends upon the following factors.

(*a*) Capacity of individual to work
(*b*) Nature of work
(*c*) Definite and clear responsibilities
(*d*) Place of work

Thus the ratio between supervisor and subordinate may vary from 1:4 to 1:5 at higher level of management and 1:15 to 1:20 at lower level of management.

36.3.2. Scalar principle

When the level of authority arranged in structure from the chief executive at the top to the workers at the bottom, the system is known as *scalar principle*. This principle holds that each successive level down wards represents a decreasing amount of authority. Consequently the position holders at each such levels have a lower status. In other words in this principle a line of authority from top to bottom results in efficient working.

36.3.3. Delegation of authority and responsibility

1. Authority. For performing a job properly, it is essential that every body must know his task and powers or authority clearly. When ever a person is assigned any task, he should be given sufficient powers to achieve his task.

2. Responsibilities. It is the obligation of a subordinate to perform any task given to him by the superior. Thus in order to exercise effective control over the work, it is necessary to fix the responsibilities of all concerned by the higher management. Thus the authority and responsibility both go together. Unless a person is given necessary authority to perform certain duties or job, he can not be held responsible for his failures.

(*a*) Aspects of delegation process. Following are the aspects of delegation process:

(*i*) Assignment of duties by an executive to his immediate subordinate.

(*ii*) Granting of necessary authority to his immediate subordinates to make commitments, use of resources and to take other actions to perform his duties.

(*iii*) To fix responsibility of each subordinate executive for the satisfactory performance of the job.

(*b*) Principles related to delegation. Following principles are related to delegation:

(*i*) Responsibility can not be delegated.

(*ii*) Avoid duel subordination.

(*iii*) Avoid coequality of authority and responsibility.

36.3.4. Unity of Command

Under this principle, each employee should know clearly to whom he is answerable and who are answerable to him. The principle under which one person has to report only to one boss is known as the *unity of command*. At each level there should be one boss. This establishes definite line of command. In this system there is no confusion and instructions are understood clearly.

36.3.5. Contact

The organisation should allow complete coordination of each branch of work. The performance of each worker of every unit should be economically related to all units keeping in view the policies of the organisation.

36.3.5. (*a*) Unity of assignment

Functions of similar jobs in different departments should be related with in the organisational structure. Functions assigned to each position should be adjustable which reasonably demand equal skill. While assigning the job, following points should be kept in mind.

(*i*) Few jobs should be assigned to an individual, preferably one job at a time.

(*ii*) Assignments of similar nature in different departments should be more or less of the same skill, so that workers may be interchanged if need arises.

(*iii*) Assignments of an individual should be of similar nature and few in number.

36.3.6. Job definition

The work amongst the workers should be allotted very carefully on the basis of their skill, experience, and ability to do that work. For this purpose department must have following informations for identifying the job:

(*a*) Name of the job
(*b*) Code of the job
(*c*) Code number of job if any
(*d*) Jobs relationship
(*e*) Shift if any
(*f*) Name of department and the section in which the job is to be performed.

36.3.7. Interrelationship

The organisational structure should clearly show the relation between superior, equal and subordinate. Each employee of the organisation should known his relative position, his superior boss and subordinates in the organisation.

36.3.8. Communication

In any organisation the number of supervisory staff must be as small as possible, so that the line of communication for passing on information and instructions from top to lower level workers is the shortest and the temptation of "short circuit" the system by jumping the supervisory level is done away with.

36.3.9. Flexibility

The organisation should be flexible to allow some changes and expansions etc. where ever necessary and it should be capable of adjusting its urgent demands. Further a good organisation should be capable to control wastage of labour, money, and material. It should minimise the labour trouble, increase production and improve the quality of production.

36.4. CHARACTERISTICS OF AN ORGANISATION

Following are the characteristics of an organisation:

1. It should have a common goal.
2. It should clearly fix the activities and responsibilities for everyone in the organisation and associated with it.
3. It should have a set structure and there should be good coordination between different departments of the organisation. In different departments there should be a set of personnel.

36.5. TYPES OF ORGANISATIONS

The distribution of authority and responsibility in any undertaking amongst its members depends upon the type and magnitude of the work involved. Depending upon the manner in which the authority and responsibilities in an undertaking are distributed, the organisational set up can be divided into the following categories.

1. Line or military organisation
2. Line and staff organisation
3. Functional organisation
4. Matrix organisation

36.6. LINE OR MILITARY ORGANISATION

This is the earliest, simplest and most important form of organisation. In this type of organisation, the authority descends from the top of the structure to its bottom level step by step through a down ward delegation of authority. All major decisions are taken by the executives at the top and passed on to their immediate subordinates for necessary action at their level. Thus a direct relationship of authority and responsibility is established between the superiors and subordinates.

This type of organisation is based upon earlier military formation. As in the army, commander in chief has full control over the entire army of the country through his major generals and area commanders and so on. Exactly the same pattern *i.e.* line organisation is followed in undertakings. The same pattern of organisation is followed in public works departments as shown in Fig. 36.1.

36.6.1. Advantages of Line Organisation

1. It is simple to work and easily understood by the employees.
2. It is most effective and economical.
3. There is unity of authority and control.

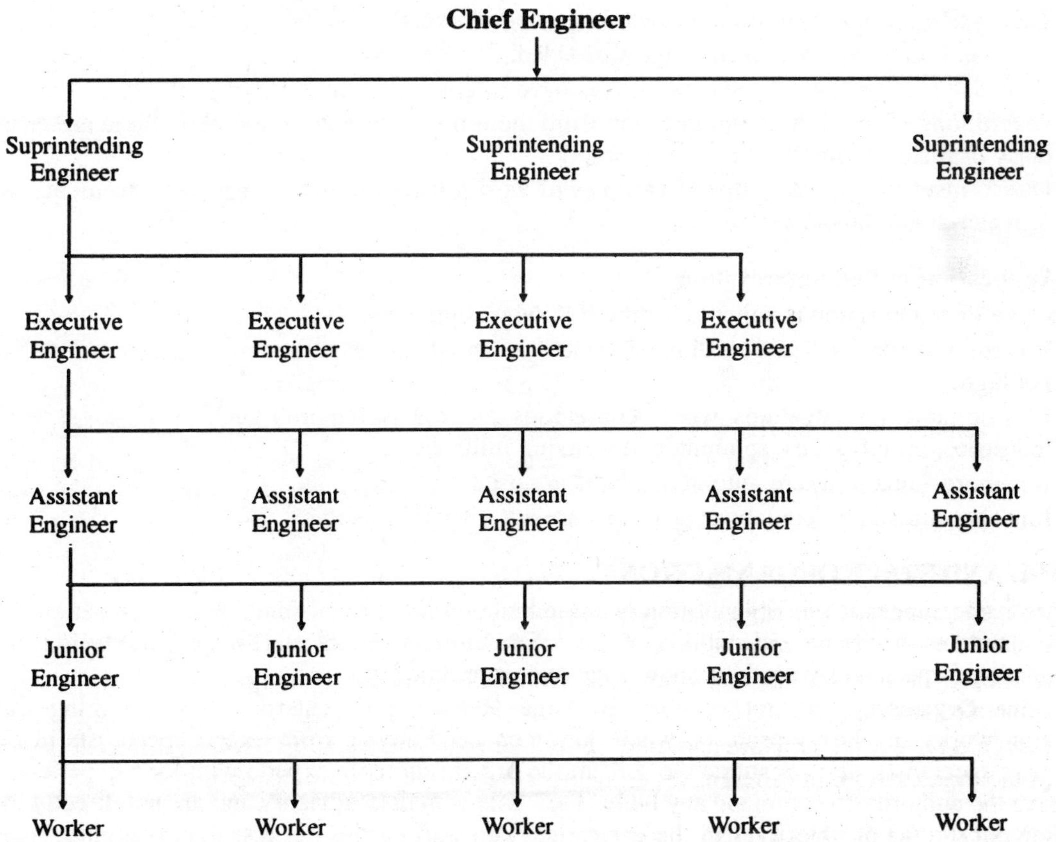

Fig. 36.1. Line organisation

4. It provides strong discipline.
5. Decisions can be taken quickly.
6. Responsibility is fixed and every body knows to whom he is responsible and who are responsible to him.
7. The system has flexibility and persons may be moved from one position to another with out difficulty.
8. It provides effective coordination with in each department.

36.6.2. Disadvantages of Line Organisation

1. The top executive tends to be overloaded with work, as all decisions have to be taken by him. The progress of work may suffer as he is left little time to look after the progress of work and its improvement. Thus the efficiency of the organisation depends upon the quality of work of the senior executives.
2. The organisation is inflexible and rigid.
3. Generally there is inadequacy of communication from lower levels to upwards, though there is good communication from top to bottom. Thus in line organisation the feed back is not received by top executives which affects the progress of the whole work.
4. In this system, it is not possible to take advice from experts. Hence all decisions have to be taken by the person incharge himself.
5. Top executive and key men are over loaded.
6. The loss of one or two capable persons may affect the whole organisation badly.
7. This system has no provision of rewarding good workers.
8. Good and trust worthy persons are over loaded.
9. Expertise is not attained as the executives have to deal different types of problems.
10. Due to long channel of communication from the top executive to the worker, there are chances of delay or distortion in the message or orders.
11. Due to insufficient knowledge of all types of works, there are more chances of accidents, wastage of material and labour etc.

36.6.3. Application of line organisation

This type of organisation is suitable for the following situations:

1. It is suitable for small and medium size factories in which the subordinate operational staff ratio is not high.
2. It is suitable for situations where continuous process is required such as in sugar and paper industries, oil refineries, spinning and weaving mills etc.
3. It is more suitable where automatic plants are used.
4. It is also suitable where labour problems are not difficult to solve.

36.7. LINE AND STAFF ORGANISATION

As the name suggests, this organisation is a combination of line and functional organisation. The line authority maintains discipline and stability of the organisation while the staff responsibility is carried out by the functional specialists with their knowledge and experience.

The line Organisation is not suitable for large and complex enterprises undertaking the large construction works and heavy projects, where key men need advice from expert specialists in different fields. These specialists who constitute the staff in the organisation are experts with long experience. They do not have the authority to command any body. Their role is mainly advisory and are not directly involved in carrying out the major objectives of the enterprise. The staff carries out research, planning, scheduling and recording of progress and the work is executed by line authority.

36.7.1. Advantages of line and staff organisation

The line and staff organisation has a definite improvement over the line organisation. It has the following advantages:

1. It is a planned and specialised system, where advice of expert specialists is available.
2. The project can be executed with better quality product.
3. It gives increased economy and efficiency, though extra expenditure has to be incurred on staff experts.
4. Staff personal carryout specialised work as per their skill. Thus the line personal get sufficient time to devote to achieve the objectives of the enterprise.
5. It provides more job opportunities.
6. Discipline problems are solved by line authority.

36.7.2. Disadvantages of line and staff organisation

1. As staff personnel do not have direct authority to enforce their decisions, some of their ideas may not be implemented.
2. Possibilities of conflict between line staff and functional staff are there as the responsibilities and authority are not well defined.
3. The expert advice available is conveyed to workers through the line authority, which is a quite lengthy route. Thus there is likelyhood of misinterpretation and misunderstanding.
4. The over head cost of the product will increase due to high salaries of staff personnel.
5. The slackness of any section will affect the whole system. It also generates poor discipline amongst the workers due to lack of responsibility at higher level.

36.7.3. Application of line and staff organisation

This type of organisation is preferred for medium and large scale industries depending upon the internal structure, and nature of production activities. It is applied to automobile and other intermittent industries. The line and staff set up is shown in Fig. 36.2.

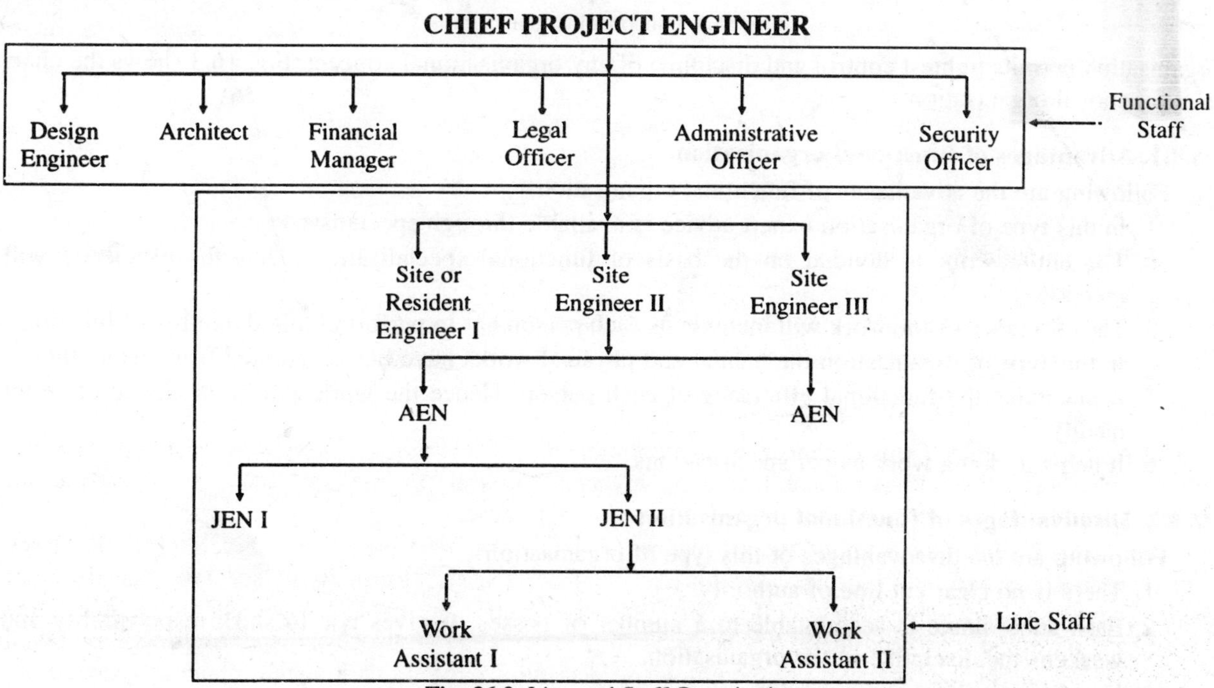

Fig. 36.2. Line and Staff Organisation

36.8. FUNCTIONAL ORGANISATION

In this type of organisation the whole work is divided in such a way that each supervisory personnel has to perform a minimum number of functions and is fully responsible for the functions assigned to him. All similar and related works are grouped together under the charge of one person. However a subordinate in any section of the organisation will be commanded directly by a number of superior officers having authority in their field. The functional organisation can be useful when the owner himself acts as the manager of the project with a minimum staff depending upon others for functional expertise. This type of

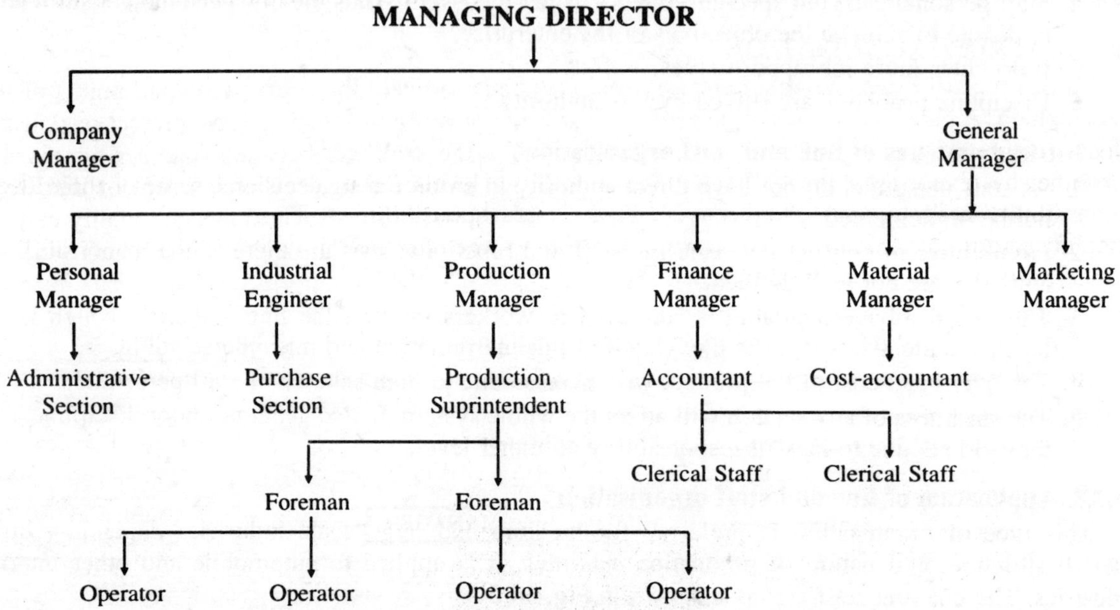

Fig. 36.3. Functional Organisation

organisation permits tightest control and discipline of any organisational concept. Fig. 16.3 shows the chart of a functional organisation.

36.8.1. Advantages of functional organisation

Following are the advantages of functional organisation:

1. In this type of organisation expert advice is available through specialists.
2. The entire work is divided on the basis of functional specialisation. Thus the efficiency will increase.
3. The efficiency of the work will increase as each person has to perform limited number of functions.
4. In this type of organisation the mental and physical works have been separated from each other.
5. It maintains the functional efficiency of each person. Hence the work will be produced of better quality.
6. It helps in doing work as per specifications.

36.8.2. Disadvantages of functional organisation

Following are the disadvantages of this type of organisation:

1. There is no clear cut line of authority.
2. Each subordinate is accountable to a number of bosses. It gives rise to shirk responsibility and weakens the discipline in the organisation.
3. It is difficult to fix responsibility.

4. Due to overlapping authority, friction is likely to be developed between different staff members.
5. Individual specialists may over emphasize their particular specility. It will prove detrimental to the over all performance of the project.
6. The system is too complicated. It is unsuitable for lower level departments of the organisation.

36.8.3. Application of functional organisation

Now a days this pattern is followed in all government and private concerns where much complicated operations are involved as in chemical plants, steel plants, electricity board and other big undertakings etc.

36.9. MATRIX ORGANISATION

In this type of organisation an attempt has been made to retain the strong and good points of line and staff method. A balanced matrix organisation divides the power into functional and project responsibilities. This structure of the organisation endeavours to solve the conflicts between line personnel and staff personnel by opening up lines of communication at all levels through the assignment of dual reporting responsibility to the subordinate managers. Functional responsibilities such as design, quality control, and internal enterprise policies have been entrusted to the functional personnel or staff and project responsibilities such as cost, schedules etc. have been given to the chief project manager. The matrix set up is shown in Fig. 36.4.

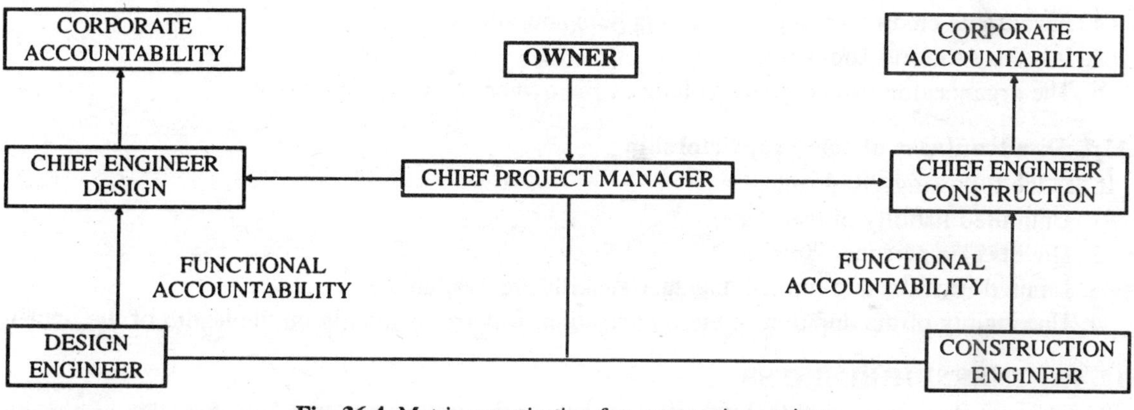

Fig. 36.4. Matrix organisation for construction project

36.9.1. Advantages of matrix organisation

1. This pattern removes some of the weakness of line and staff organisation.
2. In this pattern the functional personnels get equal powers to enforce the compliance of the concepts to improve the design and quality of work etc. with their specialised skill.
3. This concept or pattern is best suited in case the project authority and functional authority is well defined and clearly divided.

36.9.2. Disadvantages of matrix organisation

1. In comparison to other types of organisations, the overall management and administrative cost will be higher.
2. It is difficult to precisely define the accountability of the functional and project managers.

36.10. TYPE OF BUSINESS ORGANISATIONS

For carrying out different types of construction activities, construction managers may carry out the work individually or in association with other persons may from an organisation. Some construction managers form consultancy Organisation. Thus business or contracting organisations may be classified as follows:

1. Sole proprietorship
2. Partnership business
3. Private limited companies or Joint stock company
4. Cooperative societies

36.11. SOLE PROPRIETORSHIP

As the name suggests, it is wholly owned and operated by an individual. It is the oldest, simplest and the most common form of organisation. The owner of the organisation invests his own capital and uses his own intelligence and skills in the management of the business. He may get the assistance of his employees. Thus the owner is personally responsible for all liabilities of the business operations. Profits from business are taken as his personal income and taxed as his individual income. There is no government regulations. This type of organisation is suitable for small works.

36.11.1. Advantages of sole proprietorship

It has following advantages

1. It is simple and easy to form and dissolve.
2. Quick decision making and flexibility of operation.
3. Strict secrecy can be maintained.
4. Favourable credit standing among suppliers and others.
5. It is easy to form and dissolve.
6. The organisation can continue as long as the owner wants to continue it.

36.11.2. Disadvantages of sole proprietorship

It has the following disadvantages:

1. Unlimited liability of the owner.
2. High tax on personal income.
3. Limited finances and limited managerial skills are available.
4. Uncertainty of the duration of the organisation. It depends mainly on the health of the owner.

36.12. PARTNERSHIP BUSINESS

When more than one individual agree to pool their resources and work together, this arrangement is known as partnership concern. The partner who though contributes his capital, but does not participate in the running of the business is known as *sleeping partner*. A legal agreement is necessary between the partners, specifying clearly their capital contribution, nature and extent of their personal efforts and distribution of profits and losses.

36.12.1. Advantages of partnership business

It has the following advantages:

1. It is easy to form. It is also quick in decision making.
2. Larger resources are available to carry out the work.
3. It has flexibility in working and has reduced risk.
4. Balanced judgment is possible.

36.12.2. Disadvantages of partnership business

It has the following disadvantages:

1. Unlimited liabilities of each partner.
2. High taxes are levied as profit is taken as personal income.
3. Mistrust is likely to develop between the partners due to lack of understanding.

4. Instability due to likely mistrust and limited resources due to limited number of partners.

36.13. JOINT STOCK COMPANY OR PRIVATE LIMITED COMPANY

This type of concern or body is formed by registration of a limited company under the provisions of the companies act by its share holders. The liability of each share holder is limited to the value of shares owned by him. The shares are transferable. The company pays dividends to the share holders out of its profit. There are many big construction companies like Larson and tourbo, Gammon India, Hindustan Construction, Deawoo International company etc. This is the best form of organisation for carrying out major construction projects both within and out side the country.

36.13.1. Advantages of joint stock company

This system has the following advantages:

1. The liability of each share holder is limited to the extent of shares held by him.
2. Larger funds are available for executing the work.
3. Loans can be raised from banks and other financial institutions.
4. Tax rate on corporate sectors is lower than individual personal income.
5. Many other concessions are available for the developmental and other activities of the company.
6. Even if some share holders withdraw from the company, the activities of the company will continue.

36.13.2. Disadvantages of joint stock company

Following disadvantages have been observed.

1. The management of the company remains in the hands of the share holders, who have different interests.
2. It lacks the personal interest as that of sole proprietorship.

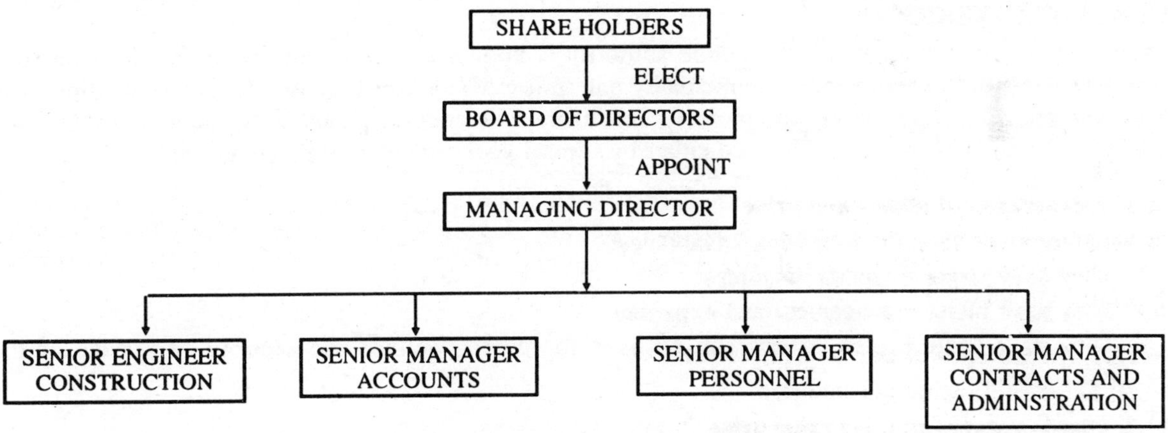

Fig. 36.5. Joint stock company

The company management for construction is shown in Fig. 36.5.

36.14. COOPERATIVE SOCIETIES

A cooperative society is the group or association of persons who join voluntarily to achieve a common economic goal under the provision of cooperative societies act. The membership of such societies is limited to actual workers only. Such societies are eligible for assistance from cooperative banks and have great potential if managed properly.

36.14.1. Advantages of cooperative societies

The advantages of cooperative societies are found as follows:

1. It removes the middle brokers and agents.
2. It does not need any publicity and advertisements.
3. It can pay better wages to workers.
4. It can produce better quality products.

36.14.2. Disadvantages of cooperative societies

Following disadvantages have been observed:

1. It has limited finances.
2. Availability of expert services is limited.
3. Generally it fails to fulfill the expectations of the common man.

The structure of cooperative organisation is shown in Fig. 36.6 below:

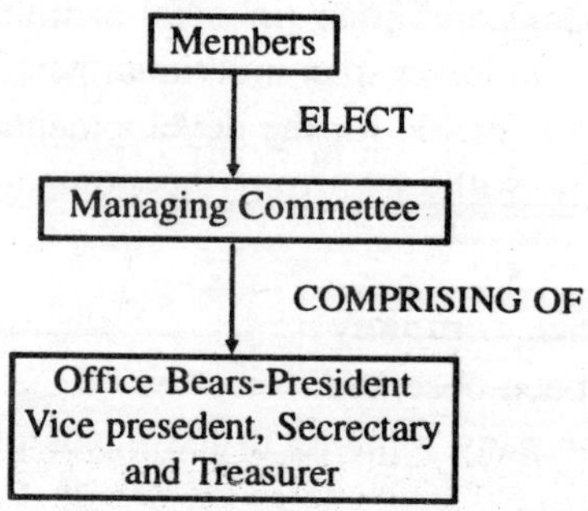

Fig. 36.6. Structure of cooperative society

36.15. STATE ENTERPRISE

A business owned and run by any public authority is known as a state enterprise. It may be a state government or central government or municipality enterprise. Major construction works like multipurpose hydropower projects, Thermal power projects, fertilizers and chemical industries, steel industries and nuclear power projects have been executed either by central government or state governments.

36.15.1. Advantages of state enterprise

State enterprises have the following advantages:

1. They have larger financial resources.
2. They have better management and expertize.
3. They have large profits, which can be used for public welfare and security of service of the employees.

36.15.2. Disadvantages of state enterprise

1. It has lack of personal interest and responsibility of the work.
2. Delay in execution due to red tapism at every level.

36.16. SITE ORGANISATION

To execute the works of different nature in a big project, site organisation is required. Small works do not require site organisation whether the work is done departmentally or through contractor. For medium and large works site organisation is required.

36.17. Types of site organisation

Usually site organisations are of the following types:

1. Site organisation of a private party
2. Site organisation of contractor
3. Site Organisation of engineer

1. Site organisation of a private party. This organisation is very small consisting of one foreman, two to three well trained and experienced craftsman as carpenter or mason and labours as per need. The structure of site organisation is shown in Fig. 36.7.

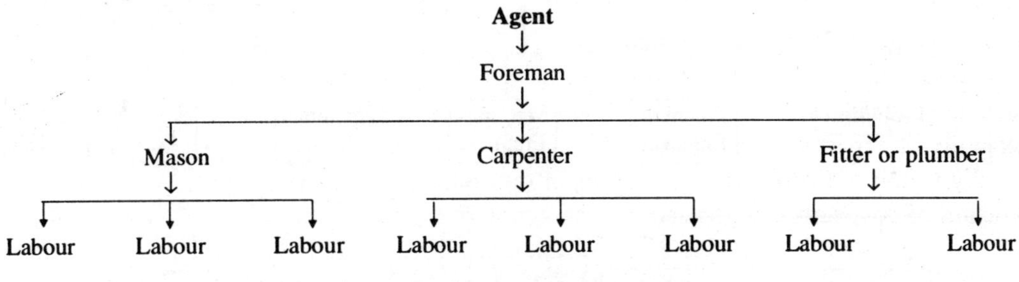

Fig. 36.7. Organisation of Private party

2. Site organisation of contractor. To get his work executed a contractor may have his organisation in many forms. One of the site organisation of a contractor is shown below in Fig. 36.8.

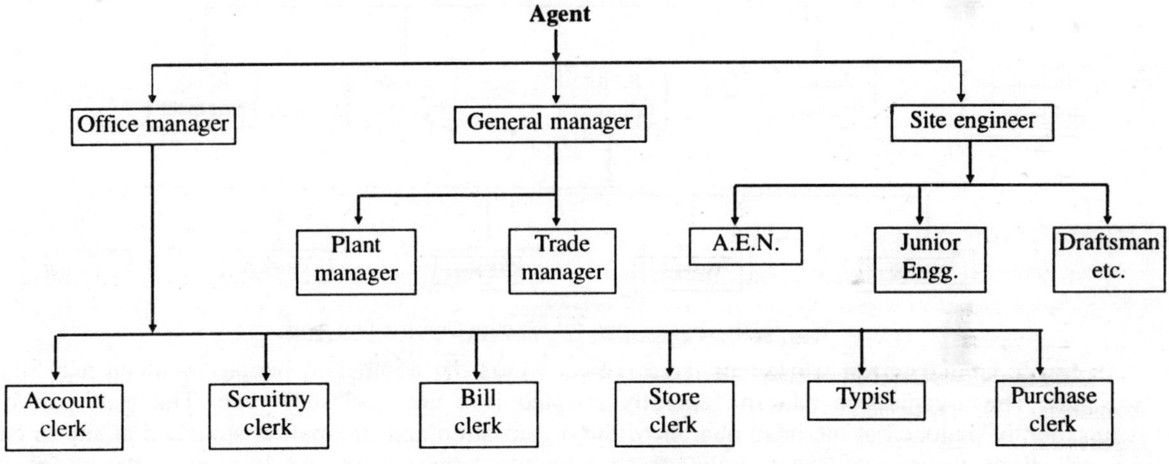

Fig. 36.8. Organisation of contractor

3. Engineer's organisation. A typical site organisation of a assistant engineer for small works is shown below in Fig. 36.9.

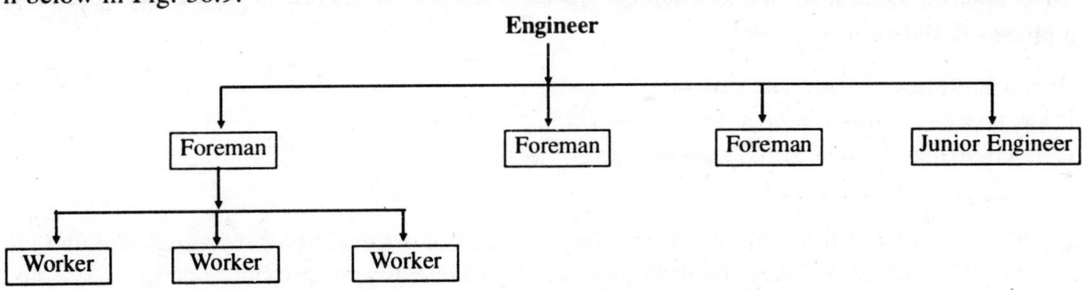

Fig. 36.9. Engineers organisation for small work.

36.18. SUITABILITY OF ORGANISATION FOR CONSTRUCTION INDUSTRY

1. Small works. For small works a simple line type of Organisation is most suitable. In such cases the engineer incharge exercises full authority and is responsible for economical and timely execution of the work in accordance with the laid down specifications. A site organisation of an engineer for a small work is shown in Fig. 36.9.

2. Medium sized works. For medium sized works a more elaborate organisation is required. For such works generally line and staff pattern of organisation is needed as shown in Fig. 36.10.

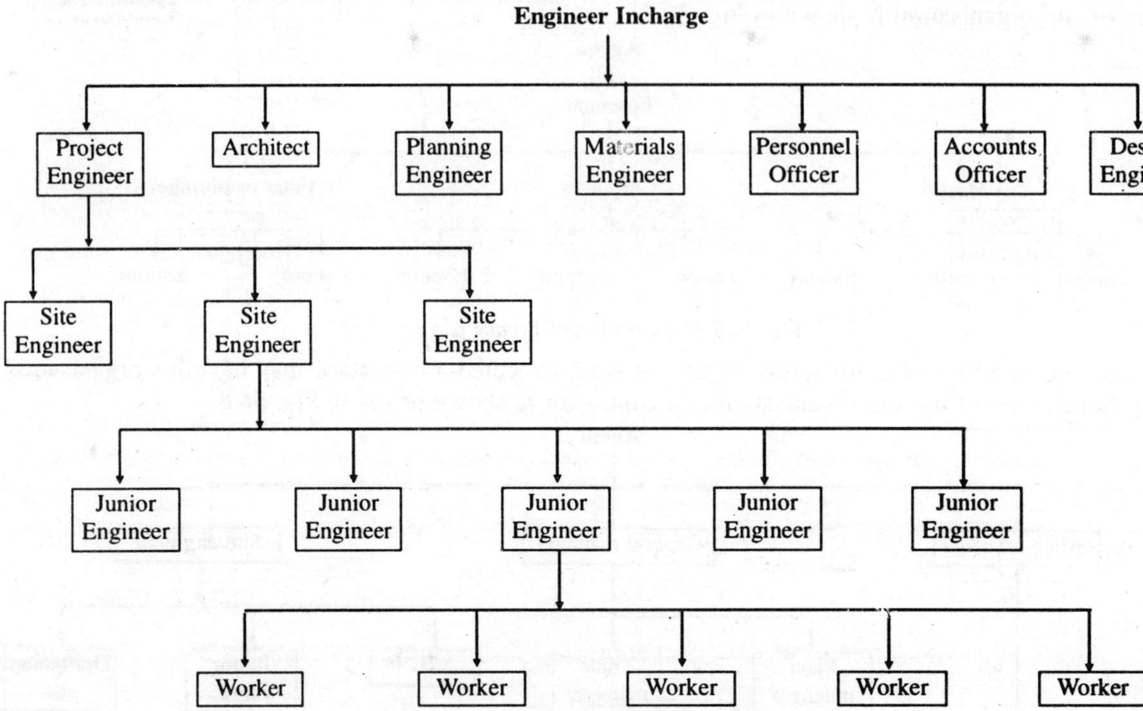

Fig. 36.10. Organisation for medium Construction work

3. Large Construction work. For large project works the number of people involved may run into thousands. The organisation pattern generally adopted is a line and staff type. The staff part of the organisation is stationed at the head quarter of the organisation and line part is stationed at site to control the work. Each departmental head looks after a particular aspect of the work, such as design, planning, purchase of materials and arranging the personnels to execute the work. They are assisted in their work by a team of subordinate staff grouped under the charge of different heads. In the field the grouping is done on the basis of work as civil works, mechanical works, electrical works etc. A typical organisational chart of a big project is shown in Fig. 36.11.

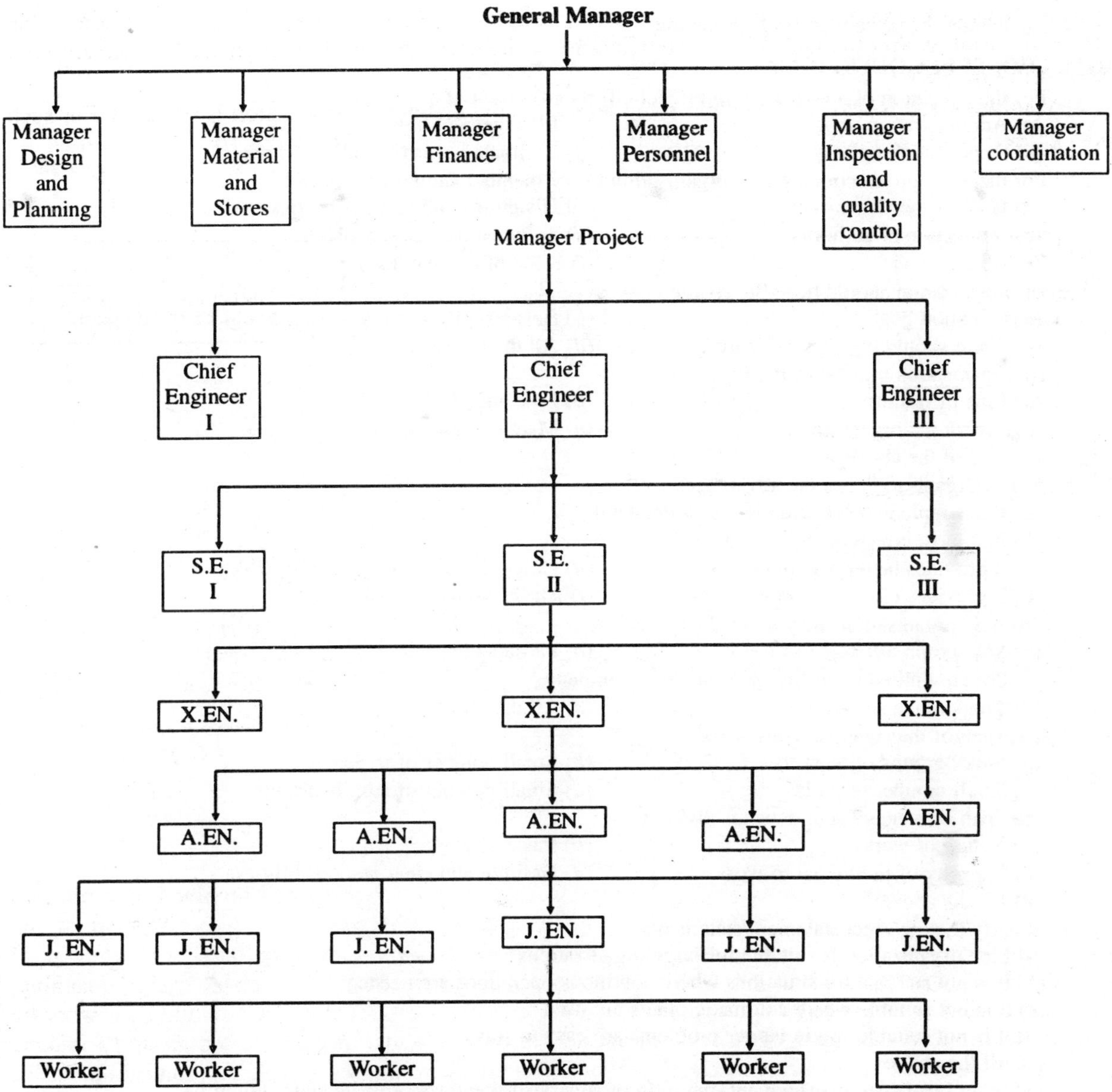

Fig. 36.11. Organisation for a large construction project

QUESTIONS

1. Explain the importance of organisation in the construction industry.
2. Enumerate the general principles to be followed in forming an organisation system.
3. Name different types of organisations and describe one of them fully indicating its merits and demerits.
4. Under what conditions the functional organisation is suitable for construction management.
5. Discuss the line Organisation fully giving its advantages and disadvantages.
6. Discuss the superiority of line and staff Organisation over other systems.
7. Explain the matrix Organisation giving its merits and demerits.
8. For the construction of a multipurpose project across a big river, suggest suitable construction organisation to be formed.

9. Enumerate the principles of Organisation.

OBJECTIVE TYPES QUESTIONS

1. For the execution of a construction project efforts are essential of
   (*a*) Administration only (*b*) Management only
   (*c*) Organisation only (*d*) Combined efforts of all the three
2. For the efficient functioning of a organisation every member should understand
   (*a*) Goal of the Organisation (*b*) His duties and responsibilities
   (*c*) Delegation of authority (*d*) To when one is responsible
   (*e*) All the above (*f*) None of the above
3. An organisation should have the characteristics:
   (*a*) Common goal (*b*) Responsibility of every one should be fixed clearly
   (*c*) There should be a set structure (*d*) All the above
4. An organisation may be of the type
   (*a*) Line or military (*b*) Line and staff
   (*c*) Functional organisation (*d*) Matrix Organisation
   (*e*) Any of the above
5. A line Organisation has the advantages
   (*a*) It is simple to work and easy to understand
   (*b*) It is most effective and economical
   (*c*) It provides better discipline (*d*) Quick decision taking and flexible
   (*e*) It provides effective coordination (*f*) All the above
6. Business organisations may be of the type
   (*a*) Sole proprietorship (*b*) Partnership
   (*c*) Private limited company or Joint stock company
   (*d*) Cooperative societies (*e*) All the above
7. The span of management consists of
   (*a*) Small groups of workers (*b*) Small number of trades
   (*c*) Small number of tools (*d*) Small number of administrators
8. The span of management depends upon
   (*a*) Nature of work (*b*) Place of work
   (*c*) Capacity of individual to work (*d*) Definite and clear responsibilities
   (*e*) All the above
9. Identify the incorrect statement/statements
   (*a*) Line organization is suitable for large organizations
   (*b*) It is not suitable for situations where continous operations are needed
   (*c*) It is not suitable where automatic plants are used
   (*d*) It is not suitable where labour problems are easy to solve
   (*e*) All the above
10. In higher level span management, the ratio of supervisory and subordinate staff should be
    (*a*) 1:2 to 1:3 (*b*) 1:4 to 1:5
    (*c*) 1:6 to 1:8 (*d*) 1:9 to 1:12
11. At lower level of management, the management to subordinate ratio should be
    (*a*) 1:10 to 1:15 (*b*) 1:30 to 1:35
    (*c*) 1:15 to 1:20 (*d*) 1:40 to 1:45

ANSWERS:

1. (*d*)	4. (*e*)	7. (*a*)	10. (*b*)
2. (*e*)	5. (*f*)	8. (*e*)	11. (*a*)
3. (*d*)	6. (*e*)	9. (*e*)	

37

Construction Labour and Relevant Labour and Industrial Laws

37.1. INTRODUCTION

In India Construction is one of the largest industry and employees about forty million (four crores) of workers, most of them being unskilled labourers. The nature of construction work is temporary, hence the jobs in the construction industry are also temporary. The workers are hired as and when needed for the execution of work and removed when no longer needed.

37.2. CONDITION OF CONSTRUCTION LABOUR IN INDIA

Construction labour is most disorganised in India. In the present social set up, the dignity of labour has not attained the desired status in this country. Due to this condition labourers move from place to place in search of work as they can not take manual labour in their own villages. India is an agricultural country and most of the people belong to the landless category. They are not in a position to earn their living wages when they are not required for cultivation work. Hence they move from place to place in search of their livihood.

The economic plight of construction labour is worst in India due to their illiteracy, lack of bargaining power and uncertainty of continuous employment. This class of labour being temporary has no organisation. Hence they are not cared for by local political forces. The employer does not care even to provide the basic amenities like shelter, drinking water, sanitary facilities etc. Maternity and child welfare conveniences are unknown to them. No body cares for the education of their children.

The construction labour could not organise itself to the extent as Labour in factories and other organised sectors of trade and industry has done. This is due to the fact that construction labourers do not have permanent place of work. They have extremely poor collective bargaining power and the impact of their movement is hardly felt.

Though the construction labour in India is cheapest in the world, but his output is very low due to illiteracy and improper training of work. A korean construction worker is able to read drawings, interpret specifications and carryout the work independently, where as an Indian worker needs a supervisor to guide and help to do this work.

To remedy this situation, the government of India has brought laws from time to time to improve the lot of labour in industrial and business establishments. However enlightened employers in the construction industry have also provided some welfare benefits to their labourers.

37.3. TYPE OF CONSTRUCTION LABOUR

Broadly construction labour can be divided into two groups as follows:

1. **Causal labour.** This class of labour is also called daily labour. They are employed as and when required for the execution of work. Payment is made on the basis of number of days they work. There is no provision of leave except weakly holiday.
2. **Regular establishment.** Staff required for more or less continuously during the construction period is included in the regular establishment. They are paid monthly wages and are entitled for leave and other benefits. These employees may be permanent or temporary. Permanent employees have greater security of service and are entitled for more service benefits than temporary employees.

37.4. WAGES OF LABOUR

Wages paid to workers may be classified into two groups:

1. **Nominal wages.** The remuneration paid to the worker in the form of money in liue of labour done by him is called nominal wages. In does not include the value of any benefit that may be provided.
2. **Real wages**. Real wages include the value of other benefits such as leave, medical care, house rent allowance, bonus etc. in addition to nominal wages. Thus real wages include the value of other benefits in addition to the nominal wages.

37.5. PAYMENT OF WAGES TO LABOUR

The payment of wages to workers is done on the following basis:

37.5.1. Time rate basis

In this system of wages payment, a suitable rate of payment is fixed per unit of time devoted by the labourer. The unit of time can be hours, days, weeks or month. Usually the rate of payment for causal labour is fixed per day and for regular employees per month.

37.5.1.1. Advantage and disadvantages of time rate system

Advantages

This system has the following advantages:

1. It is simple and easily understood by labourers as the payment to all workers of the same category is paid at the same rate.
2. The quality of work is good as the workers do not have the tendency to show increased out put at the cost of quality.
3. Workers are not strained as they do not try to increase their output beyond a certain limit.
4. This method specially is useful in situations where the measurement of output is not feasible and work is of artistic nature.

Disadvantages

Following draw backs have been observed of this method:

1. As all workers of the same category are paid at the same rate, there is no incentive for higher out put and to honest worker.
2. As the workers are assured of their wages irrespective of output, their output is low.
3. To extract work from labourers, constant supervision is necessary.
4. Effective cost control cannot be ensured due to varying productivity.

37.5.2. Piece rate system

In this system, the payment to the worker is made on the basis of his output. The work done by each labourer is measured and payment made at the agreed rate. The rate of each item of work is fixed on the basis of past record of output.

Advantages

This method has the following advantages:

1. Workers with higher output get higher wages.
2. Due to greater efforts of workers, over all productivity is increased.
3. Less supervision is required.
4. Effective cost control can be ensured.
5. The relations between the employer and employees remain cordial.
6. The system is fair for both employer as well as employees.

Disadvantages

1. There are no guaranteed wages for the workers.
2. Workers are over strained in an effort to get more money for increased output, which affect their health.
3. This system is suitable only for works which can be measured.
4. In order to increase the output, workers ignore the quality of the work. Hence in this system quality of work suffers.
5. The system is quite cumbersome as record of output of each worker is to be maintained.

Thus whatever may be the mode of payment, it should be based on real wages and should be fair for all.

37.6. LABOUR LAWS

Construction workers also come under the purveiw of labour and industrial laws. Thus in order to improve and regulate the working conditions of labourers in different industrial and business establishments the central and state legislatures have enacted a number of laws. The total number of laws may be more than one hundred. Here only few of them which concern mainly to construction labour have been discussed. The Labour and industrial laws can be broadly classified into the following three categories.

1. Laws relating to the payments of wages.
2. Laws relating to the working conditions of the labourers.
3. Laws relating to the social security and civil rights of the labourers

37.7. PAYMENT OF WAGES ACT 1936

For the first time, in India payment of wages act was enacted in 1936. This act specifically includes construction activities with in its jurisdiction. This act is applicable to employees whose salary is less than Rs. 1000/- (one thousand per month). After its enactment this act has been amended many times as in 1957, 1962, 1976 and 1977.

Wages. As per this act, the wages are defined as the salary including all allowances, bonus, compensation, incentive and reward etc. However wages do not include the value of the housing accommodation, medical aid, water and electricity supply, provident fund, travailing allowance and pension if applicable.

Wage period. This act prescribes the maximum wage period as one month. The payment of wages should be made by 7th of the following month by firms employing less than 1000 workers and by the 10th of the following month by firms employing 1000 or more than one thousand workers. The wages should be paid in the form of currency. In case a worker is terminated, his all wages should be paid with 48 hours of his termination.

37.7.1. Deductions from wages

Following deductions only can be made from the wages of the worker:

1. Dues due to absence of duty
2. Fines
3. House rent
4. Water and electricity charges

5. Provident fund dues
6. Income tax
7. Contribution to cooperative societies
8. Insurance premium
9. Subscription to government sureties
10. Recoveries on account of damages and losses due to his negligence
11. Recoveries on account of advance payment

37.7.2. Safe guards

This act provides following safe guards against deductions from the wages of the worker:

1. No fine can be imposed on children below the age of 15 years.
2. The amount of fine imposed on a worker due to any reason should not be more than one day wages of the worker.
3. The fine money should be deposited in a separate fund. This money should be used for the welfare of the workers.
4. The deductions for losses or damages should only be made if it occurred due to the negligence of the worker. The amount of deduction should not be more than the loss incurred to the establishment.
5. The house rent, water and electricity dues deductions should be acceptable to the workers.

According to the payment of wages act, the property of the employer can be attached if on the appeal of the worker, court is satisfied that employer is evading payment. The provisions of this act vary from state to state. Thus state governments are responsible for the administration of the act. Inspectors are also authorised to inspect any relevant records and present himself during the payment of wages.

37.8. MINIMUM WAGES ACT 1948

The aim of this act is social justice. The minimum wages act was passed in 1948 for the welfare of labourers of the country which is a labour surplus country.

This act provides for fixing minimum wages of labourers. The minimum wage is defined as the amount of money to be earned by a worker, which is sufficient to fulfill his normal needs and give him reasonable comforts of living in a civilized society. The money of wages should be enough to keep his body and soul together. Due to local conditions, it differs from place to place. The act aims at making provisions for statutory fixation of minimum rate of wages in a large number of industries where there are much chances of exploitation of labourers.

37.8.1. Provisions of the act

The main provisions of this act are as follows:

1. Under the provision of this act, to fix the minimum wages, a board consisting of representatives of government, employer and employees may be formed.
2. Under this act daily working hours, holidays and over time payments can be fixed. Proper record of payment to workers must be maintained by the employer on the prescribed forms. This record can be checked by any authorised person.
3. The employer will not pay wages less than minimum wages fixed for any particular class of workers under his employment.
4. The wages shall be paid in cash and the wage period will be one month.
5. If any labourer is employed on any day for less than the normal day duration, the labourer will be entitled for full day wages.
6. The normal working hours per day will be as follows:

   (*a*) For a adult labourer : 9 hours per day

(*b*) For a child labourer : $4\frac{1}{2}$ hours per day

The working period for adult worker inclusive of rest interval will not exceed 12 hours on any day.

7. Every worker will be allowed a day's rest with full wages every week.
8. If any worker works on his rest day, he will be entitled for wages for that day at the rate of over time and shall be allowed a substitute rest day with full wages.
9. If a worker works more than 9 hours on any day, he will be paid double the ordinary wages for the over time period.

37.8.2. Deductions

Some deductions can be made from the wages of a worker as discussed in article 37.7.

37.9. WORKMEN'S COMPENSATION ACT 1923

The workmen's compensation act was passed in 1923 for the first time and has been amended in 1959 and 1976.

37.9.1. Objects of the act

The object of the act is to protect and provide relief to workers and their family who become victims of accidents and lose their earning capacity due to accidents while on duty. On the one hand this act forces the employer to take all possible safety measures and on the other hand it forces the worker to work carefully and with full responsibility.

37.9.2. Scope of the act

This act covers all the persons employed in any capacity in a hazardous occupation including construction work as specified in the schedule II of the act and whose wages are less than Rs. 1000/- (one thousands) but people engaged in clerical or administrative work are excluded from the preview of this act. This act provides for payment of compensation in case of accident on site of work. The cover of compensation starts immediately on joining the employment. The employer is liable to pay compensation to a worker under the following conditions.

1. The personal injuries resulting in temporary or permanent disabilities or death.
2. Injuries took place by accident while on duty.

Conditions under which compensation is not payable:

(*a*) Injuries due to negligence or disobedience.

(*b*) Worker being under the influence of liquor or other intoxicant.

(*c*) Willful removal of safety guards or willful non observance of safety measures.

(*d*) Due to disease with which the worker was suffering before joining the employment.

However in case of death compensation has to be paid under all circumstances.

37.9.3. Causes of accidents

Causes of accidents may be classified into the following groups:

1. Personal causes. Under this head following causes may be grouped:

(*a*) Poor eye sight (*b*) Worry

(*c*) Restlessness (*d*) Fatigue

(*e*) Muscular weakness (*f*) Effect of intoxication

2. Mechanical causes. Following causes can be grouped under this head:

(*a*) Inadequate safety devices like safety guards.

(*b*) Faulty lifting and hauling equipment.

(*c*) Unreliable centering and scaffolding.

(*d*) Live electrical equipment etc.

3. Environmental causes. Under this head following causes are grouped:

(*a*) Poor lighting and ventilation
(*b*) Restricted working space
(*c*) Excessive heat and noise etc.

37.10. TYPE OF INJURIES

The compensation amount is to be paid on the type and extent of the injury. The details of injury and amount of compensation are shown in schedules I and IV of the act. The injuries may be classified into the following categories:

1. Temporary disablement which may be partial or total. As this disablement reduces the working capacity of the worker, the compensation equal to half the monthly pay of the worker is paid to him. The temporary disablement compensation can be paid upto a maximum period of 5 years.

2. Permanent disablement. This disablement renders the worker incapable of doing any work in any employment. The act specifies following injuries as total disablement.

(*a*) Total disablement.
(*b*) Loss of one hand and one foot.
(*c*) Amputation of one leg and loss of foot of the other.
(*d*) Loss of eye sight of both eyes.
(*e*) Very severe facial disfigurement
(*f*) Absolute deafness.

3. Permanent partial disablement. As per this act a large number of injuries come under this head, which reduce the earnings of the worker. The percentage loss of earning capacity due to injuries is shown in Table 37.2.

4. Death. In case of fatal accidents the amount of compensation varies from 7200 to 30,000 depending, upon the wages of the worker. The amount of compensation shown in table 37.1 is original. Amount of compensation as workmen's compensations act 1923 as shown in Table 37.1.

Table 37.1. Rate of Compensation

Monthly wages	*Amount of Compensation*		*Half Monthly comprsation of temporary disablement half montly wages*
	Death	*Permanent disability*	
0 – 60	7200	10080	36.60
60 – 90	9720	14608	42.0
90 – 120	11520	16128	48.75
120 – 150	13500	18900	60.0
150 – 200	16800	23520	82.50
200 – 300	18000	25200	82.50
300 – 400	19200	26880	100.00
400 – 500	21000	29400	118.75
500 – 600	21600	30240	135.0
600 – 700	23100	32340	148.75
700 – 800	24000	35600	160.00
800 – 900	27000	37800	168.75
900 – 1000	30,000	42000	175.0

Note: The above figures are original. They are subject to change as per government orders.

Actually the compensation to be paid can be estimated from the schedules of the act. It is the duty of the employer to pay compensation to the worker as it becomes due. In case of dispute the employee may accept the amount with out losing his right to claim further damages under the act. If the dues are not paid

Table 37.2. List of injuries deemed to result in permanent disablement

S. No.	*Description of injury*	*Percentage loss of earning capacity*
1.	Loss of both hands or emputation at higher sides	100
2.	Loss of one hand and one foot	100
3.	Loss of eye sight of both eyes rendering him unable to perform any work	100
4.	Very severe facial disfigurement	100
5.	Absolute deafness or double emputation through leg or thigh	100
6.	Amputation of shoulder joint	90
7.	Ampulation of hip joint or both foot	90
8.	Ampulation below shoulder	80
9.	Ampulation through both feet	80
10.	Ampulation below hip	70
11.	Loss of one hand or thumb and fore fingure of a hand	60
12.	Amputation below middle thigh	60
13.	Loss of four fingers of one hand	50
14.	Loss of thumb	30
15.	Ampulation of one foot	30
16.	Loss of three fingures of one hand	30
17.	Loss of two fingures of one hand	20
18.	Loss of all toes of one foot	20
19.	Loss of partial vision one eye	10
20.	Loss of index dingure	19
21.	Loss of middle fingure	12
22.	Loss of big toe	14
23.	Loss of little fingure	7
24.	Loss of other toe	3

with in one month, the commissioner may impose penalty and interest over and above the principal amount. The penalty will not exceed fifty percent of the principal amount. The employer may submit the compensation directly to the concerned commissioner instead of the employee.

The employer is obliged to send the detailed report of fatal accident or serious injury with in a weeks time to the appropriate commissioner. The failure to inform the commissioner about the accident is punishable with a fine. When the employer works through contractors, even then the liability to pay compensation is thrown upon the principal. The worker is entitled to claim compensation either from the principal or the contractor. However principal will not be liable to pay compensation to the contractor's workmen, over which he has no control. For details consult Act 1923.

37.11. FACTORS FOR WORKING OUT LUMPSUM AMOUNT FOR COMPENSATION

As per revesion of 1923 compensation act in 1924 the factor for calculating the compensation is given in Table 37.3.

As per rules of 1924 of workmen compensation act 1923, factor for working out the lumpsum equivalent of compensation is shown in table 37.3. This amount is payable in case of permenent disadbement or death.

37.12. CONTRACT LABOUR (Regulation and Abolition) ACT 1970

In certain cases, the principal contractors engage labour through sub contractors. This practice is quite common in the construction industry. The payment to the sub contractor is paid on the basis of

Table 37.3. Factors for calculating lumpsum amount

S. No.	*Completed years of age on the last birth day of the worker immediately preceeding the date on which compensation fall due (Age in years)*	*Factor*	*S. No.*		*Factor*	*Remark*
(1)	(2)	(3)	(1)	(2)	(3)	
1.	Not more than 16	228.54	26	41	181.37	(*a*) When the death occurs due to injory, the amount of compensation will be 50% of wages of the deceased worker multiply by the relevant factor or fifty thousand which ever is more.
2.	17	227.49	27	42	178.49	
3.	18	226.38	28	43	175.54	
4.	19	225.22	29	44	172.52	
5.	20	224.00	30	45	169.44	
6.	21	222.71	31	46	166.29	
7.	22	221.37	32	47	163.07	
8.	23	219.95	33	48	159.80	
9.	24	218.47	34	49	156.47	
10.	25	216.91	35	50	153.09	(*b*) In case of total permanent disablement results from the injory in that case the amount of compensation will be 60% of the monthly wages multiplied by relevent factor or sixty thousands which ever is more
11.	26	215.28	36	51	149.67	
12.	27	213.57	37	52	146.20	
13.	28	211.79	38	53	142.68	
14.	29	209.92	39	54	139.13	
15.	30	207.98	40	55	135.56	
16.	31	205.95	41	56	131.95	
17.	32	203.85	42	57	128.33	
18.	33	201.65	43	58	124.70	
19.	34	199.40	44	59	121.05	
20.	35	197.06	45	60	117.41	
21.	36	194.64	46	61	113.77	
22.	37	192.14	47	62	110.14	
23.	38	189.56	48	63	106.52	
24.	39	186.90	49	64	102.93	
25.	40	184.17	50	65 or above	99.37	

measurement of work at site. The quantum of labour put in by the workers has been ignored. To minimise the labour cost and to boost his profit, the sub contractor adopts un lawfull measures and violates a number of labour laws. Thus to regulate and in some cases to abolish the contract labour, an act was enacted in 1970. This act also deals with provision of improving the service conditions of the contract labour.

The contract labour central rule 1971 lays down the procedure for the implementation of the act. This act is very important for construction industry where most of the works are executed through contractors or contract labour. In India construction industry employs about 40 million workers. The act provides for the constitution of a central advisory contract labour board under central and state governments. This board is to advise the central and state governments on matters arising out of the administration of the act to carry out the functions assigned to it under the act.

37.12.1. Scope of the act

1. According to the act the principal employer ultimately is responsible to the labourers in respect of payment of wages and providing welfare facilities. The labourers are to be paid in time according to the provisions of the act.

2. The act is applicable to all type of business establishments who employ twenty or more than twenty workers to carry out unskilled, semiskilled or skilled, technical, manual or supervisory and clerical work etc.
3. Persons engaged in supervisory or managerial capacity earning more than Rs. 500/- per month do not come under the preview of this act.
4. This act also does not apply to those workers who are not directly under the control of the management of establishment concerned.
5. This act also is not applicable to establishment of causal nature. The establishments in which work has not been performed for more than 120 days in the preceding 12 months are called causal establishments. In case of seasonal work if work is done for less than 60 days in the 12 preceding months, the work is also known as of casual nature and this act is not applicable in both cases.

37.13. MAIN PROVISIONS OF THE ACT

Followings are the main provisions of this act:

1. Registration of the establishment. Every individual or establishment who intends to employ contract labour is required to apply on prescribed form to the registration officer for the registration of his establishment. Form I is used for this purpose.

2. Licence for Contractors. Every contractor who executes any work through contract labour has to apply on prescribed form IV to the competent authority for obtaining licence to carryout the contract labour work. The licence will be issued on the payment of prescribed fee of Rs. 30/- per worker subject to such conditions as hours of work, fixation of wages and essential amenities to the contract labour.

3. Maintenance of registers.

(*a*) The principal employer should maintain a register on prescribed form concerning contractors. From XII is used for this register.

(*b*) *Register of present employees.* This register on form XIII should be maintained by the contractor.

(*c*) *Employment card.* This card is to be issued to each worker with in 3 days of employment by the contractor in form XIV.

(*d*) *Service certificate.* This certificate is issued by the contractor on termination of employment in form XV.

37.13.1. Registers to be maintained by Employer

Under the minimum payment of wages act and payment and wages act following registers must be maintained by the employer.

(*a*) Muster roll
(*b*) Register of wages
(*c*) Register of deductions
(*d*) Register of over time
(*e*) Register of fines
(*f*) Register of advances

37.13.2. Emenities for Contract labour

Under the provision of contract labour act 1970 following emenities should be provided to the contract labour by the employer:

(*a*) If the work is likely to continue for more than 90 days (3 months) and where the worker is required to stay at night in connection with the work, the workers should be provided rest rooms by the contractor or owner. Women workers should be provided separate rest room. This arrangement must be done with in 15 days of the execution of the contract. Each worker should be provided at least 1.1 m^2 floor area in the rest room.

(*b*) The rest room should be well ventilated and lighted.

(*c*) The rooms should have concrete flooring and should be well protected from rain, heat, and wind etc.

(*d*) There should be proper and sufficient arrangement of potable water for drinking and other purposes.

(*e*) The rest rooms should be situated at convenient distance from the site of work.

37.13.3. Sanitary Services

1. (*a*) There should be at least one latrine for every 25 male workers.
   (*b*) Similarly there should be one latrine for every 25 women workers.
   (*c*) If there are more than 100 workers, in that case at least one latrine per 50 workers should be provided.
   (*d*) There should be separate arrangement of bath rooms for male and female workers.
   (*e*) There should be canteen facility. It should be provided with in 60 days of the contract.
   (*f*) For every family of the labourer, one hut should be provided. The area of the hut should not be less than 2.8 m^2 and height 2.2 m. The distance between the huts should not be less than 6.0 m. There should be separate arrangement of cooking in the huts.
2. For works likely to continue for more than 180 days and the number of workers is more than 100. In that case along with above provisions, adequate provision of canteen for labourers must be there. The canteen must be run on no loss. no profit basis. The details of providing canteen are given in the contract labour control rule 1971.
3. First aid box should be provided in every establishment.

37.14. EMPLOYEES STATE INSURANCE ACT 1948

To provide certain 'benefits' to employees, this act was enacted in 1948. This act covers all employees including engaged in physical works and whose remuneration is not more than Rs. 1000/- per month. This act empowers the government to implement the provisions of the act in stages to any class of commercial business. At present this act is not applicable to the construction site workers. However the act is applicable to any establishment that comes under the preview of the factory act and covers construction related works such as precast units and structural fabricators.

For the implementation of the act, the act provides the establishment of an corporation to be known as "Employee's state Insurance Corporation". The board's directors shall be nominated by members of parliament, central and state governments and some will be representatives of employers, employees, and medical practioners.

Powers of Corporation. The corporation has powers to take measures for the improvement and welfare of the insured persons and to establish and maintain state hospitals and dispensaries.

37.14.1. Benefits from the act

The act provides following benefits to the insured employees:

1. Benefits for sickness
2. Maternity
3. Disablement
4. Dependent's benefits
5. Medical and funeral

1. Sickness benefits. An insured person can get cash payment for his sickness if certified by a duly appointed medical practictitioner for the purpose by the competent authority. An insured person is entitled for sickness benefits after paying contribution for thirteen weeks. The maximum duration of the benefits is fifty six days. The first two days shall not be taken for the calculations of the benefits. The daily rate of benefits to be given to a insured person shall be standard benefit rate corresponding to average daily wages of that person as given in the first schedule of the act.

2. Maternity benefits. An insured women after thirteen weeks of work is eligible for the maternity benefits for illness due to pregnancy. The period of benefits is normally 12 weeks. The daily rate of benefits is twice the amount of standard benefit rate corresponding to average daily wages of that women as per 1st schedule of the act.

3. **Disablement benefits.** These benefits consist of periodical payment to an insured person suffered disablement due an injury while on duty. A disabled person shall be paid benefit both for temporary and permanent disablement according to rates mentioned in the 1st schedule of the act. To determine the extent of disablement an medical board is consistuted. The amount of benefits will be twenty five percent more than the standard benefit rates corresponding to the average daily wages of that person as per first schedule of the act. The minimum period for disablement benefits is 3 days. An insured person who is getting disablement benefits under this act can not receive benefits from other statute body like workmen compensation act. Upon the death of the insured person, these benefits will be paid to his dependents.
4. **Dependent's benefits.** The dependent's benefits of an insured person become payable to his dependents, on the death of the person while on duty. Normally widow and children receive these benefits. The amount of benefit will be twenty five percent more than the standard benefits mentioned in first schedule of the act. The widow receives 60% and children receive 40% of the benefits as long as they are minors.
5. **Medical benefits.** Medical benefits are payable to the insured person or to a member of his family. The benefits may be provided as out door patient or indoor patient. A insured person is entitled only to medical benefits as provided by the corporation. He can not claim for reimbursement of medical expenses except provided by the regulations. Under the act contributions are to be paid by employer and employee both at the rates specified in the schedule of act.

Under this act disputes and claims will be settled by a special court known as Employee's "Insurance Court". Lower civil courts than high court have no jurisdiction over such matters. However appeal against special court's judgment can be made in high court.

37.15. BONUS ACT 1965

In order to provide some financial benefits to the workers, government enacted a bonus act in 1965. This act deals with payment of annual bonus in industries. Similar to the payment of wages act, this act specifies a minimum amount of bonus payable to the workers.

This act specifies minimum and maximum amount of bonus to be paid to its employees. To qualify for the payment of bonus a worker should have worked at least for 30 days in a year in the establishment.

An dismissed employee from service due to fraud, theft, violent behaviour etc. is not qualified for the bonus payment. On the other hand an employee subjected to other punishments as fine, etc., is eligible for bonus payment. In such a case the employer is entitled to deduct any loss suffered from the bonus amount of the employee.

According to this act an employee is entitled for 8.33 percent of his salary or rupees one hundred which ever is higher each year irrespective of the profit or loss of the company.

37.16. BONUS ACT AMENDMENT 1980

In 1980 an amendment was made to the bonus act of 1965. According to this amendment the bonus shall be calculated according to *available surplus*, which is derived from the audited accounts of the company.

Available surplus = Gross profit as per balance sheet – All deductions as per income tax provisions

(All deductions include depreciation, development rebates, income tax, and other taxes shown in schedule III of the act.)

The available surplus is distributed amongst the employees as bonus subject to minimum and maximum conditions.

The maximum amount of bonus payable to an employee shall not exceed 20% of his annual wages. If an employee is getting a salary more than Rs. 750/- but less than Rs. 1000/- in that case his salary will be taken as Rs. 750/- for the purpose of calculating his bonus.

An employee getting more than Rs. 1000/- pr month as salary is not eligible to get bonus under the act. For calculating the bonus, the salary is taken as the wages plus dearness allowance and food allowance. House rent, travelling allowance, medical benefits and employer's contribution to provident fund are not included in salary for calculating the bonus amount.

Normally bonus is to be paid with in eight months from the close of the accounting year. Under this act competent authority may appoint inspectors to examine the relevant papers and to inspect the premises of companies to ensure the proper implementation of the act.

37.17. EMPLOYEE'S PROVIDENT FUND (and miscellaneous provisions) ACT 1952

To improve the financial position of workers Government enacted the provident fund act in 1952. This act is applicable to any industry or factors employing more than 20 worker as specified in first schedule of the act. Under this act construction industry is required to maintain a provident fund for his employees. This fund is administered by a board of trustees appointed by the government. For the administration of the provident fund central and state governments have appointed their boards.

37.17.1. Contribution

Under the act both the employer and the employee have to contribute 6.25% of the basic wages of the employee. The basic wages include salary plus (dearness allowance, house rent allowance, bonus and over time allowance). However travelling and food allowance is not included in it. In certain cases government may raise the contribution to 8%. The employer is required to deposit the contribution of both by the 15th day every month. In turn employer may deduct the employees share of contribution from his salary.

37.18. FAMILY PENSION SCHEME

To provide support to the family of workers who die prematurely, a new scheme called family pension scheme has been introduced. This scheme is similar to provident fund. This scheme provides family pension and life insurance benefits to the employees. Similar to provident fund, both employer and employee have to contribute to this scheme, but the amount of contribution is 25% of the amount payable in provident fund scheme.

37.19. EMPLOYEE'S DEPOSIT LINKED INSURANCE SCHEME

To provide benefits to workers another scheme was launched in 1976, which is known as "employee,'s deposit linked insurance scheme." Under this scheme both employer and employee have to contribute at the rate of 1% of basic wages of the employee as premium. This scheme works as life insurance for the employees. In the event of death of the employee, the nominee of the employee will get a sum not exceeding Rs. 1000/- depending on the balance accumulated in his account of the fund.

The amount accumulated in this fund is not liable to be attached under any decree of a court. Also the amount in the fund can not be claimed by any creditor of an insolvent person.

37.20. PAYMENT OF GRATUITY ACT 1972

A lump sum amount payable to an employee on retirement or on termination of service by the employer for reasons other than disciplinary action is known as gratuity. This act applies to factories and other establishments notified by the government that employs more than ten persons.

According to the act, the gratuity is payable to an employee after 6 years of service on retirement, disablement, death or termination of services. After the death, the gratuity amount of the employee shall be paid to the nominee of the employee. In case nominee has not been mentioned, the gratuity payable to the employee shall be paid to his heirs. An employee is eligible for gratuity for any disablement caused either due to accident or by disease that does not allow him to perform his duties.

The employee is entitled to get gratuity at the rate of fifteen days salary per annum or part there of in excess of six months of service rendered by him. The gratuity amount is paid on the basis of salary last drawn by the employee. The travelling allowance or over time allowances is not taken into account for calculating the gratuity amount.

For piece rate employees, the gratuity shall be calculated on the basis of average of the last three months salary. The rates indicated for gratuity are considered as minimum. In case the service of an employee is terminated due to misconduct, the employer is entitled to recover the loss from gratuity. In case the service of an employee is terminated due to violent behaviour or disorderly conduct, his total gratuity shall be forfeited. However the gratuity payable under the act is not liable to attachment by the order of civil, revenue or criminal court.

37.21. FACTORIES ACT 1948

The aim of this act is to protect welfare of workers. The construction workers, working at the site of the work are not covered under this act. However construction work places such as fabrication of steel structures, prefabricated R.C.C. members and other building component manufacturing units are treated as factories and their workers are covered by this act.

Factory. According to the definition of this act a premises where ten or more than ten persons are engaged in any manufacturing process with the aid of power or premises where twenty or more than twenty persons are engaged in the manufacturing process with out the aid of power are called factories.

Every factory needs a licence from the government to operate. The act has empowered the state government to make rules and appoint inspectors to regulate the working of the factories. The failure to obtain the licence before the start of the factory is punishable with imprisonment for a maximum period of three months. The factory act is a comprehensive one having control over several aspects of the factory management as health, safety and welfare of the workers.

37.22. WELFARES OF WORKERS

Under the head welfare of workers they should be provided following facilities.

(*a*) **Housing.** The workers should be provided proper housing facilities at the site of the work. The accommodation should have proper lighting and ventilation arrangement. A controlled level of dust, fumes and temperature be maintained. For each worker at least a space (volumes of 500 cu. ft. (14.16 m^3) should be provided.

(*b*) **Drinking water.** There should be adequate arrangement of good potable water for drinking. The drinking water place should be at least 20 ft. (6.1 m) away from latrine or washing place. Factories employing more than 250 people, in summer season arrangement of cool drinking water should be made.

(*c*) **Sanitation.** Usually there should be 1 latrine for every 25 persons and there should be separate latrines for male and female workers at the same rate or as specified by the government. Along with latrines, there should be adequate number of bathing rooms separate for male and female workers.

(*d*) **Medical facilities.** There should be proper and adequate medical facilities for workers and their families. First aid boxes and trained attendant must be provided.

(*e*) **Educational facilities.** There should be adequate educational facilities for the children of the workers.

(*f*) **Transport facilities.** In case workers have to travel much distance to reach their place of work, there should be proper arrangement of their transportation. It will not only help the workers, but out put of the work will also increase.

(*g*) **Food services.** There should be canteen at the site of work, which may provide eatables and tea to workers at cheaper rates. A canteen is necessary where more than 250 workers work.

(*h*) **Recreational facilities.** There should be recreational facilities at the site of work as cinema house, indoor and out door games, reading room and library facilities.

(*i*) **Lunch and rest rooms.** There should be lunch and rest rooms where workers may take their lunch and take rest in time available to them. It is compulsory for a factory employing more than 150 workers.

(*j*) **Creche facility.** There should be creche's facility where women workers may leave their children. It is compulsory for a factory employing more than 30 women workers.

37.23. SAFETY MEASURES

There are many provisions dealing with safety of the workers:

(*a*) All machines should be fenced adequately. Safe guarding of machines is compulsory.

(*b*) The maintenance and lubrication of machines while in motion should be done only by trained and experienced workman, specially appointed for this work.

(*c*) To cut off the power immediately from the moving parts, only approved devices should be used.

(*d*) Hoists and lifts should be checked every six months by competent persons.

(*e*) Cranes and lifting machines should be checked once a year.

(*f*) The rotating wheels of machines such as cutting tools and grinders etc. should not be revolved more than the specified speed.

(*g*) In a factory ways and stairs should be provided with proper foot holds and hand rails to avoid slips and accidents.

(*h*) The tanks or sumps should be kept covered.

(*i*) No. employee be allowed to move excessive weight which may be injurious to health.

(*j*) Operators working on welding and grinding machines should be provided effective screens and goggles to protect their eyes.

37.24. FIRE FIGHTING

(*a*) In every factory there must be proper and adequate arrangements of fire fighting.

(*b*) In every factory fire escapes with proper sign posts and free from obstacles should be provided.

(*c*) Doors and windows that might be used during fire, should not be kept under lock and key. Fire fighting equipment and fire alarms should be in adequate number.

(*d*) Factories which employ more than 20 persons, fire drills should be compulsory for them.

37.25.WORKING HOURS

(*a*) The maximum daily work period should not exceed 9 hours.

(*b*) Maximum working hours per week can not exceed 48 hours.

(*c*) There must be a 30 minutes break after a period of 5 hours.

(*d*) One day rest is to be provided to each worker weekly.

(*e*) For over time work, the worker is entitled at the rate of 1.5 times of is normal wages.

(*f*) A register showing personal information of each worker as nature of work entrusted to him, shift in which he has to work, his personal information etc. should be maintained in each factory.

(*g*) After putting 24 days service in a year each worker is entitled for earned leave at the rate of 1 day for each 20 days of work. The wages for earned leave will be equal to the average wages earned in the month immediately preceding the leave.

37.26. TRADE UNIONS AND THEIR ROLE

Organised labour has developed from a modest organization into one of the most powerful groups in our society. Labour unions have become an integral part of our management. Hence as such they should be recognised, under stood and dealt with effectively.

Thus trade unions are voluntary organisations of workers formed with the primary objective of protecting the interests of the labourers. In European countries labour unions exist according to craft such as carpenter or mason unions. A "trade union" means any combination of employees whether temporary or permanent formed for regulating the relations between the employers and workers or between the workers themselves or for imposing restrictive conditions on the conduct of any trade etc.

37.26. FUNCTIONS OF TRADE UNIONS

The main functions of a trade union are as follows:

1. Establishing a bargaining platform for negotiations with employers.
2. Improving wages and working conditions of the workers.
3. To promote the welfare schemes for workers.
4. To establish cordial relations between the employers and workers.
5. To provide legal assistance to workers when ever necessary.
6. To maintain necessary funds for the relief of workers in the hour of their need such as during their illness, injury and other such needs.
7. In India for the first time a trade union was formed in a textile mill in Ahmedabad (Gujrat) in 1918 and trade union movement was started.

37.27. IMPORTANT TRADE UNIONS OF INDIA

Following are the important trade unions in India:

1. All India trade union congress (AITUC). This union was formed in 1919 by congress party, but at present it is under the influence of communist party of India.
2. Indian National Trade Union Congress (INTUC). This union was set up under the patronage of Indian congress.
3. United Trade Union Congress (UTUC). This union was formed in 1949 under the patronage of leftist parties.
4. Hind Majdoor Sabha (HMS). This union was formed in 1948 by the Praja Socialist Party. It is under the influence of socialist groups.
5. Centre of Indian Trade Unions (CITU). This union is under the influence of CPI(M).
6. Bhartya Majdoor Sanght (B.M.S.) This union was started under the patronage of Jansangh party.

37.28. INDIAN TRADE UNION ACT 1926

The first Indian trade union act was passed in 1926 with the aim to allow the registered trade unions to carry out their activities and to protect the office bearers against the law suits that may be initiated by the employers. Minor amendments were made in this act in 1928, 1942 and 1947. The main provisions of the act are as follows:

1. Registration

A trade union can be registered only under the trade union act. No other registration act like cooperative societies or companies act etc. shall be applicable to it. Any seven or more members of a trade union can apply for the registration to the registrar. On verifying the information provided in the application of registration, he will issue a certificate of registration. The registrar has the power to withdraw or cancel the registration under certain conditions. A worker more than 18 years of age and not related to the establishment can be a member of any trade union subject to certain rules. At least fifty percent of the office bearers of a union should be actually engaged in that firm. Legally it is not necessary for a union to be registered. A registered union can enter into contracts and can own movable or unmovable properties. The registrar under the act is appointed by the state government.

2. Rights and Privileges

(*a*) The members and office bearers of a trade union can not be punished for criminal conspiracy until they do not intend to commit an offence.

(*b*) Peaceful strikes and demonstrations can be organised by the union with legal immunity.

(*c*) Legal proceedings against a union is not admissible in a civil court as long as the subject matter falls in the area or sphere of a trade dispute.

(*d*) For breach of any agreement legal proceedings can not be started in a civil court for the recovery of damages suffered due to breach of agreement.

(*e*) The union has the right to administer its affairs with out the interference of the employers.

(*f*) It is binding on employers to recognise the union, reply their letters and grant them interview.

3. Obligations and liabilities.

(*a*) The trade union must have some name.

(*b*) It must define its objective.

(*c*) The general funds of the union are permitted to be spent for the following purposes:

(*i*) For the salaries of the office bearers of the union.

(*ii*) Expenditure on administration of the union.

(*iii*) Expenditure on legal proceedings concerning the union.

(*iv*) Expenditure to fight the trade disputes.

(*v*) Compensation to members on losing the trade dispute.

(*vi*) Publication of periodicals.

(*vii*) For welfare activities of the members of the union.

(*viii*) The accounts of the union must be audited at least once a year by chartered auditors.

(*ix*) The executive committee should meet at least once in six months.

4. Restraints

1. No expenses can be met for political purposes from the union's funs. However a separate fund for political purposes may be maintained. This separate fund may be utilised to support any condidate for election and organise political meetings etc.
2. The act prohibits to compel any member to contribute to the political fund.
3. Contribution to political fund is not a precondition for the admission to the union.

5. Disqualification

1. Any member of the union can be disqualified from holding any office of the union if he has not attained the age of 18 years.
2. If he has been convicted by a court of law for moral turpitude and sentenced to imprisonment for any other offence. How ever he can be eligible to hold office after 5 years of his release.

37.29. AMENDMENT TO TRADE UNION ACT.

As stated earlier minor amendments were made to this act in 1928, 1942 and 1947. Due to certain unfair practices noticed in the act, it was amended in 1947 last. In this amendment following clauses were added for employer and employees both.

1. Employers

(*a*) As per the amendment of 1947 to the union act, it will be a binding on the employer to recognise the union, reply their letters and grant them interviews.

(*b*) The management will not interfere in the administration of the union.

(*c*) For being a member of the union, no discriminating action will be taken against any member of the union.

2. Employees

(*a*) No member of the union will participate in illegal strikes.

(*b*) No wrong statement shall be submitted by any member of the union.

37.30. INDUSTRIAL DISPUTE ACT 1947

After independence to maintain peace in industrial establishments an act was enacted. The objectives of this act are as follows:

1. To maintain cordial relations between the management and employees.
2. Settlement of all disputes amicably.
3. Prevention of collective strikes and lock outs.
4. Relief to workers during lay off and retrenchments.
5. To deal with collective bargaining etc.

37.30.1. Definition

The trade or business where employers and employee organise together to create wealth for human needs in called industry. The construction activities also fall under industry, hence the industrial act is applicable to construction activities also.

37.31. MEASURES TO PREVENT INDUSTRIAL DISPUTES

In order to prevent the industrial disputes the act specifies the following measures:

1. Formation of work committees
2. Formation of board of conciliation
3. Formation of labour courts
4. Formation of industrial tribunals

1. Formation of work committee. In industries employing more than one hundred people, the competent authority is empowered to order for the formation of work committee. The committee is composed of equal numbers of representatives from both sides *i.e.* employer and employees.

The work committee normally is concerned with the day to day problems to maintain cordial relations and communication between the management and workers. Legally the decisions of the work committee are not binding on either party, but normally its decisions are honoured by both the parties.

2. Formation of Conciliation board. To settle the industrial disputes, the competent authority under industrial dispute act can constitute a conciliation board or appoint an officer for the purpose. The board or the officer shall work as mediator between the parties rather than to find the legality of the dispute. In case of successful settlement of the case, the board or the officer as the case may be shall send a report including the memorandum of dispute to the competent authority. In case of failure, the board or the officer shall send report about the case to the competent authority. Legally parties are not bound or obliged to settle the dispute through the conciliation process. In such situations the competent authority may refer the dispute to labour court or tribunal having judicial authority to the disputes not settled through a conciliation process.

3. Constitution of labour court. Central and state governments both have powers to constitute labour courts. Labour courts have powers to decide all cases except certain items mentioned in the third (III) schedule of the act of industries employing less than 100 workers. Normally matters related to interpretation of standing orders, legality of strike or lock out and dismissal of worker are decided by labour courts.

4. Constitution of tribunals. Central and state governments have powers to constitute tribunals also. The tribunals have more powers than labour courts. A tribunal is entitled to decide judicially all matters including items mentioned both in schedules II and III of the act of industries employing any number of workmen. Some of the matters specified in schedule III are as wages, working hours, bonus, lock out or closure and discipline rules etc.

The disputes involving workmen of large organisations or interstate workers matters are referred to a National tribunal appointed by the central government. The industrial disputes normally be settled by above mentioned methods as an ordinary civil court has no jurisdiction over industrial disputes.

Strikes and lockouts are the final resort or final means to achieve their goals for employees and employers respectively. The industrial dispute act does not deny these rights, except in special cases like in public utilities. Strikes and lock outs do not require prior notice even under the act.

Strikes and lock outs can not be initiated under the following conditions:

1. When proceedings in the office of labour court or tribunal or reconciliation are in progress.
2. In case of breach of contract.

In these conditions the strikes and lock outs become illegal and are punishable offence.

Industries which are not of intermittent nature and employ more than 50 workman are liable for payment of lay off and retrenchment compensation to the workmen. To be eligible for compensation at least one year service is compulsory.

37.32. RATE OF COMPENSATION

1. **In case of layoff.** Fifty percent of wages are to be paid to the workmen.
2. **In case of closure.** In case of closure other than the site office of a construction firm sixty days notice in prescribed manner has to be given to the workmen and government both. In case of construction work of the undertaking is closed down due to completion of work with in two years no compensation is to be paid.
3. If the construction work is not completed within two years, the compensation shall be payable for every additional year or any part in excess of six months. The rate of compensation will be 15 days wages for every one year service of the retrenched worker.

QUESTIONS

1. Define nominal and real wages.
2. Enumerate different systems of wages of payment and discuss their merits and demerits.
3. What deductions are allowed from the salary of a worker under payment of wages act?
4. What is a contract labour? What important facilities are to be provided to the contract labour?
5. Discuss the rules for determining the amount to be paid to a worker under the minimum wages act.
6. Discuss the basic provisions of the Employees state insurance act.
7. Under what conditions an employer is liable to compensation under the compensation act.
8. Enumerate the basic provisions of payment of bonus act.
9. Define gratuity and give procedure to determine it.
10. How a factory is defined under the factory act? What are the basic provisions in the act with regard to the safety of the workers?
11. What is registered trade union? What immunities are granted to its members under the trade union act.
12. How the disputes can be settled as per industrial dispute act?
13. What is meant by labour wellfare? Discuss the facilities to be provided to workers under the welfare law.
14. Discuss the causes of poor conditions of construction labour in India.
15. Discuss the following acts in brief:
    (*a*) Minimum wage act (*b*) Workmen's compensation act
    (*c*) Contract labour act (*d*) Payment of wages act
    (*e*) Industrial dispute act (*f*) Trade union act
    (*g*) Factories and gratuity acts

OBJECTIVE TYPE QUESTIONS

1. The economic condition of construction labour in the India is
   (*a*) Worst (*b*) Best
   (*c*) Average (*d*) None of the above
2. In India the payment of wages act was enacted for the first time in
   (*a*) 1923 (*b*) 1936
   (*c*) 1948 (*d*) 1942
3. The minimum wages act was enacted in
   (*a*) 1935 (*b*) 1942 (*c*) 1948 (*d*) 1952
4. The main provisions of the minimum wages act are
   (*a*) To fix the minimum wages to be paid to a worker

(*b*) Wages less than the minimum shall not be paid
(*c*) The wages shall be paid in cash
(*d*) Every worker will be allowed a weekly rest
(*e*) The working hours of an worker will not be more than 9 hours
(*f*) All are correct

5. For the first time in India workers compensation act was enacted in
(*a*) 1917 (*b*) 1923
(*c*) 1929 (*d*) 1935
6. In India contract labour act was enacted in
(*a*) 1965 (*b*) 1947
(*c*) 1970 (*d*) 1981
7. Employees state Insurance act was enacted in
(*a*) 1937 (*b*) 1948
(*c*) 1957 (*d*) 1981
8. The benefits of state Insurance act are
(*a*) Benefits for sickness (*b*) Maternity benefits
(*c*) Disablement (*d*) Dependent's benefits
(*e*) Medical benefits (*f*) All the above
9. Bonus act was enacted in
(*a*) 1942 (*b*) 1951
(*c*) 1965 (*d*) 1976
10. Payment of gratuity act was enacted in
(*a*) 1942 (*b*) 1952
(*c*) 1962 (*d*) 1972
11. Factories act was enacted in
(*a*) 1937 (*b*) 1945
(*c*) 1948 (*d*) 1957
12. The Important trade unions of India are:
(*a*) All India trade union congress (AITUC) (*b*) Indian National Trade Union Congress (INTUC)
(*c*) United Trade Union Congress (UTUC) (*d*) Bhartya Majdoor Sabha (BMS)
(*e*) Hind Majdoor Sabha (HMS) (*f*) Centre of Indian Trade Union (CITU)
(*g*) All the above
13. Industrial dispute act was established in
(*a*) 1927 (*b*) 1937
(*c*) 1947 (*d*) 1957
14. Measure to prevent disputes are
(*a*) Formation of work committees (*b*) Formation of board of conciliation
(*c*) Formation of labour courts (*d*) Formation of industrial tribunals
(*e*) All type above
15. In case of lay off a workmen has to be paid wages at the rate of
(*a*) 20% (*b*) 35% (*c*) 50% (*d*) 75%
16. As per wages act 1936, wages include
(*a*) Pension benefits (*b*) Travelling allowance
(*c*) Provident fund (*d*) Medical aid
(*e*) Housing accommodation value (*f*) None of above
17. As per gratuity act an employee is entitled for it after a service of
(*a*) 6 years (*b*) 12 years
(*c*) 30 years (*d*) After retirement only

ANSWERS:

1. (*a*)	4. (*f*)	7. (*b*)	10. (*d*)	13. (*c*)	16. (*f*)
2. (*b*)	5. (*b*)	8. (*f*)	11. (*c*)	14. (*e*)	17. (*a*)
3. (*c*)	6. (*c*)	9. (*c*)	12. (*g*)	15. (*c*)	

38

Construction Disputes And Their Settlement

38.1. INTRODUCTION

When two individuals or parties work together for a common goal, development of disputes is a natural phenomenon. It can be between family members, between neighbours, between colleagues and between employer and employees. In construction industry disputes mainly arise between the client and the contractor. Generally conflicts develop between two colleagues who work for the same common goal to accomplish the desired end results due to difference of opinion. Development of disputes give rise to the creation of claims. The settlement of claims is essential for the progress of the work.

Every project manager has to face legal problems at one time or the other. The problem may arise at any point during the process of construction or after its completion. Generally a good contractor avoids litigation of any kind at all costs, but some times he is forced in litigations. If a project manager is familiar with legal process and its terminology and doing proper documentation of the progress of the work then he is better prepared to face inevitable legal disputes.

38.2. DEVELOPMENT OF DISPUTES

Most of the happenings that could occur during the period of actual execution can not be foreseen and no set rule can be established or postulated to foretell their effects on the work. However their effects can be minimised by adopting ethical practices and managing it in an unemotional manner. Generally disputes arise in the interpretation of contract clauses, difference of opinion regarding the execution of the work, effects of unforeseen problems as sub soil condition, natural calamities, and strikes etc. These problems should be solved expeditiously and judiciously as and when occur.

The client rightfully may demand the completion of work by the contractor in time, despite the latter's petitions against unforeseen problems. The client may stop the work and get the remaining work done either departmentally or by an other contractor.

38.3. TYPES OF DISPUTES

Construction disputes may be categorised as follows:

1. Contractor's claims against the client.
2. Client's claims against the contractor.

1. Claims of contractor against client. A contractor may have following claim's against the client.

(*a*) Claims for refund of money wrongly deducted.

(*b*) Claims for extra amount on petty grounds.

(*c*) Claims for compensation for losses suffered by the contractor due to the delay in supply of construction materials, delay in sanction or some breaches committed by the client.
(*d*) Claims on other accounts under the contract such as extra payment due, or balance payment due on various grounds.
(*e*) Interest on delayed payments.
(*f*) Interest on other claims amount.

2. Claims of client against contractor

(*a*) Claims for defective work done by the contractor.
(*b*) Claims for over payments made to the contractor.
(*c*) Claims for expenditure incurred in getting the work done in case of incomplete or abandoned work through other agencies.
(*d*) Claims for liquidated damages for delays caused by contractor in completing the work.
(*e*) Interest on amounts claimed by the client.
(*f*) Other compensation claims for delays caused by the contractor.

38.4. MODES OF SETTLEMENT OF DISPUTES

In construction contracts the mode of settlement of disputes mainly depends on the provisions provided in the contract. Normally in construction contracts provisions are included for the settlement of disputes by arbitration. When such provisions are not provided in contracts, then disputes arising in the completion of work, the disputes generally are settled by direct negotiations between the contractor and client or through civil courts. Thus the modes of settlement of disputes in construction contracts may be classified as follows:

1. By direct negotiations between the client and the contractor.
2. Through civil courts.
3. Settlement by arbitration.

30.4.1. Settlement by direct negotiations between the client and the contractor

This is the easiest and most advisable method of settlement of disputes. The majority of construction disputes are finalised and settled by this method. Even if there are clauses of arbitration in the contract, such clauses do not prevent the parties from settling amicably the dispute directly. If the disputes have been settled by direct negotiations, then arbitration clauses cease to exist. When parties do not come to terms by direct negotiations, they may go to court or for arbitration. The mode of settlement by arbitration should be reduced to the barest minimum. It is in the interest of both parties.

38.4.2. Settlement through arbitration

Definitions

1. Arbitration. The process of settlement of a dispute by the decision of one or more than one person chosen by the parties concerned with the dispute is known as *arbitration*. Thus arbitration is a domestic court where the abitrator acts as a judge of the court.

2. Arbitrator. A person chosen by the concerned parties themselves to pronounce the judgment on the dispute and agreed to abide his judgment is known as a *arbitrator*. He pronounces his judgment judicially based on facts.

When both parties agree on the name of a single person to act as a judge and appoint him for this purpose, then he is known as *sole arbitrator*. In case both parties do not agree on a single name and each party appoints his own arbitrator, in that case there are two arbitrators and known as joint abritrators. In case of joint arbitrators a third arbitrator is chosen with the consent of both the parties, who acts as a umpire in case of difference of opinion of the two arbitrators and the decision of the umpire becomes binding on the parties concerned.

3. Need for arbitration. The present day judicial system is complex and out dated. It is extremely time consuming. In certain cases the judgment comes even after 30 to 40 years. Thus to expedite the settlement of the dispute at an early date with less expenses there is need for arbitration.

4. Who can be appointed as an arbitrator. The disputes from construction industry are generally technical in nature. In such cases a technical person as Engineer or an architect who is conversant with such works and contracts should be appointed as an arbitrator.

In disputes pertaining to buildings and engineering contracts following type of persons normally be appointed as arbitrators.

1. An employee Engineer of the owner may be appointed as arbitrator. There is no objection to such an appointment.
2. An architect of the organisation may some times be appointed as an arbitrator. In such situations he will work as architect to the work as well as arbitrator to settle the dispute arising out of the contract.
3. It should be provided in the arbitration agreement that if need arises, the arbitrator will be nominated and appointed by the person as designated in the orbitration agreement. In central public works department, post and telegraph construction contracts, it is provided that Chief Engineer of the department will nominate and appoint the arbitrator. In Railway contracts, the General Manager is the authority to nominate and appoint an arbitrator.
4. In certain state public works department and industrial development corporations, the Chief Engineer of the state P.W.D. or of corporation Chief Engineer by designation will act as an arbitrator. Such a practice is followed in Maharastra corporations and Kerala public works departments. In such cases problem does not arise on transfer or death or retirement of the present incumbent as Chief Engineer. The person occupying the chair of the Chief Engineer will act as arbitrator in the matter.
5. In certain cases parties empower the owner to act as a arbitrator himself in the matter. Though it is valid provision and has been accepted by courts, but it is not a good practice. No one should be the judge in his own case.
6. When an arbitrator is appointed through the court under section 20 of the arbitration act, generally a single arbitrator is appointed by the court. Generally courts appoint the person as an arbitrator on whose name both parties agree, but in case the parties are not agreeing on one name, then court appoints the arbitrator of his own choice. In technical cases, courts also usually appoint technical person as a arbitrator.
7. In cases like International Competitive Bidding (ICB), contracts of the world bank aided projects as major irrigation works like Gujrat irrigation department, three arbitrators are to be appointed one each by each party and the third arbitrator by the chairman of central water commission. New Delhi. In such cases the award of the majority shall prevail as per section 10(2) of the arbitration act.
8. In certain contracts, the person to be appointed as arbitrator in the matter is not specifically mentioned in the arbitration clause, but only it is provided that disputes and differences arising out of the contract are to be sorted out by arbitration as per provisions of the arbitration act. In such cases at the time of disputes parties have to agree on an agreed name for the arbitrator. If the parties do not agree on a name then court will appoint the arbitrator on his own as per section 20 of the arbitration act.
9. Though there are innumerable methods of appointment of arbitrators in construction disputes provided in arbitration act, but they have only slight variations of methods as discussed above.

Restrictions on the persons to be appointed as arbitrator

Following restrictions are provided in various arbitration agreements:

1. Contract form of agreement of the Indian Institute of Architects provides that in case an dispute

arises out of the contract, the dispute shall be referred to two arbitrators, one nominated by each party with the restriction that both arbitrators should be fellows of the Indian Institute of Architects.

2. Certain other contracts provide that both the arbitrators should be fellows of the Indian Institute of Engineers.
3. Gujrat Public works department contracts provide that the arbitrator shall be a retired officer of the Gujrat PWD having held the post not less than an Superintending Engineer (S.E.).

38.5. ARBITRATION ACT 1940

An arbitration act was enacted in 1940 to consolidate and amend the law relating to arbitration to make it more comprehensive and effective. This act is applicable through out the country except Jammu and Kashmir.

38.5.1. Powers of an arbitrator as per 1940 act

This act bestowes the following powers to an arbitrator unless a different intention is expressed in the agreement.

1. To administer the Oath to the parties and the witnesses appearing in the dispute.
2. To state a special case for the opinion of the court or any question of law involved or to state the award wholly or in part in the form of a special case of such questions for the opinion of the court.
3. To make the award conditional.
4. To correct any clerical mistake in the award arising due to accidental slip or omission.
4. To administer to any party to the arbitration if found necessary in the opinion of the arbitrator or an umpire.

38.6. SETTLEMENT THROUGH COURTS

Settlement through the court of law is the last resort and usually it takes number of years to settle the dispute. In case contractor strongly feels that he is sure to win his case and injustice has been done to him at the direct negotiations or arbitrator level, then and then he should go to the court of law. Court action will require the engagement of legal aid who has some experience of construction industry disputes. As it is a long battle, it will require prolongned attention and physical presence of contractor himself or his top personal. Thus their services will be diverted away from their real business. This will be extremely costly and humiliating.

QUESTIONS

1. Disputes in construction contracts are inevitable. Discuss.
2. Discuss the factors which lead to disputes in the execution of construction projects.
3. Enumerate the different kinds of disputes in construction industry.
4. The easiest and most advisable method of settlement is by direct negotiations. Discuss the rational of this statement.
5. Write short notes on the followings:
   (*a*) Arbitration (*b*) Arbitrator
   (*c*) Settlement through courts
6. Explain fully as who can be appointed as an arbitrator.
7. Discuss the 1940 arbitration act. What powers this act bestowes on the arbitrator.

39

Total Quality Management (T.Q.M)

39.1. INTRODUCTION

Total quality management may be defined as the process in which the top management along with other people of the organisation works to improve the quality of the product and work environment continuously at all stages and at all levels with the aim to improve the satisfaction of the customers and employees. T.Q.M. is the application of scientific principles and artistic skills to improve the product and services rendered to an organisation, all the processes within an organisation and the degree to which the needs of the customer are met now and in future.

Quality became an important business issue after the fall of American competitiveness in the world market. The use of T.Q.M is increasing day by day in organisations to improve their operations and processes in all their functional areas of their organisations. T.Q.M has gained popularity due to the fact that it attempts to improve the product and service quality, productivity and competitiveness by improving the communication with customers and suppliers and with in the organisation.

Thus TQM is a quest for excellence, creating right attitudes. It controls and prevents the possible defects and optimizes the customer's statisfaction by increasing the efficiency and effectiveness. It is an approach to improve the effectiveness and flexibility of the business as a whole. Essentially it is a system of organizing and involving the whole organisation at every level. The concept of T.Q.M. and responsibilities of different levels of management are shown in Fig. 39.1.

39.2. ELEMENTS OF TOTAL QUALITY MANAGEMENT

Following are some of elements of T.Q.M.:

1. **Leadership.** The first step to attain the excellence is the major decision to provide leadership for quality as a basic strategic goal.
2. **Leadership commitment.** The total commitment of the top management is the key factor in implementing the T.Q.M. All top members of the management must lead the T.Q.M. efforts.
3. **Recognition and rewards.** Recognition is the process of acknowledgment of employee's outstanding performance by the management. It is essential to boost the morale of the employees. Recognition helps them to find themselves in a winning role. Rewards encourage them to give their best to the organisation, by way of increased productivity and quality of work.
4. **Education and training.** For successful implementation of T.Q.M. education and training of all employees from top to boom is essential.
5. **Customer orientation.** In business, the customer is the king. Customer is the purpose for the existence of the business. Customer wants product at a reasonable price.
6. **Team work and Employee empowerment.** To achieve a common goal, the involvement of all employees in a process is the main aim of team work. If the individual and inter departmental

conflicts are eliminated much more can be attained at less cost.

7. **Feed back mechanism.** For the success of total quality management program, the development of feed back mechanism for both internal and external customers is essential.
8. **Statistical process control.** Variation is an natural phenomenon. To understand the nature of the variations and estimating the capabilities of the process will help the organisation to reduce the inspection and improve the quality.

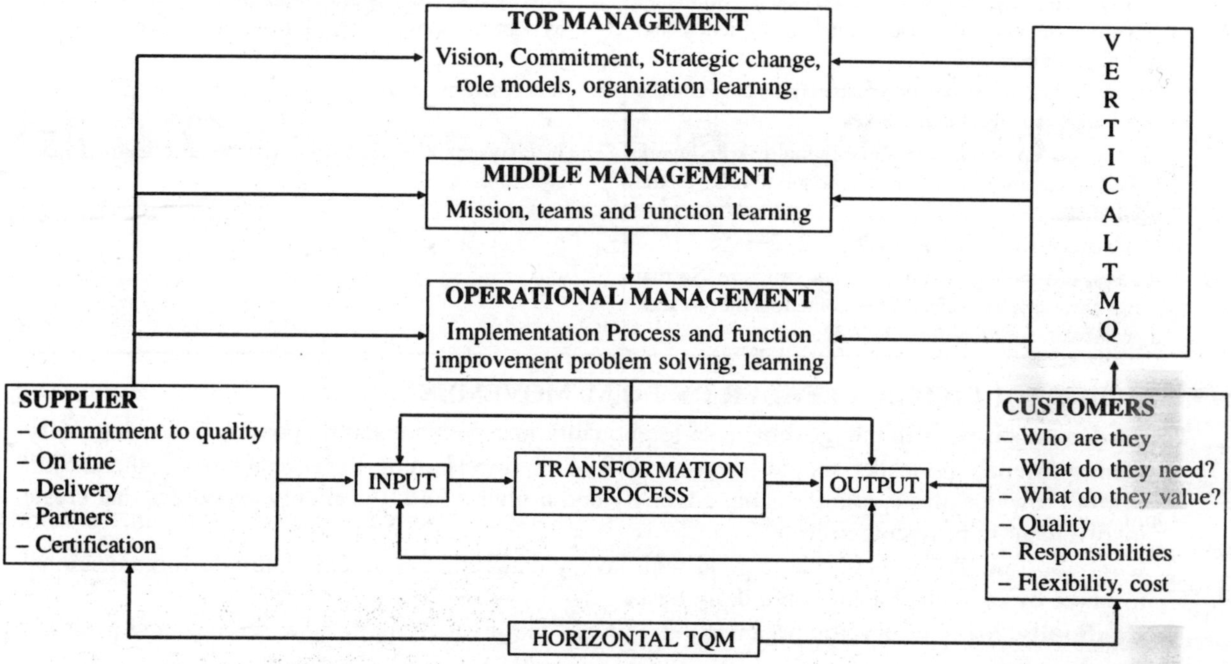

Fig. 39.1. Definition of T.Q.M.

39.3. APPROACH TO TOTAL QUALITY MANAGEMENT

1. Adoption to total quality management requires significant changes.
2. Adoption to total quality management needs opportunity to improve.
3. Adoption to total quality management needs to react to competitive threats.
4. Adoption to total quality management needs prevention of error.
5. Adoption to total quality management needs problem solving focus.
6. Adoption of total quality management needs understanding by complete organisation.

39.4. DIFFERENCE BETWEEN TRADITIONAL AND TOTAL QUALITY MANAGEMENT

The total quality management concepts have developed mainly due to the changes in industry practices with reference to the requirements of the market. The major differences between T.Q.M. and traditional management are shown in tabular form in Table 39.1.

Table 39.1.

S.No.	*T.Q.M.*	*Traditional management*
1.	It views the customers as the dominent resource.	1. In its view quality is not the gurantee of profit.
2.	It takes the view that profit follows quality.	2. In this management the scale of economy is seen as a desirable objective characterized by long prodcution runs, to incur low cost and achieve high efficiency.

S.No.	*T.Q.M.*		*Traditional management*
3.	It its view quality is composed of multi dimensional attributes.	3.	In this system high volumes, long runs and maximum products are considered desirable.
4.	In T.Q.M. economy of time and economy of scope are purssued.	4.	This system considers that workers must work and managers must manage. There is no need to develop connections between them and customers.
5.	In T.Q.M. quality, flexibility and service are dominant objectives in place of cost, technical efficiency and partial productivity.	5.	This system emphasizes on the division of work force by separating manual work from mental work.
6.	T.Q.M. is directed to develop connections between the customers, managers and workes.	6.	It is result oriented.
7.	This system emphasizes on flexible multi skilled work force that can move easily from one job to other as the need arises.	7.	It advocates a hierachical and vertical organizational structure.
8.	It is a process oriented approach.		
9.	It advocates the creation of network structure. So that teams from different disciplines come together to seek a permanent solution of each problem.		

39.5. SKILLS REQUIRED IN A LEADER OF T.Q.M. MOVEMENT

The leader associated with the movement of total quality management should possess following skills:

1. **Commitment.** The leader should have the skill of sharing learning experiences with others. Skill to work towards ideals, jointly facing adversity and bringing forth the energy, resources that create involvement in providing service.
2. **Contribution.** Skills to contribute good will, love and affection as an community or organizational resource by individual action on a daily basis.
3. **Continuity.** Skills to develop organisational image and diversifying to new services and practices and customers.
4. **Collaboration.** Skills to provide reliable interdependence, acting autonomously for the common welfare, meeting and communicating face to face and creating a net of trust through personal relationship.
5. **Conscience.** Skills involving guiding principles, ethics, values of actions and decisions etc.
6. **Conversation.** Skills of dialogue for evolving collective action, use of personal and electronic medium to enable members to share learning, to create innovating products and services and to collaborate on continuous improvement.

39.6. TOTAL QUALITY MANAGEMENT IN CONSTRUCTION INDUSTRY

As already discussed total quality management is a approach that focuses more on problem solving where as the traditional management focuses more on monitoring and inspection. T.Q.M. concept focuses on improving a process by elimination or reducing the defects and low value tasks. The aim is to strive for continuous improvement in the process through analysis and measurement, implementation of new ideas and procedures for improvement and again repeat of analysis and measurement. Thus the cycle of improvement goes on.

In an effort to improve the quality of a process there is need to identify the external and internal customers of the process. The improvement in the process may also be attained by getting the input of employees. The aim or objective of T.Q.M. is to change the mind set or attitude of the employees from only monitoring the process to look for continuous improvement.

In recent past the construction industry also has paid its attention to the implementation of total quality management. The project owners have started adopting the process of T.Q.M. The construction process is highly competitive and is hurt by adverse relationship, low morale, absenteeism and high turn over. Thus construction industry can use the T.Q.M. to improve the construction process.

39.7. WHY T.Q.M. APPLIES TO THE CONSTRUCTION PROCESS

Usually the construction process and industry is full of problems of disputes, legal suits, escalation of cost and time. Thus the construction process is very complex and requires the use of many labour skills, different materials, and complex technical and management systems. In addition to this the uncertain weather conditions and regulations etc. made it very difficult to control the construction project results. Very often it is read in the news papers that a certain project has prolonged too long with the cost going many folds that of the original estimated cost. Some times project comes under disputes and needs their settlement through the arbitration or court. It is also seen that the cost of the project increases many fold, but the productivity remains stagnant.

Some authorities relate these ills primarily to the failure of the construction industry not to adopt the following principles of total quality management system.

1. The construction industry has not focused on the detailed needs of the customer *i.e.* the end use of the project.
2. The construction industry has not fully utilized all the existing resources of the project as available man power skill etc. Secondly the various management know how and technical skill of different parties involved in the construction process have not been integrated into a common approach to solve the problems.
3. The construction industry has not implemented many industrial Engineering and measurement techniques such as statistical sampling.

Thus it can be said that the industry lacking this measurement does not have effective means of improvement. Instead of focusing on causes of problems and processes, the industry has focused on inspections and monitoring of results. As an example, in a construction project the amount of time and money wasted on non productive items, number of incidences of redoing a particular work and number of days taken in completing various tasks are not monitored. This lack of measurement leads to accept the defect. In total quality management approach the causes of these defects are searched or quantified and analysed. Thus in total quality management approach focus is on elimination or removing the causes of the defects.

39.8. CONSTRAINTS TO THE USE OFF T.Q.M. IN THE CONSTRUCTION PROCESS

Some people say that total quality management process does not apply to the construction process due to some unique characteristics of the construction industry. These unique characteristics are as follows:

1. Usually the construction duration is relatively short, one year or less. Due to this short term characteristic, it is difficult to realise the benefits that may be of long term nature.
2. On a construction project usually large percentage of labour works only for a short period only. This can be taken as a transient labour force. Thus it becomes difficult to empower them and get them committed to a team process.
3. Usually construction projects are unique, each project being different from the other. This may reduce the ability to implement the continuous improvements.
4. Generally the owners attempt to control their projects imposing penalties for non performance. They focus on monitoring the results through inspection.

These constraints relate to the application of T.Q.M. to the construction industry, but arguments given in article 39.7, why construction industry needs T.Q.M. over shadow these constraints. Thus is is suggested that some modifications may be adopted in TQM process to recognize the unique characteristics of the construction process.

QUESTIONS

1. Define the total quality management and give its various elements.
2. Discuss the application of T.Q.M. in the construction industry.
3. Discuss the constraints to the use of TQM in construction process.
4. Why T.Q.M. should be applied to the construction industry.
5. Discuss the difference between traditional management and total quality management.
6. What skills are needed in a leader of T.Q.M. movement.

OBJECTIVE TYPE QUESTIONS

1. The disputes in construction industry develop due to
   (*a*) Interpretation of contract clauses
   (*b*).Effect of unforeseen problems as sub soil condition
   (*c*) Natural calaminities
   (*d*) Strikes
   (*e*) All the above
2. The best method of construction dispute settlement is
   (*a*) By direct negotiations between the client and the contractor
   (*b*) Through courts
   (*c*) Through arbitration
   (*d*) All the above
3. Disputes between the client and contractor are
   (*a*) Claim for refund of many wrongly deducted by the client
   (*b*) Claim for extra payment by the contractor
   (*c*) Claims for losses
   (*d*) Interest on delayed payments
   (*e*) All the above
4. Settlement of disputes through the courts is except
   (*a*) Most expredious
   (*b*) It takes un duly long time
   (*c*) More expensive
   (*d*) It should be the last resort
5. The T.M.Q. approach is used for
   (*a*) To improve the operations
   (*b*) To improve the process
   (*c*) Both are correct
   (*d*) Both are incorrect
6. T.M.Q. has attained popularity as it attempts to
   (*a*) Improve the product
   (*b*) Improve the service quality
   (*c*) Improve productivity
   (*d*) Improve competitiveness
   (*e*) All the above
7. The approach of T.M.Q. is
   (*a*) To focus more on problem solving
   (*b*) It does not focus on monitoring and inspection
   (*c*) It focusses on improving the process through reduction of defects and low cost
   (*d*) It aims continuous improvement in a process
   (*e*) All the above

ANSWERS:

1. (*e*)
2. (*a*)
3. (*e*)
4. (*a*)
5. (*c*)
6. (*e*)
7. (*e*)

APPENDIX

TABLE 1. S.I. and Derived units

S. No.	*Quantity*	*S.I. Units*	*Symbol*
1.	Acceleration	metre/second square	m/sec^2
2.	Angular acceleration	Radians/second square	radian/sec^2
3.	Angular momentum (Moment of momentum)	Kilogram metre square per second	kg-m^2/sec.
4.	Angular velocity	Radian per second	radian/sec
5.	Area	metre square or milimetre square	m^2 or mm^2
			K-N-m^2
6.	Elastic modulic (E, G or K)	Kilo-newton per metre square newton per milimetere	N/mm^2
7.	Density	Kilogram per cubic metre	kg/m^3
8.	Force	Newton or kilo newton	N or kN
9.	Impulse	Newton-sec.	N- sec.
10.	Momentum of force (B. M., torque)	Newton-metre or kilo newton metre	N-m or kN-m
11.	Mass	Kilogram or tonnes	Kg,t
12.	Moment of inertia	metre^4, milimiter^4	m^4, mm^4
13.	Momentum	Kilogram-metre per second	kg-m/sec.
14.	Power		
15.	Pressure	Watt or kilo watt	W or kW
		Newton per milimiter square or kilo newton per metre	N/mm^2 or kN/m^2
16.	Stress	Kilo Newton per metre square or Newton per milimetre square	kN/m^2 or N/mm^2
17.	Section modulus	Milimetre cube	mm^3
18.	Velocity	Metre per second or kilo metre per hour	m/sec or kmph
19.	Work	Newton metre or kilo Newton metre	N-m or kN-m
20.	Work	Metre cube or milimetre cube	m^3 or mm^3
21.	Length	metre or milimetre	m, km or mm

TBALE 2. Conversion factor from M.K.S. to SI units

S. No.	*Quantity*	*M.K.S. Units*	*S.I. Units*	*Conversion factor*	
				M.K.S. to S.I.	*S.I to M.K.S.*
1.	Length (L)	Metre m	Metre (m)	1	1
2.	Mass (m)	Slug (metric)	Kilogram (kg)	9.81 (10.0)	0.102 (0.1)
3.	Force (F)	kgf	Newton (N)	9.81 (10.0)	0.102 (0.1)
4.	Work (W) Energy (E)	kgf-m	Joul (J)	9.81 (10.0)	0.102 (0.1)
5.	Power (P)	kgf-m/sec	Watt (W)	9.81 (10.0)	0.102 (0.1)
		H.P. metric	Kilo watt (K.W.)	0.73575	1.359
6.	Moment (M) Torque (T) couple	kgf-m	Newton metre (N-m)	9.81 (10.0)	0.102 (0.1)
7.	Density (ρ)	Slug/m^3	Kg/m^3	9.81 (10.0	0.102 (0.1)
8.	Specific weight (γ)	kgf/m^3	N/m^3	9.81 (10.0)	0.102 (0.1)

S. No.	*Quantity*	*M.K.S. Units*	*S.I. Units*	*Conversion factor*	
9.	Pressure (P)	kgf/m^2 or kg/cm^2	N/m^2 or KN/m^2	9.81 (10) 98.1 (.00)	0.102 (0.1) or 0.01202 or (0.01)
10.	Dynamic viscosity (μ)	kgf sec/m^2 or Poise (p)	N-s/m^2 N-s/m^2	9.81 (10) 0.1	0.102 (0.1) 10.0
11.	Kinematic viscosity (α)	m^2/sec, stock (st)	m^2/s	1.0	1.0
12.	Surface tension (σ)	kgf/m	N/m	9.81 (10.0)	0.102 (0.1)
13.	Freqeuncy (f)	CPS (cycles per second)	Hertz	1.0	1.0
14.	Momentum	Slug m/s	kg-m/s	9.81 (10.0)	0.102 (0.1)
15.	Gas constent (R)	kgf m/kgf.K.	J/kg-K	9.81 (10)	0.102 (0.1)

TABLE 3. Decent Multiple and sub multiples

S. NO.	*Factor by which the unit is multiplied*	*Prefix*	*Symbol*	*Example*
1..	One million million (10^{12})	Tetra	T	1 Tm = 10^{12} m
2.	One thousand million (10^9)	Giga	G	1 Gm = 10^9 m
3.	One million (10^6)	Mega	M	1 Mm = 10^6 m
4.	One thousand (10^3)	Kilo	K	1 Km = 10^3 m
5.	Unity			1 m
6.	One thousanth (10^{-3})	Milli	m	1 mm = 10^{-3} m
7.	One millonth (10^{-6})	Micro	μ	1 μ m = 10^{-6} m
8.	One thousand millinth (10^{-9})	Nano	n	1 nm = 10^{-9} m
9.	One million millionth (10^{-12})	Pico	p	1 pm = 10^{-12} m

1 Pascal = 1 N/m^2 or 10^6 N/mm^2 = 1 Pa, 1 Kg/cm^2 = 0.1 N/mm^2

$\therefore$ 1 MPa = 1 N/mm^2

TABLE 4. Some other important conversions for F.P.S. units to M.K.S. units

S. No.	*Quantity*	*F.P.S. Units*	*To M.K.S. units*	*Symbol*	*Multiplying factor*
1.	Area	Acre	Square metres	m^2	$\frac{4.047 \times 10^3}{3} = 0.0929$
2.	Area	Foot square	Square metres	m^2	
3.	Volume	Aere foot	Cubie metre	m^3	1.233×10^3
4.	Volume	Cubic foot	Cubic metres	m^3	0.02831
5.	Volume liquid	Gollons (U.S.)	Cubic metre	m^3	0.003785
6.	Volume liquid	Inch cubic	Cubic metre	m^3	0.00001639
7.	Volume liquid	Cubic yards	Cubic metres	m^3	0.765
8.	Weight	Pound	Kilogram	kg	0.4534
9.	Weight	Pounds per cubic yards	Kilogram per cubic metre	kg/m^3	0.5933
10.	Weight	Pounds per cubic foot	Kilogram per cubic metre	kg/m^3	1.60×10
11.	Area	Aere	Hectare	m^2	0.4047 (100 × 100) m
12.	Vol.	U.S. Gallon	litres	lit.	3.785
13.	Pressure	Pounds per Square inch	Kilogram per Centemetre square	kg/cm^2	0.0703
14.	Vol.	U.S. Gallon	Imperial gallon	—	0.833